Sustainable Futures in the Built
Environment to 2050

# Sustainable Futures in the Built Environment to 2050

## A Foresight Approach to Construction and Development

*Edited by*

**Tim Dixon, John Connaughton and Stuart Green**

*University of Reading, UK*

*Registered Offices*
John Wiley & Sons, Inc., 111 River Street, Hoboken, NJ 07030, USA
John Wiley & Sons Ltd, The Atrium, Southern Gate, Chichester, West Sussex, PO19 8SQ, UK

*Editorial Office*
9600 Garsington Road, Oxford, OX4 2DQ, UK

For details of our global editorial offices, customer services, and more information about Wiley products visit us at www.wiley.com.

Wiley also publishes its books in a variety of electronic formats and by print-on-demand. Some content that appears in standard print versions of this book may not be available in other formats.

*Library of Congress Cataloging-in-Publication Data*

Names: Dixon, Timothy J., 1958– editor. | Connaughton, John E., editor. | Green, Stuart, 1958– editor.
Title: Sustainable futures in the built environment to 2050 : a foresight approach to construction
    and development / edited by Tim Dixon, University of Reading, Whiteknights, Reading,
    Stuart Green, University of Reading, Whiteknights, Reading, John Connaughton, University of Reading,
    Whiteknights, Reading.
Description: Hoboken : Wiley-Blackwell, 2018. | Includes bibliographical references and index. |
Identifiers: LCCN 2017033420 (print) | LCCN 2017056900 (ebook) | ISBN 9781119063803 (pdf) |
    ISBN 9781119063827 (epub) | ISBN 9781119063810 (paperback)
Subjects: LCSH: Sustainable development. | Construction industry–Management. | BISAC: BUSINESS &
    ECONOMICS / Development / Sustainable Development.
Classification: LCC HC79.E5 (ebook) | LCC HC79.E5 .S8627 2018 (print) | DDC 338.4/7624–dc23
LC record available at https://lccn.loc.gov/2017033420

Cover design: Wiley
Cover image: IJland - Almere Buitendijks - seen at night, a new town in Almere, the Netherlands.
© West 8, MVRDV, WMcDonough+Partners and the municipalities of Almere and Amsterdam

Set in 10/12pt Warnock by SPi Global, Pondicherry, India

Printed in Singapore by C.O.S. Printers Pte Ltd

10  9  8  7  6  5  4  3  2  1

# Editorial Board

## Editors

**Tim Dixon** is Professor of Sustainable Futures in the Built Environment at the University of Reading (School of the Built Environment). With more than 30 years' experience in education, training and research in the built environment, he leads the Sustainability in the Built Environment network at the University of Reading and is co-director of the TSBE doctoral training centre (Technologies for a Sustainable Built Environment). He has co-led major UK research council research projects on brownfield land and urban retrofit, and is currently working with local and regional partners to develop a Reading 2050 smart and sustainable city vision, which also connected with the UK BIS Future Cities Foresight Programme. Recently he has worked on funded research projects on smart cities and big data, smart and sustainable districts, and social sustainability for housebuilders. Tim is a member of the Climate Change Berkshire Group, and a member of the All Party Parliamentary Group on Smart Cities and UK Stakeholders' Group on Smart Cities. He is also a member of the editorial boards of four leading international real-estate journals, a member of the Advisory Board for Local Economy, a member of the review panel for Commonwealth Scholarship Commission, a mentor for the Villiers Park Educational Trust, and a member of the review panels of EPSRC and the RICS Research Paper Series. He was also a member of the international scientific committee for the national Visions and Pathways 2040 Australia project on cities. He has written more than 100 papers and books about the built environment.

**John Connaughton** is Head of Construction Management and Engineering and Professor of Sustainable Construction at the University of Reading (School of the Built Environment). John has worked in the construction sector for over 37 years, 30 of which have been spent in management and related consultancy. Prior to joining the University of Reading in 2012, John was a partner in Davis Langdon, one of the world's largest construction cost and project management companies, where he has spent most of his professional career. He was head of the firm's management consulting group from 2005 and has worked extensively on improving construction procurement and management processes. He was lead author on a range of industry guides produced by the UK Construction Industry Board following the Latham Review of UK Construction in 1994, and was one of the founding members of the UK Board of the Movement for Innovation (M4I). His involvement in sustainability in construction dates from the mid-1980s when he was involved in the UK Department of Energy's Passive Solar Design

Studies Programme, and subsequently was responsible for the development of Davis Langdon's Sustainability Services, with a particular focus on material resource efficiency. At the University of Reading, John is currently involved in funded research on new models of construction procurement and on energy use in office buildings. He is currently Chair of the Executive Board of the UK Construction Industry Research and Information Association.

**Stuart Green** is Professor of Construction Management in the School of the Built Environment at the University of Reading, UK. Stuart enjoys extensive policy connectivity within the UK construction sector and is frequently invited to contribute to industry debates. From 2007 to 2013 Stuart served as a core commissioner with the Commission for a Sustainable London 2012 which provided assurance to the Olympic Board and the public on how the delivery agencies performed against their sustainability commitments. From 2011 to 2016 he chaired the Chartered Institute of Building's Innovation and Research Panel. Stuart has extensive experience of construction-related research leadership and has been principal investigator on Engineering and Physical Sciences Research Council (EPSRC) research awards totalling in excess of £7.5 million. Stuart originally studied civil engineering at the University of Birmingham. Following graduation in 1979 he worked for a national contractor on a range of construction projects throughout the UK. He was subsequently seconded for a year to an engineering consultancy where he gained the necessary design experience to become a chartered engineer. Stuart returned to academia to study for a master's degree at Heriot-Watt University in Edinburgh, prior to joining the University of Reading as a lecturer in 1987. He completed his PhD in 1996 and was promoted to professor in 2002. While based in Reading he has travelled extensively and has held numerous international advisory and consultancy roles in a variety of different locations. He is a visiting professor at Chongqing University and Xi'an University of Architecture and Technology, China.

# Contents

# List of Contributors

Janet F. Barlow
Modassar Chaudry
Phil Coker
Joe Doak
Ian J. Ewart
Lorraine Farrelly
Andy Ford
Aaron Gillich
Jim Hall
Gerard Healey
Adrian J. Hickford
Will Hughes
Graeme D. Larsen
Robert Nicholls
Gavin Parker
Li Shao
Constance Smith
Stefan Thor Smith
Bob Thompson
Jacopo Torriti
Martino Tran
Jorn van de Wetering
Geoff Watson
Saffron Woodcraft

# Note on Contributors

**Professor Janet F. Barlow** is in the Department of Meteorology at the University of Reading and does research in urban meteorology, natural ventilation and renewable energy. She was a Board member of the International Association for Urban Climate, and is currently on the Steering Committee for the UK Wind Engineering Society. She is also on the Met Office Scientific Advisory Committee.

**Dr Modassar Chaudry** is a Senior Research Fellow in the School of Engineering at Cardiff University. His expertise covers a range of energy topics, in particular modelling (optimisation) and analysis of gas, electricity and heating supply systems. He has co-authored a number book chapters and journal papers on integrated energy network modelling and analysis.

**Dr Phil Coker** is a Lecturer in Renewable Energy in the School of the Built Environment, University of Reading. Following 15 years as an engineer in the UK gas industry, he has spent the last decade researching the impacts of variability in low-carbon energy systems. Current projects range from helping the system operator respond to increased intermittent renewables, through assessing the system value of hydrogen to supporting development of a commercial vehicle-to-grid solution.

**Joe Doak** is Associate Professor of Urban Planning and Development at the University of Reading. He has undertaken major research into the formulation and implementation of regional, strategic and local planning policies, and was a senior planning officer at county and district levels of UK local government.

**Dr Ian J. Ewart** is an anthropologist and engineer, and currently Lecturer in Digital Technologies in the School of the Built Environment, University of Reading. His research focus is on the perception and application of technologies, the practices these influence, and how these inform the real, social experience of the world.

**Professor Lorraine Farrelly** is an architect and head of the new Architecture School at the University of Reading. The ambition for the new School is to relate the education experience to current professional practices in architecture, and to develop a collaborative education model that positions architecture within the built environment professions. She has written several books considering relationships between architecture and urban design.

**Professor Andy Ford** is the Director of Research at London South Bank University. He has worked extensively on innovative building throughout his career and contributed to many award-winning designs. Andy is the founder of Fulcrum Consulting. Andy's long-term interest in knowledge transfer led to academia in 2013 following the sale of Fulcrum Consulting to Mott MacDonald.

**Dr Aaron Gillich** has a BEng in Aerospace Engineering from Carleton University, an MSc in Astronomy and Physics from St Mary's University, and a PhD in Architecture from the University of Cambridge. He is currently a Senior Lecturer at London South Bank University. His research focuses on the energy trilemma of delivering a low-cost, low-carbon, secure energy system.

**Professor Jim Hall** is Director of the Environmental Change Institute and Professor of Climate and Environmental Risks at the University of Oxford. His research focuses on management of climate-related risks in infrastructure systems, in particular relating to various dimensions of water security, including flooding and water scarcity. He leads the UK Infrastructure Transitions Research Consortium (ITRC), which has developed the world's first national infrastructure simulation models for appraisal of national infrastructure investment and risks. His book *The Future of National Infrastructure: A System of Systems Approach* was published by Cambridge University Press in 2016.

**Dr Gerard Healey** is a sustainable built environment practitioner with over 10 years' experience. He has worked for design firm Arup and currently is Manager – Sustainable Campus Design for the University of Melbourne. Gerard's PhD investigated socio-technical transitions for sustainability and he brings this multi-disciplinary perspective to his practice.

**Adrian J. Hickford** is Senior Research Assistant in the Transportation Research Group at the University of Southampton. As well as his recent work on implementing strategic change to infrastructure provision, he has been involved in a number of projects aiming to increase the use of sustainable travel, and enhanced practices of traffic accident data gathering and use.

**Professor Will Hughes** is Professor of Construction Management and Economics at the School of the Built Environment, University of Reading. His research is positioned in the construction sector, focusing on the business of construction in relation to contracting, management, organisation and procurement. His current research is on modelling construction procurement decisions and contributing to national and international standards drafting.

**Dr Graeme D. Larsen** is an Associate Professor in Construction Management and Innovation at the University of Reading. He held the position of School Director of PhD Research Studies at the School of the Built Environment for 8 years. Dr Larsen is a Fellow of the Chartered Institute of Building (CIOB). His research interests include innovation diffusion, networks of firms, sustainability, communication networks, innovative methods in niche markets and sports venues. Dr Larsen has secured funding for research projects with such names as Silverstone Circuits Limited, published over 30 research articles and successfully supervised a number of PhD candidates.

**Professor Robert Nicholls** is Professor of Coastal Engineering at the University of Southampton. His research is focused on coastal impacts and adaptation to climate change from local to global scales. More broadly, he is also interested in integrated assessment problems analysing complex systems subject to multiple drivers such as infrastructure.

**Professor Gavin Parker** is Professor of Planning Studies at the University of Reading, UK and for a period he was a director of the Royal Town Planning Institute (RTPI). He is a chartered town planner and researcher who has written extensively on planning, land and citizenship. His books include *Key Concepts in Planning* (Sage, 2012), written with Joe Doak.

**Professor Li Shao** is based at the School of Construction Management and Engineering at the University of Reading, UK. He is a Director of the EPSRC Engineering Doctorate Centre Technologies for Sustainable Built Environments. He specialises in building energy management and climate change adaptation, including the integration of green space in the built environment.

**Dr Constance Smith** is a Hallsworth Research Fellow in Social Anthropology at the University of Manchester. She works on the anthropology of urban planning and architecture. She has conducted extensive fieldwork in African cities and, more recently, on urban change and placemaking in London.

**Dr Stefan Thor Smith** is a Lecturer in Energy Systems and the Built Environment within the School of the Built Environment, University of Reading. His research is focused on energy use and climate within an urban context, anthropogenic influence on urban environments and resilience of city infrastructure to climate change.

**Bob Thompson** is a Director of Remit Consulting specialising in research and strategy, with a special interest in the impact of technological change on all aspects of real estate. Recent publications include *The Building Machine* (Parkside, 2014), *The Role of Cloud Computing in Commercial Property* (with Andrew Waller, RICS, 2011) and *The Role of Social Media in Property* (RICS, 2009). In total, he has produced over 250 publications across all channels since 1985.

**Dr Jacopo Torriti** is an Associate Professor in Energy Economics and Policy in the School of the Built Environment at the University of Reading, with previous roles at the London School of Economics, University of Surrey, European University Institute and the Massachusetts Institute of Technology. He is author of more than 50 publications in the area of energy demand, economics and policy, including the book *Peak Energy Demand and Demand Side Response*, and sits on DEFRA'S Economics Advisory Panel.

**Dr Martino Tran** is Assistant Professor in Urban Systems at the University of British Columbia and Research Associate at the University of Oxford. He has broad interests in complexity, resilience and risk, and has published widely on modelling the performance of future technology and infrastructure. He has advised governments and industry on major infrastructure investments in energy and transport.

**Dr Jorn van de Wetering** is a Lecturer in Real Estate Appraisal at Real Estate & Planning in the Henley Business School at the University of Reading. He holds a PhD in Real Estate Economics. His research interests include property market adoption patterns of eco-certification and the financial performance of environmentally and energy-efficient office space.

**Geoff Watson** is a Senior Research Assistant in the Infrastructure Research Group in the Faculty of Engineering and the Environment at the University of Southampton. He is working on the modelling of future infrastructure requirements for the UK solid waste sector. He also contributed to the infrastructure chapter on the second UK Climate Change Risk Assessment. He has also been involved in research in waste mechanics and rail infrastructure.

**Saffron Woodcraft** is a Research Associate at the Institute for Global Prosperity at UCL. She leads the Institute's research on developing new models and measures of sustainable local prosperity in East London. She has conducted extensive academic and applied fieldwork with communities and built environment professionals engaged in large-scale urban development and regeneration programmes. She is a PhD candidate in anthropology at UCL, where her research focuses on London's Olympic regeneration legacy and new communities. Saffron co-founded of Social Life, a social enterprise established to examine how local communities are affected by urban development and regeneration.

# Foreword by Sir Terry Farrell[1]

In downtown Newcastle, the city where I lived during my teens and twenties, a commemorative pavement inscription honours the 19th century builder and developer Richard Grainger. The words of dedication read 'The past is my present to your future', which expresses the city's gratitude to him as he knew that what we do in the present affects the quality of life for future generations. This quote echoes the 1987 Brundtland Report's definition of sustainable development as 'development that meets the needs of the present without compromising the ability of the future generations to meet their own needs' (Brundtland Report, 1987: 16). This far-reaching report has directed and shaped sustainability agendas and goals for 30 years and is also known as *Our Common Future*. I feel this subtitle to be increasingly more relevant to all of us living in a globalised and interconnected world, but perhaps for the professionals working within the built environment is it particularly significant. As the report states:

> '*Our Common Future* is not a prediction of ever increasing environmental decay, poverty, and hardship in an ever more polluted world among ever decreasing resources. We see instead the possibility for a new era of economic growth, one that must be based on policies that sustain and expand the environmental resource base. And we believe such growth to be absolutely essential to relieve the great poverty that is deepening in much of the developing world.' (Brundtland Report, 1987: 11)

The significance for today's globalised and multidisciplinary built environment community of developers, architects, master planners, engineers, construction industries and occupancy managers is that collaborative work practice has become more established to a point where a range of different professionals can work together with a unified and coordinated vision of a sustainable future. Connectivity between and amongst specialist teams is an approach we valued in the government initiated Farrell Review (2014), which drew together a multidisciplinary team to consider the present and future state of British architecture and masterplanning. Described as an example of 'futures thinking', the Farrell Review used an approach outlined in the introductory chapter to this book of collecting input to see what was going on, analysing what seemed to be happening, interpreting what was really happening and then prospecting or recommending ideas for improvement.

---

1 In collaboration with food anthropologist Bee Farrell.

The power of futures thinking may not be in the solutions we gain from horizon scanning. The micro management of potential future scenarios will not be what guarantees sustainable futures, but the connectivity, communication and creativity inherent in the cross-connectivity of many hands and minds working together is. As an immersive practitioner, I am action-orientated yet I am also stimulated by the evolution of my thoughts and ideas when I work across disciplines and with others from the built environment community. Like many others, I am stimulated by the cross-fertilisation of ideas as I dip in and out of the parallel universes of academia and industry. I feel that in some ways my voice and observations can hold a valued place in these other realities and, in turn, I am energised by the work being done in other disciplines, professions and fields.

Perhaps inherent in the notion of this philosophy of futures thinking is the belief that we can still control our destiny and our dominant place in the natural world. Many great scientists and thinkers recognise that change is part of a natural order. The natural plant and animal world thrives on change and adaptation, as humankind has also done for 200,000 years. However, I return to the point of the process of working together being perhaps more of an enabler of a sustainable future than the possible tangible outcomes we strive for, as explained by John Thakara, who celebrates the value of our connectivity when we look ahead together as:

> 'When change and innovation are no longer about finely crafted "visions" and the promise of a better reality described in some grand design for some future place and time. Change is more likely to happen when people re-connect – with each other, and with the biosphere – in rich, real-world, contexts.' (Thakara, 2016)

What we have craved for the past 200 years is some certainty that we are going to live comfortably and forever. But, as Colin Fournier believes, is there a 'necessary unpredictability of change' (Fournier, 2011: 9–11) so can we think our way out of the challenges of the unknown? Despite the abundance of literature on sustainability there is little that fully captures the messy complexity of the predicaments and possibilities we face, but the efforts and skills that work towards the capture and analysis are significant as we are unified in thinking and acting upon our common future.

Cities are made by many different people, whether they are organic cities like London, 'artificial' cities such as Milton Keynes or cities formed under governance like Paris. Each built environment continues to evolve by incorporating and utilising technology, assessment tools, frameworks, strategies, policies, local and global economies, and the relationship of its inhabitants with their places of work, study and family. The ability to adapt and thrive is held in our propensity to think across cultures and beyond past socio-economic models.[2]

So, who are the built environment clients? In a world of finite resources, increasing numbers of urban and world population, climate change, food shortages, unstable global economics, volatile political governance and the mitigation of migration, one

---

2 Farrell recently revised the 2009 sustainability approach to one which we hope will animate productive sustainability dialogues and invigorate sustainable design. Adaptive Communities, researched and designed by food anthropologist Bee Farrell is a catalyst for rethinking and communicating internally and externally a holistic and place-specific approach.

client is undeniably the future generation. The other 'client' is Earth's ecosystem as we begin to embed the natural environment and resource stewardship into our built environment planning, design, build and habitation through such innovations as closed-loop technology systems or urban greening.

Many of the fine essays in this book are a testament to biocultural knowledge, hard and soft scientific expertise, and a belief that connectivity and creativity play an ever more valuable role in reaching the 2050 carbon-reduction targets. But maybe it is time to flip the perspective around completely and view humankind as the client of Earth's ecosystem? As Austrian architect and artist Hunderwasser wrote in the 1970s we should behave like a good guest of nature. What is clear is that the fusion of eco-centric social and technological innovation and activity makes sense economically, environmentally and socially. Improving the quality of urban life for ordinary people is an exciting and multifaceted task for modern-day built environment visionaries.

## References

Brundtland Commission (1987) *Our Common Future: Report of the 1987 World Commission on Environment and Development.* Oxford University Press, Oxford.

Farrell, T. (2014) *The Farrell Review of Architecture and the Built Environment.* Available at: http://www.farrellreview.co.uk/ (accessed February 2017).

Fournier, C. (2011) The Legacy of Post-Modernism, in Farrell, T. (ed.) *Interiors and the Legacy of Post-Modernism.* Laurence King.

Thakara, J. (2016) Manifesto For Utopias Are Over: Cities Are Living Systems, John Thakara blog, September 19. Available at: http://thackara.com/place-bioregion/manifesto-for-utopias-are-over-cities-are-living-systems/ (accessed February 2017).

# Preface

The inspiration for this book came through our increasing realisation that there was a deficit in *current* thinking about how not only the built environment, but also the real estate (or property), construction and development sectors could, and should, evolve now and into the *future*. As we sit at the cusp of a hugely important time for the world, both environmentally and politically, it is tempting to think that just solving the short-term problems that we face is enough to soak up and even nullify our capacity to think and act. Yet this ignores the importance of the long-term view and thinking about the sort of world we, and our children and grand-children, want to inhabit in 2050 and beyond. In a sense, the importance of overcoming the disconnection that exists between relatively short-term political and planning perspectives and longer-term environmental change has never been greater. We strongly believe that futures thinking and foresight need to be part of this movement and change in our thinking.

The construction and development sectors matter because the built environment, or the buildings and hard infrastructure we see in our cities and urban areas, matter too. In our world, both construction and real estate play a big role in contributing to carbon emissions and resource depletion, but the deployment of new technologies, the emergence of new business and financial models, and changing professional roles in the built environment are also a vital means of ensuring we use and manage the sectors to make a positive difference in achieving a sustainable future by 2050.

However, we face huge challenges in tacking these issues at scale. Although many heralded the Paris Climate Change Agreement of 2015 as a huge step forwards, as governments agreed to limit warming to well below 2 degrees, the following statistic gives us a sense of the huge challenges which still remain: based on expected GDP growth of approximately 3% each year and the requirement to stay within the 2 degrees warming target, on average countries will need to reduce their carbon intensity (t$CO_2$/\$m GDP) by 6.5% every year from now to 2100.[1]

To achieve this sort of reduction target requires us to mobilise action within the built environment in a concerted and orchestrated way. Thinking 'across scales', so we understand the lessons already learned that apply at building scale, neighbourhood level and city level, and between those scales is therefore vital to understand how the real estate and construction and development sectors need to change. Moreover, to tackle the

---

1 PwC (2016) *The Paris Agreement: A turning point? The Low Carbon Economy Index 2016*. PwC. Accessed February 2017: http://www.pwc.com/ee/et/publications/pub/low-carbon-economy-index-2016.pdf

'wicked', complex and interrelated problems surrounding climate change and resource depletion we also need to think about how we can overcome the fragmented and often complex nature of the construction and real-estate sectors. In what are essentially 'conservative' industry sectors, which are often criticised as lacking 'innovation', it is also important to understand how we need to change ourselves, and 'walk the talk' in client-led advice, and in our professional and academic roles. This also means not only adopting a truly interdisciplinary-led approach to our understanding of the future of the built environment, which interweaves a range of disciplines in a common thread of expert-led knowledge and research, but also creating the space to produce solutions which truly are 'sustainable', 'smart' and 'resilient', as well as scalable.

This book also comes at a time when we have restructured our thinking in a new, overarching School of the Built Environment at the University of Reading, which brings together the long-established Department of Construction Management and Engineering with a new Department of Architecture. The School of the Built Environment is an interdisciplinary centre of excellence in research and education with a strong orientation towards societal aspirations for a more sustainable built environment, and with strong links to other departments at the University of Reading (including Real Estate and Planning and Meteorology). Expertise in sustainability ranges across the scales from individual buildings to city-scale urban metabolism, and our coverage includes thermal and energy simulation of buildings, the impact of urban microclimate on energy demand, indoor environment quality and green infrastructure, and our work on smart cities extends from innovation diffusion to the implications of emerging digital technologies for evolving patterns of sustainable living.

Our other, related, inspiration for this book was to develop a project which brought together the range of experts with whom we work with at University of Reading and in our new School of the Built Environment, together with other international academic experts and practitioners. The aim is to focus on a common goal: thinking about how we can transition to a sustainable built environment to 2050, what is influencing and inhibiting change to this goal, and what the future might look and feel like. This book therefore focuses on three key dimensions to future change in the built environment to 2050:

- sustainability and the built environment
- changing professional practice
- transformative technologies and innovation.

Primarily using a foresight-based approach, but with a more qualitative and 'provocative' practitioner-based element to supplement the specific thinking on professional practice, the chapters seek to focus on both construction and development issues as key elements in the built environment to 2050. Thinking about the future in a fresh and innovative way has never been more important. As Nicholas Taleb[2] wrote:

> 'If the past, by bringing surprises, did not resemble the past previous to it (what I call the past's past), then why should our future resemble our current past?'

We hope you enjoy reading the book.

---

2 *Fooled by Randomness* (Penguin, 2007).

# Acknowledgements

Tim Dixon would like to thank all his family for their love, patience and support during the writing of this book. He would also like to thank his colleagues and all the contributors to the book for their hard work, without whom the project would not have been possible. Finally, he would like to dedicate the book to his first friend and mentor at Reading: Professor Peter Byrne, Real Estate and Planning, University of Reading (1946–2015), who had a keen interest in technology applications in real estate.

John Connaughton is grateful for the valuable contributions made by all those involved in this book, both directly – as co-editors, authors and those involved in production and publication – and indirectly – as supportive family, friends and colleagues.

Stuart Green would first and foremost like to thank his co-editors who have undoubtedly carried the bulk of the work in putting this volume together. He would also like to thank his colleagues in the School of the Built Environment whom it was his privilege to lead as Head of School from 2010–2017. But if authorship is about anything, it is about creating a narrative around what is already happening and projecting it into the future. Hence the substantive credit belongs with my past and present colleagues with whom we have worked.

*Tim Dixon, John Connaughton and Stuart Green,*
*February 2017 (University of Reading).*

# Book Endorsements

There is much to recommend in this book for those looking for new pathways capable of transforming the built environment by mid-century and understanding the more innovative roles that the property development and construction industries will need to play in this process. The book is also a far-sighted manifesto developed by the new School of the Built Environment at Reading, therein constituting a challenge to other university faculties and schools in the field of Built Environment and Design world-wide to similarly define the strategic agendas for their research and teaching programs.

**Professor Peter Newton**, *Centre for Urban Transitions, Swinburne University of Technology, Australia*

The scale and breadth in achieving sustainable cities by the middle of this century is huge and will require massive change in the attitude and practice of the construction industry and its professions. Tim Dixon and his co-authors bring together current thinking across a range of issues relating to what our future cities may look like and what industry is needed to achieve the transition. Some thirty or so contributors deal with the themes of sustainability in the built environment, the changing industry, future viewpoints, and transformative technologies and innovation. In dealing with the uncertainties of the future, this thought- provoking book may also help us address the increasing uncertainties of the present. Thoroughly recommended!

**Professor Phil Jones**, *Welsh School of Architecture, Cardiff University*

The people who live, work and play in cities, and society as the collective, provide the ultimate client for the civil engineer, and the construction industry is the vehicle to deliver their creations, and what they create is expected to function effectively into the far future. The material that is covered in this book, which quite properly combines these perspectives, represents essential reading for those engaged in delivering a built environment that is fit for the (far) future.

**Professor Chris Rogers**, *Department of Civil Engineering, University of Birmingham*

An important and timely analysis of the critical challenges facing the real estate and construction sector, now and in the future. Crucially, this book demonstrates that a foresight approach can not only help practitioners and policy-makers mitigate risk, but actively exploit the many opportunities that arise from the necessary transformation to a sustainable built environment. Essential reading for all those striving to change the sector from within.

**John Alker**, *Campaign & Policy Director, UK Green Building Council*

There are few topics more important today than the sustainable future of the built environment. Urban development over the coming 30 years will be providing living space for a further 3 billion urban dwellers. It is happening when the challenges of climate change and resource scarcity will be providing severe tests for humanity. We have now the opportunity to future-proof these new developments. This book brings together essays by key players in the field, and will be very widely read and used.

**Sir David King**, *The Foreign Secretary's Special Representative for Climate Change and Chairman of the Board of Future Cities Catapult (2013–2017), Partner, SYSTEMIC (from 2017)*

We build for the requirements of today, often with the methods of yesterday – but what we build is likely to be around for our grandchildren, and possibly theirs too. Futures evidence, debate, learning and skills – summed up in the foresight approach – are much needed in UK construction, but so far there is a great blank area on the map. This book opens up that area. It provides the beginnings of roadmaps for infrastructure, planning, energy and other crucial themes. It should help many others to explore in more detail the peril and promise of uncertain times.

**Dr Joe Ravetz**, *Co Director, CURE (Collaboratory Urban Resilience & Energy), University of Manchester*

If debate about sustainable futures is to be more than abstract and utopian it must be rooted in the present and be able to demonstrate how future scenarios could realistically be achieved. This book makes an all-important, original contribution to this effort, especially by leading an in-depth discussion of how professional practice will need to evolve to meet the demands for a more sustainable built environment. Ultimately, it is within this practice context that real change towards sustainable futures will occur.

**Professor Simon Joss**, *Professor of Science & Technology Studies, University of Westminster*

A series of enlightening contributions make this an engrossing, concerning and poignant text which presents important viewpoints from which practitioners and scholars, at all stages of their careers, may cast their gaze into the not-too distant future. The comprehensive range of essays, while embedded in future studies, serve to highlight the challenges that must be faced today for the built environment of tomorrow - whether in classroom discussions, midst laboratory experiments, at onsite deliberations or within the market place.

**Dr David Howard**, *Associate Professor in Sustainable Urban Development, University of Oxford*

# 1

# Introduction: Foresight and Futures Studies in Construction and Development

*Tim Dixon, John Connaughton and Stuart Green*

> *'It is far better to foresee even without certainty than not to foresee at all.'*
> Henri Poincare, mathematician, 1854–1912 (Poincare, 1013: 129)

## 1.1 Background and context

Despite the impact of the Great Recession the construction industry[1] remains a vital and important part of the UK economy. For example, in 2014 construction contributed £103 billion in economic output, which is 6.6% of the total UK output, and 2.1 million jobs, or 6.2% of total jobs in 2015 (Rhodes, 2015). Recent research (GCP Global & Oxford Economics, 2015) suggests that the importance of the construction industry globally is set to grow by 85% to $15.5 trillion by 2030, with three countries (China, the USA and India) leading the way and accounting for 57% of all global growth. Continued high levels of investment are also expected to contribute to a growing built asset value globally. In 2012, the combined stock of built asset wealth in the 30 largest economies totalled $193 trillion, and this is set to grow to $261 trillion by 2022 at a rate of 35% in real terms, with 30–40% of GDP attributable globally to built asset wealth (HM Government, 2015a). With continued growth in the UK operations and facilities management sector, and a growing smart cities market there is also considerable potential in the UK construction industry.

This provides rich opportunities for UK construction, with exports in construction contracting and design services growing fast and worth more than $3.5 billion in 2013 (Jermey, 2015). The UK also has a comparative advantage in several sectors, primarily engineering, architecture and low-carbon environments, and over the last few years as part of the previous Construction 2025 strategy (HM Government, 2015b) the UK has placed the development of Level 2 building information modelling (BIM) programme centre stage as it aspires to develop the Digital Built Britain Level 3 platform for the 2020s (HM Government, 2015a).

---

1 In some parts of this book the term 'architecture, engineering and construction (AEC) sector' is used to more explicitly include design, engineering and project management consultancies in addition to the contracting firms which comprise Division 45 of the Standard Industrial Classification (SIC) developed by the UK Office for National Statistics.

*Sustainable Futures in the Built Environment to 2050: A Foresight Approach to Construction and Development*, First Edition. Edited by Tim Dixon, John Connaughton and Stuart Green.
© 2018 John Wiley & Sons Ltd. Published 2018 by John Wiley & Sons Ltd.

Recent analysis in the Construction 2025 report (HM Government, 2015b) also confirmed this view of opportunities and growth, and highlighted the strengths of UK construction. In particular, the report focused on its key economic role and wider economic significance, the internalised UK supply chain accounting for some £124 billion of intermediate consumption, the UK's world-class design skills in architectural design, civil engineering and sustainable construction, and low entry cost and low capital, which benefit small firms and promote competition in the sector. The more recent Government Construction Strategy 2016–20 (Infrastructure Projects Authority, 2016) also builds on this analysis and reinforces the UK Government's commitment to procurement innovation, BIM, skills development and whole-life sustainability. The opportunities in overseas markets are also clear as a result of rapid growth in BRIC markets, but also the continuing demand for low-carbon construction. For example, green building is now about 25% of total global construction activity (Dodge Data and Analytics, 2016). We are also seeing the development of BIM in the UK and overseas, which is likely to improve productivity and lower costs because of improved information flow and greater collaboration.

Despite the continued focus on UK construction through reports such as Latham (1994), Egan (1998) and Wolstenholme (2009), there is a recurring tendency for the construction industry to be criticised for its lack of forward thinking, poor performance and lack of innovation (Fernie *et al.*, 2006; Goodier, 2013). Indeed, the Construction 2025 report also highlighted supposed weaknesses in the sector, including the lack of sector integration in the supply chain and a reliance on sub-contracting, which can often lead to a disconnection and fracturing between design and construction management, leading in turn to a lack of innovation (HM Government, 2015b). Generally, construction is perceived as having low levels of investment in research and development and new processes because of uncertain demand for new goods and limited collaboration. This lack of collaboration and limited knowledge sharing from previous projects, which are team-based, often results from the break-up of teams when projects are completed, and this therefore compounds a lack of technology transfer. Also, in the UK construction costs are relatively high in comparison with overseas competitors and this is driven by inefficient procurement and processes rather than material costs (HM Government, 2015b). This is also compounded by a frequent lack of access to finance, poor skills levels and a high degree of fragmentation relative to other sectors and other countries. Indeed, the *Farrell Review of Architecture and the Built Environment* (Farrell, 2014) also highlighted the fragmentation of policy making across the field and the skills challenges facing all built environment professionals.

Nor are these issues peculiar to the UK; to take the example of a typical building supply chain, there is typically fragmentation and non-integration, and even the largest players in the supply of buildings are relatively small by international standards, with such companies tending to be international rather than multinational (WBCSD, 2008; Green, 2011). There are also many stakeholders in the building supply chain with complex relationships between them, which can result in functional gaps and management discontinuities between the professional and trade responsibilities and the building delivery process. This creates 'operational islands', characterised by ineffective co-ordination and poor communication (WBCSD, 2008).

It is perhaps surprising therefore that there have been relatively few forward-thinking long-term studies (30 years or more) which have attempted to examine and analyse how the role of the construction industry in the UK and internationally is shaping the built environment of the future (Chan and Cooper, 2011; Goodier, 2013). This is perhaps partly influenced by the reluctance within the industry to plan for the long term because of market volatility, but also a lack of perceived control over external organisational factors (Goodier, 2013). The UK construction industry, however, faces several key strategic challenges as it seeks to set out a long-term vision (HM Government, 2015b).

- *The emergence of smart construction and digital design*: There is a growing convergence between different data sets and different technologies in the digital economy and through a focus on *Digital Built Britain* (HM Government, 2015a). For example, the growth of open data (i.e. data that can be freely used, shared and built on by anyone, anywhere, for any purpose) and big data (i.e. very large, complex and rapidly changing datasets), and the development of the Internet of Things (i.e. the network of physical objects – devices, vehicles, buildings and other items embedded with electronics, software, sensors, and networks – that enables these objects to collect and exchange data) are creating substantive opportunities for innovation. For example, the potential for embedding new technologies in buildings to create 'intelligent assets', where the performance of a building and its components can be constantly monitored and so create more efficient asset management and facilities management (Ellen MacArthur Foundation, 2016). Understanding asset performance will be improved therefore during both construction and throughout the design phase and this could potentially lead to smarter design and more efficient construction, with fewer materials and improved resilience of assets. This is also connecting through the 'smart cities' debate which has gained traction globally (Dixon *et al.*, 2015).
- *The growth of low-carbon and sustainable construction*: The global green and sustainable building industry is set to grow at a rate of 23% as a result of increasing regulatory requirements around low carbon and an increasing demand for greener products (HM Government, 2015b). This has been recognised by the UK Green Construction Board, which has developed a low-carbon route map for the built environment to meet the UK's national carbon emissions target by 2050 (Green Construction Board, 2016). There are clear, identifiable opportunities for retrofitting and other activities at building, neighbourhood and city scale, and across both the domestic and non-domestic property sectors in operational and capital terms (with the latter especially important in infrastructure terms) (Arup, 2015). For example, the construction industry has a critical role to play in meeting climate change targets. Globally, buildings contribute to approximately one-third of global final fuel and power consumption whilst emitting 8.1 Gt of $CO_2$ per year (Jennings *et al.*, 2011). Similarly, in the UK research (BIS, 2010) has shown that the amount of $CO_2$ emissions that construction can influence is significant, covering design, manufacture, distribution, and assembly on site, in use and refurbishment/demolition, and accounting for almost 47% of total $CO_2$ emissions in the UK. Much remains to be done here, however, as a recent report (Arup, 2015) revealed that in 2012 emissions had increased relative to 2009, primarily through increased gas consumption for heating buildings in the UK. If the UK is to achieve its ambitions of a 50% reduction on 1990 levels by 2025 (and ultimately a reduction of 80% by 2050) there needs to be a further 39% reduction by 2025 against the 1990 baseline (Arup, 2015).

- *Growth through improved trade performance*: The UK construction industry is more fragmented than other countries, such as the USA and Germany, and there is only one UK firm in the top 10 European contractors and housebuilders, and only two in the top 20 (HM Government, 2015b). Despite the UK's strong reputation for design and construction services, construction still accounts for only 2% of UK exports. A key challenge facing the UK construction industry is how to take a lead role on overseas projects and compete more effectively in those markets.

These strategic concerns for the UK construction industry are also underpinned by a complex mixture of drivers, or 'megatrends', which are shaping the world in which we live (Ernst and Young, 2015). For example, the growth of digital technologies and the rise of entrepreneurship are creating an increasingly globalised market place. Urban growth continues to be dramatic, with more than 50% of the world's population living in cities today, and this is expected to grow to 66% by 2050 (UN, 2015). Rapid urban population growth in China and India, and further demographic changes to 2050, will produce challenges and opportunities for the global construction industry. This also comes at a time when the built environment professions and their institutions are facing flux and change with increasing challenges to their value and criticism for perceived protectionism, resistance to change, the reinforcement of silos and the preservation of hierarchies (Morrell, 2015).

So now, perhaps more than ever, there is a need for the construction industry, and the related built environment professions, to take a considered long-term view, and look at what sort of future we will see in 2050 in terms of (i) the future shape and form of the built environment, (ii) how the construction industry will need to evolve and change to meet these challenges, and (iii) what the response of the built environment professions should be to these challenges and opportunities. This book therefore aims to address the gap in futures studies in construction by drawing together a wide range of chapters which focus on these three aspects of future change using a foresight-based approach.

## 1.2 Sustainable futures in the built environment: some important definitions

Before we review the positioning of this book within the wider discourse of futures (and foresight-based) studies in construction, it is helpful to define our field of study and what boundaries we draw in defining the focus for the book. We will therefore define the following terms:

- construction and development
- built environment
- sustainable development
- sustainable futures
- foresight studies.

First, our focus is primarily on the construction and development industries. In statistical (and process-based) terms the UK construction industry can be defined as including general construction and allied construction activities for buildings and civil engineering works. It includes new work, repair, additions and alterations, the erection of prefabricated buildings or structures on the site and constructions of a temporary nature (ONS, 2009). In contrast, a recent UK Department for Business Innovation and Skills report (BIS, 2013) suggested that the UK construction sector[2] was composed in company-based terms of (i) the construction contracting industry, (ii) the provision of construction-related professional services and (iii) construction-related products and materials. Clearly definitions vary, but in this book we are interested in the way in which construction is positioned within the wider development process. For example, for Harvard (2008), property development is taken to be a process 'that involves the transformation of property from one state to another', and for Wilkinson and Reed (2008) it is a process that 'involves changing or intensifying the use of land to produce buildings for occupation'. This invites us to think in a more integrated fashion about the 'real estate' lifecycle (RICS, 2015a) so in this book we take 'construction and development' to be a process which encompasses planning and acquisitions, development, and operations.

Second, our focus is on the built environment context of construction and development. The built environment has been defined in a variety of ways by different researchers. In general, it is defined as the part of the physical environment that is constructed by human activity. In one definition, for example, the built environment consists of the following elements: land use patterns, the distribution across space of activities and the buildings that house them; the transportation system, the physical infrastructure of roads, sidewalk and cycle paths, as well as the service this system provides; and urban design, the arrangement and appearance of the physical elements in a community (Handy *et al.*, 2002). The Smart Cities Council (2015) define built environment as comprising buildings, parks and public spaces, and other components such as streets and utility infrastructure are seen as part of energy and transportation. In this book, we adopt the following definition (Health Canada, 2002, quoted in Srinivasan *et al.*, 2003):

> 'The built environment includes our homes, schools, workplaces, parks/recreation areas, business areas and roads. It extends overhead in the form of electric transmission lines, underground in the form of waste disposal sites and subway trains, and across the country in the form of highways. The built environment encompasses all buildings, spaces and products that are created or modified by people. It impacts indoor and outdoor physical environments (e.g., climatic conditions and indoor/outdoor air quality), as well as social environments (e.g., civic participation, community capacity and investment) and subsequently our health and quality of life.'

Third, we adopt the premise that sustainable development is an area of major concern for the construction and development industries primarily because of the substantive role it plays in producing operational and capital (embodied) carbon emissions. In this sense, a good starting point for understanding what is meant by 'sustainable

---

2 We use the terms 'sector' and 'industry' interchangeably in this book. Some chapters also focus on what is referred to as the architecture, engineering and construction sector (see footnote 1). These terms should all be treated as synonymous with the wider aspirations of the book, which is to focus on construction and development within the built environment.

development' is the Brundtland Commission definition, which defines the term as (Brundtland Commission, 1987: 27):

> '...development that meets the needs of the present without compromising the ability of future generations to meet their own needs. It contains within it two key concepts:
>
> - the concept of needs, in particular the essential needs of the world's poor, to which overriding priority should be given; and
> - the idea of limitations imposed by the state of technology and social organization on the environment's ability to meet present and future needs.'

This thinking has been at the heart of government policies relating to sustainable development globally, and has been re-emphasised in the UK with policy which has highlighted the importance of improving quality of life for people (e.g. UK Government's *A Better Quality of Life* Report (HM Government, 1999)). As the Pearce (2003) report *The Social and Economic Value of Construction* noted, sustainable development is a process which ensures a rising per capita quality of life over time, and this is reflected in per capita real incomes, better health and education, improved quality of both natural and built environments, and enhanced social stability. For Pearce, sustainability, as the goal of sustainable development, is generated through the possession of four main types of capital assets to advance productivity through technological change:

- human capital, or labour force
- man-made capital, or the built assets
- natural capital, or the environment
- social capital, or interpersonal relationships.

This has also been framed within a 'triple bottom line' approach to sustainable development (Elkington, 1997), which highlights the importance of social, economic and environmental sustainability, underpinned by appropriate governance structures. In this sense, sustainable development can be seen as a pathway to future 'sustainability', and this was at the heart of the UK Government's *Sustainable Development Strategy* report (DEFRA, 2005), which highlights five guiding principles for sustainable development:

- living within environmental limits
- ensuring a strong, healthy and just society
- achieving a sustainable economy
- promoting good governance
- using sound science responsibly.

Fourth, this leads us to the concept of 'sustainable futures'.[3] The Pearce report (Pearce, 2003) highlighted the important role that construction plays in contributing to sustainable development, and the importance of the built environment, as built assets, in the world of construction. In this book, we are interested in highlighting how a sustainable future built environment might look and feel like in 2050, focusing on the physical built

---

3  See also the discussion on the sustainable built environment in Chapter 17.

environment, the new processes and techniques that are becoming more and more important to understand, and the changing roles that construction and development professionals (and other built environment professionals) will face. In other words, if we use a normative lens for seeing the future in sustainable terms, what are the forces driving these changes, and what are the likely outcomes by 2050?

Fifth, in bringing these concepts of 'built environment', 'construction and development', and 'sustainable development' together within the normative vision of a sustainable future, we have used a conceptual framework for the chapters based on a foresight approach. In the *Oxford English Dictionary* 'foresight' has the following alternative definitions:

- 'The ability to predict what will happen or be needed in the future'
- 'The front sight of a gun'
- 'A sight taken forwards' (in surveying).

For Loveridge (2009: 12) foresight is 'essentially practical and qualitative anticipation' and should be distinguished from the institutional foresight of policy and planning circles. In this sense foresight can also be thought of a conceptual framework involving a range of forward-looking approaches of informed decision-making that include considerations and views of the long term (Kubeczko *et al.*, 2011). Conway (2014) also helpfully distinguishes foresight from futures studies. For Conway (2014: 2) foresight is:

> '…the capacity to think systematically about the future to inform decision making today. It is a cognitive capacity that we need to develop as individuals, as organisations and as a society. In individuals, it is usually an unconscious capacity and needs to be surfaced to be used in any meaningful way to inform decision making, either as individuals or in organisations. It's a capacity we use every day.

In contrast, the term 'futures' refers to (Conway, 2014: 2):

> '…the broad academic and professional field now developing globally as well as research, methods and tools that are available to us to use to develop a foresight capacity. The term "futures" should be viewed as a collective noun, in the same way that we talk of "economics" or "politics". The term is always plural, because there is always more than one future to consider.'

Foresight methodologies can be classified into four levels (Voros, 2003), each with its own guiding questions (Figure 1.1) (Conway, 2014):

- Input: What is going on?: information is gathered on the current environment.
- Analytical: What seems to be happening?: trends and patterns in society are analysed.
- Interpretive: What's really happening?: interpretive methods make sense of the information that has been collected in an in-depth way.
- Prospective: What might happen?: alternative views of the future are identified.

In this book we are interested in addressing all of these questions in relation to sustainable futures in the built environment, looking ahead to 2050. We have therefore commissioned authors using a foresight framework, and in a number of chapters alternative futures are considered. This is important because a lot of thinking about

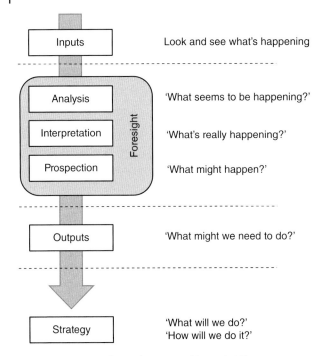

**Figure 1.1** Generic foresight process (Voros, 2003).

sustainability is shaped and influenced by the future implications of today's actions. Adopting a precautionary focus also plays to the notion that we should think about desirable future states for our world and the built environment, which brings concepts such as future studies more into focus.

## 1.3 Futures studies in construction: an overview and critique

### 1.3.1 Overview of futures studies

The global construction industry has traditionally taken a relatively short-term view of the future. As Goodier (2013: 7) states:

> 'The global construction industry needs to expand its planning horizons to pre-pare for potential future events, trends and operating environments...yet con-struction companies appear reluctant to engage in planning beyond a few years, or past the next project, and there is little evidence of a formal process in the formulation of long term strategies.'

This may partly explain the relatively few reports which have focused on long-term trends and the future shape of the industry. There are exceptions, however, which have been reviewed by authors such as Harty *et al.* (2007) and Chan and Cooper (2011),

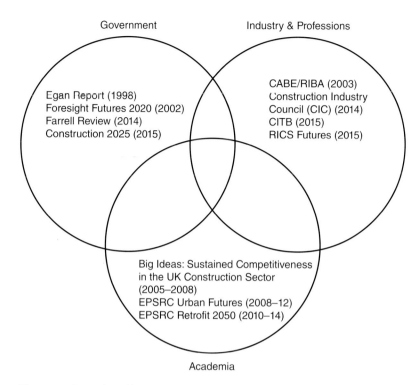

**Figure 1.2** Examples of futures studies relating to UK construction and the built environment.

although the studies covered by these authors have tended not to look further ahead than 10–20 years.

There are three main types of futures studies in construction which can be categorised by source (Figure 1.2). First, there are futures studies (which may also have elements of foresight) stemming from government commissioned reviews: examples here include the Egan Report (Egan, 1998), the Fairclough report (Fairclough, 2002), the Foresight Futures report (DTI, 2002), the Farrell review (Farrell, 2014) and the Construction 2025 report (HM Government, 2015b). Second, there are studies which have stemmed primarily from industry and the professions. Examples here include the Commission for Architecture and the Built Environment/Royal Institute of British Architects (CABE/RIBA) review (CABE/RIBA, 2003), the Construction Industry Training Board (CITB) Construction 2030 and Beyond (CITB, 2015), the Royal Institution of Chartered Surveyors (RICS) Futures programme (RICS, 2015b; Cook, 2015) and the Construction Industry Council (CIC) Built Environment 2050 (CIC, 2014). Third, a number of studies have focused primarily on (i) the future of construction and the challenges and opportunities facing it over the next 10–20 years, and (ii) the built environment at city level to identify its future shape and form and the implications of sustainable development for cities. Relevant programmes here include the Big Ideas Sustained Competitiveness in the UK Construction Sector programme (a collaborative programme between the universities of Reading, Loughborough and Salford) and EPSRC Retrofit 2050 and the EPSRC Urban Futures programmes (other examples are covered in Fernandez-Guell and Gonzalez-Lopez (2014)) This latter group of futures studies also has synergy with some of the ideas explored in the futures thinking of Arup at city level (Arup, 2013, 2014).

Figure 1.2 focuses on the UK, but there are other national studies from the USA, Germany and Australia which can be categorised in a similar fashion (see, for example, work referenced in Chan and Cooper (2011) and also Bok *et al.* (2012) and McGrail and Gaziulusoy (2014)). More recently GCP Global and Oxford Economics (2015) have produced global forecasts of the construction industry looking ahead to 2030. Such studies also differ in the way that they approach futures thinking. Harty *et al.* (2007), for example, suggests as far as the first two groups are concerned, that they involve workshops, interviews/consultations, individual or organisational speculation, or reviews of past work. The third group of academic-based studies has used foresight methods (including backcasting techniques) to construct visions and scenarios for cities (Dixon *et al.*, 2014) for example, whilst the Big Ideas research used workshops, causal maps and scenarios (Goodier *et al.*, 2007).

The use of scenarios is an important element in some studies. Definitions of scenarios vary but Godet and Roubelat (1996: 166) understand a scenario as 'a description of a future situation and the course of events, which allows one to move forward from the original situation to the future'. A study by Sami Consulting/Experian (2008) for the CITB, which looked at the future of UK construction to 2020, used four scenarios (based on the UK foresight national 2020 scenarios): 'World Markets' (a world driven by wealth and aspirational values with limited government in a heavily globalised world), 'National Enterprise' (aspirations of personal independence and wealth but rooted within a national context), 'Global Responsibility' (aspirations of high levels of welfare with shared values and equal opportunities) and 'Local Stewardship' (aspirations of sustainable levels of welfare within federal and network communities).

Similarly, a Foresight Project on Intelligent Infrastructure Systems (IIS) included four scenarios (Curry *et al.*, 2006). The IIS project set out to examine the challenges and opportunities for the UK in bringing 'intelligence' to its infrastructure, that is, the physical networks that deliver such services as transport, telecommunications, water and energy. In particular, the project explored how, over the next 50 years (to 2055), science and technology can be applied to the design and implementation of intelligent infrastructure for robust, sustainable and safe transport, and its alternatives. The scenarios comprised 'Perpetual Motion' (a society driven by constant information, consumption and competition), 'Urban Colonies' (investment in technology focuses mainly on minimising environmental impacts), 'Tribal Trading' (a world that has been through a sharp and savage energy shock) and 'Good Intentions' (a world in which the need to reduce carbon emissions constrains personal mobility).

Scenarios therefore have tended to be used in some studies to analyse the possible effect of one particular driver or theme such as sustainability or climate change, and those that offer a more complex mix of factors to develop the scenario (Harty *et al.*, 2007). In contrast, the EPSRC Retrofit 2050 work used backcasting techniques. This is a way of defining a desirable future and then working back to the present to identify policies and practices that will enable the future to be a reality (Eames *et al.*, 2013a). In EPSRC Retrofit 2050[4] a set of three visions (or shared expectations of a desirable future)

---

4  See www.retrofit2050.org.uk.

was developed, based on retrofitting cities (Eames *et al.*, 2013a,b). This research scoped out three generic visions:

- *Vision I 'Smart-networked city'*: The city as a hub within a highly mobile and competitive globally networked society. Pervasive, information-rich virtual environments integrate seamlessly with the physical world. ICTs provide real-time information to drive efficiencies through automation and intelligent control, and advanced market-oriented solutions allow for the internalisation of environment costs. This is an open, outward-looking society in which the mobility of people, goods and services remains high.
- *Vision II 'Compact city'*: The city as a site of intensive and efficient urban living. Urban land use, buildings, services and infrastructure provision are optimised to create dense urban settlement forms that encourage reduced demand and more efficient use of energy and resources. Concentration in urban centres reduces pressures on the periphery. Significant efficiencies are obtained through systems integration and re-design.
- *Vision III 'Self-reliant green city'*: The city as a self-reliant bio-region, living in harmony with nature. A self-replenishing, largely self-reliant system of circular metabolism, where resources are local, demand is constrained, and the inputs and outputs of the city are connected (cradle to cradle). In many ways this is an inward-facing society, but one conscious of its global responsibility to 'live within its limits'.

In the Urban Futures programme of work scenarios were applied to city regeneration projects and an interactive tool developed for futures thinking to help urban designers analyse the resilience of their sustainability solutions[5] (Rogers *et al.*, 2012).

But what do the various futures studies tell us about the key drivers for change associated with the construction industry? These are many and various but Goodier (2013) suggests (based on previous research and existing knowledge) that the main forces for change which affect the construction industry are climate change, energy demand and supply, resilience (the ability to bounce back from extreme shocks), sustainability, and the take up of new technologies, materials and methods. Similarly, Harty *et al.* (2007) provided a helpful taxonomy of these 'issues and drivers' from previous studies, covering the period 1998–2005, and classified them as 'technological', 'environmental', 'human', 'economic', 'governance' and 'other' (Table 1.1).

More recently, the CITB (2015) study identified 10 drivers of long-term change in the construction industry (Table 1.2). These drivers also link quite closely with the five priority areas identified as being crucial to long-term success in the UK's Construction 2025 Vision (HM Government, 2015b):

- people: an industry that has a talented and diverse workforce
- smart: an industry that is efficient and technology advanced
- sustainable: an industry that leads in low carbon and green construction exports
- growth: an industry that drives economic growth
- leadership: an industry with strong leadership from the Construction Leadership Council.

---

5  See http://designingresilientcities.co.uk/.

**Table 1.1** Key issues and drivers in UK futures studies in construction (1998–2005) (Harty *et al.*, 2007).

| Group | Specific issues |
| --- | --- |
| Technological | Increased standardisation and offsite construction |
| | Increased use of common ICT and information-sharing platforms |
| | Increased automation and use of robotics |
| | Increased use of 3D technology (virtual reality, CAD) |
| | New/smart construction materials |
| Environmental | Increased importance of sustainability |
| | Climate change/global warming/extreme weather |
| | Resources/energy conservation |
| | Oil depletion/energy crisis |
| | Reduce waste and pollution/increased recycling |
| | Increased urbanisation |
| | Demographics changes |
| Human | Reduction of skilled trades/consolidation of professions |
| | Shift education and training requirements |
| | Improved health and safety, welfare and working conditions |
| | Flexible working |
| | Smaller households |
| | Changing healthcare needs and requirements |
| | Vulnerability and security |
| Economic | More profitable, efficient and competitive construction industry |
| | Increased foreign competition and globalisation |
| | Consolidation and de-fragmentation of construction industry |
| | Increased use of whole-life costing, PPP and PFI initiatives |
| | Increase gap between rich and poor |
| Governance | Changes in government policy |
| | Increased or alignment of legislation and regulation |
| Other | Wild cards |
| | Major shocks |

ICT, information and communications technology; CAD, computer aided design; PPP, private and public partnership; PFI, private finance initiative.

The timelines of such studies also vary. Generally speaking, government and industry/professions-based studies have taken a view to 2020 or 2030. Occasionally 2050 has been the focus of study, for example the CIC (2014) study on Built Environment 2050 takes a long-term look to 2050 to examine construction's digital future. This work was partly driven by the BIM2050 group and focuses on education and skills, technology and process, and the culture of integration, and divided the timeline for digital futures into four waves corresponding to specific time horizons (Table 1.3). A longer-term perspective has also been seen in the work of academia in both the UK and Australia looking ahead to 2050 (see, for example, Dixon *et al.* (2014), McGrail and Gaziulusoy (2014) and Alford *et al.* (2014)).

**Table 1.2** Drivers of long-term change in UK construction (CITB, 2015).

| Driver | Comments |
| --- | --- |
| Economy | The construction industry is sensitive to the level of economic growth and is vulnerable to a cyclical economy. The rate of economic growth and its direction are key to demand within the different subsectors and will determine the demand for the number of trainees and the type of skill required. |
| Market sector conditions | The level of activity in each of the main market sectors of the industry – defined for this research as new housing, new building, infrastructure and repair and maintenance – will have a significant impact on training needs as each has its own requirements for skills. |
| Demography and migration | The population in Britain is growing and changing rapidly, causing demand for infrastructure, homes and public buildings. The population is becoming more diverse. Immigration has recently become important to the construction industry in supplying labour. Migration patterns could provide significant shocks to skills supply. |
| Sustainability | The issues of climate change and carbon mitigation and adaption are important as a source of work and employment. They will affect the legislation imposed on the industry and attitudes within it. |
| Technology and innovation | Changes in technology have the possibility of significantly changing the industry. They are primarily digital technology, notably BIM, and off-site construction processes |
| Relationship with government | Government is construction's largest customer and as a smart customer has the capability to help the industry develop and improve. A good relationship with government is necessary to ensure that regulation is supportive and appropriate. |
| Business model-direct employment | A significant change within the industry over the past decade has been the shift from direct employment to self-employment and sub-contracting. This has had an impact on training and implications for the relevance of government skills policy. |
| Business model supply chain | The British legal system and construction's adversarial contracts are considered to be a significant cause of the ills of the industry. Moves toward collaborative contracts have only been moderately successful. A change in the current model would stimulate change within the industry, improving innovation and margins, and demanding new skills. |
| External image | The external image of the industry is important in recruitment and in relationships with clients and government. The current image is poor, due to the lack of technology, poor quality, a poor health and safety record, and precarious employment terms. |
| Internal attitudes | While flexibility and problem solving abound in the industry, its resistance to change, macho image, confrontational attitudes up and down the supply chain, sexism and prejudice are recognised as being deterrents to efficiency, recruitment and diversity. |

Some of these recent studies also link back to current UK government policy on construction. As far as UK government policy on construction is concerned, the Construction 2025 strategy should also be seen in the context of its links with the Business and Professional Services strategy, the Smart Cities strategy and the Information Economy strategy, all of which are brought together with the Digital Britain strategy

**Table 1.3** Timelines for feedback wave cycles: digital future in construction (adapted from CIC (2014)).

| Wave | Period | Characteristics |
|---|---|---|
| Wave 1: Analogue decisions | 2010–2020 | At key stages (Capex/Opex) |
| Wave 2: Digital decisions | 2020–2030 | Converging information Performance/operation |
| Wave 3: Predictive digital | 2030–2040 | Emerging information Social outcomes |
| Wave 4: Artificial intelligence | 2040+ | Adaptive and agile |

(HM Government, 2015a). The Construction 2025 strategy (HM Government, 2015b) also summarises the work that the Government will undertake to achieve its overall ambitions, which are focused on (Rhodes, 2015; Hansford, 2014):

- a 33% reduction in both the initial cost of construction and the whole-life cost of assets (from 2010/09 levels)
- a 50% reduction in the overall time from inception to completion for new-build and refurbished assets (based on industry standards in 2013)
- a 50% reduction in greenhouse gas emissions in the built environment (compared to 1990)
- a 50% reduction in the trade gap between total exports and total imports for construction products and materials (from February 2013 deficit of £6 billion).

The recent *Government Construction Strategy 2016–20* report (Infrastructure Projects Authority, 2016) also focuses on more immediate, shorter-term steps, including improving government capability in construction 'clientship', the industry-wide adoption of BIM and the development of appropriate workforce capacity and skills.

### 1.3.2 A critique of future studies in construction

A major weakness of many of these futures studies is that they tend to extrapolate current trends rather than reimagine a radically transformed future (Harty *et al.*, 2007). Often the terms that are used are also not unpacked or defined, for example the many differing interpretations of 'sustainability' can impact and be perceived differently by different stakeholders in the built environment. Sustainability will also mean different things to different people in national contexts: what is sustainable in a developed world city (e.g. smart metering) may have no place in a developing world city struggling to provide basic utilities.

Moreover, the studies we have examined also often assume internal drivers and external drivers do not interact together, rather they operate independently. So, for example, demographic changes are assumed to configure and drive change in the sector without an examination of how this impacts and interacts on the organisation of the sector or the long-term skills requirements for the sector (Harty *et al.*, 2007). Moreover, these internal and external drivers can be seen as effects and causes of change, for example technology can be a driver pushing construction professionals towards greater reliance on ICT for design construction and management but also utilised as a response to cost reduction or the need to compete in a global market. Therefore, it is the interconnectivities and interrelationships between drivers that are important to understand, but they are often overlooked in construction futures studies.

Chan and Cooper (2011) also point to a great deal of convergence within futures studies in construction as they have tended to examine changes faced by society across social, economic, political and environmental dimensions during a particular time period of change (i.e. the last 20 years or so). However, as the nature of the main participant stakeholders changes over time, and as power relations shift, there may be a possible divergence of views which is important to capture. What might be true for one generation may not be true for the next. Furthermore, as was seen in the previous section, construction futures studies tend to take a short/medium term view of the future, looking 10–20 years ahead, at most. The advantage of a longer time frame to 2050 is that this opens up a 'possibility space', or freedom to think outside current constraints, and can help overcome the disconnection that exists between short-term planning horizons and longer-term environmental change (Eames *et al.*, 2013a,b).

There is also a tendency to see futures studies in construction as produced by 'committee' and so lacking a personalised view of the world (Chan *et al.*, 2005; Chan and Cooper, 2011). As Chan and Cooper (2011: 21) state:

> 'It is our suspicion that foresight reports are just simply crystal-balls for future gazing; it is probably difficult, and indeed a futile exercise, to figure out what real action exactly derives from which report. If foresight studies were to realise their intentions of engendering change in industry and society, there is a pressing need to personalise "futures thinking".'

Ultimately, we must also think about the context of futures studies, and what they mean for the construction industry (Harty *et al.*, 2007). First, defining what we mean by 'construction' is important, and who comprises the target audiences of the futures studies. Second, the futures set out in such studies have different implications for different stakeholders. A future based on a highly regulated and standardised sector, with a strong focus on environmentally sound buildings, not only needs to consider the important potential social impacts caused by employment shifts, but also the resultant aesthetics and design of such buildings. Finally, what will be the potential differential impact of particular scenarios on small firms and larger firms? Who will be the winners and who will be losers? We should not shy away from answering these sorts of questions.

Despite these criticisms, futures studies can help us develop a clearer understanding of the complexities of change in an uncertain world. Futures studies help us challenge our existing assumptions and explore ways in which the future might be different from the present. This implies that by understanding the future better, we can make 'better' decisions now, either by avoiding ones that are not future proof or at least bringing about better or improved futures (Coyle, 1997). This book is therefore an attempt to bring together thinking from leading academics and practitioners within a foresight framework to understand future changes in construction and development. Learning from the shortcomings of previous futures studies in construction, we take a long-term perspective to 2050 and adopt a multidisciplinary approach in exploring a range of related interdependent, and cross-cutting, themes.

## 1.4    Conceptual framework for the book

The starting point for our book is the built environment in 2050, focusing on a sustainable future. The date is important, not only because it is a mid-century point, but also because it represents a key date in the UK's national strategy to address greenhouse gas emissions, namely that by 2050, under the Climate Change Act (2011), there is a primary target to reduce national greenhouse gas emissions by 80% from their 1990 baseline levels. It also represents a longer-term view of construction and development than has been the case in the majority of futures studies.

This book is also founded on a foresight approach to thinking about the future. In this sense, we adopt the Miles and Keenan (2002:15) view of foresight as describing:

> '...a range of approaches to improving decision making...Foresight involves bringing together key agents of change and sources of knowledge in order to develop strategic visions and anticipatory intelligence. Of equal importance, foresight is often explicitly intended to establish networks of knowledgeable agents.'

Foresight techniques also include 'horizon-scanning', which aims to gather a wide range of evidence and information about upcoming trends, ideas and events (Habegger, 2009). This also underpins the rationale for compiling the chapters in this book, which are written by experts in each field and address developments that inform each particular subject area (cf. Dixon *et al.*, 2014). The chapters in this book were therefore commissioned on the basis of highlighting, where appropriate, for each topic:

- data and trends (including historical data and UK and international case studies)
- policies or government legislation/programmes related to the field
- the current state of understanding
- key challenges
- key advances (including disruptive and systemic technological innovations)
- change issues and critical uncertainties
- future visions and scenarios.

However, it should be noted that in some chapters a more discursive, critical approach is adopted to offer an academic counterpoint and critique of current thinking (see, for example, Chapters 15 and 16). Also, to build on this and to offer a 'practice-based' perspective, we have commissioned two chapters in Part 3 of the book which are practitioners' viewpoints, 'provocations about the future'. These are less formal in their approach to foresight and are designed to provide a provocative counterpoint to the more formal foresight chapters in the rest of the book.

In methodological terms, the authors were identified because they had substantive knowledge in the field and because of their ability to think in terms of the future (cf. Loveridge, 2009). The overall aim of the book therefore, within an integrated programme of foresight thinking to 2050, is to bring together leading thinking on:

- issues of new professional practice
- the future of a sustainable built environment.

The book focuses on both construction and development issues as key elements in the built environment. The majority of the chapters have a 'construction' focus but importantly some chapters also have a 'development' focus, for example around sustainable real estate, sustainable communities and planning.

In summary, the book focuses on how we can transition to a sustainable future by 2050, bringing together leading research and practice. The book examines how emerging socio-economic, technological and environmental trends will influence the built environment of the future, covering both the built environment (across the scales of buildings, communities and cities) and how professional practice will need to adapt to these trends. This broader context is underpinned by an analysis of emergent technologies, business models and shifting requirements for expert advice from clients within the relevant chapters.

## 1.5   Overview of book

The book is structured into four main parts as follows.

### Part 1: Sustainability and the Built Environment

In the first part of the book, the chapters cover the interface between sustainability and the built environment.

In Chapter 2 Barlow, Li Shao and Smith examine the complexities of the relationship between climate change, resilience and the built environment. This chapter considers the current use of dynamic thermal simulation software, its fitness for purpose in predicting future building performance, and new approaches arising from the application of climate science.

In Chapter 3 van De Wetering examines sustainable buildings and looks at some of the important key trends and drivers and barriers influencing the take-up of sustainability, particularly in relation to commercial property markets.

In Chapter 4 Woodcraft and Baldwin examine sustainable communities. In the UK there is growing interest in measuring the social outcomes of regeneration and urban development from property developers and local government, and this chapter offers a critical perspective on how the 'sustainable community' is defined, operationalised and measured in planning policy and urban development.

Dixon looks at the emergence of smart and sustainable cities in Chapter 5. This chapter reviews the growth of the 'future cities' agenda in the UK and internationally, and examines the implications for the construction and development professions. The chapter also looks at how cities may evolve in the future if they are to be smart and sustainable, and what the challenges and opportunities will be looking ahead to 2050.

Tran *et al.* examine sustainable infrastructure in Chapter 6. As they point out, infrastructure systems (energy, transport, water and digital communications) are vital for modern economic activity, but are also major sources of carbon emissions and environmental impacts. The chapter reviews the state-of-the-art on infrastructure modelling and assessment for futures studies, and provides key insights for policy makers and practitioners for the analysis of sustainable infrastructure futures.

In Chapter 7 Farrelly examines sustainable design. In this chapter Farrelly offers examples of an approach to design which encourages new and reactive solutions to designing for the built environment of the future, and how design relates to its surrounding community. The chapter also touches on the nature of 'defuturing' in design.

### *Part 2: Changing Professional Practice*

This part of the book examines the way in which professional practice in the built environment, in its widest sense, is changing as technology, new business models and interpretations of sustainability evolve now and into the future.

In Chapter 8 Parker and Doak review the concept of sustainable planning, exploring its roots in planning policy and practice, its emergence as an overarching discourse and its possible trajectories into the future. The chapter provides a critique of the concept of sustainability as deployed in planning theory and practice, drawing out its definitional flexibility, contested nature and core principles.

Green examines sustainable construction in Chapter 9 and offers a critical review of key concepts in the context of contested knowledge and the decline of professionalism. In this chapter, Green reviews definitions of 'sustainable construction', 'sustainability' and the notion of 'systems thinking' in a critical vein. The chapter shows how sustainability is ultimately about making difficult trade-offs. It further recognises that making meaningful progress despite transient and conflicting objectives is an inevitable part of the work of a professional.

Connaughton and Hughes look at sustainable procurement in Chapter 10. This chapter examines the role of procurement in sustainable construction and development in terms of both buyer and supplier responsibility and governance, and in the context of recently published standards and guidance. It focuses in particular on the construction supply chain and the challenges to more sustainable procurement raised by the contemporary practice of competitive buying/contracting through multiple tiers of suppliers. The chapter envisions a future for sustainable construction by 2050 in which procurement focuses more on understanding and meeting client requirements through innovation rather than through the provision of low-cost labour and materials.

Thompson examines the changing role of social media in construction and real estate in Chapter 11. As the chapter points out, if Facebook were a country, at the start of 2015 it would be the same size as China. This indicates that social media is no longer a fringe activity for any company in any sector, but few companies have an understanding of exactly how social media interacts with consumers to expand product and brand recognition, drive sales and profitability, and engender loyalty. This chapter therefore catalogues the contribution that the different threads of social media can make to a sustainable built environment now and in the future.

### *Part 3: Provocations about the Future: Practitioners' Viewpoints*

In this part of the book practitioners set out their personal viewpoints on changing professional practice.

In Chapter 12 Ford and Gillich look at sustainable and collaborative working. The built environment established players are realising that the effective separation that has for so long served their needs may be at a tipping point. Up until now construction has delivered profit through a simple project focus, but new types of professional are required who are able to work across industries and established professions, translating and working together with a concentration on the customers' long-term experience. This chapter examines how collaboration is playing out in the design and construction professions, and the role of academia in facilitating sustainable change.

In Chapter 13 Healey examines the built environment professions and their relation-ship with the sustainability agenda. The chapter summarises why traditional economic, moralistic and information-based approaches can be inadequate to engage clients. The chapter draws upon literature from behavioural economics, judgement and decision making, green buildings and sustainability communication, as well as the author's expe riences as an engineer and sustainable building practitioner to propose a broader range of communication tools for pitching sustainability initiatives to decision makers.

### Part 4: Transformative Technologies and Innovation

Coker and Torriti examine energy and the built environment in Chapter 14. They suggest that the ways that we access, transport and use energy are changing dramati-cally in the face of technological advancement and the policy imperatives of afforda-bility, security and decarbonisation, and that variable renewable energy sources will provide a significant share of cities' energy needs by 2050. Together, these trends bring many challenges for built environment professionals, who must be able to navigate this complexity.

Larsen looks at sustainable innovation in construction and development in Chapter 15. This chapter takes the stance that transitioning to a sustainable built environment by 2050 will require innovation and change within current materials, digital technologies, processes and working practices in the construction sector. Central to the chapter is the notion that firms are rarely innovative in isolation and that for the uptake of an innova-tion to be sustained, networks of stakeholders must work together, either knowingly or unknowingly. It is then essential to gain a greater understanding of how all associated stakeholders operate in a market network and the potential impact these have on the uptake of innovations.

In Chapter 16 Ewart looks at the importance of humanising digital practices in con-struction. The chapter first explores the process of social incorporation of new tech-nologies, how they transfer from one community to another and the opportunities for innovation this presents. Second, the chapter focuses on the vast proliferation of data generated by digital technologies and the need to reframe this at a human scale to make it meaningful. In both cases Ewart suggests that the AEC sector can make a significant and optimistic contribution to our digital future.

### Part 5: Conclusions and Common Themes

Finally, in Chapter 17 we draw together the main themes and findings of the book, and anchor these against an appraisal of foresight techniques and views on the future. The chapter covers three main themes:

- *Understanding the future*: explores the nature of technology disruption and conver-gence, and the interaction with 'megatrends' to 2050, with a particular focus on their impact on construction and development.
- *What lies ahead for the built environment?*: explores the emergent lessons from the chapters in this book.
- *Shaping the future: techniques, practice and policy*: examines the importance of futures-based techniques and 'black swans', and discusses the policy and practice implications of foresight in helping to shape the built environment of the future.

# References

Alford, K., Cork, S., Finnigan, J., Grigg, N., Fulton, B. and Raupauch, M. (2014) The Challenges of Living Scenarios for Australia in 2050. *Journal of Futures Studies*, March, 18(3), 115–126.

Arup (2013) *It's Alive: Can you imagine the urban building of the future?* Arup, London.

Arup (2014) *Cities Alive: Rethinking Green Infrastructure.* Arup, London.

Arup (2015) *Green Construction Board Low Carbon Routemap for the Built Environment: 2015 Routemap Progress – Technical Report.* Arup, London.

Bok, B., Hayward, P., Roos, G. and Voros, J. (2012) *Construction 2030: A Roadmap of R&D Priorities for Australia's Built Environment.* Sustainable Built Environment National Research Centre, Brisbane. Available at: http://www.sbenrc.com.au/wp-content/uploads/2013/11/construction_2030_fullreport_4dec12.pdf (accessed March 2016).

Brundtland Commission (1987) *Our Common Future: Report of the 1987 World Commission on Environment and Development.* Oxford University Press, Oxford.

BIS (2010) *Estimating the Amount of $CO_2$ Emissions that the Construction Industry Can Influence: Supporting Material for the Low Carbon Construction IGT report.* Department for Business Innovation and Skills, London.

BIS (2013) *UK Construction: An Economic Analysis of the Sector.* Department for Business Innovation and Skills, London.

CABE/RIBA (2003) *The Professionals' Choice: The Future of the Built Environment Professions.* Commission for Architecture and the Built Environment/Royal Institute of British Architects, London.

Chan, P., Abbott, C., Cooper, R. and Aouad, G. (2005) 'Building future scenarios: a reflection for the research agenda', in Khosrowshahi, F (ed.), *21st Annual ARCOM Conference, 7–9 September, SOAS, University of London.* Association of Researchers in Construction Management, Vol. 2, pp. 709–19. SOAS, London.

Chan, P., and Cooper, R. (2011) *Constructing Futures: Industry Leaders and Futures Thinking in Construction.* Wiley-Blackwell, Oxford.

CIC (2014) *Built Environment 2050: A Report on Our Digital Future.* Construction Industry Council, London.

CITB (2015) *Construction 2030 and Beyond: The Future of Jobs and Skills in the UK Construction Sector.* Construction Industry Training Board, London.

Conway, M. (2014) *Foresight: An Introduction – A Thinking Futures Reference Guide.* Thinking Futures: Melbourne. Available at: http://thinkingfutures.net/wp-content/uploads/TFRefGuideForesight1.pdf (accessed March 2016).

Cook, D. (2015) RICS futures: turning disruption from technology to opportunity. *Journal of Property Investment & Finance*, 33 (5), 456–464.

Coyle, G. (1997) The nature and value of futures studies or do futures have a future?. *Futures*, 29 (1), 77–93.

Curry, A., Hodgson, T., Kelnar, R. and Wilson, A. (2006) *Intelligent Infrastructure Futures: The Scenarios – Towards 2055.* DTI, London.

DEFRA (2005) *Sustainable Development Strategy.* Department for Environment, Food and Rural Affairs, London.

DTI (2002) *Foresight Futures 2020 Revised Scenarios and Guidance.* Foresight/Department of Trade and Industry, London.

Dixon, T., Barlow, J., Grimmond, S. and Blower, J. (2015) *Smart and sustainable: Using Big Data to Improve Peoples' Lives in Cities*. Discussion Paper. University of Reading, Reading. ISSN 2058-975.

Dixon, T., Eames, M., Lannon, S. and Hunt, M. (eds) (2014) *Urban Retrofitting for Sustainability: Mapping the Transition to 2050*. Routledge, London.

Dodge Data and Analytics (2016) *World Green Building Trends*. Dodge Data and Analytics, Bedford, MA.

Eames, M., Dixon, T., May, T. and Hunt, M. (2013a) City futures: exploring urban retrofit and sustainable transitions. *Building Research and Information*, 41 (5), 504–516. ISSN 1466-4321.

Eames, M., Hunt, M., Dixon, T. and Britnell, J. (2013b) *Retrofit city futures: visions for urban sustainability*. Report. University of Cardiff, Cardiff.

Egan, J. (1998) *Rethinking Construction: Report of the Construction Taskforce*. Department of the Environment, Transport and the Regions, London.

Elkington, J. (1997) *Cannibals with Forks: the Triple Bottom Line of 21st Century Business*. Capstone, London.

Ellen Macarthur Foundation (2016) *Intelligent Assets*. Ellen Macarthur Foundation.

Ernst and Young (2015) *Megatrends 2015: Making Sense of a World in Motion*. Ernst and Young, London.

Fairclough, J. (2002) *A Review of Government Policies and Practices*. Department of Trade and Industry, London.

Farrell, T. (2014) *The Farrell Review of Architecture and the Built Environment*. Farrells, London. Available at: http://www.farrellreview.co.uk/.

Fernandez-Guell, J. and Gonzalez Lopez, J. (2014) Cities Futures: A Critical Assessment of How Future Studies are Applied to Cities, *5th International Conference on Future Oriented Technology Analysis (TFA – Engage Today to Shape Tomorrow)*, Brussels, 27–28 November.

Fernie, S., Leiringer, R. and Thorpe, T. (2006) Change in construction: a critical perspective. *Building Research and Information*, 34(2), 91–103.

GCP Global/Oxford Economics (2015) *Global Construction 2030: A Global Forecast for the Construction Industry to 2030*. GCP Global/Oxford Economics, London.

Godet, M. and Roubelat, F. (1996) Creating the future: The use and misuse of scenarios. *Long Range Planning*, 29(2), 164–171.

Goodier, C.I. (2013) The future(s) of construction: a sustainable built environment for now and the future, in Soutsos, M., Goodier, C., Le, T.T. and Van Nguyen, T. (eds) *The International Conference on Sustainable Built Environment for Now and the Future*, Hanoi, Vietnam, 26–27 March 2013, pp. 27–36.

Goodier, C.I., Soetanto, A., Austin, S. and Price, A. (2007) A competitive future for UK construction? *Construction Information Quarterly*, 9(4), 169–174.

Green, S.D. (2011) *Making Sense of Construction Improvement*. Wiley-Blackwell, Oxford.

Green Construction Board (2016) *Low Carbon Routemap for the Built Environment*. Green Construction Board, London. Available at: http://www.greenconstructionboard.org/index.php/resources/routemap (accessed March 2016).

Habegger, B. (2009) *Horizon Scanning in Government: Concept, Country Experiences and Models for Switzerland*. Center for Security Studies, Zurich.

Handy S.L., Boarnet M.G., Ewing R. and Killingsworth, R.E. (2002) How the built environment affects physical activity: views from urban planning. *American Journal of Preventive Medicine*, 23, 64–73.

Hansford, P. (2014) How Britain's construction industry will be transformed by 2025 – and the reasons why, *Civil Engineering*, 167(Feb), 9.

Harty, C., Goodier, C., Soetanto, R., Austin, S., Dainty, A. and Price, A.D.F. (2007) The futures of construction: A critical review of construction future studies. *Construction Management and Economics*, 25(5), 477–493.

Harvard, T. (2008) *Contemporary Property Development*. RIBA, London.

Health Canada (2002) *Natural and Built Environments*. Division of Childhood and Adolescence, Health Canada, Ottawa.

HM Government (1999) *A Better Quality of Life*. HM Government, London.

HM Government (2015a) *Digital Built Britain: Level 3 Building Information Modelling – Strategic Plan*. HM Government, London.

HM Government (2015b) *Construction 2025*. HM Government, London.

Infrastructure Projects Authority (2016) *Government Construction Strategy 2016–20*, March 2016. Infrastructure Projects Authority (Crown Copyright), London.

Jennings, M., Hirst, N. and Gambhir, A. (2011) *Reduction of Carbon Dioxide Emissions in the Global Building Sector to 2050 – Grantham Institute for Climate Change Report GR3*. Grantham Institute, London.

Jermey, D. (2015) Global markets: constructing a sustainable future worldwide, in *Building Better: Recommendations for a More Sustainable UK Construction Sector*. Westminster Sustainable Business Forum, London.

Kubeczko, K., Ravetz, J., van der Giessen, A. and Weber, M. (2011) *Screening Urban Foresights and Studies Supporting Forward Activities: What can we learn for a JPI-Urban Europe 2050+ Foresight*. European Foresight Platform, Brussels.

Latham, M. (1994) *Constructing the Team: Joint Review of Procurement and Contractual Arrangements in the United Kingdom Construction Industry*. HMSO, London.

Loveridge, D. (2009) *Foresight: The Art and Science of Anticipating the Future*. Routledge, London.

McGrail, S. and Gaziulusoy, A.I. (2014) *Using futures inquiry to create low-carbon, resilient urban futures: a review of practice, theory and process options for the Visions and Pathways project*. Working paper for the Visions and Pathways project, March 2014. V & P 2040, Melbourne. Available at: http://www.visionsandpathways.com/wp-content/uploads/2014/06/McGrail_Gaziulusoy_Futures_RB.pdf (accessed March 2016).

Miles, I. and Keenan, M. (2002) *Practical Guide to Regional Foresight in the United Kingdom*. European Commission.

Morrell, P. (2015) *Collaboration for Change: The Edge Commission Report on the Future of Professionalism*. Ove Arup/The Edge, London.

ONS (2009) *UK Standard Industrial Classification of Economic Activities 2007 (SIC 2007) Structure and explanatory notes*. Office for National Statistics, London.

Pearce, D. (2003) *The Social and Economic Value of Construction: The Construction Industry's Contribution to Sustainable Development*. nCRISP, London.

Poincare, H. (1913) *The Foundations of Science: Science and Hypothesis, The Value of Science, Science and Method (English translation)*. Science Press, London.

Rhodes, C. (2015) *Construction Industry: Statistics and Policy Briefing Paper Number 01432, 6 October*. House of Commons Library, London.

Rogers, C., Leach, J., Lombardi, D. and Cooper, R. (2012) The urban futures methodology applied to urban regeneration. *Proceedings of the Institution of Civil Engineers Engineering Sustainability*, 165(ES1), 5–20.

RICS (2015a) *Competency Framework and Real Estate Lifecycle*. Royal Institution of Chartered Surveyors, London.

RICS (2015b) *RICS Futures: Our Changing World – Let's Be Ready*. Royal Institution of Chartered Surveyors, London.

Sami Consulting/Experian (2008) *2020 Vision: The Future of Construction*. SAMI/Experian, St Andrews. Available at: http://www.cskills.org/uploads/2020VisionScenarios forconstructionskills_tcm17-11077.pdf (accessed March 2016).

Smart Cities Council (2015) *Smart Cities Readiness Guide*. Smart Cities Council, Redmon, WA.

Srinivasan, S., O'Fallon, L. and Deary, A. (2003) Creating healthy communities, healthy homes, healthy people: initiating a research agenda on the built environment and public health. *American Journal of Public Health*, 93(9), 1446–1450.

UN (2015) *World Urbanization Prospects: the 2014 Revision*. United Nations, New York.

Voros, J. (2003) A generic foresight process framework. *Foresight*, 5(1), 10–21.

Wilkinson, S. and Reed, R. (2008) *Property Development*. Routledge, London.

Wolstenholme, A. (2009) *Never Waste a Good Crisis: A Review of Progress since Rethinking Construction and Thoughts for Our Future*. Constructing Excellence, London.

WBCSD (2008) *Energy Efficiency in Buildings*. World Business Council for Sustainable Development, Geneva.

**Part 1**

**Sustainability and the Built Environment**

# 2

# Climate Change, Resilience and the Built Environment

*Janet F. Barlow, Li Shao and Stefan Thor Smith*

## 2.1 Introduction

In the fight against climate change it has been claimed that 'the built environment is in the front line of the battle to cut carbon emissions as far as possible, and as fast as possible' (UK-GBC, 2008). The built environment and the professions that create and manage it face many challenges: growing and ageing populations, water and energy shortages, air quality, a globalised and increasingly competitive construction sector, changing governance and increasing reliance on ICT infrastructure. Adapting to or mitigating against climate change can be hard to define, let alone act on, and industry leaders have been sceptical about a 'low-carbon agenda' (Chan and Cooper, 2010).

While future climate predictions will always be uncertain, present-day weather extremes cause big problems requiring swift action and serious reflection on city system management processes. Cities regularly grind to a halt due to flooding, wind storms, heavy snowfall, etc. but it is high temperatures that particularly depend on building design. The widespread European heatwave of summer 2003 caused the deaths of at least 35,000 people, many of whom lived in large cities, 2000 being UK nationals. It was deemed to be the worst natural disaster for 50 years, but given the recognition that poor-quality buildings in large urban areas played a significant role, it resulted from a combination of both natural and man-made factors. Certainly, the event prompted a mass of research and policy-making to analyse which elements of built infrastructure cause widespread overheating, and how overheating can be mitigated or adapted to. Aside from global climate change, it is increasingly being recognised that expansion or densification of cities can also cause warming due to microclimate change.

As large amounts of energy are used in heating and cooling buildings, any options for adapting the built environment to a warmer future should also mitigate against further climate change. This chapter describes dynamic thermal simulation (DTS) as a modelling tool to aid building design and adaptation planning, and latest developments to integrate it within long-term city master-planning tools.

*Sustainable Futures in the Built Environment to 2050: A Foresight Approach to Construction and Development*, First Edition. Edited by Tim Dixon, John Connaughton and Stuart Green.
© 2018 John Wiley & Sons Ltd. Published 2018 by John Wiley & Sons Ltd.

## 2.2   Hot in the city: urbanisation and changing urban climates

The built environment is of increasing importance because the majority of the world's population now lives in urban areas. From 2008 onwards, more than 50% of the world's population was urban and by 2050 this figure is estimated to rise to 67% (UN_DESA, 2015). Economic factors drive urbanisation, and most of the world's activities generating gross domestic product (GDP) are also concentrated in urban areas (Satterthwaite *et al.*, 2010). Thus, cities provide enormous opportunities for tackling climate adaptation and mitigation due to their resources and relatively agile governance, but due to large populations and concentration of assets, the exposure to climate risk is large (Field *et al.*, 2014). In the UK, the population is highly urbanised already, being 83% in 2015 (UN_DESA, 2015), but major cities are expected to expand further. For example, Greater London's population was 8.2 million in 2011, estimated to rise to 9.2 million by 2021, and to 10.7 million by 2041 (GLA, 2015a).

In the UK, the Climate Impacts Programme (UKCIP; Hedger *et al.*, 2006) has provided a means for understanding the implications of climate projections. The climate projections used are due to the UK Met Office Hadley Centre for Climate Research, running their HadGCM model (Murphy *et al.*, 2007, 2009). In turn, the Climate Change Risk Assessment (CCRA) is done every 5 years to assess in which sectors and on what timescale climate change will have an effect (DEFRA, 2012). Despite uncertainty in climate change projections, there are certain trends for the UK that are anticipated and concomitant risks that are a high priority. The UK will continue to be vulnerable to extreme weather events such as severe winters, heatwaves, flooding and storms. Summer temperatures for the south-east of England are set to increase by 1 to 8 °C by 2080s, depending on the assumed emissions scenario (Murphy *et al.*, 2009). Winter rainfall is projected to increase, in particular the number of days with heavy rain. Sea level in the vicinity of London could increase by 20–70 cm, and potentially by as much as 190 cm. The CCRA has also been done on a regional basis to take account of variations in climate and risk: for London, urban overheating and surface water flooding due to heavy convective rainfall are the biggest climate risks at the present time (ClimateUK, 2012).

The other important trend for the UK concerns the building stock. 26 million buildings existed in 2008: by 2050 it is estimated that 75–85% of the current building stock will still be in use (Dowson *et al.*, 2012). This shows that the main challenge will be adaptation of existing buildings, rather than redesigning new buildings (although this is also important). The emphasis on UK dwelling refurbishment to date has concentrated on reducing energy use and $CO_2$ emissions during the heating season, for example by increasing loft and wall insulation. However, there has been increasing evidence pointing to the need for a more holistic approach. Climate change projections show an increase in both the frequency and severity of extreme weather events, including heatwaves. Future retrofit planning therefore needs to take account of not only winter thermal performance and associated $CO_2$ emissions, but also the need to reduce summer overheating to provide a safe and comfortable environment in a changing climate.

While climate change on a regional scale around a city might cause warming, city expansion or densification will also cause microclimate change. Buildings don't just withstand climate, they create it. Luke Howard was the first scientist to discover the urban heat island (UHI) (Howard, 1833): the average temperature between 1801 and 1841 in London was approximately 1 °C above the rural temperature. He also correctly identified some of the mechanisms causing it: materials such as stone and brick absorb the sun's heat during the day and release it slowly at night, heat is trapped/re-radiated between buildings, and wind that could remove heat is slowed by the city.

London's UHI was studied again in the 1960s (Chandler, 1965), prompted by concern about the toxic London smogs of the early 1950s that led to the Clean Air Act in 1956. Chandler drove a vehicle with meteorological equipment across London overnight, allowing contour maps of temperature to be constructed. They showed a strong relationship with land use, with more densely developed areas showing the highest temperatures, but also that the city centre was warmer than the sub-urban perimeter. For a city the size of London, the intensity of the UHI (measured in degrees difference from a rural site) was related to its size, a feature later quantified by Oke (1973) in terms of population and building density. Recognising that building designers needed hard data on London's UHI, the Building Research Establishment (BRE) conducted measurements of temperature at 80 sites across the city in 1999–2000 (Watkins *et al.*, 2002). During heatwave conditions the city was up to 6 °C warmer than the rural surroundings, and identical houses across London were shown to perform differently in terms of the balance of heating and cooling energy use.

## 2.3 Policies and guidelines in the UK relating to climate change and the built environment

With expanding urban populations and the threat of climate change at global and regional scales, it has been clear in the UK that re-design and adaptation of urban areas is a key priority not only for government, but also architects, engineers, urban planners and the general population.

### 2.3.1 Climate change policy at national and city scale

In the UK there have been various policies to reduce $CO_2$ emissions from the built environment sector. The Climate Change Act of 2008 was world-leading in committing the UK to 80% reduction (relative to a 1990 baseline) in $CO_2$ emissions by 2050, and at least 34% by 2020. At the COP21 Climate Summit in Paris in December 2015, 195 countries (including the UK) signed an agreement which aims to limit global warming to 2 degrees. The Climate Change Act led to responsibility for the Department for Environment, Farming and Rural Affairs (DEFRA) to perform the CCRA, to be updated every 5 years (DEFRA, 2012). Table 2.1 outlines the development of policy related to the built environment with respect to climate change mitigation measures.

In 2014 the Adaptation Sub-Committee of the UK Committee on Climate Change (CCC) highlighted overheating buildings as a growing risk: one-fifth of current homes in the UK had potential to overheat, with apartments at particular risk, having increased from 15% in 1996 to 40% of new builds. Care homes and hospitals were also found to be overheating in the present climate. The CCC's Progress Report to Parliament in July 2015

**Table 2.1** UK national policy measures influencing the energy efficiency of buildings and climate change mitigation.

| Year | Law/policy/regulation/report | Outcome |
| --- | --- | --- |
| 2006 | Climate Change and Sustainable Energy Act | Energy efficiency of buildings, cutting $CO_2$ emissions |
| 2006 | Building Regulations | Extended to include Eurocodes requiring building energy to be measured |
| | | New approved documents for Parts F and L |
| 2006 | Code for Sustainable Homes | Government announces all domestic new buildings to be zero carbon by 2016 (level 6) |
| 2006 | Review of the sustainability of existing buildings | DCLG report identifies lack of adequate insulation in UK dwellings |
| 2007 | Building a Greener Future: Policy Statement | Progressive tightening of building regulations to achieve 2016 goal: 25% by 2010, 44% by 2013 |
| 2008 | Climate Change Act | Binding national targets for $CO_2$ emission reduction |
| 2008 | Budget | Government announces all non-domestic new buildings to be zero carbon by 2019 |
| 2010 | Building Regulations | Rewritten |
| 2012 | Energy Performance of Buildings (England and Wales) | National Calculation Method for buildings other than dwellings |
| 2015 | Fixing the foundations: creating a more prosperous nation | 'Allowable solutions' carbon offsetting scheme and 2016 target for level 6 homes scrapped |

DCLG, Department of Communities and Local Government.

called for a new standard to prevent overheating in new homes and to introduce passive cooling measures in existing buildings.

However, in summer 2015 the UK government under the Conservative Party published *Fixing the foundations: creating a more prosperous nation*, in which the 2016 target for all new domestic buildings to be zero carbon and 'allowable solutions' carbon off-setting schemes were scrapped. The reason given by the Department for Communities and Local Government was that new housing developments would be accelerated, given the housing crisis at the time (Pickles, 2015). The UK Green Building Council and BSRIA Ltd[1], as well as 200 signatories to an open letter sent to the Chancellor, were highly critical of the move as industry had geared up to producing energy-efficient homes over the previous decade. In April 2016 the House of Lords voted in favour of an amendment in the new Housing and Planning Bill that would effectively revive the zero-carbon homes standard by requiring the government to ensure 'all new homes in England built from 1 April 2018 achieve the carbon compliance standard'. The Chief Executive of the Federation of Master Builders, Brian Berry, saw such regulation as 'heavy-handed' and suggested that further $CO_2$ reduction onsite

---

1 BSRIA Ltd is an organisation that provides testing, instrumentation and research consultancy to construction and building services.

would be 'difficult-to-impossible to achieve', amounting to a tax to enable off-site $CO_2$ emission mitigation and therefore burdensome to SME house builders. When the Bill returned to the House of Commons in May 2016, the Government sought to reject the carbon compliance amendment, and the House of Lords insisted on keeping it. The impasse was resolved with the Government proposing to take on a statutory duty to undertake a review of energy standards in new homes, and the Bill became an Act of Parliament in May 2016.

Governance at city scale can lead to stronger policy actions: cities with mayors such as London have developed adaptation strategies with constraints on development that might worsen the UHI. Following the 2003 heatwave, the Greater London Authority commissioned research leading to a report on London's UHI (GLA, 2006). Subsequently, there was greater recognition that the so-called Central Activity Zone (CAZ) of the city, where buildings are most densely packed, requires amended planning guidelines to deal with higher temperatures. A Climate Change Action Plan followed in 2007 (GLA, 2007), leading to an adaptation strategy in 2011 that included a target to increase urban vegetation by 10% in the CAZ as a cooling strategy. The adaptation strategy was cited several times in the Intergovernmental Panel on Climate Change (IPCC) report of 2015 (Revi *et al.*, 2014) as a good example of megacity action on climate change. In 2011 a climate change mitigation strategy (GLA, 2011) was also published, focusing on the future energy system for the city, followed by 2015's Energy Planning report (GLA, 2015b). The latter included a 'cooling hierarchy' that ranked measures to reduce energy demand for cooling, from reducing internal heat gain and using passive design with mechanical ventilation as a last resort. It was also recognised that waste heat from air-conditioning units can raise urban temperatures, and thus outlets were to be placed above roof level. Much of the research highlighted in Section 4 influenced these measures and the use of DTS to assess overheating risk was strongly encouraged.

### 2.3.2 Guidelines relating to the built environment

The extent to which city infrastructure is resilient to climate change depends on the success of implementing mitigation and adaptation plans. As an example, certification schemes for benchmarking sustainability of construction have been developed (LEED (US) and BREEAM (UK)) and adopted worldwide to encourage greater whole lifecycle resource efficiency. In the UK the Simplified Building Energy Model (SBEM) is a software tool developed by the BRE (BRE, 2013) that calculates monthly energy use and $CO_2$ emissions of a building given a description of the building geometry, construction, use, heating, ventilation and air conditioning (HVAC), and lighting equipment, and compares the output with a notional building. The SBEM is used for non-domestic buildings in support of the National Calculation Methodology (NCM), the Energy Performance of Buildings Directive (EPBD) and the Green Deal policies. Currently (2016) the tool is used to determine $CO_2$ emission rates for new buildings in compliance with Part L of the Building Regulations (England and Wales) and equivalent regulations in Scotland, Northern Ireland, the Republic of Ireland and Jersey. It is also used to generate energy performance certificates for non-domestic buildings on construction and at the point of sale or rent. As such, it is a compliance procedure and not a design tool, that is, it cannot predict the internal temperatures of a building.

## 2.4 Climate adaptation options: modelling tomorrow's buildings today

To test building performance in terms of thermal comfort, DTS models allow interior temperatures to be simulated, given external weather conditions, and are typically run for a year. As they include heating and cooling elements, the resulting energy use can also be estimated. DTS is incorporated in the LEED and BREEAM certification schemes, not only to demonstrate an effective and efficient heating and cooling design, but also to understand the adaptive capacity of design and operation under climate change. This section outlines the basic principles of DTS, reports on a case study of building adaptation for London in a heatwave, and considers how the effects of climate change and urban heat islands can be taken into account.

### 2.4.1 DTS for building design

#### 2.4.1.1 Physical processes captured in DTS modelling approaches

Figure 2.1 shows the heat flows between a building and its environment that control indoor temperature. In any DTS model it is likely that conduction through the building fabric, solar gain and heat loss by radiation, convection of heat away from external surfaces, internal heat sources (e.g. people), air infiltration, ventilation, and heating and cooling systems are represented to determine the temperature and humidity within a building, as well as the energy used to obtain comfortable indoor conditions. Heat and mass transfer (i.e. moisture) processes are the fundamental building blocks of any DTS, but the way in which they are represented in a model varies from detailed analytical representations of heat transfer to simplified models that 'lump' building components together and use the theory of electrical resistance and capacitance as an analogy to thermal resistance and thermal store.

Underwood and Yik (2004) provide a detailed account of the physical processes captured by DTS and the different modelling approaches used in available tools.

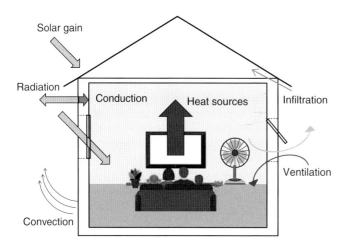

**Figure 2.1** Schematic of heat flows in a building.

In Chapter 7 of their book the different methods are clearly summarised by range of application (utility), detail needed for modelling (rigour) and computational expense (cost). A review of the capabilities of 20 of the most comprehensive models (Crawley *et al.*, 2008) showed varying capability, even between tools that superficially state the same capability. Given this variability in DTS models, one recommendation was that using a suite of tools would provide a more robust methodology in energy and comfort assessment over the current practice of using a single tool.

### 2.4.1.2 Input weather data for DTS models

DTS models require hourly weather data as inputs to calculate heating and cooling loads over a whole year. To evaluate building performance under current climatic conditions, at least 30 years of data from meteorological observation sites are required. Statistically representative, artificial weather years are generated to provide typical conditions or highlight years with high-impact weather events, such as heatwaves (Levermore and Parkinson, 2006). The climatological average is captured in typical meteorological years (TMYs) or test reference years (TRYs), and extreme heat in design summer years (DSYs). TRYs are intended for simulations to assess annual energy consumption, whereas DSYs are used to test overheating risk in naturally ventilated and passively controlled buildings.

Longstanding, high-quality observation sites are limited in number and usually situated outside cities in order to meet World Meteorological Organisation (WMO) standards. To increase the geographical coverage of weather data, observational records with fewer than 30 years have been used, with ASHRAE[2] in the US providing over 3000 weather files for energy calculation across the world (Huang *et al.*, 2014).

### 2.4.1.3 Taking climate change into account in DTS: 'morphing' and climate projections

The use of artificial weather years based on present-day climate statistics is increasingly of limited value as the climate changes. Buildings constructed today are likely to be in use for several decades, and so will be operating in a significantly changed climate. How can climate change influenced weather files for DTS modelling be generated?

Climate model data such as the UKCIP 2002 projections (released as UKCP02; Hulme *et al.*, 2002) can be used to develop future climate weather files for building energy simulation using a technique known as 'morphing'. Morphing uses regional monthly climate change factors for given weather variables and applies them to weather files representing the baseline climate. This is done by 'shifting' (where the monthly mean is increased by an absolute value), 'stretching' (where monthly mean and variance are multiplied by a change factor) or a combination of the two (Belcher *et al.*, 2005).

While such work leads to much-needed design data, it is acknowledged that uncertainty is inherent in climate projections and is an important consideration in impact and resilience assessment (Mastrandrea and Schneider, 2004). Subsequent advances in climate modelling (Collins, 2007) have enabled probabilistic climate change risk assessment. Probabilistic projections result from carrying out an ensemble of climate model

---

2 ASHRAE is the American society that leads through its membership on issues of building development, services and wider built environment sustainability issues (https://www.ashrae.org/about-ashrae). ASHRAE used to be an acronym, but it isn't any longer.

runs, each one perturbing model parameters by a likely error, as well as running multiple climate models to account for different modelling approaches. The uncertainty in $CO_2$ emissions into the future is kept separate, with projections being produced for low, medium and high emissions scenarios (Meehl *et al.*, 2007) and for seven overlapping 30-year time-slices (2020s through to 2080s). In 2009, UKCIP were the first to provide probabilistic climate projections, known as UKCP09. This probabilistic approach was intended for decision-makers, designers and planners to account for risk and uncertainty in the resilience of systems undergoing impact assessment (Jenkins *et al.*, 2009). Tools such as the US Climate Resilience Toolkit and those in Europe found under the European Climate Adaptation Platform (http://climate-adapt.eea.europa.eu) help to highlight the risks of climate change to our built infrastructure.

Under the UK Adaptation and Resilience in the Context of Change (ARCC) Coordination Network (http://www.arcc-network.org.uk), approximately 30 research projects have been using the probabilistic climate change projections to understand the implications for the built environment. These projects range from city level resilience to overheating risk in buildings, with some projects focusing on health and well-being impacts. When considering the resilience of city infrastructure the spatial and temporal scales relevant to system behaviour must be considered (Dawson, 2015). For example, modelling a district heating network requires representation of the weather across the city on an hourly timescale. For the case of UKCP09, hourly weather data is produced by using a statistical weather generator based on data interpolated to a resolution of $5 \times 5$ km grid-squares from observation sites across the UK (Perry *et al.*, 2005). However, the heterogeneity of cities makes it very difficult for interpolation to capture accurately different microclimates within cities, and very few city observations exist (Smoliak *et al.*, 2015).

Using a weather generator to provide a 30-year baseline climate to which projections can be applied means that data are not spatiotemporally consistent (i.e. weather files at different locations are not realistically correlated). If spatiotemporal consistency is required then applying the projections to observed data would be one option, the main limitation here being the spatial resolution of observations. However, if looking at isolated buildings, the combination of weather generator and projections is appropriate.

#### 2.4.1.4 CIBSE and GLA guidelines on weather data

Probabilistic climate change projections represent a significant step forward in climate impact assessment. There is still an underlying question of whether industry can yet use probabilistic projections effectively. Two key factors to address are (i) the supporting infrastructure to handle and analyse large data sets, and (ii) the appropriate expertise to properly evaluate and communicate the statistical output of probabilistic analysis. Although risk assessment is a core process in financial and insurance services, engineering firms are often guided by thresholds and best practice as set out by professional bodies. In terms of overheating buildings, two UK institutions played a significant role in this regard.

In the UK, weather files have been supplied by the Chartered Institution for Building Service Engineers (CIBSE). Due to growing recognition of climate change during the lifetime of a building, the question arose as to how to modify the weather files. CIBSE published a Technical Memorandum (TM36) in 2005 (CIBSE, 2005) that presented a morphing methodology, combining existing weather data with increasing temperatures as given in UKCIP scenarios (Belcher *et al.*, 2005). The work behind TM36 included simulations of future internal temperatures assuming different adaptation interventions, to assess energy use and overheating exposure (Holmes and Hacker, 2007). In 2009 CIBSE issued TM48, in which future weather files were made available for the UK following the morphing methodology.

The GLA also recognised that these weather files were still not sufficient in capturing London's UHI. The city centre could be 4 °C warmer than the edge on a warm summer evening, and up to 10 °C warmer during a heatwave. A piece of commissioned research resulted in additional guidance for London (TM49; Hacker *et al.*, 2014), where analysis of existing weather data led to the recommended use of three sites across London representing rural, sub-urban and central urban temperatures. It was also deduced that the DSY of 1989 was reasonable in terms of the degree of thermal discomfort likely to be experienced, but that its return period in the future was likely to be too small, and that 1976 and 2003 were also to be considered.

### 2.4.2 Using DTS to study building adaptation to climate change: the CREW project

As part of the ARCC network, a recently completed UK research project called Community Resilience to Extreme Weather (CREW) (Hallett, 2013) used DTS to quantify the effect of a range of single and combined passive adaptations on thermal comfort during a heatwave period, as well as minimising winter heating energy and considering retro fit cost. The DTS model EnergyPlus (Crawley *et al.*, 2008; DoE, 2016) was used to assess and rank the effectiveness of passive adaptations (interventions) for a range of common UK dwelling types, as shown in Figure 2.2: a 19th century Victorian terraced house, a 1930s semi-detached house, 1960s blocks of flats and a modern detached house built to 2006 Part L building regulations. Building orientation to the sun and occupancy profiles were also tested, namely, daytime-occupied dwellings (e.g. those used by elderly people or carers with children) or daytime-unoccupied (e.g. a family where all members leave the house for work or school each weekday).

Three options were considered for weather files: (i) future weather data, developed using a morphing methodology as used in CIBSE TM36, (ii) actual weather data from a warmer European city, to approximate the predicted future UK climate, and (iii) data from actual UK heat wave periods from 1976, 1995 and 2003 (Porritt *et al.*, 2012). The results below are based on the third option, using 2003 weather data, because using European weather data was not acceptable as certain aspects of the data, for example

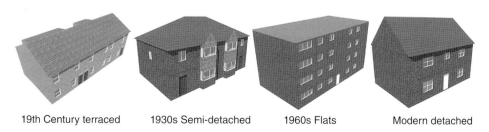

| 19th Century terraced | 1930s Semi-detached | 1960s Flats | Modern detached |

**Figure 2.2** UK dwelling types simulated during the CREW project using DTS model EnergyPlus.

solar altitudes, were not appropriate for the UK. In addition, methodology 1 as used in CIBSE TM36 is in need of further improvement as it did not yield a heatwave as severe as that of 2003.

### 2.4.2.1 Effectiveness of single adaptation measures in reducing overheating exposure

There are two 'tiers' of building types in terms of overheating exposure. Tier 1 includes the 1930s, 1960s and 19th century houses. Figure 2.3 shows that Tier 1 buildings typically experience less than half the overheating exposure of Tier 2 buildings, which include the 1960s top-floor flat and the modern detached house. It is not surprising for the top-floor flat to overheat significantly but it is not satisfactory for the modern building to perform badly. It has been suggested that improved insulation and air tightness regulations guard well against cold but can lead to overheating.

Across all building types studied, daytime-occupied dwellings experienced much higher overheating exposure than those occupied only in the evenings. This difference in overheating exposure is greater in Tier 1 building types. The overheating exposure associated with daytime occupancy was up to twice as much as for daytime-unoccupied dwellings. This makes the elderly and infirm more vulnerable. The results also suggest that it would be better to avoid housing the elderly and infirm in dwellings vulnerable to overheating.

Many passive methods and technologies exist to help adapt dwellings to minimise overheating exposure. The CREW project found that external shutters are the single most effective adaptation for almost all house types considered, resulting typically in a 50% reduction of overheating exposure. External shutters should be integrated in future window designs and installed systematically at the time of window replacement. Figure 2.4 shows that the only exception was daytime-unoccupied terraced

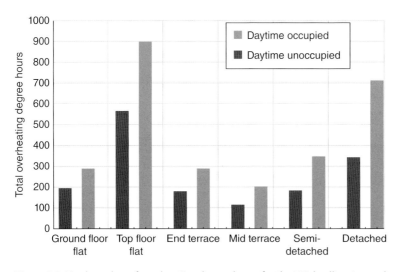

**Figure 2.3** Total number of overheating degree hours for the UK dwelling types shown in Figure 2.2. Two types of occupant behaviour are tested: daytime occupied (e.g. carers at home with children, elderly people) and daytime unoccupied (e.g. people out at work or school).

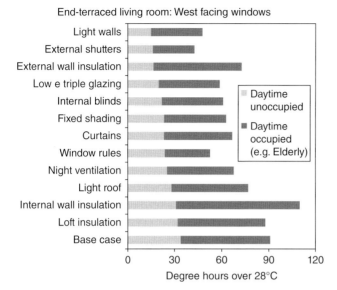

**Figure 2.4** Comparison of overheating exposure (measured in degree hours over threshold temperature) for single adaptation interventions with the base case with no adaptations at the bottom of the chart. Example is for an end-terraced house living room with west-facing windows and ordered in terms of daytime unoccupied results.

houses: their solid walls facilitate conduction of solar heat inwards and so highly reflective, light-coloured walls could be more effective than shutters.

The CREW results also demonstrate the value of behavioural (zero cost) adaptations. Figure 2.4 shows that 'window rules', whereby the building users refrain from opening windows when the outside temperature is higher than the indoor temperature, could result in a 30% reduction in overheating exposure for daytime-occupied dwellings compared to the base case with no intervention. Other behaviour-related adaptations include closing internal blinds or curtains and using night ventilation. Their effectiveness depends on correct operation, which may require education.

Caution is needed in the selection of insulation for future retrofit projects. External insulation consistently outperforms internal insulation in reducing overheating exposure for all considered dwelling types, occupancies and orientations. Furthermore, Figure 2.4 shows that internal insulation could lead to worse overheating for the daytime-occupied case than the base case with no adaptation. However, internal wall insulation is still useful if combined with other adaptations, and is considered in the next section.

### 2.4.2.2 Contrasting effectiveness and cost of combined passive adaption measures

Figure 2.4 shows that no single adaptation measure can eliminate overheating exposure. All compatible combinations (approximately 100,000 in total) of the passive adaptations were simulated. The process was automated through a parametric control interface (jEPlus), using a cluster of parallel processors.

For Tier 1 dwelling types, it was found that overheating could be eliminated using certain combinations of adaptations, although low-cost interventions often led to greater winter energy use. However, certain win–win combinations were also identified. For example, for a semi-detached house combined adaptations costing £3k resulted in an 85% reduction in overheating and up to 20% reduction in winter heating energy use. Better performance is achievable through more expensive interventions, for example combined adaptations costing £10k resulted in a 95% reduction in overheating and over 40% reduction in winter heating energy use. Costs and performances were broadly similar for other Tier 1 buildings.

The performance of adaptations applied to Tier 2 buildings is dramatically different. Generally, Tier 2 buildings are harder to treat. Overheating exposure could not be eliminated using any of the combined adaptations. The modern detached house is already well insulated and it is much harder to find adaptations that would lead to a reduction in winter heating energy use: indeed, most adaptations resulted in greater winter energy use. Furthermore, adaptation costs are much higher than for Tier 1. For example, adaptations achieving similar overheating reduction cost £23k for the detached house compared with only £3k for the semi-detached house.

DTS permits analysis of the main design elements causing overheating (Porritt *et al.*, 2012). Top-floor flats overheat due to solar gain through the roof, which is understandable. More surprising is how much the modern houses overheat due to heat being trapped internally. High levels of insulation should be retained for energy efficiency, although the appropriate type should be adopted, together with solar control and other measures. This prompts the question that if older houses were retrofitted to reduce $CO_2$,

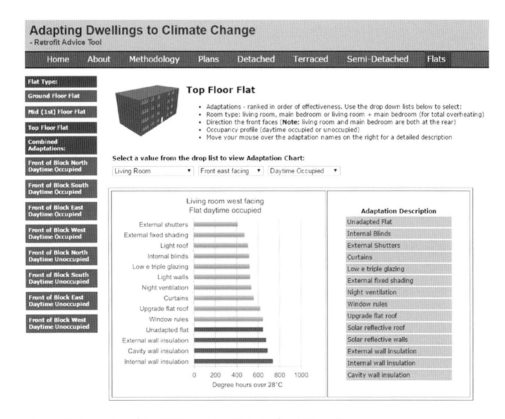

**Figure 2.5** Screenshot of the CREW project online retrofit advice toolkit.

for example by having comparable standards of thermal insulation and air tightness as modern detached houses, would they overheat as much? CREW simulations have indicated that this is indeed the case (Hallett *et al.*, 2013). It follows that unless adaptation is integrated with mitigation in the retrofit of existing dwellings, the result could be a building stock that overheats and becomes harder and more expensive to treat. Worse, if occupants of overheating dwellings opt for energy-intensive air conditioning as a quick (and often cheaper) fix, the mitigation objective would be compromised too.

For occupants weighing up options in the face of competing factors, including their own experience of heatwaves, making choices that also mitigate climate change is very difficult. An interactive retrofit advice toolkit was developed through the CREW project and is available at www.iesd.dmu.ac.uk/crew to allow informed selection of optimal adaptations for dwellings. Figure 2.5 shows a screenshot of the toolkit, which allows a user to navigate thousands of simulation results in a relatively simple way. By selecting a dwelling type and orientation, the effect of single adaptations on overheating can be compared. For example, the top and ground floors of the same block of flats would require different solutions.

An important part of the web-based toolkit is the scatter plots, as illustrated in Figure 2.6, which can be used to assess the best combined adaptations in terms of cost and energy use. To reduce overheating users should choose points in the area under the

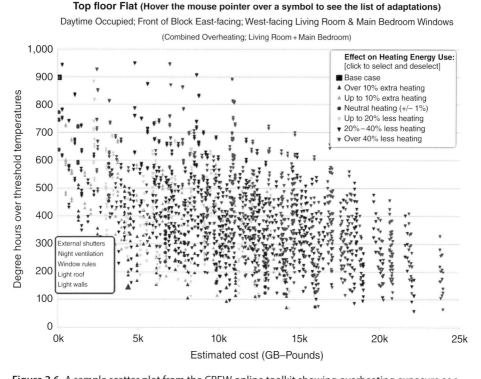

**Figure 2.6** A sample scatter plot from the CREW online toolkit showing overheating exposure as a function of cost for a large range of combined adaptations. Heating energy use change is indicated by marker type. The base case is the black square in the top left corner. Each point is one possible set of adaptations: in the interactive online version, the text box in the bottom left is revealed when the mouse hovers over a point.

grey band, which includes the best performing adaptations at various costs. Each point is a set of combined adaptations, the detail of which is revealed when the mouse is hovered over the point. To avoid additional winter heating, only points indicated as 'neutral heating' or 'less heating' should be chosen. The toolkit thus provides insights into the relationships between overheating exposure, adaptation performance, cost, construction type, occupancy and orientation.

### 2.4.3 Active but climate appropriate technologies: mechanical cooling

Designing buildings to minimise mechanical cooling requirements through passive design measures has to be offset by the need for buildings to be energy efficient and comfortable under current climate conditions. Such mixed-mode control depends not only on the passive design elements, but also the mechanical cooling technology (Smith *et al.*, 2011).

Hanby and Smith (2012) noted that the UKCP09 climate projections showed not only a rise in temperature for south-east England by 2050, but a concomitant decrease in relative humidity. In certain locations a decrease in relative humidity provides the opportunity for low-energy evaporative cooling technology to be used. Water scarcity might be a constraint but the study shows that both passive *and* active cooling technologies benefit from climate-sensitive design.

Mechanical cooling typically has a shorter life expectancy than passive design measures and so as the climate changes mechanical cooling technology may be updated. Assessing the changes in operational advantage of some technologies over others helps to inform on innovation for resilience, policy and appropriate government support for future low-energy technology.

## 2.5 New approaches: combining city growth, weather and building energy models

### 2.5.1 Simulating the UHI

DTS has become embedded as a tool to simulate individual buildings or classes of buildings scaled up to the entire building stock (Mavrogianni *et al.*, 2012). However, DTS cannot replicate the impact of the buildings themselves on the local microclimate. If a building façade is made more reflective, solar radiation is redirected towards ground level or other buildings, leading to heat gains. If air-conditioning units are installed, waste heat can raise temperatures within a neighbourhood. A different modelling approach is needed to simulate the microclimatic impact of buildings.

Global climate models (GCMs) that generate climate change projections incorporate the physical processes of heat transfer at the Earth's surface: incoming solar radiation is conducted into the ground, evaporates water and drives plant growth. In turn, the warmed ground heats the air above, driving convection, which influences cloud formation. Some materials with high heat capacity, such as stone or concrete, can store heat to re-radiate as longwave radiation later into the night. These processes are modelled using surface energy balance schemes, models capturing similar physical processes to those present in DTS models at the scale of a single building, and yielding surface temperature as an output.

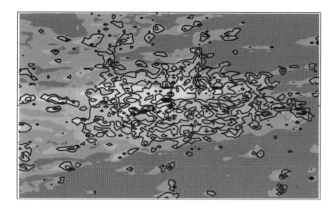

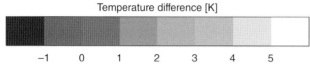

Temperature difference [K]

−1  0  1  2  3  4  5

**Figure 2.7** London's UHI, as simulated using the UK Met Office forecast model. Shades of grey show the difference (in degrees Kelvin) between a simulation with and without London. Contours indicate the built-up fraction in each 1 km² model grid-box from 0 to 1 in increments of 0.2.

GCMs are designed to capture the world's weather in a computer program that is efficient enough to be run on a daily basis by major meteorological services. The models have to be run with a coarse grid resolution of order 50–100 km, and thus cities are barely resolved. Numerical weather prediction (NWP) models are run several times per day on a more limited domain but with higher resolution to capture the weather at the scale of individual countries. Model resolution is typically 1–10 km, and with increasing computing power is resolving much finer features. London, which is 50 km across, is now well resolved in the daily weather forecast from the UK Met Office, which has a grid resolution of 1.5 km, and its UHI is clearly visible (Barlow *et al.*, 2015).

Through the LUCID project (Davies, 2010), simulations of London's UHI were carried out using a modified version of the UK Met Office's NWP model, the unified model (Bohnenstengel *et al.*, 2011). Complex heat exchange between the urban surface and the atmosphere was simplified enough to be included (Harman *et al.*, 2004; Harman and Belcher 2006; Porson *et al.*, 2010). The resulting simulations showed the UHI to be highly dynamic, changing throughout a diurnal cycle and dependent on weather conditions. Figure 2.7 shows a snapshot of London's UHI at 8pm on 7 May 2008, when there was an easterly wind: it can be seen that whilst warmer temperatures are associated with the most built-up areas, towns and villages to the west of London are also affected by heat blown downstream, showing that large megacities can produce regional climate change. The model was used to explore the reduction in UHI achievable using different policy scenarios of city greening.

Increase in model resolution has driven much activity in developing urban surface energy balance schemes for better urban weather forecasting. A recent international intercomparison of around 30 such schemes (Grimmond *et al.*, 2010, 2011) showed that much progress has been made in capturing the radiative impact of the urban surface, but that urban vegetation could be better represented, as could heat release due to traffic and HVAC systems. Given that models are currently weak in areas where policies are popular (e.g. increasing urban vegetation to provide cooling), model development and testing remain a high priority.

### 2.5.2   Coupling building energy models and numerical weather prediction

In recent years there has been increasing use of high-resolution NWP models as tools in city master planning for climate adaptation, allowing policies to increase greening (Bohnenstengel, 2011) or implement cooling ventilation pathways (Chen *et al.*, 2011) to be tested quantitatively. The European 2003 heatwave disaster drove research into how mass uptake of air conditioning could affect future heatwaves in Paris. Given the positive feedback that arises as more people retrofit HVAC that expels waste heat, warms neighbourhoods and thus makes it harder to cool buildings, how much was the city likely to warm, in particular during heatwave scenarios? Also, air conditioning is certainly effective for relieving heat stress, but how much additional energy would be consumed?

Very simple representations of this positive feedback were included in modelling work by Kikegawa *et al.* (2003). They estimated increases in urban street temperatures in Tokyo of 7–9 °C per unit area and kilowatts of expelled heat from HVAC systems. Their model was necessarily simple and could not include passive design measures such as shutters on windows or more sophisticated HVAC systems. The Town Energy Balance (TEB) surface scheme (Masson, 2000) was coupled to a mesoscale model (MESO-NH) to estimate the impact of different air-conditioning scenarios in Paris (Tremeac *et al.*, 2012; De Munck *et al.*, 2013a). Energy demand was simply modelled by a constant indoor temperature of 26 °C, with additional HVAC heat being added directly. Similar to earlier studies (Kikegawa *et al.*, 2003; Salamanca *et al.*, 2014) different HVAC systems led to an increase in street-level temperature of between 0.5 and 2 °C. Scenarios included a doubling of dry air conditioning, a combination of dry and wet cooling towers, and a district cooling system where waste heat was delivered into the ground or into the river Seine.

*En route* to simulating climate adaptation in Paris using a fully coupled BEM-TEB-Meso-NH system, several steps were taken by Bueno and co-authors. Initially coupling TEB to EnergyPlus (Bueno *et al.*, 2011), simulations of energy demand for heating and cooling were evaluated against data measured for Toulouse (Pigeon *et al.*, 2007). Simplifying the BEM was necessary for integration with both surface scheme and mesoscale models (Bueno *et al.* 2012a,b), with a final version including simplified versions of five different types of residential building commonly found in Paris (Pigeon *et al.*, 2014). Alongside the development of coupled BEM-TEB, the TEB model was modified to include green roofs (De Munck *et al.*, 2013b).

Such consistent development of modelling tools permits the latest, state-of-the-art models to quantify the impacts of urbanisation alongside climate change adaptation. Masson *et al.* (2014) proposed a fully integrated modelling environment, coupling economy, urban planning and architectural models with TEB, BEM and a simplified model of the boundary layer (Bueno *et al.*, 2013) instead of the full mesoscale model. This is a more sophisticated approach than using fixed scenarios for city growth and modelling only their climatic impacts. Careful validation of each component model was performed as far as available data would allow. Energy use data for Paris was available from 1998 to 2008 and the modelling system captured total annual energy use to within 5%, as well as capturing year-to-year variability due to climate fluctuations.

In addition to studying Paris, Masson *et al.* (2014) used Toulouse (in the south of France) for an adaptation study to 2100 under the assumption of 2, 4 or 6 °C of warming. Seven systemic scenarios were devised, showing different city development pathways in terms of economy, attractiveness, population, technology (including uptake of HVAC), retrofit and occupant energy behaviour. The study found that reduction of energy use for winter heating outweighs any increase due to summer cooling, leading to lower consumption overall in the future, although the shift from multiple energy sources for heating to increasing reliance on electricity for cooling would require substantial adaptation of the electricity transmission system.

## 2.6 Prospects and challenges for constructing resilient built environments

It can be seen that designing and operating buildings that are robust and comfortable throughout their lifetimes is a challenge. Doing this and achieving the larger goal of reducing $CO_2$ emissions is even more difficult, requiring consistency of international, national and local governance. Mostly technical challenges around keeping buildings cool have been explored in this chapter, but it has been clear that scientists, policy-makers and built environment professionals need to work in step with each other. Given the national policy aim of reducing $CO_2$ emissions drastically by 2050, what lies ahead for these three groups until then?

Scientific research in the built environment needs to cut across disciplinary boundaries. The UK Government recently completed a Foresight project on the Future of Cities (Government Office for Science, 2016), covering economy, governance, infrastructure, city metabolism, form and lifestyles. Areas for future urban science research are inherently interdisciplinary and driven by an overarching need for systems analytics of cities. Urban economies are interconnected at global and regional scale, so elements such as workforce mobility and housing market evolution need further study. Seeing a city's metabolism holistically – use of water, materials, energy – can lead to enhanced sustainability, for example by integrating blue/green/grey (water/vegetation/built) infrastructure. Modelling tools such as Masson *et al.* (2014), with DTS at their heart, are assisting city decision-makers by providing quantitative information for different development scenarios to support investment and policy-making. Other urban science revolutions are taking place, with more data and monitoring of disparate parts of the city system than ever before: traffic counts and air quality, building information modelling being increasingly mandated in construction, mining of social media data for useful information in an emergency. In addition, infrastructure is increasingly seen as being interconnected (Hall *et al.*, 2016): transport relies on good energy infrastructure and ICT underpins all elements. Making sense of the complexity of modern, globally connected cities requires as much model development as data collection and is a huge challenge to engineering approaches requiring codification based on past data.

The Foresight project also identified a lack of long-term thinking within governance: methods to encourage and integrate foresighting techniques (such as creating city visions) into local governance and policy-making were recommended (Government Office for Science, 2016). Recognising the importance of cities at a global level, the IPCC highlighted the need for joined-up policy-making: climate change mitigation and adaptation, urban regeneration and planning, sustainable development and economic development (both of which are heavily dependent on energy costs and policy). Given that politics always governs policy-making, this chapter has highlighted how changes in national government can cause sharp policy U-turns at odds with long-term, globally important goals. The national referendum in June 2016 resulted in a decision that the UK should leave the European Union, which changes the context of every conceivable policy area for the country. However unpredictable national politics might be, increased emphasis on city-level governance could provide more stability: cities form networks such as the C40 group championing sustainability (http://www.c40.org/), sharing best practice, economic co-operation and plans for effective resilience. The Zero Carbon Hub may no longer exist in the UK, but its resources on low-energy buildings and cities still support globally relevant work on carbon reduction in the built environment (Zero Carbon Hub, 2015). Cities of the 21st century will form an ecosystem of their own.

The increasingly global connectivity of the built environment will force professional institutions to have an international perspective: there is an urgent need to include a focus on sustainability and resilience. The IPCC has made the point that whilst most urbanisation in the 19th and 20th centuries was in prosperous nations, in the 21st century almost three-quarters of the world's urban population lives in low- to middle-income countries. The resources and knowledge of how to adapt the built environment are therefore not necessarily in the places that need them most. In his 2014 review of architecture and the built environment, Sir Terry Farrell highlighted the opportunity for UK experts across built environment professions to lead urban development at international level (Farrell, 2014). The newest generation of professionals *will* see significant and potentially devastating climate change in their lifetimes: it will change their lives. In embracing a low-carbon transition, they would be part of an industry which 'stands on the threshold of great opportunities…to export products and skills of a modernised industry; to play its part in readying society for a resource efficient future; and to excite future generations of potential recruits into an industry with a noble cause and a secure future' (BIS, 2010).

## 2.7   Conclusions

This chapter has considered the technical and political challenges of designing energy-efficient and comfortable buildings that will be capable of withstanding climate change. A specific focus has been on designing buildings resilient to overheating, a growing risk in urban areas due to climate change and increasing urbanisation. DTS and the weather files needed for it have been discussed, as well as emerging modelling approaches at the interface between engineering, planning and climate science. Such modelling tools can be used not only for single building but entire city design and management. Prospects for designing sustainable future cities, fit to withstand 21st century climates, have been outlined.

## Acknowledgements

The authors would like to acknowledge helpful comments from the editors. Dr Sylvia Bohnenstengel is thanked for her help in producing Figure 2.7.

## References

Barlow, J.F., Halios, C.H., Lane, S.E. and Wood, C.R. (2015) Observations of urban boundary layer structure during a strong urban heat island event. *Environmental Fluid Mechanics*, 15, 373–398.

Belcher, S.E., Hacker, J.N. and Powell, D.S. (2005) Constructing design weather data for future climates. *Building Services Engineering Research and Technology*, 1, 49–61.

BIS (2010) *Low carbon construction Innovation and Growth Team – final report* (online). Department for Business Innovation and Skills. Available at: https://www.gov.uk/government/publications/low-carbon-construction-innovation-growth-team-final-report (accessed 24 August 2016).

Bohnenstengel, S.I., Evans, S., Clark, P.A. and Belcher, S.E. (2011) Simulations of the London urban heat island. *Quarterly Journal of the Royal Meteorological Society*, 137(659), 1625–1640.

BRE (2013) *Simplified Building Energy Model (SBEM)*. Building Research Establishment, London. Available at: https://www.bre.co.uk/page.jsp?id=706.

Bueno, B., Norford, L., Pigeon, G. and Britter, R. (2011) Combining a detailed building energy model with a physically-based urban canopy model. *Boundary-Layer Meteorology*, 140(3), 471–489.

Bueno, B., Pigeon, G., Norford, L.K., Zibouche, K. and Marchadier, C. (2012a) Development and evaluation of a building energy model integrated in the TEB scheme. *Geoscientific Model Development*, 5(2), 433–448.

Bueno, B., Norford, L., Pigeon, G. and Britter, R. (2012b) A resistance-capacitance network model for the analysis of the interactions between the energy performance of buildings and the urban climate. *Building and Environment*, 54, 116–125.

Bueno, B., Hidalgo, J., Pigeon, G., Norford, L. and Masson, V. (2013) Calculation of air temperatures above the urban canopy layer from measurements at a rural operational weather station. *Journal of Applied Meteorology and Climatology*, 52, 472–483.

Chan, P. and Cooper, R. (2010) *Constructing Futures: Industry leaders and futures thinking in construction*. Wiley-Blackwell.

Chandler, T.J. (1965) *The Climate of London*. Hutchinson of London, 289pp.

Chen, F., Kusaka, H., Bornstein, R. *et al.* (2011) The integrated WRF/urban modelling system: development, evaluation, and applications to urban environmental problems. *International Journal of Climatology*, 31, 273–288.

CIBSE (2005) *TM36 Climate change and the indoor environment: impacts and adaptation*. Technical Memorandum. Chartered Institution for Building Service Engineers. ISBN 9781903287507.

ClimateUK (2012) *A Summary of Climate Change Risks for London* (online). Available at: http://climatelondon.org.uk/wp-content/uploads/2012/01/CCRA-London.pdf (accessed 4 August 2016).

Collins, M. (2007) Ensembles and probabilities: a new era in the prediction of climate change. *Philosophical Transactions. Series A, Mathematical, Physical, and Engineering Sciences*, 365(1857), 1957–1970.

Crawley, D.B., Hand, J.W., Kummert, M. and Griffith, B.T. (2008) Contrasting the capabilities of building energy performance simulation programs. *Building and Environment*, 43, 661–673.

Davies, M. (2010) *LUCID – ARCC* (online). Available at: http://www.arcc-network.org.uk/project-summaries/lucid/#.V6hz-lf4PHg (accessed 4 August 2016).

Dawson, R. (2015) Handling interdependencies in climate change risk assessment. *Climate*, 3(4), 1079–1096.

De Munck, C., Pigeon, G., Masson, V. *et al.* (2013a) How much can air conditioning increase air temperatures for a city like Paris, France? *International Journal of Climatology*, 33(1), 210–227.

De Munck, C.S., Lemonsu, A., Bouzouidja, R., Masson, V. and Claverie, R. (2013b) The GREENROOF module (v7.3) for modelling green roof hydrological and energetic performances within TEB. *Geoscientific Model Development*, 6(6), 1941–1960.

DEFRA (2012) *UK Climate Change Risk Assessment: Government Report* (online). Department for Environment, Food and Rural Affairs, London. Available at: https://www.gov.uk/government/uploads/system/uploads/attachment_data/file/69487/pb13698-climate-risk-assessment.pdf (accessed 4 August 2016).

DoE (2016) *EnergyPlus simulation software* (online). Department of Energy, London. Available at: http://apps1.eere.energy.gov/buildings/energyplus/ (accessed 4 August 2016).

Dowson, M., Poole, A., Harrison, D. and Susman, G. (2012) Domestic UK retrofit challenge: drivers, barriers and incentives leading into the Green Deal, *Energy Policy*, 50, 294–305.

Farrell, T. (2014) *The Farrell Review of Architecture and the Built Environment: 'Our future in place'* (online). Available at: http://www.farrellreview.co.uk (accessed 4 August 2016).

Field, C.B., Barros, V.R., Dokken, D.J. *et al.* (eds) (2014) *Climate Change 2014: Impacts, Adaptation, and Vulnerability. Part A: Global and Sectoral Aspects. Contribution of Working Group II to the Fifth Assessment Report of the Intergovernmental Panel on Climate Change*. Cambridge University Press, Cambridge, and New York,1132 pp.

GLA (2006) *London's Urban Heat Island: A summary for Decision Makers*. Greater London Authority, London.

GLA (2007) *London's Climate Change Action Plan*. Greater London Authority, London.

GLA (2011) *Delivering London's Energy Future. The Mayor's Climate Change Mitigation and Energy Strategy*. Greater London Authority, London.

GLA (2015a) *2015 round population projections (online)*. Greater London Authority, London. Available at: http://data.london.gov.uk/dataset/2015-round-population-projections (accessed 24 August 2016).

GLA (2015b) *Energy Planning: Greater London Authority guidance on preparing energy assessments (April 2015)*. Greater London Authority, London.

Government Office for Science (2016) *Future of cities: science of cities* (online). Available at: https://www.gov.uk/government/publications/future-of-cities-science-of-cities (accessed 24 August 2016).

Grimmond, C.S.B., Blackett, M., Best, M.J. *et al.* (2010) The international urban energy balance models comparison project: First results from phase 1. *Journal of Applied Meteorology and Climatology*, 49(6), 1268–1292.

Grimmond, C.S.B., Blackett, M., Best, M.J. *et al.* (2011) Initial results from Phase 2 of the international urban energy balance model comparison. *International Journal of Climatology*, 31, 244–272.

Hacker, J.N., Belcher, S. and White, A. (2014) *TM 49: Design Summer Years for London.* CIBSE, London.

Hall, J.W., Tran, M., Hickford, A.J. and Nicholls, R.J. (2016) *The future of national infrastructure: a system-of-systems approach.* Cambridge University Press, Cambridge, 318pp.

Hallett, S. (ed.) (2013) *Community Resilience to Extreme Weather – the CREW Project: Final report.* 110pp. Available at: www.extreme-weather-impacts.net.

Hanby, V.I. and Smith, S.T. (2012) Simulation of the future performance of low-energy evaporative cooling systems using UKCP09 climate projections. *Building and Environment*, 55, 110–116.

Harman, I.N. and Belcher, S.E. (2006) The surface energy balance and boundary layer over urban street canyons. *Quarterly Journal of the Royal Meteorological Society*, 132, 2749–2768.

Harman, I.N., Best, M.J. and Belcher, S.E. (2004) Radiative exchange in an urban street canyon (pdf). *Boundary-Layer Meteorology*, 110, 301–316.

Hedger, M.M., Connell, R. and Bramwell, P. (2006) Bridging the gap: empowering decision-making for adaptation through the UK Climate Impacts Programme. *Climate Policy*, 6(2), 201–215.

Holmes, M.J. and Hacker, J.N. (2007) Climate change, thermal comfort and energy: Meeting the design challenges of the 21st century. *Energy and Buildings*, 39(7), 802–814.

Howard, L. (1833) *The Climate of London* (online). Available at: http://urban-climate.com/wp3/wp-content/uploads/2011/04/LukeHoward_Climate-of-London-V1.pdf (accessed 4 August 2016).

Huang, Y.J., Su, F., Seo, D. and Krarti, M. (2014) Development of 3012 IWEC2 Weather Files for International Locations (RP-1477). *ASHRAE Transactions*, 120(1), NY–14–029.

Hulme, M., Jenkins, G.J., Lu, X. *et al.* (2002) *Climate Change Scenarios for the United Kingdom: The UKCIP02 Scientific Report.* Tyndall Centre for Climate Change Research, School of Environmental Sciences, University of East Anglia, Norwich, 120 pp.

Jenkins, G.J., Murphy, J.M., Sexton, D.M.H., Lowe, J.A., Jones, P. and Kilsby, C.G. (2009) *UK Climate Projections: Briefing report.* Met Office Hadley Centre, Exeter.

Kikegawa, Y., Genchi, Y., Yoshikado, H. and Kondo, H. (2003) Development of a numerical simulation system toward comprehensive assessments of urban warming countermeasures including their impacts upon the urban buildings' energy-demands. *Applied Energy*, 76(4), 449–466.

Levermore, G.J. and Parkinson, J.B. (2006) Analyses and algorithms for new Test Reference Years and Design Summer Years for the UK. *Building Service Engineering Research and Technology*, 27(4), 311–325.

Masson, V. (2000) A physically based scheme for the urban energy budget in atmospheric models. *Bound.-Layer Meteor*, 94, 357–397.

Masson, V., Marchadier, C., Adolphe, L. *et al.* (2014) Adapting cities to climate change: A systemic modelling approach. *Urban Climate*, 10, 407–429.

Mastrandrea, M.D. and Schneider, S.H. (2004) Probabilistic integrated assessment of "dangerous" climate change. *Science*, 304(April), 571–575.

Mavrogianni, A., Wilkinson, P., Davies, M., Biddulph, P. and Oikonomou, E. (2012) Building characteristics as determinants of propensity to high indoor summer temperatures in London dwellings. *Building and Environment*, 55, 117–130.

Meehl, G.A., Stocker, T.F., Collins, W.D. *et al.* (2007) *Global Climate Projections. In: Climate Change 2007: The Physical Science Basis. Contribution of Working Group I to the Fourth Assessment Report of the Intergovernmental Panel on Climate Change*, Solomon, S., Qin, D., Manning, M. *et al.* (eds), Cambridge University Press, Cambridge and New York.

Murphy, J.M., Booth, B.B.B., Collins, M., Harris, G.R., Sexton, D.M.H. and Webb, M.J. (2007) A methodology for probabilistic predictions of regional climate change from perturbed physics ensembles. *Philosophical Transactions. Series A, Mathematical, Physical, and Engineering Sciences*, 365(1857), 1993–2028.

Murphy, J.M., Sexton, D.M.H., Jenkins, G.J. *et al.* (2009) *UK climate projections science report: Climate change projections.* Met Office Hadley Centre, Exeter.

Oke, T. (1973). City size and the urban heat island. *Atmospheric Environment Pergamon Press*, 7, 769–779.

Perry, M. and Hollis, D. (2005) The generation of monthly gridded datasets for a range of climatic variables over the UK. *International Journal of Climatology*, 25, 1041–1054.

Pickles, E. (2015) Department for Communities and Local Government and The Rt Hon Sir Eric Pickles MP, Written statement to Parliament, Planning update. Available at: https://www.gov.uk/government/speeches/housing-and-planning (accessed 6 July, 2017).

Pigeon, G., Legain, D., Durand, P. and Masson, V. (2007) Anthropogenic heat release in an old European agglomeration (Toulouse, France). *International Journal of Climatology*, 27, 1969–1981.

Pigeon, G., Zibouche, K., Bueno, B., Le Bras, J. and Masson, V. (2014) Improving the capabilities of the Town Energy Balance model with up-to-date building energy simulation algorithms: An application to a set of representative buildings in Paris. *Energy and Buildings*, 76, 1–14.

Porritt, S.M., Cropper, P.C., Shao, L. and Goodier, C.I. (2012) Ranking of interventions to reduce dwelling overheating during heat waves. *Energy and Buildings*, 55, 16–27.

Porson, A., Clark, P.A., Harman, I.N., Best, M.J. and Belcher, S.E. (2010) Implementation of a new urban energy budget scheme in the MetUM. Part I: Description and idealized simulations. *Quarterly Journal of the Royal Meteorological Society*, 136(651), 1514–1529.

Revi, A., Satterthwaite, D.E., Aragón-Durand, F. *et al.* (2014) *Urban areas. Climate Change 2014: Impacts, Adaptation, and Vulnerability. Part A: Global and Sectoral Aspects. Contribution of Working Group II to the Fifth Assessment Report of the Intergovernmental Panel on Climate Change*, Field, C.B., Barros, V.R., Dokken, D.J. *et al.* (eds), Cambridge University Press, Cambridge and New York, pp. 535–612.

Salamanca, F., Georgescu, M., Mahalov, A., Moustaoui, M. and Wang, M. (2014) Anthropogenic heating of the urban environment due to air conditioning. *Journal of Geophysical Research : Atmospheres*, 119, 5949–5965.

Satterthwaite, D., McGranahan, G. and Tacoli, C. (2010) Urbanization and its implications for food and farming. *Philosophical Transactions of the Royal Society of London. Series B, Biological Sciences*, 365(1554), 2809–2820.

Smith, S.T., Hanby, V.I. and Harpham, C. (2011) A probabilistic analysis of the future potential of evaporative cooling systems in a temperate climate. *Energy and Buildings*, 43(2–3), 507–516.

Smoliak, B.V., Snyder, P.K., Twine, T.E., Mykleby, P.M. and Hertel, W.F. (2015) Dense Network Observations of the Twin Cities Canopy-Layer Urban Heat Island. *Journal of Applied Meteorology and Climatology*, 54, 1899–1917.

Tremeac, B., Bousquet, P., de Munck, C. *et al.* (2012) Influence of air conditioning management on heat island in Paris air street temperatures. *Applied Energy*, 95, 102–110.

UK-GBC (2008) *Zero Carbon Task Group Report: Definition of Zero Carbon*. The UK Green Building Council. Available at: http://www.ukgbc.org/sites/default/files/Definition%2520of%2520Zero%2520Carbon%2520Report.pdf (accessed 6 July 2017).

Underwood, C.P. and Yik, F.W.H. (2004) *Modelling Methods for Energy in Buildings*. Blackwell Publishing.

UN_DESA (2015) *World Urbanization Prospects: The 2014 Revision, Highlights (ST/ESA/SER.A/366)*. United Nations, Department of Economic and Social Affairs: Population Division.

Watkins, R., Palmer, J., Kolokotroni, M. and Littlefair, P. (2002) The balance of the annual heating and cooling demand within the London urban heat island. *Building Services Engineering Research & Technology*, 23(4), 207–213.

Zero Carbon Hub (2015) *Zero Carbon Compendium 2015* (online). Available at: http://www.zerocarbonhub.org/resources/reports/zero-carbon-compendium-2015 (accessed 24 August 2016).

# 3

# Sustainability in Real Estate Markets

*Jorn van de Wetering*

## 3.1   Real estate and sustainability

As the awareness of environmental issues and the perceived need for action to tackle negative environmental impacts has increased, there has been a response from within the property industry, where sustainability has emerged as an area of focus for real estate developers, architects, investors, occupiers and consultants. Driven by legislation and reputational requirements, but also by financial benefits, environmental issues and social issues have become more important in decision-making processes.

Although there is still a lack of consensus on how sustainability should be defined overall, there are clear drivers that explain why sustainability concerns have gained such a foothold alongside traditional property issues. This chapter investigates how emerging environmental and social issues have fundamentally changed, and are continuing to alter, the outlook for the real estate industry now and in the future, particularly until 2050. It will investigate the rationale for adoption and how these changes have affected the behaviour of key stakeholders, with a particular focus on property investors and property occupiers.

### 3.1.1   Reputational drivers

Corporate social responsibility or corporate responsibility signifies the adoption of environmental and social elements into business models so that their emphasis shifts beyond the traditional economic focus. It is a way for organisations to demonstrate good practice across their activities. Such a focus can be traced to different motivations, which can include traditional corporate philanthropy, whereby organisations want to be seen to be doing good, risk management, whereby organisations want to minimise existing or new risks that can be associated with environmental or social performance, and value creation, whereby the focus on new environmental and social issues can be a way to add value for staff, clients, shareholders and other stakeholders (*The Economist*, 2008).

The balanced approach towards environmental, social and economic issues is also commonly referred to as the triple bottom line (TBL). To investors who hold buildings

*Sustainable Futures in the Built Environment to 2050: A Foresight Approach to Construction and Development*, First Edition. Edited by Tim Dixon, John Connaughton and Stuart Green.
© 2018 John Wiley & Sons Ltd. Published 2018 by John Wiley & Sons Ltd.

as real estate investments, whether direct or indirect, the demonstration of a commitment to socially responsible investment (SRI) requirements which are linked to the TBL has become increasingly important. Such organisations have started to measure their environmental and social performance and publish statistics on this performance on their websites, in annual reports or even in separately published sustainability reports and other relevant publications.

Investors benefit from available guidance, standards and indices. The UN Principles for Responsible Investment[1] offer a set of environment social governance (ESG) principles that property investors can adhere to. These cover the incorporation of ESG issues into investment analysis, decision-making processes, and ownership policies and practices. They also require investors to seek appropriate disclosure of ESG issues by the entities in which they invest, and promote acceptance and cooperation towards implementation in the investment industry. Investors should also report on their activities towards meeting the principles. Additionally, indices such as the Dow Jones Sustainability Index[2] and the FTSE4Good index[3] measure the ESG performance of companies with a strong focus on sustainability issues and can be used by market participants who wish to inform themselves regarding the sustainability performance of companies.

From the perspective of occupiers of property, which can include both tenants and owner-occupiers, the occupation of green buildings can similarly lead to financial and reputational benefits. Some of these benefits are discussed in more detail in section 3.4. As before, there is an increasing need to demonstrate to customers, clients and staff that social and environmental issues are actively addressed. The demand for environmentally superior real estate products has been explicitly stated by some market participants. For instance, UK Government procurement policies for buildings dictate that public sector bodies must achieve minimum building environmental assessment method standards in new buildings and major refurbishments (Green Government Unit – Cabinet Office, 2011).

In addition to such public sector requirements, which effectively lead to a semi-mandatory push towards buildings with superior environmental credentials for investors who do not wish to exclude sought-after public sector tenants, there is a demand from private sector tenants as well. For instance, a number of large retailers have implemented comprehensive environmental plans to demonstrate their environmental and social credentials to their customers. These environmental plans frequently extend to the buildings that these retailers occupy. For instance, Marks & Spencer's Plan A includes several ethical and environmental goals, which include the environmental performance of buildings. The organisation also monitors progress towards meeting these. Retailers such as Asda, Aldi, Waitrose, John Lewis, Lidl, Morrison's, Sainsbury's and Tesco also target buildings with superior environmental performance credentials. This is the case in other sectors too, such as the office sector, where there is a growing demand for environmentally efficient buildings and services from professional services firms. In the education sector this demand exists as well, highlighting that the extent to which environmental concerns are addressed may be of interest to prospective applicants to universities, colleges and schools.

---

1 http://www.unpri.org/.
2 http://www.djindexes.com/sustainability/.
3 http://www.ftse.com/products/indices/FTSE4Good.

As mentioned before, many organisations have started to report their sustainability performance to key stakeholders and this includes the performance of the buildings that they own or occupy. Typically, sustainability reporting involves outlining the general sustainability strategy of each organisation and the setting of targets for sustainability performance which can then be linked to key performance indicators (KPIs), as well as monitoring the progress that is made towards meeting these KPIs. Sustainability reports also tend to highlight key areas of good practice performance and report progress towards meeting targets in areas which include environmental themes such as energy consumption, $CO_2$ emission impacts, water consumption and waste management, but also social areas such as staff development, tenant engagement and local community engagement.

Particularly in the case of investors in property, reports also contain information on the performance of the organisation in external benchmarking methods, such as the Global Real Estate Sustainability Benchmark (GRESB), the Building Research Establishment Environmental Assessment Method (BREEAM) and Leadership in Energy and Environmental Design (LEED), which will be discussed in section 3.2.2. The Global Reporting Initiative (GRI)[4] offers sustainability standards for reporting to businesses, governments, civil society and citizens. Companies can also use ISO 14000 standards to measure and manage their environmental performance.[5] Some investors have even introduced their own internal environmental management system (EMS) that can be used to benchmark their overall current performance against their own past performance, as well as that of their peers. The reports are generally aimed at shareholders or other stakeholders, so that these can monitor the steps that organisations are making towards addressing environmental concerns and risks in their portfolios.

The demand for sustainability assessment at the asset or portfolio level has also resulted in the availability of a range of sustainability services for property owners and occupiers from real estate consultancies. These services include monitoring and benchmarking of sustainability performance, and also reporting and communicating this performance to external stakeholders. Property consultants can also provide advice on how to manage buildings more sustainably through sustainable facilities management. Furthermore, in line with the reporting of performance by occupiers and investors, these consultants have started to report their own internal ESG performance as well.

### 3.1.2 Regulatory drivers

The pace of regulatory change towards minimising environmental impacts is one of the most significant challenges that the real estate sector has to address. As such, it is a driving force behind the shift towards sustainable best practice. Much of the national and international policy focus is on energy efficiency and reducing greenhouse gas (GHG) emissions. At the COP21 summit in Paris a deal was agreed between 195 nations to attempt to limit the rise in global temperatures to well below 2 °C (UNFCCC, 2015). The EU had previously set itself a 20% energy savings target by 2020 when compared to the projected use of energy in 2020 and EU member states have agreed on an energy-efficiency target of 27% or greater by 2030 (European Commission, 2016). In the UK, the

---

4  https://www.globalreporting.org/Pages/default.aspx.
5  http://www.iso.org/iso/iso14000.

Climate Change Act 2008 (HM Government, 2008) has committed the government to a net carbon amount by 2050 of at least 80% lower than the 1990 baseline. This will be achieved through reductions in net carbon dioxide emissions and other GHG emissions.

These requirements for the reduction of carbon and GHG emissions, alongside a commitment towards efficient energy consumption patterns, have resulted in modifications to the legislative framework that affects the built environment. At a European level, this has resulted in significant pressure for improving the fabric of buildings. The Energy Performance of Buildings Directive (EPBD) stipulates that all EU member states must put in place Energy Performance Certificates (EPCs), which must be included when marketing buildings when they are sold or let. More detail on EPCs can be found in section 3.2.1. Member states must also establish inspection schemes for heating and air-conditioning systems.

Stricter legislation aimed at improving the energy fabric and specification of buildings has also been put in place. Under the EPBD, EU member states must ensure that all new buildings are nearly zero energy by 31 December 2020 (public buildings by 31 December 2018), and set minimum energy performance requirements for new buildings, for the major renovation of buildings and for the replacement or retrofit of building elements. They must also draw up lists of national financial measures to improve the energy efficiency of buildings. In addition, building construction standards have become more stringent over the years, which is reflected in tighter energy performance standards for new and existing buildings in Part L of the building regulations in the UK (DCLG, 2016a).

In addition to changing building standards to strengthen energy-efficiency requirements and making the energy performance of buildings more transparent with building energy assessment methods, providing financial incentives can also play a role in a shift towards more energy-efficient buildings, such as those proposed by the EPBD. In Germany, the government-owned KfW development bank offers loans with relatively low interest rates which can be used to improve the energy fabric of homes. In the commercial sector in the UK, under the Enhanced Capital Allowances Scheme, organisations can write off the total cost of energy-efficient equipment against their taxable profits (CCC, DEFRA, DECC and EA, 2016).

Conversely, the regulatory framework may be adjusted to penalise energy-inefficient behaviour, by levying fines or charging higher taxes or business rates. A clear example from the UK is the CRC Energy Efficiency Scheme, which stimulates a better understanding of energy consumption by requiring large private and public sector organisations to report their energy consumption levels, but also buy allowances for every tonne of carbon that they emit. Penalties included in the UK Energy Act 2011 (HM Government, 2011), which sets minimum performance standards for buildings, as stipulated by the Minimum Energy Efficiency Standard (MEES; see section 3.3.1), is also putting the onus on property owners to improve the energy efficiency of their stock when it is let to tenants.

### 3.1.3 Barriers for adoption

One of the most generally cited barriers to the adoption of green buildings or green features in buildings is the additional cost that is commonly associated with constructing or retrofitting to superior environmental standards. A study by Kats *et al.* (2003), for instance, aggregated the costs and benefits of a small sample of 33 green buildings and found a cost premium of slightly less than 2% for green buildings. Kats (2013), in a sample of 170 buildings in the USA and 10 non-US buildings, found that the majority of reported premiums for constructing green were between 0% and 4%, with a median of 1.5%. The author contrasts this finding with the perception that business leaders have, who believe such a premium to be around 17% (as found in WBCSD (2008)), highlighting that although there can be higher costs, there may also be mismatch between perceptions of cost for green constructing and the actual cost for doing so. A study by Davis Langdon (2004) found that, although there is no one-size-fits-all solution, the majority of buildings that were studied were able to achieve their LEED aspirations without additional funding. A follow-up study confirmed that many projects were achieving LEED within their budgets, and were in the same cost range as non-LEED projects (Davis Langdon, 2007). Conversely, the Building Research Establishment (BRE) Trust and Cyril Sweett (2005) found in a series of case studies that to achieve a BREEAM 'Excellent' rating would add to construction costs for both naturally ventilated and air-conditioned offices types.

There are also variations in the level of engagement of real estate market participants. The profile of each investor and their investment outlook are important factors that determine their commitment to sustainability concerns. For institutional investors, such as pension funds and insurance companies who operate life bonds, the ability to maintain constant income security with low levels of volatility and release capital over longer periods of time is likely to be of greater importance. These investors tend to be risk averse and will wish to minimise any future threats that can damage their security, which includes any structural sustainability risks. For more opportunistic and risk-seeking investors, a long-term horizon may be of lesser importance, although the inclusion of sustainable building features may be an opportunity for adding additional value.

From the perspective of the occupiers of commercial buildings, sustainability tends to rank lower on a list of overruling preferences which can include the location of the building and its proximity to clients, staff and suppliers, lease terms, the building's overall aesthetic and whether it offers the facilities that an organisation needs to run (see, for instance, Van de Wetering and Wyatt, 2011). The environmental and social performance of buildings may fit in to this list of requirements, but may ultimately only be a secondary consideration which will be relevant only after other, overruling considerations are met.

The many permutations of ownership, management and use of property can make achieving energy-efficiency measures challenging (JLL, 2014). A separation of ownership and occupation, which characterises buildings that are held as real estate investments, complicates the adoption of sustainable practices. In tenanted properties, improving the performance of buildings may not be straightforward. Split incentives exist between landlords and tenants, whereby the tenant pays for energy consumed in the building but it is the landlord who would have to pay for improvements to the building. If landlords invest in improving the energy performance of buildings, the financial benefits of investment in improved energy performance would go the tenant. Smaller tenants in particular may only have a low degree of control over what they can ask their landlord to do. Even if tenants have a higher level of control and are interested in putting in place energy improvements, there will still be only a limited incentive for investments in features that would result in an improvement of the energy performance of buildings when the long-term payback periods for such technologies exceed the lease term for which they have signed up.

A lack of information transparency, which is required to address poor performance at the operational stage of a building lifecycle, may be another barrier (Van de Wetering and Wyatt, 2011). For instance, energy consumption information may be provided too infrequently to allow for real-time performance improvement or information provision may be minimal and lacking sufficient detail to accurately improve performance, which reduces the ability for tenants to monitor, manage and reduce their energy consumption if they should wish to do so. The installation of smart meters and additional sub-meters may help to overcome this information barrier.

The implementation of green leases can go some way towards addressing these issues. In green leases, targets for the reduction of energy efficiency and other environmental gains can be agreed between the landlord and the tenant, and responsibilities for meeting these targets can be clearly allocated between them. This can help to ensure that energy-efficient best practice becomes more firmly entrenched. Active asset management with incentives for reductions in energy consumption can similarly result in savings.

The benefits of saving energy can, however, be complicated by rebound effects, whereby financial savings in energy consumption can lead to a demand for alternative products, the production of which generates additional $CO_2$, thus effectively undoing many of the benefits that have been achieved. Set institutional requirements similarly limit the potential for making savings. For instance, certain office occupiers require energy-intensive heating, ventilation and air-conditioning (HVAC) systems, which may have a higher energy demand than natural ventilation systems. In the retail sector, the current trend towards smaller food shops with smaller cooling systems undoes some of the energy-efficiency economies of scale that were previously achieved in larger, centralised locations.

## 3.2 Building environmental assessment methods

Buildings are heterogeneous and possess unique features, especially in the non-domestic sector. As such, it is difficult to formulate a single definition of a green or sustainable building. Each building presents unique challenges which can relate to its inherent features, such as its location, intended use, size and design specification. Consequently, there may be trade-offs and even sustainability paradoxes that prevent one-size-fits-all solutions.

Rather than a restrictive definition, there is a set of commonly accepted principles that can be used to define sustainability. Such principles are promoted by building environmental assessment methods that can be used to improve the environmental and social performance of buildings and make their performance transparent. They offer a commonly accepted and applied classification of the wider sustainability performance of buildings.

### 3.2.1 Mandatory methods

As previously stated, the EPBD requires European member states to implement EPCs. In the UK, EPCs assess the *intrinsic* performance of buildings based on the various attributes which contribute to their overall energy consumption. One of the aims of the

EPBD is to provide market participants with information regarding the energy performance of buildings when they seek to lease or purchase a building. EPCs in the UK are therefore a requirement when a building is constructed, sold or let and they are valid for 10 years. For non-domestic buildings, an EPC assessor collects information on the building's *construction*, including the thermal performance of walls, floors, roofs, doors and glazing, the building's *geometry*, assessing elements of zoning in the building, including configuration of the building envelope, doors and windows, as well as building *services*, including heating, ventilation and air-conditioning systems, hot water systems and renewable energy features of the building. This information is then used to generate the EPC rating in the iSBEM software package. For domestic buildings, the SAP method is used, which assesses similar elements. The assessment that EPCs provide is therefore based on standardised assumptions of conditions and building features and is entirely theoretical. The assessment of non-domestic buildings is generally more onerous due to the larger degree of heterogeneity that such buildings typically display.

In addition, the UK has also introduced Display Energy Certificates (DECs), which assess the operational performance of buildings as recorded through metered energy consumption. They are required for an occupier subset of public authorities and institutions providing public services to a large number of persons, who occupy space in a building with a total useful floor area greater than $250\,m^2$. The ORCalc methodology is used to calculate these certificates. Whereas EPCs are valid for 10 years, DECs need to be renewed annually and include indicators of year-on-year energy performance. In the UK, DECs need to be clearly displayed in the public building or space in the building that is assessed so that building users can see how the building is performing.

### 3.2.2 Voluntary methods and approaches

Whereas mandatory EPCs and DECs focus on the assessment of energy consumption, further voluntary methods focus on other environmental and social areas as well. Although a large number of methods now exist, only a smaller number have seen significant levels of adoption by the real estate industry. Among the more widely used ones are BREEAM in the UK and LEED in the USA. BREEAM is managed by the Building Research Establishment (BRE), and LEED is managed by the US Green Building Council (USGBC). Both methods are balanced scorecards which can be used to assess how green or how sustainable an asset or group of assets is likely to be.

At its most basic level, environmental performance tends to be defined in these building environmental assessment methods across themes which include issues such as management, energy, water, waste, materials, transport, pollution and site ecology. They also assess social building indoor health and well-being issues. Within these themes, they propose various criteria which include specific measures that can be taken to improve the sustainability performance of a building or group of buildings. Such measures are linked to credits, which can be scored. The measures, criteria and total scoring vary, reflecting the priorities that are defined for each method. They do tend to contain country- and region-specific aims and criteria, which limits their direct comparability.

Performance across these measures is then assessed and the outcome leads to a total score. In some methods, this score is weighted by thematic area to calculate a final result. As with the total credits achievable in the assessment categories, these requirements display differences between each methodology, further reflecting the priorities of each method. A third party BREEAM or LEED assessor will certify that this result has actually been achieved in the building through an inspection. The final assessment outcome result tends to then be expressed on a scale which provides an indicator of the building's overall sustainability performance and which is normally expressed using a label that clearly separates poor performance from superior performance. To minimise the selective cherry picking of credits that can be easily achieved, some methods include minimum thresholds or mandatory criteria that must be met before certain performance outcome levels can be awarded.

The methods are generally used in the design and construction phases of buildings in the office, retail and industrial sectors, but can also extend to uses such as healthcare, education and prisons. Generally, performance in themes is assessed at the project level, which can range from individual buildings to entire neighbourhoods. A publication by the Royal Institute of Chartered Surveyors (RICS) (2015) shows how total certifications under BREEAM and LEED, and also the French method Haute Qualité Environnementale (HQE) and the German method Deutsche Gesellschaft für Nachhaltiges Bauen (DGNB), are distributed across Europe, with BREEAM and LEED seeing the most significant levels of adoption overall.

A shift is also visible towards voluntary assessment of other building lifecycle stages, such as operational measurement and refurbishment. The DGNB building environmental assessment method, for instance, focuses more explicitly on the life cycle assessment (LCA) of buildings. The RICS SKA rating and LEED Interior Design and Construction can be used to assess the sustainability performance of fit outs.[6] BREEAM In Use is an operational method that can be used to assess the sustainability performance of a building in its operational phase, as well as how the building is managed and how occupiers use it. In the Netherlands, the government uses the Milieuprestatie van gebouwen, an LCA approach which assesses the environmental impacts of materials used in the construction of buildings (Rijksoverheid, 2017).

Increasingly, there is also a move among property investors towards methods which have been designed to assess performance of entire portfolios, rather than individual assets. An example of this is GRESB, which is used by investors, including those with real estate portfolios and infrastructure assets, to assess and benchmark the ESG performance of real assets globally using a questionnaire.[7] The Real Estate Environmental Benchmark[8] can be used by investors to compare the energy, water and waste performance of their own buildings. The lower level of granularity required for these assessments tends to make them less onerous than methods designed to assess the performance of individual buildings.

### 3.2.3 Building environmental assessment methods: discussion

Building environmental assessment methods create transparency in the performance of buildings and allow for a direct comparison of sustainability performance. Yet although methods such as BREEAM and LEED are viewed as *de facto* standards for reporting the

---

6 http://www.rics.org/uk/knowledge/ska-rating-/.
7 https://www.gresb.com/.
8 http://www.jll.co.uk/united-kingdom/en-gb/pages/real-estate-environmental-benchmark.aspx.

sustainability performance of buildings, as voluntary methods they have not seen the adoption levels of mandatory EPCs (the adoption rates for these are examined in section 3.3.1) and, to a lesser extent, DECs. They are generally applied to the top end of commercial Grade A properties in the UK and are often reported as part of the marketing particulars of buildings. Moreover, investors can use methods such as GRESB to benchmark their performance against that of key competitors and report their progress towards meeting their sustainability aspirations to relevant stakeholders.

Although these methods have provided a useful starting point for raising awareness and providing transparency, they are also subject to certain limitations. Several studies have reported signs of mismatches between hypothetical energy consumption as expressed by ecolabels and the operational energy that is consumed in reality. For instance, studies by Majcen *et al.* (2013a,b) found differences between theoretical energy use and actual energy use. Newsham, Mancini and Birt (2009) found little correlation between the levels of LEED certification or energy credits achieved in design and measured energy performance. If the information that goes into the assessment is incomplete, imprecise or, in the worst case, incorrect, the rating will not accurately reflect the building's operational performance, for obvious reasons.

Striking a balance between short-term and long-term requirements can also be complicated. Methods that assess the wider environmental performance of buildings incentivise their users to tackle a large number of themes, but this holistic approach can divert at least some attention away from reductions in energy and GHG emissions. Conversely, EPCs only make an estimate of the theoretical energy that can be directly associated with the day-to-day operation of a building; they are not a predictor of actual operational energy performance. They also do not include estimates of transportation energy consumption emissions that are an indirect result of the location of the building, nor do they include inputs for embodied energy, which can be associated with the construction, refurbishment or redevelopment of buildings.

Although the weighting of environmental issues is designed to reflect current priorities, such priorities tend to change. As methods are adjusted to meet the most up-to-date environmental needs, differences start to emerge between various iterations of methods that make them not necessarily compatible and can make some past methodologies seem arbitrary in retrospect. BREEAM versions 2006, 2008, 2011 and 2014 each include different ways of assessing some of the same issues, for instance in measuring the expected energy performance of buildings. The definition of environmental efficiency thus undergoes changes, indicating that the path to sustainable development is still undergoing revisions at this stage, some of which can be significant.

## 3.3 Sustainability risks

Regulation and CSR requirements have changed property standards and the challenge for investors is to manage their expectation of property risk accordingly. More stringent mandatory environmental standards can introduce new risk, particularly affecting properties which were never constructed with environmental considerations such as energy efficiency in mind. In some cases, additional investment may be required to alter the services or the fabric of buildings to bring them in line with new occupational or regulatory requirements. In the worst case, the introduction of new environmental requirements or changing weather patterns can make a building in its entirety technically or functionally obsolete. The risk profile of properties may also be affected in locations that are particularly exposed to a risk of flooding, wildfire or other environmental disasters. Investors may decide to minimise such risks, mitigate their impacts or avoid them altogether. This section looks at two examples of the most significant environmental risks that investors in property will have to address in the future.

### 3.3.1 Risk example 1: Minimum Energy Efficiency Standard

As previously discussed, the Energy Act 2011 (HM Government, 2011) sets minimum performance standards for buildings. It includes a section which states that landlords in both the domestic and non-domestic sector will not be able to let private rented properties to tenants unless relevant energy-efficiency improvements have been made. The Minimum Energy Efficiency Standard (MEES) sets the threshold for such improvements at a minimum EPC E rating or higher for properties in the domestic sector and all categories of non-domestic property (DECC, 2015). From 1 April 2018, this will apply when a lease is granted to either a new tenant or an existing tenant. From 1 April 2023, the regulations will be extended to apply to all privately rented property, including those where a lease is already in place and that are already occupied by a tenant.

For many investors, the MEES has resulted in data collection exercises to identify exposure to future risk and decide whether they should make improvements to underperforming properties or, in the worst case, dispose of them. To illustrate the scale of this challenge in the UK commercial property market, Figure 3.1 shows non-domestic EPCs for properties in England and Wales by energy performance asset rating.

Between 2008, when EPCs were first introduced, and 2015, the total number of non-domestic assessments that resulted in an F rating was 47,204 (8.22% of the total) and the total number of assessments that resulted in a G rating was 56,868 (9.91% of the total). The remaining assessments outperform the minimum threshold of E or higher. Looking

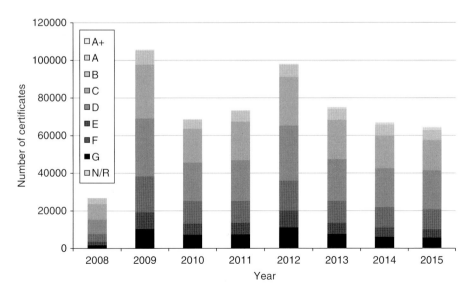

**Figure 3.1** Distribution of non-domestic EPCs (number of certificates by year) (DCLG, 2016b).

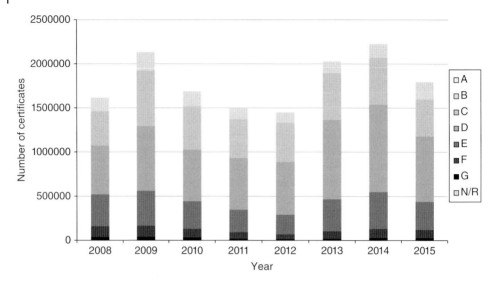

**Figure 3.2** Distribution of domestic EPCs (number of certificates by year) (DCLG, 2016c).

year by year, the percentages of the combined total of F- and G-rated certifications vary from a minimum of 13.07% in 2008 to a maximum of 20.37% in 2012.

Figure 3.2 includes a breakdown of EPCs by energy-efficiency rating for all dwellings in England and Wales.

Between 2008 and 2015, the total number of assessments for dwellings that resulted in an F rating was 745,099 (5.16% of the total) and assessments resulting in a G rating totalled 221,105 (1.53% of the total). Between 2008 and 2012, the percentages of the combined total of F- and G-rated certifications varied from a minimum 4.71% in 2012 to a maximum of 9.80% in 2008.

These statistics show that a significant portion of buildings may be affected by the MEES, although it is unclear which proportion of these certificates can be linked to lease transactions. Overall, it would appear that the percentage of properties that may be in the category that is at risk of the MEES is lower for domestic buildings on average, although in absolute terms the number exceeds that of non-domestic buildings. Dwellings tend to be much smaller in unit size than commercial buildings, however. A few things should be pointed out. First, as EPC ratings are a requirement when a building is being constructed, sold or let, it means that these assessments can reflect the intrinsic performance of both entire buildings and parts of buildings. The assessment figures do not reveal how much of a percentage of total floor space is assessed and they also do not reveal the extent of dual certification; possibly some properties may have been certified twice because information was imperfect or because the property or section within the property underwent a significant refurbishment and achieved a different second EPC as a result.

The exact nature of any financial consequences is at this stage still unclear, although non-compliance with the standard will automatically result in financial penalties. Costs are likely to extend to energy-efficiency improvements needed to improve the fabric and energy-consuming features of buildings to address the cause of the poor EPCs. The regulations will require improvements that are permissible, appropriate and cost-effective, and they will contain safeguards to ensure this. There are also exceptions where only minimal or no improvements are required, although the earlier discussed mismatch between the theoretical energy consumption as estimated by EPCs and actual operational energy consumption is a factor that should be carefully considered as well.

The Investment Property Databank (IPD, 2013) has estimated that in 2013, 13% of total estimated rental value (ERV) in their Eco-Portfolio Analysis Service (EcoPAS) investment tool was obtained from units that were F and G rated. This ERV totalled £1.1 billion. This count of units with an EPC rating represented 43.2% of the total number of units for which EPC information was known, so the total ERV may be much higher if all units are counted.

Uncertainty about the actual direction that legislation will take and a past inconsistency or lack of legislation enforcement explain the reluctance of investors to take a strong lead. If regulatory requirements are not heavily enforced, resources could be allocated more efficiently elsewhere. A precedent of a sudden but significant change in the direction of government policy implementation is provided by the Green Deal, a scheme under which the UK government lent money through the Green Deal Finance Company to make improvements to dwellings. Although the original intention was to extend this scheme to non-domestic buildings, it was instead cancelled in 2015. However, even if the MEES will not be implemented and enforced to its maximum potential in the near future, properties with F and G ratings have now been identified as potential long-term liabilities.

### 3.3.2 Risk example 2: climate change impacts

Climate change will also affect the physical built environment in which people live and work. A report by the MET office highlights that the UK could be exposed to more extreme weather in the future, that is, colder winters, but also hotter summers with more heatwaves (Met Office, 2015). In addition to stricter requirements for energy performance, buildings must therefore simultaneously also be made to be more adaptable to extreme weather patterns. Climate change can increase the likelihood that average temperatures may be lower or higher than they have been historically. As with energy efficiency, this particularly presents challenges for a legacy of existing buildings that were never designed with changing requirements in mind. A further complexity is that it is difficult to predict exactly how climate change will affect local weather patterns in the short to long term.

The MET report also highlights the possibility for more extreme rainfall in autumn and wetter than average summers in the future. The last few years have illustrated the damage that the resultant flooding can inflict. The Association of British Insurers estimates that total pay-outs for the floods in 2016 will equal approximately £1.3 billion (ABI, 2016). Estimates by the Local Government Association indicate that the damage to infrastructure caused by flooding equalled almost £250 million in 2016 alone (LGA, 2016).

Statistics from the Department for Environment, Food and Rural Affairs (DEFRA, 2011) show that in 2011, out of 2.74 million residential and non-residential properties, 19.9% were at significant (greater than 1 in 75 chance in any given year) risk of flooding from rivers and sea, 31.1% at a moderate risk (1 in 75 to 1 in 200 chance in any year) and 48% were at a low risk of flooding (less than 1 in 200 chance in any year); 1% of properties yielded no result. The IPD has also monitored environmental risks of properties in the EcoPAS investment tool. Of the properties in this data set, 5.8% were at a significant risk of floods, 6.6% at moderate risk of floods and 10.8% were at low risk of floods; the remainder of properties were at a flood risk classified as nil or unknown (IPD, 2013). The capital value of the combined significant and moderate risk properties was estimated to be £5.8 billion.

Insurers are now taking steps to identify and address environmental issues in the stock that they own. The Association of British Insurers has identified two types of risk that can be associated with flooding (ABI, 2014). First, flooding can increase the risk and costs of insurance pay-outs, which means that investors have to carefully examine their exposure to such properties among their policyholders. Second, flooding can impact on the quality of their investments; this latter issue is relevant to all investors who hold property among their assets.

Flooding can have a myriad of negative financial impacts, as well as other disruptive and undesirable effects. It can cause physical damage to buildings, thus accelerating their deterioration process or, in the worst case, destroying them. If floods are severe, homeowners or commercial property occupants may be forced to temporarily relocate to alternative accommodation, which can lead to significant additional costs. If, in addition, substantial property damage has been caused and the property needs to be repaired, there will be a cost of repair and more permanent alternative accommodation has to be found until the property can be used again. In the worst case, a property is destroyed entirely and occupants have to relocate permanently. Relocation may not be an option for all property occupants. For retailers, an inaccessible property can result in lost trading hours and lost income. Industrial property occupiers may similarly not be able to relocate their activities to another location.

The owners of domestic and non-domestic buildings in areas of higher flood risk are exposed to the added risk that insurers will require substantial premiums and may even refuse insurance in some cases. This would have a significant impact on the market value of these properties. The value of such properties may then fall to reflect the reduced ability or even the inability to insure them. On a global level, an increasing risk of droughts, wildfires and storms may similarly expose buildings and infrastructure to additional risk and uncertainty. The United States Office for Disaster Risk Reduction already monitors floods, storms, droughts and extreme temperatures to better understand the cost and impacts of such disasters.[9] On a European level, the promotion of better decision-making and action by Member States is now encouraged with a view towards adapting to the impacts of climate change, particularly in vulnerable areas (European Commission, 2013).

## 3.4   Green value

The ownership and occupation of buildings with sustainability attributes can yield positive benefits. A significant number of empirical studies have established a relationship between superior environmental certification of buildings and measurable financial rewards.

---

9  https://www.unisdr.org/we/inform/disaster-statistics.

The rationale behind the existence of a premium for green products can be linked to the intrinsic benefits that they offer, which has translated into additional demand for them. Such additional demand can also translate into an increased implicit willingness to pay (WTP). Sale and rent premiums may be a necessary compensation for the higher construction costs of such buildings. Fuerst and McAllister (2011a) discuss how, in the short term, higher costs of construction to superior environmental standards, such as BREEAM and LEED, requires developers to obtain higher prices, causing supply to become inelastic. Occupiers may be expected to pay more to compensate for certified products and this can lead to a new supply and demand equilibrium for certified compared to non-certified stock. The marginal WTP is expected to decrease as supply increases and costs of construction decrease. When large quantities are consumed, the premium may disappear altogether. Aroul and Hansz (2012) elaborate on this by theorising that the implementation of mandatory green building programs leads to an increased demand for green buildings in the short term, which results in a price premium compared to non-certified buildings. The authors also theorise that although this premium will continue to exist in the long term, as supply is brought in line with demand the premium is reduced to lower levels.

### 3.4.1  Sustainability value

Some of the clearest evidence for the positive financial benefits of, and indeed the business case for, green buildings emerges from several studies conducted using property data from the USA. These studies have investigated the link between superior environmental performance as assessed by building environmental assessment methods and rental income and property value. They generally look at the pricing impacts of a set of traditional hedonic property attributes and test the impact of the introduction of superior environmental certification. The introduction of labels that express the environmental performance is often tested against a control sample of non-assessed buildings *ceteris paribus*, that is, keeping all else equal. Using hedonic modelling the impact of various independent variables, often a bundle of typical property characteristics, is tested on a dependent variable, such as rents or sale prices.

#### 3.4.1.1  Value of LEED

Based on a sample of 8105 CoStar US observations Eichholtz *et al.* (2010) found a statistically significant rent premium of 3.3% for Energy Star-rated buildings compared to non-rated buildings, *ceteris paribus*. Looking at 1813 sale price observations, they also found a significant premium of 19.1% for Energy Star-rated buildings. Fuerst and McAllister (2011a) also used CoStar US data and, based on 10,970 observations, they found significant rent premiums of 4% for Energy Star-rated buildings and 5% for LEED-rated buildings. Using 6167 observations, the authors also found sales price premiums of 26% for Energy Star-rated buildings and 25% for LEED-rated buildings. Wiley *et al.* Johnson (2010) looked at CoStar data for 7308 properties in 46 office markets in the USA and found, depending on the specification, significant rent premiums of 7.3–8.9% for Energy Star-rated buildings and 15.2–17.3% for LEED-rated buildings, as well as sales price premiums for Energy Star- and LEED-rated buildings. Reichardt *et al.* (2012) identified comparatively lower, albeit positive premiums. The authors found that Energy Star certification increases rents by 2.5% and that LEED certification increases rents by 2.9%, averaged over all the time periods they included. The authors also found that the Energy Star premium peaked between Q4 in 2006 and Q2 in 2008, and decreased in subsequent periods.

#### 3.4.1.2 Value of BREEAM

Similar impacts have also been identified in the UK. Chegut *et al.* (2012) looked at a sample of 1149 transactions and found rent premiums for BREEAM-rated buildings of 28–31% and, based on a sample of 2019 observations, sale price premiums that range from 26% to 38%, depending on the specification. The authors add that the value appears to be conditional on the economic conditions at the time. Fuerst and van de Wetering (2015) looked at a sample of 19,509 observations and found an achieved rent premium that, depending on the specification, ranges from 23% to 26% for BREEAM-rated buildings compared to non-BREEAM rated buildings.

#### 3.4.1.3 Value of EPCs

There is also evidence of an impact of mandatory labels. Using a sample of 31,993 domestic housing transactions in the Netherlands, Brounen and Kok (2011) found, after controlling for building quality characteristics, that EPC A-, B-, or C-rated buildings transact at an average transaction price premium of 3.6% compared to the remainder of labels. Fuerst *et al.* (2015) looked at 333,095 dwellings in England sold at least twice in the period from 1995 to 2012 and found a positive relationship between the energy-efficiency ratings of dwellings and transaction prices.

Evidence of premiums for mandatory labels has also been found for non-domestic buildings. Fuerst and McAllister (2011b) used IPD UK data and found that equivalent yields are impacted by EPC ratings, although the authors found no significant impact on market rent or market value. Kok and Jennen (2012) looked at 1100 commercial real estate leasing transactions and found that labels of D or lower commanded a discount of 6.5% compared to A–C, *ceteris paribus.*

### 3.4.2 Discussion of value impact

These studies and many others have found evidence to suggest positive and significant relationships associated with superior environmental performance, although the interpretation of the coefficients is subject to a number of caveats. The first concern relates to the use of data. The accuracy of the data that was used to generate these results may not be optimal; this is an issue that is commonly associated with property data sets. Some of these studies have also used comparatively small samples, which may limit the ability to accurately test wider impacts.

A lack of suitable control variables is another limitation. Buildings with superior environmental performance may be located in superior locations and may be constructed to higher specifications and design standards. Without adequate controls for location such premiums may not be accurately captured, especially at the micro location level (Fuerst and McAllister, 2011a). Furthermore, without suitable variables that can be used to accurately capture building quality it may be difficult to separate the superior specifications and design quality of buildings from their superior environmental performance.

Many of these studies have used asking rent as a pricing indicator, whereas it would be preferable to use headline rents. Even then, without accurate information on tenant covenant strength and additional lease structure information, including variables such as the lease length, rent review structure, break clauses and any other incentives such as rent-free periods, it may be more difficult to capture impacts accurately in the coefficients. It is also assumed that tenants will have a higher WTP, but rather than paying a direct financial premium, occupiers may be willing to forego favourable lease terms such as rent-free periods and shorter leases with more flexibility in exchange for superior environmental or social performance credentials in the building. Instead, they may be willing to sign up for longer leases, or have fewer break clauses or shorter rent-free periods in exchange for the benefits that sustainable buildings can provide. In such cases a premium would not be captured.

Indeed, the existence of such premiums and, if they do exist, whether they display the magnitude identified in these studies, remains a contested issue within the real estate industry and the validity of these findings is frequently challenged. It should be understood that the inclusion of additional environmental efficiency features does not by default result in a realisation of positive financial impacts on market rents and sale prices. Fuerst and McAllister (2011b) suggest that the role of EPCs is limited when the information is not provided when it should be. They discuss that there is evidence of lack of compliance with legislation, as well as reporting of EPCs after the marketing stage, when heads of terms have already been agreed. In such cases, there would be no role for EPCs in informing market participants about the energy performance of buildings and they consequently cannot capitalise them into their decision-making process. Conversely, the identification of financial benefits based on the superior environmental performance of buildings may create opportunities for those investors who can accurately identify assets that have been mispriced.

Adopting a long-term perspective, an accurate and exact view of the future impact of sustainability issues on the performance of buildings may be difficult to obtain. If green premiums are identified, they may not be maintained over time, especially as sustainability definitions are continuously altered to reflect current concerns, which continue to shift. Current legislation does, however, signpost the direction with a focus on minimising energy consumption and GHG emissions, as well as addressing the wider environmental impacts of buildings. Rather than a 'green premium', a 'brown discount' may emerge, which means that buildings that do not meet expected sustainability standards or requirements may sell or rent for less compared to those that do (WGBC, 2013). This can also result in faster depreciation over time of 'brown' assets compared to 'green' ones,[10] for instance in the case of energy-efficient buildings which are able to consistently meet or outperform energy standards. Such buildings, which have been effectively future-proofed, are likely to be increasingly sought after and see higher levels of rental growth, while their yields will stay at lower levels compared to their non-green counterparts.

The RICS is the leading organisation in the world for professionals in property, land and construction. In that capacity, it sets, maintains and regulates standards. The organisation has provided valuation surveyors with recommendations in an RICS professional guidance standard on sustainability and commercial property valuation (RICS, 2013).

---

10  C. Strathon (2014) Sustainability and Value, Jones Lang LaSalle, presentation delivered on 20th November 2014.

In this document, the RICS stresses the importance of the role of valuers, who should reflect markets in valuations and not lead them. It advises valuers to approach the valuation of superior environmental performance with caution and to collect evidence where necessary. Sustainability characteristics should only be built into a report on value where market evidence supports their impact. At the same time, the RICS states that valuers should have an awareness of sustainability features in the short, medium and longer term. As such, they should collect any appropriate sustainability data for future purposes.

### 3.4.3   Additional sustainability value impacts

Although the extent to which superior environmental credentials result in observable higher rents and sale prices has been the basis for much research, there are many other benefits which have been linked to green or sustainable buildings. Fuerst and McAllister (2011c) mention widely cited advantages, which include reduced utility costs, improved productivity and reputational benefits. Many of these benefits are explored in more detail in a report by the World Green Building Council (WGBC, 2013) on the business case for green buildings.

Higher occupancy levels are found by Wiley *et al.* (2010), who identified higher occupancy rates of 10–11% in Energy Star-rated buildings and 16.2–17.9% in LEED-rated buildings. Reichardt *et al.* (2012) also found statistically significant higher occupancy rates for Energy Star-rated buildings. Fuerst and McAllister (2009) found that occupancy rates are approximately 3% higher in Energy Star-rated buildings and 8% higher in LEED-rated buildings compared with non-rated buildings, although the authors stated that these effects may be concentrated in certain market segments. In addition, superior green credentials may help to attract more favourable tenants with a stronger covenant, such as the previously discussed public sector bodies and large private sector occupiers. They may be easier to let as space is absorbed more quickly, and may be associated with higher levels of tenant retention.

Sustainable buildings can also yield significant benefits from an occupational perspective. During the use phase of a building, the energy-efficiency features of green buildings may immediately result in lower operating costs or service charges and may also provide protection from rising energy costs in the future. Water-efficient features can help to save on water costs and the provision of facilities that improve waste sorting and recycling can help to reduce the cost of waste disposal. Because of their future-proofed design, through a prescribed use of materials that are more resilient and have a longer lifespan, the need for renovations, refurbishments or retrofits may also be reduced, which can help save costs, especially for tenants on full repairing and insuring leases. If designed and constructed with future adaptability in mind, the building fabric may be more easily re-usable for alternative uses.

As previously highlighted, ecolabels such as BREEAM and LEED also advocate specific health and well-being measures which focus on optimising lighting and temperature conditions in buildings whilst minimising visual and acoustic intrusions. They therefore promote an optimal working environment for staff that can translate into such benefits as reduced absenteeism, a more productive workforce and even a higher retention of talented staff, *inter alia* (Fuerst and McAllister, 2011a). As staff wages are often the most significant component of the overhead of any organisation, any productivity gains can be highly beneficial. Particularly in office space, new working practices are emerging that are challenging perceptions of workplace conventions. Companies such as Google are taking a lead in offering their staff new features, such as gaming zones and nap pods, but are also rethinking the traditional ways in which space is organised and used in a bid to appeal to their staff.

Companies may also be able save on their overheads by introducing a more flexible working environment in which fewer desks are assigned. The adoption of more flexible ways of using offices may help to minimise environmental impacts, including eliminating the need to travel by offering staff the opportunity to work from home more often, as well as meeting clients by using teleconferencing facilities rather than through physical travel. Care should be taken to involve staff in the transition to any new working practices and arrangements, by actively consulting them and monitoring their satisfaction.

## 3.5  Conclusion

This chapter has looked at the impacts of sustainability issues on the property industry, how they have evolved and what direction they will take in the future. Over the last decade there has been a shift towards the measurement, monitoring and assessment of sustainability performance by property investors and occupiers which is likely to continue to strengthen. Mandatory methods such as EPCs and DECs, as well as voluntary methods such as BREEAM, LEED and GRESB, offer definitions for sustainability in buildings that can be used when they are designed and constructed, but also throughout the rest of their lifecycle.

The most significant challenge will be reducing the intrinsic and operational carbon emissions that are directly attributable to buildings. 2050 falls within the lifecycle of many buildings that exist today. International and national commitments towards achieving GHG emissions have already led to the introduction of new mandatory energy standards in property markets, such as those required from 2018 by the MEES in the UK. In order to meet the requirements of the Climate Change Act 2008 (HM Government, 2008), the energy consumption profile of domestic and non-domestic real estate in the UK will need to be altered significantly to lower the net carbon amount by 80% compared to the 1990 baseline by 2050. Of particular concern is the performance of existing, older buildings, which were built at a time when environmental issues were of little or no concern and which were never designed or constructed with current energy standards in mind. The legislative focus is also likely to shift towards other environmental areas where the built environment generates significant environmental impacts, such as waste disposal and water consumption. New regulations introduce new risk components to property investments, and may accelerate the depreciation of buildings that do not meet the required higher standards.

This can be further compounded by uncertainty and risk caused by future changes in the global climate, the full impacts of which are currently unknown. A report by the European Environment Agency (EEA, 2016) has estimated that annual flood losses across Europe may increase five-fold by 2050 and up to 17-fold by 2080. This makes buildings in areas with a lower risk of floods more desirable and buildings in areas with high flood risk more vulnerable. Forzieri *et al.* (2016) found that, particularly along coastlines and in floodplains, Europe will likely face a progressive increase (the authors identify a prominent spatial gradient towards south-western regions) in overall climate hazard such as windstorms and floods, which will be mainly driven by the rise of heat waves, droughts and wildfires. Buildings with an in-built resilience to extreme temperatures are likely to depreciate more slowly, and buildings in areas with a lower risk of wildfires or other natural disasters that are enhanced or accelerated by climate change will be in higher demand.

JLL (2014) has estimated that property owners and operators who have not yet started reducing their energy consumption will need to meet an annual carbon emissions reduction target of 3.5% to achieve the 80% reduction target by 2050. This will require decarbonising the energy supply, but it can also be achieved through improving the energy-efficiency fabric of buildings and reducing operational energy consumption by setting KPIs and measuring, managing and monitoring these. But this may not be straightforward. Landlords and tenants are known to have conflicting or even adversarial interests, which has resulted in significant challenges for a more widespread adoption of sustainable best practice in the built environment. For both property owners and property occupiers, environmental and social issues need to be ranked among more traditional property decision-making priorities, which currently still tend to overrule any concerns regarding the sustainability performance of buildings. There is, however, much evidence of sustainability leadership and there are many examples of best practice efforts and sincere commitment to improving the overall sustainability performance of buildings, whether from an investment or occupational point of view.

Sustainability drivers include reputational benefits linked to CSR, as well as higher financial returns. From the perspective of property investors, financial benefits linked to the superior environmental performance of buildings include higher rents, higher sale prices and improved occupancy rates. For occupiers, occupying buildings can result in cost savings and productivity benefits. Energy-efficient buildings also offer protection from rising energy prices and penalties which can be levied against inefficient stock. Such drivers can provide a strong incentive towards a continued adoption of environmental and social best practice in green buildings.

## References

ABI (2014) *Topics and issues – Climate Change*. Association of British Insurers. Available at: https://www.abi.org.uk/Insurance-and-savings/Topics-and-issues/Climate-Change.

ABI (2016) *New figures reveal scale of insurance response after recent floods*. Association of British Insurers. Available at: https://www.abi.org.uk/News/News-releases/2016/01/New-figures-reveal-scale-of-insurance-response-after-recent-floods.

Aroul, R.R. and Hansz, J.A. (2012) The Value of 'Green': Evidence from the First Mandatory Residential Green Building Program. *Journal of Real Estate Research*, 34(1), 27–49.

BRE Trust and Cyril Sweett (2005) *Putting a price on sustainability*. BRE Trust, Watford.

Brounen, D. and Kok, N. (2011) On the economics of energy labels in the housing market. *Journal of Environmental Economics and Management*, 62(2), 166–179. doi:10.1016/j.jeem.2010.11.006.

CCC, DEFRA, DECC and EA (2016) *Policy paper. 2010 to 2015 government policy: energy demand reduction in industry, business and the public sector*. Available at: https://www.gov.uk/government/publications/2010-to-2015-government-policy-energy-demand-reduction-in-industry-business-and-the-public-sector/2010-to-2015-government-policy-energy-demand-reduction-in-industry-business-and-the-public-sector.

Chegut, A., Eichholtz, P. and Kok, N. (2012) *Supply, Demand and the Value of Green Buildings*. Available at: http://www.rics.org/site/download_feed.aspx?fileID=11662&fileExtension=PDF.

Davis Langdon (2004) *Costing Green: A Comprehensive Cost Database and Budgeting Methodology*. Available at: http://www.davislangdon.com/upload/images/publications/USA/2004%20Costing%20Green%20Comprehensive%20Cost%20Database.pdf.

Davis Langdon (2007) *Cost of Green Revisited: Reexamining the Feasibility and Cost Impact of Sustainable Design in the Light of Increased Market Adoption*. Available at: http://www.davislangdon.com/upload/images/publications/USA/The%20Cost%20of%20Green%20Revisited.pdf.

DCLG (2016a) *Conservation of fuel and power: Approved Document L*. Department for Communities and Local Government, London. Available at: https://www.gov.uk/government/publications/conservation-of-fuel-and-power-approved-document-l.

DCLG (2016b) *Table A – Non Domestic Energy Performance Certificates for All Properties: Number of Non-Domestic Energy Performance Certificates lodged on the Register in England & Wales by Energy Performance Asset Rating - in each Year/Quarter to 31 December 2015*. Department for Communities and Local Government, London. Available at: https://www.gov.uk/government/statistical-data-sets/live-tables-on-energy-performance-of-buildings-certificates.

DCLG (2016c) *Table D1 – All Dwellings in England & Wales – Number of Energy Performance Certificates lodged on the Register by Energy Efficiency Rating in each Year/Quarter to 31/12/2015*. Department for Communities and Local Government, London. Available at: https://www.gov.uk/government/statistical-data-sets/live-tables-on-energy-performance-of-buildings-certificates.

DECC (2015) *Private Rented Sector Minimum Energy Efficiency Standard Regulations (Non-Domestic)*. Department for the Environment and Climate Change, London. Available at: https://www.gov.uk/government/uploads/system/uploads/attachment_data/file/401378/Non_Dom_PRS_Energy_Efficiency_Regulations_-_Gov_Response__FINAL_1_1__04_02_15_.pdf.

DEFRA (2011) *Number of properties at risk of flooding from rivers and sea, 2011*. Department for Environment, Food and Rural Affairs, London. Available at: https://data.gov.uk/dataset/number-of-properties-at-risk-of-flooding, accessed 18 July 2016.

EEA (2016) *Flood risks and environmental vulnerability Exploring the synergies between floodplain restoration, water policies and thematic policies*. Available at: http://www.eea.europa.eu/publications/flood-risks-and-environmental-vulnerability.

Eichholtz, P., Kok, N. and Quigley, J.M. (2010) Doing Well by Doing Good? Green Office Buildings. *The American Economic Review*, 100, 2492–2509.

European Commission (2013) *The EU strategy on adaptation to climate change*. Available at: http://ec.europa.eu/clima/publications/docs/eu_strategy_en.pdf.

European Commission (2016) *Energy Efficiency – Saving energy, saving money*. Available at: https://ec.europa.eu/energy/en/topics/energy-efficiency.

Forzieri, G., Feyen, L., Russo, S. *et al.* (2016) Multi-hazard assessment in Europe under climate change. *Climatic Change*, 137(1), 105–119. doi:10.1007/s10584-016-1661-x.

Fuerst, F. and McAllister, P. (2009) An investigation of the effect of eco-labeling on office occupancy rates. *Journal of Sustainable Real Estate*, 1(1), 49–64.

Fuerst, F. and McAllister, P. (2011a) Green noise or green value? Measuring the effects of environmental certification on office values. *Real Estate Economics*, 39(1), 45–69. doi:10.1111/j.1540-6229.2010.00286.x.

Fuerst, F. and McAllister, P. (2011b) The impact of Energy Performance Certificates on the rental and capital values of commercial property assets. *Energy Policy*, 39(10), 6608–6614.

Fuerst, F. and McAllister, P. (2011c) Eco-labeling in commercial office markets: Do LEED and Energy Star offices obtain multiple premiums? *Ecological Economics*, 70(6), 1220–1230.

Fuerst, F. and van de Wetering, J. (2015) How does environmental efficiency impact on the rents of commercial offices in the UK? *Journal of Property Research*, 32(3), 193–216. doi: 10.1080/09599916.2015.1047399.

Fuerst, F., McAllister, P., Nanda, A. and Wyatt, P. (2015) Does energy efficiency matter to home-buyers? An investigation of EPC ratings and transaction prices in England. *Energy Economics*, 48, 145–156. doi:http://dx.doi.org/10.1016/j.eneco.2014.12.012.

Green Government Unit – Cabinet Office (2011) *Greening Government Commitments – Guidance on measurement and reporting.* Available at: https://www.gov.uk/government/uploads/system/uploads/attachment_data/file/61172/Greening_20Government_20Commitments_20-_20guidance_20on_20measurement_20and_20reporting.pdf.

HM Government (2008) Climate Change Act 2008, Chapter 27. HM Government, London. Available at: http://www.legislation.gov.uk/ukpga/2008/27/pdfs/ukpga_20080027_en.pdf.

HM Government (2011) Energy Act 2011, Chapter 16. HM Government, London. Available at: http://www.legislation.gov.uk/ukpga/2011/16/enacted.

IPD (2013) IPD EcoPAS Q3 results (PowerPoint presentation). Investment Property Databank. Available at: http://www.klgates.com/files/Publication/166f3ffb-9505-4778-90ec-396dcdb19d7f/Presentation/PublicationAttachment/13917155-22bb-48f9-81c0-39e4f16351f1/IPD_EcoPAS_Q3_Results_2013-Jess_Stevens_13112013.pdf.

JLL (2014) *3.5% – the path to 2050? What the commercial property sector needs to do to meet the UK Government's greenhouse gas emissions reduction target.* Available at: http://www.jll.co.uk/united-kingdom/en-gb/Research/path-to-2020.pdf.

Kats, G. (2013) *Greening Our Built World: Costs, Benefits, and Strategies.* Island Press, Washington.

Kats, G., Alevantis, L., Berman, A., Mills, E. and Perlman, J. (2003) *The Costs and Financial Benefits of Green Buildings – A Report to California's Sustainable Building Task Force.* Available at: http://www.calrecycle.ca.gov/greenbuilding/design/costbenefit/report.pdf.

Kok, N. and Jennen, M. (2012) The impact of energy labels and accessibility on office rents. *Energy Policy*, 46(0), 489–497. doi:10.1016/j.enpol.2012.04.015.

LGA (2016) *Winter flooding: Nearly £250 million damage caused to roads and bridges, new survey reveals.* Local Government Association. Available at: http://www.local.gov.uk/media-releases/-/journal_content/56/10180/7754074/NEWS.

Majcen, D., Itard, L.C.M. and Visscher, H. (2013a) Actual and theoretical gas consumption in Dutch dwellings: What causes the differences? *Energy Policy*, 61, 460–471. doi:http://dx.doi.org/10.1016/j.enpol.2013.06.018.

Majcen, D., Itard, L.C.M. and Visscher, H. (2013b) Theoretical vs. actual energy consumption of labelled dwellings in the Netherlands: Discrepancies and policy implications. *Energy Policy*, 54, 125–136. doi:http://dx.doi.org/10.1016/j.enpol.2012.11.008.

Met Office (2015) *From global carbon budgets to food security – Highlights of research into our changing climate*. Available at: http://www.metoffice.gov.uk/media/pdf/s/f/Highlights_of_research_into_our_changing_climate_for_COP21.pdf.

Newsham, G.R., Mancini, S. and Birt, B.J. (2009) Do LEED-certified buildings save energy? Yes, but. *Energy and Buildings*, 41(8), 897–905.

Reichardt, A., Fuerst, F., Rottke, N.B. and Zietz, J. (2012) Sustainable Building Certification and the Rent Premium: A Panel Data Approach. *Journal of Real Estate Research*, 34(1), 99–126.

RICS (2013) *RICS Professional Guidance, Global – Sustainability and commercial property valuation*, 2nd edn. Royal Institution for Chartered Surveyors, London.

RICS (2015) *Going for Green, Sustainable Building Certification Statistics, Europe 2015*. Royal Institution for Chartered Surveyors, London. Available at: http://www.breeam.com/filelibrary/BREEAM%20and%20Value/Gr-n-kommt--2015.pdf.

Rijksoverheid (2017) *Duurzaam bouwen en verbouwen – Milieuprestaties van gebouwen meten*. Avaiable at: https://www.rijksoverheid.nl/onderwerpen/duurzaam-bouwen-en-verbouwen/inhoud/duurzaam-bouwen/milieuprestaties-van-gebouwen-meten.

*The Economist* (2008). Just good business. Available at: http://www.economist.com/node/10491077.

UNFCCC (2015) *Historic Paris Agreement on Climate Change – 195 Nations Set Path to Keep Temperature Rise Well Below 2 Degrees Celsius*. Press release, United Nations Framework Convention on Climate Change. Available at: http://newsroom.unfccc.int/unfccc-newsroom/finale-cop21/.

Van de Wetering, J. and Wyatt, P. (2011) Office sustainability: occupier perceptions and implementation of policy. *Journal of European Real Estate Research*, 4(1), 29–47.

WBCSD (2008) *Facts & Trends – Energy Efficiency in Buildings. Business realities and opportunities*. Full Report. World Business Council for Sustainable Development Available at: http://www.wbcsd.org/pages/edocument/edocumentdetails.aspx?id=13559.

Wiley, J., Benefield, J. and Johnson, K. (2010) Green design and the market for commercial office space. *Journal of Real Estate Finance and Economics*, 41(2), 228–243. doi:10.1007/s11146-008-9142-2.

WGBC (2013) *The Business Case for Green Buildings – A Review of the Costs and Benefits for Developers, Investors and Occupants*. World Green Building Council, London. Available at: http://www.worldgbc.org/sites/default/files/Business_Case_For_Green_Building_Report_WEB_2013-04-11-2.pdf.

# 4

# From the 'Sustainable Community' to Prosperous People and Places: Inclusive Change in the Built Environment

*Saffron Woodcraft and Constance Smith*

## 4.1   Introduction: The 'sustainable community' in crisis

Creating sustainable communities has been at the forefront of planning policy since the New Labour era. In this chapter, we argue that the 'sustainable community' is no longer a meaningful or productive planning goal. We draw on new qualitative data from two research projects in East London: one exploring what the idea of a sustainable and prosperous community means to people living and working in three neighbourhoods in and around the Queen Elizabeth Olympic Park[1] and a second with a team of architects, planners, house builders and regeneration practitioners engaged in planning and designing a new urban neighbourhood (Woodcraft, 2016). We argue that the term 'sustainable community' has become so elastic and ambiguous it is now frequently used to describe development models that are *un*sustainable in local terms. We examine how people living through change and regeneration in three East London neighbourhoods experience conflicts between planning policy that promises sustainability and day-to-day realities of unaffordable housing, insecure employment and anxieties about displacement. Our research shows these conflicts often centre on questions of value: What value does change in the built environment generate? Who benefits and how? How can the 'social value' of a strong and inclusive community be reconciled with the economic value generated by rising land and property values?

We argue that to take seriously the question of sustainable futures in the built environment, policymakers and practitioners must confront the tensions and conflicts inherent in current models, which are undermining trust in the planning system. We need new ways of thinking and working that are more closely aligned with lived experience and which take into account communities' own aspirations. We present a 'prosperity model' as a way to challenge current thinking about what constitutes sustainable and prosperous communities and to identify new pathways to sustainable futures. Grounded in the day-to-day experiences and aspirations of people living in East London, the model

---

1  The Prosperity in East London pilot study is a mixed methods research programme carried out by UCL's Institute for Global Prosperity, in partnership with London Legacy Development Corporation (LLDC). The purpose of the study was to develop new ways of conceptualising and measuring progress towards the creation of sustainable and prosperous communities in East London. The research was carried out in 2015.

*Sustainable Futures in the Built Environment to 2050: A Foresight Approach to Construction and Development*, First Edition. Edited by Tim Dixon, John Connaughton and Stuart Green.
© 2018 John Wiley & Sons Ltd. Published 2018 by John Wiley & Sons Ltd.

represents the conditions and aspirations that research participants say they, and their communities, need to prosper. This work clearly shows sustainable and prosperous communities are understood as places that support people to flourish and thrive in diverse ways that go far beyond orthodox notions of prosperity as wealth creation and economic growth. We argue for the adoption of 'prosperity' as a guiding principle to building equitable, sustainable futures (Moore, 2015). Understood as diverse, inclusive forms of human flourishing within sustainable environmental limits, prosperity offers new ways of thinking about the built environment holistically, as a long-term social good rather than as short-term financial gain. Using the qualitative findings of our East London research, and based on the experiences of the research participants, we develop a scenario of a sustainable and prosperous community in 2050. Using backcasting techniques, we then identify pathways that can lead from current experience towards the realisation of this future scenario.

## 4.2 Sustainable communities: an ambiguous goal in an unsustainable system

In 2003, the Labour government launched the Sustainable Communities Plan (Office of the Deputy Prime Minister, 2003). This defined the 'sustainable community' as a socio-economic model of place in which aspirations to create socially inclusive and economically thriving communities were integrated with good quality housing and infrastructure. The Sustainable Communities Plan listed 12 of the 'most important requirements of sustainable communities', four of which referred to social aspects: strong leadership to respond positively to change; effective engagement and participation by local people, groups and businesses in long-term stewardship of their community; a diverse, vibrant and creative local culture, encouraging pride in the community and cohesion within it; and a 'sense of place' (Office of the Deputy Prime Minister, 2003: 5).

New housing and neighbourhood regeneration were established as the main policy instruments for delivering this vision. Under the plan, new social housing and social infrastructure were to be funded through the development and sale of private housing, which established a new reliance on partnerships between government and private-sector house builders (Raco, 2005). In the subsequent 13 years, an extensive body of literature has questioned how effective this policy agenda has been at creating places that are inclusive and sustainable in social and economic terms. Critics argue that estate regeneration, most notably in urban areas, has tended to displace low-income populations and undermine local social cohesion (Lees, 2008, 2014). New house building, meanwhile, often fails to provide homes that are genuinely affordable in local terms, pricing local people out of the market and producing social and financial exclusion of a different kind.

In this section, we explore the shifting political and economic conditions that have seen the 'sustainable community' evolve from a holistic policy goal to a fragmented idea used by house builders to demonstrate competitive advantage. We describe what the sustainable community has come to mean in practice, drawing on in-depth interviews with a house builder and team of architects and regeneration practitioners working on the planning, design and construction of a new neighbourhood in East London, and in-depth interviews with house builders, planners and architects working separately on urban regeneration and estate renewal programmes in London (Woodcraft, 2016).

In 2004, the Egan Review was commissioned to conduct an assessment of the professional built environment skills needed to develop the then Labour Government's sustainable communities agenda. The Egan Review called for a holistic and joined-up approach to delivery involving a range of governmental, private sector and civil society actors (DCLG, 2004: 37). However, since 2010, financial and institutional support for the sustainable communities agenda has gradually been withdrawn. This retraction has undermined institutional capacity, in local government in particular, to deliver on the Egan Review and subsequent strategies. Meanwhile, planning reform and the introduction of the National Planning Policy Framework (NPPF) have moved away from the former holistic approach and strengthened the link between planning, development and economic growth, as this extract from the NPPF clearly shows (DCLG, 2012: i):

> 'Sustainable means ensuring that better lives for ourselves don't mean worse lives for future generations. Development means growth. So sustainable development is about positive growth – making economic, environmental and social progress for this and future generations.'

This shift towards sustainability-as-economic-growth illustrates the elasticity that the term 'sustainable' has acquired. This ambiguity has created a discursive space in which the 'sustainable community' can be reimagined and reinterpreted by house builders, planners and sometimes communities themselves. Woodcraft's research (2016) shows that one consequence of this reinterpretation has been the fragmentation of the holistic 'sustainable community' into distinct elements. This extract from an interview with a major house builder illustrates the operational distinctions made between the social, economic and environmental dimensions of sustainability:

> 'Environmental sustainability is a hygiene factor now everybody else is doing it. It doesn't mark you out at all and you have no choice anyway. Being sustainable…in future, it won't be about environmental. That leaves economic: not easy to deliver but easy to define and count jobs, apprenticeships, and you have to do it. And social: hard to count, hard to define, not assumed to be our expertise.'

As this interview makes clear, environmental sustainability is now highly institutionalised and a taken-for-granted element of planning, architecture and construction. This is in part because it has become defined and understood in terms of environmental assessment frameworks such as the Code for Sustainable Homes, first launched by New Labour in 2007.[2] Social sustainability, on the other hand, lacks such institutionalised frameworks, and is much more amorphous and open to interpretation. One house builder described how it is regarded in the sector as 'unclaimed territory'; a new space for architects, planners and developers to signify innovative practices and differentiate themselves in a highly competitive market. As such, the 'social' aspects of sustainable communities – such as the presence of community groups, positive relationships with neighbours, community events that make people feel involved, included and belonging

---

2  The Code for Sustainable Homes was withdrawn in March 2015 and replaced with the Home Quality Mark, which measures a home's environmental footprint as well as other indicators (see https://www.bre.co.uk/academy/page.jsp?id=3600).

to a place – are increasingly recognised by house builders as having financial value, even if is difficult to establish exactly how to quantify that value. In this sense, recognising the value of social sustainability to built environment initiatives follows a logic already established by the value-generating potential of the 'environmental'. Several authors have described the emergence of entrepreneurial modes of urban governance in the UK during the 1990s and 2000s, which saw cities competing to attract investment (While *et al.*, 2004; Cugurullo and Rapoport, 2012; Brand and Thomas, 2013). Urban (environmental) sustainability has figured significantly in this space, in particular landmark projects like eco-cities or sustainable architecture (see, for example, While *et al.* (2004)). Cugurullo and Rapoport (2012: 2), for example, observed how many urban sustainability projects sought to fit environmental considerations into 'a tool that is largely about property development' and were ideologically grounded in the belief that sustainable development 'can and should be a profit-generating activity'.

In consequence, professional perspectives on what constitutes the 'social' in 'social sustainability', and who should take responsibility for it, are often highly selective. Academic literature describes social sustainability as a product of the relationship between change in the built environment – specifically regeneration and new housing development – and the creation of well-being, social capital and certain practices of citizenship at the neighbourhood level (Colantonio and Dixon, 2010; Dempsey *et al.*, 2011; Weingaertner and Moberg, 2011; Magee *et al.*, 2012; Murphy, 2012). By contrast, Woodcraft's research suggests that in practice many house builders de-limit their responsibility for the social aspects of sustainability by distinguishing between 'place-making' activities and public services. For example, high levels of health and education are understood by house builders to be essential aspects of sustainable communities but, as public services, they are regarded as the remit of local government. Instead, 'placemaking' projects – interventions that support community engagement or foster a sense of belonging – have become a popular way for house builders to indicate that their projects can contribute to sustainable communities. These projects can take a range of forms, including timebanks, street parties, pop-up cafes or community gardens. They can be useful ways to build community interaction and local participation, but are not able to address more deep-seated community concerns. In this way, the social aspects of the sustainable community – originally defined as social cohesion, inclusion and belonging – are broken down into 'deliverable' categories that can be operationalised as part of development and regeneration programmes.

Over the last decade, the holistic definition of the 'sustainable community' has slowly disintegrated, with the social dimensions gradually being separated out and reinterpreted. Our research shows that the terms 'sustainable community' and 'social sustainability' are used loosely, interchangeably and in ambiguous ways. Increasingly, social sustainability is being reconfigured as a value-generating practice. This has had the effect of hollowing out the 'sustainable community' as a policy goal. We argue the very elasticity of 'the sustainable community' in discourse, policy and practice has allowed its application to *un*sustainable models of development, from regeneration programmes that displace homeowners and tenants to the rise of affordable housing policy that bears no relation to median household incomes. It is clear from these accounts that policymakers and practitioners need to acknowledge these tensions and reconfigure both what we mean by sustainable futures and the most appropriate methods of arriving there.

## 4.3 Local perspectives on sustainable and prosperous communities

The language of sustainability is not merely an academic concern, it has material repercussions in everyday life. As the previous section shows, the discursive framing of the sustainable community determines the parameters for action and works to 'transform the perceptible into non-obvious meanings' (Rydin, 1999: 467). In this section, we examine what a sustainable and prosperous community means to people living in three East London neighbourhoods and how these meanings are mediated by rapid changes in the built environment. The accounts we present demonstrate how interviewees – despite their different circumstances – described a shared understanding of the conditions needed for people and places to prosper, and how these conditions vary in each neighbourhood to produce different experiences of change. Building on these accounts, we develop a 'prosperity model' as a tool to consider alternative pathways to sustainable futures, which we argue are more meaningful and productive because they are grounded in lived experience.

In 2015, the authors were part of a research team at University College London (UCL)'s Institute for Global Prosperity (IGP) working on a pilot study exploring new ways of thinking about, and measuring, the development of sustainable and prosperous communities in East London. The pilot study sought to respond to the tensions and shortfalls revealed in studies of the sustainable communities policy agenda by developing two new strands of thinking. First, to explore what a sustainable and prosperous community means in local terms, particularly in the context of the rapid social and economic change underway in East London that is associated with the Olympic Legacy and wider processes of urban expansion. Second, based on these accounts, to develop new tools for conceptualising and measuring sustainable prosperity that, crucially, reflect local experience, priorities and aspirations. The pilot focused on three case areas: East Village; new neighbourhood directly adjacent to the Queen Elizabeth Olympic Park (QEOP); part of a neighbourhood in Stratford and part of Hackney Wick. The research team included academics and ten community researchers who live and work in the areas of study (see Figure 4.1). The local knowledge of the community researchers was invaluable, and they participated from the outset in designing research questions and developing methodologies.

### 4.3.1 Pioneers and paninis: local narratives of change

Each research site has its own distinct experience and narrative of change, which shapes how people living and working locally feel about regeneration in East London. The diversity of individual experience was considerable – the pathways that had led interviewees to start a life in East London had, unsurprisingly, taken enormously divergent trajectories. Yet despite this, there were interesting commonalities across the study sites. The majority of interviewees, regardless of social or ethnic background, housing tenure or employment status, said they welcome investment in housing, transport and the public realm. Yet at the same time, almost all felt anxious and uncertain about the likelihood of 'local' people and organisations being able to benefit from new housing, facilities and employment. A common theme was the sense that urban development in

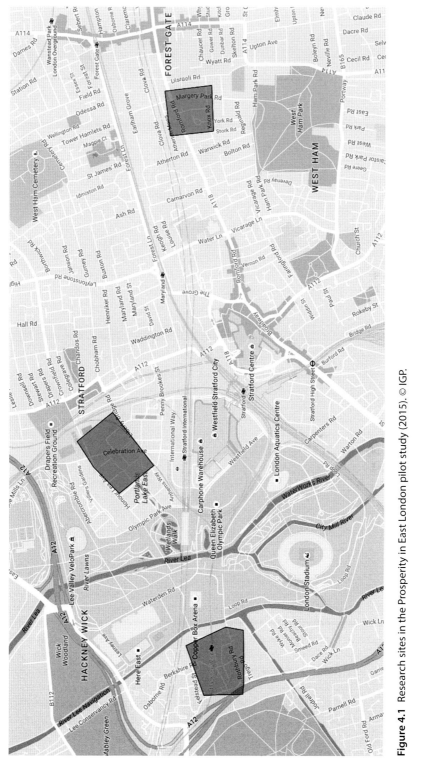

**Figure 4.1** Research sites in the Prosperity in East London pilot study (2015). © IGP.

East London is an unstoppable process – a 'tsunami', as one interviewee said – that local communities feel they have little power to influence. This was not only reported by those who had lived in low-income neighbourhoods in East London for many years, but by those who had recently moved to new housing developments. Though interviewees had had different experiences of change and regeneration, their perspectives about the opportunities represented by such changes did not correlate with their class, culture, profession or length of residence in East London.

What was clear from the study was that very few of our interviewees felt secure amid the changes that were underway in their neighbourhoods. The confluence of rising housing costs, changing working practices, urban development and wider economic conditions affects people from a variety of backgrounds. Young professionals living in East Village were as likely to share anxieties about the pressure of rising housing costs and the prospect of being priced out of the neighbourhood as long-term social housing tenants in Stratford and Hackney Wick. Many interviewees were frustrated at the lack of scope for communities to shape planning or have a stake in future development, and were keen to see alternative housing and development models alongside conventional, private-sector-led schemes. Urban development models that focus on generating short-term economic value for private corporations were generally felt to be at odds with a much broader, local notion of prosperity that prioritises social and economic inclusion, and where the benefits of investment can be recouped by existing communities.

People living in East Village – previously the Olympic Athletes' Village of QEOP – are Olympic Legacy 'pioneers' and our interviewees frequently described themselves in those terms. They are the first group of people to experience the day-to-day reality of life in the Olympic Park. Being an Olympic pioneer brings with it a strong sense of belonging to the neighbourhood. People frequently expressed excitement at being part of something new and described how this feeling is translated into everyday social interactions in the neighbourhood. This quote from Lucy, who had lived in East Village for a year at the time of our interview, best describes this feeling:

> 'It's almost like the normal rules of city living don't apply to the East Village…we have met people we would never have met if we lived on a normal suburban street in London. The only connection we had was that we were all living in the spirit and that was enough to start friendships with people.'

Nevertheless, interviewees of diverse backgrounds also described concerns about the way inequalities can be entrenched, rather than ameliorated, by new housing development in East Village and East London more widely. East Village residents described how tensions emerged between people living in private and affordable housing over housing management rules. Different categories of resident were subject to different restrictions, such as whether or not they were allowed to keep bicycles inside or dry laundry on their balconies. Community events were also not always inclusive of residents in different types of tenure. Irrespective of their tenure type – private rental, affordable rental or shared ownership – our research participants felt that such rules and restrictions worked to draw attention to social and economic differences in a way that undermined other types of community connection. Some interviewees also felt that residents had little influence over the future of East Village, and did not feel able to contribute to the future shape of their community. Developers who are currently building new housing in and around East Village were perceived as having 'a free rein to do as they wish'. Although developers are clearly subject to planning regulations, this perception of unaccountability and lack of public engagement is important, as it helps to shape community sentiment and experiences.

Generally, East Village residents described themselves as feeling prosperous – in the sense of having a very good quality of life and opportunities – but that this prosperity was not secure. Few interviewees felt able to make plans to stay longer than a year or two. The high costs of housing and management fees were reported as the main reasons why people are likely to move on, conditions that interviewees recognised as likely to undermine the sense of community that is so highly prized by pioneer residents. One resident, who lives in what is officially designated as 'affordable' housing, told us:

> 'It's hard to make it sustainable because I pay such a premium to live here…If prosperity is living in a great place, having a fantastic school and great quality of life then I am prosperous. But it's a struggle to hold on to this, to pay for it…You can get on if you can afford to live here.'

Interviewees in the study site in Stratford, on the other hand, had a different experience of regeneration. Participants here described regeneration as either 'something that is passing us by' or as synonymous with 'gentrification' and the departure of longstanding residents from local communities and the borough as a whole. Sometimes referred to as 'old Stratford', this site is relatively further from the recent radical reshaping of the QEOP, as well as related investments such as Westfield and multiple new housing developments. Seeing few material improvements in the immediate neighbourhood, many residents described a sense of exclusion from the Olympic Legacy. The dilapidated public realm, sex workers on local streets, and poor quality and overcrowded housing were cited as evidence that the Olympic Legacy was yet to reach them. A feeling of exclusion was compounded by the sense that local amenities and spaces were under threat from the development of new high-end shops at Westfield and luxury housing in the Olympic Park, which were not intended to appeal to local people. One interviewee who has worked in Stratford for more than 20 years made this clear when she described Stratford High Street and Stratford Shopping Centre as symbolic of the social divide between the 'new and old East End':

> 'They have a view of a middle class, upper class set of people who are gonna move into these homes…Not everyone can afford to shop at Westfield. The idea was Stratford Shopping Centre would close, but it holds its own cos people can't afford to eat at Westfield…Legacy should be about incorporating the past as well as the present…[but now] it's all about elitism and not fitting in with the existing community…I wish we had the old cafes, that part of East London has gone… now it's all paninis. It's a shame.'

The site in Hackney Wick was particularly varied in terms of the diversity of residents and types of housing. Our pilot study interviewed a range of residents, from long-term tenants of a former council estate (now a mix of housing association tenants, privately rented and privately owned households) to artists sharing informal live–work units in ex-warehouses to owners of new residential flats. What was notable was that despite their socio-economic background and form of residency, many interviewees felt that their life in Hackney Wick was precarious, though this precarity was experienced in different ways. Many were concerned about the poor quality of local housing, rising housing costs and social rented housing being replaced with new private or 'affordable' housing as a consequence of new development. Job security, household security and opportunities for work and education were also discussed in anxious terms. Interviewees in shared live–work units were concerned about short-term leases that threatened their capacity to continue to live and work in the neighbourhood, while those from the former council estate described how it was particularly difficult for young people from working class and minority ethnic backgrounds to access employment. Interviewees felt that East London's renaissance was not making the local community more sustainable, rather it was further exposing already vulnerable and disadvantaged areas through rapid changes to the social mix and intensifying competition for local resources. A long-term resident of Hackney Wick who runs a charity based in East London described this feeling of insecurity:

> 'The situation is precarious for people around here. The combination of unaffordable housing, zero hours contracts, portfolio careers…people have no security. This is a toxic mix…there are local kids who can't get a foothold in the local job market regardless of their work experience. They are on zero hours contracts so they can't get a house, and if they can't get a house they won't be able to stay locally.'

Across the three sites, prosperity for our interviewees was understood to mean flourishing, thriving and doing well in a very broad sense. Material security – in the sense of quality employment and housing – was recognised as an essential foundation of prosperity, but it was felt that the current focus on wealth creation and economic growth was only delivering this security to a tiny minority. Indeed, current regeneration practices were felt to be increasing tenancy insecurity, population churn and anxiety about the future. Our interviewees' remarks about employment contracts, tenure types, leisure opportunities and the importance of history and belonging demonstrated their understanding that building sustainable communities requires the intersection of many complex factors. In the full interviews, the importance of social networks, healthy environments, personal development, time for family and friends and maintaining a work/life balance were also emphasised. We collated these reported factors and used them as the basis for a 'prosperity model', which we describe in the next section.

### 4.3.2 Sustainable and prosperous communities: a local model

We have argued that local meanings and aspirations for sustainable places are in conflict with current planning policy and development practice. Analysis of our interview data shows that almost 100% of the 256 people who participated in the pilot study felt that East London's regeneration strategies are not creating communities that are sustainable or prosperous in terms that are meaningful to local people. Tensions revolve around different economies of value and their place in hierarchies of power. The critiques of the 'sustainable community' presented here are a further contribution to a wider body of literature examining the social consequences of urban planning and development (Lees, 2008; Lupton, 2008; Lupton and Fuller, 2009; Cohen, 2013; Watt, 2013). East London has a particularly rich history of sociological work that dates back to Charles Booth's Poverty Maps (Young, 1934; Young and Willmott, 1957; Dench *et al.*, 2006). The question of sustainable futures in the built environment is therefore neither new nor lacking examination. The challenge is to move beyond well-rehearsed arguments to identify credible and viable pathways to change. IGP's prosperity model is directly intended to address this.

Despite their diversity of experience, our interviewees showed considerable commonality in terms of what sustainable prosperity means to them and the factors that are important or essential to achieving it. We use these factors as a basis for developing a prosperity model to advance thinking about developing new pathways to sustainable prosperity for local communities. At the time of writing, this work is still in development as the findings of the pilot study are translated into a conceptual model and a set of prosperity measures capable of tracking progress towards, or away from, local visions of prosperity.[3] A close examination of the interview data revealed 16 general factors that interviewees in all three research sites described as the conditions people and places need to prosper. The relative importance of these factors varied depending on the individual circumstances of interviewees, but they were sufficiently consistent to represent a set of conditions that can be generalised to other neighbourhoods. The 16 factors were grouped to reflect the way interviewees had described the relationships and overlaps between different aspects of prosperity. This enabled us to produce a model with five high-level dimensions (see Table 4.1) articulating what sustainable prosperity means in local terms.

Analysis of the interview data using these categories identified that concerns associated with socially inclusive change and value creation were the most pressing in all three research sites. Good quality and secure local employment, housing that is affordable in local terms, improved local economic development with opportunities for local businesses and the meaningful involvement of local communities in decisions about change were the issues our research participants felt were most important to the prosperity of their local communities. Yet in many cases, these issues were also identified as the most vulnerable to pressure from planning and development that seeks to maximise financial returns on local land and assets. Rising land values, commercial rents and housing costs, in conjunction with financial models that rely on private sector investment to provide affordable housing are felt, as one long-term Hackney Wick resident described, to privilege 'outsiders over locals'.

IGP's prosperity model has been designed to respond directly to these concerns about value. What frustrated many people was the lack of scope for alternative economies of value that reflect local priorities that could co-exist with dominant models. Cafes, pubs, low-cost workspace and neighbourhood shops are what our interviewees described as 'ordinary' places, which are important sites for social life in the neighbourhood. Such spaces are often viewed in planning terms as 'under-utilised', 'under-developed' or 'under-capitalised', yet have social and symbolic value that matters as much as their

---

3 IGP established the London Prosperity Board (LPB) in 2016. The LPB is a cross-sector partnership, including government, public agencies, communities, third-sector organisations and businesses, which will oversee the development of new prosperity measures based on learnings from the Prosperity in East London pilot study.

**Table 4.1** Sustainable prosperity: contributory factors identified in the Prosperity in East London Pilot Study (2015) © IGP.

| Dimension | Description | Required conditions |
|---|---|---|
| Socially inclusive and sustainable value creation | Material security (in terms of secure and good-quality work, secure, affordable and good-quality housing, and social support in the neighbourhood) and socially inclusive economic and political systems and processes of change that generate opportunities for local communities and businesses to create, retain and curate value in the neighbourhood. | Good-quality and secure employment<br>Household security and affordability<br>Local value creation<br>Support for local innovation and enterprise |
| Health and healthy environments | This dimension conceptualises the close relationships between physical and mental health and environmental conditions (including decent housing, good-quality and safe public realm, clean air and energy, food and nutrition, social relationships and well-being). | Healthy bodies and healthy minds<br>Healthy, safe and secure neighbourhoods<br>Access to care and public services |
| Opportunities and aspirations | This dimension describes opportunities for good-quality basic education, lifelong learning and personal development, alongside rewarding, good-quality and secure work, which could be paid or unpaid, and wider aspirations for personal freedoms and work/life balance. | Good-quality basic education<br>Lifelong learning<br>Autonomy and freedom |
| Belonging, identities and culture | This encompasses various expressions of inclusion and belonging that contribute to a sense of identity and cultural belonging. These include local social cohesion, civic involvement, social and financial inclusion. | Social inclusion and cohesion<br>Sense of community<br>Inclusive identities and cultures |
| Networks, connectivity and relationships | This dimension integrates various forms of networks and connectivity that contribute to a sense of prosperity, including social relations (e.g. family, friends, associations, professionals, faith), transport connectivity and digital networks, and global connections. | Social and support networks<br>Power, voice and influence<br>Global networks and connectivity |

practical and economic contributions to the neighbourhood. A long-time community activist working in Hackney Wick had this to say about the importance of 'ordinary' places in maintaining a sense of inclusion for long-term residents:

> 'We don't need more health food…no bulgar wheat or soy latte…we need normal food at decent prices so older people can afford a cup of tea or young people, who frankly have nowhere else to go, can find somewhere to get together.'

All this suggests that understanding what prosperity means, and identifying how to move towards it, needs to be a localised effort. It is at the local level that policymakers, businesses and communities can interrogate what it means to live a good life and intervene to improve opportunities and conditions. In the next section, we use foresight methods to develop ideas for policies and practical interventions that can help to realise what our interviewees' aspirations for truly sustainable, locally meaningful, community prosperity might look like.

## 4.4    Connecting the future and the present

In this section, we build on the accounts of research participants in IGP's 2015 Prosperity in East London pilot study to develop a future vision. We use two foresight methods, scenario planning and backcasting, to construct a scenario of a sustainable and prosperous East London community in 2050. We then use backcasting as a method to suggest possible pathways, models and policy directions needed to make this future possible. Backcasting is a technique to connect future scenarios to present conditions by identifying possible causal relationships between pathways and outcomes. Well-established in foresight studies, backcasting is a popular approach in planning for sustainable development. In such studies, a future vision or outcome is imagined from which researchers or planners work backwards to identify the steps needed to make such a vision a reality (Carlsson-Kanyama *et al.*, 2008). In this case, we use backcasting as a tool to contemplate the changes necessary to catalyse new approaches to urban development that are genuinely inclusive and socially sustainable.

The 2050 scenario we are working with in this paper is unusual in the sense that it is primarily grounded in qualitative data about lived experience and relies less heavily on macro socio-economic trends data than is commonly used for scenario planning. In addition, we are working with one scenario that articulates 'sustainable futures' from the perspective of research participants, rather creating a group of scenarios to 'future proof'[4] a particular strategy. This decision is intentional. Our 2050 scenario seeks to challenge normative practices and open up space for thinking about alternative models of urban living.

### 4.4.1    Scenario: East Town, 2050 – A model for sustainable and prosperous urban development

It is 2050, 38 years after the London Olympics, and 20 years after the conclusion of the city's Olympic legacy regeneration programme. East Town exemplifies innovative and experimental approaches to housing, urban development and regeneration in East London. East Town's inclusive model of sustainable development was made possible by East Borough's adoption of a Prosperity Innovation Strategy in 2016. The Prosperity Innovation Strategy to 2050 was produced in response to London's 2015 work and housing crisis. It observed that pressure on wages, zero-hours contracts, poor educational attainment, entrenched poverty, rising housing costs and increasing pressure on inner-London neighbourhoods from global buy-to-let investors, combined with

---

4  Future proofing is commonly understood to be a process of anticipating future social, economic, environmental and technological changes that have the potential to transform society. The goal is to minimise the impact and shocks to business and policy. In the UK, it is a futures technique used in industry and government.

continued public sector spending cuts were forcing residents and employers to relocate and thereby threatening the stability and future prosperity of the borough.

The Prosperity Innovation Strategy recognised that fundamentally different ways of thinking about work, housing and education had to be developed to address these threats. East Borough set goals to develop socially and economically inclusive models of development and service delivery that recognised work, housing and education as inter-related and inter-dependent foundations of sustainable and equitable prosperity. The borough established cross-sector and cross-disciplinary partnerships tasked with identifying global best practice and bringing innovative thinking and approaches from business, the community and academia to bear on challenges related to work, housing and education. One such initiative is the Urban Development Innovation Institute – a partnership between East London councils, universities, developers and employers that was established to drive experimentation and test new approaches to urban regeneration.

As part of the Prosperity Innovation Strategy, the council adopted a Diversified Development Programme (DDP) to provide housing and work space that is genuinely affordable in local terms. It also enables the council and local communities to capture the value of local development and to recycle the surplus into research and innovation, services and projects. The aim of the DDP is to encourage new development models that create inclusive, sustainable and prosperous communities with a mix of housing tenures and live–work spaces to rent or own.

The DDP has encouraged a number of new development vehicles, including a council-owned development company to construct new housing and workspaces that are offered at 'East Town living rents'. These were introduced in 2018 to ensure housing costs are no higher than 30% of median household incomes for the neighbourhood rather than the discounted market rent offered at the peak of London's 2015 housing crisis. A Community Land Agency has also been established, with the remit to bring forward parcels of land for community-led development by co-operatives, land trusts or community co-living companies, and to build innovative 'self-finish' apartment blocks as low-cost home ownership options for housing associations and community co-operatives. These vehicles operate alongside conventional developer-led models offering private, for-profit housing for sale. Together these measures have reduced the ratio of median household earnings to house prices from the peak of 10.10 in 2015 to the 1999 ratio of 3.64.[5]

Sharing economy principles are embedded in new housing and commercial developments. New communities have food gardens – a mixture of individual allotments, community growing spaces and food business spaces – to localise food production and make fresh food more accessible in low-income neighbourhoods. Local planning policy ensures car and bicycle schemes are expanded for every additional 100 new households in the borough (including the conversion of existing houses into apartments by individual landlords) and developments above 50 new households include car share membership in the rent or sale price.

Olympicopolis, the Olympic Park's cultural and educational quarter, has become established as the capital's innovation, research and creative industries hub. Establishing

---

5 The figures used in the scenario are median household earnings to house price ratios for the London Borough of Newham as reported in *Median and Lower Quartile Ratio of House Prices to Earnings* (DCLG, 2015).

a light industrial zone in the neighbourhood has protected East London's long-established manufacturing businesses. East Borough's council-owned development company purchased a portfolio of warehouse and workshop spaces that are now held in a Community Enterprise Trust to offer 'East Town working rents' – rents set to reflect the turnover of local businesses – in perpetuity for local creative and artistic enterprises. Affordable workspaces have enabled East London's arts and creative industries to remain in the area, build new links with incoming major cultural institutions and develop educational outreach and apprenticeship programmes that now provide proven pathways to employment in creative industries for young people in East London.

East Borough has established a number of council-owned social enterprises. An example of these is a neighbourhood retrofit company that runs a programme to replace windows on social and private housing and commercial premises across the borough with energy-generating solar glass. The company is part of a green-tech R&D partnership working from Olympicopolis that provides jobs, training and apprenticeships to local people. The neighbourhood retrofit company is the first of its kind in the capital and generates revenue by providing services to other councils and private developers.

This scenario may sound idealistic in the context of the critiques described earlier in this chapter. Yet people's aspirations for secure and good quality employment, decent schools and life chances, affordable and stable housing are not – or should not be – utopian. For our research participants, the absence of these aspects in their daily lives shapes their vision for individual and community prosperity. Furthermore, though this scenario might sound like a distant vision, in fact there are many innovative small-scale projects across London and the UK that are experimenting with alternative ways to create inclusive change and local value. Though small-scale, these projects nevertheless provide a basis from which to consider the pathways and policy directions that could connect the East Town 2050 scenario to the present. In the next section we propose three such pathways: first, a new national conversation about value and prosperity in the built environment that re-frames how we understand and balance social, economic and environmental needs; second, catalysing social innovation in the housing sector to bring new thinking to the complex problem of equitable and inclusive development; and third, developing new methods for understanding and measuring the relationship between local prosperity and change in the built environment.

## 4.5  Building prosperity: re-thinking value and innovation in the built environment

### 4.5.1  A new conversation

The first step towards creating sustainable futures in the built environment is a new type of conversation between government, citizens, policymakers and built environment practitioners. By asking new questions from different angles, it becomes possible to gain fresh perspective on seemingly entrenched problems. This conversation must address fundamental questions about the kinds of futures that are valued and how building sustainable and prosperous places is integral to achieving this vision. Crucially, this debate needs to take place not only within boardrooms, design studios or council offices, but with and among communities themselves. It is, we argue, only when communities' own experiences are properly engaged in every stage of urban development – from planning to evaluation – that key problems can be identified, and vital feedback loops and processes of learning can be integrated.

Our research identifies a disconnect between current approaches to urban development, which are highly fragmented and prioritise return on investment, and local notions of sustainability, which communities know from experience is shaped by a complex set of intersecting factors. This disconnect is, in part, a consequence of starting from the wrong problem. Rather than innovating for environmental integrity and human well-being, too often in urban development the primary concern is to maintain the status quo – and the bottom line. How do we look beyond urban development models founded in profit and economic growth to realise a form of planning that addresses social progress, quality of life, opportunity and aspiration? These are difficult questions, yet it is clear the current growth-focused, market-led mode of development is a major obstacle to genuinely prosperous future communities. Failing to address such fundamental tensions will only continue to entrench issues of social and financial exclusion.

There is growing consensus that orthodox economic growth models are unsustainable, not just in a context of finite planetary resources but because the forms of development they have delivered are acutely unevenly distributed (Eisler, 2008; Jackson, 2017; Gower *et al.*, 2012; Mason, 2015). Jackson (2017) has argued that prosperity without growth is not only possible, but desirable; it entails a shift in perspective that puts people's everyday lives back at the heart of economic planning and policy. Moore argues for the adoption of 'prosperity' – rather than 'development' – as a guiding principle for change. Understood as 'diverse forms of human flourishing', prosperity encompasses the health of society, inclusive models of development, civil liberties and active citizens who are involved in co-producing their equitable futures within sustainable limits of the planet's resources (Moore, 2015: 804, 811). These kinds of debates about the social sustainability of economic models are re-evaluating some long-held assumptions about what constitutes national and international development and how we think about successful countries. We understand the challenge now to be how to expand on these conversations to rethink urban development policy, planning and practice. In short, to imagine a 'new normal' for urban development that moves away from a singular notion of 'value' towards a plurality of 'values'.

In the scenario above, we imagined how 2015's housing crisis might catalyse such fundamental debates. In our vision for East Town, these conversations initiated a systemic refiguring of what delivering 'sustainable urban futures' might look like. This was a deliberate attempt to rethink the kinds of reactions the crisis has provoked thus far. London's unaffordable rents and skyrocketing house prices – and in particular high-profile cases such as the New Era housing estate and the controversial redevelopment of the Heygate Estate – have indeed attracted considerable public comment.[6] Yet the official response has been short-sighted and far from comprehensive. In an attempt to relieve the pressure on housing and increase supply, the government is investing in expanding the private rented housing sector. Two publicly-funded schemes are intended

---

6  See, for example, Oliver Wainwright and Stephen Moss writing about the Heygate Estate for the *Guardian* (Moss, 2011; Wainwright, 2016), Kate Allen's review of regeneration and rent control on the New Era Estate for the *Financial Times* (Allen, 2015) and the *Independent's* review of the Cereal Killer café protests (Mortimer, 2015).

to stimulate development of 10,000 new private rented homes: the £1 billion Build to Rent Fund and the Private Rented Sector Debt Guarantee Scheme to support low-cost private sector borrowing (DCLG, 2015: 9, 10). Such schemes, instead of analysing the roots of the crisis and tackling unaffordable housing by looking for new ways to radically cut housing costs, continue to entrench issues of affordability by replacing one increasingly unaffordable form of tenure (owner-occupation) with another (private renting).

We use our 2050 scenario to illustrate an alternative future. In doing so, our aim is to illuminate tensions and contradictions with current policy and to identify potential pathways to change in order to begin new conversations. Such conversations are not easy to have and they do not deliver quick answers. But if future investments in the built environment are to support sustainable long-term and inclusive prosperity, then it is crucial that policymakers start from the experiences of the communities whose prosperity is at stake. The East Town 2050 scenario is based on our qualitative research with residents in East London, in which, together with local community researchers, we started by asking fundamental questions about what prosperity means to them, and what kind of changes need to happen to realise such futures. This has initiated a very different vision, one that recognises how an apparently discrete issue like unaffordable housing intersects with other factors like employment insecurity and poor educational and health indicators. And, just as importantly, how local prosperity is shaped by economic and political systems that are outside the neighbourhood.

### 4.5.2 Catalysing social innovation

As we work back from this scenario to develop pathways to sustainable community prosperity, it is crucial that we keep such conversations in focus. This requires a multi-sectoral response and a diverse set of models, strategies and interventions that are grounded in local realities. This is why our imagined 'prosperity innovation strategy' engages councils, developers, employers and researchers, as well as communities themselves, in working together on situated responses.

The second proposed pathway towards our Scenario 2050 moves from the discursive transformations described above to look at tangible, practice-led innovations needed to deliver equitable and inclusive change in the built environment. As our scenario makes clear, not only should new conversations about prosperity and value be rooted in communities, but new practices and methods of developing social change can be generated from the bottom up, led by communities themselves as they respond creatively to the challenges they experience. This form of social innovation, defined as new approaches to addressing social needs, will be crucial to testing new ways of working towards the built environments of the future, as we develop processes of urban change that are comprehensive, evidence-based and responsive to community needs. Catalysing these kinds of social innovation cannot be left solely to civil society alone, however. For innovative practices and processes to effect wider change requires inter-sectoral support as well as financial and legislative capacity.

As we backcast from our Scenario 2050 to develop the pathways that can enable social innovation to occur at scale, there are examples around the UK from which we can learn. Innovative projects from housing co-operatives to community land trusts, self-build communities, co-living, printing houses using 3D printers and new forms of modular architecture are growing in frequency, and showing how community groups can work with designers, engineers, councils and businesses to meet the challenges of different localities. Many of these models are conceived as inclusive forms of development and set out to give people a stake in housing projects, tackle the lack of affordable housing or find ways for the financial gains from development to be retained and managed by local communities. Examples from London include innovative community-led projects such as the self-build housing at Angell Town in Brixton[7] and the London Community Land Trust (CLT), the first CLT in London to sell affordable housing that is linked to local earnings. The CLT's first development at St Clements Hospital in East London will sell homes at approximately one-third of the open market value. The CLT model is designed to enable local organisations to use assets in the community to meet local needs. Land, buildings, workspace or housing are acquired – often below market rate – and held in perpetuity by the CLT for the community. In this way, the value of the land and gains from development are retained for the benefit of the local community.

A rare, but promising, recent example of inclusive development can be found in Brixton, South London in Lambeth Council's partnership with Ovalhouse Theatre and Brixton Green – a community-owned mutual benefit society – to redevelop Somerleyton Road. Lambeth Council's wider record on estate regeneration and new housing development has been much criticised by residents, housing commentators and housing activists, in particular for its decision to demolish Cressingham Gardens Estate in South London.[8] Such criticisms are justified, but with Somerleyton Road, Lambeth has rejected the conventional approach where a leasehold on the land is sold to a private developer and income from the sale of private housing is used to subsidise affordable housing. Instead, following an extensive consultation process, they adopted an innovative development model that has enabled the council to retain full ownership of the development site, borrow money for the development and procure a development partner to manage and build the project. Different financial scenarios were prepared to examine rental income from private rental, affordable rental and mixed tenure schemes. The council determined that by borrowing £43 million at an interest rate of 4.5% it could pay off the total debt by 2060 from rental income of £60 million earned from mixed-tenure properties. This option was chosen over the £250 million that could be earned from a private-rented property (Melhuish, 2015: 23). This project demonstrates how communities and councils can collaborate to address difficult questions about the different forms of value produced by change in the built environment and develop socially inclusive and financially viable alternatives to dominant models. It shows how it is both practical and possible for local government to make responsible trade-offs between public – more specifically local – good and maximising private profit.[9]

--------

7  The regeneration of Angell Town Estate in Brixton, South London, included 10 'self-build' homes. Residents worked closely with the contractor Higgins, who provided training to enable people to decorate and fit their own kitchens and bathrooms (see http://www.mode-1.co.uk/242_EcoHomes%20Fact%20Sheet.pdf).
8  Cressingham Gardens is a post-war housing estate in Tulse Hill, South London. Residents have led a high-profile campaign to protest against Lambeth Council's plans to demolish their homes (Hill, 2015).
9  There are other notable examples, including the St Anne's Regeneration Trust (StART), a CLT led by a group of Haringey residents. They are organising an alternative to the planned redevelopment of the St Anne's Hospital site, which would see only 14% of new homes classed as 'affordable'. Instead, StART seek to acquire two-thirds of the site for a community-led housing development which will meet the needs of local people and be truly affordable in local terms (see http://www.startharingey.co.uk/).

### 4.5.3   Towards sustainable and prosperous places: new measures of change and progress

The East Town Scenario is a tool for imagining pathways to alternative futures. A crucial element of this process is to develop new methods of evaluation. Urban development projects need to be reflexive, responding constructively to feedback loops and enabling new indicators of change and success to be built in. Therefore, the third proposed pathway towards our Scenario 2050 is to develop new locally situated measures of change and progress. There is no doubt that indicators are powerful tools of governance (Davis *et al.*, 2012) and audit (Strathern, 2000), yet evidence shows that clear links between indicator development and meaningful change are hard to identify (Holman, 2009; Scott and Bell, 2013; Turcu, 2013). To address this deficit, we argue that to identify pathways to sustainable and prosperous futures, new measures should draw on both qualitative and quantitative data and, crucially, must be grounded in local lived experience.

IGP is currently developing a dashboard of prosperity measures to connect the East Town Scenario to the contemporary accounts of change and broad notions of prosperity described by our interviewees in East London. Working with community researchers and local stakeholders, the research team has translated the 16 headline indicators in the prosperity model outlined in section 4.3 into 50 discrete measures of subjective experience. Developing these new measures requires extensive testing and refinement, and this work is still in progress. The final dashboard will not be released until after further research and evaluation, taking place in 2017–18. Ultimately, it is envisaged that IGP's prosperity model will enable researchers, regeneration practitioners as well as communities in Stratford, Hackney Wick and East Village to monitor how urban development projects and interventions come together to effect change in the area.

We argue this work is both conceptually and methodologically innovative. Conceptually, our focus on prosperity as 'diverse forms of flourishing', rather than fixating on wealth creation and economic growth, creates space for local meanings to emerge. As our East London work shows, applying this prosperity lens to local experience reveals the importance of socially inclusive change and challenges existing planning policy. By taking account of lived experience, local conditions and real constraints, we can conceptualise and measure prosperity in local terms that are both meaningful and actionable. This attention to and evaluation of subjective experience means that our approach enhances the wide range of existing measures that report on local social and economic conditions, such as the UK's Indices of Multiple Deprivation. More importantly, however, our holistic approach challenges conventional modes of categorising and organising the world. Instead of replicating the normative, yet artificial, distinctions between social, economic and environmental domains of life that characterise governance frameworks and public policy measures, we have designed measures that reflect how these domains are in practice mutually constitutive.

Methodologically, our focus on co-producing measures with community researchers and local people has proven to be essential to identifying measures that resonate with local experience. Moving forward, IGP will collect new quantitative data to produce small-area statistics about subjective experiences of place. We argue that this methodology is critical to identifying viable pathways to change because, as a comparative framework, it can identify how effects and experiences are distributed within and between neighbourhoods. This differentiates our approach from other subjective measurement frameworks, such as the UK's National Well-Being framework (Hicks *et al.*, 2013), which reports on levels of well-being at local authority and regional level, and other indices that compare global performance at the state level using secondary data (Social Progress Imperative, 2016; Legatum Institute, 2015) but do not draw on ethnographic or experiential methods.

It is important to acknowledge that indicators, while critical to planning, decision-making and evaluation, are not sufficient in themselves to bring about lasting change. Sustainability, well-being, resilience and quality of life indicators have proliferated since the 1990s, along with an extensive literature critiquing their construction, limitations and practical application to policy and decision-making (e.g. Turcu, 2012). For example, the field of sustainability measurement is now so extensive that there is not scope in this chapter to account for all the conceptual and methodological frameworks that are employed, nor to describe the numerous sub-fields (such as urban sustainability, social sustainability and resilience) and the various geographies at which indicators work (for a detailed description see Holman (2009)). Yet despite this proliferation of metrics, the widening gap between rich and poor, unequal service delivery and rising child poverty rates – to indicate just a few markers – suggest that our established methods of measurement are not increasing our capacity to tackle complex global issues such as social inequality, depleted ecological resources or the delivery of inclusive economic models.

To be effective, new measures must be meaningful, operational and, most importantly, situated in policy environments and stakeholder partnerships that can activate change. Our East Town Scenario identifies a cross-sector partnership of citizens, government, business and local organisations as one form of local governance that can build sustainable futures. In real life, the new forms of measurement initiated by IGP are already directly activating change, as we seek to make the forms of partnership imagined in Scenario 2050 a reality. IGP has established the London Prosperity Board, a partnership between universities, government, business, civil society and East London communities. The board will begin the new conversation we describe in this chapter, starting the work of catalysing social innovation and developing further measures in a responsive and iterative model of urban change.

## 4.6 Conclusion

Contemplating socially sustainable futures in the built environment to 2050 is necessarily a speculative exercise, one with no certain outcomes and with a large degree of unpredictability. It is nevertheless vital to conceptualising, planning, implementing and evaluating what we mean by truly prosperous people and places. We have argued in this chapter that the notion of 'sustainable communities' has become so amorphous as to be no longer fit for purpose, allowing a reconfiguration of sustainability as a for-profit practice that undermines social cohesion, quality of life and resilient community prosperity. Related categories such as 'affordable' housing have similarly come to lose all meaning in relation to lived experience. Government responses to the recent housing crisis have been short-sighted and have tended to reinforce growth-based models of urban development, in which the generated value is not retained for the local community.

In response, we have used a diverse, inclusive and sustainable understanding of 'prosperity' as a guiding principle to consider alternative models of urban change. Steered by IGP's findings in East London and the experiences and perspectives of the residents who participated in the research, we imagined a 2050 Scenario in which current challenges were understood as a critique of established models, stimulating creative and constructive alternatives from local authorities, businesses, charities, education providers and civil society working in partnership. We propose that the pathways needed to make such scenarios a realistic, viable alternative can be divided into three new approaches. First, we need to not only acknowledge that current models are not working for communities, but to think about entrenched problems in fresh ways that holistically consider what it takes to enable communities to flourish. Second, we need to foster social innovation, finding new techniques, processes and practices that can initiate social change from the grassroots, but in an environment of supportive policy and governance that enables successful interventions to be scaled up. Third, we need to embed new forms of measurement and evaluation based on reported experiences of change as well as statistical data. These need to be actionable, setting in motion iterative processes of learning through ongoing critique and refinement. Fundamentally, we suggest, building the sustainable, prosperous communities of the future relies on moving away from growth-based models of development and instead initiating strategies and methods that are underpinned by a plurality of forms of value.

## References

Allen, K. (2015) High-profile hoxton rebels given means-tested rents, *Financial Times*, August 17. Available at: http://www.ft.com/cms/s/0/ed095a0c-44c7-11e5-af2f-4d6e0e5eda22.html (accessed 2 August 2016).

Brand, P. and Thomas, M. (2013) *Urban Environmentalism: Global Change and the Mediation of Local Conflict*. Routledge.

Carlsson-Kanyama, A., Dreborg, K.H., Moll, H. C. and Padovan, D. (2008) Participative backcasting: A tool for involving stakeholders in local sustainability planning'. *Futures*, 40(1), 34–46.

Cohen, P. (2013) *On the Wrong Side of the Tracks? East London and the Post-Olympics*. Lawrence & Wishart, London.

Colantonio, A. and Dixon, T. (2010) *Urban Regeneration & Social Sustainability: Best Practice from European Cities*. John Wiley & Sons.

Cugurullo, F. and Rapoport, E. (2012) *Between the global and the local: The ideologies and realities of sustainable urban projects*. University College London, London.

Davis, K., Kinsbury, B. and Engle Merry, S. (2012) *Governance by Indicators: Global Power through Classification and Rankings*. Oxford University Press.

Dempsey, N., Bramley, G., Power, S. and Brown, C. (2011) The Social Dimension of Sustainable Development: Defining Urban Social Sustainability. *Sustainable Development*, 19(5):289–300.

Dench, G., Gavron, K. and Young, M. (2006) *The New East End: Kinship, Race & Conflict*. Profile Books.

DCLG (2004) *The Egan Review: Skills for Sustainable Communities.* Department for Communities and Local Government, London. Available at: http://www.communities. gov.uk/publications/communities/eganreview (accessed 28 September 2012).

DCLG (2012) *National Planning Policy Framework.* Department for Communities and Local Government, London. Available at: http://www.communities.gov.uk/ planningandbuilding/planningsystem/planningpolicy/planningpolicyframework/ (accessed 28 September 2012).

DCLG (2015) *Accelerating Housing Supply and Increasing Tenant Choice in the Private Rented Sector: A Build to Rent Guide for Local Authorities.* Department for Communities and Local Government, London. Available at: https://www.gov.uk/government/uploads/ system/uploads/attachment_data/file/416611/150323_Accelerating_Housing_Supply_ and_Increasing_Tenant_Choice_in_the_Private_Rented_Sector.pdf (accessed 28 March 2016).

Eisler, R.T. (2008) *The Real Wealth of Nations: Creating a Caring Economics.* Berrett-Koehler Publishers.

Gower, R., Pearce, C. and Raworth, K. (2012) Left behind by the G20. How inequality and environmental degradation threaten to exclude poor people from the benefits of economic growth. Oxfam policy and practice. *Agriculture, Food and Land*, 12(1), 35–80.

Hicks, S., Tinkler, L. and Allin, P. (2013) Measuring subjective well-being and its potential role in policy: Perspectives from the UK Office for National Statistics. *Social Indicators Research*, 114(1), 73–86.

Hill, D. (2015) A time for trust at Lambeth's Cressingham Gardens estate. The Guardian, 8 March. Available at: https://www.theguardian.com/uk-news/davehillblog/2015/ mar/08/a-time-for-trust-at-the-cressingham-gardens-estate.

Holman, N. (2009) Incorporating local sustainability indicators into structures of local governance: A review of the literature. *Local Environment*, 14(4), 365–375.

Jackson, Tim. (2017) *Prosperity without Growth: Foundations for the Economy of Tomorrow.* 2nd edition. Abingdon, Oxon; New York, NY: Routledge.

Legatum Institute (2015) *The 2015 Legatum Prosperity Index.* The Legatum Institute. Available at: http://www.prosperity.com/#!/ (accessed 2 August 2016).

Lees, L. (2008) Gentrification and social mixing: Towards an inclusive urban renaissance? *Urban Studies*, 45(12), 2449–2470.

Lees, L. (2014) The death of sustainable communities in London? In Imrie, R. and Lees, L. (eds) *Sustainable London? The future of a global city.* Policy Press.

Lupton, R. (2008) *Neighbourhood Effects: Can We Measure Them and Does It Matter?* Social Science Research Network, Rochester, NY. Available at: http://papers.ssrn.com/ abstract=1158964 (accessed 22 April 2013).

Lupton, R. and Fuller, C. (2009) Mixed communities: A new approach to spatially concentrated poverty in England. *International Journal of Urban and Regional Research*, 33(4), 1014–1028.

Magee, L., Scerri, A. and James, P. (2012) Measuring social sustainability: A community-centred approach. *Applied Research in Quality of Life*, 7(3), 239–261.

Mason, P. (2015) *Postcapitalism: A Guide to Our Future.* Allen Lane.

Melhuish, C. (2015) *Lambeth Council, Brixton Green and Ovalhouse Theatre in South London: A Co-Operative Community-Led Development in Inner London.* UCL Urban Lab. Available at: https://www.ucl.ac.uk/urbanlab/docs/case-study-5-lambeth-council (accessed 28 March 2016).

Moore, H.L. (2015) Global prosperity and sustainable development goals. *Journal of International Development*, 27(6), 801–815.

Mortimer, C. (2015) Cereal Killer Cafe Attacked in 'Anti-Gentrification' Protest. *The Independent*, September 27. Available at: http://www.independent.co.uk/news/uk/anti-gentrification-protesters-attack-cereal-killer-cafe-with-paint-a6668886.html, (accessed 2 August 2016).

Moss, S. (2011) The Death of a Housing Ideal. *The Guardian*, March 4. Available at: http://www.theguardian.com/society/2011/mar/04/death-housing-ideal (accessed 2 August 2016).

Murphy, K. (2012) The social pillar of sustainable development: A literature review and framework for policy analysis. *Sustainability: Science, Practice, & Policy*, 8(1), 15–29.

Office of the Deputy Prime Minister (2003) *Sustainable Communities Plan*. Available at: http://webarchive.nationalarchives.gov.uk/20060502043818/http://odpm.gov.uk/pub/872/SustainableCommunitiesBuildingfortheFutureMaindocumentPDF2121Kb_id1139872.pdf (accessed 20 April 2013).

Raco, M. (2005) Sustainable development, rolled-out neoliberalism and sustainable communities. *Antipode*, 37(2), 324–347.

Rydin, Y. (1999) Can we talk ourselves into sustainability? The role of discourse in the environmental policy process. *Environmental Values*, 8(4), 467–484.

Scott, K. and Bell, D. (2013) Trying to measure local well-being: indicator development as a site of discursive struggles. *Environment and Planning C: Government and Policy*, 31(3), 522–539.

Social Progress Imperative (2016) *2016 Social Progress Index*. Available at: http://www.socialprogressimperative.org/global-index/ (accessed 2 August 2016).

Strathern, M. (2000) *Audit Cultures: Anthropological Studies in Accountability, Ethics, and the Academy*. Routledge.

Turcu, C. (2013) Re-thinking sustainability indicators: Local perspectives of urban sustainability. *Journal of Environmental Planning and Management*, 56(5), 695–719.

Wainwright, O. (2016) Revealed: How Developers Exploit Flawed Planning System to Minimise Affordable Housing. *The Guardian*, June 25. Available at: http://www.theguardian.com/cities/2015/jun/25/london-developers-viability-planning-affordable-social-housing-regeneration-oliver-wainwright (accessed 2 August 2016).

Watt, P. (2013) It's Not for Us. *City*, 17(1), 99–118.

Weingaertner, C. and Moberg, A. (2011) Exploring social sustainability: Learning from perspectives on urban development and companies and products. *Sustainable Development*, 22(2), 122–133.

While, A., Jonas, A.E.G. and Gibbs, D. (2004) The environment and the entrepreneurial city: Searching for the urban 'sustainability fix' in Manchester and Leeds. *International Journal of Urban and Regional Research*, 28(3), 549–569.

Woodcraft, S. (2016) Reconfiguring 'the social' in sustainable development: community, citizenship and innovation in new urban neighbourhoods, in Murphy, F. and McDonagh, P. (eds) *Envisioning Sustainabilities*: *Towards an Anthropology of Sustainability*. Cambridge Scholars Publishing.

Young, T. (1934) *Becontree and Dagenham: The Story of the Growth of a Housing Estate*. Samuel Sidders and Son.

Young, M. and Willmott, P. (1957) *Family and Kinship in East London*, rev. edn. Penguin.

# 5

# Smart *and* Sustainable?: The Future of 'Future Cities'

*Tim Dixon*

## 5.1   Introduction

We live in the age of the city. A majority of the world's population (3.9 billion or 54%) lives in cities and this is set to grow to 66% by 2050. Much of this growth is occurring in developing countries and through the increasing number of mega-cities (or cities of more than 10 million). On the one hand this unprecedented urban growth presents us with huge opportunities because cities can act as vibrant hubs of innovation, enterprise and jobs growth, and as places which create economies of scale in technology deployment. On the other hand, but it can also present us with substantial challenges because as urbanisation continues rapidly it creates more greenhouse gas emissions, depletes resources, consumes more energy and can create socio-economic polarisation (Dixon, 2015).

Today therefore, more than ever, there is a strong practice and policy focus on cities, not only in the UK, but internationally as well. In the UK, for example, we have seen the emergence over the last few years of the UK Department of Business, Innovation and Skills (BIS) Smart Cities initiative, the UK government's funding of the Future Cities Catapult (one of a number of centres designed to transform the UK's capability for innovation in specific areas and help drive future economic growth) and the UK Government Office for Science Future Cities Foresight programme, and we have also seen an increasing policy focus on providing greater devolved funding powers for cities across the political spectrum. Also, internationally, the recent IPPC report on climate change pointed to the key role that cities will play in tackling future climate change (Van Staden, 2014), and initiatives such as the Rockefeller Resilient Cities and the C40 Cities Climate Disclosure programmes have placed city actions centre stage.

This chapter discusses why it is important to think about cities, and how the future cities discourse has evolved from its historic roots in utopic thinking. The coming together of 'smart' and 'sustainable principles' is then discussed, and what this means in theory and in practice. The chapter addresses the driving forces and the barriers for smart and sustainable cities, and concludes by posing four questions:

- What will be the key driving forces and trends that will impact on such cities to 2050?
- What will these cities look like in 2050?

*Sustainable Futures in the Built Environment to 2050: A Foresight Approach to Construction and Development*, First Edition. Edited by Tim Dixon, John Connaughton and Stuart Green.
© 2018 John Wiley & Sons Ltd. Published 2018 by John Wiley & Sons Ltd.

- What will these cities be made of in 2050?
- How can such cities best plan for the future?

## 5.2   Why is thinking about cities important?

As we shall see later in this chapter, thinking about the future of cities is not new. But why do we need to think about cities today and in the future, perhaps more than ever before? Moreover, what are the possible ramifications of this growing importance of cities on our professional work in the built environment disciplines?

First, we need to think about the rapid urbanisation that has, and will continue to have, a global impact. The world has gone through a process of rapid urbanisation over the past 60 years: in 1950, more 70% of people lived in rural settlements globally and less than 30% in urban settlements. In today's increasingly global and interconnected world, more than half of the world's population (54%) lives in urban areas although there is still substantial variability in the levels of urbanisation across countries. Indeed, in 2007, for the first time in history, the global urban population exceeded the global rural population, and the world population has remained predominantly urban thereafter (Figure 5.1). The next 30–40 years will see further profound changes in the size and spatial distribution of the global population. The continuing urbanisation and overall growth of the world's population is projected to add 2.5 billion people to the urban population by 2050, with nearly 90% of the increase concentrated in Asia and Africa (and India, China and Nigeria expected to account for 37% of the world's projected urban population growth to 2050). At the same time, the proportion of the world's population living in urban areas is expected to increase, reaching 66% by 2050 (UN, 2015). Although there will be an increase in the number of mega-cities (cities with more than 10 million population) to 41 from the current 28, the fastest growing urban

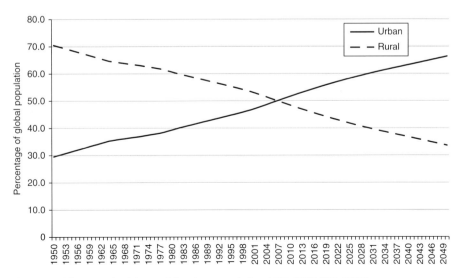

**Figure 5.1**  The growth of the world's urban population 1950–2050 (UN, 2015).

**Table 5.1** City challenges and opportunities in the 21st century (Walt *et al.*, 2014).

| Challenges | Opportunities |
| --- | --- |
| Population growth and stressed infrastructure | Political autonomy and collaboration |
| Resource efficiency and low carbon growth | Information and communication technology to optimise city systems |
| Resilient systems | Efficiency and economies of scale |
| Income inequality | Prosperity and innovation |
| Demographic change and disease | Civic engagement and social movement |

centres will be medium- and smaller-sized cities, particularly in Asia and Africa. Indeed, in 2030, about 45% of people will still live in smaller cities (cities of less than 500,000) (UN, 2015).

Second, we need to think about cities because they face an increasing mix of challenges and opportunities. After all, some 70% of greenhouse gas emissions are created by cities and they consume some 60–80% of energy globally (UN, 2011). It is the cities in the developing world that will face the toughest challenges as they will see the majority of this growth and experience a huge amount of change, but with low levels of resource and limited institutional capacity. Similarly, the competition for scarce resources and inward investment means increasing competition between cities nationally and internationally.

This powerful duality of increasing urbanisation and globalisation means that cities also face a number of important challenges relating to climate change, population growth and migration (Table 5.1). For example, cities will need to deal with rapid growth but also maintain their built environment, transport, communications and other infrastructure without increasing congestion. Yet cities also present us with great opportunities: they act as hubs and centres of enterprise, innovation and social learning, and can provide economies of scale in tackling many of these problems. So, for example, devolving powers to cities (as is happening in the UK) can, in theory, enable city governments to focus more closely on taking responsibility for spending and tackle the big urban challenges such as climate change at city scale.

Thirdly, we need to think about cities because our view about them has changed, and this opens up possibilities and potential for new markets and new urban innovations, in which built environment professionals can play a key role. Recently, for example, the 'smart city' model has gained traction, as commercial companies have seen a growing market for the future development of smart city technologies and the supply of 'big data' (or huge, rapidly changing and dynamic datasets) has increased (Dixon *et al.*, 2015). Proponents of the smart city model argue that technology can be leveraged to enhance economic development and the quality of life, and that the increasing availability of 'big data' and its integration, can be used to underpin these goals. Information for decision-making at a range of scales is therefore vital, and further enhanced by the rapid development of pervasive technologies, such as mobile devices and ubiquitous computing, in cities and individuals' daily lives. The RICS Futures Programme, for example, highlights the importance of 'big data' to property and construction professionals in terms of mobile applications, asset management and BIM (RICS, 2015).

A further dimension to our changing view of cities is provided by the increasing focus on a 'science of cities', or cities as 'complex adaptive systems' (Batty, 2008, 2013a). This thinking has been behind the establishment of the Future Cities Catapult in the UK, but also the recent Government Office for Science Future of Cities Foresight Programme. Both place an emphasis on seeing cities as urban systems, represented as a set of interacting subsystems or their elements (Batty, 2008). This builds on the work of Wiener (1948) and others, such as von Bertalanffy (1969), who has promoted a general systems theory which could, in their view, be applied to natural and human phenomena. We can see cites today as a set of interlinked systems. As Walt *et al.* (2014: 8) suggest:

> 'Cities are complicated and messy systems. Urban problems are the result of multiple factors with far-reaching impacts involving complex feedback loops. Traffic congestion, for example, could be the result of increasing population, decreasing household size, expensive public transport, a lack of parking or the city's layout. In turn, congestion can lead to poor air quality and high noise levels, increased health risks, less enjoyable public spaces, reduced productivity and fewer tourists in the city. Each urban problem is part of an intricate system of interactions.'

As a result of this we can really only 'understand' cities if we recognise their complexity, or the notion that cities grow from the bottom up as the product of millions of 'quasi- independent' decisions, yet they hang together in highly ordered ways that tend to defy traditional understanding (Batty, 2013b). From this understanding, but also the development of smart city models and big data, we have also seen the development of 'urban informatics' or, in fairly loose terms, the application of computers to the functioning of cities. More specifically this can be seen as the ways in which computer hardware and software are being embedded into cities to make service delivery functions more efficient through sensor-based technologies but also through improved analytics and understanding of the city (Batty, 2013b).

The implications of these changing understandings of the city are also important because they require different ways of working and interdisciplinary teams, such as spatial, design-led solutions, physical infrastructure-led service providers, digital and data analytics specialists to derive new insights into a city's form and evolution, commercial finance and business service-led providers (to enable more integrated forms of urban development), and social innovators (to develop better citizen engagement, information sharing and user centred design) (Walt *et al.*, 2014). Understanding how cities evolved, how they are today and how they will evolve in the future is vital if the built environment profession is to continue to flourish to 2050.

## 5.3   The evolution and growth of the future cities discourse: from garden cities to smart cities

Thinking about the future of cities, of course, is not new. Writers, philosophers, scholars, planners and architects have been thinking about how we might live in 'future cities' for many hundreds of years. Early writers such as Plato (380 BC) and Thomas More (1516) were contemplating future cities long before more recent thinkers such as

**Table 5.2** Future cities: conceptions of success.

| Environmental | Social | Economic | Governance |
|---|---|---|---|
| Garden cities | Participative cities | Entrepreneurial cities | Managed cities |
| Sustainable cities | Walkable cities | Competitive cities | Intelligent cities |
| Eco cities | Integrated cities | Productive cities | Productive cities |
| Green cities | Inclusive cities | Innovative cities | Efficient cities |
| Compact cities | Just cities | Business friendly cities | Well-run, well-led cities |
| Smart cities | Open cities | Global cities | Smart cities |
| Resilient | Liveable cities | Resilient cities | Future cities |

(*Source:* Moir *et al.*, 2014a)

Ebenezer Howard (1898) wrote *Garden Cities of Tomorrow*. So, 'future cities' has a specific meaning and context; as Moir *et al.* (2014a: 7) suggest:

> 'Future cities is a term used to imagine what cities themselves will be like, how they will operate, what systems will orchestrate them and how they will relate to their stakeholders (citizens, governments, businesses, investors, and others).'

Today, many terms and concepts make up the idea of future cities, all of them reflecting different perspectives from interest groups and stakeholder groups. Moir *et al.* (2014b) see these as also representing 'conceptions of success' based on whether they relate to environmental, social, economic or governance dimensions (Table 5.2). Within the discourse on future cities therefore we see a strong emphasis on environmental issues, hence the emergence of the concept of 'sustainable cities', particularly following the Brundtland Commission's report on sustainable development in 1987 (Brundtland Commission, 1987).

Today the emphasis in future cities is very much on 'smart cities', with a strong focus on technology. The concept of a smart city is not new, however. For example, Angelidou (2015) suggest the origins of smart cities can be found within two strands of thinking. Firstly, an 'urban futures' strand, with its origins in the thinking of early urban visionaries such as Ebenezer Howard, Garnier and Le Corbusier leading to more recent work in the 1960s, 1970s and 1980s to 'wired cities', 'information cities' and 'network cities' (Batty *et al.*, 2012). In essence, in many of these visions of urban futures, technology is seen as a key driver in creating modern and healthy environments and democratic governance, although research has questioned whether the smart cities movement now being promoted is itself a strategic vision for the future rather than a reality (Wolfram, 2012; Angelidou, 2015). Secondly, Angelidou (2015) (see also Kitchin, 2014) also sees a 'knowledge and innovation' strand of thinking based on ideas which emerged in the second half of the 20th century, and with knowledge and innovation as assets which underpin creative competitive advantage in a city (or indeed an organisation or company).

There are a very large number of definitions for 'smart city', which not only reflects the differing origins of the term, but also the varying disciplinary and institutional lenses through which a city can be viewed (Moir *et al.*, 2014a; Kitchin, 2015; Glasmeier and Christopherson, 2015; Albino *et al.*, 2015). For example, some define the smart city as an urban environment that is alluring and more liveable than the complex, messy environments we inhabit today. For others, the smart city provides a new market for urban management and an opportunity to sell technology-led solutions to city authorities facing environmental, economic and social challenges (Glasmeier and Christopherson, 2015).

The term 'smart city' can be broadly related to two distinct understandings of what makes a city smart (Kitchin, 2014, 2015). First, the term 'smart city' is often used to focus on the increasing extent to which cities are composed of pervasive and ubiquitous information and communications technology (ICT) embedded in the urban fabric (e.g. fixed and wireless telecoms networks, sensor and camera networks, and building management systems) (Townsend, 2013). In a smart city, these are used to monitor, manage and regulate real-time date flows and processes as people in the city move around, interact and use mobile devices. By connecting up, integrating and analysing this 'everyware' technology, a more cohesive and better understanding of the city can be developed, it is argued by smart city advocates. This can not only help cities provide more effective and efficient governance to benefit their citizens, but also a better and 'smarter' understanding of how data can be used to analyse processes and outcomes in a city (Kourtit *et al.*, 2012).

Second, 'smart city' has also been used to refer to the wider economic and innovation benefits that can be gained by developing and enhancing the knowledge economy in a city region. In this view of smart cities ICT is seen as a platform for bringing together ideas and innovations, especially with regard to professional services. The focus, however, is not on ICT in its own right, but rather on how networked technology infrastructures can provide a platform for innovation and creativity in a city, and therefore facilitate social, environmental, economic and cultural development (Logan and Molotch, 1987).

## 5.4 Being 'smart and sustainable': what does it mean for a city?

Despite the growth of the smart city movement, the concept has not been without criticism (Marvin *et al.*, 2016). The emerging critique relates to the politics of smart cities (a critical analysis of the promises and potential of smart cities), the capacities and capabilities of smart cities (examining the specific techniques, technologies and dominant configurations) and ways of knowing and seeing the city (relating to visual and technology dominated interfaces within cities) (Marvin *et al.*, 2016; Kitchin, 2014).

For example, Adam Greenfield's (2013) work, which focuses on Masdar City, Songdo International Business District and the Living PlanIT project in Portugal suggests that we should be wary of the allure of a neo-liberal ideology which can be seen as mixing technocratic governance with mass surveillance. Townsend (2013) argues for a more socially inclusive notion of a smart city, with a more important focus on 'bottom-up' innovation, driven by citizens themselves instead of a one size fits all approach from technology companies and consultants.

Nesta (2015) also highlights what it considers to be four practical flaws with the smart city concept. First, work on smart cities has often been technology led, so the question has been, what uses can be found for cutting edge technologies? Instead, in commissioning projects, cities need to understand that technology is only part of the answer.

Second, there is still insufficient evidence to suggest that smart city solutions help cities address real-world problems. Installing infrastructure sensors throughout the city might potentially make cities more efficient and sustainable but costs might also out-weigh the savings. Third, there is little transfer of learning between smart city projects, and, finally, many smart city projects offer citizens little opportunity to engage directly in the design and deployment of new technologies. The idea that no size fits all applies to smart cities and, for Goodspeed (2015), IT can often be fundamentally ambivalent and evolve in different directions in cities. Therefore, private companies may not under-stand local contexts and conditions. This means that bottom up community-driven and experimental projects may offer cities better opportunities to help address what ultimately are 'wicked' problems in an urban context.

In other instances, it has been argued, as part of the 'critique' of smart cities, there is a danger that smart cities do not necessarily produce sustainable outcomes, unless this is also stated as an explicit part of the smart city 'vision' (Dixon and Cohen, 2015). A simple example of where 'smart' is not necessarily 'sustainable' highlights the impor-tance of these two elements within a city, that is, a smartphone application for finding car parking spaces is a short-term solution, whereas providing a sustainable transport system is a longer term and potentially smarter and more sustainable solution. A smart and sustainable city can be defined as (ITU, 2014a: 3):

> 'An innovative city that uses information and communication technologies (ICTs) and other means to improve quality of life, efficiency of urban operation and ser-vices, and competitiveness, while ensuring that it meets the needs of present and future generations with respect to economic, social and environmental aspects.'

This definition identifies a series of key attributes that are intrinsic to this notion, most notably:

a) **Sustainability:** This is related to the city's infrastructure, governance, energy and climate change, pollution and waste management, socio-economic aspects and health provision.
b) **Quality of life:** A crosscutting issue, the quality of life of the citizens and the initia-tives in place to continuously improve it are vital to the strategic vision and identity of a smart and sustainable city.
c) **Intelligence or smartness:** A smart city exhibits implicit or explicit ambition to improve economic, social and environmental standards. Commonly quoted aspects in definitions reviewed in the report include smart economy, smart people, smart governance, smart mobility, smart living and smart environment.

These attributes are present across four intersecting dimensions of complex urban systems, where smart and sustainable functionalities take place (Figure 5.2) (ITU, 2014a):

- *Societal*: The city is for its inhabitants (i.e. the citizens).
- *Economic*: The city must be able to thrive – create and sustain jobs, growth, finance.
- *Environmental*: The city must be sustainable in its functioning for future generations.
- *Governmental*: The city must be robust in its ability to administer and implement policies, and bring together different actors.

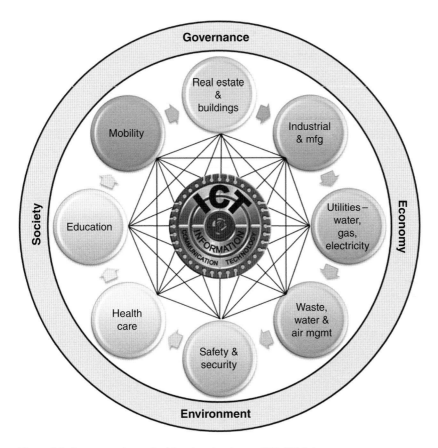

**Figure 5.2** A smart and sustainable urban landscape (ITU, 2014a).

These functionalities within a smart and sustainable city encompass a number of activity areas ranging from mobility through to healthcare, safety and security, for example, with ICT linking these activities through a central hub (see Box 5.1).

This focus on smart and sustainable is important at EU level, for example Europe 2020 sets out Europe's strategy for smart, sustainable and inclusive growth, where Europe's economy is based on knowledge and innovation, is more resource efficient, greener and economically competitive, and where there is high employment, social and territorial cohesion (European Commission, 2010; EIB, 2012). This has also been supported with the recent establishment of the European Innovation Partnership on Smart Cities and Communities in 2012, which brings together European cities, industry leaders and representatives of civil society to develop smart and sustainable solutions for Europe's cities. The policy goals are the EU 20/20/20 energy and climate targets. By 2014 the partnership had received 370 commitments focused on smart city projects and solutions covering more than 3000 partners across 31 countries (European Commission, 2016).

Following the growth of interest and development of smart cities there have also been moves to develop standards. In the UK, for example, BIS commissioned the British

---

**Box 5.1 What might a smart and sustainable city look like (EIB, 2012)?**

'…city residents, businesses, and visitors use their smart phones and other smart devices to access data, information and services wherever they are. City authorities and other public service agencies are able to connect directly with residents and businesses to inform public service delivery and allow for increased efficiency, targeting, and reduced costs, and contribute to citizen engagement in issues that affect their quality of life…'

'…city transport authorities predict the demand for public transport and anticipate road traffic, people work at home and remotely, reducing city congestion and easing the flow of traffic, and allowing the provision of up to the second travel and routing information to people on foot, cycling, using public transport and electric vehicles…'

'…sensors within your energy efficient home allow you to remotely manage your energy use, with automated systems automatically switching your electric vehicle to charge when electricity is in lowest demand, and providing renewable energy back into the grid as its generated…'

'…all powered by advances in technology, allowing cities to operate 'smarter', and providing opportunities for economic growth and development, reduction in carbon emissions, and socially inclusive cities.'

---

**Table 5.3** Examples of BSI smart city standards.

| Standard | Focus |
|---|---|
| PAS 180 | The development of a standard on smart city terminology |
| PAS 181 | The development of a smart city framework standard |
| PAS 182 | The development of a data concept model for smart cities |
| PD 8100 | A smart city overview document |
| PD 8101 | A smart city planning guidelines document |

Standards Institution (BSI) to develop a standards strategy for smart cities in the UK.[1] The strategy identifies the role of standards in accelerating the implementation of smart cities and providing assurance to citizens that the risks are being managed appropriately. More recently, the Cities Standards Institute has been launched, a joint initiative of the BSI and the Future Cities Catapult, brings together cities and key industry leaders and innovators to work together in identifying the challenges facing cities, providing solutions to common problems and defining the future of smart city standards.[2] The current standards (Table 5.3) include terminology, common concepts, data and city planning.

---

1  China, Korea and Germany are also working on relevant smart city standards, as is the European Commission (ISO/IEC, 2014).

2  Other related smart and sustainable cities and communities standards include (i) an indicator reporting standard for quality of life and services in cities (BS ISO 37120), (ii) research on smart infrastructure projects (PD ISO/TR 37150) and (iii) a specification for key performance indicators for smart infrastructure projects (PD ISO/TS 37151) (see http://www.bsigroup.com/en-GB/smart-cities/Smart-Cities-Standards-and-Publication/).

Similar moves internationally have been made to scope out standards, for example ISO/IEC (2014) has produced a preliminary report on smart cities. We have also seen the emergence of a World Council on City Data standard (ISO 37120) for the sustainable development of communities (WCCD, 2014) which identifies smart city services and quality of life indicators.

Further work by BSI/Imperial College (2014) distinguishes a variety of existing standards relevant to smart cities: technical (what needs to be done in terms of implementation and operation, 43 standards), process (how steps are being taken, 29 standards) and strategic (why standards are needed at a planning/management level, 17 standards).

The concept of being smart and sustainable also implies measurement of performance in achieving the ambitions and goals of a particular city. A recent exploratory framework (ITU, 2014b) suggested that there should be six dimensions to measuring performance:

- information and communication technology
- environmental sustainability
- productivity
- quality of life
- equity and social inclusion
- physical infrastructure.

These are shown in more detail in Table 5.4. However, globally there are some 200 city indices measuring (through different types of indicators in aggregated form) a variety of aspects of cities from quality of life to culture and environment and sustainability (JLL, 2015). This suggests there is some way to go to reach an agreed international standard in smart and sustainable city measurement.

## 5.5 Driving forces for smart and sustainable cities

Despite the continuing issues over standards and measures, whilst estimates of the 'market' for smart cities vary, the figures are substantive. Navigant (cited in NESTA, 2015) puts the current figure for the smart cities global market, in terms of services and technology solutions, at $8.8b. BIS assessed the market for smart technology solutions (deployment and rolling out of technology) in five main sectors (water, energy, transport, waste and assisted living) and estimated the value to be $400b by 2020, of which 10% represented the UK market share (BIS, 2013). Frost and Sullivan (2014) forecast a market for smart city services and solutions of $1.565 trillion by 2020, with energy a particularly important focus.

The creation of 'big' data sets (or very large, complex and rapidly changing datasets), generated primarily by the decentralised nature of computing, and the ability to connect and analyse the huge amounts of data created through pervasive and ubiquitous ICT networks and mobile devices, has created powerful possibilities and challenges for cities (Dixon *et al.*, 2015). Data lies at the heart of the smart and sustainable city concept because city governments and businesses require data and information to be able to provide appropriate and timely services and products to their citizens and customers. Therefore, the increasing availability of big energy data, construction data, transport and environmental data, and indeed the opening up of some datasets by city

**Table 5.4** Sub-dimensions to KPIs for smart and sustainable cities (ITU, 2014b).

| Dimension | Dimension | Sub-dimension | Sub-dimension |
|---|---|---|---|
| D1 | Information and communication technology | D1.1 | Network and access |
| | | D1.2 | Services and information platforms |
| | | D1.3 | Information security and privacy |
| | | D1.4 | Electromagnetic field |
| D2 | Environmental sustainability | D2.1 | Air quality |
| | | D2.2 | $CO_2$ emissions |
| | | D2.3 | Energy |
| | | D2.4 | Indoor pollution |
| | | D2.5 | Water, soil and noise |
| D3 | Productivity | D3.1 | Capital investment |
| | | D3.2 | Employment |
| | | D3.3 | Inflation |
| | | D3.4 | Trade |
| | | D3.5 | Savings |
| | | D3.6 | Export/import |
| | | D3.7 | Household income/consumption |
| | | D3.8 | Innovation |
| | | D3.9 | Knowledge economy |
| D4 | Quality of life | D4.1 | Education |
| | | D4.2 | Health |
| | | D4.3 | Safety/security public place |
| | | D4.4 | Convenience and comfort |
| D5 | Equity and social inclusion | D5.1 | Inequity of income/consumption (Gini coefficient) |
| | | D5.2 | Social and gender inequity of access to services and infrastructure |
| | | D5.3 | Openness and public participation |
| | | D5.4 | Governance |
| D6 | Physical infrastructure | D6.1 | Infrastructure/connection to services – piped water |
| | | D6.2 | Infrastructure/connection to services – sewage |
| | | D6.3 | Infrastructure/connection to services – electricity |
| | | D6.4 | Infrastructure/connection to services – waste management |
| | | D6.5 | Connection to services – knowledge infrastructure |
| | | D6.6 | Infrastructure/connection to services – health infrastructure |
| | | D6.7 | Infrastructure/connection to services – transport |
| | | D6.8 | Infrastructure/connection to services – road infrastructure |
| | | D6.9 | Housing – building materials |
| | | D6.10 | Housing – living space |
| | | D6.11 | Building |

authorities and national governments has paralleled the development of smart cities (BSI/ONS, 2016).

Broadly speaking, the smart city arena can be seen as being shaped by two distinct forces (Angelidou, 2015). First, the 'technology push' of new supply-side solutions, and, second, the 'demand pull' of solutions/products being produced as a result of scientific research and innovation responding to demand in cities. On the supply side, for example, there have been an increasing number of transport, energy, healthcare, water and waste solutions and products being delivered to assist in urban management. Technology vendors and consultancies have therefore responded, driven by other stakeholders such as global forums, academic research groups, and local and global policymaking institutions and their funding streams. On the demand side, the growth of interest in smart cities has been driven by increasing urbanisation and an increasing recognition that city authorities need to do more to tackle climate change and resource depletion issues. In an increasingly globalised world there is also increasing recognition that cities need to compete for skilled labour and investment, so having a more effective and efficient city government can potentially offer a better service for those the city is seeking to attract. This is being driven and enhanced by grassroots movements of local technology applications and software developer specialists, as well as public and non-profit organisations such as the World Bank.

In the UK, recent work by Policy Exchange (2016) suggests that city devolution could be a key driver for smart and sustainable cities. Cities have been at the heart of the UK government's policy agendas since 2010, and in May 2015 the government introduced the Cities and Local Government Devolution Bill, which opened the way for cities to have greater powers over investment and spending in return for new devolved governance structures. Ultimately this is designed, in the eyes of the government, to promote regional economic growth and to innovate in the provision of public services. Greater Manchester is the first major city to complete a settlement of these new powers: a new mayor will be elected in 2017 to represent the city region and new powers will include investment in transport and housing, the setting of local planning strategy, greater powers over land development, and control of police and fire services. The mayor will also be able to control borrowing against future increases in local business rates.

Currently within the smart city movement in the UK the government is using a market-making approach by trying to create conditions conducive to business uptake (Centre for Cities, 2014). The government therefore acts as a co-ordinator through initiatives such as the Smart Cities Forum and Future Cities Catapult, as a funder through Innovate UK and as a regulator by working with such bodies as the BSI. The government has also supported smart cities through the establishment of a Smart Cities Forum and a number of large UK cities have benefited from UK government and EU funding for smart city projects (e.g. Bristol, Milton Keynes and Manchester).

However, to tackle the barriers that exist at city and data level, Policy Exchange (2016) suggest that as a pre-condition for receiving devolved powers that each city should develop an Office of Data Analytics (ODA), based on the concept of the Mayor's Office of Data Analytics[3] in New York City. The ODA would be responsible for helping the elected mayor and the city's public bodies use data analytics to help tackle the city's

---

3 http://www1.nyc.gov/site/analytics/index.page.

problems in a unified and strategic way. This would also be underpinned by the development of a city data marketplace (CDM), which is a virtual platform at city level connecting creators and users of data.

Funding of projects globally has also been bolstered by special development funds. A sample of 15 smart cities by Frost and Sullivan (2014), for example, found that some 40% of projects were funded in this way, with 37% from public–private partnerships, 22% self-financed form public budgets with national government support and only 1% from private investment. Looking more widely, the Centre for Cities (2014) suggests that although there is no single route to becoming a smart city, those cities that have made the most progress have tended to use three general principles to help shape and drive their smart city agendas:

- *Integration* with economic development and public service delivery plans: rather than starting from scratch, cities have looked at how new technologies can help them achieve their existing goals, for example Bristol is becoming smart by focusing on smart technologies that help it reach its long-term carbon reduction goals.
- *Pragmatic focus*, with the bulk of investment being spent on practical, achievable and financially viable projects.
- *Participation* of community representatives, local business and residents to ensure that plans are relevant to the city's opportunities and challenges, for example the Smart London and Smart Birmingham projects both involve a range of academics, civil servants and private/third-sector organisations.

## 5.6 Smart and sustainable cities in practice

Smart cities come in a range of types, sizes and with different characteristics. Not only is the concept a broad one, but understanding the particular context is also important as some smart city projects are new, greenfield cities whilst many others use smart city concepts within existing cities. Also, as Zegras *et al.* (2015) point out, in some of the biggest cities in the world, such as Dhaka, Bangladesh, something as simple as a transit map is not available. What is 'smart' for one city may already be available in another (Glasmeier and Christopherson, 2015). In other words, there is no one size fits all blueprint for a smart and sustainable city.

According to Lee *et al.* (2014) there were 143 ongoing or completed self-designated smart city projects globally in 2012, divided between Europe (47 projects), North America (35 projects), Asia (40 projects), South America (11 projects) and Middle East/Africa (10 projects). Much depends on definition of course, and recent research within the EU (Directorate General for Internal Policies, 2014) identified 240 cities (out of 468 EU-28 cities with at least 100,000 population) with significant and verifiable smart city activity, with particular hotspots in the UK, Spain and Italy.

Recently there has been a particular emphasis in the BRIC countries on developing smart cities. For example, according to the Chinese Smart Cities Forum (Liu and Peng, 2013) six provinces and 51 cities have included an emphasis on smart cities, with 36 under construction. These are primarily technology focused with relatively less attention focused on environmental and social issues. As Albino *et al.* (2015) report, a number of South-East Asian cities, such as Singapore, South Korea, Taiwan and Hong

Kong, are following a similar path, promoting economic growth through smart city programmes. These include Singapore's IT2000 plan to create an 'intelligent island' and Taoyuan's E-Taoyaun and U-Taoyaun projects. In India, there are plans to create 100 smart cities at a cost of £445 billion. Several of these projects have been started, including Kochi smart city and Naya Raipur smart city (UKTI, 2015). The Indian government plans to develop these as satellite towns of larger cities and by retrofitting existing medium-sized cities so that both will act as magnets for investment and development.

The majority of smart city projects tend to be based on existing brownfield cities rather than new greenfield cities, although in the Middle East, India and South-East Asia new smart city projects are more commonplace than in the rest of the world. For example, in the United Arab Emirates Masdar City is being promoted as a smart and sustainable city (Albino *et al.*, 2015). In Korea, Songdo is a new city built over the last decade to house 75,000 people at a cost of $35 billion (Albino *et al.*, 2015). However, these new projects are the exception rather than the rule, so in understanding smart cities it is more productive to focus on the implementation of smart cities in existing places (Shelton *et al.*, 2015: 14):

> 'Rather than the construction of new cities from scratch or the wholesale importation of universal ideals into existing cities, the smart city is assembled piecemeal, integrated awkwardly into existing configurations of urban governance and the built environment.'

In the UK, recent research by Centre for Cities (2014) suggests that smart city projects can be classified according to whether they are top down or technology focused. In this model cities become smart by integrating data gathered from different kinds of sensors into a single platform to manage operations more effectively (e.g. Glasgow). New smart city projects such as Songdo and Masdar are also adopting this approach, although recently Masdar announced a substantial scaling back in its ambitions (Goldenberg, 2016). In the UK, the majority of smart city projects have been developed through bottom-up approaches using new technologies and new data to enable stakeholders to develop solutions. These initiatives include open data platforms (Centre for Cities, 2014).

Those existing cities which appear to be combining smart and sustainable practices successfully tend to be those which have strong 'visions' (or shared expectations about the future), strong leadership and have pursued a high level of participatory engagement in developing their programmes and projects (Dixon and Cohen, 2015). Copenhagen is an example of such a city. Copenhagen is the largest city in Denmark with about 600,000 inhabitants in its city area and almost 2 million in its greater metropolitan area. The capital is generally considered to be very technologically advanced and with excellent quality of life, as shown in 2014 when Copenhagen won the prestigious World Smart Cities Award in Barcelona for the concept Copenhagen Connecting and was also the European Capital in the same year (Arup, 2016).

Copenhagen has a target within its city vision to be carbon neutral by 2025, which is an ambition supported by the CPH 2025 Climate Plan and adopted by the city in 2009. A mid-term goal of a 20% reduction in carbon emissions by 2015 has already been achieved and since 1995 Copenhagen has reduced carbon emissions by 50%. The CPH 2025 Climate Plan focused on four main areas: energy consumption, energy production, green mobility and city administration. For example, since 2005, one billion DKK has been invested in bike lanes and super cycle highways, with 45% of people cycling to work or school every day. Also, 98% of households are connected to the district heating system (State of Green, 2016). Building on this sustainable face to the city Copenhagen has also begun to develop digital infrastructure across the city through its Copenhagen Connecting project, with the socio-economic benefits of the project estimated at 4.4 billion DKK. This is being supported by the Copenhagen Solutions Lab, which was set up in 2014 and has begun to develop smart solutions for transport, energy and environment. Finally, the city has begun to open up data through an open data portal with more than 100 data sets, and Hitachi is establishing a big data platform for the city (Arup, 2016).

## 5.7 What is the future for 'future cities'?

Smart and sustainable cities are a very important and growing part of the future cities debate (PwC, 2015). If we accept that cities globally need to be both smart and sustainable, what is the future for them and how will they achieve their ambitions? What might they look and feel like in 2050? This section of the chapter aims to answer four key questions, drawing on current research, futures studies and related literature:

- What will be the key driving forces and trends that will impact on such cities to 2050?
- What will these cities look like in 2050?
- What will these cities be made of in 2050?
- How can such cities best plan for the future?

### 5.7.1 Driving forces and trends to 2050

The dominant trends in urbanisation seem likely to continue to 2050. This means that the world's global cities will continue to build greater economic power and wealth, opening up greater potential inequalities. Currently the world's 750 biggest cities account for 57% of global GDP. By 2030 they will contribute 61% of global GDP. By 2030 the world's 750 biggest cities will also gain an additional 220 million additional middle-class consumers and form 60% of total global spending. This will also be paralleled by a rapid expansion of young people in Africa, for example, with other older cities (e.g. in Europe and Japan) shrinking in size and perhaps influence (Oxford Economics, 2014; Ernst and Young, 2015). We will also see these continuing rapid urbanisation trends interacting with the continuing growth of digital technologies (particularly through the growing focus on big data, open data and the Internet of Things, the growth of entrepreneurial activity in cities and further globalisation).

Alongside these interrelated driving forces, many existing cities, if they are to become smart and sustainable, will need to scale up building and neighbourhood actions across city level. This is likely to be influenced by capacity, resource and skills constraints (Dixon *et al.*, 2014), but there are recognisable sustainability trends to 2050 at city level which also need to be understood, including (Forum for the Future, 2011):

- climate change adaptation and mitigation
- continued resource scarcity: energy, water and food, for example
- growth of smart digital infrastructure

- personal mobility and modal split in transport: a move towards more sustainable forms of transport
- growing citizen empowerment through web and social media
- growth of green buildings and the green built environment movement.

### 5.7.2 What will cities look like in 2050?

Smart and sustainable cities in 2050 may take a variety of forms. Cities in the future will need to look very different from cities today if they are to address the challenges of rapidly rising urban populations, and climate change, and provide highly integrated solutions for everything from energy provision to transport (Arup, 2013; Samsung, 2016). Therefore, we may see some of the following elements in our cities by 2050 (Figure 5.3):

- *Green infrastructure and biophilic/biomimicry design*: We will see a stronger emphasis on vertical farming with green roofs and walls more commonplace than today. Extensive blue–green networks will link through our cities with permeable paving and sustainable drainage systems. We may see biophilic design and intelligent and adaptable buildings (e.g. algal biofuels embedded within buildings as part of the façade) and self-cleaning reactive buildings (Arup, 2013). Digital technologies will be at the heart of this revolution.

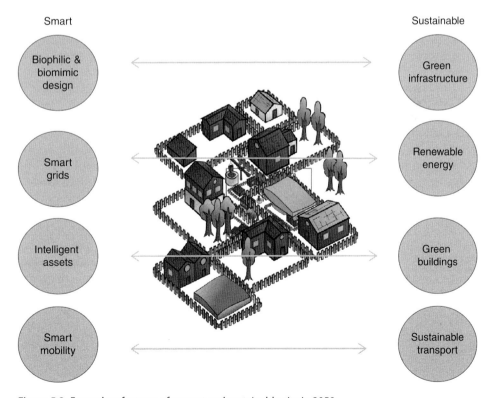

**Figure 5.3** Exemplary features of a smart and sustainable city in 2050.

- *Renewable energy and smart grids*: Cities will focus on renewables deriving power from solar, wind and other forms of renewable energy. Smart grids will use technology to balance demand and supply more accurately and energy metering will be pervasive.
- *Green buildings and intelligent assets*: Today markets in green buildings vary in maturity. More mature markets such as the USA and the EU will continue to grow and it is likely developing countries will also scale up actions as green assessment standards gain greater consistency across national boundaries (Dodge Data and Analytics, 2016). There will be a strong focus on intelligent assets (which are physical objects that are able to sense, record and communicate information about themselves and/or their surroundings) (Ellen Macarthur Foundation, 2016). This concept is at the heart of the circular economy and is predicated on providing knowledge and information about the location, condition and availability of assets (e.g. predictive maintenance and performance models for buildings).
- *Sustainable transport and smart mobility*: Cycling and walking in cities will continue to gain momentum and public transport systems will be based on renewable power and sustainable energy supplies, with a stronger focus on city level actions and self-sufficiency for the city as a whole (IPPR, 2014).

### 5.7.3   What will cities be made of in 2050?

Despite the need to retrofit and re-engineer many of our cities, it is unlikely that the bulk materials mix in cities will change significantly (Purnell and Roelich, 2015). A typical city contains at least 1 million tons of construction materials per square mile (equivalent to more than 100 tons per person) and this has been the case for more than 100 years, but continued pressure on resources and changes in infrastructure and building design are likely to mean a more widespread use of recycled and recovered resources. Advanced materials are also likely to become more important, such as insulation materials, including aerogels, and phase change materials which can store heat (Dixon *et al.*, 2014; Purnell and Roelich, 2016). The use of functional materials for ICT and energy generation and supply within cities will also become even more important, but perhaps with the additional risks associated with critical supply disruptions in an uncertain world. Therefore 'technodiversity' to prevent lock-in to particular technologies will be very important in smart and sustainable cities, perhaps with 'urban mining' becoming a more important way of deconstructing existing assets to release valuable materials.

### 5.7.4   How can cities plan for a smart and sustainable future?

Planning for the future is vital if cities are to overcome the disconnection between long-term environmental change and the relatively short-term planning horizons that exist today. Within the future cities debate there has been an increasing emphasis on how cities can create visions to anchor their plans and actions against a shared expectation of a desirable future for the city. Many cities have therefore created visions for their cities which are more than simply branding exercises but are designed to (Dixon *et al.*, 2014):

- provide a sense of purpose
- underpin vitality and belief systems

- address the question of what sort of future we want
- promote discussion and debate
- mobilise resources around desired futures.

Thinking about the future therefore opens up the possibility for discussion and debate, free from the constraints of short-term thinking. There has also been a move towards co-creation of visions (Dixon and Cohen, 2015). In this sense, 'co-creation' in some cities sees universities being positioned as key stakeholders and facilitators in helping develop a valid city vision (Trencher *et al.*, 2013; Goddard and Vallance, 2013) This perspective has also found translation through the development of urban transition laboratories (Nevens *et al.*, 2013) and opens up possibilities for exhibition spaces or 'urban rooms' promoted by Terry Farrell and exemplified by projects such as Newcastle's City Futures (Farrell, 2014; Tewdr-Jones *et al.*, 2015).

In the UK, for example, Bristol's 2020 vision, and its smart city vision, is based on 'people, place and prosperity', a desire to be a 'Global Green Capital', and an aspiration to be a centre for smart city thinking. In Canada, Vancouver aims to be the world's greenest city by 2020 with tough targets set for greenhouse gas emissions and a desire to create a city which is resilient to climate change. Looking further ahead into the future, Glasgow has developed a vision for 2061 that is now also underpinned by its aspiration to be a leading 'future city' with smart technology at its core. Smaller urban areas have also developed visions. In the UK, for example, Milton Keynes is working with business and other stakeholders to develop a Smart 2020 Vision with a strong focus on electric vehicles and smart technologies. More recently the UK Government Office for Science Foresight programme on Future Cities has placed a strong emphasis on the co-creation of city visions, and UK cities have engaged in this process in a variety of ways through scenario development, exhibition spaces and design challenges (Government Office for Science, 2016). To connect with this work, the University of Reading partnered with Barton Willmore and Reading UK CIC (the economic development company for Reading) to develop a Reading 2050 vision (Dixon and Cohen, 2015: Dixon and Montgomery, 2015). However, a vision on its own will not supply the answer to the problems that cities face. This requires strategic thinking and an action plan that tackles a complex range of interrelated issues (Eames *et al.*, 2014).

## 5.8 Conclusions: opportunities and challenges to 2050

The cities which are leading the smart and sustainable development agenda internationally (e.g. Copenhagen, Bristol and Barcelona (CATR, 2014; Burdett, 2015: Dixon and Cohen, 2015)) are those which have developed a clear, forward-thinking and participatory vision for the future. Although every city is different, this means developing an integrated approach to tackle climate change linked with long-term planning for the future. It also means developing cohesive partnerships for action, new and scaled-up financing mechanisms (e.g. city carbon bonds), as well as setting clear targets for emissions by sector, including the built environment. Yet we must also recognise the differences and distinctions between cities. Recent research (Shell, 2015) has identified six city archetypes globally: underdeveloped urban centres, developing mega-hubs, underprivileged crowded cities, sprawling metropolises, prosperous communities and urban powerhouses, each of which corresponded to particular demographics and energy use. These will require different solutions, applications and inputs to help address the challenges they face.

These developments also open up two possibilities in the developed world because cities have the potential to grow as major procurers in their own right (Dixon, 2015). First, the UK's expertise in construction and smart city technologies offers a real global growth opportunity in both smart construction (including offsite) and digital engineering (including BIM), not only in existing cities but also in new city development projects. For example, the UK BIS estimated the global market for smart solutions across five sectors (water, energy, transport, waste and assisted living) will be worth $440 billion by 2020, of which 10% could be potential UK business, and it is also estimated that at least $40 trillion will need to be invested in urban infrastructure over the next 20 years. This is also in the context of a global construction industry set to grow by 4.3% per annum until 2025, with much of this growth in the emerging economies.

Second, given the fact that in the developed world the majority of existing buildings will still be standing in 2050, there is also a valuable potential retrofit market in our cities. Recent research by the Institute of Sustainability, for example, has suggested there is a £500 billion market of UK domestic retrofit involving 20 million homes over a 40-year period, and DECC's Low Carbon Innovation Coordination Group (LCICG) recently highlighted that the low-carbon design services and low-carbon materials and components sectors are set to be worth approximately £488 billion by 2050.

Although there is exciting potential around future cities, there are also concerns about the proliferation and fragmentation of bottom-up experiments in both smart thinking and retrofit projects in the UK. For example, market weaknesses (which include lack of risk financing, problems in working across departments, and privacy and security concerns) are inhibiting the growth of smart and sustainable city thinking in the UK, where the current market-led approach needs better co-ordination and direction. Moreover, scaling up retrofit actions at city scale involves substantial challenges, including the reconciliation of disparate stakeholder perspectives (both public and private), as well as developing new access to green finance which takes us beyond the recent failure of the Green Deal. Again, however, in the urban retrofit arena, although we see pockets of innovation in terms of neighbourhood and community retrofit programmes, city-wide retrofit on a grand scale continues to elude us (Dixon *et al.*, 2015; Eames *et al.*, 2017).

The policy changes to help tackle these big issues require a much stronger focus on long-term 'city thinking' from government, local government, and the construction and property industry. They also require us as built environment professionals to understand city scale thinking and how we can respond to the complex urban challenges we face globally. This will require new ways of thinking and of doing business, and new skills if we are to create cities that truly are smart and sustainable. In particular, built environment professionals and supply companies will need to ensure their in-house and supply-based systems have full interoperability with the new digital infrastructure networks and the right interdisciplinary blend of skills to meet the new challenges (CIC, 2013).

# References

Albino, V., Berardi, U. and Dangelico, D. (2015) Smart cities: definitions, dimensions, performance and initiative. *Journal of Urban Technology*, 22, 1–19.

Angelidou, M. (2015) Smart cities: a conjuncture of four forces. *Cities*, 47, 95–106.

Arup (2013) *It's Alive: Can you imagine the urban building of the future?* Arup, London.

Arup (2016) *Growing Smart Cities in Denmark*. Arup, London.

Batty, M. (2008) The size, scale, and shape of cities. *Science*, 319(5864), 769–771.

Batty, M. (2013a) *The New Science of Cities*. MIT Press, Cambridge, MA.

Batty, M. (2013b) *Urban Informatics and Big Data: A report to the ESRC Cities Expert Group*, ESRC Paper. Available at: http://www.spatialcomplexity.info/files/2015/07/Urban-Informatics-and-Big-Data.pdf (accessed March 2016).

Batty, M., Axhausen, K.W., Giannotti, F., Pozdnoukhov, A., Bazzani, A., Wachowicz, M., Ouzounis, G. and Portugali, Y. (2012) Smart cities of the future. *European Physics Journal Special Topics*, 214, 481–518.

BIS (2013) *The Smart City Market: Opportunities for the UK*. Department for Business, Innovation and Skills, London.

Brundtland Commission (1987) *Our Common Future*. United Nations, New York.

BSI/Imperial College (2014) *Mapping Smart City Standards*. British Standards Institution, London.

BSI/ONS (2016) *City Data Survey Report*. British Standards Institution/Office for National Statistics, London.

Burdett, R (2015) *Innovation in Europe's Cities*. London School of Economics, London. Available at: https://files.lsecities.net/files/2015/02/Innovation-in-Europes-Cities_Bloomberg-Mayors-Challenge1.pdf (accessed March 2016).

Centre for Cities (2014) *Smart Cities*. Centre for Cities, London.

CATR (2014) *Comparative Study of Smart Cities in Europe and China White Paper*. China Academy of Telecommunications Research, Beijing. Available at: http://eu-chinasmartcities.eu/sites/default/files/Smart_City_report_draft%20White%20Paper%20_%20March%202014.pdf (accessed March 2016).

CIC (2013) *Built Environment 2050: A Report on our Digital Future*. Construction Industry Council.

Directorate General for Internal Policies (2014) *Mapping Smart Cities in the EU* European Parliament.

Dixon, T. (2015) Future cities: urbanisation and the impact on the construction and property sector in *Building Better: Recommendations for a More Sustainable Construction Sector*. Westminster Sustainable Business Forum, London, pp. 23–25. Available at: http://www.policyconnect.org.uk/sites/site_pc/files/report/605/fieldreportdownload/wsbf-buildingbetter.pdf (accessed March 2016).

Dixon, T. and Cohen, K. (2015) Towards a smart and sustainable Reading 2050 vision. *Town and Country Planning*, January, pp. 20–27.

Dixon, T. and Montgomery, J. (2015) *Towards a smart and sustainable Reading UK 2050: Full report*. Project Report. Barton Willmore, pp54. ISBN 9780993318801. Available at: www.reading2050.co.uk (accessed March 2016).

Dixon, T., Eames, M., Lannon, S. and Hunt, M. (eds) (2014) *Urban Retrofitting for Sustainability: Mapping the Transition to 2050*. Routledge, London.

Dixon, T., Barlow, J., Grimmond, S. and Blower, J. (2015) *Smart and sustainable: using Big Data to improve peoples' lives in cities. Discussion Paper.* University of Reading, Reading. ISSN 2058-9751. Available at: https://www.reading.ac.uk/web/FILES/cme/cme-Dixon_SCME_big_data_paper_AS_v_11_WEB_(1).pdf (accessed March 2016).

Dodge Data and Analytics (2016) *World Green Building Trends.* Dodge Data and Analytics, Bedford, MA.

Eames, M., Lannon, S., Dixon, T. and Hunt, M. (2014) Financing, managing and visioning the urban retrofit transition to 2050 in Dixon, T., Eames, M., Lannon, S. and Hunt, M. (eds.) *Urban retrofitting for sustainability: mapping the transition to 2050.* Routledge.

Eames, M., Dixon, T., Hunt, M. and Lannon, S., (eds) (2017) *Retrofitting cities for tomorrow's world.* Wiley-Blackwell, Oxford, pp. 288. ISBN 9781119007210 (in press).

Ellen Macarthur Foundation (2016) *Intelligent Assets.* Ellen Macarthur Foundation.

Ernst and Young (2015) *Megatrends 2015: Making Sense of a World in Motion.* Ernst and Young, London.

European Commission (2010) *EUROPE 2020: A strategy for smart, sustainable and inclusive growth.* European Commission, Brussels.

European Commission (2016) *Smart Cities* (website). Available at https://ec.europa.eu/digital-single-market//en/smart-cities (accessed March 2016).

EIB (2012) *JESSICA for Smart and Sustainable Cities.* European Investment Bank, Brussels. Available at: http://www.eib.org/attachments/documents/jessica_horizontal_study_smart_and_sustainable_cities_en.pdf (accessed March 2016).

Farrell, T. (2014) *Our Future in Place: Farrell Review of Architecture and the Built Environment.* Available at: http://www.farrellreview.co.uk/ (accessed October 2014).

Forum for the Future (2011) *Sustainable Urban Enterprise: Creating the Right Business Environment in Cities.* Forum for the Future, London. Available at: https://www.forumforthefuture.org/project/sustainable-urban-enterprise-creating-right-business-environment-cities/overview (accessed March 2016).

Frost and Sullivan (2014) *Strategic Opportunity analysis of the Global Smart City Market. Presentation.* Available at: http://www.slideshare.net/FrostandSullivan/smart-city-perevezentseveng (accessed February 2016).

Glasmeier, A. and Christopherson, S. (2015) Thinking about smart cities. *Cambridge Journal of Regions, Economy and Society*, 8, 3–12.

Goddard, J. and Vallance, P. (2013) *The University and the City*, Routledge, London.

Goldenberg, S. (2016) Masdar's zero-carbon dream could become world's first green ghost town. *Guardian*, 16 February. Available at: http://www.theguardian.com/environment/2016/feb/16/masdars-zero-carbon-dream-could-become-worlds-first-green-ghost-town (accessed March 2016).

Goodspeed, R. (2015) Smart cities: moving beyond urban cybernetics to tackle wicked problems. *Cambridge Journal of Regions, Economy and Society*, 8, 79–82.

Government Office for Science (2016) *Future of Cities Foresight Webpage.* Available at: https://www.gov.uk/government/collections/future-of-cities (accessed March 2016).

Greenfield, A. (2013) *Against the Smart City (The City is Here for You to Use).* Do Projects, New York.

Howard, E. (1898) *Garden Cities of Tomorrow.* Swan Sonnenschein & Co., London.

IPPR (2014) *City Energy: A New Powerhouse for Britain.* Institute for Public Policy Research, London.

ISO/IEC (2014) *ISO/IEC JTC 1: Smart Cities – Preliminary Report.* International Organization for Standardization/International Electrotechnical Commission.

ITU (2014a) *An Overview of Smart Sustainable Cities and the Role of Information and Communication Technologies.* International Telecommunications Union, Geneva.

ITU (2014b) *Overview of key performance indicators in smart sustainable cities.* International Telecommunications Union, Geneva.

JLL (2015) *The Business of Cities.* Jones Lang LaSalle, London.

Kitchin, R. (2014) The real-time city? Big data and smart urbanism. *GeoJournal*, 79, 1–14.

Kitchin, R. (2015) Making sense of smart cities: addressing present shortcomings. *Cambridge Journal of Regions, Economy and Society*, 8, 131–136.

Kourtit, K., Nijkanp, P., Arribas-Bel, D. (2012) Smart cities perspective: a comparative European study by means of self-organising maps. *Innovation*, 25(2), 229–246.

Lee, J., Hancock, M. and Hi, M. (2014) Towards an effective framework for building smart cities: Lessons from Seoul and San Francisco. *Technological Forecasting & Social Change*, 89, 80–99.

Liu, P. and Peng, Z. (2013) *Smart Cities in China, IEEE Computer Society Digital Library.*

Logan, J. and Molotch, H. (1987) *The City and Growth Machine – Urban Fortunes: The Political Economy of Place.* University of California.

Marvin, S., Luque-Ayala, A. and McFarlane, C. (eds) (2016) *Smart Urbanism: Utopian Vision or False Dawn?* Routledge, Oxford.

Moir, E., Moonen, T. and Clark, G. (2014a) *What are Future Cities? Origins, Meanings and Uses.* Future Cities Catapult/Government Office for Science, London.

Moir, E., Moonen, T. and Clark, G. (2014b) *The Future of Cities: What is the Global Agenda?* GoS Foresight Future of Cities, London.

Nesta (2015) *Rethinking Smart Cities from the Ground Up.* Nesta, London.

Nevens, F., Frantzeskaki, N., Gorissen, L. and Loorbach, D. (2013) Urban Transition Labs: co-creating transformative action for sustainable cities. *Journal of Cleaner Production*, 50, 111–122.

Oxford Economics (2014) *Global Cities 2030.* Oxford Economics, Oxford.

Policy Exchange (2016) *Smart Devolution: why smarter use of technology and data are vital to the success of city devolution.* Policy Exchange, London.

Purnell, P. and Roelich, K. (2015) *What will cities of the future be made of?* GoS Foresight Future of Cities, London.

PwC (2015) *Connecting the Dots: Smart and Sustainable Cities.* Price Waterhouse Coopers, Delhi.

RICS (2015) *Our Changing World: Let's Be Ready.* Royal Institution of Chartered Surveyors, London.

Samsung (2016) *Smart Things Future Living Report.* Samsung, London.

Shell (2014) *New Lenses on Future Cities.* Shell, London.

Shelton, T., Zook, M. and Wiig, A. (2015) The 'actually existing smart city'. *Cambridge Journal of Regions, Economy and Society*, 8, 13–25.

State of Green (2016) *City of Copenhagen Website.* Available at: https://stateofgreen.com/en/profiles/city-of-copenhagen (accessed March 2016).

Tewdr-Jones, M., Goddard, J. and Cowie, P (2015) *Newcastle City Futures 2065: Anchoring Universities in City Regions through Urban Foresight.* Newcastle University. Available at: http://www.newcastlecityfutures.org/NewcastleCityFutures2065Report.pdf (accessed March 2016).

Townsend, A. (2013) *Smart Cities*. W.W. Norton & Company, London.

Trencher, G.P., Yarime, M. and Kharrazi, A. (2013) Co-creating sustainability: cross-sector university collaborations for driving sustainable urban transitions. *Journal of Cleaner Production*, 50, 40–55.

UKTI (2015) *India's Smart Cities Programme*. United Kingdom Trade and Investment, London.

UN (2011) *Cities: Investing in Energy Efficiency and Resource Efficiency*. United Nations, New York.

UN (2012) *Challenges and Way Forward in the Urban Sector*. United Nations, New York.

UN (2015) *World Urbanization Prospects: the 2014 Revision*. United Nations, New York.

von Bertalanffy, L. (1969) *General System Theory – Foundations, Development, Applications*. George Braziller, New York.

Van Staden, R. (2014) *Climate Change: Implications for Cities – Key Findings from the Intergovernmental Panel on Climate Change Fifth Assessment Report*. ICLEI & University of Cambridge, Cambridge. Available at: http://www.cisl.cam.ac.uk/business-action/low-carbon-transformation/ipcc-briefings/pdfs/briefings/IPCC_AR5__Implications_for_Cities__Briefing__WEB_EN.pdf (accessed March 2016).

Walt, N., Doody, L., Baker, K. and Cain, S. (2014) *Future Cities: UK Capabilities for Urban Innovation*. GoS Foresight Future of Cities, London.

WCCD (2014) *ISO 37120 Sustainable Development of Communities: Indicators for City Services and Quality of Life*. World Council on City Data, Toronto.

Wiener, N. (1948) *Cybernetics*. MIT Press, Cambridge, MA.

Wolfram, M. (2012) Deconstructing smart cities: an intertextual reading of concepts and practices for integrated urban and ICT development, in Schrenk, M., Popovich, V., Zeile, P. and Elisei, P. (eds) *REALCORP 2012 Proceedings*. CEIT Alanova, Vienna, pp. 171–181.

Zegras, C., Eros, E., Butts, K., Resor, E., Kennedy, S., Ching, A. and Mamum, M. (2015) Tracing a path to knowledge? Indicative user impacts of introducing a public transport map in Dhaka, Bangladesh. *Cambridge Journal of Regions, Economy and Society*, 8, 113–129.

# 6

## Sustainable Infrastructure

*Martino Tran, Jim Hall, Robert Nicholls, Adrian J. Hickford, Modassar Chaudry
and Geoff Watson*

## 6.1   Introduction

National Infrastructure (NI) provides the foundation for economic productivity and human well-being, and is the cornerstone of modern industrialised society. NI provides the energy and water resources that all societies need to function, and enables people, information and goods to move efficiently and safely. Further, NI shapes the interactions between human civilisation and the natural environment. Whilst infrastructure is humanity's most visible impact on the environment, modern sustainable infrastructure is also essential to minimising human impacts on the environment. In developing economies, providing infrastructure is the key challenge, while in developed countries, maintaining existing infrastructure, which is ageing, is a major challenge.

Infrastructure systems (including energy, transport, water, waste and digital communications) are vital for modern economic activity, but are also major sources of carbon emissions and environmental impacts. New policies and technologies are therefore needed to enable a transition to more sustainable infrastructure systems. However, these need to take into account the long-term risks due to increasing infrastructure interdependency, which are not well understood.

This chapter aims to consider sustainable infrastructure in an increasingly complex world with a focus on more developed countries drawing on the experience of the Infrastructure Transitions Research Consortium (ITRC) (Hall *et al.*, 2016). In this context we consider 'infrastructure' to be those assets which comprise the various supply systems for energy, transport, water and waste, while 'sustainable infrastructure' is that which contributes towards a future where limited resources are managed responsibly, perhaps through demand management, with minimal impact on the natural surroundings and climate. For example, in energy this is a future emphasis on increased use of renewable energy and decarbonisation of current energy generation; for waste, this implies reduction of waste arisings, with more efficient reuse and recycling.

Throughout this chapter we use the colloquial term 'Britain' due to spatially different data sets; the energy sector encompasses the United Kingdom while the waste sector focuses on England. This chapter begins with a discussion on the need to transition to more sustainable infrastructure, including policy initiatives and key challenges.

*Sustainable Futures in the Built Environment to 2050: A Foresight Approach to Construction and Development*, First Edition. Edited by Tim Dixon, John Connaughton and Stuart Green.
© 2018 John Wiley & Sons Ltd. Published 2018 by John Wiley & Sons Ltd.

Second, we describe an innovative national infrastructure systems model, and assess the energy and solid waste sectors in Britain, a country where rapid decarbonisation policies are in place. This includes analysis of the long-term (to 2050) performance of these sectors. Finally, we close with reflections on future uncertainties and strategic opportunities for achieving more sustainable infrastructure.

## 6.2    Infrastructure policy

The provision of resilient, effective NI systems has become a policy focus for advanced as well as emerging economies. Investments for a reliable and resilient NI facilitate economic competitiveness and positively impact growth (Aschauer, 1989; Munnell, 1992; Gramlich, 1994; CST, 2009). In many ways, infrastructure defines the boundaries of national economic productivity. It is often cited as a key ingredient for a nation's economic competitiveness (Urban Land Institute and Ernst and Young, 2011). The World Economic Forum (WEF), for example, lists infrastructure as the second 'pillar' in its Global Competitiveness Index, a measure of national competitiveness (WEF, 2011, 2012, 2013). Investments to increase the resilience of infrastructure against the impacts of climate variability and climate change can serve as a competitive international advantage. Public investments in infrastructure generally have a positive impact on economic growth, and there is a strong positive relationship between the growth rates of public capital and GDP. All this suggests that significant long-term investment in infrastructure is a desirable outcome for government and society as a whole.

However, public funds for infrastructure investment are limited, especially during times of fiscal austerity. Therefore there is growing interest in the potential to attract private investment into national infrastructure around the world. To attract these investments in an increasingly competitive global economy, it is essential to have coherent long-term goals for infrastructure provision and a policy and regulatory framework sufficiently stable for infrastructure providers to take investment and operational decisions consistent with these goals. This framework needs to include co-ordination mechanisms to ensure that different policy objectives are taken into account (e.g. energy security, affordability and sustainability) and that interactions between infrastructure sectors are considered. It also needs to include appropriate mechanisms for learning from both success and failure (NAO, 2013).

Whilst such a long-term approach is attractive in principle, there are significant practical challenges. For example, risk-conscious investors could be discouraged from investing in infrastructure associated with a low-carbon economy (i.e. green infrastructure), since the economic viability of such investments relies heavily on long-term policies. Policy frameworks such as the UK Climate Change Act (2008) are seeking to deal with such challenges, but as has been the case recently, shorter term disagreements within government about policy priorities can still have a detrimental effect on investment commitments to infrastructure. Further, investments in innovative technologies such as offshore wind are considered higher risk as these infrastructure assets lack a credible investment performance track record in most countries, reflecting that there is considerable learning and rapid technical change occurring, and developers have been historically over-optimistic about costs and performance. This can often serve to discourage investors in these areas (Hall *et al.*, 2014).

## 6.3 Key challenges

In more developed countries, infrastructure systems face a number of serious challenges (Hall *et al.*, 2016): (i) an increased demand for infrastructure services from a growing and ageing population, (ii) ageing infrastructure assets in need of replacement or rehabilitation, (iii) risks of infrastructure failure, in particular from climatic extremes and security threats, (iv) significant investment requirements to counter the vulnerabilities, capacity limitations and supply insecurities associated with an ageing infrastructure system, (v) the increasing complexity, diversification and interdependence of infrastructure networks, and (vi) a widespread desire to maintain and improve environmental standards, including decarbonisation across infrastructure sectors. These challenges threaten the ability of NI to continue to provide the essential services that support nearly all aspects of daily life in advanced societies. Meanwhile, massive infrastructure investments are taking place in emerging economies, which may be locking in patterns of unsustainable development. Less developed countries have the greatest deficit in their stock of infrastructure assets and are particularly vulnerable to shocks from natural disasters and conflict, which can devastate fragile infrastructure systems.

Increasing infrastructure interdependencies can introduce layers of complexity, uncertainty and risk to NI planning and design. Over the last 50 years, infrastructure has shifted from unconnected independent systems to interconnected national networks (CST, 2009). This shift has important implications for the resilience of infrastructure sectors. For example, a power failure in 2011 at a major exchange in Birmingham resulted in the temporary loss of broadband service for hundreds of thousands of customers across Britain, particularly affecting business customers (BBC, 2011). These interdependencies are only likely to grow.

Even small, temporary failures can have significant effects on economic productivity. In the long term, these risks intensify as systems become larger and increasingly interdependent. The combined effect of ageing infrastructure, growing demand (nearing capacity limits) from social and economic pressures, interconnectivity and complexity leads to systematic weakening of the resilience of infrastructure systems (CST, 2009). Climate-related extremes have also caused major service interruptions in recent years (e.g. floods and major snowfall). Climate change is increasing the risk of extreme events (Field *et al.*, 2012) and hence infrastructure failures.

The changing patterns of demand also influence different infrastructure sectors in rather similar ways, providing a further source of interdependence in the long term. In Britain, for example, if it is possible to reduce domestic demand for water this will have implications not only for water supply, but also for energy (as 18% of household energy is used for heating water (DECC, 2011)) and wastewater treatment. Moreover, one infrastructure sector can be a major component of demand for another sector, for example the transport sector represents 34% of energy demand, whilst electricity generation is responsible for 32% of all non-tidal water abstractions (DEFRA, 2009).

Infrastructure in many industrialised countries is ageing, which can negatively impact the efficient and reliable delivery of services. Taking Britain as an example, the existing infrastructure stock was built in the 19th century or early 20th century (HM Treasury and Infrastructure UK, 2010): this can cause supply insecurities.

Consider, for example, the 31,000 km of water mains in London, where nearly half (44%) are over 100 years old. Thames Water has replaced over 2,000 km of London's mains since 2003, at a cost of £650 million, reducing leakage by 27% (Thames Water, 2011).

In the case of transport, the last 15 years have seen growing demand across all modes of travel for long-distance trips (over 160 km). This growth is expected to continue, with the Department for Transport (DfT) forecasting that between 2008 and 2043 there will be an increase of 36% in the total number of long-distance road, rail and air trips per person (DfT, 2011). For digital communications, the infrastructure is new and rapidly evolving, but change in demand is dramatic. The number of households with access to the internet continues to increase, 86% in 2015, compared to 57% in 2006 (ONS, 2015), with 78% of all adults accessing the internet every day on average in 2015 (compared with 35% in 2006) and 68% using a mobile phone, portable computer and/or handheld device (ONS, 2014). Significant levels of investment are needed to address the challenges of ageing infrastructure and growing demand.

## 6.4   Planning for uncertainty

Overcoming these multiple challenges requires a long-term strategic view on infrastructure provision, especially given the long lifespan (many decades or longer) of many physical infrastructure assets (particularly in water, transport and energy), and the long lead time to effect change in these systems (ICE, 2009, 2010, 2014; Hall *et al.*, 2016). However, the feasibility of such planning is challenged by future uncertainties associated with demographic, economic and environmental changes, as well as uncertainties about the nature of technological change, all of which are likely to influence the demands and requirements of NI systems.

In addition, there are uncertainties about the approach to governance arrangements for infrastructure that influences decision-making by infrastructure providers (Hiteva and Watson, 2016). It is essential to take a long-term view in planning for the replacement of infrastructure nearing the end of its life, and for the additional capacity that is required to meet increasing demands (HM Treasury and Infrastructure UK, 2010).

Whilst a long-term view helps ensure new NI will meet current and future demand, anticipating future demand is challenging due to the high degree of uncertainty in the long term (HM Treasury and Infrastructure UK, 2010). Moreover, infrastructure provision can encourage patterns of development and land use that become practically irreversible. Choices about technologies can lock in patterns of behaviour and economic activity. Complex interdependencies between infrastructure sectors can intensify uncertainty in the long-term planning of infrastructure. Hence, when predicting future demand for a given infrastructure sector, the demands from other sectors must be considered (e.g. the need for transportation services to provide fuel sources to the energy sector or the necessity for energy supply for digital communications). Thus, evaluating the demand for a given sector in the long term requires a coordinated planning effort across infrastructure sectors to balance these dependencies.

## 6.5  Infrastructure systems modelling

Historically, policies and decisions regarding individual infrastructure sectors have been made in isolation with little regard for other interconnected infrastructures. Levels of investment in infrastructure have been influenced by the perceived political and economic importance of individual sectors, and such investments have fluctuated over time (Helm *et al.*, 2009; Marshall, 2010). This highlights the increasing importance for taking a long-term and cross-sectoral view of infrastructure provision, including how future investment strategies will interact between sectors.

The Infrastructure Transitions Research Consortium (ITRC) (Hall *et al.*, 2016) has developed a process to appraise the long-term performance of infrastructure policy. This starts by asking a range of high-level questions such as:

1) How much are we prepared to invest from public and private sources?
2) How committed are we to environmental objectives?
3) To what extent are we willing to reduce demand for infrastructure services through price mechanisms, technology, land use changes and changes in behaviour?
4) On what timescales should we plan?

Commitments to economic and environmental policy objectives will determine how much room there is to manoeuvre in devising long-term pathways for transforming the provision and use of infrastructure services.

Long-term strategic analysis requires data and models to appraise options and evaluate system performance under a range of possible future conditions. Simulation modelling provides the ability to analyse in a virtual environment the long-term performance of infrastructure investment strategies across a wide range of possible futures. This can provide insight and evidence concerning benefits and costs, and help safeguard against future risk and systems failure. The ITRC has developed a national assessment and modelling capability for Britain to address this challenge termed the National Infrastructure System Model (NISMOD) (Hall *et al.*, 2016). The approach is generic and transferable, assuming that appropriate data is available.

NISMOD comprises spatially and temporally resolved capacity and demand models that characterise five different infrastructure sectors in Britain: energy, transport, water, wastewater and solid waste. The aim is to inform decisions for planning by evaluating the performance of different strategies for providing infrastructure services under a wide range of future conditions.

As part of this modelling activity, we have developed an ensemble of national infrastructure scenarios for Britain that capture exogenous variables that are external to infrastructure systems but nonetheless influence their performance. These include: (i) demographic change, which affects demand for infrastructure services, (ii) economic change, which affects the demand for infrastructure services, both in final household demand and industrial sectors, (iii) global fossil-fuel costs, which affect both operating costs and transport costs in particular (some national policy measures may affect these costs, but these are assumed to be exogenous to the models) and (iv) environmental change where climate change can affect resources for water and demand for energy. These scenarios are used as direct data inputs for each sector model, ensuring consistent national assumptions (Otto *et al.*, 2014; Hall *et al.*, 2016).

There are many possible strategies for the provision of future infrastructure services (Hickford *et al.*, 2015). Strategies may combine measures to increase the structure or capacity of national infrastructure networks and manage demand. Supply and demand-side measures are becoming increasingly integrated, for example through the development of smart grid networks. Each sector has developed strategies that simulate decisions that can change the infrastructure performance of each sector. These strategies are introduced by input variables representing (i) social and behavioural change (i.e. changes in demand), (ii) technological change (i.e. changes to technology efficiency and costs) and (iii) systemic change within the physical system of infrastructure assets (i.e. changes to the configuration and capacity of infrastructure networks).

This separation of changes to the system through decisions (strategies) and external future conditions (scenarios) enables us to evaluate the performance of infrastructure systems for a specific strategy across a wide range of possible future scenario conditions. A particular scenario/strategy combination will comprise (i) the exogenous assumptions about the socio-economic and environmental context in which national infrastructure is operated, (ii) the high-level assumptions which determine the willingness to invest in new infrastructure assets, (iii) the environmental ambition to decarbonise and mitigate other environmental impacts resulting from infrastructure operation and (iv) the level of commitment to demand management via strong price signals, consumer technology and level of decentralisation (Hickford *et al.*, 2015).

The scenario and strategy modelling outputs are then entered into a common database, which is used for post-processing and visualisation of data outputs. This also allows centralised sampling of model runs and collection of model results. Importantly, this integrated framework allows us to assess total system performance and sectoral interdependencies (Barr *et al.*, 2016). Figure 6.1 illustrates how the various modelling components are linked together.

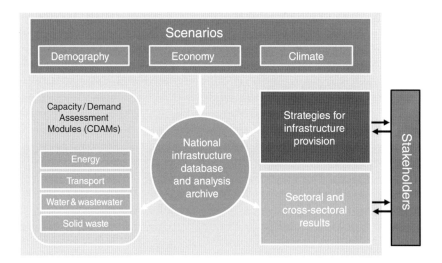

**Figure 6.1** Implementation structure of the general model framework; consisting of capacity and demand modules (CDAMs) for each NI sector, socio-economic models to define possible future demographic and economic conditions, the central database, and the routines for sampling, post-processing, and visualisation across the different infrastructure strategies.

## 6.6   Analysing future infrastructure choices: examples from the energy and solid waste sectors

Here we illustrate the NISMOD framework with an application to Britain's energy and solid waste sectors. There are interesting interactions between these two sectors, which will change with time depending on the future investment strategy taken within each sector. Solid waste infrastructure currently uses energy in the form of electricity, gas and liquid fuels. For example, the failure of the electricity or loss of fuel supply could affect waste treatment, possibly necessitating the storage or stockpiling of waste or disposal to landfill. It could also prevent leachate pumping in landfills, increasing the risk of pollution events. This risk can be mitigated through the use of on-site generators. Energy infrastructure also receives energy from waste by combustion, recovery of high calorific materials such as plastic and paper in the form of fuels and the generation of electricity from landfill gas or biogas from anaerobic digestion (AD).

While energy generated from waste forms, at present, a very significant portion of renewable energy, the overall contribution of renewables to the energy sector is small. However, it may become more important in the drive to increase the use of renewable fuels. In addition, recycling saves energy in comparison with the use of virgin material, but this will only affect Britain directly if the recycled materials are reused here (i.e. closed-loop recycling). Energy outputs are primarily electricity with heat, biogas (from AD or landfill) and syngas (from gasification or pyrolysis) becoming potentially more important in the future. Energy also contributes to the cost of solid waste services for the collection, transportation and processing of wastes (Watson *et al.*, 2016).

Future interactions between the energy and solid waste sector will be influenced by how each infrastructure system evolves with time. Below, we first describe the current energy and solid waste systems, and then present future strategies and model results for alternative infrastructure investment in each sector.

### 6.6.1   Energy

Major investments are anticipated in Britain's energy system to maintain and increase capacity, meet greenhouse gas emission reduction commitments and address EU directives. The main energy networks in Britain are the gas and electricity systems. Gas and electricity networks are very similar, in that they are both designed to transport energy from remote locations to demand centres, often separated by considerable distances. It is this geographical separation that results in the transmission business being of such high national importance. Generally, both gas and electricity energy systems can be structured into the following categories: (i) fuel sources (coal, gas oil, uranium, etc.) and power generation, (ii) transmission (high-voltage power network, high-pressure gas network), (iii) distribution (medium/low-voltage power network, medium/low-pressure gas network) and (iv) consumers (electricity/gas demand) (Chaudry *et al.*, 2008).

However, there are differences between these two networks. Natural gas constitutes a primary form of energy that comes from gas fields, while electrical energy is a secondary form of energy, which is formed by the transformation of primary energy (fuel) in a power plant. Gas is transported from the gas fields (suppliers) to customers through pipelines while electricity is transmitted through power circuits. Additionally, gas networks can store natural gas to be used at peak load periods while electricity cannot be stored efficiently or economically (although future electricity storage technologies may emerge).

There has been rapid increase in renewable capacity (mainly wind) in recent years to meet binding renewable (EU) targets. Renewable generation capacity was at 30 GW in 2015 and the share of total electricity generation from renewables has increased from ~7% in 2010 to ~25% in 2015. As renewable generation capacity deployments continue to increase there will be a requirement for greater electricity transmission capacity, such as the under-construction UK HVDC western link that will help bring renewable energy from Scotland to England and Wales. Additionally, as more wind capacity gets connected to the electricity network there will be a need for flexible plants, mainly in the form of combined cycle gas turbines (CCGTs) for energy-balancing purposes.

### 6.6.1.1 Strategies for energy security in Britain

Britain has committed to decarbonising its energy system by around 80% by 2050 from 1990 values (Committee on Climate Change, 2008). Here we analyse the impacts of imposing a carbon price on the electricity and gas networks under different future scenarios of economic and population growth, including a high-growth scenario (D), medium-growth scenario (A) and a low-growth scenario (F) (Thoung *et al.*, 2016).

This minimum policy intervention (MPI) strategy introduces a carbon price floor for 2013 (£16 $tCO_2^{-1}$), 2020 (£30 $tCO_2^{-1}$) and 2030 (£70 $tCO_2^{-1}$) out to 2050. We assume there is no significant strengthening of climate policies and therefore longer-term targets are not necessarily met. As a result, the optimal generation mix and expansion of the gas and electricity infrastructure is determined based on cost minimisation and subject to limitation of resources and meeting gas and electricity demands.

Concerns about energy security continue and ensure that there is sufficient investment to provide reasonable levels of energy security. Existing long-term trends in demand continue with upward pressures from population and economic growth offset by improvements in energy efficiency, but only limited improvements in regulatory standards, some tax incentives and limited support programmes. Smart meters are rolled out, but there is no need for significant use of demand response.

Consequently, the energy supply sector changes rather slowly, with continued dominance of large-scale investments by large companies. There is no significant investment in nuclear or carbon capture and storage (CCS). Renewables investment continues as costs fall, but capacity increases only slowly. Power sector investment continues to rely largely on CCGTs with gas supplies from imported, but diverse, sources. Heat remains largely dependent on gas although with continued efficiency improvements. Transport fuel supply remains largely oil dependent with some slow penetration of biofuels and electricity (Baruah *et al.*, 2016).

### 6.6.1.2 Model results

The generation capacity mix for MPI-A with and without carbon price floor is shown in Figure 6.2. In the MPI-A strategy with no carbon floor price imposed, CCGT capacity increases from under 30 GW in 2010 to 55 GW by 2050 and accounts for ~60% of total capacity. CCGT capacity is built mainly due to low capital and fixed operating and maintenance costs, and also because of favourable fuel price variations (lower gas price in summer) compared with other fuels. New coal plants are built to compensate for decommissioning of old coal plants, therefore this maintains coal capacity at around

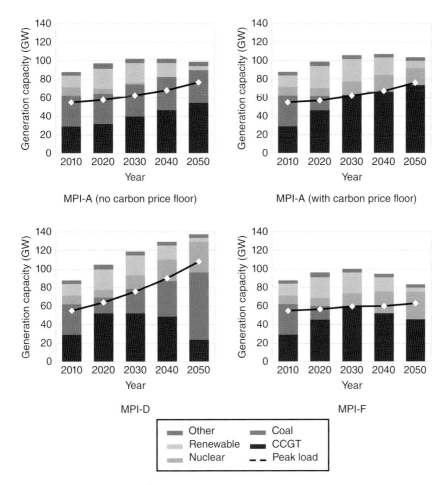

**Figure 6.2** Generation mix for MPI strategies.

35 GW (36% of total capacity in 2050). Coal plants have an overall load factor of 80% by 2050 while CCGT load factor is 39% by 2050. Due to gas price variations in 2050, CCGT load factor during summer/intermediate periods is much higher than the annual value of 39%. CCGTs provide the reserve capacity required to maintain the security of the power system.

Imposing a carbon price floor (£16/tonne in 2014, £30/tonne in 2020 and £70/tonne in 2030 and beyond) makes coal power plants more expensive to run, and therefore less economic compared to CCGT and even nuclear. CCGT capacity increases from under 30 GW in 2010 to 73.5 GW by 2050 and accounts for ~70% of total capacity. New nuclear plants become economically attractive from 2030s onwards as the carbon price floor increases to £70 per tonne.

Total generation capacity for MPI-D in the period between 2020 and 2050 is higher than the generation capacity in MPI-A due to a rise in the electricity demand as higher GDP and population growth was assumed alongside a fall in fuel prices. Capacity of CCGTs increases from roughly 30 GW in 2010 to 52 GW in 2020 and then falls to 24 GW by 2050.

Despite the adverse impact of the carbon price floor on the competitiveness of coal plants, the capacity of coal plants reaches 73 GW by 2050. This is due to a decrease in coal price that makes generation from coal economically viable.

In MPI-F there is lower electricity demand due to a decrease in the GDP and population growth alongside a rise in fuel prices. CCGT capacity at 46 GW and nuclear with 30 GW are the predominant generation technologies in 2050. High coal prices, in addition to a carbon price floor, make it expensive for coal plants to be built after existing plants are decommissioned by 2030.

For the gas network, major investment in new liquefied natural gas (LNG) capacity was predicted in all MPI strategies due to a decline in gas supply from the UK Continental Shelf (UKCS) and to meet increasing gas demand in 2050 (Figure 6.3). Import dependency grows from 55% in 2010 to more than 90% by 2050 for all strategies. The annual gas demand in the MPI-A strategy for residential, commercial and industrial sector grows from 71 bcm in 2010 to 84 bcm by 2050; the rest of the gas demand is from the power sector (CCGTs). The MPI-D and MPI-F strategies have annual gas demands in 2050 (excluding gas for power generation) that are approximately 35% higher and 10% lower than MPI-A, respectively.

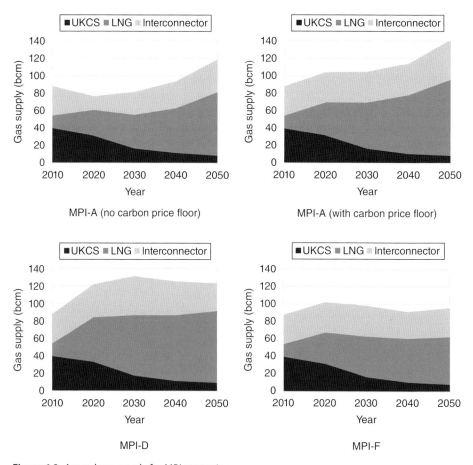

**Figure 6.3** Annual gas supply for MPI strategies.

Gas demand for generation constitutes a significant part of the total gas demand in MPI-A. Gas demand for power generation in MPI-D decreases significantly by 2050 due to the cost competitiveness of coal and nuclear power plants. A considerable amount of investment is required for expanding gas import capacity (LNG and inter-connector) to meet gas demand and to provide enough capacity to satisfy 1-in-20 peak day demand. The 1-in-20 peak day demand is the level of demand that, in a long series of winters, with connected load held at the levels appropriate to the winter in question, would be exceeded in one out of 20 winters (Baruah *et al.*, 2016). The largest investment in gas supply infrastructure is predicted for MPI-D due to higher annual and peak gas demand (517 mcm/day excluding gas power demand).

### 6.6.2   Solid waste

Britain's solid waste infrastructure system covers both waste gong to landfill and resource management whereby resources are reclaimed by recycling and processing. The infrastructure comprises (i) transfer stations for sorting, recovering and con-solidating waste prior to onward processing or disposal, (ii) material recovery facilities (MRFs), where waste is sorted prior to transport for recycling, (iii) recycling or other processing facilities (e.g. AD), (iv) incinerators, where waste is combusted usually to produce electricity, and (v) landfill. There are three main sub-systems: collection, treatment and final disposal.

Britain's solid waste sector deals with approximately 300 million tonnes of waste annually. The construction and demolition (C&D) sector is the largest producer of waste in the UK, producing typically 100 Mt a year (DEFRA, 2015a) of which about 55% is excavation waste. As part of the EU Waste Framework Directive (WFD), the UK has an obligation to recover 70% of C&D waste by 2020. The latest figures show that 86.5% of non-hazardous C&D waste was recovered in 2012 (DEFRA, 2015b). However, there is room to improve as, for example, the London 2012 Olympic Park managed to reuse, recycle or recover 98% of its construction waste (Jackson *et al.*, 2011) and 98.5% of its demolition waste (Carris, 2011). There is relatively little data on C&D arisings and little has been done to forecast future arisings but with best practice recovery levels, design for reuse, and using better design and construction practice to reduce arisings (Barrit, 2016), the environmental impact of the construction sector should continue to reduce.

In the last decade, the sector has transformed rapidly, responding to EU and national legislation. This has increased the amount of waste recycled, composted or reused and nearly halved waste going to landfill. Historically, economic growth and household waste generation were coupled, but there is some evidence that this may no longer be true. National and EU directives for reducing solid waste (e.g. the proposed EU target to increase recycling to 70% by 2030 (EC, 2014)) will affect the levels of investment needed in the near term. There is the possibility of a complete paradigm shift towards solid waste becoming a resource recovery industry, which is explored to varying degrees in the following section for the four investment strategies (Watson *et al.*, 2016):

1) the minimum intervention strategy
2) the new capacity strategy
3) the closed loop strategy
4) the demand reduction strategy.

#### 6.6.2.1   Strategies for solid waste: towards a circular economy?

In a minimum intervention strategy, existing waste, reuse and recycling targets for household, commercial and industrial (C&I), and C&D wastes are met by continuing the current trends and building new infrastructure, particularly energy from waste (EfW) and AD plant as required. There is a steady improvement in the performance of the waste sector and the amount of waste being landfilled continues to fall due in part to increases in landfill tax.

We also explore the implications of a new capacity strategy, where developments in materials separation and recovery technologies mean that wastes require minimum source separation. For householders, this means two bins – food and green wastes, and everything else. Consumers disengage from concerns about waste and recycling but despite this, rates of recycling and composting/AD continue to rise as does the overall waste production. The materials left over from materials recovery are used for fuels in EfW plant.

The above strategies are compared against two related strategies driven by environmental policy and lifestyle changes: closed loop, where there is a move from consumption to leasing with products designed for long life, easy repair and remanufacturing (D4R), and demand reduction, in which waste arisings are reduced by increasing prices for waste disposal and increasing the involvement of the third sector in refurbishing of unwanted goods. In both strategies, there is little investment in waste infrastructure. Changes are driven by cultural and behavioural change in the latter and by changes in the philosophical approach in manufacturing and design required to transition to a circular economy in the former (Watson *et al.*, 2016).

#### 6.6.2.2   Model outputs

The capacity of the existing, under-construction and consented residual waste (residual waste is the waste remaining after recyclables and material for biological treatment have been removed) treatment facilities (excluding landfill) is modelled for the nine English Government regions. In the North-West, Yorkshire and Humberside, and Eastern regions there is currently insufficient capacity for all of the strategies. Figure 6.4 shows the data from Yorkshire and Humberside as an example, where the only successful strategy is demand reduction, which reduces waste arising below existing and consented capacity by 2040.

Figure 6.5 shows the data for the North-East region. In the North-East, the capacity of the existing, under construction and consented residual waste (residual waste is the waste remaining after recyclables and material for biological treatment has been removed) treatment facilities (excluding landfill) are below the projected residual waste arisings until 2020. After that time, there is excess capacity in all strategies except for the new capacity strategy, which focuses on building additional capacity without initiatives to reduce demand and invest in recycling. For the other strategies, spare capacity may enable other regions to meet their 2020 targets (although with potentially high transport costs).

Figure 6.6 shows the data for the South-East region as an example of a region in which there is a large continuing requirement for landfill void space due to the shortfall in alternative residual waste treatment capacity.

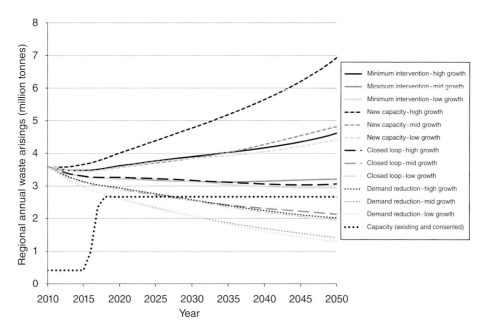

**Figure 6.4** Graph of residual waste arisings for the Yorkshire and Humberside government region. It shows the residual waste arisings for the three scenarios with four different strategies. The difference between arisings and the available capacity line is the excess waste, which will need to be disposed of to landfill or treated out of region.

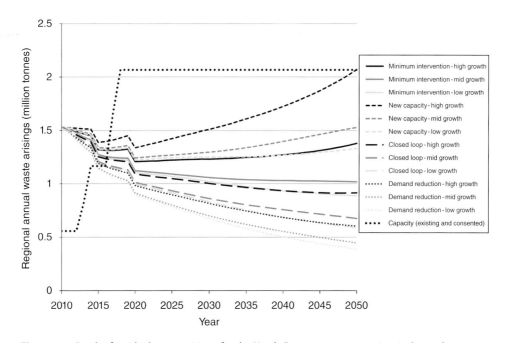

**Figure 6.5** Graph of residual waste arisings for the North-East government region. It shows the residual waste arisings for the three scenarios with four different strategies. Data above the capacity line indicate a treatment shortfall, the excess waste from which will need to be disposed of to landfill. Where the capacity line is above the arisings line, this indicates excess capacity, which could be used to treat arisings from outside the region.

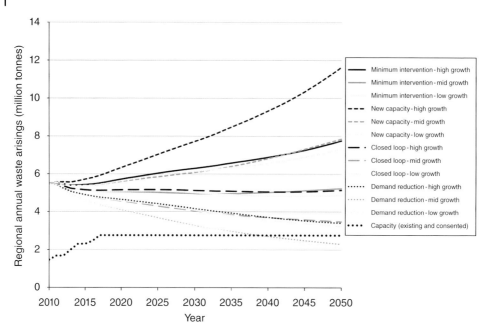

**Figure 6.6** Graph of residual waste arisings for the South-East government region. It shows the residual waste arisings for the three scenarios with four different strategies. The difference between arisings and the available capacity line is the excess waste, which will need to be disposed of to landfill or treated out of region.

Although not shown here, in the remaining five government regions (the South-East, the South-West, London, the West Midlands and the East Midlands), the capacities of the existing, under construction and consented residual waste treatment facilities (excluding landfill) are, in most cases, insufficient to deal with any scenario and strategy combination until mid-century, when the closed-loop scenarios A and F have led to sufficient per capita waste reductions that, coupled with low economic and population growth, there is sufficient residual waste capacity. The gap between the residual waste arisings and the treatment capacity will need to be filled by landfill. However, it should be noted that in England and hence in some or all of the regions, the 2013 biodegradable municipal waste diversion and recycling and composting targets were met in 2010, showing that the recycling and composting targets were exceeded rather than just met.

Figure 6.7 is an example for the Yorkshire and Humberside regions showing the minimum requirement for recycling and composting based on the Environment Agency's existing targets for MRFs and composting facilities (EA, 2010). It should be noted that the capacities shown will not necessarily capture all recycling operations, for example household recyclables that are collected through a kerbside sorted collection do not require an MRF. The same is true for household waste disposed of through household waste recycling centres (which will typically have a recycling rate of over 50% and account for about 10–20% of household waste) and waste disposed of through bring banks.

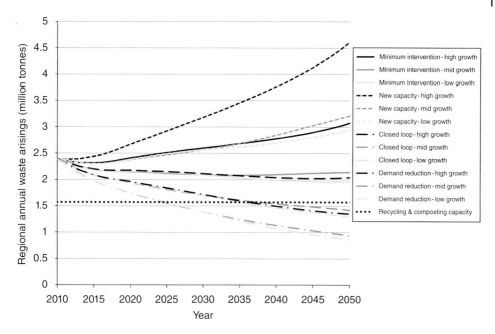

**Figure 6.7** Graph of recycling and composting for the Yorkshire and Humberside government region. Data are shown for the three scenarios with three different strategies.

## 6.7 Critical uncertainties

As discussed above, there are multiple challenges that infrastructure systems face around the world. Given the long lifetime of these systems, we have argued for the need for a long-term strategic planning approach. However, there are inherent uncertainties in the long-term performance of these systems, driven by changes in technological innovation and resulting in a range of alternative investment strategies that critically depend on which technologies become technically and economically viable. There are also major uncertainties in future demand patterns, which depend on macro level drivers of change such as macroeconomic growth and demographic changes across different regions. These critical uncertainties are highlighted below.

### 6.7.1 New technologies

For the energy sector, current trends indicate an increased uptake of information and communication technologies (ICT). New information technologies can potentially transform the current energy system, as it becomes integrated through the supply chain all the way to the final consumer. This includes its use in embedding distributed renewable energy generation sources into the grid and balancing international energy flows in transmission from reserved power sources (Wissner, 2011). It is also becoming more central to the actual distribution of energy on the demand side, via price and incentive-based mechanisms, and improving the amount of information available to both operators and consumers (Wissner, 2011).

An impact of ICT is that it cuts across supply and demand, and will therefore shape investment needs for capacity provision and potentially alter future demand trends. For example, there are particularly strong interdependencies between energy and transport, with the EU and UK implementing policies to encourage investment into smart network architecture and mass roll out of smart meters by 2020. It is believed that there is potential to increase overall system efficiency by better matching energy demand and supply through improved data monitoring and information feedback. For example, network operators will get more detailed information about supply and demand improving management of the system such as shifting demand to off-peak times. As a result, a smart network will be able to better accommodate mass penetration of intermittent renewables and electric vehicles. However, there are many unanswered questions surrounding the system-wide impacts on the energy system from mass uptake of ICT.

For the solid waste sector, there are a number of new technologies that may influence the future performance of the system:

1) *Mechanical heat treatment facilities*: In this technology the mixed residual waste is heat-treated for sanitisation. Outputs include recyclables, solid recovered fuel (SRF) and a residual waste fraction to landfill.

2) *Advanced thermal treatment (ATT)*: This is a group of related thermal processes that can be combined with an MRF to recover recyclables prior to thermal treatment. Gasification may be combined with an MRF or use refuse-derived fuel or SRF as the fuel. Waste is heated to 700 °C with a controlled amount of oxygen, without allowing combustion. Outputs include syngas (mainly CO and $H_2$) that is usually combusted on site to generate electricity (and heat), slag and ash. Pyrolysis may be combined with an MRF or use SRF as the feedstock. Waste is heated to high temperatures in the absence of oxygen. Outputs may include char (a carbon-rich solid fuel), liquid or gaseous fuels depending on processing temperature (Williams and Barton, 2011), recyclables and ash as well as $CO_2$ and nitrous oxides. Plasma arc gasification may be combined with an MRF or use SRF as a feedstock. Waste is heated in a low-oxygen atmosphere using a plasma torch. Outputs include syngas, which maybe combusted on site to produce electricity (and heat) and vitrified slag (Watson *et al.*, 2016).

These treatment technologies are relatively new to Britain. Although more experience is available elsewhere (e.g. two municipal solid waste plasma gasification plants at commercial scale in Japan), there is still some debate about the large-scale future of all of these technologies, fuelled by the continuing failure (at the time of writing) of any of the ATT plants to deliver as promised (Goulding, 2016). It is possible that further funding support for these technologies will be required due to the reluctance of banks to finance new technology for waste management infrastructure, although Goulding (2016) would seem to contradict this. This tends to force operators to propose more commercially proven recycling, composting or waste to energy technologies that may not always be the most effective solutions for maximising utility from waste.

It is well known that changes in collection strategy for household waste (e.g. fortnightly refuse collection) can significantly increase the amount of recyclables that is collected. Refinement of collection strategies may help optimise material recovery.

### 6.7.2   Alternative investment strategies

When comparing across alternative strategies, we see important differences in infrastructure performance. It is also important to recall that each sector strategy will be influenced by the economic and demographic assumptions that have been developed into future scenarios. For the economic scenarios alone there are a possible 72 possible future projections that can be developed with different impacts on the performance of sector level strategies.

Also, alternative demographic projections tend to have the following effects: (i) a larger population tends to increase expenditure by households across the economy, (ii) a larger population also increases the size of the workforce, permitting higher employment (a higher availability of labour may also curb wage growth) and (iii) a larger population will also raise demand for government goods and services, and therefore the requirement for necessary infrastructure to support such services.

The impacts of scenario variation can be seen in the solid waste sector at the regional level, giving insight into capacity constraints and necessary investment strategies. For instance, for all but the highest growth scenario (scenario D), current residual waste treatment capacity in the South-East region is sufficient from 2020 until 2035. For the central and low-growth assumptions, the current capacity is sufficient until beyond 2070. For the energy sector, we can see the important differences in both total electricity capacity and the resulting impacts on the gas supply network as a function of different population and economic growth scenarios. At the strategy level, we see the influence that different carbon prices have on the generation mix by 2050.

When we therefore account for the influence of macro level demographic and economic scenarios combined with sector-specific strategies, the space of alternative future outcomes opens up even more. This highlights the importance of investment decisions we make today, and how this will impact on future infrastructure performance.

We can also see the cumulative effects of our decisions such that the differences between strategy outcomes are even greater as we look further out in time. However, the range of possible strategy outcomes also implies that we may not be as locked in as we think. This should incentivise us to plan and invest into infrastructure provision over a far longer time horizon than is conventionally done today.

## 6.8   Conclusions

The planning of future infrastructure systems is challenged by critical uncertainties associated with demographic, economic and environmental changes, as well as uncertainties about the nature of technological change, all of which are likely to influence the demands and requirements of NI systems. Moreover, infrastructure provision can encourage patterns of development and land use that can become irreversible, and new technologies can alter consumer behaviour and demand. Moreover, new technologies such as ICT and increasing cross-sector demand will increase interdependencies between infrastructure sectors, which can intensify uncertainty in the long-term planning of these systems.

These are considerable challenges. However, we have demonstrated an approach for assessing the future performance of infrastructure that systematically addresses some of these challenges. For example, to attract investment, it is necessary to have coherent long-term policies and regulatory frameworks to minimise risk for potential investors. Our methods for analysing the long-term performance of infrastructure systems across a range of future scenarios and strategies can inform policies and regulations to incentivise necessary investments. Our methods have been illustrated using the energy and waste sectors in Britain. These types of results can be used to inform decision-making and policy formulation by evaluating the performance of alternative strategies for providing infrastructure services under a wide range of future socio-economic and environmental conditions.

These methods are generic and could be applied widely in other developed national economies facing similar challenges such as in Europe and North America. With suitable modification, these methods are suitable in emerging economies. In this case, rather than transform an existing infrastructure system, the goal is to greatly enhance and expand such systems. The issues of long-term performance are still pertinent and such analysis will provide insight about the key choices that exist and their potential trade-offs.

## Acknowledgements

All chapter authors acknowledge funding of the work by the Engineering and Physical Sciences Research Council of the UK under Programme Grant EP/I01344X/1 as part of the Infrastructure Transitions Research Consortium (www.itrc.org.uk).

## References

Aschauer, D.A. (1989) Is public expenditure productive? *Journal of Monetary Economics*, 23(2), 177–200.

Barr, S., Alderson, D., Ives, M.C. and Robson, C. (2016) Database, simulation modelling and visualisation for national infrastructure assessment in Hall, J.W., Tran, M., Hickford, A.J. and Nicholls, R.J. (eds) *The future of national infrastructure: a system-of-system approach*. Cambridge University Press, Cambridge.

Barritt, J. (2016) An overview on recycling and waste in construction. *Proceedings of the Institution of Civil Engineers – Construction Materials*, 169, 49–53.

Baruah, P., Chaudry, M., Qadrdan, M., Eyre, N. and Jenkins, N. (2016) Energy systems assessment in Hall, J.W., Tran, M., Hickford, A.J. and Nicholls, R.J. (eds) *The future of national infrastructure: a system-of-system approach*. Cambridge University Press, Cambridge.

BBC (2011) *BT suffers huge broadband failure*. Available at: http://www.bbc.co.uk/news/technology-15154020.

Carris, J. (2011) *Learning Legacy: Demolition Waste Management on the Olympic Park*. Available at: http:// learninglegacy.independent.gov.uk/documents/pdfs/sustainability/15-demolition-waste-aw.pdf (accessed 1 June 2016).

Chaudry, M., Jenkins, N. and Strbac, G. (2008) Multi-time period combined gas and electricity optimisation. *Electric Power Systems Research*, 78, 1265–1279.

Climate Change Act (2008) Climate Change Act 2008. HM Government, London.

Committee on Climate Change (2008) *Building a low-carbon economy – the UK's contribution to tackling climate change.* TSO, London.

CST (2009) *A national infrastructure for the 21st century.* Council for Science and Technology, London.

DECC (2011) *Digest of UK Energy Statistics (DUKES).* Department of Energy and Climate Change, TSO, London.

DEFRA (2009) *Estimated abstractions from all sources (except tidal), by purpose and Environment Agency region: 1995–2008, England and Wales.* Department for Environment, Food and Rural Affairs, London.

DEFRA (2015a) *Digest of Waste and Resource Statistics – 2015 Edition.* Department for Environment, Food and Rural Affairs, London.

DEFRA (2015b) *UK Statistics on Waste.* Department for Environment, Food and Rural Affairs, London.

DfT (2011) *Future demand for long distance travel: scheme development – high speed rail consultation.* Department for Transport, London.

EA (2010) *Waste infrastructure report 2010.* Environment Agency, Bristol.

EC (2014) Higher recycling targets to drive transition to a Circular Economy with new jobs and sustainable growth [online]. Available at: http://europa.eu/rapid/press-release_IP-14-763_en.htm. (accessed 10 July 2014).

Field, C.B., Barros, V., Stocker, T.F., Qin, D., Dokken, D.J., Ebi, K.L., Mastrandrea, M.D., Mach, K.J., Plattner, G.-K., Allen, S.K., Tignor, M. and Midgely, P.M. (eds) (2012) *Managing the risks of extreme events and disasters to advance climate change adaptation.* A Special Report of Working Groups I and II of the Intergovernmental Panel on Climate Change. IPCC, Cambridge and New York, 582pp.

Goulding, T. (2016) *Is large-scale gasification viable?* Available at: http://www.letsrecycle.com/news/latest-news/is-large-scale-gasification-viable/ (accessed 31 March 2016).

Gramlich, E.M. (1994) Infrastructure investment: a review essay. *Journal of Economic Literature*, 32(3), 1176–1196.

Hall, J.W., Henriques, J.J., Hickford, A.J., Nicholls, R.J., Baruah, P., Birkin, M., Chaudry, M., Curtis, T.P. Eyre, N., Jones, C., Kilsby, C.G., Leathard, A., Lorenz, A., Malleson, N., McLeod, F., Powrie, W., Preston, J., Rai, Street, R., Stringfellow, A., Thoung, C., Tyler, P., Velykiene, R., Watson, G. and Watson, W.J. (2014) Assessing the long-term performance of cross-sectoral strategies for national infrastructure. *Journal of Infrastructure Systems*, 20(3), 04014014.

Hall, J.W., Tran, M., Hickford, A.J. and Nicholls, R.J. (2016) *The future of national infrastructure: a system-of-systems approach.* Cambridge University Press, Cambridge.

Helm, D., Wardlaw, J. and Caldecott, B. (2009) *Delivering a 21st Century infrastructure for Britain.* Policy Exchange, London.

Hickford, A.J., Nicholls, R.J., Otto, A., Hall, J.W., Blainey, S.P., Tran, M. and Baruah, P. (2015) Creating an ensemble of future strategies for national infrastructure provision. *Futures*, 66(Feb), 13–24.

Hiteva, R. and Watson, J. (2016) Governance of interdependent infrastructure networks in Hall, J.W., Tran, M., Hickford, A.J. and Nicholls, R.J. (eds) *The future of national infrastructure: a system-of-system approach.* Cambridge University Press, Cambridge.

HM Treasury and Infrastructure UK (2010) *Strategy for national infrastructure.* HM Treasury. London.

ICE (2009) *State of the Nation: defending critical infrastructure.* Institution of Civil Engineers, London.

ICE (2010) *State of the Nation: infrastructure 2010*. Institution of Civil Engineers, London.

ICE (2014) *State of the Nation: infrastructure 2014*. Institution of Civil Engineers, London.

Jackson, R., Bonard, C., Bold, N. *et al.* (2011) *Learning Legacy: Construction Waste Management on the Olympic Park*. Available at: http://learninglegacy.independent.gov.uk/documents/pdfs/sustainability/16-const-waste-aw.pdf (accessed 1 June 2016).

Marshall, T. (2010) *Planning and infrastructure sectors – a history*. UK Working Paper. Department of Planning, Oxford Brookes University, Oxford.

Munnell, A.H. (1992) Policy watch: infrastructure investment and economic growth. *Journal of Economic Perspectives*, 6(4), 189–198.

NAO (2013) *Planning for economic infrastructure*. National Audit Office, London.

ONS (2014) *Internet access – households and individuals, 2014: Statistical bulletin*. Office for National Statistics, Cardiff.

ONS (2015) *Internet access – households and individuals, 2015: Statistical bulletin*. Office for National Statistics, Cardiff.

Otto, A., Hall, J.W., Hickford, A.J., Nicholls, R.J., Alderson, D. and Barr, S. (2014) A quantified system-of-systems modelling framework for robust national infrastructure planning. *IEEE Systems Journal*, 99, 1–12.

Thames Water (2011) *Investing in our network: Replacing London's Victorian water mains*. Available at: https://corporate.thameswater.co.uk/About-us/Investing-in-our-network/Victorian-mains-replacement (accessed 3 June 2011).

Thoung, C., Beaven, R., Zuo, C., Birkin, M., Tyler, P., Crawford-Brown, D., Oughton, E.J. and Kelly, S. (2016) Future demand for infrastructure services in Hall, J.W., Tran, M., Hickford, A.J. and Nicholls, R.J. (eds) *The future of national infrastructure: a system-of-system approach*. Cambridge University Press, Cambridge.

Urban Land Institute and Ernst and Young (2011) *Infrastructure 2011 – a strategic priority*. Urban Land Institute, Washington DC.

Watson, G.V.R., Stringfellow, A.M., Powrie, W., Turner, D.A., and Coello, J. (2016) Solid waste systems assessment in Hall, J.W., Tran, M., Hickford, A.J. and Nicholls, R.J. (eds) *The future of national infrastructure: a system-of-system approach*. Cambridge University Press, Cambridge.

WEF (2011) *The global competitiveness report 2011–2012*. World Economic Forum, Geneva.

WEF (2012) *The global competitiveness report 2012–2013*. World Economic Forum, Geneva.

WEF (2013) *The global competitiveness report 2013–2014*. World Economic Forum, Geneva.

Williams, P.T. and Barton, J. (2011) Demonstration scale flash pyrolysis of municipal solid waste. *Proceedings of the ICE – Waste and Resource Management*, 164(3), 205–210.

Wissner, M. (2011) The Smart Grid – A saucerful of secrets? *Applied Energy*, 88(7), 2509–2518.

# 7

# Sustainable Design of the Built Environment

*Lorraine Farrelly*

## 7.1   Introduction

There are a range of initiatives that consider the idea of improving the quality of design and the experience of place making, and which implicitly highlight the importance of sustainable design. The Farrell Review, led by Farrell Architects (Farrell, 2013), was a national review of architecture and the built environment. One of its themes was design policy and it suggested that strong leadership is needed at local authority level to encourage a collective community-led approach to improving the quality of the built environment. It also suggested that all government decision-making panels for major infrastructure reviews should have design professionals represented. The idea of the design review panel, a group of professionals from disciplines across the built environment from architects to landscape specialists, environmental engineers, transport engineers, was supported as a way to ensure that the design of the built environment is considered by a range of professional perspectives. This approach meant there was an objective debate around design quality that informed the planning process.

In response to the Farrell Review, there was a proposal that all towns and cities should have an 'urban room', a place to encourage discussion around place-making and the quality of townscape and urban environments and cities. A group of academics and professionals have established Place Alliance. This is an alliance chaired by Professor Matthew Carmona and hosted by UCL University that comprises universities and other organisations who are involved in the education and delivery of building places or spaces. All the contributors want to improve the quality of public space and the built environment.

This emphasis on quality of design in the built environment is therefore a driving force in ensuring we create sustainable places to live now and in the future to 2050. This chapter therefore considers how sustainable design in relationship to architecture and the built environment can be described and defined. This could be in terms of a building or space, or the relationship to cultural and social expectations and regulations. The chapter also looks at a range of examples of sustainable buildings and places to define the policies and issues that inform the design of sustainable built environments. However, to understand how places should be designed for the future, we also need to understand the social production of space, place and environment, and the role of

*Sustainable Futures in the Built Environment to 2050: A Foresight Approach to Construction and Development*, First Edition. Edited by Tim Dixon, John Connaughton and Stuart Green.
© 2018 John Wiley & Sons Ltd. Published 2018 by John Wiley & Sons Ltd.

community and critical regionalism in setting the concept of place in context. The chapter therefore begins by placing sustainable design in a wider context of social and cultural values.

## 7.2   The social production of space, place and environment

The idea of sustainable design for buildings and cities can exist at a range of levels, from the specification of the materials used in a building to the infrastructure within which it is placed. This may offer opportunities for the users of the building to use sustainable transport systems, such as buses powered from hybrid energy or an integrated set of cycle pathways. Sustainability needs to work at all levels, from the individual who may want to use a sustainable system of transport, to the client and contractor responsible for specifying materials and finishes for the final building so that they can be recycled and are from sustainable sources. The starting point for any sustainable building should therefore be part of a planning and masterplanning approach that considers holistically how people will live, work, travel and socialise, and the masterplanning framework supports that approach.

When designing architecture, consideration of sustainability is implicit for the architecture to be relevant culturally and socially. It affects the design of the building itself in terms of relationship to site, use of materials and relationship to infrastructure, such as public transport, as well as being part of a larger context, for example of a sustainable community. The impact that architectural design itself has on sustainable communities is an important consideration, not only for architects, when they react to a project brief, but also for the 'success' of the community. To understand this impact, it is important to determine what is a sustainable community and what is good architectural design within that context.

The issues that surround sustainable design are driven not only through social and cultural expectations, but also regulatory requirements for designing buildings, which now require consideration of materials and energy use to certain standards so that they can comply with building regulations. In terms of a definition of 'sustainable design', Jarzombek (2003) promotes a holistic idea of sustainability, bridging technology-driven approaches and socio-political point of views. This moves away from a singular definition of sustainability, and allows sustainability to be more meaningful for design, aligned to a range of approaches and more flexible.

As Pyla (2008) suggests: 'Sustainability should not become a totalizing concept that subsumes crucial design questions about the social, the cultural, the political, the aesthetic and the physical, which, incidentally, are not unambiguous categories. Maybe it is good that sustainability does not have a fixed or coherent definition.' This definition 'will threaten to reduce design to a series of small decisions on materials, energy or feasibility, that will ultimately have less to do with design and more with management or with political correctness.'

Similarly, Hagan (2008) suggests that sustainable architecture can only arise by bridging the gap between environmental practice and digital architecture. She points to the gap between the environmentally inclined architects and builders on the one hand, and the digital design 'avant-garde' on the other. For Hagan, the first group base their sustainable ambitions on the idea that we should use natural ecosystems and try to reproduce them in our own built world (i.e. 'desire to replicate in the built world, the waste-not-want-not efficiencies of natural ecosystems' (Hagan, 2008)), whilst the second are pursuing the development of innovative forms, structures and new striking aesthetics. Respecting nature and seeking for the new and innovative are necessary to achieve this idea of sustainable architecture.

In summary, sustainable architecture can be innovative in terms of its form and also distinctive aesthetically, driven by the possibilities of using advanced computer systems. It can also be designed in a more simplistic way, using traditional design methods which produces a less distinctive visual expression of the built form, utilising traditional design approaches and passive systems such as maximising natural light or using natural ventilation systems.

## 7.3  Sustainable community

The concept of a sustainable community is also fundamental to understanding sustainable design. A sustainable community can be defined in many ways (some of these are explored in more detail in Chapter 4). In general terms, it can be seen as a community that has been designed to encourage and promote sustainable living. In a holistic sense, sustainable living involves a strategy to encourage a community to live in this way easily, and has the infrastructure and governance to support the vision of the community. There are many approaches to the idea of creating a sustainable community or place and these shape the subsequent design strategy of an individual building or place. The role of architectural design in sustainable communities is therefore also a key factor for its success, particularly as the design process should be seen as a 'collaborative' experience that brings together different perspectives from a range of professional contributors. A well-designed environment is holistic and will take into consideration a range of issues around context, including physical, cultural and social characteristics. The impact that carefully considered design has on such environments will have a legacy on future generations. The design process is also about the engagement of stakeholders, whether a client, a local community or the end users. For design to have an impact on sustainability, it must be relevant to these users and it must meet the needs of the user and be adaptable and flexible to their current requirements and future needs.

The implicit definition of 'sustainability' adopted here relates then to a design response that is durable and can adapt over time to the changing needs of the community. There are many factors of design that can impact sustainability. For example, good design can improve the energy efficiency of buildings, even by considering existing buildings and re-designing their energy use. It can impact on lifestyle, creating healthier lifestyles and happier, more connected communities through careful location of key facilities such as shared recreation and community space, neighbourhood shops and schools.

There are many exemplars of sustainable communities encouraging this holistic approach, which identifies values for a community as well as design parameters. One of the most influential examples in the UK is BEDZED. Designed by Bedford Zero Energy Development with Bill Dunster Architect in 2002, it was the result of a collaboration between Peabody Trust, a social housing provider, Arup Engineers and Bioregional, an organisation which works with different groups to develop sustainable living projects.

This was one of the first mixed-use communities with a range of innovative approaches to housing, offices and social and community facilities. Its intention was to develop a carbon-neutral community, reducing carbon use in the materials used for the building design and the energy used by the community. One of the innovations in the design strategy was the idea that live and work spaces could be co-designed in an integrated way. These typologies had generally been considered separately and often zoned in different parts of town and cities, so promoting what was often considered unsustainable travel from one zone to another. The BEDZED approach was to discourage travel across zones and design a 'live–work' approach, in other words a place that doesn't separate, but encourages mixing of activities. This approach created its own challenges, however, because as people work and live in the same physical space, there are few spaces for social interaction to occur.

Other innovations on the BEDZED project included using energy from renewable sources generated on site, using building materials that were recycled or from local-sourced sites, and having an eco-friendly approach to transport by considering cycleways, encouraging the pedestrian and using public transport. The detailed and explicit consideration of journeys to work, cycle ways, pathways and play spaces can therefore create an integrated and more sustainable community.

The idea of a sustainable community must have an infrastructure that supports reducing energy use through a carefully designed integrated transport system. For example, in his book *Cities for People*, Jan Gehl (2010), a Danish architect and urban designer, tries to reclaim the territory of the city back for people by taking it away from the car. He has been influential in the complete reorganisation of Copenhagen, transforming the city into a zero-carbon community where the bicycle and the pedestrian have priority.

The design implication of these innovations (i.e. route ways and cycle ways) is that public spaces, the streets and the squares, become more important, encouraging people to walk or cycle and use these spaces. However, this requires detailed planning and design considerations. Good sustainable design should therefore start with a masterplan, which includes a strategy for people to move around a place effectively, and a strategy for clean, sustainable energy use that people can identify with from the start. It also needs to have a strong community ethos that takes responsibility for shared spaces and engages with managing those spaces effectively.

An example of this shared community ethos was developed though the garden city concept developed by Ebenezer Howard in *Garden Cities of Tomorrow* (Howard, 1902). The wider garden city movement continues to have an impact today. For example, the Town and Country Planning Association, in their publication *Creating Garden Cities and Suburbs today: A Guide to Councils* (TCPA, 2013), suggested that the following concepts were essential for a successful community:

- strong vision, leadership and community engagement
- land value capture for the benefit of the community
- community ownership of land and long-term stewardship of assets
- mixed-tenure homes and housing types that are affordable for ordinary people
- beautifully and imaginatively designed homes with gardens in healthy communities
- a strong, local jobs offer in the garden city itself and within easy commuting distance of homes

- opportunities for residents to grow their own food, including allotments
- generous green space, including a surrounding belt of countryside to prevent sprawl, well-connected and biodiversity-rich public parks, high-quality gardens, tree-lined streets and open spaces
- strong local cultural, recreational and shopping facilities in walkable neighbourhoods
- integrated and accessible transport systems.

The idea of the garden city has inspired new thinking around the types of community that can use the idea of shared space to live, work and plan as a backdrop to a more sustainable community. For example, the UK government announced in January 2017 the idea of a new set of 14 'garden villages', communities similar in principle but smaller is scale than garden cities, and which will be developed in the next few years. Whatever the merits or problems with this new initiative it is important to recognise that, in theory, although a sustainable community can be located anywhere, it needs to be supported by a group of people who want to put the foundations of community in place and contribute to the formation of that structure and community. Moreover, for it to be truly sustainable it needs to respond to local context, and climate and environmental issues above all else.

## 7.4  Architectural design

For architectural design to be considered of the highest quality, it must relate to its context and be fit for purpose to address the expectations of social, cultural and legislative requirements. These requirements include responding to the planning and building regulation policy agenda for sustainable design as a minimum, but also the cultural expectations to use energy and materials responsibly and appropriately.

There are many documents that act as reference points for sustainable design. An important report in this context is *Our Common Future*, written in 1987 by the United Nations World Commission on Economic Development, otherwise known as the Brundtland report. The report (Brundtland, 1987) has an important definition of sustainable development:

> 'Sustainable development is development that meets the needs of the present without compromising the ability of future generations to meet their own needs.'

This is a clear statement that can be applied in an architectural context to the use of materials and the use of energy. Therefore, sustainable building design requires an approach to efficiency, particularly energy and material efficiency. Building design reacts to this by considering a range of spatial construction and energy efficiency issues, which also has impact through an 'aesthetic' response. An example of this is 'high tech', which was characteristic of the architects Foster, Rogers and Grimshaw from the 1980s onwards, where aspects of construction and energy efficiency affect the visual effect of the architecture. An impressive and memorable example of 'high tech' is the Pompidou Centre in Paris, a cultural and exhibition centre designed in 1977 by engineer and architect Renzo Piano and Richard Rogers. It is a building where the technology has impacted on its visual appearance, and it has become expressed in and on the elevation, with the building presented as a 'machine' in the cityscape.

Another architect who has responded to technology to develop a particular aesthetic is the Malaysian architect Ken Yeang, who has developed an approach to bioclimatic design. This is an approach where the design of the architecture is responding to local climatic conditions. Essentially, successful bioclimatic design uses such conditions to ensure the building conserves energy by using design strategies such as the orientation of the building to optimise its performance.

The design of the iconic skyscraper has also been affected by approaches to create low-energy buildings. Architects have developed mechanisms such as environmental filters that act as solar shades, and innovations such as vertical farms and planted sky terraces to offer a tantalising glimpse of futuristic 'green' skyscrapers. These concepts have dramatically affected the resultant architectural expression.

All of these new approaches to design have produced a range of technological innovations around building skins and cladding, but also servicing approaches to buildings. They have created a resultant architectural expression and form. For example, the use of green roofs or roof gardens and balconies, or green 'living' walls have offered architects new approaches to cladding, where the surfaces are dynamic and grow (Wilkinson and Dixon, 2016). In this context, the French designer Patrick Blanc has been an innovator of the 'living wall', for example the vertical garden of the Caixa Forum in Madrid. These walls are designed as a system of plants and an integrated irrigation system to support the 'living wall'.

The use of solar energy has also produced new types of glass, and the inclusion of photovoltaics in cladding systems has produced some impressive façade responses. These ideas have also had impact in basic design considerations for buildings, for example by designing in a way to react to the site and local climatic conditions, allowing solar gain to provide energy use. The technology has resulted in a new aesthetic that has had tremendous impact on design in both planning and strategic terms, but also in in the resultant visual effect of the architecture. The idea of the modernist approach to architecture (or *form following the function*) was originally described by Louis Sullivan, the American Architect who pioneered the skyscraper in the late 19th century in *The Tall Office Building Artistically Considered* (Sullivan, 1896), and is part of this approach to architecture. The building design is responding to the function, and the ambition is to create buildings which are intrinsically sustainable in their approach to energy use.

Climate-responsive architecture was pioneered by Reyner Banham. In *Architecture of the Well-Tempered Environment* (Banham, 1969), he advocates a conscious architecture which should be able to identify and solve the unique solution to specific problems. There is also a related approach to design, where the building is seen as an eco-system in itself, responding to nature, using renewable natural materials and low-technology approaches to solve problems, and reducing the need for energy waste systems. There can be a dependency on a centralised system for energy use in buildings by going off the main grid or electricity supply. There are also related examples in the USA, such as architect Samuel Mockbee's idea, rural studio, where communities build their own places to live using recycled materials, but also develop an ethos so a sustainable environment is created. These communities are interested in the social sense of working together to develop, and build the places that they live and work. This concept is also part of the Auburn University architecture programme, which encourages students to become involved in design build projects and to understand the building system, its materials and also ways to be sustainable in energy use and production.

Finally, in design terms, multi-functional buildings that can perform a range of functions or uses can be seen as being truly sustainable because, potentially, they can have a lifetime of several hundred years. Buildings designed for one use, which cannot adapt to future needs, are therefore unsustainable. The idea of building re-use or retrofitting existing buildings is now an important aspect of adapting an existing community of buildings to become sustainable in energy use for today and tomorrow. We cannot just create new communities using new systems of building and new materials: we also need to consider the fabric of cities, towns and communities that exist already and upgrade those environments so that they use less energy, are well insulated and can cope with the requirements and expectations of a 21st century community. In short, we should understand that the idea of good architectural design is influenced by a range of factors. It needs to be fit for purpose, it needs to be adaptable to the users' needs and it needs to respond to the context, which is cultural and social, but also environmental.

## 7.5  Impact of architectural design

Vitruvius, a Roman architect and author in the 1st century BC, in his text *Ten Books of Architecture* (Vitruvius *et al.*, 1914), considered the ideas of 'commodity', 'firmness' and 'delight' as the main considerations for architecture – in a contemporary sense this could be considered as 'function', 'material' and 'form'. The best architecture works across all three elements by balancing the issues of use with material appropriateness and the physical shape and aesthetics of the building.

Following Vitruvius' early thinking, the architecture profession today is aware that defining 'good' architecture and design is something that is challenging, but also necessary so that the public and communities who work with design professionals can create appropriate responses to their needs. The value of good architecture and design is that it can provide the client and the community with an innovative response that adapts to their needs and is a sustainable and long-term solution.

There have been a range of publications that have tried to define the idea of good design. One example is *Good Design: It All Adds Up*, the good design guide by RIBA (2011). This stresses the importance of good design and that it should also consider lifestyle and health. As the guide states (RIBA, 2011: 4–5):

> 'For thousands of years, people have designed and built their own habitats, to fit their own needs. Today, when our homes and neighborhoods are created independently of us, they can often fail to provide the flexibility, functionality, comfort, privacy or freedom that we need, and our quality of life can suffer. And if a home fails to withstand the test of time – and of market changes – that negative impact on our lives can be prolonged.'

'Design quality indicators' have also been developed as a system to measure the quality of design embodied in the product and the buildings themselves (Gann *et al.*, 2003). This system was developed to measure the quality of design in buildings to try to bring a common language to the conversation around design quality in architecture (Samuel and Odgers, 2010) and support the construction industry to define good design across a range of sectors from education buildings to mixed-use development. The design quality indicators are based on the Vitruvian principles of functionality, quality and impact. The process requires assessment at a series of stages of a project's lifecycle, and it is carried out by an independent assessor working with the client and all stakeholders of the project. It is a useful process as it works with the users' requirements, but also measures a project's progress against agreed benchmarks and can measure the effectiveness of a project.

Of course, badly designed homes have a negative impact on society and on the success of the community. There is research by the Building Research Establishment (Roys *et al.*, 2010) which indicates that there are over 4 million homes in the UK which are so badly designed that they are causing health risks such as asthma and cardio respiratory disease. The impact of good design on educational spaces (CABE, 2005) has also been found to be very powerful, indicating that better-designed spaces encourage children to learn and become more actively engaged citizens, therefore creating healthier future communities. This is true from kindergarten to higher education learning spaces. Better designed spaces, with careful consideration of lighting, ventilation as well as material choices, will be more attractive spaces to work. Indeed, innovative ideas about social learning and group activity spaces can spark new approaches to group engagement and facilitate collaborative approaches to work, which can be transferable to employment and society as a whole. The best designed spaces are therefore fit for purpose and for their users.

Most important in any well-designed community is the consideration of context. To design appropriately the existing context must be understood so there can be a positive reaction to it. This can be the physical context, that is, the surrounding buildings, climate and microclimate, and the concept of 'ecological urbanism' (Mostafavi, 2010), where, in industrial locations, new buildings benefit from the context of the site that is under development. An example is the forum areas of the north-east coastal park in Barcelona by Abalos and Herreros. This development combines the infrastructure and public space with a municipal waste management complex on the site of an artificial landfill. It is argued by Mostafavi that the site for this project acts as a 'mnemonic device' establishing new memories and experience. The final result is relational between the terrain or ground, the built form and the viewer and their participatory experiences.

The context of a place can also be a cultural and social context that needs to be respected and understood. The analysis of existing aspects of a context is an important part of architectural design. For example, to be relevant, a building or community needs to react to 'place'. It should add to the identity of a place, develop that identity, offer new opportunities and experiences for the users of that place, and ensure that there is a vision or a sustainable approach to the activities that define it. The work of Kevin Lynch is important in understanding place identity. Lynch (1981: 126) defined 'place identity' as: 'The extent a person can recognize or recall a place as being distinct from other places, as having a vivid or unique, or at least particular character of its own.'

Finally, in understanding architectural design, there is an idea of 'genius loci', which can be described also the 'spirit of place' or Zeitgeist, which refers to the idea that a concept or design relates to a current issue relevant to a particular period. Genius loci has been used in many references to architecture and urban design, and its origins are Roman in reference to religious iconography. In contemporary architecture, it has been part of a set of ideas developed by the Italian modernist architect Giuseppe Terragni, and also Christian Norberg Schulz in his text 'Towards a Phenomenology of Architecture' from the book *Genius Loci* (Norberg-Schulz, 1980). This concept describes how an important approach to good design is to really understand the spirit, the identity of the place, so that any proposed architectural intervention is a positive reaction to that. All the parameters that inform good urban and architectural design need careful strategic consideration before something is proposed. The sensory aspects of design around touch, smell and visual impact need to be considered, as well as the use of local materials to ensure that the proposal 'fits' to the local environment.

## 7.6   Critical regionalism

Although local place identity is important, we also need to understand design in the context of wider global concepts of place and architecture. We must therefore also consider a regionalist approach to design where architects react to the place, the site and the context using local materials and approaches to a building which have adapted to climate and place, but set in a more global context.

The idea of 'critical regionalism', which tries to mediate between local and more global concepts of architecture and place, is part of what might be termed a 'contemporary dilemma'. How can we identify with place locally within a global context? For this to happen we need to inhabit and engage physically with wider spatial contexts of place. This concept was described by Kenneth Frampton in *Towards a Critical Regionalism* (Frampton 1983), and was seen as requiring a reaction to the particularity of a place as can be described by the building forms, materials, the vernacular and typology of the place, as well as the people and cultures that inhabit and define it.

For urban designers and architects the planning legislation and building codes of an area are also part of the context that both restrict and connect the architecture to its locality. There are various schemes that have been used in the UK to inform designers, developers, contractors and ultimately users of the homes, of the quality of these places about the design of our communities and how to measure the success of that design. For example, Building for Life is a 12-point scheme that considers aspects of character, transport, community and design and construction for homes in the UK. The Design Council, CABE, the House Builder's Federation and the Design Council all support the scheme, which attempts to consider the idea of good design holistically around three categories: 'integrating into a neighbourhood', 'street and home' and 'creating a place'. The intention is to interpret a series of important considerations for new housing and new communities being developed across the UK and offer national standards and descriptors to measure them against.

The Building for Life Code uses the same categories to support the idea of responding to place-making by reacting to the existing context and also trying to ensure that proposed communities are new places with character, with spaces to play and live comfortably, and with the infrastructure, such as public transport, to support sustainable new communities and future expectations.

To create sustainable solutions for buildings and places there are a range of UK government requirements concerning sustainability. For example, environment impact assessments are part of the UK Town and Country Planning Regulations 2011. They apply to a certain type and scale of development to protect the environment and require a description of the full predicted impact of a development on a local area. This has to be disclosed as part of the planning application so that it informs any decision making about a proposed project. An environmental statement considers information to explain the impact which (DCLG, 2011: Schedule 4 Part 1, paras 3 and 4):

> '...includes population, fauna, flora, soil, water, air, climatic factors, and material assets, including the architectural and archaeological heritage, landscape and the inter-relationship between the factors. Consideration should also be given to the likely significant effects resulting from the use of natural resources, the emission of pollutants, the creation of nuisances and the elimination of waste.'

This legislative requirement to accompany all planning applications demonstrates the importance of sustainability to architecture, as it needs to be part of the process of any new building. A good example of this kind of thinking is the self-sustainable neighbourhood of Buiksloterham in Amsterdam and the work of the Dutch architecture and urban practice Space & Matter. Their work includes the development of a manifesto for circular urbanism and climate-proof cities based on a high level of community engagement. The Amsterdam site was developed on a disused ship-building yard across the river from the main station at Amsterdam. It has been developed through changing the use of the site from industrial to live–work and other uses, allowing for an organic development of the site, led by the community for the community.

## 7.7   Future vision case studies

To describe various approaches to sustainable built environments two case studies are now considered which have responded to two very different physical environments. In each scheme innovative design has had an impact on the success of the architecture and the project as a 'sustainable community'.

The first project is Park Hill in Sheffield, which is a renovation of a housing scheme demonstrating the reinvention of a building and the development of a new community within a completely revitalised environment that was designed in the 1960s and had become a failing housing estate until it was redesigned by Hawkins Brown Architects.

The second scheme is Almere, in the Netherlands, which is a project by West 8, MVRDV and McDonough partners. It is a truly collaborative architecture and engineering project. The site comprises a reclaimed piece of land to the east of Amsterdam that required some imaginative responses to energy use, but also incorporated community-led design. This is a completely new community with innovative approaches to the building and design of the community.

### 7.7.1   Park Hill in Sheffield

This is an example of retrofit or building re-use, which is an important issue when considering our existing building stock: how do we make it fit for purpose through careful re-design, keeping the fabric of the structure and therefore preserving the material substance of the building to produce a sustainable approach?

This housing estate was designed in 1960 in Sheffield by architects Ivor Smith and Jack Lynn to replace back-to-back housing in one of the great post-war visions to

**Figure 7.1** Elevation of Park Hill before, during and at completion of the new facade. Images depicting the building before work started, following strip out and following its reinvention. Reproduced by permission of Hawkins\Brown, © Richard Hanson.

regenerate Britain. It had some real innovations in housing, with deck access to the new homes, which were described as 'streets in the sky'. The Victorian terraced streets of the original community were replaced by open access as wide as a traditional street in the new housing development. The regeneration concept was to allow neighbours from the original community to be re-housed next to one another to ensure continuity. As a result of a series of issues, including unemployment as local industries collapsed and a lack of maintenance, the development had become severely dilapidated as people moved out, and it ultimately became derelict. It was designated a Grade II Listed Building in 1998 and purchased by the regeneration company Urban Splash in collaboration with English Heritage.

Working with architects Hawkins Brown and Egret West, Urban Splash developed an approach to completely reinvent the building by carefully re-designing its interior spaces with contemporary approaches to living spaces and considering the external landscape spaces for use at all times of the day and for all seasons. The intention was to attract a new community to the building and area, a mixed set of uses around living, community space and business offering a mixed-use approach to reinvent the site.

Park Hill was selected for the RIBA Stirling shortlist in 2013 for Building of the Year, and offers a really important exemplar of sustainable re-design, which is about the focus of the project as a re-use of an existing structure. This is in itself a sustainable approach using existing structures and materials. It is, therefore building a new community on the site, and providing one which is offering a mixed approach to 'live', 'work' and 'lifestyle'. The retrofit of the site has upgraded the building fabric as well as heating and other systems to provide in energy use a much more sustainable architectural solution (Figures 7.1–7.3).

### 7.7.2 Almere self-build in the Netherlands

In the Netherlands there has traditionally been a challenge for any new development to be engineered to cope with the low-lying land, much of which is below sea level.

1:2500 @A3

**Figure 7.2** Landscape masterplan showing the extent of first-phase works at Park Hill, including landscape works to South Street Park and the central courtyard. Reproduced by permission of Hawkins\Brown, © Hawkins Brown.

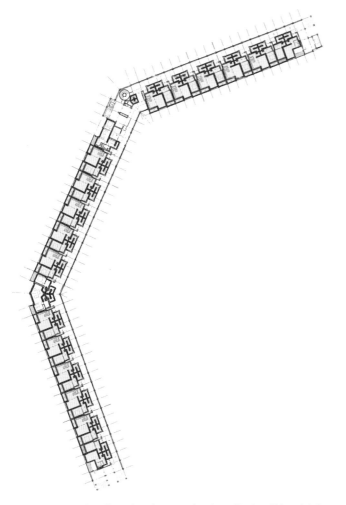

**Figure 7.3** Level 12 floorplan showing the three flanks of Norwich Street completed as part of the first-phase works. Reproduced by permission of Hawkins\Brown, © Hawkins Brown.

This challenge has resulted in innovative solutions in engineering terms, requiring the design of any community to involve engineers working to develop a new infrastructure. This approach is based on integrating, for example, drainage and flood barriers and prioritising the design of the road and transport infrastructure before the housing, business and other commercial and community buildings are designed.

Ijland in Almere, the newest city in the Netherlands, which has been built on reclaimed land, represents an iconic new community project. The vision for Almere started in the 1950s when the first piece of land was reclaimed. The first house was built in 1976 and the population is now nearly 200,000 with a plan for expansion to 350,000 by 2030. A road infrastructure, cycleways and station were all put in place once the land had been reclaimed. The new community proposal for Ijland was for a mixed-use community combining living, working and recreational environments amongst the natural wetlands of the Netherlands just to the east of Amsterdam.

Ijland is the result of a collaboration between West 8, MVRDV, WMcDonough + partners and the municipalities of Almere and Amsterdam. It combines rail connectivity, ecology, recreation and unique living environments with 5000–10,0000 houses. The new development is only possible because there has been so much pre-planning and strategic thinking and commitment to the project. On the south side of Ijmeerbaai is the waterfront, which will provides recreational amenities such as a pier, sports facilities, hotels, cafes, restaurants and shops. It is a haven for water-sports lovers on the Ijmeer. This new waterfront will offer Ijland space for new housing and (regional) facilities. Further from the centre there is room for low-density housing.

The innovation for the new community project came through the planning and design process itself. The design was developed from a top-down government-led initiative, but it was also driven from the bottom up by local people using a community-led approach. The idea was to empower people to make the city, and conceptually the design was developed by creating a new physical landscape to connect people to nature.

The local community have also been part of the physical making of the landscape through a self-build initiative, and the local council installed all the infrastructure. The intention is for 3000 self-build homes to occupy a 250-acre section of the site. Some of these areas are 'live–work' areas, encouraging not only housing, but also employment on the site. As well as individual plots for self-builders, there are also sites for developers to bring together groups of self-builders and facilitate a new approach to building. The resultant architecture in Ijland has therefore been diverse, as this individual and mixed approach encourages individual design thinking and ideas. The intention has been to make self-build affordable, developing diverse approaches to both the development of the community and the physical response with architectural expression (Figures 7.4 and 7.5).

**Figure 7.4** Almere new town in the Netherlands as seen at night. Developed by West 8, MVRDV, WMcDonough+ partners and the Municipalities of Almere and Amsterdam. Reproduced by permission of West 8, © West 8.

**Figure 7.5** The waterfront view of the Almere new town developed on reclaimed land to the east of Amsterdam, the Netherlands. Reproduced by permission of West 8, © West 8.

## 7.8   The future

It is clear that good sustainable design will have an important impact on the future of a sustainable built environment to 2050. The process needs to involve experts from a range of disciplines to work together to inform the design from the start. Truly sustainable environments will adopt this collaborative approach to design. The spaces, places and buildings that we provide for people and communities to live in to 2050 will need to be well designed. This means good design which is adaptable, responsive to change and offers a sustainable lifestyle for future societies. It needs to respond to the quality of life indicators around functionality, form and impact.

Effective sustainable design for 2050 should also have an awareness of materials that are produced, sourced and manufactured appropriately. It should be designed to limit the use of energy and use appropriate technologies to support energy efficiency, and it should react to a brief not for an immediate need but that accommodates change; this adaptability will provide intrinsic sustainability, reducing the need for more buildings using yet more resources.

When considering the impact of architectural design for a sustainable environment in 2050 it should be considered as part of a holistic idea for design, including measurable energy, which affects factors such as thermal comfort, but also an idea of place-making for communities which encompass social and cultural values. Sustainable design is inclusive, and to continue to be relevant it must be adaptable to change. There is always a delay as policy catches up with the consensus view about how we need to live now and in the future to 2050.

Perhaps somewhat controversially, the idea of 'holistic' design, as described by Fry (2008), uses the idea of 'defuturing', which questions the role of design and the responsibility of designers to facilitate the ability to sustain. According to Fry (2008: 6): 'Design is everything, everything is designed.' The future is seen as being a rationale to occupy space and develop place as space. However, the idea of defuturing proposes an alternative agenda of thinking, to create a way of making and living that recognises that the future is not a void, but a time and place operating in the past and present, which flows into the future. Defuturing is therefore about understanding the historical nature of the unsustainable and the possible consequences of using our resources, which are finite.

In reality, as Fry suggests, there is a crisis surrounding resource depletion, and we currently have an unsustainable approach, where we are using finite natural resources that cannot be replenished. It is therefore argued by Fry that we need a new design philosophy that is not about resource depletion, but about creating innovative ways to regenerate resources, whether that is energy or materials. In this regard, Fry's concern is that there is no singular solution to 'the crisis of resource depletion' (Fry, 2008).

In conclusion, it is perhaps fair to suggest that true 'sustain-ability' is an action, or the ability to sustain, as referred to by Fry (2008: 7) (i.e. a response to everything that is unsustainable). Therefore, the concept needs to be constantly updated and informed by current and future thinking about new technologies and new materials. Design is about choice, a reaction to a condition or a problem, so sustainable design must react to the issues that face us in today's 'unsustainable' environment. There must be a new design philosophy that changes our perception of the inter-related issues of energy use, material use and human behaviour: only then can we create truly sustainable design for 2050 and beyond.

# References

Banham, R. (1969) *The architecture of the well-tempered environment.* Architectural P, London.

Brundtland, G.H. (1987) Our common future – call for action. *Environmental Conservation*, 14(4), 291–294.

CABE (2005) *Design with distinction: The value of good building design in higher education.* CABE, London.

DCLG (2011) *The Town and Country Planning (Environmental Impact Assessment) Regulations 2011.* Department for Communities and Local Government, London.

Farrell, T. (2013) *The Farrell Review.* Department for Culture Media and Sport, London.

Frampton, K. (1983) Towards a critical regionalism: Six points for an architecture of resistance, in Foster, H. (ed.) *The Anti-Aesthetic: Essays on Postmodern Culture.* Bay Press, Port Townsend.

Fry, T. (2008) *Design Futuring, Sustainability, Ethics and New Practice.* Berg, Oxford.

Gann, D., Salter, A. and Whyte, J. (2003) Design quality indicator as a tool for thinking. *Building Research & Information*, 31(5), 318–333.

Gehl, J. (2010) *Cities for people.* Island Press, Washington, DC.

Hagan, S. (2008) *Digitalia. Architecture and the Digital, the Environmental and the Avant-Garde.* Routledge, London, New York.

Howard, E. (1902) *Garden Cities of Tomorrow.* S. Sonnenschein & Co., London.

Jarzombek, M. (2003) Sustainability: fuzzy systems and wicked problems. *Blueprints*, 21(1), 6–9.

Lynch, K. (1981) *Good City Form*. MIT Press, Cambridge, MA.

Mostafavi, M. (2010) *Why Ecological Urbanism? Why Now?* in Mostafavi, M. and Doherty, G. (eds) *Ecological Urbanism*, Lars Müller Publishers, Cambridge, p. 12–51.

Norberg-Schulz, C. (1980). *Genius Loci*. Rizzoli, New York.

Pyla, P. (2008) *Counter-Histories of Sustainability*. Archis Volume 18, Special issue on sustainability, "After Zero" Archis Volume 18, pp 14–17.

RIBA (2011) *Good design: it all adds up*. RIBA Publishing. Available at: https://www.architecture.com/files/ribaholdings/policyandinternationalrelations/policy/gooddesignitalladdsup.pdf (accessed 3 February 2017).

Roys, M., Davidson, M., Nicol, S., Ormandy, D. and Ambrose, P. (2010) *The Real Cost of Poor Housing*. BRE Trust Report FB23, BRE Press.

Samuel, F. and Odgers, J. (2010) Designing in quality in Dutoit, A., Odgers, J. and Sharr, A. (eds) *Quality Out of Control*, Rootledge, pp 41–54.

Sullivan, L.H. (1896) The Tall Office Building Artistically Considered. *Lippincott's Magazine*, March, 403–409.

TCPA (2013) *Creating Garden Cities and Suburbs today: A Guide to Councils*. Town & Country Planning Association, London.

Vitruvius, P., Morgan, M. and Warren, H. (1914) *Vitruvius, the ten books on architecture*. Harvard University Press, Cambridge, MA.

Wilkinson, S.J. and Dixon, T. (eds) (2016) *Green roof retrofit: building urban resilience*. Wiley, London, p. 288.

**Part 2**

**Changing Professional Practice**

# 8

# Planning for Sustainability: Reflections on a Necessary Activity

*Joe Doak and Gavin Parker*

## 8.1 Introduction

The concept of sustainable development has had significant import for the policy and practice of spatial planning over the last three decades in the UK. Although there is debate about the extent of tangible or substantive change generated by the emergence of sustainability, there is little doubt that it has transformed the rhetoric that permeates international, national and local policy. This chapter reviews that emergent policy and practice, and maps out the main facets of sustainability that can be used to underpin the development of spatial planning responses into the future. In doing this we argue that an appropriately sensitive and embedded planning ethos is critical to the joining up of different components of sustainable city development.

Planning provides an organising lens through which a range of built environment policy and practice can be effectively debated, orchestrated and implemented, with sustainable development playing a central role as an organising concept or 'metanarrative' (Law-Yone, 2007). As a result, the concept of environmental, social and economic sustainability has long been something that planners have included in their visions, plans and programmes but wider aims of planning practitioners to ensure well-being and efficient resource predates current terminology. The following UK examples from the pre-Brundtland commission era illustrate the range of issues and areas that planning has historically been drawn into to manage economic 'externalities' and deliver an 'efficient' use of land and resources:

- the breadth of *material considerations* in development control decision-making, covering environmental impact and resource efficiency/conservation
- the *conservation of open land*, including national parks, green belts, metropolitan open space, other valued landscapes (e.g. areas of outstanding natural beauty, heritage coasts), historic built environments (e.g. conservation areas/listed buildings/ scheduled ancient monuments) and habitats (e.g. sites of special scientific interest/ nature reserves), both as amenity and environmental resources
- *environmental improvements*, for example in river valleys, on the urban fringe and in areas of dereliction

*Sustainable Futures in the Built Environment to 2050: A Foresight Approach to Construction and Development*, First Edition. Edited by Tim Dixon, John Connaughton and Stuart Green.
© 2018 John Wiley & Sons Ltd. Published 2018 by John Wiley & Sons Ltd.

- *regional policy/distribution*: policies and funds directed towards growth and investment
- *new towns* and other large self-contained communities drawing in principles of integration and juxtapositioning of compatible uses
- *public consultation* on policies and proposals (relating to the principle of participation in the shaping of futures).

The concern with preserving nature, enhancing the quality of life and aiding economic development existed as priorities long before the formal introduction of a planning 'system' in the UK 70 years ago. Indeed the 'ecological' dimensions of human communities and their prosperity have been written about for centuries and have formed important parts of numerous religious canons. Sustainability is not a new concept, even if the word itself, the label, is of relatively recent origin. Robert Nisbet dedicates a whole chapter of his book *The Social Philosophers* (1973) to the idea of 'the ecological community'. As he points out, the roots of sustainability thinking in the global north go back some considerable way: 'the first expression of the ecological community in the West after the downfall of Rome is the monastic order that began in the sixth century with the remarkable Saint Benedict of Nursia' (Nisbet, 1973: 324). He then goes on to examine 14 centuries of ecological thinking that have led us, with many historical feedback loops, to the contemporary concept of 'sustainable development'. This historical perspective reminds us that the planning of environmental resources is something that is necessary for all societies at all times: planning as forethought, orchestration and regulation is therefore a necessary set of activities if sustainability goals are to be achieved.

The (post)modern idea of 'sustainable development' was developed during the 1970s and was first used in 1980 when the World Conservation Strategy reconceptualised conservation as 'the management of human use of the biosphere so that it may yield the greatest sustainable benefit to present generations while maintaining its potential to meet the needs and aspirations of future generations'. As part of this 'development' was said to involve (IUCNI *et al.*, 1980: 34):

> 'the modification of the biosphere and the application of human, financial, living and non-living resources to satisfy human needs and improve the quality of human life…For development to be sustainable it must take account of the social and ecological factors as well as economic ones: of the living and non-living resource base, and of the long-term as well as the short-term advantages and disadvantages of alternative actions.'

The standard definitional statement about sustainable development derives from the Brundtland Report (WCED, 1987). The fuller version of the concept is outlined in page 9 of the report and carries several facets:

> 'The ability of humanity to ensure that it meets the needs of the present without compromising the ability of future generations to meet their own needs. Sustainable development is not a fixed state of harmony, but rather a process of change in which the exploitation of resources, the direction of investments, the orientation of technological development and institutional changes are made consistent with future as well as present needs.'

The report emphasises these facets as certain key principles, such as meeting *needs* (not unlimited demands), considering and providing for future needs (the *futurity* principle) and sustainability as a process of change (of *development*). It is clearly anthropocentric in its approach (i.e. human needs come first) and this is true of most policy definitions. Many academic critiques of the concept (e.g. Atkinson, 1991; O'Riordan and Rayner, 1991; Dobson, 2007) have pointed out that different definitions of sustainability fit along a philosophical continuum from 'light' green to 'deep' green. This is useful in that it helps us appreciate the variety of ideas that exist *within* the sustainability discourse and which have also led some to claim that sustainability as a concept is rather an empty signifier (e.g. Davidson, 2010; Swyngedouw, 2010).

A useful graphic is the often-used Venn diagram of sustainability, which is based on the inter-linking of environmental, economic and social aspects of the concept. This emphasis rests on a *holistic* approach and this is potentially one of the most radical aspects of the concept and has led to sustainability being posited as the metanarrative guiding planning practice. The requirement to *integrate* these aspects is a defining characteristic of sustainability and one that challenges the established practice of planners in trying to balance or trade-off (rather than integrate) these dimensions. Of course, it is no accident that the rise of the sustainability agenda has been accompanied by a shift from the (more narrowly defined) 'land-use planning' tag to the (more holistic) 'spatial planning' label.

A combination of policy pressure coming from the EU (mostly through regularly updated Environmental Action Plans) and direct action and lobbying by the environmental movement (particularly Greenpeace and Friends of the Earth) has pushed the UK government into incorporating sustainable development overtly into national policy. Ironically it was Margaret Thatcher, that fierce proponent of the free market (see Thornley, 1993), that introduced the first UK Sustainable Development Strategy (DoE, 1990). However, the principles of sustainability used in this document clearly placed it more at the 'dry green' end of the definitional continuum (DoE, 1990: 3):

> 'Sustainable development means living on the earth's income rather than eroding its capital. It means keeping the consumption of renewable natural resources within the limits of their replenishment. It means handing down to successive generations not only man-made wealth, but also natural wealth, such as clean and adequate water supplies, good arable land, a wealth of wildlife, and ample forests.'

The incoming Labour Government of Tony Blair (1997–2008) did not make much effort to move the definition, saying that sustainable development (HM Government, 1999: para. 1.2):

> '...means meeting four objectives at the same time, in the UK and the world as a whole:
>
> - social progress which recognises the needs of everyone;
> - effective protection of the environment;
> - prudent use of natural resources; and
> - maintenance of high and stable levels of economic growth and employment.'

In 2005, the then Labour Government in the UK responded to critics who argued that unbridled economic 'growth' was not compatible with sustainable economic 'development'. Their version of the UK Sustainable Development Strategy revised the guiding principles of sustainability to cover (HM Government, 2005: 16):

- living within environmental limits
- ensuring a strong, healthy and just society
- achieving a sustainable economy
- promoting good governance
- using sound science responsibly.

The latest swing in political orientation and emphasis has come about from the recent Conservative/Liberal Democrat coalition administration (2010–2015), which placed more emphasis on economic growth and market-led forms of development. The definition used in the current version of the National Planning Policy Framework (DCLG, 2012) illustrates this point, when it says that (DCLG, 2012: i):

> 'Sustainable means ensuring that better lives for ourselves don't mean worse lives for future generations. Development means growth. We must accommodate the new ways by which we will earn our living in a competitive world. We must house a rising population, which is living longer and wants to make new choices. We must respond to the changes that new technologies offer us. Our lives, and the places in which we live them, can be better, but they will certainly be worse if things stagnate.'

Given the brief history of the concept above, it is not surprising that one of the key features of sustainable development is its contested nature. This arises because the term 'sustainable development' was created by people to encompass a set of ideas about the way that human beings should/could live their lives in relation to other human beings and the physical world, and this, it hardly needs saying, covers very many things. Although those ideas were created on the basis of people's experience of living with each other and the physical world, the term sustainable development is, ultimately, a socially constructed device. Furthermore, once a term like this comes into existence, it is then deployed and re-created on a daily basis and is not only socially-constructed but subject to political manipulation. The social re-construction and contestation of the concept and its components is an ongoing process, drawing in a very large range and number of actors who reinforce and alter the spaces for sustainable development.

As suggested above, this contestation has an important implication for the way we should approach the concept of sustainable development in planning and development practice and research. Thus, there can be no one absolute definition of sustainability and any attempt to impose one is doomed to perish on the rocks of social diversity and conflicting interpretations. An effective and critically aware approach to this problem is to accept the diversity of definition and meaning underpinning the concept of sustainability and to build from a broad definition that allows the exploration of this diversity in an explicit and critical way. In doing this we should accept that terms (and whole discourses) like 'sustainability' are deployed by people in different ways to achieve different objectives. The concept needs to be kept open so that the different ideas that are wrapped up in the term are transparent, problematised and debated.

Having emphasised the malleability of the concept, we have suggested elsewhere (Parker and Doak, 2012: 61–66) that certain core principles or components tend to surface during any debate about sustainability. At the heart of sustainability lie five principles, some emphasised by Brundtland. The first is *futurity*, which takes a long-term view of development and considers the impacts of current decisions on future generations. *Environmentalism* introduces the underlying ecological focus of sustainable development which requires decision-makers at all levels to take into account the environmental implications of their actions. The idea of *development* has featured explicitly already and this has been heavily promoted in the various governmental statements mentioned above. However, the narrow interpretation of this word as 'economic growth' latterly promoted ignores the wider conception emphasised by Brundtland and others, who see economic development as a basis for providing for people's needs and overall quality of life. Two other socio-political aspects were forcefully inserted into the frame of reference during the 1992 Rio Earth Summit (UNCED, 1992). Many NGOs representing the interests of the global south demanded that sustainable development should also be based on social *equity* and that the meaningful *participation* of all stakeholders should be a core component of processes of determining future action.

These five key facets, futurity, environmentalism, development, equity and participation, provide a useful evaluative lens through which planning practice can be organised, shaped and critically assessed. Indeed, these make for touchstones of sustainable development and have already permeated planning policy and practice, interweaving themselves with existing planning ideas to produce the policy package or assemblage we have today. We will return later in the chapter to the implications of these five for the development of future policy and practice, but it is useful now to outline how these facets have contributed to our current ideas about sustainable place-making and to critically review recent attempts to deliver sustainable outcomes in line with these organising principles.

## 8.2   Sustainability and planning

During the 1990s the sustainability agenda was formally embedded into planning practice and many of the policies/initiatives above were re-defined or developed into a package of policy prescriptions or practices that sought to make planning outcomes more sustainable. These have included a concern with:

- compact city strategies, to minimise resource use and enable better quality services
- mixed use development, to integrate uses and therefore patterns of living and movement
- brownfield redevelopment and related housing targets
- urban densification
- integrated public transport
- creation of (green) travel plans
- congestion charging, to effect behavioural change towards more sustainable transport and improve air quality
- urban (later Millennium) village and sustainable urban neighbourhood (sun) initiatives
- sustainability appraisal and strategic environmental assessment (SEA)

- use of the sequential approach in development control decision-making to ensure that the most sustainable option was considered first
- contaminated land reclamation
- environmental (and then also sustainability) assessment
- sustainability checklists for development control decision-making
- green development or developer guides
- increasing inclusion of sustainability elements in S106 Agreements
- sustainable urban drainage (SUDS)
- community engagement through Local Agenda 21 (and, more recently, sustainable community strategies)
- establishment of (sustainability/regeneration) partnerships
- use of sustainability indicators to measure/monitor progress
- waste minimisation and recycling
- encouragement of renewable energy schemes
- sustainability codes or standards (for housing and other types of development)
- creation of sustainable communities
- eco-towns and transition towns
- (most recently) neighbourhood planning and development (the 'new localism').

Each of these policies or initiatives has had its own trajectory, criticisms, problems and successes. They are connected by aims that relate to environmental, social and economic sustainability in some way or measure. In broad terms, they are the manifestation of the growing discourse of sustainability in planning policy and practice. Possibly the most all-encompassing policy packages have been aimed at delivering sustainable communities. This has taken a number of forms over recent years as successive governments have sought to badge their own (or other people's) initiatives with suitably populist labels such as 'urban villages', 'Millennium communities', 'sustainable urban neighbourhoods', 'sustainable communities', 'eco-towns', 'transition towns', 'resilient communities' and 'localism'. The evidence of success has been variable, with academic critiques (e.g. Biddulph *et al.*, 2003; Raco *et al.*, 2006; Parker *et al.*, 2015) pointing towards significant warping of the stated sustainability principles; as policy implementation processes mobilise a range of actors towards policy delivery. The inevitable negotiations and re-formulations between sets of inter-dependent organisations and interests have left certain policy priorities sidelined whilst others have been reasserted or retracked and realised in development outcomes.

Two examples of this corruption or marginalisation of sustainable development in planning practice are provided by the urban village story and the current government's promotion of the localism agenda through neighbourhood planning. Urban villages were an early attempt to operationalise an expression of sustainability in the planned environment after the publication of the Brundtland Report. Research by Biddulph and colleagues (Biddulph *et al.*, 2002, 2003) showed how the conception of urban villages drew upon and blended a range of other ideas, including neighbourhood planning, urban social geography, urban design and sustainability. Initiated by the Prince of Wales, this development concept was 'fixed' (but not without some debate) by the development principles established by the Urban Villages Group/Forum (see Aldous, 1992). Figure 8.1 illustrates how the concept then became 'unfixed' or destabilised during policy implementation as it collided with other discourses, local structures and actors.

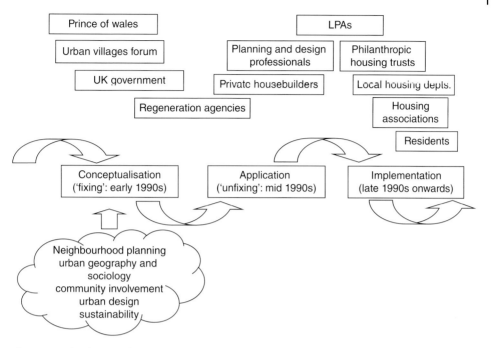

**Figure 8.1** The dynamic 'fixing' and 'unfixing' of the urban village idea (after Biddulph *et al.*, 2003).

Biddulph and his team concluded that 'the urban village concept was constructed differently and to different degrees of refinement by different interests, with no shared or immutable meaning. Thus, both meaning and application are rendered contradictory and contested, resulting in a fluidity of interpretation' (Biddulph *et al.*, 2002: 14). This correlates with our view of sustainability as a contested concept that is recursively negotiated on a daily basis. The variable development outcomes of urban village policy implementation are outlined in Table 8.1, showing how far the urban village development principles were in evidence in the development outcomes from three local case studies. The research team observed that (Biddulph *et al.*, 2002: 21):

> '...the extent to which the urban village concept was drawn upon and modified in each case study location varied according to the historical and topographical context, the local structures (development industry, planning regimes, community/social structures) and agents (developers, architects, etc.). In this way, the urban village concept as an idealised notion gets transformed through the process of alignment by agents working within local areas, structures and regimes.'

This kind of conclusion alerts us to the importance of building shared understanding and, where possible, common interest around the principles and policy objectives of sustainability, but also a tolerance of the inevitable variety of local conditions and, by implication, outcomes that might arise from sustainable planning practice.

The localism agenda pursued by the UK government since 2010 is one of the latest policy packages being deployed to achieve wider stakeholder participation in the planning process, with the intention of achieving sustainable forms of development

**Table 8.1** Variable implementation of the urban village development principles in three case study areas (after Biddulph *et al.*, 2003).

| Fixing concept: development principles | 'Un-fixing' during implementation process | | |
| --- | --- | --- | --- |
| | Bordesley | Garston | West Silverton |
| *Urban design* | x | x | √ |
| *High-density development* | x | x | √ |
| *Identity and place-making* | √/x | √ | √ |
| *Community involvement* | √/x | √ | x |
| *Environmentally-friendly design* | x | x | √ |
| *Open space* | √/x | √/x | √/x |
| *Mixed use* | √ | √/x | √/x |
| *Mixed tenure* | √/x | √/x | √/x |
| *Local community facilities* | √ | √ | √ |
| *Public transport* | √/x | √/x | √ |
| *Self-sufficiency* | n/a | n/a | √/x |
| *Social sustainability* | √/x | √/x | x |

√, yes; x, no.

(see Smith, 2016; Locality, 2012). Although subject to considerable critique (see Davoudi and Madanipour, 2013; Parker *et al.*, 2015; Williams *et al.*, 2014) the identification of local communities as being an important part of shaping sustainable development is significant and reflects a revival in communities helping set agendas. In particular, the creation of formal neighbourhood plans, which enable neighbourhoods to take a lead in deliberating on their futures and to take some ownership of how and what development will be realised in their own neighbourhood, has clear promise (see Bradley and Brownill, 2016; Parker, 2012). Yet the structures and processes involved in linking types of knowledge and understanding across scales has yet to be convincingly resolved. If neighbourhood planning is generating interest and debate about development at the community scale, it is less clear how on the one hand communities are sufficiently empowered to make more radical plans, but on the other how to ensure that such plans are sufficiently deliberative, as well as coordinated with wider evidence, need and policy direction from above. This brings into view the need to reflect not only on participation as if it is an end of itself but also that the participation actively and deliberatively reflects on the options, issues and other, sometimes apparently competing, facets of environment, development, equity and futurity.

Thus, as the neighbourhood scale is becoming a more important locus for decision-making and deliberation, much more attention is needed to help develop the understanding required to bring the facets and implications of integrated sustainable development policy together, and how to apply such considerations responsibly at the neighbourhood scale without displacing local voices entirely. Indeed, findings from research looking at neighbourhood plans indicate how much help has been needed from the public and private sector in support of neighbourhoods (Parker *et al.*, 2014, 2015) and moreover how many neighbourhood plans are not pushing the sustainability agenda very strongly – if anything government has acted to deter such behaviour for fear of preventing growth. This is another example of sustainable development practices being pushed back and contained in a narrow or 'drier' container.

## 8.3   Future trends and opportunities

This discussion of planning in relation to sustainable communities leads us towards the contemplation of possible future scenarios. The idea of building an integrated planning response remains an essential component of the advocates of sustainability in the face of the grand challenge that the demands of climate change, economic growth (and recurrent crises), resource uncertainty, rapid technological innovation and demographic restructuring present. To be effective the response would need to reflect and address the multi-scalar nature of social, economic and environmental entities and processes. The response also requires a more nuanced conception of planning, drawing upon the lessons that have been learned from past attempts to plan and develop sustainable communities. Such a conception is one in which the definitions of the planner and the planned are blurred and decentred, and what constitutes 'planning' itself becomes more embracing (or indeed open): in the future, we should take a cue from the historical perspective that all societies need to plan and manage the environmental and other resources they are dependent upon and in a way which allows them to adapt to the climatic and other conditions they face.

An effective approach towards sustainability therefore requires some fundamental rethinking of the purpose of planning and subsequent development outcomes. This is where the five facets of sustainability mentioned earlier usefully come back into play: for us an effective transition to sustainable development requires a much clearer embedding of environmentalism, futurity, development, equity and participation within place-making policy and practice. How can future patterns of development deliver against these fundamental tests to provide for the needs of current and future generations? We use these components as the analytical lens for mapping the future of planning. The particular means of achieving these aspects (e.g. solar panels, neighbourhood plans or electric vehicles) are almost certain to change and evolve through time, but the underpinning requirements of sustainable development will remain relatively intact. We explore the nature of a future-oriented planning approach below and provide tentative examples of the types of policy and implementation tools that could be deployed to secure sustainable planning outcomes.

*Environmentalism* calls for a clear priority to be placed on the essential role of the ecological system in maintaining the necessary conditions for life on the planet. Destruction or significant erosion of the 'web of life' compromises the choices and opportunities of current and future generations. As a society, we are tied to that web, we need to undertake a number of actions to maintain and improve the ecological (ecosystem) services that sustain life. Here we can roll forward the historic role of planning in protecting against and allocating land for development, conserving critical environmental capital and maintaining/managing the use of environmental resources. However, these actions need to be undertaken with a mindset that treats the 'human' and 'natural' worlds as one entity, each inter-dependent on the other. Land designations and environmental assessment methods will need to adapt and evolve to capture this 'systems' view of the mankind-environment relationship. Recent moves towards one-planet living and eco-footprinting illustrate the kind of approach which integrates environmental resources/capacities into development trajectories. Similarly, the basic idea of eco-system services is a tool that could, with cautious application, provide a way of planning the protection and enhancement of essential environmental assets and it is noticeable that the idea has gained traction in recent years (Gómez-Baggethun and Barton, 2013), with some local plans beginning to adopt green-living-type testing, for example Stroud, Gloucestershire (see SDC, 2015).

A number of spatial planning tools can help embed the need for *futurity* in societal decision-making. At its most prosaic, planning is about making future plans. Without a clear vision of a desired future and a set of objectives and policies to secure that future, sustainable development remains a vague aspiration. Indeed, one of the strengths of open and democratic plan-making is that it provides a space in which the contested nature of sustainability can be debated and conflicting interests can be mediated. Although many have raised questions about the darker side of this process (e.g. Flyvbjerg, 1996; Yiftachel, 1998), the fact remains that some sort of spatial and sectoral integrated plan-making is required to build consensus and map out the needs and priorities of current and future generations. How such visions are shaped and con-structed remains a pivotal issue, as often the interests of those living and those with voice marginalise those absent and without voice.

Such plan-making needs to be constructed within an ethos that can support the pro-cesses of experimentation and transition in sustainable development. Given future plan-making requires a framework of firm goals and objectives (based on the five facets of sustainable development), there will also need to be some flexibility about the par-ticular *means* organised to achieve those goals. If sustainability is a learning process, then the plan can help set the curriculum for that study and achievement.

The debates around the type, amount and form of *development* are also part of the plan-making process. This cannot just be left to the vagaries of a catch-all term and its consequences, such as 'market demand', but should be defined in terms of a set of social and environmental 'needs' that become the end-points of the planning and develop-ment process. Markets are as much an assemblage of people, institutions and discourses as any other aspect of material life, so they can be shaped and orchestrated in certain directions to achieve preconceived visions and objectives. That is what the 'plan' for sustainable development should really be about: shaping and facilitating transitions towards more sustainable forms of development. Inevitably that shaping process will require a package of regulative constraints and facilitative supports to move develop-ment outcomes in line with agreed goals and policies. Persistent and patient movement in the right direction will be important and again the sight of the big picture must be retained and its priority over short-term or narrow thinking asserted.

The emphasis placed on social *equity* also challenges much of the market rhetoric promulgated in recent governmental policy documents. The evidence accumulated over decades is such that markets, if unregulated, will not act to manage the future sustainably. The provision for social needs (of current and future generations) makes us think about the hierarchy of material, psychological and social needs depicted by Maslow (1954), which stresses the multi-dimensional nature of those needs, only some of which, for some people, are delivered through market processes. The inequality in many market outcomes, such as housing provision, adds a further cautionary perspective on the reliance of 'unburdened' markets as a goal of sustainable development. To deliver social equity, therefore, the 'plan' for sustainable development must seek support from non-market tools such as public funding, government agencies, NGO and voluntary sector initiatives, market regulation and forms of partnership working.

For these four components of sustainable development to be debated, orchestrated and implemented appropriately, a *participatory* approach to future development is required. This needs to build on and utilise the tapestry of social and other networks that exist within and between communities to proactively plan for and incorporate the actor networks that negotiate and shape planning practice. In doing this, we need to plan like communities, acknowledging that planning takes place on a daily basis, and is undertaken by a whole host of groups and organisations. Figure 8.2 illustrates our thinking in this area. This depicts the various stakeholders (individuals or organisations) that interact with each other within any given community. These actors both create and draw upon a range of resources to further their particular objectives (illustrated by the 'wells' of capital in the diagram). In any community, there are some actors who operate as key nodes (shaded in the diagram), bringing different actors together to negotiate common objectives, orchestrate different resources and build/extend network relations. Accepting and using this process of community network building, an effective approach to planning a sustainable community would seek to both map this capital-network and shape it towards sustainability objectives that are both relevant to the network and agreed by the stakeholders. These objectives would populate an overarching sustainability strategy and a set of formal or informal partnerships that would

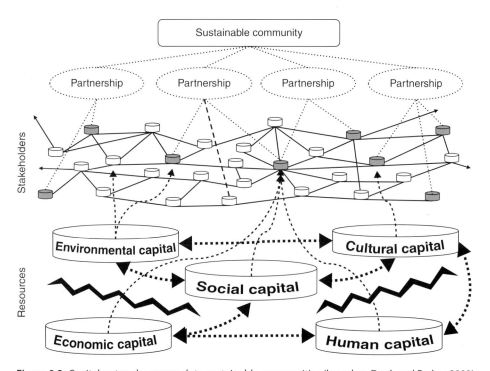

**Figure 8.2** Capital-networks approach to sustainable communities (based on Doak and Parker, 2002).

mobilise the actor-network towards more effective forms of policy implementation than hitherto witnessed in many of the sustainable community initiatives attempted in the UK or other locations. Indeed, some of the more bottom-up arrangements, such as the transition town initiative (Hopkins, 2008; Bulkeley *et al.*, 2010), have echoed this kind of model. However, they have often lacked a multi-scalar dimension to their operation (something the community strategy programme of the previous Labour Government tried to incorporate; see Raco *et al.*, 2006), so an explicit 'follow the network' approach is needed to address the 'glocal' (i.e. global *and* local) nature of issues like climate change, economic resilience, infrastructure provision and demographic movements.

This kind of model for embedding (negotiated) sustainability components into co-produced planning frameworks sits quite comfortably with some of the eco-city ideas that have been developed over the last 20 years. The more nuanced approaches have accepted and worked with the need for an overtly political (i.e. power-aware) dimension to the process. Building on earlier work undertaken for the OECD on ecological cities (CAG Consultants and Land Use Consultants, 1994) and by the EU Expert Group (EC, 1996), Joe Ravetz worked with a team from the Town and Country Planning Association to produce a book entitled *City Region 2020* (Ravetz, 2000). It was based on action-research in the north-west emanating from a debate and campaign aimed at supporting eco-city planning in the UK. The book, like the earlier OECD and EU reports, is underpinned by a systems and networked view of urban regions. There are a number of related themes running through the book, including integration of sectors, activities and organisational policies (and of space and time at different spatial levels), and a process, over time, of re-engineering the city-region. It contains a comprehensive consideration of different aspects or sectors (six in total) and contextual factors like funding constraints, political power, the centrality of the economy, globalisation and spatial variations in policies and outcomes, resembling a PESTLE analysis.

The chapter outlining the political metabolism (Ravetz, 2000: 250–270) sets a context for the political mobilisation of sustainable development and stresses the role of structure and agency in constructing a new political order (arguing for a form of Third Way or democratic renewal). It incorporates the argument for the network-based set of political processes required to challenge dominant discourses and negotiate sustainability strategies. Ravetz argues that multi-sectoral partnership working is necessary to address eco-city challenges and achieve appropriate sustainable outcomes. He suggests that each sector and each geographical scale (neighbourhood through to region) should construct interlocking '2020 development strategies'. The capitals-networks model discussed above provides the kind of detailing that could operationalise these strategic ideas for eco-city building and help construct the kind of strategies Ravetz is seeking.

## 8.4   Conclusion

This chapter has emphasised the contested and socially contingent nature of the definition and interpretation of sustainable development, and the emergence of certain key principles from that (contested) process. We have also shown how much activity and many mechanisms have been mobilised by planners over time. There is evidence of a rich history of sustainability thinking in planning practice and wide experience of the difficulties inherent in multi-stakeholder and multi-scalar policy making and implementation processes. It has been argued that sustainable forms of urban development need to take their cue from the key components of sustainability which we have explained above and that a planning framework is central to engaging with, mediating and coordinating the range of actors that produce and use the built environment.

That necessary planning process needs to work in an adaptable and multi-scalar way, embedding key agents of change and sources of knowledge to develop strategic visions and anticipatory intelligence. In a world formed by assemblages of networked relations (De Landa, 2006; De Roo and Hillier, 2016), planners (broadly defined) need to work with the grain to restructure the network-building processes that currently often lead to unsustainable forms of development. Using a capitals-network approach would allow communities to map those networks, and the available resources and resource barriers that exist, to negotiate more sustainable policy objectives and development outcomes. Rather than be knocked-off course by the dark side of existing actor networks, such as happened in relation to urban villages and may well be taking place with the new localism, a power-aware approach would explicitly engage with the political metabolism of those networks and encourage stakeholder interests to broker multi-scaler sustainability strategies and deliver the agreed objectives/principles in a more open and democratic way.

Once the visions and goals have been negotiated and arranged into future-making plans, a whole (new and old) set of implementation tools can then be drawn on to help deliver outcomes in line with the needs of current and future generations. The market can and indeed should be shaped and orchestrated through facilitation, regulation, taxation, funding, negotiation and partnership working, whilst other resources and forms of knowledge will come from non-market groupings such as NGOs, community enterprises, governmental agencies and social movements. To shape this constellation of actors, powers, resources and institutional arrangements in a consistent and purposeful way towards the facets of sustainable development, a clear and consistent line of guidance is required. It can certainly learn from the implementation process and be flexible on details, but it needs the political support that only effective multi-scaled governance structures can play in legitimising the agreed plans and strategies developed through the community planning processes outlined above. With that broad planning framework in place and structured according to sustainability principles, the transition to a sustainable built environment has a chance of being realised.

# References

Aldous, T. (1992) *Urban Villages: A Concept for Creating Mixed-Use Urban Developments on a Sustainable Scale*. Urban Villages Group, London.

Atkinson, A. (1991) *Principles of Political Ecology*. Belhaven, London.

Biddulph, M., Franklin, B. and Tait, M. (2002) *The Urban Village: a real or imagined contribution to sustainable development*. Cardiff University, Cardiff.

Biddulph, M.J., Franklin, B. and Tait, M. (2003) From concept to completion: A critical analysis of the urban village. *Town Planning Review*, 74(2), 165–193.

Bradley, Q. and Brownill, S. (eds) (2016) *Neighbourhood Planning and Localism: Power to the People?* Policy Press, Bristol.

Bulkeley, H., Broto, V., Hodson, M. and Marvin, S. (eds) (2010) *Cities and Low-carbon Transitions*. Routledge, London.

CAG Consultants and Land Use Consultants (1994) *OECD Ecological Cities – UK National Overview: Summary, Conclusions and Recommendations.* Draft report to the Department of the Environment for the OECD Ecological City Project. CAG Consultants, London.

Davidson, M. (2010) Sustainability as ideological praxis: The acting out of planning's master-signifier. *City*, 14(4), 390–405.

Davoudi, S. and Madanipour, A. (2013) Localism and neo-liberal governmentality. *Town Planning Review*, 84(5), 551–562.

DCLG (2012) *National Planning Policy Framework.* Department for Communities and Local Government, London.

De Landa, M. (2006) *A New Philosophy of Society: Assemblage Theory and Social Complexity,.* Bloomsbury, London.

De Roo, G. and Hillier, J. (2016) *Complexity and Planning: Systems, Assemblages and Simulations.* Routledge, London.

Doak, J. and Parker, G. (2002) Pre-Plan Mapping, Networks, Capital Resources and Community Strategies in England. *Working Papers in Real Estate & Planning,* No. 08/02. University of Reading, Reading.

Dobson, A. (2007) *Green Political Thought*, 4th edn. Routledge, London.

DoE (1990) *This Common Inheritance: Britain's Environmental Strategy.* Department of the Environment, London.

EC (1996) *European Sustainable Cities: Report by the Expert Group on the Urban Environment.* European Commission, Brussels.

Flyvbjerg, B. (1996) The dark side of planning: Rationality and 'realrationalität' in Mandelbaum, S., Mazza, L. and Burchell, R. (eds) *Explorations in Planning Theory.* CUPR, New Brunswick, NJ, pp. 383–394.

Gómez-Baggethun, E. and Barton, D. (2013) Classifying and valuing ecosystem services for urban planning. *Ecological Economics*, 86, 235–245.

HM Government (1999) *A Better Quality of Life: A Strategy for Sustainable Development for the United Kingdom.* TSO, London.

HM Government (2005) *Securing the Future: A Sustainable Development Strategy for the UK.* TSO, London.

Hopkins, R. (2008) *Transition Handbook. From Oil Dependency to Local Resilience.* Green Books, Cambridge.

IUCNI, United Nations Environment Programme, World Wildlife Fund, Food and Agriculture Organization of the United Nations, and UNESCO (1980) *World Conservation Strategy: Living Resource Conservation for Sustainable Development.* International Union for Conservation of Nature and Natural Resources, Gland (Switzerland).

Law-Yone. H. (2007) Another planning theory? Rewriting the meta-narrative. *Planning Theory*, 6(3), 315–326.

Locality (2012*) Neighbourhood Planning Roadmap.* Locality, London.

Maslow, A. (1954) *Motivation and Personality.* Harper, New York.

Nisbet, R. (1973) *The Social Philosophers: Community and Conflict in Western Thought.* Heinemann, London.

O'Riordan, T. and Rayner, S. (1991) Risk management for global environmental change. *Global Environmental Change*, 1(2), 91–108.

Parker, G. (2012) Neighbourhood planning: precursors, lessons and prospects. *Journal of Planning & Environment Law*, 40, OP139.

Parker, G. and Doak, J. (2012) *Key Concepts in Planning*. Sage, London.

Parker G., Lynn, T., Wargent, M. and Locality (2014) *User Experience of Neighbourhood Planning in England.* Locality, London.

Parker, G., Lynn, T. and Wargent, M. (2015) Sticking to the script? The co-production of neighbourhood plans. *Town Planning Review*, 86(5), 519–536.

Raco, M., Parker, G. and Doak, J. (2006) Reshaping spaces of local governance: community strategies and the modernisation of local government in England, *Environment and Planning C*, 24(4), 475–496.

Ravetz, J. (2000) *City-Region 2020: Integrated Planning for a Sustainable Environment.* Earthscan, London.

SDC (2015) *Your District, Your Future*, Stroud District Local Plan, November 2015. Stroud District Council, Stroud.

Smith, L. (2016) *Neighbourhood Planning.* House of Commons Library briefing paper No.05838 July 2016. Available at: http://researchbriefings.files.parliament.uk/documents/SN05838/SN05838.pdf.

Swyngedouw, E. (2010) Impossible sustainability and the post-political condition in Cerreta, M., Concilio, G. and Monno, V. (eds) *Making Strategies in Spatial Planning Knowledge and Values.* Springer, Dordrecht, pp 85–205.

Thornley, A. (1993) *Planning and Thatcherism: The Challenge of the Market.* Routledge, London.

UNCED (1992) *Agenda 21: Programme of Action for Sustainable Development*, United Nations Conference on Environment and Development. UN Publications, New York.

Williams, A., Goodwin, M. and Cloke, P. (2014) Neo-liberalism, Big Society and progressive localism. *Environment and Planning A*, 46, 2798–2815.

WCED (1987) *Our Common Future* (The Brundtland Report). World Commission on Environment and Development, Oxford University Press, Oxford.

Yiftachel, O. (1998) Planning and social control: Exploring the dark side. *Journal of Planning Literature*, 12(4), 395–406.

**9**

# Sustainable Construction: Contested Knowledge and the Decline of Professionalism

*Stuart Green*

## 9.1   Introduction

The purpose of this chapter is to critique current notions of 'sustainable construction'. It should be recognised from the outset that universal definitions remain stubbornly elusive (as was alluded to in Chapter 1). There are also difficulties in terms of the levels at which the sustainability debate takes place. Agreements which take place at the inter-governmental level at United Nations summits do not translate easily to the sectorial level within developed domestic economies such as the UK. But even the 'best practice' advice which is offered at the level of the construction sector is often of little use to individual firms engaged in the localised challenges of sustainable construction. It will be argued in this chapter that sustainability is ultimately about making difficult trade-offs, and the knowledge on which such trade-offs depend is not so easily 'commodified'. It should also be recognised that at the lowest level are individual construction profes-sionals seeking to balance a wide range of conflicting interests on a day-to-day basis; sustainability in no small way is about the recognition that such conflicting objectives are an inevitable part of the work of a professional.

Much of the current advice offered on sustainable construction is contestable, calling into question the validity of the underpinning knowledge base. The concept is further distorted by the repeated exhortations that it should be justified with reference to the 'business case'. The danger in always insisting on a supporting business case is that sustainability only becomes adopted if it replicates and reinforces existing practice. What does become clear is that the available guidance on 'sustainable construction' in itself is not going to result in any radical shift in the way the industry currently operates. Such guidance can play an important role in raising awareness, and, of course, this can only be a good thing. The question then becomes one of what construction professionals do that would make their practices more 'sustainable' as a result of this raised awareness.

The adopted perspective is underpinned by a belief that concepts such as sustainability are grounded in broader processes of social and political change. The chapter primarily focuses on the evolution of sustainability within the specific context of the UK construc-tion sector. Nevertheless, many of the parameters that shape current interpretations of sustainability also have global resonance; readers from other countries will therefore be able to make their own comparisons.

*Sustainable Futures in the Built Environment to 2050: A Foresight Approach to Construction and Development*, First Edition. Edited by Tim Dixon, John Connaughton and Stuart Green.
© 2018 John Wiley & Sons Ltd. Published 2018 by John Wiley & Sons Ltd.

The term 'sustainable construction' is indicative of an explicit recognition that the construction sector has a responsibility to reflect broader societal concerns regarding the attainment of sustainability. There are of course two significant difficulties here. The first relates to the continuing ambiguity of what sustainability means in operational terms; the second relates to whether the construction industry is an entity that is capable of bearing responsibility. Given its heterogeneous nature – and plethora of representative bodies – the latter point can by no means be taken for granted.

The argument is structured as follows. The discussion starts with the Brundtland Report *Our Common Future*, published in 1987 (Brundtland Commission, 1987), and its less well-known successor *Caring for the Earth*, published in 1991 (IUCN/UNEP/WWF, 1991). From the outset, it is necessary to recognise that debates about sustainable development have long-since been the subject to deep-rooted tensions between the Global North and the Global South. The discussion progresses to consider the merits and limitations of systems thinking as a means of understanding sustainability. It is tentatively suggested that sustainability is best understood as a 'hologram' which shows different faces to different interest groups. The arguments are then embedded within the context of the UK construction sector, taking due account of the dynamics of structural change and recurring debates about industry improvement. It is suggested that sustainability is best understood as a 'wicked problem', which is forever destined to defy technological solution.

Attention thereafter is directed towards a detailed critique of the UK government's strategy for sustainable construction, published in 2008. The parameters of this strategy continue to influence current debates about the operationalisation of sustainable construction. It is also argued that there is a danger in sustainable construction being adopted as yet another dimension of best practice which is evaluated on the basis of the business case. The chapter draws to a close with a discussion of the battle lines which characterise the quest for sustainable construction. In contrast to other sources, the battle lines are drawn between long-established notions of professionalism and the ever-encroaching and corrosive logic of managerialism. Finally, some thoughts are offered on the future of sustainable construction and the skills which are required if societal aspirations for continued action are to be satisfied to 2050 and beyond.

## 9.2 Our common future

It is important to acknowledge from the outset that the concept of sustainability is not new. The hunter-gatherer people of the Mesolithic period undoubtedly understood the importance of sustainability – at least on an intuitive level if not self-consciously (Hill and Bowen, 1997). The fact that we find it necessary to talk about sustainability is in itself indicative that something has gone wrong. But very few of us would wish to return to the quality of life which was on offer prior to the Neolithic Revolution – even if this were possible. The Neolithic Revolution saw many human societies transition from a lifestyle of hunting and gathering to one centred on agriculture and settlement. It was a transition which involved often radically modifying the natural environment within which we live. The impact on the natural environment grew exponentially as a result of the Industrial Revolution, which many developing economies are still experiencing. Yet the pressure for a stronger focus on sustainability developed within the post-industrial West; and here lies an ongoing source of tension whenever sustainability is debated on the international stage. The very meaning of sustainability is invariably a hugely politicised issue, especially when played out across the global north–south divide.

Most discussions of sustainability commence by quoting the definition of sustainable development offered by *Our Common Future* authored by the United Nations World Commission on Environment and Development (WCED) in 1987:

> '...development that meets the needs of the present without compromising the ability of future generations to meet their own needs'

For many who operate in the commercial environment of the construction sector the above definition may seem hopelessly idealistic. Yet for others the exhortation to think about the needs of future generations offers a timely reminder of their responsibilities as professionals. To understand the arguments offered by *Our Common Future* (otherwise known as the Brundtland Report) it is necessary to understand it was authored by the United Nations WCED. Its purpose was to harness international support based on multilateralism and the interdependence of nations. Its achievement as an act of international negotiation was to promote the co-existence of environmental, social and economic concerns. It was this line of argument which led to the so-called three pillars of sustainability which still pervade so many conversations about sustainability. The three pillars relate to social, environmental and economic aspects of sustainability. This 'triple bottom line' has since become essential to the lexicon of sustainable construction.

The Brundtland Report was also important in paving the way for the 1992 Earth Summit and the adoption of Agenda 21, the Rio Declaration and the Commission on Sustainable Development. Discussion at these various international venues were invariably dominated by climate change and how humankind could better protect the long-term future of the planet through limiting the use of fossil fuels. The impact of fossil fuels of course is not constrained by international boundaries. Hence the importance of the principle of multilateralism. But the difficulty here is that mitigating actions take place in localised contexts. The debate about fossil fuels has long since been characterised by a suspicion on the part of developing countries that their development was being unreasonably constrained by policies developed in the West (i.e. the 'Global North'). The persistent difficulty is that meeting the 'needs of the present' translates to different imperatives in different places. For much of the world's population the most immediate need relates to the alleviation of poverty. Maslow's (1954) hierarchy of needs has become a tired cliché, but the point remains that we cannot expect those living on (or below) the poverty line to spend too much time worrying about climate change. The priorities of sustainable development when viewed from the leafy suburbs of Berkshire in the UK tend to look very different from those which prevail in sub-Saharan Africa. The moral imperatives are fundamentally different, but the basic argument holds true if affluent shire towns are compared with the sink estates of inner London, or the neglected post-industrial wastelands of Lancashire. Marshalling support for a 'common future' is rendered much more problematic by the absence of any sort of 'common past', and the present only ever exists as a point of connection between the past and the future.

The subsequent report *Caring for the Earth* (IUCN/UNEP/WWF, 1991) is less well-known than the Brundtland Report, but is arguably of equal importance. The report was published in partnership by the World Conservation Union (IUCN), the United

Nations Environment Programme (UNEP) and the World Wide Fund for Nature (WWF). Of particular note is the way the *Caring for the Earth* report criticised 'sustainable development' as being ambiguous and contradictory (Hill and Bowen, 1997). The term was also often used interchangeably with 'sustainable growth', a concept which was held to collapse too easily down to a single economic dimension. The report notably offered an alternative definition of 'sustainable development' as that which 'improves the quality of human life while living within the carrying capacity of supporting eco-systems'. To position the quality of human life at the centre of the sustainability debate was for many an important step forward. Most pertinently, within the context of the current chapter the revised definition resonates with the notion of professionalism which continues to survive in the construction sector, despite trends towards more narrowly defined 'managerialism' (cf. Green *et al.*, 2008). Yet the *Caring for the Earth* report was ultimately unable to alleviative long-standing tensions between the global north and south in terms of who was inflicting the most damage to the world's eco-systems and who should pick up the bill. The lesson is that reaching a consensus on such issues is rather less important than arriving at a pragmatic accommodation.

It should further be recognised that the world has changed since 1991. One important change is the increased prevalence of the neoliberal consensus in favour of laissez-faire economic policy. But perhaps the biggest material change relates to the associated rapid increase in globalisation, especially in terms of the parameters of trade, finance and the growth of international companies. Equally evident has been the rapid growth in urbanisation such that the percentage of the world's population living in urban areas is expected to increase to 66% by 2050 (UN, 2014). Support services derived from the world's eco-systems – such as food production – remain critically important. But development on the global scale has become increasingly synonymous with urban development. The conversation therefore shifts to notions of urban metabolism, otherwise construed as the flows of materials and energy within cities. Cities are thereby themselves viewed as ecosystems which are dependent upon the flow of materials and energy, but also crucially water, food and people. Such issues may seem a long way removed from the remit of the construction sector as traditionally conceived, but the more forward-looking firms are increasingly positioning themselves in these terms. They are also committed to acquiring the required expertise. Urban metabolism models rest on the metaphor of cities as living organisms, and conversations about sustainability increasingly draw from the intellectual framework offered by systems thinking. Indeed, in some circles, systems thinking is being positioned as if it were a panacea for the complex, multi-dimensional challenges of sustainability (e.g. Godfrey, 2010). Such acclaimed panaceas will inevitably disappoint as the challenges of sustainability ultimately defy technical solution. But this does not mean that systems thinking cannot help in developing a more nuanced understanding of the complexity of sustainability, and the inherent interconnectedness of its constituent elements.

## 9.3 Systems thinking for sustainability

Systems thinking originally came into vogue during the late 1960s. Its advocates started to conceptualise businesses as open systems that engage in a dynamic interaction with the broader environment. Systems thinking, and the need to adapt to the prevailing social environment, underpinned much of the prevailing management literature during the late 1960s and early 1970s (cf. Berrien, 1976; Burns and Stalker, 1961; Rice, 1963). Lawrence and Lorsch (1967) were especially influential in arguing that organisations engage in a dynamic interaction with their broader environment. Kast and Rosenzweig (1970) crystallised much of this thinking in focusing on the relationship between businesses and the societal environment within which they operate:

> 'Organizations are subsystems of a broader suprasystem – the environment. They have identifiable but permeable boundaries that separate them from their environment. They receive inputs across these boundaries, transform them, and return outputs. As society becomes more and more complex and dynamic, organisations need to devote increasing attention to environmental forces.'

It is important to recognise that 'environmental forces' does not refer specifically to the environment as it is commonly understood within the scientific community. But over time systems thinking provided much of the lexicon through which the debate about balancing the three pillars of sustainability was conducted. Others would talk in quasi-mystical terms of the need to live in 'harmony' with nature. But the difficulty again is how this plays out in localised contexts where different groups of stakeholders have very different priorities. Commentators such as Prince Charles make much of the notion of harmony when outlining their vision for a sustainable future, but for those struggling to escape from the trap of poverty it is easy to understand how 'harmony' may fall below food and shelter in the list of priorities. Maslow's (1954) hierarchy of needs is perhaps still of direct relevance here. Certainly, it is persuasive to suggest that the need for harmony usually only kicks in when (almost) all other needs have been met. This argument of course would not be accepted by those idealists who privilege environmental activism over-and-above any recognition of the role of economic activity in improving the quality of life. But such activists are not very often embraced by the mainstream.

Leaving aside quasi-mystical notions of harmony, those in search of a 'scientific' basis for sustainability habitually revert to the tradition of systems thinking. The systems thinking as advocated by Kast and Rosenzweig (1970) undoubtedly resonated with the more widespread social idealism which prevailed during the 1960s and 1970s. The imperative was that businesses are not expected to confine their attention to narrowly construed notions of profit maximisation – such a unidimensional focus was seen to be inherently unsustainable. The pursuit of profit without regard to broader externalities was equated to 'closed-systems' thinking. Closed-systems thinking was considered unsustainable in the long term and was commonly associated with the optimisation algorithms of operational research. Both were seen to share the same myopic perspective.

The corollary to closed-systems thinking is of course 'open-systems' thinking, which emphasises the importance of understanding how firms operate within a broader context or, to use the jargon, the 'environmental supra-system'. Systems thinking undoubtedly continues to have its advocates, but it has never quite managed to shrug off the criticism that it is useful for the purposes of 'understanding', but rather less useful for the purposes of guiding meaningful action. However, if the contribution of systems thinking is to encourage managers to be thoughtful and hence less constrained by short-term financial targets then its legacy is secure. But here again we run the risk of projecting arguments on the basis of how we think human endeavour *should* operate, rather than an understanding of how it operates in reality. There is a parallel here with the musings of Leon Trotsky (1924) in respect of the new 'Communist Man' upon whom the supposed utopian society of 'pure communism' depended. Leaving aside the lack of emphasis on gender equality, the new Communist Man of the future was apparently required to raise himself to a new plane of consciousness together with a new ethical outlook. For the likes of Trotsky, the selfishness of 'Economic Man' was deemed to be a product of a flawed system. It was hence argued that once the enhanced level of consciousness was achieved the new socio-economic system would reproduce itself accordingly. Stalin was to subsequently re-work the same idea in the form of 'New Soviet Man' (with a rather different storyline for the 'New Soviet Woman'). Needless to say, this particular social experiment ultimately ended badly.

Idealism was once again on the march in the 1960s, and systems thinking promoted a new challenge to Herbert Simon's narrowly rationalistic model of 'Economic Man'. 'Holistic Man' was seen to be the answer to the reductionism which too often prevailed. The argument was that if only people would think more holistically then sustainability would become the norm rather than the exception. Such debates played out in the United Nations, as they continue to play out across numerous national, regional and localised contexts. But the difficulty is that different stakeholders frequently struggle to agree on the 'systems' which should be of primary concern. In many respects, sustainability exists (and perhaps only exists) as a hologram at the very nexus of these overlapping perspectives.

## 9.4   Meanwhile back in the UK construction sector

Debates within the corridors of the United Nations are of course hugely important in terms of building an international consensus in favour of more sustainable ways of living. However, they are somewhat removed from the policy-level debates which shape the UK construction sector. At the time *Our Common Future* was published in 1997 Margaret Thatcher was coming towards the end of her second term as UK Prime Minister. Thatcher was not especially renowned for her environmental concerns, but she was steadfast in her adherence to economic neoliberalism, perhaps initially primarily in terms of rhetoric, but progressively thereafter in terms of the material reality of her policies. The bundle of neoliberal economic policies pursued by Thatcher marked a dramatic end to the social-democratic consensus whereby the post-war Beveridge settlement was abandoned in favour of the enterprise culture (cf. Keat and Abercombie, 1991; du Gay and Salaman, 1992).

Thatcher remains vilified by those on the Left, but she could not have won three successive general elections had she not enjoyed some degree of popular support. What cannot be denied is that she was a divisive leader. Key policy dimensions included privatisation, deregulation, reduction of trade union power, removal of council houses from public ownership and the lowering of direct taxes. The accepted euphemism for such trends is the 'flexible economy'.

This shift in the prevailing political climate questioned the very existence of 'society' and emphasised evermore strongly that the primary responsibility of firms is to make a profit.

Hence storylines advocated by the likes of Kast and Rosenzweig (1970) became ever less popular. Systems thinking fell victim to the changing times – in much the same way as sociology. Thatcher, of course, was not responsible for the time-space compression of globalisation. These forces were generated externally and progressively became irresistible. Competitiveness was the new mantra of the enterprise culture, and progressively sustainability was (bizarrely) re-conceptualised amongst business leaders as a means of remaining competitive over time.

The idea that competitiveness lies at the core of sustainability is not a million miles away from the definition of sustainability offered in the *Caring for the Earth* report (IUCN/UNEP/WWF, 1991). Competitiveness is seen to be the primary mechanism for improving the quality of human life. The challenge therefore becomes how to be competitive as a business while living within the carrying capacity of the supporting eco-systems. This is a definition that most construction professionals would feel eminently comfortable with, not least because it negates any need to regress back to Mesolithic models of hunter-gathering (for which we should be thankful).

But competitiveness is voracious, and unconstrained competition can too easily translate into a 'race to the bottom'. There is a persuasive argument that this accounts in part for the heavily fragmented structure of the UK construction sector. Major contractors have progressively divorced themselves of responsibility for the physical task of construction, preferring instead to outsource work to the 'supply chain' (Green, 2011). In essence, the construction sector's competitive model is primarily governed by risk management. When faced with a recurring stop–go economic cycle it makes good 'survivalist' business sense for firms to limit their exposure to the costs of direct employment. Hence the sustained shift to a business model whereby almost all the work is routinely subcontracted. In the mid-1970s direct labour organisations (DLOs) accounted for over 15% of the industry's workforce, thereby providing islands of stability for training and skills development. At least in terms of new build, at the time of writing DLOs are just about non-existent. The demise of the DLOs was inevitable once they were exposed to the market rigours of compulsory competitive tendering (CCT). For many organisations – public and private alike – it became progressively untenable to invest in training and skills development.

Slowly but surely a critical tipping point was reached whereby a reliance on subcontracting become the dominant model. The subcontractors themselves followed suit, such that multi-tiered chains of subcontracts became the norm rather than the exception. At the bottom of these chains, the employment status of a casualised workforce is often difficult to ascertain, even for the operatives themselves. Labour-only subcontractors blur into bogus self-employment and transient labour-supply agencies. The long-term impact of the enterprise culture on the UK construction sector has been to progressively replace contracts of employment with contracts of service. The accumulative effect of this is well-described in the Donaghy Report' (Donaghy, 2009: 21):

> 'The Construction Industry generally is modelled to provide maximum flexibility. Consequently the majority of functions are contracted out and at least 40% pf workers are self-employed or CISs. The advantages are obvious in that it reduces overheads. Some but not all argue that it improves profitability and productivity. The disadvantages are that it becomes more difficult for a safety culture to flourish, worker engagement is weak, employment security and continuity is minimal and skills training is at best patchy.'

Although Donaghy's (2009) main focus of interest was health and safety, the same argument can also be made about sustainability. It has become especially popular to talk about the need to promote 'green skills' if the industry is to become more sustainable (e.g. HM Government, 2011). In truth, the problem is not limited to green skills, it extends to skills more generally. Of particular concern is the lack of on-site supervisory skills, and indeed the dissipated responsibility for supervision that results from the fragmented nature of the construction supply chain. If on-site construction operations are not properly supervised, the industry is unlikely ever to bridge the much heralded 'performance gap' between the energy use of buildings predicted during design and that subsequently achieved in practice. It is relatively easy to call for ever more sophisticated energy models, or indeed for increased involvement from social scientists in terms of a better understanding of post-occupancy user behaviour. Ensuring that mundane tasks such as the installation of cavity insulation are properly supervised is infinitely less glamorous, but is ultimately at least of equal importance. It is notable that the recently published *Farmer Review of the UK Construction Labour Model* (Farmer, 2016) blames the industry's skills crisis on the industry's labour model. He also suggests that the sector is close to reaching a tipping point if it fails to modernise. The sad reality is that all the evidence points to a tipping point being reached 20 years ago.

## 9.5 Modernisation of the construction sector

There is a long-standing myth that the construction sector is slow to change and consistently underperforms. The *Farmer Review* is one of a long sequence of reports which continues to propagate this myth. The reality, however, is that the construction sector underwent considerable change over a 20-year period commencing in the mid-1970s. It was over this period that the sector implemented its strategic model of structural flexibility in recognition that it could no longer rely on government to provide continuity of demand. The retreat of government as a mass provider of housing was just one policy signal amongst many which was difficult to ignore. One of the supposed root causes of the industry's failings suggested by the *Farmer Review* was its 'survivalist' shape, structure and associated commercial behaviours. Farmer is right up to a point in suggesting that the shape of the industry has developed to cope with an unforgiving market environment characterised by low capital reserves and chronically volatile demand. But the 'survivalist' metaphor is interesting. Not least in the imagery of the sector as a living organism which evolves in accordance with an ever-changing external environment. This ability to evolve in response to external stimuli is a central condition of sustainability, and also entirely consistent with open-systems thinking. Closed systems are ultimately unsustainable for the very reason that they fail to respond to external stimuli.

The above argument also extends to the values which are held by those who work in the construction sector. Too often it is suggested that people who work in the construction sector are isolated from the rest of society, both in terms of their 'adversarial' working practices and lack of orientation towards collaborative working. Those who work in construction have on occasion even been cast in the role of dinosaurs, suggesting an aversion to change which is not supported by the facts (Fernie *et al.*, 2006).

The *Farmer Review*'s approach to addressing the construction industry's problems is further underpinned by an unfortunate medical analogy: the diagnosis is that the industry is ill and urgently needs treatment. 'Modernise or die' is the strap-line. Scary stuff indeed. For Farmer, the features of the industry are synonymous with a sick, or even dying, patient. Construed rather differently, it could be said that the construction sector has been at the vanguard of modernisation in leading the UK towards its apparent destiny as a 'gig economy'. Whether or not this is something to be proud of is a moot point. But it is difficult to see how this trend could be seen to contribute positively to the cause of sustainability. Certainly, it does nothing for the cause of sustainable jobs, or to long-term skills development (green or otherwise).

The Egan report *Rethinking Construction* (Egan, 1998) played an important role in the legitimisation of the construction sector's labour model which is rarely acknowledged. To understand the significance of the Egan report it is necessary to place it in the context of Tony Blair's New Labour government, which had taken office the previous year. It was the Deputy Prime Minister (John Prescott) who commissioned Sir John Egan to conduct a review of the construction sector, or at least to put his name to the report.

In comparison to previous government-sponsored reports on industry reform, the Egan report was cobbled together with almost irresponsible haste. There was no real review of how the industry worked, and neither was there any significant degree of consultation with key stakeholders. The key message was pre-determined and was eminently clear for those who wished to read between the lines. The headline message was that the newly elected New Labour government would not be reverting to the command-and-control policies so favoured by previous Labour governments. There was to be no construction sector nationalisation nor any return to the discredited policies of demand management. In other words, there would be no departure from the enterprise culture. The Egan report was notably heavy on the rhetoric of customer satisfaction and on the need to add value through efficiency improvement. Given Egan's background with Jaguar Cars, it was perhaps inevitable that the report should look to the car industry for inspiration. What was less easy to understand was Egan's naïve faith in supposedly 'modern' management techniques such benchmarking, total quality management (TQM) and partnering.

But the most important contribution of *Rethinking Construction* was its implicit legitimisation of the industry's strategic model of structural flexibility (euphemistically known as 'lean construction'). It further served to undermine long-established notions of professionalism in the construction sector in favour of narrowly defined managerialism and a naïve reliance on instrumental toolkits. It was especially light on sustainability; it offered no definition nor any meaningful guidance on how it should be operationalised. To say that the Egan report paid lip-service to sustainability would be to overstate the case.

In summary, there is a prevailing myth that the UK construction sector is slow to change despite extensive re-structuring since the mid-1970s. There is also a prevailing misconception that the sector's fragmented structure is in some way independent of four decades of government policy. The current structure of the construction sector owes much to the prolonged incentivisation of self-employment through the tax and national insurance system. The industry's fragmented structure is therefore at least in part the product of a politicised policy agenda. It has further been suggested that the Egan report was implicit in the legitimisation of the structural changes that had taken place over the preceding 20 years. These changes culminated in the dominance of the 'hollowed-out firm' with direct adverse consequences for skills development and health and safety. Sources such as the *Farmer Review* (Farmer, 2016) argue that the current construction labour model is economically unsustainable. In no small part this a failure not only of government policy but also the industry's leadership.

## 9.6   Sustainable construction as a 'wicked' problem

There are very few sources which offer meaningful advice on how sustainable construction should be operationalised. Hill and Bowen (1997) make the point that optimisation of the listed principles is not always possible, and that trade-offs and compromises may be necessary. In truth, trade-offs and compromises are always necessary. Notions of optimisation should be left to those who seek elegant solutions to relatively unimportant problems. However, those who deal with the messy problems of the real world need to look elsewhere for inspiration.

Sustainability is undoubtedly a messy problem. The intractability of such problems has been recognised for some considerable time, certainly pre-dating the popularity of sustainability. Ackoff (1979: 97) offers an explanation of a messy problem which should be recognisable by all those who seek to progress sustainable construction:

> 'Managers are not confronted with problems that are independent of each other, but with dynamic situations that consist of complex systems of changing problems that interact with each other. I call such problems messes. Problems are abstractions extracted from messes by analysis; they are to messes as atoms are to tables and chairs.'

Rittel and Webber (1973) had previously set out a similar logic in drawing their famous distinction between tame and wicked problems. 'Tame' problems are seen to be those which can be specified in advance, in a form agreed by relevant parties. They are further seen to be problems which remain unchanged throughout the process of analysis. Tame problems may be technically very complex, but they do at least lend themselves to solution on the basis of 'good engineering'. 'Wicked' problems in contrast comprise multiple interpretations of what the problem is, such that the multiple interpretations themselves become a very central part of the problem. In contrast to tame problems, wicked problems cannot be separated from the interpretation of interested parties. But even more crucially, wicked problems change as a direct consequence of analysis, that is, they take on new manifestations because interested parties *learn* as a result of the analysis. Hence their interpretative perspective changes, as does the collective understanding of the problem which needs to be addressed. It is this very intractability that makes sustainable construction such a challenging concept. It further becomes apparent that the various strategies for achieving sustainable construction tend over time to become part of the problem which needs to be addressed.

The important point here is not to draw supposed distinctions between 'wicked' problems and messes, but to recognise that the challenges of sustainable construction are not susceptible to technical solution. It is possible of course to extract a well-defined problem from the broader 'mess' and to subject it to scientific analysis. But the solution then just becomes another part of the mess, not least because others will question why this particular abstraction has been privileged over others.

## 9.7  Strategy for sustainable construction

Given the fact that sustainability is a contested concept, it is perhaps unsurprising that approaches to developing coherent strategies for sustainable construction are fraught with difficulty. A relatively early attempt to realise a strategy for sustainable construction in the UK was published by HM Government (2008) in association with the now defunct Strategic Forum for Construction. The strategy appeared just as the global economy slipped into severe recession and the UK Government's priorities very quickly re-focused on keeping the economy afloat. Striving for a balance between economic, social and environmental goals consistently plays out well when the economy is growing, but in times of recession it seems that economic priorities are consistently privileged. This lack of continuity of emphasis continues to plague the sector's commitment to sustainability.

The *Strategy for Sustainable Construction* commences by emphasising the economic contribution of construction, and the importance of an efficient infrastructure as a driver of national productivity. Interestingly, the rate at which resources are used falls within the category of 'other economic effects'. The strategy is clearly intended to keep the corporate readership on side from the outset; there is little emphasis on the need to make difficult trade-offs. Buildings are seen to account for almost half of the UK's carbon emissions, half of our water consumption and almost a third of landfill and one quarter of raw materials. But the emphasis lies on running the Strategy alongside a strong business case for the sustainable construction agenda, based upon:

- increasing profitability by using resources more efficiently
- firms securing opportunities offered by sustainable products or ways of working
- enhancing company image and profile in the market place by addressing issues relating to corporate social responsibility.

There is little evidence here of even the rudiments of systems thinking, let alone quasi-mystical notions of harmony. The stated purpose of the Strategy was to provide clarity around the existing policy framework and to signal the future policy direction. The clarity on offer was in truth stark: 'increasing profitability in the market place' is what seems to be really important.

In terms of delivery, the *Strategy for Sustainable Construction* abounds with the targets so beloved by the New Labour government at the time. The overarching targets related to the identified 'means' and 'ends'. The 'ends' related directly to sustainability issues such as climate change and biodiversity; the 'means' related to the processes through which the ends were to be achieved. If the suggestion was that there was some sort of casual relationship between means and ends then this was by no means made clear in the report.

### 9.7.1  The 'means' through which sustainable construction is achieved

The *Strategy for Sustainable Construction* identifies five 'means' through which sustainable construction should be achieved: (i) procurement, (ii) design, (iii) innovation, (iv) people and (v) better regulation. It is appropriate to comment on each, and to update on how thinking has developed since the strategy was published.

### 9.7.1.1 Procurement

The advocated target for procurement is to improve 'whole life value through the promotion of best practice construction procurement and supply chain integration'. This was safe ground at the time for the Strategic Forum and provided strong continuity with preceding initiatives. Reference was made to the 'construction commitments' that were championed at the time by the Strategic Forum (HM Government, 2008: 12):

> 'A successful procurement policy requires ethical sourcing, enables best value to be achieved and encourages the early involvement of the supply chain. An integrated project team works together to achieve the best possible solution in terms of design, buildability, environmental performance and sustainable development.'

The suggestion that sustainable procurement has an ethical dimension which extends beyond legal requirements is of interest not least in extending the 'wickedness' of the problem with which the industry is expected to engage.

Thinking on sustainable procurement has been more recently updated by DEFRA (2013), largely on the basis of the lessons learned by the Olympic Delivery Agency (ODA) in procuring the infrastructure for 2012 London Olympics. Of particular note is the derivation of the eight principles to inform procurement (see Box 9.1 and also Chapter 10).

The extent to which the eight principles in Box 9.1 offer new knowledge is debatable, but certainly they provide few insights into what sustainability objectives should look like. The advice seems to be limited to the delivery of 'specific, clear and challenging objectives'. Precisely what the objectives should be and how uncomfortable trade-offs might be achieved remains as opaque as ever. There is vague advice on the use of a 'balanced scorecard'. All tenders on the Olympic Park apparently had a set of award criteria that included sustainability, but ultimately they were seemingly evaluated on the basis of most economically advantageous tender (MEAT). The balanced scorecard was perhaps not as 'balanced' as might have been expected.

---

**Box 9.1  Eight principles to inform sustainable procurement (DEFRA, 2013: 4–8)**

1) Seek a clear and public commitment to sustainability at the highest level of the organisation.
2) Prepare thoroughly: early consideration of sustainability.
3) Set specific, clear and challenging targets from the outset.
4) Be an intelligent client: get the right people on board, define the project and set the budget.
5) Embed sustainability objectives throughout the team and supply chain.
6) Identify and use low-impact, responsibly sourced products and materials, and ensure good supply-chain management.
7) Create a structure that supports a collaborative approach whilst maintaining an environment of challenge.
8) Organise procurement so services can be shared.

### 9.7.1.2 Design

In the case of design, the aim was 'to achieve greater use of design quality assessment tools'. Interestingly, good design was seen to be synonymous with sustainable construction by ensuring that 'buildings, infrastructure, spaces and places are sustainable, resilient, adaptable and attractive'. The identified need in all cases was to contribute to the triple bottom line of environmental, social and economic sustainability. There is a circularity of argument at work here: good design takes into account sustainability, and sustainability depends upon good design. But those looking for clear guidance on the operationalisation of sustainable construction seem destined to remain frustrated.

### 9.7.1.3 Innovation

In the case of innovation, the aim was to enhance the industry's capacity to innovate and to increase the sustainability of both the construction process and its resultant assets (see also Chapter 15). Reference was made to the *Code for Sustainable Homes* (DCLG, 2006), subsequently scrapped by the Cameron government's 'bonfire of red tape' in 2015. There was also support for the Technology Strategy Board's *Innovation Platform in Low Impact Buildings*, established with great fanfare in 2008 and recently re-launched as *Future Building: The Low Impact Building Innovation Platform* (Innovate UK/Technology Strategy Board, 2014). Of primary interest here is the way that sustainable construction began to shrink in scope following the 2008–2009 recession. This shift in emphasis is readily apparent in the final report of the Low Carbon Construction Innovation & Growth Team (HM Government, 2010: 2):

> 'A concentration on energy and carbon brings simplicity and rigour, and provides a new focus for action and a sense of priority; but carbon reduction is not the only critical issue for the industry, nor the only measure of sustainability, and plans across all measures, addressing both mitigation and adaptation, need to be integrated.'

The previous quest for the triple bottom line was hence progressively reduced to the concept of 'low impact'. This was in many ways a direct consequence of the age of austerity, but it was also a recognition that the 'wicked' problems of sustainability were ultimately unsolvable. Unfortunately, abstracting a specific part of the problem on the basis that it lends itself to a 'sense of priority' is a false economy in that opens up the possibility of unintended consequences (see the discussion below on climate change mitigation).

The aim of promoting innovation in respect of sustainable construction can only be construed as positive, but there is a recurring problem with insisting that innovation is subject to the 'business case'. The problem here is that the business case invariably relates to the way in which the business currently operates; rarely does it relate to the way the business might operate if the innovation were to be successful (see also Chapter 17). Hence the insistence on a narrowly defined business case is arguably counter to the cause of innovation. This applies equally to sustainability as to all other proposed innovations. A more constructive frame of reference would be to accept innovation as part of normal business, while insisting on the business case for maintaining the *status quo*.

#### 9.7.1.4  People

The next overarching target *vis à vis* the selected 'means' relates to people, with the aim of an increase in organisations committing to a planned approach in training. There is also a stated commitment to reduce the incidence of fatal and major injury accidents by 10% year on year from 2000, although there was little guidance on how this should be achieved. Quite how a reduction in fatalities provides the means of achieving some other (unstated) goal is not made clear. One would have thought keeping people alive was a worthwhile end in itself. The construction sector's failure to organise itself in terms of health and safety was soon to receive a damning incitement from Donaghy (2009), and in the context of the dominant strategic model of structural flexibility, warm words about organisations committing themselves to a 'planned approach to training' were always going to be limited in terms of impact.

#### 9.7.1.5  Better regulation

The final 'means' is a plea for better regulation, but 'better' in this case axiomatically translates to 'less'. The target is a 25% reduction in the administrative burdens affecting the private and third sectors. Once again, palatability to the corporate sector seems the most important criterion. Ultimately, the lauded *Code for Sustainable Homes* (DCLG, 2006) was deemed to be an administrative burden and was formally ditched in 2015. The fable of the man who eats himself comes to mind. Any attempt to regulate in favour of sustainable construction rapidly becomes an administrative burden, until even to think about sustainability is seen to be wasteful. This is an end point which must be avoided, and is the very antithesis of professionalism. The fact that the meaning of sustainable construction has to be socially negotiated in every specific context does not mean that it is not important; it simply shifts the focus of importance onto the process of social negotiation.

### 9.7.2  The 'ends' that the industry should be striving to achieve

The above-described 'means' through which sustainable construction is supposed to be achieved notably fall significantly short in terms of operational guidance. But perhaps rather more important are the 'ends' which the *Strategy for Sustainable Construction* is striving to achieve: (i) climate change mitigation, (ii) climate change adaptation, (iii) water, (iv) biodiversity, (v) waste and (vi) materials. It is once again appropriate to comment separately on climate change mitigation and climate change adaptation. However, the 'ends' relating to water, biodiversity, waste and materials can safely be addressed collectively given that the respective sections are so light on meaningful content.

#### 9.7.2.1  Climate change mitigation

The section on climate change mitigation begins by quoting the Government's much heralded target for $CO_2$ reduction (HM Government, 2008: 30):

> 'Reducing total UK carbon dioxide ($CO_2$) emissions by at least 60% on 1990 levels by 2050 and by at least 26% by 2020'

The targets were subsequently revised under the provisions of the Climate Change Act 2008 to 80% below base year levels by 2050 and at least 34% below base year levels by 2020. Quite why the targets published in HM Government (2008) differ from those which were made legally binding in the Climate Change Act 2008 is not clear. Nevertheless, there remains a strong scientific consensus regarding the causes of climate change and the corresponding need to reduce $CO_2$ emissions. How this relates to meaningful action for the construction sector is rather more controversial. What is widely accepted – and well-rehearsed by the *Strategy for Sustainable Construction* – is the fact that the existing building stock accounts for the majority of carbon emissions. Given that around 70% of the current housing stock will still be standing in 2050 (SDC, 2006) it is clear that this should be prioritised in terms of energy efficiency if the mandatory 80% reduction target is to be met. Hence the strong focus on the retrofit of the existing stock. But the difficulties here lie in the realisation that energy reduction in the existing building stock is not prone to technological solution. Buildings have occupiers, and such occupiers tend not to behave in ways which are subject to technological determinism.

One of the most intractable issues is how to incentivise homeowners to invest in home improvements which may realise the required energy savings. One such scheme was the ill-fated Green Deal set up in 2009 by the incoming Cameron/Clegg government. Others include the requirement for electricity companies to source an increasing proportion of electricity from renewable sources and the use of feed-in tariffs. The latter guarantee payments from energy companies for surplus electricity generated from low-carbon micro-generation technologies. Typical energy-saving improvements under the Green Deal (abandoned with much embarrassment in 2015) included the installation of traditional solutions such as insulation, draught-proofing and double-glazing in addition to rather more innovative renewable energy technologies such as solar panels and heat pumps. Such interventions are, however, notoriously prone to unintended consequences, such that the cure can on occasion be worse than the disease. Shrubsole *et al.* (2014) identify no less than 100 unintended consequences of such supposed 'solutions', many of which impact negatively on the physical and mental health of building occupants. For example, better insulated buildings can impact positively on winter mortality rates, but can also increase the potential for summer overheating. Top-floor apartments may be particularly at risk, especially in urban environments prone to urban heat island effects (Mavrogianni *et al.*, 2012).

The issue of unintended consequences raises many questions for those involved in research relating to the retrofit of the existing building stock. The notion of unintended consequences is not new: they have been recognised by economists and social scientists for centuries; but now it seems that they have been recognised by building physicists, thereby serving to make actionable advice on the reduction of $CO_2$ emissions rather more contested than is commonly recognised. This does perhaps call into question the status of 'knowledge' as it currently relates to achieving climate mitigation through sustainable construction. It also re-emphasises the need to recognise the challenges of sustainable construction as a 'wicked' problem which routinely defies technological solution.

### 9.7.2.2  Climate change adaptation

Climate change mitigation is not the only end point of sustainable construction. The *Strategy for Sustainable Construction* also alludes to climate change adaptation, with an overarching target of developing a robust approach shared across government.

Reference is made to the increased likelihood of extreme weather events such as high winds, heavy prolonged rainfall, flooding, drought and heat waves. In response, the Strategy argues that it is necessary to build the potential for adaptation into design and construction methods. The challenge is to make buildings and places resilient to the likely impacts of climate change. The danger here, of course, is that the wholesale adoption of adaptation strategies discourages people (and governments) from taking climate change mitigation seriously. However, given that global warming according to the UK Met Office has already risen by more than 1 °C since the pre-industrial era, with further increases already locked in, many are arguing that mitigation is already a lost cause. This is a highly dangerous argument. The reality is that if we fail to take climate change mitigation seriously we will be faced with potentially devastating consequences for the world's ecosystems and in all likelihood for the world's population. In reality, there is no choice other than to adopt a twin strategy of mitigation and adaptation. We need to radically reduce our reliance on fossil fuels and at the same time we need to design our infrastructure and built environment to be resilient to environmental disruption. Given such serious global challenges, the *Strategy for Sustainable Construction* seems remarkably limp. In many respects, it represents an attempt at voluntary regulation such that the industry itself is expected to carry responsibility for implementation. Unfortunately, the document routinely converges on the lowest common denominator such that none of the representative interests are overly challenged.

### 9.7.2.3    Water, biodiversity, waste and materials

The target in respect of water is to assist the Future Water (DEFRA, 2008) vision of reducing water consumption to an average of 130 litres per person per day by 2030. Vague promises are made to allow water meters in water-scarce areas, namely the south and south-east of England. Approximately half of all homes in the UK currently have a water meter, but there is no imminent prospect of them being made compulsory. In summary, there are lots of promises by Government to 'review' and 'consult' but little in the way of tangible proposals. The targets in respect of biodiversity, waste and materials are similarly vague. Numerous references are made to the Code for Sustainable Homes (DCLG), subsequently to be scrapped in 2015. Responsibility for monitoring progress for these final four 'ends' rests in part with the now defunct Strategic Forum for Construction. There is notably an absence of guidance on how to make trade-offs between competing priorities. The subsequent Construction Leadership Council (CLC) seemingly found such multi-criteria models of sustainability too difficult, and hence chose to prioritise the single aim of reducing carbon emissions in the cause of climate change mitigation.

### 9.7.3    Sustainable construction: best practice

In seeking to understand the popularised interpretation of sustainable construction it is appropriate to start with the definition published by Constructing Excellence (2004: 1):

> 'A sustainable approach takes account of the need for your company to prosper in business, without seeking profitability at the expense of the environment or society.'

The above definition is reminiscent of that previously offered by the report *Caring for the Earth* (IUCN/UNEP/WWF, 1991). Constructing Excellence make much of the triple bottom line and the need to strike a balance between objectives of economic, environmental and social sustainability. The advice is that sustainability should be considered when first deciding that a building is needed, and thereafter throughout design, construction and operation through to eventual demolition. This is good advice, but suggesting that sustainability should be 'considered' plays very much to the lowest common denominator.

Paradoxically, it is then suggested that a variety of direct financial rewards and indirect benefits can be derived from the adoption of sustainable construction. The point is illustrated by a quote from Sir Neville Simms, who was at the time Chairman of Carillion: 'Sustainability underpins future profits' (p. 1). The cynic would probably conclude that such firms are in all likelihood rather more concerned with underpinning future profits than underpinning future reductions of $CO_2$ emissions, or indeed 'underpinning' wealth and equality of opportunity in the communities within which they operate. It is important to note that this is not a criticism of Carillion, or even of construction firms generally. It is more a criticism of the way in which sources such as Constructing Excellence frame the supporting argument. Sustainability just becomes yet another dimension of best practice.

## 9.8 The battle lines for sustainability

The final issue that deserves attention is the association between sustainability and the concept of professionalism. The accepted orthodoxy throughout the 1960 and 1970s was that there is a close relationship between ethical behaviour, social responsiveness and the notion of professionalism (cf. Kast and Rosenzweig, 1985). Indeed, professionalism also extended to recognising the importance of the natural environment. However, such 'old-fashioned' notions of professionalism suffered at the hands of the advocates of the enterprise culture. Balancing different needs which do not directly serve the commercial interests of the client was seen as unreasonable arrogance. The Egan report (Egan, 1998) has already been noted for its heavy rhetoric of customer satisfaction and its ruthless focus on the need to add value through efficiency improvement. The long-established tendency of professionals to take account of externalities was hence construed as 'waste'. The advocated worldview saw such tendencies as diminishing the value which was returned to the client. The consensus became that it should be the client (i.e. the paying customer) who decides how value is defined, hence construction professionals were progressively denied the legitimacy to make trade-offs between conflicting objectives. Here lies the end point of the logic of lean construction. The aim is always to reduce the complexity of real-world problems to suit the logic which is on offer. No space here for 'wicked' problems.

It is also increasingly popular to cast professional groups as self-serving monopolies which serve the interests of neither clients nor society (cf. Flynn, 2002). Any attack on professionalism hence also becomes on attack on sustainability. It is the instrumental logic of lean construction which renders sustainability dependent upon the 'business case' of the paying customer.

The difficulty in linking professionalism to sustainability is that the former is no easier to define than the latter. Leaving aside issues of ethical behaviour and social responsibility, professionals are perhaps distinguished by the expectation that they should have an underpinning body of knowledge. It is further expected that such knowledge should be accumulated through a prolonged period of training. Entry qualifications are frequently governed by professional associations, but membership of specific professions also depends on unique social configurations (cf. Vollmer and Mills, 1966). It is this specialised knowledge which traditionally accords professionals with some degree of authority in the eyes of their clients, but 'experts' in recent years have been treated with growing suspicion (see Chapters 12 and 13). Clients who follow the advice of the Egan report would not be encouraged to rely on the judgements of professionals, and the same is true of those who read more recent reports such as those published by Wolstenholme (2009) and Farmer (2016).[1] Luckily very few clients read reports such as these, and most construction professionals are themselves knowledgeable enough not to take them entirely seriously, otherwise sustainable construction would have been a lost cause years ago.

Professionalism has always been strong in the construction sector, especially within the domains of architecture and engineering. The self-identities of practicing architects and engineers have long since been shaped by notions of serving society at large. Societal concerns *vis à vis* sustainability therefore should become the concern of professionals. The distinction between professionals and those who (supposedly) engage in commercial trade for the purposes of profit alone was forged within the parameters of the British class system (cf. Bowley, 1966). The battle lines more recently have been drawn between the conflicting doctrines of professionalism and managerialism (Fournier, 2000; Exworthy and Halford, 2002). Of particular concern is the extent to which creeping managerialism involves an ongoing attempt to replace professional knowledge with narrowly defined instrumentalism. The seemingly endless proliferation of key performance indicators arguably acts to remove professional discretion from decision making. The decline of professionalism should therefore be of direct concern to those who advocate the cause of sustainability.

It should also be recognised that professionalism in the construction sector is not the monopoly of the professional institutions. It is quite possible to commit oneself to doing a 'professional job' without being a member of a professional institution. However, it is also important to acknowledge that the professional institutions have not been exempt from criticism. Indeed, criticising the professional institutions has long since been something of a turkey-shoot. The Edge report *Collaboration for Change* (Morrell, 2015) rehearses many such criticisms, including alleged protectionism, resistance to change, the maintenance of silos and preservation of outdated hierarchies (see Chapter 17).

The argument promoted by the Edge report is in many ways parochial: it is directed at the structure of professional institutions which prevails in the UK (and selected parts of the Commonwealth). It is nevertheless a timely reminder of the responsibility of professionals to act in the public interest. And yet the report says little about the full-frontal assault on the ethos of professionalism launched in the name of the enterprise culture. This battle has ranged across the UK construction sector for over three decades, and professionalism has been in retreat. 'Acting in the public interest' is just not compatible with the logic of lean construction and the associated 'cult of the customer'. One might

---

1  See Chapter 17 for a further discussion on the role of built environment professionals.

ask where the members of the Edge Commission were when the major clients were championing the Egan report and its particular brand of instrumental logic.

The cause of sustainability is hugely conflated with the notion of public interest. Indeed, the definition of 'sustainable development' as that which 'improves the quality of human life while living within the carrying capacity of supporting eco-systems' (IUCN/UNEP/WWF, 1991) is arguably synonymous with the definition of the 'public interest'. The same dilemmas apply, and the same assumptions that there is an easy consensus to be reached on how the public interest can be identified.

Yet it must be conceded that there is something strange about having different institutional structures for different disciplines. Whatever the challenges of sustainability are, they are inherently interdisciplinary. Professionals therefore need access to different bodies of knowledge or, phrased rather differently, professionals need to be committed to learning across artificially created professional boundaries. In this regard, the Edge report's call for increased collaboration should be welcomed. As an aside, it is interesting that the Edge report refers to the gap between predicted and actual performance of built assets without commenting on the appalling lack of on-site supervisory skills. In common with most professional institutions such mundane issues seem to fall below their level of interest. The Edge report also seemingly privileges the 'impact of the built environment on climate change' rather than enter the politicised swamp of sustainability. In any real-world context action on climate change needs to be tensioned against other challenges which are often seen by those directly involved to be of equal importance. Ethical certainty remains in short supply. It is easy to agree to the need for a sustainable future, but the issues become much more complex if our horizons extend to the Global South – or even beyond the coffee bars of central London.

## 9.9   Conclusions: towards 2050 and beyond

It is undoubtedly difficult to be optimistic about the future of sustainability. One thing that is clear is that 'sustainability' is not a problem which can ever be solved. The more progress we make towards a more sustainable future, the more we will raise our aspirations for what a sustainable future looks like. If we take seriously the idea that sustainability is a 'wicked' problem, we should also accept that such problems can never be solved. The ascribed meaning of sustainability has evolved over time and will continue to do so. Commitment to sustainability will always be shaped and constrained by the prevailing political discourse. Furthermore, sustainability will continue to be enacted differently in different contexts. Grand generalisations should therefore be treated with caution. It is also necessary to recognise that the construction industry and society are not independent entities. Idealistic people who care deeply about broader society are no less likely to be found in construction firms than elsewhere. Such individuals are indeed capable of breaking out from the constraints of selfish vested interest to forge a more sustainable future to 2050 and beyond.

On a global scale, there is no doubt that meaningful progress depends on improved inter-governmental co-operation. In this respect, the ongoing weakness of the United Nations should be a primary concern. On a European level, the Brexit vote does not bode well for improved European collaboration. The election of Donald Trump as President of the USA is perhaps of even greater concern for the environmental agenda (see Chapter 17). The increasing influence of populist politicians should be of concern to all, especially in light of the emerging post-truth culture and denigration of experts. The clarion call in this respect has to be in support of evidence and rational argument. Such values continue to be held dear in scientific networks and amongst the well-educated. Unfortunately, the legacy of the Enlightenment and the triumph of rational enquiry cannot be taken for granted; it needs to be celebrated and protected.

Research and education will remain of central importance to the cause of sustainability. Education should be within reach of everyone. This is perhaps the biggest challenge in building a more sustainable future to 2050, and hence essential to the cause of sustainable construction. Science is of course of central importance to the mitigation of climate change. But the political skills of consensus building are no less important. This applies in the international debating chambers of the United Nations, but it also across the scales. We need the skills of consensus politics at the national level, we need them at the regional level and, perhaps most of all, we need then on the local level wherever construction intersects with local communities. In short, we need greater engagement with the communities within which construction takes place, and we need to identify new ways of enacting local democracy.

## References

Ackoff, R.L. (1979) The future of operational research is past. *Journal of the Operational Research Society*, 30(2), 94–104.

Berrien, F.K. (1976) A general systems approach to organization, in Dunnette, M.D. (ed.) *Handbook of Industrial and Organizational Psychology*. Rand McNally College Publishing, Chicago.

Bowley, M.E.A. (1966) *The British Building Industry: Four Studies in Response and resistance to Change*. Cambridge University Press, Cambridge.

Brundtland Commission (1987) *Our Common Future: Report of the 1987 World Commission on Environment and Development*. Oxford University Press, Oxford.

Burns, T. and Stalker, G.M. (1961) *The Management of Innovation*. Tavistock Publications, London.

Constructing Excellence (2004) *Sustainable Construction: An Introduction*. Constructing Excellence.

DCLG (2006) *Code for sustainable homes: A step-change in sustainable home building practice*. Department for Communities and Local Government, London.

DEFRA (2008) *Future Water, the Government's water Strategy for England*. Department for Environment, Food and Rural Affairs, London.

DEFRA (2013) *London 2012 Legacy: Sustainable procurement for construction projects*. Department for Environment, Food and Rural Affairs, London.

Donaghy, R. (2009) *One Death is Too Many*. Report to the Secretary of State for Work and Pensions. Cm 7657, TSO, London.

du Gay, P. and Salaman, G. (1992) The culture of the customer. *Journal of Management Studies*, 29, 615–633.

Egan, Sir John (1998) *Rethinking Construction. Report of the Construction Task Force to the Deputy Prime Minister, John Prescott, on the scope for improving the quality and efficiency of UK construction*. Department of the Environment, Transport and the Regions, London.

Exworthy, M. and Halford, S. (eds) (2002) *Professionals and the New Managerialism in the Public Sector*. Open University Press, Buckingham.

Farmer, M. (2016) *The Farmer Review of the UK Construction Labour Model: Modernise or Die*. Construction Leadership Council, London.

Fernie, S., Leiringer, R. and Thorpe, T. (2006) Change in construction: a critical perspective. *Building Research and Information*, 34(2), 91–103.

Flynn, R. (2002) Managerialism, professionalism and quasi-markets, in Exworthy, M. and Halford, S. (eds) *Professionals and the New Managerialism in the Public Sector*. Open University Press, Buckingham, pp. 18–36.

Fournier, V. (2000) Boundary work and the (un)making of the professions, in Mallin, N. (ed.) *Professionalism, boundaries and the workplace*. Routledge, London.

Godfrey, P. (2010) Using systems thinking to learn to deliver sustainable built environments. *Civil Engineering and Environmental Systems*, 27(3), 219–230.

Green, S.D. (2011) *Making Sense of Construction Improvement*. Wiley-Blackwell, Oxford,

Green, S.D., Harty, C.F., Elmualim, A.A., Larsen, G. and Kao, C.C. (2008) On the discourse of construction competitiveness. *Building Research & Information*, 36(5), 426–435.

Hill, R.C. and Bowen, P.A. (1997) Sustainable construction: principles and a framework for attainment. *Construction Management and Economics*, 15(3), 223–239.

HM Government (2008) *Strategy for Sustainable Construction*. HM Government in association with the Strategic Forum for Construction, London.

HM Government (2010) *Low Carbon Construction IGT: Emerging Findings*. Department for Business, Innovation and Skills, London.

HM Government (2011) *Skills for a Green Economy: A Report on the Evidence*. Department for Business, Innovation and Skills; Department of Energy and Climate Change; Department for Environment, Food and Rural Affairs.

Innovate UK/Technology Strategy Board (2014) *Future Building: The Low Impact Building Innovation Platform*. Technology Strategy Board.

IUCN/UNEP/WWF (1991) *Caring for the Earth. A Strategy for Sustainable Living*. Gland, Switzerland.

Kast, F.E. and Rosenzweig, J.E. (1985) *Organization and Management: A Systems and Contingency Approach*, 4th edn. McGraw-Hill, New York.

Keat, R. and Abercombie, N. (1991) *Enterprise Culture*. Routledge, London.

Lawrence, P.R. and Lorsh, J.W. (1967) *Organization and Environment*. Harvard Press, Cambridge, MA.

Maslow, A. (1954) *Motivation and Personality*. Harper, New York.

Mavrogianni, A., Wilkinson, P., Davies, M., Biddulph, P. and Oikonomou, E. (2012) Building characteristics as determinants of propensity to high indoor summer temperatures in London dwellings. *Building and Environment*, 55, 117–130.

Morrell, P. (2015) *Collaboration for Change: The Edge Commission Report on the Future of Professionalism*. Ove Arup/The Edge, London.

Rice, A.K (1963) *The Enterprise and its Environment*, Tavistock Publications, London.

Rittel, H.W.J and Webber, M.M. (1973) Dilemmas in a general theory of planning. *Policy Sciences*, 4(2), 155–169.

SDC (2006) *'Stock Take': Delivering Improvements in Existing Housing*. Sustainable Development Commission, London.

Shrubsole, C., Macmillan, A, Davies, M. and May, N. (2014) 100 Unintended consequences of policies to improve the energy efficiency of the UK housing stock. *Indoor and Built Environment*, 23(3), 340–352.

Trotsky, L. (1924) *Literature and Revolution*. International Publishers, New York [English translation].

UN (2014) *World Urbanization Prospects: the 2014 Revision*. Department of Economic and Social Affairs, United Nations, New York.

Vollmer, H.M. and Mills, D. (eds) (1966) *Professionalization*. Prentice-Hall, Englewood Cliffs, NJ.

Wolstenholme, A. (2009) *Never Waste a Good Crisis*. Constructing Excellence in the Built Environment, London.

# 10

# Sustainable Procurement
*John Connaughton and Will Hughes*

## 10.1 Introduction

Around the world, construction is a significant industrial sector, typically accounting for 5–15% of GDP, depending on the stage of economic development in any particular country. Construction is a relatively labour-intensive process and the sector employs a similarly significant proportion of the economically active population (UNEP, 2007). It is also a major consumer of raw materials and a generator of waste. Notably, the sector accounts for some 40–50% of total world resource consumption by volume, including some 30% of global timber consumption (UNEP, 2007).

In recent years there has been a good deal of attention devoted to improving the sustainability of construction output. However, sustainability in the construction sector is seen principally in terms of the energy performance of buildings and their effect on the well-being of users and occupants. The emphasis is typically on designing (and, to a lesser extent, constructing) the built environment to reduce its reliance on greenhouse gas (GHG)-producing energy sources. While some attention has been paid to the procurement of material resources for construction, including, for example, the sustainable procurement of timber (Auld *et al.*, 2008), the procurement of other resources, including labour, and the wider role that procurement has in supporting more sustainable construction and development has attracted less interest.

Procurement is a wide-ranging concept and may refer to any of the strategic processes of funding, organising, managing and decision-making in a construction project (or programme) at all stages of development. This includes the creation, management and fulfilment of contracts for construction work, consultancy and advice throughout the supply chain networks that collectively achieve construction output. Essentially, we are interested in the commercial processes of structuring, negotiating, recording and enforcing business deals for the acquisition of construction.

This chapter examines the role of procurement in supporting sustainable construction and development. We consider procurement from two key perspectives: 'client-side' (i.e. on behalf of construction clients who purchase construction services and projects from the construction industry) and 'supply-side' (i.e. on behalf of construction companies and suppliers who supply to construction clients). In turn, they purchase

*Sustainable Futures in the Built Environment to 2050: A Foresight Approach to Construction and Development*, First Edition. Edited by Tim Dixon, John Connaughton and Stuart Green.
© 2018 John Wiley & Sons Ltd. Published 2018 by John Wiley & Sons Ltd.

resources and services from other companies and suppliers along their supply chain. We also consider procurement as having various objectives. On construction projects, the goal is improving the performance of project processes and completed buildings and built infrastructure. In many cases there are secondary objectives, such as targeted employment. For construction organisations, the goal is improving the sustainability of business processes and organisational performance. Our review spans these different perspectives and objectives. Thus, we emphasise the significant and pervasive role of procurement in securing more sustainable construction and development through to 2050.

A comprehensive review of all these aspects is, of course, beyond the scope of this chapter. Instead, and in line with the futures focus of this book, we look ahead to 2050 to consider the sustainable procurement practices necessary to support more sustainable construction in the mid-21st century. As we will show, much of the necessary guidance and standards for more sustainable procurement already exist, but they have not yet been brought fully into mainstream practice. This is partly because they are relatively new. It is also because they do not sit comfortably with many of the more conventional and deeply embedded practices in construction. Our focus, then, is on the implications for such buyers and suppliers, in terms of their responsibilities and governance, of adopting new, sustainable procurement standards and good practice guidance against a background of deeply-rooted traditions and contemporary construction practices.

This chapter has four key parts, covering:

- construction procurement and practice – the importance of procurement from both client-side and supply-side perspectives; some important characteristics of contemporary construction practice that create challenges for more sustainable procurement
- concepts of sustainable procurement
- sustainable procurement in construction - available guidance, standards and potential 'good practice'
- looking ahead to 2050 – the implications for buyers and suppliers of adopting more sustainable procurement practices, and overcoming key challenges from contemporary practice through to 2050.

## 10.2   Construction procurement and related practices

### 10.2.1   Procurement in construction: how clients put their demand to the market

Procurement is essentially the process of acquiring goods and/or services from a supplier. While procurement in construction would seem primarily to be a demand-side activity, the emphasis in many texts tends to be on how clients mobilise the supply side to meet their requirements. Hackett and Statham (2016), for example, use *contracting methods* – fixed-price contracting, design-build, management contracting and so on – as the key to explain the various options available. However, this focuses mainly on the need for clients to understand contractual arrangements that are familiar to the supply side. It focuses far less, if at all, on the need for the supply side to understand those key client requirements that are driving the process. While some guidance recognises the primacy of understanding client needs – preferably expressed in a clear business case that informs a procurement strategy (e.g. BS 8534, BSI, 2011a) – too often procurement in construction is portrayed as a supplier-dominated contractual process. In this chapter we emphasise the need to understand client needs as an essential element in more sustainable procurement, and we return to the point below in our look ahead to 2050.

### 10.2.2 Procurement in construction: how the market responds to demand

Turning to the supply side, modern construction supply chains are long and complex. This means that much detailed procurement of the labour and material inputs to construction projects takes place across multiple tiers of subcontractors and suppliers. They each buy from and sell to one another in a series of procurement processes that bundle diverse work packages into one or more head contracts with a client. These processes can also often be overlooked in the construction procurement literature, which tends to concentrate on how the firms at the top of the supply chain deal with their clients (Hughes *et al.*, 2006). That they are overlooked, perhaps, reinforces the point that, conventionally, procurement in the literature is as much about forms of organisation and contract as it is about more fundamental issues of sourcing and buying. However, these latter issues are at the core of how procurement can support sustainable development and construction.

Further discussion of the development of construction procurement is beyond the scope of this chapter (for a more detailed treatment, see, for example, Hackett and Statham (2016) and Hughes *et al.* (2015)). However, it is important to recognise certain key features of contemporary construction practice that have, at least partly, been influenced by developments in construction procurement. These, in turn, impact on the sustainable procurement of construction. We consider five interrelated features to be particularly significant:

- a strong tradition of price competition
- the prevalence and growth of subcontracting
- the increasing casualisation of labour (the trend for labour to be employed on short-term contracts and/or on a self-employed basis, together with the use of migrant labour)
- the role of intermediaries (builders' merchants) in materials supply, and increasing consolidation among them
- the sector's predisposition to bribery and corruption.

### 10.2.3 A Tradition of price competition

Construction has long been considered a sector with very high levels of competition and low barriers to entry (see Hillebrandt, 2000; Ive and Gruneberg, 2000; BIS, 2013a). Price competition is often singled out as a major cause of problems in construction procurement. In particular, the practice of lowest-price tendering is frequently seen as a major contributor to the relatively poor performance record of construction in terms of delivery to expected price, programme and quality criteria. However, it is not at all clear that poor performance in relation to price, programme and quality can be fixed with a 'magic bullet' of changing the nature of the competition. The characteristics of construction contracts are such that construction projects tend to be expensive and protracted. Decisions at one stage in a project are often implemented much later. This means that uncertainty and change are inevitable for two reasons: (i) design and specification information is always incomplete as there is no such thing as perfect information, and (ii) as time passes, things change. In rather simple terms, of course, price-based competitive procurement tries to deal with this by passing the risk of uncertainty and the potential for change to suppliers/contractors. But is there a better way of coping with such uncertainties by rethinking how demand is put to the market? Instead, for example, of issuing incomplete and uncertain specifications to the market to secure a price, could clients think about allowing the market to develop its own specifications as the basis for solutions that are appropriate to clients' needs? We discuss this more performance-based approach to procurement below in our look ahead to 2050.

Nonetheless, in the contemporary construction sector, the selection of construction contractors and consultants on the basis of lowest price prevails. Indeed, it is known for participants at different tiers of the supply chain (see below in the section on the growth of subcontracting), especially in recessionary periods when construction work is scarce, to exploit their relative market dominance by seeking below-cost bids (Green, 2011). This is not to suggest that below-cost bids are necessarily loss-making. Indeed, many in the industry do not make their profits from simply selling buildings for more than they paid for their supplies. Construction tends to be a cash-flow business, not a trading business. In a cash-flow business, contractors can often pay for their supplies some time after being paid for work in progress (usually monthly). As long as the difference between cash in and cash out remains positive, contractors have the opportunity to generate income from the surpluses that they hold temporarily. In such trading circumstances, price considerations and the ability to manage cash flow dominate the procurement process and the opportunity to introduce other, more sustainability-focused requirements (these are discussed further in the section on sustainable procurement below) is considerably limited.

### 10.2.4   Growth of subcontracting

The prevalence of subcontracting in the construction sector is widely recognised as providing a means of managing both project risk and complexity, and the significant discontinuities in workload that are a feature of the construction marketplace (see Hillebrandt, 2000). Workload discontinuities are caused by the fact that construction contracts are relatively large, bespoke and are not generally placed in the market to provide a continuous flow of work. This means that, in an era before so-called 'zero-hours' contracts, it was very expensive for contractors to maintain their labour force from one project to the next. Winch (1998) observes how subcontracting provides flexibility to cope with such market volatility, permitting rapid expansion (via the engagement of more specialist subcontractors) and contraction in response to fluctuations in demand. Harvey (2003) and Green (2011), amongst others, have examined the growth of subcontracting in UK construction since the 1970s. Harvey (2003) describes a process of 'flexibilisation' whereby construction contracting firms downsized and outsourced key functions – and principally their direct labour – in response to competitive pressures and to shed many of the ongoing liabilities associated with employing a large workforce. Indeed, without doing this they would not remain competitive and would fail.

Similarly, Green (2011) charts the effective disappearance through the 1980s of once large construction contractors that directly employed both specialist and general labour. He notes their replacement by 'hollowed-out' construction firms in which few people are directly employed, 'other than a tight core of managerial personnel' (pp. 60–69), and the resulting supply-side fragmentation into ever smaller firms, many of which are contracting entities that undertake little or no construction work. Such supply chain fragmentation and complexity is examined further by the UK Department for Business, Innovation and Skills (BIS, 2013b), noting the multiple tiers of subcontractors on typical construction projects: these start with a main contractor (contracting directly with a client 'buyer') who subcontracts elements of the project to a range of specialist subcontractors who, in turn, subcontract to other subcontractors in a downward subcontractual cascade across four, five and sometimes more subcontracting tiers. In this scheme, procurement is not simply a buying process between a client and contractor; it is a complex, disaggregated and multi-layered network of contracts involving a large number of separate procurement exercises between buyers and sellers, many of whom perform both roles simultaneously.

### 10.2.5 Labour casualisation

The growth of subcontracting in construction has been accompanied by an increase in labour-only subcontracting. This means that construction labour is not directly employed by contractors but provided on a subcontract basis, either by individuals or subcontracting firms and agencies. This has resulted in a corresponding increase in the self-employment of construction operatives in the UK. While self-employment is not always easy to define, operatives having this status are essentially one-person trading entities. So widespread has the practice become that, in 2016, over 850,000 people (almost 40% of all UK construction operatives) were classed as self-employed in construction statistics published by the Office of National Statistics (ONS), compared to some 23% in 1980 (ONS, 2016). However, the practice is the subject of much uncertainty and some controversy: on the one hand, self-employment is believed to improve labour market flexibility and promote entrepreneurship; on the other, it is considered exploitative and a way of transferring disproportionate responsibility (for continuity and security of work, the provision of training, etc.) and risk onto the individual worker (Parker, 2004). Green (2011) has charted the industrial and policy origins of this trend, arguing that, while self-employment may offer certain advantages to operatives (principally in the form of higher wages and greater flexibility), it has significant adverse consequences for security of work, employment rights, welfare, training and personal development, and other matters (pp. 69–76). Indeed, a recent surge in the use of zero-hours contracts in other industries, such as care workers, delivery drivers and so on (Pyper and Dar, 2015), has emphasised the plight of casualised workers. These workers belong to something recently labelled the 'gig economy'. The trends that have been prevalent in construction for decades are spreading to other industrial sectors.

Another key development is construction's increasing reliance on migrant labour, partly from new accession countries in an enlarged European Union (EU) after 2004 and partly from non-EU countries with high levels of outward migration stimulated by domestic or regional unrest. Indeed, the tradition of using migrant labour in construction has its roots before the industrial revolution in the UK. For example, much of the manual labour for building canals and railways came from Ireland. Chan *et al.* (2010) discuss the long tradition of the use of migrant labour in the UK construction sector as a means by which construction firms manage market volatility. They argue that migrant labour not only provides an important supplement to domestic resources when the quantum required exceeds that available but also, just as importantly (to them: they focus on improving vocational education and training in the sector), it provides an important injection of *skills* to meet domestic deficiencies. They acknowledge also that the attractiveness of construction migrant labour for employers is at least partly because of immigrants' lower wage demands and tolerance of poorer working conditions than their domestic counterparts would accept.

There are other concerns, of course. By relying on migrant labour – especially highly skilled labour – Chan *et al.* (2010) argue that the UK is effectively exporting its education and training obligations to less wealthy countries that pay the costs for the UK to receive the benefits. The Chartered Institute of Building (CIOB, 2015) picks up this theme but focuses more on the domestic consequences, arguing that an over-reliance on migrant labour to supplement domestic shortfalls permits construction firms to avoid much needed investment in training and developing indigenous labour. More broadly, the CIOB (2015) acknowledges the domestic social and community pressures that may arise from large-scale immigration, although they argue against onerous restrictions because they may reduce the international competitiveness of construction and the freedom of UK migrants to seek work abroad. Indeed, the movement of labour has long been a characteristic of construction. Again, the scale of a construction project, as compared to singular transactions in other industry sectors, means that there are specific problems in this sector relating to the volatile demands for the supply of labour of all kinds.

Of course price/economic considerations feature as strongly in more general construction procurement as they do in the procurement of construction labour. But labour is something of a special case, raising more fundamental issues of human rights and welfare, just reward and fair working conditions, together with a range of attendant consequences for policy. It cannot be ignored in any sustainable scheme. The challenges – and opportunities – for more sustainable procurement of labour are considerable.

### 10.2.6 Intermediation and consolidation in materials supply

Construction is heavily dependent on material resources, and a sophisticated materials sourcing, production and supply infrastructure has evolved to support the procurement of materials. Some important features are particular to construction, and affect thinking about more sustainable procurement of materials. These include the role of builders' merchants in materials delivery, and increasing consolidation and concentration in the merchant sector. Agapiou *et al.* (1998) examine the role of builders' merchants as intermediaries between materials producers/manufactures and their contractor customers. Traditionally, merchants 'break bulk' by purchasing significant material/product quantities from manufacturers. These manufacturers do not have the supply infrastructure to sell in smaller volumes to a wide range and number of geographically dispersed contractors. Merchants sell these materials and components in smaller quantities to individual contractors. An important feature of merchants' practices is that they offer credit to their contractor customers based on, among other things, volumes of trade and payment history. In this sense they are often viewed as one of the 'construction industry's bankers' (Agapiou *et al.*, 1998: 360), indirectly contributing an important source of working capital for many contractors. They also operate in a very competitive marketplace, which has driven increasing consolidation in an attempt to reduce costs. Agapiou *et al.* (1998) report an increase of some 30% in market concentration (measured by the concentration ratio of the top three firms) between 1990 and 1995. While formal assessments of market concentration in this sector are not well covered in the literature, Lowe (2011) points to a greater degree of market concentration in the materials sector than in many other economic sectors, and principally in 'heavy-side' materials (including cement, sand and aggregate, and concrete; see also Hammond and Wembridge, 2011). The role of merchants in the construction supply chain is not simply about materials delivery, but is also about the provision of finance by some of these economically strong organisations to their smaller contractor customers that helps create a strong co-dependency between them.

### 10.2.7   Corruption and bribery

Tookey and Chalmers (2009), in their overview of corruption in the UK construction sector, comment on the sector's worldwide reputation for dishonesty and fraudulent practice. Corruption is difficult to define, and rather more difficult to normalise across different regions/countries – it depends on local legislative and regulatory frameworks, cultural preferences for trade and related matters, established business relationships and other socio-economic practices. The voluntary business ethics organisation, Transparency International, identifies 'construction and public works' as the leading sector in its Bribe Payers' Index (Transparency International, 2014). This index is the result of a survey of business people around the world on their perceptions of the extent to which bribes are paid to help smooth business processes, including the award of contracts in different countries and in different sectors of economic activity. While the UK is not top of the Transparency International list of bribe-paying countries, the UK construction sector is certainly not immune to corruption and fraudulent practices.

A particular problem with significant impact on procurement is collusion in tendering. The UK Office of Fair Trading (OFT) enquiry in 2009 (Europe Economics, 2010) uncovered evidence of breaches of UK competition law and fined 103 companies some £129 million. Collusive practices included 'cover pricing'. This is an illegal form of bid-rigging where a firm submits an artificially high bid so as to exclude itself from the competition and, potentially, favour another; such cover prices are typically determined by colluding with this other bidding firm. This occurred on some 199 tenders from 2000 to 2006. Compensation payments – where successful bidders pay agreed sums to unsuccessful bidders – were also discovered on a smaller number of tenders.

Tookey and Chalmers (2009) argue that the relative predisposition of construction to corruption is due to a range of factors: the ease of engaging in corrupt activities, the complexity of construction projects with multiple actors and contractual interrelationships (having opportunities for corruption at each contractual interface), and the idea that participants feel compelled to engage in corrupt activities because their competitors are doing so (pp. 128–130). The situation is not helped by the relatively large scale of payments between the parties to a construction contract that provide potentially attractive opportunities for corruption. Additionally, a tradition of non-compliant behaviour by construction companies in relation to their regulatory, taxation and other obligations underlines the sector's poor ethical performance. In the UK, for example, the government has found it necessary to develop regulations specifically for construction to minimise tax evasion: the Construction Industry Scheme (CIS) requires contractors to deduct money from subcontractors and pass it to the government as part of a subcontractor's tax obligations. A lack of transparency in many procurement and contract award processes suggests that corruption is not an exclusively supply-side malaise, but can be as much to do with failure of governance on the part of procuring authorities, particularly in the public sector (Kenny, 2010). While corruption has no place in a sustainable procurement process, the many opportunities for corrupt practices around construction projects cannot be ignored, nor can the damage corruption can cause (Peter Eigen, quoted in Transparency International, 2005: 2):

> 'Corruption in the construction sector not only plunders economies; it shapes them…The opportunity costs are tremendous, and they hit the poor hardest. Were it not for corruption in construction, vastly more money could be spent on health and education and more developing countries would have a sustainable future…'

### 10.2.8   Construction practices and sustainable procurement

These practices and developments have important consequences for sustainable construction because, in some instances, they run counter to some of the more fundamental principles of sustainable development outlined in Chapter 1. To summarise the points so far:

- Procurement is usually characterised in terms of how clients should mobilise the supply side, rather than in terms of how the supply side should understand client requirements, nor indeed how clients may best put demand to the market.
- Complex supply chains lead to networks of contracts and multi-tiered subcontracting.
- Construction work is typically price-competitive.
- The inconsistent nature of the demand for different kinds of specialist works results in a prevalence of subcontracting.
- Unskilled labour is often informal and untrained.
- Skilled labour is drawn from an international labour pool.
- The sector's intermediaries, wholesalers and distributors are always present in the supply chain and contribute to the positive cash flow of contractors by waiting for payment until weeks after supplies are incorporated into the work.
- Bribery and corruption are common, if not endemic. There are structural reasons why these poor practices are disproportionately present in the construction sector.

Before looking at how these issues might be addressed in a future where more sustainable construction procurement could prevail, we turn first to an examination of key concepts of sustainable procurement, and what these mean in a construction context.

## 10.3   Concepts of sustainable procurement

### 10.3.1   The role of procurement in sustainable development

Alongside the evolution of concepts of sustainable development since the mid to late 1980s, has come a recognition that procurement has a key role to play in the achievement of sustainability goals. Despite this, there is no single, generally accepted definition of sustainable procurement currently in use. Laryea *et al.* (2013) reviewed the literature on sustainable procurement and found a variety of concepts in use, including green procurement, responsible sourcing and even 'good procurement' (p. 1287). Such disparity has led to a broad range of definitions, many of which start with a general statement of the broad purpose of sustainability – of meeting current needs without compromising the ability of future generations to meet theirs – and view sustainable procurement as a buying process that helps achieve it. Laryea *et al.* (2013) consider that an 'essential feature' of the different definitions currently in use – in line with an important policy statement from a UK Government Department (DEFRA, 2006) – is that sustainable procurement should support social, economic and environmental goals to offer long-term benefits to society (p. 1287).

### 10.3.2   Policy development and related guidance

The idea that sustainable procurement is a key purchasing mechanism for sustainable development informs a good deal of policy development in relation to sustainability. The World Summit on Sustainable Development (WSSD) in 2002 recognised the importance of government's dual role of purchaser and regulator, combined with its leadership responsibilities. It called for the promotion of 'public procurement policies that encourage development and diffusion of environmentally sound goods and services' (WSSD, 2002: 9). In the UK, this important obligation of leadership underlined the UK government's approach when stating its goal to be one of the leaders in Europe on sustainable procurement by 2009 (DEFRA, 2005). A subsequent report by the National Audit Office (NAO, 2009a) in the UK assessed that progress had been more modest against 2006 plans and aspirations. Nonetheless, the deployment of sustainable procurement across central government departments and agencies had been well underway (Walker and Brammer, 2009), and most departments now adopt sustainable procurement policies that are broadly in line with DEFRA (2006). Sustainable procurement in UK local authorities also appears well advanced, perhaps following a lead provided by the Greater London Authority (GLA) as one of the first UK local authorities to publish a sustainable procurement policy in 2006, emphasising the role of public procurement in supporting social inclusion, equality and environmental objectives (GLA Group, 2006).

Much of this policy development is now supported by a range of publicly available guidance material (e.g. DEFRA, 2010, 2014). Similarly, developments outside the UK have given rise to further guidance on sustainable procurement across all key sectors or economic activity as well as the public sector. At the EU level the concept of 'buying green' has been used to promote sustainable procurement under a Green Public Procurement (GPP) policy which, amongst other things, recognises the role of procurement as providing a strong focus for innovation in sustainability (European Commission, 2016). More widely still, ongoing work by the UNEP, under the broad objective of Sustainable Consumption and Production (SCP), has charted the beneficial environmental and social impacts of sustainable procurement in key regions (UNEP, 2012a) and produced substantive guidance for the public sector for the development of policies and plans (UNEP, 2012b). In the UK, policies of this nature have become more than mere guidance with the Public Services (Social Value) Act 2012, which makes it incumbent on procurers in the public sector to set up their contracts with regard to the three key strands of the sustainability agenda.

Of course, sustainable procurement is not an exclusively public policy issue. Notable among the guidance available in the UK is British Standard BS 8903:2010 Sustainable Procurement (BSI, 2010a), which seeks to strengthen both the business and ethical case for procurement that leads to more sustainable outcomes. This Standard may be used in both public and private sectors. It is also important in the application of sustainable procurement in construction, and is discussed further below. Broadly, BS 8903 adopts the definition of sustainable procurement in Department of Environment, Food and Rural Affairs (DEFRA, 2006: 10) (i.e. initially developed by the UK Government's Sustainable Procurement Task Force) as:

> '...a process whereby organisations meet their needs for goods, services, works and utilities in a way that achieves value for money on a whole life basis in terms of generating benefits not only to the organisation, but also to society and the economy, whilst minimising damage to the environment.'

In particular, it emphasises the importance of organisational policy in setting the scene for sustainable development and the sustainable procurement processes that will support it. It sets out the business reasons for the adoption of sustainable procurement and identifies key enablers, including leadership and governance, people, risk and opportunity management, engagement (of suppliers) and measurement of outcomes. It also provides a detailed, seven-step generic procurement process that takes account of these enablers and is focused specifically on sustainable procurement.

Despite the intensity of policy development in the past decade or so, and the plethora of guidance currently available, evidence for take up is patchy. For example, Burke and King (2015), in analysing local authority websites, suggest that, by 2015, up to 75% of local authorities had not included reference to the Public Services (Social Value) Act or to social value in their corporate procurement strategies. More broadly, the World Economic Forum (2016) suggest that the construction sector is the top consumer of raw materials globally, that 50% of solid waste in the USA is produced by the construction industry and that 30% of global greenhouse gases are attributable to buildings (p. 12) (see also Chapter 17). The report also states that one strategic imperative for construction companies is 'to incorporate principles of sustainability into their strategies and business models' (p. 33). Clearly though, there is still a long way to go in implementing principles and policies that are widely accepted and espoused.

## 10.4   Sustainable procurement in construction

### 10.4.1   Key developments

As noted in the introduction to this chapter, a good deal of recent thinking on sustainable construction has focused on project *outcomes* and on the performance, in sustainability terms, of long-life built assets. Given this, there is a key role for procurement in helping to deliver this performance. Much of the more general policy development and public procurement guidance published in the last decade or so has touched on construction to a greater or lesser degree as a key sector and an important opportunity to improve the performance of built assets. For example, DEFRA (2006) highlight construction as a top 'priority spend area' (p. 17), guidance provided by the European Commission (2014) identifies buildings as a key GPP sector (pp. 68–69) and the UNEP (2012a) presents a study of sustainable construction in the UK as one of its sustainable procurement impact studies.

More specifically, the now defunct UK Office of Government Commerce (OGC, 2007) developed guidance on sustainable procurement in construction, focused on the delivery of sustainable development in construction through procurement. It sets out a detailed procurement process, focusing on the integration of sustainability objectives into project business needs. Further, it looks at the construction project lifecycle in its entirety, considering the long-term performance of built assets and their disposal at the end of their useful lives (pp. 6–7). However, while this process spans the construction project lifecycle, it is essentially a 'client-side' view of procurement, where the goal of sustainable procurement is to specify and procure something that may be considered sustainable in-use.

More recently, Berry and McCarthy (2011), while also considering sustainable procurement across the construction project lifecycle, supplement the client-side perspective with more of an explicit focus on the supply side. Their scheme recognises the role of procurers along the construction supply chain in procuring the human and material inputs to construction and also on the conditions under which these inputs come together and are combined in the construction process. Further, they adopt the DEFRA definition of sustainable procurement (DEFRA, 2006), which in turn provides the basis of more general guidance in BS 8903 (BSI, 2010a). Indeed, their scheme is essentially the application of BS 8903 in construction. The scheme developed by Berry and McCarthy (2011) is well-established; it focuses on procurement across the project lifecycle, and it has a dual perspective of client- and supply-side procurement along the construction supply chain. Given this, it provides a suitable basis for considering sustainable construction procurement through to 2050. In particular, as we will discuss below, it provides a useful basis for considering how current construction practices that run counter to the goal of more sustainable procurement may be met and, potentially, overcome.

### 10.4.2   An outline scheme for sustainable procurement in construction

In Figure 10.1, Berry and McCarthy (2011) illustrate the different procurement processes involved at different stages of the construction project lifecycle and across different levels of the construction supply chain. Berry and McCarthy (2011) also recognise the

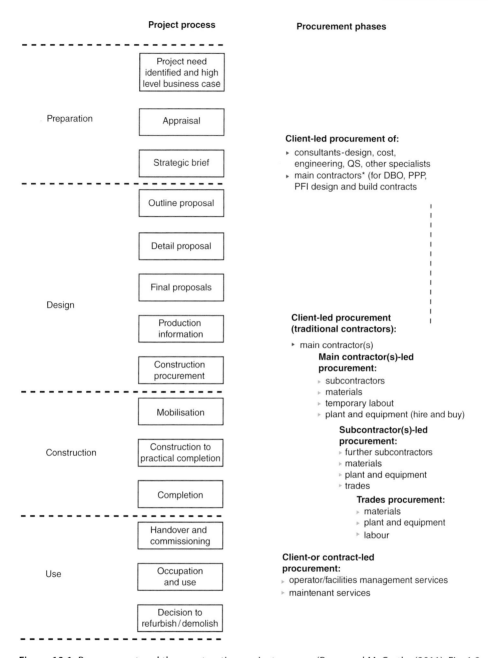

**Figure 10.1** Procurement and the construction project process (Berry and McCarthy (2011), Fig. 1.2, p. 4). DBO, design, build and operate; PPP, public–private partnership; PFI, private finance initiative; QS, quantity surveyors.

client's and relevant contractors' organisational policies in setting overall sustainability objectives (as in BS 8903:2010 and the more general procurement guidance in BS 8534:2011). In their scheme, such policies link sustainability goals to project outcomes across all key project stages. Berry and McCarthy also acknowledge that construction tends to be procured on a project-by-project basis and the unique circumstances of physical location and other matters can give rise to particular constraints as well as opportunities for action. Such circumstances cover a range of environmental, socio-economic, political and commercial issues (Berry and McCarthy, 2011) and, while present on most projects, their particular combination on individual projects is unique.

Client requirements for environmental performance and/or sustainability are often driven by the need for targeted ratings using the Building Research Establishment Environmental Assessment Method (BREEAM) or Civil Engineering Environmental Quality Assessment and Award Scheme (CEEQUAL) systems, or equivalent. They may also be driven by planning conditions. Collectively, these requirements exert a strong influence over what is being procured. The procurement scheme in Figure 10.1 also covers the 'downstream' procurement roles of contractors and suppliers. The idea of responsible sourcing is key to these roles, and new guidance for responsible sourcing in construction (BRE Global Ltd, 2014) provides a framework for this. This guidance also aims to support the certification of construction products against sustainability criteria, which are slightly adapted from those in BS8900:2006 and BS 8902:2009, and supports the achievement of BREEAM and other environmental assessment system ratings in relation to materials usage on construction projects.

### 10.4.3   Sustainable construction procurement: key elements

The seven steps in the sustainable procurement process in BS 8903 adopted by Berry and McCarthy (2011) for construction are summarised in Table 10.1.

**Table 10.1**  Key steps in the sustainable procurement process.

| Key step/stage | Aims |
|---|---|
| Identify the business need | Establish need and whether procurement can fulfil it. Identify key business and sustainability requirements and risks. Challenge recent purchases and identify potential for improvement through innovation. |
| Define the sourcing strategy | Understand the market and evaluate potentially valuable procurement solutions. Select the most appropriate procurement approach. |
| Identify suppliers and selection process/tender | Identify and, if appropriate, pre-qualify potential suppliers. Develop selection/tender processes and invite proposals/bids. |
| Evaluate and award | Evaluate proposals/bids against business and sustainability requirements. Negotiate/agree contract terms. Confirm the award. |
| Implement | Support mobilisation of the successful supplier. Confirm and establish contract management and review process, linked to sustainability requirements. |
| Manage performance and relationships | Work with suppliers to manage performance against agreed goals. Identify sustainable improvement opportunities. |
| Review and learn | Review, capture and share feedback and learning to ensure it helps improve future performance. |

Adapted from BS 8903:2010 (BSI, 2010a) and Berry and McCarthy (2011).

These steps provide a structured and managed approach for identifying and securing desired sustainable outcomes through procurement. Considerably more detailed guidance for each key step is provided in BS 8903:2010 (BSI, 2010a). As Berry and McCarthy (2011) note, 'sustainable procurement is just good procurement', embedding sustainability considerations into the process alongside others such as price and quality (p. 78).

### 10.4.4   Progress with adoption

As far as we are aware, no comprehensive assessment has yet (early 2017) been undertaken on the adoption of sustainable procurement at a national level in the UK. A number of studies have examined aspects of the implementation of sustainable procurement in, variously, the UK public sector (NAO, 2009a, 2013; Walker and Brammer, 2009), UK local government (e.g. Thomson and Jackson, 2007; Wilkinson and Kirkup, 2009), across the public sector internationally (Brammer and Walker, 2011) and also in the private sector also (e.g. Srivastava, 2007). The recent UK NAO (2013) review notes that very little information is available to measure the extent to which UK central government departments are complying with the government's procurement aims and standards. The NAO also note that these standards are not universally applied across the wider public sector. While they present some evidence of progress and good practice in key areas, the overall picture is of a partial adoption of sustainable procurement across government activities (with 9 out of 15 departments reporting compliance with government procurement standards, and only three recording the production of sustainable procurement strategy and/or guidance).

In construction, there is an emphasis on reporting case studies of sustainable procurement practice rather than more general assessments of progress with adoption across the sector as a whole. For example, Bowen *et al.* (2009) discuss the specific case of public sector procurement in South African construction as an enabling mechanism in the country's construction reform programme. Berry and McCarthy (2011) also present case studies of the identification and management of sustainability requirements on major construction projects in the UK, as well as cases covering supply chain procurement. Hartwell (2013) similarly outlines general principles of 'good' procurement practice and presents case studies of three UK construction projects to help illustrate general environmental benefits. While Jones (2014) examines the procurement policies of eight major UK-based building contractors – concluding, *inter alia*, that their adoption of sustainable procurement was driven significantly by the requirements of public procurers in particular – there appears less by way of overall assessments of sustainable procurement in construction than, say, across the public sector more generally. However, Ruparathna and Hewage (2015), in a survey of the Canadian construction industry, find limited evidence of the adoption of sustainable procurement, citing a lack of consideration of sustainability criteria in bid evaluation as a major drawback.

Of course, the development of good practice for sustainable procurement in construction is in its relative infancy, with key guidance material no more than 5 or 6 years old. In an industry not noted for its rapid adoption of innovation and new practice, it may be expected that widespread implementation of sustainable procurement will take some time yet. Indeed, the UK government, in a joint government/industry strategy to 2025 (HM Government, 2013) recognises the potential for progress and identifies 'low carbon' construction as a key strategic priority for the sector (see Chapter 1). Further, it considers improvement in client capability and procurement as a key driver of the change necessary to make progress in this priority area. For that to happen, the important features of construction identified earlier in this chapter that inhibit more sustainable practices need to be addressed. In our look ahead, not only to 2025 but beyond through to 2050, we now consider the future of sustainable construction procurement in the light of these challenges.

## 10.5    Looking ahead to 2050: meeting key challenges

### 10.5.1    Construction in 2050: a more sustainable sector?

A number of other chapters in this book identify a range of possible sustainable futures for construction to 2050. HM Government (2013) in the Construction 2025 strategy, see construction as a key driver of growth through the design, construction and maintenance of sustainable built assets that 'deliver genuine whole life value for customers' (p. 18). On a shorter time horizon, the UK Government sets out an action plan (to 2020) for its part in improving construction by developing its capability as a key industry client. They emphasise the role of 'collaborative procurement'. This involves early supply chain involvement and skills development in achieving better whole-life performance (Infrastructure and Projects Authority, 2016: 9–11[1]). The Construction Industry Training Board (CITB, 2015) echoes the Construction 2025 goal of improving the sustainability performance of built assets. With a focus on labour supply and skills development to 2030, it highlights a number of challenges to be addressed, including a shift from direct employment to self-employment, a lack of collaboration along lengthy supply chains, and a marked resistance to change across construction, among other issues. More broadly, the World Economic Forum (2016) sets out a future vision of a global construction sector that relies strongly on effective collaboration between key stakeholders to exploit new technologies to improve the lifecycle performance of built assets. The role of public procurement is key to achieving this vision, involving in particular the management of project pipelines, the implementation of transparency and anti-corruption standards, and the use of 'innovation friendly' and whole-lifecycle oriented procurement.

Clearly, different prognoses of the construction sector's future development are always likely to identify different goals and opportunities for action. However, there is considerable agreement in these positive and aspirational visions of the sector's future. Also, such agreement is not only in the broad direction of development, towards a collaborative, innovative future where construction delivers valuable built assets that perform well in sustainability terms: it is in much of the detail and in the identification of challenges to be overcome. As we argued earlier in this chapter, a construction industry that is sustainable is also an industry where:

- price is considered in the context of whole-life performance
- collaborative working along construction supply chains and across tiers of subcontracting is supported and effective

---

1  Note that the Infrastructure and Projects Authority focuses exclusively on government action and differs from Construction 2025, which is a joint industry/government strategy.

- people are treated fairly and with dignity, their personal development is addressed and they are employed on a sustainable basis
- materials are sourced responsibly, paying attention to reducing/avoiding undesirable social, environmental and economic impacts along the supply chain
- opportunities for bribery and corruption are reduced and where possible avoided altogether.

While improving the construction sector in these terms will not resolve all of its shortcomings, it would achieve very significant progress on the path to a more sustainable future. We now turn to consider how these goals may be addressed through procurement. Our specific focus is on potential improvements in the practice and governance of procurement that will help improve the sustainability of construction projects and construction businesses/organisations through to 2050.

We have noted the generally slow pace of change in many aspects of construction practice and performance in the past 50 years or so, despite repeated calls for reform (e.g. Green, 2011). Given that 2050 is, at the time of writing, just over 30 years away, it may be tempting to think that no significant change can be effected in that timescale. Certainly, many of the changes required for more sustainable procurement in construction challenge not only some of the sector's more deeply embedded practices, but also elements of its financial and contractual structures. A shift in thinking is needed in relation to construction procurement. Fundamentally, it should focus much more on what clients wish to achieve, rather than on what construction is prepared to deliver. Arguably, productivity improvement and innovation in construction have been stifled because the market has been constrained by a strong emphasis in procurement on what the supply side wishes to offer. Ways of working have evolved that have changed little in decades, although recent developments perhaps change this emphasis. For example, the Achieving Excellence guidance (OGC, 2007) as well as British Standards BS 98534 and BS 8903 (BSI, 2010a, 2011a) shift the emphasis more towards the need to *understand* client requirements, using this as the primary driver of effective procurement processes that will achieve them.

Our vision for construction in 2050 therefore is of a sector that has increasingly adopted these approaches and transformed itself into an agent for implementing change with a clear client focus, rather than one focused primarily on delivery and assembly processes involving the procurement of low-cost materials and labour. We make the following suggestions for improvement that support this vision and help address the key challenges we have identified.

## 10.5.2 Client-driven procurement policies

In any dictionary, procurement is about acquiring or buying, so it would seem that the client has a stronger role than merely supporting exhortations to conform to serious policy objectives. The calls for sustainable sourcing of materials and labour, for example, should apply primarily to the way that clients put demand to the industry. Responsible procurement requires clients of the industry to be clear about what they are willing to pay for. The tradition of selecting suppliers based on price alone was appropriate when there were no qualitative differences between suppliers. But does this still apply to the modern construction sector where contractors and specialists seek to create competitive advantage?

One aspect of the client focus is to think about demand management. To what extent does the client think about the timing of a major project in relation to how busy the market happens to be at any point in time? The UK government, for example, now publishes capital expenditure plans in advance (see, for example, Infrastructure and Projects Authority, 2016) in an attempt to help the supply side to plan for employment, training and investment. In a modern, collaborative industry, to what extent can other clients encourage sustainable behaviours by making commitments to the supply side that would enable sustainable practices? The counter argument to this is to ask how can clients possibly expect contractors, designers and specialists to build up collaborative supply chains for regular streams of work as long as they have to bid on price alone for irregular streams of work?

One key part of a vision for 2050 is the idea of all major clients, not only governments, offering clarity on their pipeline of major projects so that major suppliers can equip themselves to respond to future demand. Commitments should therefore flow in both directions.

### 10.5.3   Price and competition in the context of whole-life performance

Although lowest price tendering has long been seen as a contributor to the industry's poor performance record, it is not clear that simply changing the nature of the competition will provide a suitable panacea. Rather, it may be better to think about how clients put demand to the market than how the supply side may prefer demand to be put to it. Two approaches in particular place client need more directly at the heart of the procurement process: first, *performance-based contracting*, where the supply side is paid for the performance/outcome of what they provide, rather than what it is made of; and, second, the concept of *total cost of ownership*, which takes account of the cost of assets over their entire lifecycles. These approaches combined provide the potential to change the supply-side emphasis from the cost of what is provided to value in the client's terms.

Traditionally, construction can be procured on the basis of specifications developed at a point well before contractors and subcontractors become involved. Specifications are part of a design process that is carried out by a team that is independent of the constructors. Procurement is structured around the provision of labour and materials to meet these specifications, and construction is paid for as work progresses. Indeed, payment for work in progress has become enshrined in construction-specific legislation. Performance-based contracting in construction replaces this emphasis on supplying the specified components that go to make up a building, with a focus on meeting the need that the building is meant to fulfil. Procuring construction in this way essentially transfers the operational liability for a building to the contractor who provides it. In this way, clients are not involved in the design, specification and construction processes, but in procuring (and paying) for the required building function and operational performance only after construction has been completed and the building commissioned.

Hughes and Kabiri (2013) discuss the potential benefits of such an approach, including the potential for the supply side to be more innovative. Moreover, because contractors will have to invest more in design and construction processes before their client pays for these services, design, construction and operations become more integrated as a matter of course. Hughes and Kabiri also identify a range of challenges, including the need for the supply side to fund design and construction work (foregoing payment until the operational phase of buildings), how the supply side may need to change from product installation to service provision and what new contractual and other arrangements are required to support these changes. A key challenge is the capital required to fund design and construction, and the associated risks. In an earlier work Gruneberg *et al.* (2007) suggest that, in general, construction companies have the assets to be able to take on the risk of such performance-based contracting. Hillig and Hughes (2008) have analysed the legal position in relation to construction contracting in English law, challenging the idea that the implications for how contracting businesses are structured present insurmountable difficulties.

Of course, there are elements of performance-based contracting in the contemporary construction market, most visibly since the advent of the private finance initiative (PFI) and related arrangements (NAO, 2009b) and in other areas also, including highway maintenance work, school refurbishment and energy performance contracting. Hughes and Kabiri (2013) identify valuable insights from many of the known approaches, concluding that progress has been somewhat patchy and, crucially, has not led to significant change in how business is transacted in the construction sector. One key feature of approaches such as PFI is that they are dependent on third-party funding. The key to aligning risks and rewards with those who produce elements of buildings is in supply-side investment, rather than debt-financing for special purpose vehicles. Fundamentally, the challenges for firms to make a transition from product 'manufacturer' to service provider are considerable, not only in terms of existing organisational and contractual structures, but in access to capital and attitude to risk.

Nonetheless, the potential remains for performance-based contracting to provide a workable basis for shifting the emphasis in procurement onto what clients want. To be effective, clients need to recognise and value the potential for innovation from the supply side, seeking to benefit from this by specifying what they want to achieve rather than how it is to be provided. This would require the supply side to find a way of funding the risk of providing it. This may involve reducing the role of consultants as mediators between clients and suppliers of construction services. Looking ahead to 2050 and beyond, both need to commit to a future where procurement is about performance and benefits rather than supply and costs.

### 10.5.4 Collaborative working along the construction supply chain

The growth of subcontracting is, perhaps, an inevitable consequence of discontinuities in demand for construction work and of the technical complexity of construction projects, requiring increasing specialisation in design and manufacture/installation. Regardless, the existence of multiple subcontracting 'tiers' on modern construction projects complicates procurement and creates challenges for how the supply side might find a way to focus more on delivering performance through, for example, performance-based contracting across all of its supply tiers. Additionally, the separation of responsibilities for design and construction has long been seen as an impediment to innovation and good performance in project delivery, amongst other things.

Against this background, the need for greater collaboration, both across multiple supply/subcontracting tiers and between designers and constructors, as a key to improved performance, is widely recognised. However, simple exhortations for more effective collaboration among supply-side participants have not been sufficient to encourage the required collaborative behaviour. The sector's entrenched practices and institutions are often seen as significant barriers to improvement. While a detailed treatment of collaboration is beyond the scope of this chapter, we note one particular opportunity for improvement that lies in a new approach to liability insurance in construction, involving a shift in responsibility away from individual design and construction team members and onto the team as a whole.

Current insurance arrangements within UK design and construction teams – whereby each member is individually liable for their own negligence and error, and insures accordingly – can promote loss avoidance behaviour among them. This does not directly support team-working, problem-sharing and the joint pursuit of project goals that are believed to be essential to effective collaborative working on construction projects (Cabinet Office, 2012). A new approach to project insurance (integrated project insurance (IPI); see Integrated Project Initiatives Ltd, 2014; Cabinet Office, 2014) has the potential to encourage a more collaborative approach among team members. The IPI approach provides single insurance cover for the construction project team as a whole – designers, constructors and key specialists/suppliers – and covers all their liabilities. By bringing team members together into a virtual organisation the aim is to provide a structure within which they can work more effectively together and help unlock their collective creative and problem-solving potential.

Such single project insurance is more common outside the UK in other, mainly European construction markets that have a different legal basis for design and construction liability. Its relevance here is not only about the provision of insurance for the construction team as a 'virtual company', but primarily because it has been developed as an approach to procurement geared towards aligning supply-side members' interests with those of the client. It aims to do this by, amongst other things, selecting team members on the basis of their potential to work collaboratively, creating an 'alliance' of client and team members to oversee project delivery, supported by a form of alliance contract, and insuring the team as a single entity for all liabilities, including design, construction, defects and the potential for the project to overrun in terms of cost and/or programme (Integrated Project Initiatives Ltd, 2014).

At the time of writing (early 2017) a trial of the IPI approach is currently underway on a live construction project (Constructing Excellence, 2016) and it is too early to say how effective the approach might be. It is noteworthy, however, that the first IPI policy in the UK has been placed on this trial project, indicating a willingness by insurers to support the approach (Knutt, 2016). By shifting construction participants' individual liabilities onto the design and construction team as a whole, IPI provides a novel way of supporting more collaborative working, not only between designers and constructors, but across different levels/tiers of supply also, depending, of course, on how the alliance is constituted and how extensive it is when the project is being established. Exploiting the potential of such collaboration is crucial if construction is to make the transition from simply supplying in accordance with a specification to understanding what clients want to achieve. Making this understanding an essential pre-condition for being included in the team is one recipe for encouraging innovative thinking in relation to meeting client needs.

### 10.5.5    Treating people fairly in the context of labour casualisation

The effectiveness and development of the construction labour force is high on the agenda for debate in the UK construction sector. Concerns about productivity (Green, 2016), skill development (Institute for Employment Research, 2012; CITB, 2015) and the overall structure and performance of the sector's 'labour model' (Farmer, 2016) are all part of this agenda. Recommendations for improvement cover a broad range of opportunities for action at both policy and industry levels, but the potential role of improved procurement practices is often overlooked. Labour casualisation carries inherent risks of exploitation of vulnerable workers in terms of low pay, poor welfare conditions and limited prospects for personal development. There is a significant opportunity to address some of these key concerns by encouraging suppliers to provide improved labour conditions as a pre-cursor to doing business.

The role of procurement in helping to improve labour conditions and, ultimately, performance is not new, of course, and is widely recognised as an opportunity for public sector procurers in particular (see, for example, Bell and Usher, 2007). Recommendations tend to focus on the use of recognised, responsible sourcing and ethical procurement approaches (e.g. Fair Labor Association, 2015) that prioritise safeguarding workers' rights and welfare) and, indeed, compliance with relevant legislation, such as the UK's Modern Slavery Act 2015. These will, no doubt, help reduce the potential for worker exploitation, and we expect increasing adoption of such practices through to 2050. However, safeguarding basic rights and working conditions is not enough for a more sustainable construction sector. Of interest also is how procurement might help alleviate the lack of opportunities for personal and professional development that are brought about by excessive casualisation.

The core theme of this 'looking ahead' section – requiring a shift in emphasis in procurement onto what clients want to achieve – ultimately requires a more consolidated and collaborative response from the construction supply side. One way this may be realised is through the development of more vertically integrated supply structures either through strong collaborative arrangements across tiers of subcontracting/supply or via a single ownership structure typically found in other industries. While such vertical integration is not very common in the construction sector, the growth of off-site manufacture and prefabrication (Miles and Whitehouse, 2013) is one way in which this might be achieved, and provides a basis from which some of the negative consequences of casualisation may be avoided. Farmer (2016) acknowledges that vertical integration could help with labour force development, but notes a significant challenge in the lack of a sufficient and consistent level of demand for construction, which constrains the supply side's willingness to invest. However, larger clients are recognising the potential value to them of more strategic client/supplier alliances, and of publishing details of their forward investment programmes so that the supply side may have more confidence in future work volumes (Infrastructure and Projects Authority, 2016).

Our vision of a more sustainable construction sector by 2050 is of one where greater visibility of demand from major clients is matched by an integrated approach to supply that, amongst other things, invests in providing more secure, valuable and rewarding jobs for its workforce. This is not something that the supply side can do alone. Major clients carry a responsibility for creating a more predictable regime of demand.

### 10.5.6 Materials procurement, responsible sourcing and intermediation in materials supply

Important developments in 'responsible sourcing', with a strong focus on materials sourcing and procurement in recent years, point the way towards more sustainable approaches for the construction sector. This 'greening of the supply chain' has involved the development and adoption of largely voluntary systems of accreditation and certification designed to demonstrate good environmental management and governance in materials sourcing and production along the supply chain (see, for example, BS 8902:2009; BSI, 2009). The use of many of these schemes has been encouraged by (similarly voluntary) building-level environmental assessment and certification schemes that require the specification and procurement of materials that are produced in an environmentally friendly way. These latter schemes include BREEAM in the UK and LEED in the USA as well as a wide range of comparable schemes in other countries (for an overview see Cole, 2005). Indeed, responsible procurement guidance (such as BES 6001; BRE Global Ltd, 2014) and more general sustainable procurement guidance and standards (such as BS 8903:2010; BSI, 2010a) also support the adoption of responsible materials sourcing systems, although the extent of the use of these approaches is unclear.

The growing adoption of material/product certification schemes by consumers and procurers has led to a proliferation of schemes which should, generally, support progress towards more sustainable procurement. However, while the range of certification schemes across different material/product categories has increased, so has the number of schemes within similar categories. In some areas there are now many similar schemes for the same basic materials that differ by country of origin, industrial subsector, material form and a range of other factors. Environmental certification schemes for timber, many of which are among the more advanced for standard-setting and governance in the construction sector (Auld *et al.*, 2008) are a good example of this. Interestingly, despite such growth, the success of these schemes in developing markets for sustainable timber appears to have been somewhat limited (Irland, 2007), although it is not particularly clear whether this is related to the variety of schemes available. Regardless, the point here is that while these schemes are meant to support and simplify sustainable procurement, the range and lack of direct comparability of many of them adds complexity and, potentially, confusion to procurement decisions.

This is a significant challenge for the development of more sustainable procurement in construction as the proliferation of these largely voluntary, market- or industry-driven certification schemes and associated guidance is set to continue, creating something of a minefield for procurers. One way of addressing this could be through some form of regulatory intervention, a point returned to in the conclusions section below. Another could be through the provision of independent advice on the robustness and comparability of the different schemes. This is perhaps what the UK government had in mind when establishing a Central Point of Expertise on Timber (CPET) in 2004 to provide advice and support to public sector procurers about the sustainable sourcing of timber. The CPET regularly reviewed certification schemes (see, for example, CPET, 2010) and, while the service ended in 2016, it reflected a growing need for independent advice for procurers on the appropriateness and robustness of available certification schemes.

Looking ahead to 2050, it is possible to envisage the growing adoption of a more systematic approach to materials procurement, using recognised responsible sourcing principles (such as in BES 6001; BRE Global Ltd, 2014) that should help procurers establish basic standards to evaluate the various certification schemes available. Additionally, the provision of independent advice – possibly through procurers' own trade organisations or procurement consortia – could provide considerable support for procurement decisions. Further, a lack of comparability between certification schemes could be addressed if the organisations involved adopted more standardised approaches as envisaged under BS 8902:2009 (BSI, 2009). Indeed, there is a potentially significant role for building materials distributors ('merchants') in this future. As noted, these are increasingly large and powerful organisations providing an intermediate 'market making' function between materials/product manufacturers and building contractors. They could encourage a more consistent response from producers to the efforts of contractors to source and procure more responsibly. They could facilitate the provision of advice on many of the different certification schemes available to enable their contractor customers to make more informed and sustainable procurement decisions. They could also promote the adoption of more consistent certification approaches as envisaged under BS 8902:2009 (BSI, 2009) to help improve comparability and consistency among them. In these ways – and others – builders' merchants could reinforce the positive benefits of intermediation in materials supply and support the longer-term goal of more sustainable construction procurement.

### 10.5.7   Avoiding bribery and corruption

Looking forward to 2050, it is difficult to see the construction sector's tendency to engage in corrupt practices disappearing entirely. However, it may be expected to diminish if other improvements in construction procurement highlighted in this chapter – particularly the adoption of more sustainable procurement approaches (such as BS 8903:2010; BSI, 2010a), together with a reduction in emphasis on lowest price tendering, use of more collaborative arrangements and the adoption of responsible sourcing – can be achieved over a sustained period. Additionally, the adoption of more general guidance on good corporate/organisational governance, such as BSI's Code of Practice for delivering effective governance of organisations (BS 13500:2013; BSI, 2013) will support businesses that want to change. More specifically, it is important to recognise the threat of corruption, and to address it explicitly through new practices and management arrangements – the available guidance is extensive, including the BSI's Specification for an anti-bribery system (BS 10500:2011; BSI, 2011b) and, more specifically for construction, the Global Infrastructure Anti-Corruption Centre's (GIACC) Project Anti-Corruption System (GIACC, 2009).

The availability of voluntary guidance will help those organisations that wish to change, although they will be much less effective for those that do not recognise the need, or the benefits. Government plays a key role in this area, of course, and already there is specific anti-bribery legislation in the UK (The Bribery Act, 2010) prohibiting a range of corrupt business practices, as well as procurement legislation (principally under EU Procurement Directives) that governs many public procurement practices. In addition to enforcing compliance, government is also active in encouraging anti-corrupt business behaviour (HM Government, 2014), although this could perhaps go further in the period to 2050 to promote more sustainable procurement.

One idea is to mandate the adoption of certain practices by the supply side as a pre-condition for access to public procurement. This has been done for building information modelling (BIM), where the UK government set a target for all new public works procurement to be on the basis of BIM Level 2 (BIM Working Party, 2011) by 2016. Regardless of whether the 2016 deadline has been achieved, the BIM mandate appears to have motivated businesses to accelerate their adoption of BIM technology. Although it is not entirely clear whether this would have happened in any event, by setting a target in the foreseeable future, government has generated considerable debate and activity around preparedness for BIM adoption (but see Chapter 16 for a more sceptical perspective on progress in BIM).

A similar target for the adoption of good governance and responsible sourcing along the construction supply chain could also motivate debate and lead to action to promote more sustainable construction. Indeed, government could consider more active enforcement through the greater regulation of the public procurement process in particular, to ensure that desired standards are followed and to set an example for private procurement to follow. This point is returned to in the conclusions section below.

## 10.6   Conclusions

It is interesting to see how the sustainability agenda, among other things, has created a fundamental shift in how good business practice is defined. Not too long ago, the test of a successful business was predominantly in the measure of profits and shareholder dividends. This has changed in many industry sectors and in many businesses. Greater awareness of the need for development and growth to be sustainable, together with the growing acceptance by business of its responsibilities for the environment and to society (via concepts such as corporate social responsibility) have re-shaped business goals. These developments have also re-shaped the relationships that businesses have with their employees, shareholders, suppliers and a wider community of stakeholders.

Procurement is a key mechanism through which businesses and other organisations not only can help implement their sustainability goals, but influence the behaviour and performance of others. Especially in construction, with its traditions of price competitiveness, multi-tiered supply chains and exploitative practices, procurement – whether led by clients or by contractors/suppliers at points along the supply chain – has a crucial role to play in putting the sector on a more sustainable footing through to 2050.

Fundamental to this is a shift in emphasis in procurement that is away from delivery and assembly processes involving low-cost materials and labour, towards a focus on understanding and meeting client needs through innovation and effective service delivery. In this new world, a greater emphasis on performance as the basis for construction contracts, greater collaboration between designers, contractors and suppliers, more vertically integrated supply, the adoption of responsible sourcing, developing new methods of collaborative selection to replace traditional approaches to tendering, and renewed efforts to remove opportunities for corruption all have the potential to deliver significant improvement. Key to this is the more widespread adoption of standards for more sustainable procurement.

Good standards already exist, of course, notably BS 8534:2010 and BS 8903:2011, and a new international standard on sustainable procurement is, at the time of writing, being developed: ISO 20400 *Sustainable procurement – Guidance.* ISO 10845 (BS1 2010b, 2011c) is currently under revision to incorporate BS 8534:2010. A key question, however, is 'What will motivate adoption of these standards?' While some increasing take up may be expected as standards become established and more visible internationally, strategic intervention by government could play a significant role. Targeting the adoption of standards in public construction procurement in particular is one option, setting clear dates for achievement and precluding non-conforming participants from public construction business. Although it is tempting to think that more targeted regulation may be another, perhaps the focus should be more on individuals, business and public organisations.

In a future where the UK's position in international markets is uncertain, individuals and businesses are tending to make up their own minds about what is good for them and for society. Increasingly, buyers of all kinds of products are making ethical choices that extend beyond their immediate transactions to all of the transactions in a supply chain and in a product's lifecycle. The political scene in many regions renders calls for government intervention and market regulation hollow and ineffectual. But empowering ordinary people to make decisions about their own impact on the environment, whether locally, regionally or globally, requires transparency and influence in relation to decision-making. Construction and infrastructure affect everyone in myriad ways. The opportunities for transforming procurement that are offered in this chapter will help empower all stakeholders in the acquisition and supply of facilities. The underlying agenda brings the users and creators of built facilities closer together in a way that demands disintermediation, localism and long-term thinking. Such policies may yet enable us to witness a more productive, innovative and sustainable construction sector by 2050.

## References

Agapiou, A., Flanagan, R., Norman, G. and Notman, D. (1998) The changing role of builders' merchants in the construction supply chain. *Construction Management and Economics*, 16(3), 351–361. DOI: 10.1080/014461998372376.

Auld, G., Gulbrandsen, L. and McDermott, C. (2008) Certification Schemes and the Impacts on Forests and Forestry. *The Annual Review of Environment and Resources*, 33, 187–211.

Bell, S. and Usher, A. (2007) *Labour Standards in Public Procurement: Background paper for DFID Labour Standards and Poverty Reduction Forum, 23 May 2007.* Ergon Associates, London.

Berry, C. and McCarthy, S. (2011) *Guide to sustainable procurement in construction.* The Construction Industry Research and Information Association, London.

BIM Working Party (2011) *BIM – Management for value, cost and carbon improvement. A report for the Government Construction Client Group.* Constructing Excellence and the Construction Industry Council, London. Available at: http://www.bimtaskgroup.org/wp-content/uploads/2012/03/BIS-BIM-strategy-Report.pdf.

BIS (2013a) *UK Construction: An Economic Analysis of the Sector*, July 2013. Department for Business, Innovation and Skills, London.

BIS (2013b) *Supply Chain Analysis into the Construction Industry: A Report for the Construction Industry Strategy*, September 2013. Department for Business, Innovation and Skills, London.

Bowen, P., Edwards, P. and Root, D. (2009) Corporate social responsibility and public sector procurement in the South African construction industry, in Murray, M. and Dainty, A. (eds) *Corporate Social Responsibility in the Construction Industry*. Taylor and Francis, London, pp. 304–326.

BRE Global Ltd (2014) *BRE Environmental & Sustainability Standard. BES 6001: ISSUE 3.0 Framework Standard for Responsible Sourcing*. BRE Global Ltd, Watford.

Brammer, S. and Walker, H. (2011) Sustainable procurement in the public sector: an international comparative study. *International Journal of Operations & Production Management*, 31(4), 452–476.

BSI (2009) *BS 8902:2009, Responsible sourcing sector certification schemes for construction products – Specification*. British Standards Institution, London.

BSI (2010a) *BS 8903:2010, Principles and Framework for Procuring Sustainably – Guide*. British Standards Institution, London.

BSI (2010b) *BS ISO 10845-1:2010, Construction procurement – Part 1: Processes, methods and Procedures*. British Standards Institution, London.

BSI (2011a) *BS 8534:2011, Construction procurement policies, strategies and procedures. Code of practice*. British Standards Institution, London.

BSI (2011b) *BS 10500:2011, Specification for an anti-bribery management system*. British Standards Institution, London.

BSI (2011c) *BS ISO 10845-2, Construction procurement – Part 2: Formatting and compilation of procurement documentation*. British Standards Institution, London.

BSI (2013) *BS 13500:2013, Code of practice for delivering effective governance of organizations*. British Standards Institution, London.

Burke, C. and King, A. (2015) Generating social value through public sector construction procurement: A study of local authorities and SMEs, in Raidén, A.B. and Aboagye-Nimo, E. (eds) *Proceedings of the 31st Annual ARCOM Conference, 7–9 September 2015, Lincoln, UK*. Association of Researchers in Construction Management, pp. 387–396.

Cabinet Office (2012) *Government construction strategy: trial projects*. Cabinet Office, London. Available at: https://www.gov.uk/government/publications/government-construction-strategy-trial-projects.

Cabinet Office (2014) *New Models of Construction Procurement: Introduction to the Guidance for Cost Led Procurement, Integrated Project Insurance and Two Stage Open Book*. Cabinet Office, London. Available at: https://www.gov.uk/government/publications/new-models-of-construction-procurement-introduction.

Chan, P., Clarke, L. and Dainty, A. (2010) The dynamics of migrant employment in construction: can supply of skilled labour ever match demand?, in Ruhs, M. and Anderson, B. (eds) *Who Needs Migrant Workers? Labour Shortages, Immigration, and Public Policy*. Oxford University Press, Oxford, pp. 225–255.

CIOB (2015) *CIOB Perspectives: An Analysis of Migration in the Construction Sector*. Chartered Institute of Building, Bracknell.

CITB (2015) *Construction 2030 and Beyond: The Future of Jobs and Skills in the UK Construction Sector*. Construction Industry Training Board, London.

Cole, R.J. (2005) Building environmental assessment methods: redefining intentions and roles. *Building Research & Information*, 35(5), 455–467.

Constructing Excellence (2016) *Trial Project: Dudley Advance II: Integrated Project Insurance.* Constructing Excellence, London. Available at: http://constructingexcellence. org.uk/wp-content/uploads/2016/12/20161205-Trial-Projects-Dudley-College-Advance-ll-Case-Study-3-FINAL.pdf.

CPET (2010) *Evaluation of Category A Evidence: Review of forest certification schemes – Results.* Central Point of Expertise on Timber, London. Available at: https:// www.gov.uk/government/uploads/system/uploads/attachment_data/file/324576/2010_ Review_of_forest_certification_schemes_Final_report_December_2010.pdf.

DEFRA (2005) *Sustainable Development Strategy.* Department for Environment, Food and Rural Affairs, London.

DEFRA (2006) *Procuring the Future. Sustainable Procurement National Action Plan: Recommendations from the Sustainable Procurement Task Force.* Department for Environment, Food and Rural Affairs, London.

DEFRA (2010) *Sustainable procurement in government: guidance to the flexible framework DEF-PB13423 06/10.* Department for Environment, Food and Rural Affairs, London.

DEFRA (2014) *Guidance: Sustainable procurement tools.* Department for Environment, Food and Rural Affairs, London. Available at: https://www.gov.uk/guidance/ sustainable-procurement-tools.

Europe Economics (2010) *Evaluation of the impact of the OFT's investigation into bid rigging in the construction industry: A report by Europe Economics.* Office of Fair Trading, London. Available at: http://webarchive.nationalarchives.gov. uk/20140402142426/http://www.oft.gov.uk/OFTwork/publications/publication-categories/reports/Evaluating/oft1240.

European Commission (2016) *Buying Green! A handbook on green public procurement,* 3rd edn. Publications Office of the European Union, Luxembourg. Available at: http:// ec.europa.eu/environment/gpp/pdf/handbook.pdf.

Fair Labor Association (2015) *Principles of Fair Labor & Responsible Sourcing.* Fair Labor Association, Washington, DC. Available at: http://www.fairlabor.org/sites/default/files/ principles_fair_labor_responsible_sourcing_february_2015_0.pdf.

Farmer, M. (2016) *The Farmer Review of the UK Construction Labour Model.* The Construction Leadership Council, London. Available at: http://www.cast-consultancy. com/wp-content/uploads/2016/10/Farmer-Review-1.pdf.

GIACC (2009) *Project Anti-Corruption System.* Global Infrastructure Anti-Corruption Centre. Available at: http://www.giaccentre.org/project_anti_corruption_system_ home.php.

GLA Group (2006) The GLA Group Sustainable Procurement Policy. Greater London Authority Group, London. Available at: http://www.webarchive.org.uk/wayback/ archive/20061223120000/http://www.london.gov.uk/gla/tenders/docs/sustainable-procurement.pdf.

Green, S. (2011) *Making Sense of Construction Improvement.* Wiley-Blackwell, Chichester.

Green, B. (2016) *Productivity in Construction: Creating a Framework for the Industry to Thrive.* Chartered Institute of Building, Bracknell.

Gruneberg, S., Hughes, W. and Ancell, D. (2007) Risk under performance-based contracting in the UK construction sector. *Construction Management and Economics,* 25(7), 691–699. DOI: 10.1080/01446190601164097.

Hackett, M. and Statham, G. (2016) *The Aqua Group Guide to Procurement, Tendering & Contract Administration,* 2nd edn. Wiley-Blackwell, Chichester.

Hammond, E. and Wembridge, M. (2011) UK building materials sector faces competition probe. *Financial Times*, August 16.

Hartwell, J. (2013) Sustainable procurement, in Cotgrave, A. and Riley, M. (eds) *Total Sustainability in the Built Environment*. Palgrave-Macmillan, London, pp. 206–224.

Harvey, M. (2003) Privatization, fragmentation and inflexible flexibilization in the UK construction industry, in Bosch, G. and Philips, P. (eds) *Building Chaos: An International Comparison of Deregulation in the Construction Industry*, Routledge, London, pp. 188–209.

Hillebrandt, P. (2000) *Economic Theory and the Construction Industry*. Macmillan, London.

Hillig, J.-B. and Hughes, W.P. (2008) Ownership rights in performance-based contracting: a case study of English law, in Brown, S. (ed.) *Proceedings 2008 COBRA Conference, Dublin, Ireland, September 4–5.*

HM Government (2013) *Construction 2025. Industrial Strategy: government and industry in partnership*. HM Government, London.

HM Government (2014) *UK Anti-Corruption Plan*. HM Government, London. Available at: https://www.gov.uk/government/uploads/system/uploads/attachment_data/file/388894/UKantiCorruptionPlan.pdf.

Hughes, W. and Kabiri, S (2013) *Performance-based contracting in the construction sector: A report for Transport for London*. School of Construction Management and Engineering, University of Reading, Reading. Available at: http://centaur.reading.ac.uk/34767/1/Hughes-and-Kabiri.pdf.

Hughes, W.P., Hillebrandt, P.M., Greenwood, D.G. and Kwawu, W.E.K. (2006) *Procurement in the construction industry: the impact and cost of alternative market and supply processes*. Taylor & Francis, London.

Infrastructure and Projects Authority (2016) *Government Construction Strategy 2016–20 (March 2016)*. Infrastructure and Projects Authority (Crown Copyright), London.

Institute for Employment Research (2012) *Sector Skills Insights: Construction: Evidence Report 50*. UK Commission for Employment and Skills, London. Available at: https://www.gov.uk/government/uploads/system/uploads/attachment_data/file/304475/Sector_Skills_Insights_Construction_evidence_report_50.pdf.

Integrated Project Initiatives Ltd (2014) *The Integrated Project Insurance (IPI) Model: Project Procurement and Delivery Guidance*. Integrated Project Initiatives Ltd. Available at: https://www.gov.uk/government/uploads/system/uploads/attachment_data/file/326716/20140702_IPI_Guidance_3_July_2014.pdf.

Irland, L.C. (2007) Developing markets for certified wood products: greening the supply chain for construction materials. *Journal of Ecology*, 11(1), 201–216.

Ive, G.J. and Gruneberg, S.L. (2000) *The Economics of the Modern Construction Sector*. Macmillan, London.

Jones, A. (2014) Sustainable procurement: the challenge for contracting organisations. *Journal of TEE (Faculty of Technology, Engineering and the Environment)*, 1, 36–58. Available at: http://www.bcu.ac.uk/computing-engineering-and-the-built-environment/research/cebe-journal/issue-1.

Kenny, C. (2010) *Publishing Construction Contracts and Outcome Details: Policy Research Working Paper 5247*. World Bank, Washington, DC.

Knutt, E. (2016) Integrated project insurance: A non-confrontational approach. Construction Manager, 2 May. Available at: http://www.constructionmanagermagazine.com/agenda/integrated-project-insurance-non-confrontational-a/.

Laryea, S., Alkizim, A. and Ndlovu, T. (2013) The increasing development of publication on sustainable procurement and issues in practice, in Smith, S.D. and Ahiaga-Dagbui, D.D. (eds) *Proceedings of the 29th Annual ARCOM Conference, 2–4 September 2013, Reading, UK.* Association of Researchers in Construction Management, pp. 1285–1294.

Lowe, J. (2011) Concentration in the UK construction sector. *Journal of Financial Management of Property and Construction*, 16(3), 232–248.

Miles, J. and Whitehouse, N. (2013) *Offsite Housing Review.* Construction Industry Council, London.

NAO (2009a) *Addressing the environmental impacts of government procurement.* The Stationery Office, London.

NAO (2009b) *Performance of PFI Construction.* National Audit Office, London.

NAO (2013) *Sustainable Procurement in Government: Briefing for the House of Commons Environmental Audit Select Committee, February 2013.* National Audit Office, London.

OGC (2007) *Achieving Excellence in Construction Procurement Guide: Sustainability.* Office of Government Commerce, London. Available at: http://webarchive. nationalarchives.gov.uk/20110601212617/http://www.ogc.gov.uk/documents/ CP0016AEGuide11.pdf.

ONS (2016) *JOBS02: Workforce jobs by industry.* Available at: https://www.ons.gov.uk/ employmentandlabourmarket/peopleinwork/employmentandemployeetypes/datasets/ workforcejobsbyindustryjobs02.

Parker, S.C. (2004) *The Economics of Self-Employment and Entrepreneurship.* Cambridge University Press, Cambridge.

Pyper, D. and Dar, A. (2015) *Zero-hours contracts,* House of Commons SN/BT/6553. House of Commons Library, London. Available at: http://api.data.parliament.uk/ resources/files/50743.pdf.

Ruparathna, R. and Hewage, K. (2015) Sustainable procurement in the Canadian construction industry: current practices, drivers and opportunities. *Journal of Cleaner Production*, 109, 305–314.

Srivastava, S.K. (2007) Green supply-chain management: A state-of-the-art literature review. *International Journal of Management Reviews*, 9(1), 53–80.

Thomson, J. and Jackson, T. (2007) Sustainable procurement in practice: Lessons from local government. *Journal of Environmental Planning & Management*, 50(3), 421–444.

Tookey, J. and Chalmers, D. (2009) Corruption in the UK construction industry: Current and future effects, in Murray, M. and Dainty, A. (eds) *Corporate Social Responsibility in the Construction Industry.* Taylor and Francis, London, pp. 121–140.

Transparency International (2014) *Bribe Payers Index* 2011. Available at: http://bpi. transparency.org/bpi2011/results/.

Transparency International (2005) *Global Corruption Report 2005.* Available at: http:// www.transparency.org/news/pressrelease/a_world_built_on_bribes_corruption_in_ construction_bankrupts_countries_and.

UNEP (2007) *Buildings and Climate Change: Status, Challenges and Opportunities.* United Nations, Paris. Available at: http://wedocs.unep.org/handle/20.500.11822/7783.

UNEP (2012a) *The Impacts of Sustainable Public Procurement: Eight Illustrative Case Studies.* United Nations, Paris. Available at: http://www.scpclearinghouse.org/resource/ impacts-sustainable-public-procurement-eight-illustrative-case-studies.

UNEP (2012b) *Sustainable Public Procurement Implementation Guidelines: Introducing UNEP's Approach.* United Nations, Paris. Available at: http://www.scpclearinghouse.org/sites/default/files/10yfp-spp-guidelines.pdf.

Walker, H. and Brammer, S. (2009) Sustainable Procurement in the United Kingdom Public Sector. *Supply Chain Management*, 14(2), 128–137.

Wilkinson, A. and Kirkup, B. (2009) *Measurement of sustainable procurement.* East Midlands Development Agency, Nottingham.

Winch, G. (1998) The construction firm and the construction project: a transaction cost approach. *Construction Management and Economics*, 7(4), 99331–99345.

World Economic Forum (2016) *Shaping the Future of Construction: A Breakthrough in Mindset and Technology,*. World Economic Forum, Geneva. Available at: http://www3.weforum.org/docs/WEF_Shaping_the_Future_of_Construction_full_report__.pdf.

WSSD (2002) *Plan of Implementation of the World Summit on Sustainable Development.* United Nations, New York.

# 11

# Social Media in the Built Environment
*Bob Thompson*

## 11.1 Introduction

'Social media' is shorthand for a host of different applications, channels and platforms that facilitate interaction and networking amongst people and groups with a common interest. As an interface between consumers of goods and services and their provision, social media is about wider technological issues and how they influence the occupation and use of workspace.

This chapter explores what social media is currently and the factors affecting its rise to importance, pausing to look at the scale of the subject and how it affects the individual and the built environment. The built environment here refers to the man-made surroundings that provide the setting for human activity, ranging in scale from buildings and infrastructure to neighbourhoods and cities. The functional remit covers the entire lifecycle of a building from planning and development through design, construction, transaction and occupational management.

Historic drivers of social media are examined drawing out the links with broader technologies. Social media in its current form is then examined in more detail, breaking down the subject into different types of user interaction and exploring the growth and popularity of each.

Looking to the future, contextual analysis is undertaken to highlight the strategic issues and technologies that will affect social media in the future and future scenarios generated that challenge the technology.

### 11.1.1 What are social media?

Social media includes computer-mediated tools that allow the creation, sharing or exchange of information in virtual communities and networks. Kaplan and Haenlein (2010: 61) define social media as 'a group of internet-based applications that build on the ideological and technological foundations of Web 2.0, and that allow the creation and exchange of user-generated content'.

Social media depends on technology to create highly interactive platforms through which individuals and communities are able to share, discuss and modify user-generated

*Sustainable Futures in the Built Environment to 2050: A Foresight Approach to Construction and Development*, First Edition. Edited by Tim Dixon, John Connaughton and Stuart Green.
© 2018 John Wiley & Sons Ltd. Published 2018 by John Wiley & Sons Ltd.

content. Kietzmann and Hermkens (2011) suggest that it introduces substantial and pervasive changes to communication between businesses, organisations, communities and individuals.

Traditional media operates under a monologic transmission model (one source to many receivers). Social media operates in a dialogic transmission system (many sources to many receivers). This is important in that it facilitates and encourages individual, hitherto receivers of information to become initiators and providers of information.

### 11.1.2   The personal paradox

Social media platforms are essentially personal, but individuals are employed by companies, which may also have a social media presence. Personal branding describes the process by which individuals differentiate themselves by identifying and articulating their unique value proposition and then leveraging it across platforms with a consistent message and image. Research by Thompson (2014) amongst real-estate researchers found that 80% felt that their personal brand was important to their career, 71% to their professional status and 59% to their next job.

However, the overwhelming majority of people working in the built environment are discouraged by policy or contractually constrained from publishing opinion different to that of their employer. Companies, aware of the Dutch maxim that 'reputation arrives on foot but departs on horseback', are nervous about giving free rein to their employees or contractors to express their opinions freely.

It is instructive that only 36% of the real-estate researchers responding felt that they were trusted as ambassadors of the corporate brand (Thompson, 2014) and 48% did not know whether they were or not. Unsurprisingly only 38% of employers had a social media policy and only 22% actively encouraged staff to use social media.

### 11.1.3   Social media take-up

Research from Ofcom, the UK agency responsible for telecommunications, shows that more than seven in 10 adult internet users (72%) have a social media profile, and social media use is correlated to age. A majority of internet users aged 16–24 (93%), 25–34 (90%), 35–44 (80%) and 45–54 (68%) have a social media profile, such as a Facebook or Twitter account. This compares to 49% of 55–64-year-olds and 28% aged 65+ (28%) (Ofcom, 2015).

In addition to having the highest reach, Facebook has the highest frequency of use. A fifth of Facebook users (19%) claim to use the site over 10 times daily. Over 10% of Snapchat, Twitter and WhatsApp users also claim to use these sites over 10 times a day.

Young adults aged 16–24 make extensive use of social media. The majority (97%) of all adults aged 16+ with a social media profile say they use Facebook, and close to half (48%) of those with a profile say they have one only on Facebook.

There is significant take-up of social networking platforms among 12–15-year-olds. A significant proportion of teens aged 12–15 have used YouTube (81%), Facebook (72%), Instagram (55%), Snapchat (53%) and WhatsApp (48%).

The almost ubiquitous presence of social media underpins the use of these tools in almost all areas of business for communication with stakeholders but also to provide access to applications.

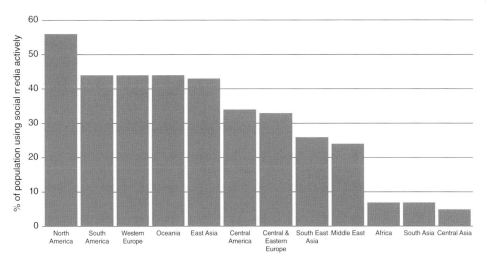

**Figure 11.1** Social media penetration by region, 2015 (Thompson (2014) using WeareSocial data).

Given the dominance of US products, the fact that social media penetration is highest in North America should be no surprise. Research from WeareSocial (2015) shows 29% of the world population are active users of social media but penetration in North America is as high as 56% and as low as 5% in Central Asia. Figure 11.1 shows social media penetration by region.

### 11.1.4  Social media and the built environment

Social media has had a profound effect on many aspects of how business is conducted and this has had an impact on how space is developed, transacted, occupied and managed. It is relevant to the built environment because it allows professional, functional and social networks to be built and sustained virtually, that is, without any spatial imperative. Using a networking platform, for example, it is possible to present content, discuss it and comment on it using a global network of professionals in real time, hardly incurring any environmental penalty at all.

The penetration of social media in the built environment varies markedly according to company and platform. Nor is it sufficient just to have a presence; to contribute, it needs to be used actively. Pauley (2014), for example, reports that 90% of the top 15 construction companies are active users of Twitter while only 45% are active on Linkedin and 30% on Facebook. Azhar and Abeln (2014) found construction companies to be using social media in the areas of recruitment, disseminating news, client networking, raising brand awareness and showcasing innovations. However, they also found that most companies had not explored the potential of social media and were only using it for sporadic, one-way communication. Brown (2012) reports that the biggest barrier to social media take-up lies at board and director levels. Most staff within organisations in the built environment will use social media in some personal capacity, which is a skill that should be harnessed corporately.

Some social media platforms are being used by some companies to improve the functionality of the built environment:

- **Rated People:** Founded in 2005, Rated People is an UK online trade recommendation service that connects homeowners with local tradesmen. Homeowners who are in need of a tradesman can post jobs free of charge and receive quotes from interested tradesmen. Homeowners who have found their tradesman through Rated People can leave ratings, so they are always based on genuine experiences from previous customers. These ratings allow other homeowners to hire a tradesman they can trust. The tradesmen can in turn use their ratings on Rated People to build their reputation and portfolio of local clients. The construction industry generally is beginning to use sites like this to find reputable tradesmen for commercial developments.
- **Facebook:** Although Facebook has evolved as an essentially personal networking system, it also contains many examples of Facebook sites set up to act as a focal point for information and communication about a particular physical building or service. For example, Aberdeen Universities Living in Halls Facebook page provides information on maintenance issues, events and living in student accommodation generally. Alternatively, the Empire State Building Facebook page gives general information about the attraction and is a gateway to purchasing tickets.
- **Linkedin:** LinkedIn's focus on professional networking makes it a natural home for construction and real-estate professionals networking within groups of interest. In February 2016, there were over 16,000 real-estate related groups on Linkedin. Many of these are in active use for referrals, transactions, research and recruitment.
- **Youtube:** Launched in May 2005, YouTube is a library of user-generated videos. The site provides a forum for people to connect and acts as a distribution platform for original content creators and advertisers. As of February 2016, YouTube has over a billion users and real-estate content ranging from 'How to get rich in real estate' through to training videos for real-estate managers, corporate promotional content and buildings for sale. The physical nature of the construction process makes the sector fertile ground for video. The Danish Construction channel, for example, hosts weekly updates of construction-related films.
- **Wikipedia:** In many respects Wikipedia has become a symbol of Web 2.0 – a collaborative project that has developed around the world to compile the knowledge and expertise of everyone. The software that underpins Wikipedia and any number of close copies are in use capturing industry and person-specific knowledge into a structured form for sharing. WikiRealty is an example of a wiki developed to provide hyper local information to buyers of real estate. As well as market information the site delivers news and user-generated content, and acts as a platform for listing property. Designing Buildings Wiki puts construction industry knowledge in one place and makes it freely available.

### 11.1.5 Social media and the workplace

The interaction between workplace and workspace has been the coal face for technology-enabled change. As individuals and work have become mobile, so workplaces have changed to accommodate the ideas of personal workspace. The key difference between workplace and workspace is that the latter is personal and therefore mobile, whereas the former is collective and fixed. By making this distinction, the old certainties of the workplace begin to break down. If work itself is mobile and can be undertaken anywhere, the role and organisation of a fixed workplace is called into question.

Despite increasing levels of mobility, workplaces that support the co-location of teams are still important for firms of any size. However, these spaces may not be owned or occupied on conventional lease terms, particularly by small companies. Social media in the workplace provides an additional layer of communication both internally and with external stakeholders. This is particularly relevant to a mobile workforce that may not be gathered in the same place at the same time.

## 11.2   Historic trends

There are five key trends that have combined to make the exponential growth of social media possible.

### 11.2.1   Web 2.0

The internet itself continues to evolve. In 2004, the term Web 2.0 was given form by Dale Dougherty as a new paradigm that was driving the post dot com structure forward. Social media makes heavy use of Web 2.0 principles. Web 2.0 is best described by a set of characteristics and principles that shape the way the whole internet is used. The web is seen as a platform for the delivery of services rather than just the delivery of information. At its heart is data that is dynamic and which can be recombined into different views depending on the user, the context or the transaction required.

This is important in that it is dialogue rather than monologue. Not only do users have the ability to put up content on their own behalf, but they have the ability to respond to content that they find either directly or through rating or recommendation. This is also a stern test of the quality of the content being produced since any flaws can be exposed instantly to a large, responsive audience outside the control of the content producer.

Because applications are entirely web based, it becomes much easier to share content, for example documents often have many authors. Collaboration tools are used to share texts in a shared environment for editing. This replaces an email to all the authors with the attendant problems of version control.

Web 2.0 democratises access: the same resources are available to all users. The one-person company has access to the same tools as the large corporation. Typically, these tools will appear as small applications that can be combined to suit individual circumstances. Because it is data-based, typical applications deliver better functionality the higher the critical mass. Networking websites would be fairly useless without a critical mass of networkers, for example.

### 11.2.2   Accessibility

UK data from Ofcom (2015) shows that the proportion of UK homes taking broadband services had grown to 78% by mid-2015. The same report shows that two-thirds of adults had a smartphone in 2015, compared with 39% in 2012. Fifteen per cent of all households in 2015 were mobile only, that is, they had no landline telephony at all.

Nearly a third (30%) of UK adults had access to 4G, the fourth-generation mobile communications standard. 4G users show significantly different online behaviour: they are more likely to go online more often, be more attached to their smartphones and do more 'data-heavy' activities online more often. 4G users are also more likely than smartphone owners without 4G access to use mobile internet outside the home.

### 11.2.3 Bandwidth

The availability of broadband to an ever-wider population has been an important trigger in the growth of the internet. In 2015, 83% of UK premises were able to receive a superfast broadband service. In the six years to November 2014 average actual fixed broadband speeds increased at an average annual rate of 36% per year, from 3.6 Mbit/s in November 2008 to 22.8 Mbit/s in November 2014 (although they are still lower in rural areas).

### 11.2.4 Mobility

The delivery of web services via mobile telephony and the rise in wifi coverage in urban areas have been important drivers. In 2015, the smartphone overtook the laptop as the device internet users say is the most important for connecting to the internet. Thirty-three per cent of internet users said their smartphone is the most important device for getting online, compared to 30% who cited their laptop. This marks a clear shift since 2014, when 23% cited their phone and 40% preferred their laptop.

Overall in 2015, smartphone users spent nearly 2 hours (114 minutes) using the internet on their mobile phone, nearly twice as much time as the average time spent going online via a PC or laptop (69 minutes). Ofcom report that smartphones are used for a range of non-communication based activities, including watching short video clips (42%), streaming television programmes or films (21%), making purchases online (45%) and online banking (44%).

### 11.2.5 Cultural change

Ofcom research (Ofcom, 2015) has been tracking internet use in the UK for 10 years. Over the decade to 2016 the time adults spend using the internet has increased substantially, both at home and elsewhere. The estimated number of hours spent online per week has more than doubled since 2005, from around 10 to over 20 hours.

Take-up of most online activities has increased since 2005. For example, there has been a noticeable increase in the use of the internet at least weekly for news (25–42%), and for banking and paying bills (31–42%).

A majority of internet users claim confidence in finding information on the internet and understand how search engines operate. The proportion of internet users who agree that they are confident at finding things online has remained the same since 2007 (91% vs 92%). Six in ten (60%) adults believe that some websites will be accurate and unbiased, while others won't be, close to the 2009 figure (54%).

The majority of internet users say they would share personal information online, but there is evidence of added caution in doing this over the 10 years of tracking. For example, six in 10 (60%) internet users say they would give out their home address online but have concerns about doing so, compared to 46% in 2005.

## 11.3   Classifying social media

In analysing the different components of what is described as social media, it becomes clear that there is often an overlap between functions that does not fit any rigid taxonomy easily. This is even less easy at the level of individual websites since, very often, they offer multiple facilities. Figure 11.2 describes the social media universe.

### 11.3.1   Content creation

#### 11.3.1.1   Blogging

Blogging simply allows the creation of content for publication and a platform upon which to publish. It has grown to become a powerful platform for placing corporate or personal opinions online.

Far from being hidden away in the back reaches of the net these blogs are indexed by the major search engines and therefore are firmly in the public eye to the point where, in some industries, bloggers themselves have become celebrities. In practice the whole range of quality is explored by these systems from the vacuous to the insightful.

Blogging is widely regarded as the future of journalism. The next generation of magazines, for example, is likely to be run by collections of bloggers working towards a central editorial theme rather than a team of traditional paper-based journalists. To manage the burgeoning universe of blogs, aggregation platforms have sprung up that index and group blogs by categories of interest.

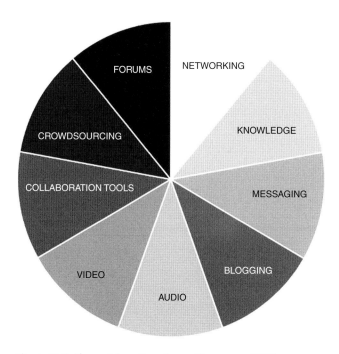

**Figure 11.2**   The social media universe (Thompson, 2014).

#### 11.3.1.2  Messaging

Instant messaging is a complex area in its own right, yet can be very powerful and influential. Most networking platforms have their own messaging capability but there are also standalone messaging services. Perhaps the best known of these are Twitter and Snapchat.

These two typify the different types of messaging. Twitter allows private messaging between individuals or broadcast messaging. The messages are retained. This makes it a useful platform for dissemination of information quickly and concisely. For example, Bruns and Burgess (2013) catalogue the use of Twitter as a primary source of information on the ground during the Christchurch earthquakes and the Queensland floods.

Snapchat also allows private messaging but is unique in that all photos and videos only last a brief amount of time before they disappear forever, making the app ephemeral in nature. As of May 2014, Snapchat users were sending 700 million snaps a day.

#### 11.3.1.3  Images

The history of moving pictures over the last 100 years is that they moved from being essentially amateur productions produced by enthusiasts to professionally produced movies, creating a whole industry in the process. The advent of cheap video cameras, by default included in a mobile phone, has moved the volume of content back in favour of the amateur. This is not necessarily a good thing, as the quality of much publicly available content shows, but it has changed the expectation of the audience.

The fact that video has become a commodity also has the effect of reducing production costs significantly, putting professional video within the reach of relatively small companies. Typically, it is difficult for the indexing engines to pick up video content, which has led to the growth of specialist video indexes such as YouTube that facilitate the use of video in viral marketing campaigns.

Sites such as Instagram serve the same function for still images. Here, the smartphone self-portrait or 'selfie' has established itself a form of self-expression. The Pew Research Center (2014) found 55% of US millenials had posted a selfie in the last year.

#### 11.3.1.4  Sounds

The sharing of music was, in many ways, the start of social media. Music had moved progressively from physical media such as records and tapes onto digital media like DVD and online but until 1999 the industry had managed largely to keep control of its distribution and therefore the usage royalties on which the industry was based – a classic monologic process. In 1999, the file-sharing system Napster was launched, allowing people to share their music files, and within a year the service had over 20 million users – dialogue had replaced monolog. The anarchy of the early file-sharing systems fitted in well with the purists' vision of Web 2.0 in which all resources are available to everyone at no cost. Now that music downloading has become institutionalised through sites like iTunes, pure audio is finding it difficult to compete with video. Podcasts have a ready outlet for portable delivery of information in circumstances where video is inappropriate. Again, to be useful, these need to be produced professionally.

## 11.3.2 Knowledge sharing

Sharing of knowledge is at the heart of Web 2.0 and manifests itself in the form of the generic Wiki in social media. A Wiki is a piece of software that allows users to create and edit Web page content using any Web browser.

### 11.3.2.1 Wiki

Wiki supports hyperlinks and has a simple text syntax for creating new pages and crosslinks between internal pages. Wikipedia is the best large example, but the principle is used to create special interest databases by allowing individuals to post content.

Clearly the quality of content can be an issue since many wikis are self-policing without any independent oversight. In his 1995 design ideas for wiki, Cunningham states:

> '**Trust** – This is the most important thing in a wiki. Trust the people, trust the process, enable trust-building. Everyone controls and checks the content. Wiki relies on the assumption that most readers have good intentions.' (Cunningham, 1995)

Wikis are cheap, extensible and easy to implement, and they don't require a massive software rollout. They also interface well with existing network infrastructures. Furthermore, wikis are Web-based and thus present little or no learning curve in the adoption cycle, and they allow the user to determine the relevancy of content rather than being dependent upon a central distribution centre or a linear distribution chain. After the initial setup, users, not administrators, control a wiki, to the benefit of both.

A major benefit of many wikis is their ability to organise themselves organically. In other words, users can create their own ontology, rather than have it imposed on them by the developers of content management software.

Wikis are best used by people with a shared cultural language so that the ontology and navigation make sense to everybody. Wikis are well-suited to the workplace because a common corporate language is already in place.

### 11.3.2.2 Crowdfunding

Crowdfunding is a form of alternative finance that has emerged outside of the traditional financial system. Crowdfunding is an initiative undertaken to raise money for a new project proposed by someone by collecting small investments from a crowd of other people (Ordanini, 2009). The growth in worldwide crowdfunding is shown in Figure 11.3.

Different players are involved in crowdfunding models:

- The proposers of projects to be funded. These want to use crowdfunding to get direct access to the market and to gather financial support.
- The crowd that decide to support these projects financially, risking capital in expectation of a return.
- The crowdfunding organisation that brings together the proposers and the crowd of potential investors using a social media platform.

Crowdfunding worldwide rose exponentially from under $1 billion in 2011 to over $34 billion in 2015 (Massolution, 2015). In 2014, the World Bank estimated that

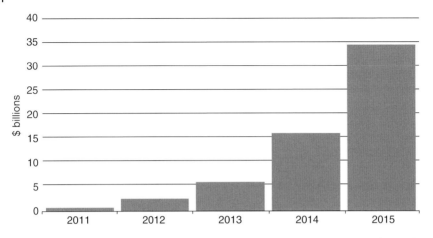

**Figure 11.3** Growth in worldwide crowdfunding (Thompson (2014) using Massolution data).

crowdfunding would reach $95 billion by 2025; on current rates of growth this would appear to be an underestimate.

Construction and real-estate examples of crowdfunding abound. CrowdProperty, for example, is a peer-to-peer lending platform designed to facilitate loans between private individuals and professional property businesses securing any loan by a registered first legal charge against the property.

BD Bacatá is a 67-storey hotel in Bogata, Colombia. By the time construction started in 2013, $170 million had been raised from 3800 investors to build what will be Colombia's tallest structure. This was the world's first crowdfunded skyscraper. Each of the investors in BD Bacatá owns equity shares in the project, and some have received returns exceeding 40% of their stakes.

### 11.3.2.3 Crowdsourcing

Crowdsourcing is where social media and the collaborative economy overlap. In its broadest sense, crowdsourcing is a distributed problem-solving model. Problems are broadcast to an unknown group of people – the crowd – who then submit potential solutions. The crowd can also rank the solutions. It is this ranking function that is most prevalent in social media, with sites that allow users to present and classify information that is then presented in rank order. TripAdvisor, for example, which encourages hotel users to review their stay, has become a key influencer in the industry.

Crowdsourcing is becoming a valuable tool in research and data collection. JISC (2016), in association with King's College, have developed the Strandlines project. This assembles documents that articulate the history of one of London's streets, The Strand. This site is an archive from which crowdsourced experiences, memories and reflections can be retrieved, a gallery where photographs, drawings and films can be viewed, and also a place where residents, workers and visitors can engage with one another by sharing stories and images.

Greenlancer provides online access to the solar system designs needed to build and install residential solar electric systems. The platform allows contractors to manage projects, get quotes and order services from one centralised place. For installers of solar energy systems, GreenLancer provides high-quality designs more quickly and cost-effectively than conventional design firms and works by pulling together designs from a specialist crowd of designers working on a project-by-project basis.

### 11.3.2.4 Forums

Forums and bulletin boards have been a feature of the internet since the early days of web sites. They have limited applications for soliciting crowd responses to specific questions – IT problems, for example – but general open-ended fora have never reached critical mass.

### 11.3.2.5 Networking

Networking is about building and maintaining a personal brand. While content creation is about the substance of the brand, networking is about the linkages that help to propagate it. When personal and corporate objectives are in alignment this is an extraordinarily powerful process. However, in the event of discord, it has the potential to be equally destructive.

The key point is that networking is under the control of the individual not the company. Consequently, a common corporate response is to bar employees from accessing networking sites in case they 'waste time'. However, this hides a number of other, more deeply rooted problems. First, applications such as Facebook or Linkedin are much more functional than the majority of internal networking applications. Their interfaces also tend to be in a different league, making them easier to use. Clearly there is an argument for embracing these tools rather than banning them. If, as a company, the expectation is that all employees are brand ambassadors, then this function should be encompassed within their job description.

However, this gives rise to the second problem – trust. Do companies trust their employees to be effective brand champions? Personal networking is not controllable at a corporate level but may be influenced by company behaviour. If companies treat employees well, the expectation would be that this would be reflected in personal networking. Similarly, employees who feel badly treated are unlikely to present a favourable image of their employer.

Different networking sites have evolved in different directions. Facebook and Myspace have grown as personal, fun sites on which to interact with friends. LinkedIn has grown to be much more commercially focused. All provide the functionality to build personal networks and participate in interest groups.

## 11.4 Future context

The context to the future growth of social media is one of change. Innovation in the provision of access to information and tools has accelerated genuinely disruptive change and in many cases social media platforms are the agents of that disruption. This is expected to accelerate over the next decade with social media representation of the trends in policy, economics, the social environment and technology all acting as drivers of change.

### 11.4.1 Policy

The relevant policy context for social media is that surrounding regulation of communications. Eric Schmidt, co-founder of Google, calls the internet 'the world's largest ungoverned space' and 'an experiment in anarchy' (Schmidt and Cohen, 2013: 1). It should be axiomatic that such a ubiquitous source of information should, at 25 years old, have matured into a controlled economic space. At one level, despite serious attempts to limit its content or access to it in different parts of the world, the internet remains a noisy anarchic teenager providing a rich virtual landscape of opportunity. The downsides are pornography and terrorist chatrooms.

In fact, the internet is a controlled economic space. The internet is operated by a conglomerate dominated by governments. In the 1990s, the US government set up the Internet Corporation for Assigned Names and Numbers (ICANN) to run the internet. It now keeps track of who owns which domain names and maintains various systems that underpin the internet. Nevertheless, a spirit of anarchy still remains.

Attempts to control the internet have always been contentious. In the UK, a new draft Investigatory Powers Bill makes explicit in law security services powers for the bulk collection of personal communications data. It also creates explicit powers to hack into and bug computers and phones. Further, it places a new legal obligation on companies to assist in these operations.

In the USA, the latest in a series of failed attempts to reform cybersecurity, the Cybersecurity Information Sharing Act, grants broad latitude to tech companies, data brokers and anyone with a web-based data collection to mine user information and then share it with 'appropriate Federal entities', which themselves then have permission to share it throughout the government.

The main policy challenges revolve around censorship, particularly by governments. However, censorship is a spectrum. It is difficult to object to the UK's practice of blocking child pornography but easier to decry the banning of websites showing political cartoons (India) or the blocking of any information critical of the regime (China).

Social media plays a role in circumventing censorship. Because of its distributed, local, mobile nature it is difficult to track or block. As a consequence, it is the protestor's tool of choice, facilitating the release of live information from any situation.

The internet is the theatre for economic competition, crime, conflict and struggles for basic rights such as privacy and expressive liberty. In response, governments and companies have struggled over the shape of the internet, promoting prescriptions that suit their particular interests and agendas. The policy paradigm for the internet is as a free, open and secure space.

In June 2008, ministers and stakeholders from OECD countries met in Seoul to consider the social, economic and technological trends shaping the development of the internet. They forged broad principles that can provide an enabling policy environment for the internet economy. This has become known as *The Seoul Declaration for the Future of the Internet Economy* (OECD, 2008). It outlines the basic principles that will guide further development of the internet economy.

The Seoul declaration was important because it recognised the pivotal role of the internet globally and its role in the generation of growth and opportunity across borders. Since 2008, the internet has grown and diffused rapidly across the globe. In parallel, social media platforms are transforming how social interactions, business and personal relationships are conducted.

In 2014, in response to pressure from the internet community, the US Government announced that it planned to transfer ICANN oversight to a group of international stakeholders by September 2015.

Underlying this initiative is the fundamental need to preserve the openness of the internet. The concept of an open platform where all the stakeholders work together to develop applications and services is at the heart of the development of social media. However, in recent years concerns have emerged that the open and decentralised architecture of the internet and the free flow of data across borders is not necessarily serendipitous, as the use of the internet by terrorist groups exemplifies. These concerns are likely to be important drivers of policy over the next decade and may act as a brake on the development of infrastructure, particularly in regions controlled by the more regressive regimes.

An open internet is of great importance to the built environment. Data has always played a profound role in the decision-making and engineering management processes within the built environment, whether at building, community or city scale. The interaction of people, places and processes is enhanced and accelerated by the provision of internet infrastructure.

## 11.4.2   Economy

The economic context for social media is complex. Clearly, access to the internet is often a function of affordability and there are many regions where that affordability is the preserve of very few of the population. Nevertheless, the globalisation of trade, information flows and technology has increased significantly. Barber (2016) points out that at the end of the Cold War in 1980 around 1 billion people lived in market economies. By 2016 that had grown to nearly 4 billion. Globalisation has made borders porous to information, foreign investment and popular culture, and social media has been both a promoter and beneficiary of this change.

Using social media in this environment means local interaction with data centers physically located in different countries and even different continents. Currently, Microsoft alone operates 22 data centres around the world, supporting its Cloud infrastructure. Posting a comment on Facebook in London implies a data transaction with Luleå in Sweden and probably one with San Francisco.

Not only does social media use a wider spatial context than real estate is used to but it implies different economic models as well. The collaborative economy involves using internet technologies to connect distributed groups of people to make better use of goods, skills and services. According to Botsman and Rogers (2010), it is built on 'distributed power and trust within communities as opposed to centralised institutions', blurring the lines between producer and consumer.

Social media, allied to the internet, has been a powerful driver of collaboration for two main reasons:

- It allows producers and consumers to communicate peer to peer. A knitter of socks can sell them directly to people with cold feet, for example, without going through a distributor – consumers needing lime green socks fashioned from alpaca wool can order them directly from a producer;
- It facilitates communication around a transaction. If a crowd is funding a project, progress updates can be sent or suggestions solicited with ease. Crowdfunding property investment, for example, is growing and is already prevalent in alternative investments such as car parking and hotels.

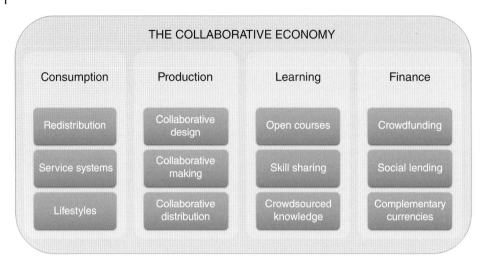

**Figure 11.4** The four pillars of the collaborative economy (Thompson (2014) after Stokes *et al.* (2014)).

These characteristics have facilitated the construction of collaborative businesses. In many cases, these involve connecting distributed people or assets without reference to a central organisation. In others, spare capacity, which would otherwise stand idle, can be made accessible and used more effectively.

The ability to share information easily makes it possible to generate trust. In its simplest form, this involves rating systems that allow hosts to vet their guests and guests their hosts, for example, building and maintaining reputation. But it can be more sophisticated too, for example crowdsourcing design ideas.

None of this is new in concept. Direct sales to consumers predate the industrial revolution and unhappy customers have always been able to write a letter of complaint. However, social media makes the process easier and more efficient as well as synchronous. Figure 11.4 shows the four pillars of the collaborative economy.

Stokes *et al.* (2014) propose a list of five collaborative economy traits:

1) enabled by internet technologies
2) connecting distributed networks of people and/or assets
3) making use of the idling capacity of tangible and intangible assets
4) encouraging meaningful interactions and trust
5) embracing openness, inclusivity and the commons.

The same research sets out a taxonomy for the collaborative economy comprising four pillars:

**Pillar 1: Collaborative consumption** Gaining access to goods or services through renting, lending, trading, exchanging, reselling or swapping.

- **Redistribution markets:** Reselling things from where they are not needed to where they are wanted. The London Re-use Network, a consortium of charities and social enterprises, re-routes furniture and other bulky items from the waste stream and redeploy them. Freecycle, run by volunteers, does much the same on a global scale.

- **Product service systems:** Paying to access goods, instead of owning them outright. Two specific built environment examples are Airbnb and Office Genie. Airbnb is a community marketplace for people to list, discover and book accommodation around the world, allowing individual owners to monetise spare rooms. Office Genie matches producers needing desk space with spare desks posted by companies with spare capacity.
- **Collaborative lifestyles:** People share and exchange intangible assets, such as time, skills, money and space. Justpark, for example, brings together motorists and private parking spaces on unused driveways. Hub Culture offers collaboration tools, support and pop-up pavilions in major urban areas.

**Pillar 2: Collaborative production** Groups or networks of individuals collaborate to design, produce or distribute goods.

- **Collaborative design:** People work together to design a product or service. GrabCAD began as a community where engineers could upload and download models from a free CAD library. In 2013, GrabCAD released Workbench, a free Cloud-based collaboration solution that helps engineering teams manage, share and view CAD files. Workbench allows multiple engineers to work on the same files at the same time without overwriting each other's work. Workbench also lets engineers share files externally and with non-CAD users.
- **Collaborative making:** People connect outside of formal institutions or organising structures to collaborate on making projects and products. OpenStreetMap, for example, is a collaborative project building a free-to-use, open-source editable map of the world.
- **Collaborative distribution:** Peer-to-peer distribution of goods. Applications like Nimber and uberRUSH match delivery requests to journeys already being made, thus sharing resources.

**Pillar 3: Collaborative learning** Learning experiences that are open to anyone and where people share resources and knowledge to learn together.

- **Open courses and courseware:** Courses, lectures and educational content can be made freely and openly available to anyone. Massive open online courses (MOOCs) are evolving from being a one-way transfer of information to incorporate individual learning needs. So-called MOOC 2.0 reflects a bottom-up approach sensitive to local cultural and social drivers, enabling individuals to select relevant content.
- **Skill sharing:** Experts offer to teach or share a skill. MOOCs are also moving from being the exclusive preserve of universities to a platform for the individual transfer of skills.
- **Crowd-sourced knowledge:** Aggregation of knowledge to solve problems collectively. Silberzahn and Uhlmann (2015) postulate that crowdsourcing research can balance discussions, validate findings and better inform policy, citing their research into racism using multiple researchers and a common dataset.

**Pillar 4: Collaborative finance** Funding, lending and investment services offered outside of traditional financial institutions.

- **Crowdfunding:** Groups of people contribute directly to a specific project's funding goal. Fundrise, for example, is a platform for crowdfunding real-estate investment.

- **Peer-to-peer lending:** People with money to invest are connected directly with people looking to borrow funds. Zopa peer-to-peer lending, for example, brings together individuals who have money to lend, and individuals or companies who wish to borrow money.
- **Complementary currencies:** Alternatives to state-managed legal tender that enable different ways for groups to measure value. Bitcoin is a prominent example in this area, but there are other more local examples, such as Economy of Hours (ECHO), which matches skills with demand in 'echos', with 1 Echo being the equivalent of 1 hour.

Collaboration implies sharing – of space, of infrastructure, of information and much more besides. It also changes the nature of competition fundamentally. The implications for the built environment are potentially disruptive.

Collaborative production could revolutionise manufacturing space, for example. It is already happening: Hax is a hardware accelerator based in Silicon Valley and Shenzhen in China. The company provides entrepreneurs with enough workspace, mentoring and finance to prototype hardware products and bring them to market; Wholly owned by the Canary Wharf Group, Level39 is a technology accelerator space for finance, cyber-security, retail and smart-city technology companies. Since 2013, it has grown from a simple idea into a three-floor, 80,000 square foot accelerator space occupying the 39th, 24th and 42nd floors of One Canada Square in London's Docklands.

In a technology enabled economy the relatively low costs and high impact of technologies mean that digital companies have marginal costs that tend towards zero and 'information goods' being sold have storage and distribution costs that are virtually nil. The built environment develops over time to best service the economy. Just as traditional economies are disrupted by technology, so is the built environment.

### 11.4.3    Social context

#### 11.4.3.1    Individual values

It has already been noted that social media platforms are essentially personal and encourage individual participation in communal ventures. Growth in social media has coincided with a surge in creative output around the world. Statistics from YouTube, for example, show that, at the end of 2015, 300 hours of video was being uploaded to the platform each minute.

It has become commonplace to review facilities that have been used, for example the travel site TripAdvisor has garnered over 320 million reviews of hotels and restaurants. These are influential to the extent that there have been instances of hotel owners reviewing their own properties in glowing terms and guests demanding discounts on pain of a poor review.

Social media has brought the level of customisation and customer service at which a customer feels that he or she is an exclusive or preferred customer of the firm much closer, but there remains a long way to go before individual occupiers of space in the sustainable built environment feel their opinions and feedback are valued by building owners and managers.

### 11.4.3.2  Communal culture

Communal culture is best described by example. The Maker Movement is a coming together of artisan workers around the world. Its main principle (it has a manifesto) is that each person should be a creative, inventive, productive individual and that through making, we learn.

The Maker Movement manifests itself in a number of different ways:

- Fablabs: short for Fabrication Laboratories, their purpose is to make cutting edge tools (like 3D printers) available to anyone.
- Maker faire: the movement magazine (MAKE) established the Maker faire, which is an event where people can exhibit their creations and co-create with others.
- Makerspaces are commercial spaces that provide digital fabrication tools such as 3D printers, laser cutters and design software. The tools are available for a small fee to users.
- Hackerspaces are community-driven spaces for software developers and experts to share ideas and collaborate.

Although individual creativity is the driver, the culture is communal and supported by Facebook groups and websites that act as a showroom for goods and communal use of tools.

## 11.4.4  Technology context

The pace of change in technology is very fast indeed by comparison with the built environment. Mainstream companies grow to prominence very quickly (and sometimes disappear even more quickly). Most mainstream social media platforms are in their mid-teens and even companies like Apple and Microsoft are only around 30 years old. By contrast, British Land, one of the UK's leading property companies, was 160 years old in 2016.

This relatively fast pace of change applies at a product level as well. The Royal Exchange in the City of London dates to 1844 and was rebuilt on the site of two previous exchanges going back to 1566. This contrasts with a product lifecycle of between nine and 18 months reported by Burruss and Kuettner (2003) for Hewlett Packard printers. Although there are examples of relatively short lifecycles in the built environment – temporary 'pop-up' shops perhaps – for technology products iterations are generally measured in days rather than months.

The impact of technology on the built environment has changed everything about buildings from their location, through their design and construction to how they are used, managed and transacted. For example, high-rise office buildings would never have been conceived without elevator technology. This change is an ongoing feature of the sector and it is expected that new and changing technologies will continue to have a significant impact.

As technology transforms business models and processes, it is also changing the way employees work. McKinsey research (Chui *et al.*, 2015) found that already-proven technologies could automate as much as 45% of the tasks individuals are currently paid to perform.

Existing manifestations of technology like Cloud computing and social media are expected to continue to reflect changing patterns of use over the next decade but there are four key areas of technology that will have a significant impact over this timeframe:

- the Internet of Things (IoT)
- machine learning and robotics
- building data
- distributed ledger technology.

### 11.4.4.1 The internet of things

The IoT is the network of physical objects – devices, vehicles, buildings and other items – into which electronics, software, sensors and network connectivity have been embedded that enables these objects to collect and exchange data. The IoT allows objects to be sensed and controlled remotely across existing network infrastructure.

Each device is uniquely identifiable through its embedded computing system and is able to operate within the existing internet infrastructure. Macauley *et al.* (2015) estimate that the IoT will consist of almost 50 billion objects by 2020. Each of these objects will be addressable and, in theory, could have its own Facebook page or Twitter feed.

The history of the IoT mirrors that of the internet itself. The first 'thing' connected to the internet was probably the Coke machine at Carnegie Mellon University in the late 1980s, but in 2016 'things' refers to a wide variety of devices that collect useful data and then autonomously flow the data between other devices, facilitating real-time control.

The IoT is massively relevant to the realisation of a sustainable built environment. As well as being at the heart of building management systems, the IoT is one of the platforms that underpins the smart city and smart energy management systems. The city of Nice, for example, is building smart city solutions to further advance the potential impacts of the IoT for cities. The project's main objectives are to test and validate a technology architecture and economic model, as well as to determine the social benefits of the IoT.

The project includes four city services that can rapidly demonstrate the benefits and value of the IoT for both residents and city leadership. These services include:

- smart circulation
- smart lighting
- smart waste management
- smart environment monitoring.

As these solutions are implemented, Nice are assessing how captured data can be treated to make information context-specific and useful across different services. For instance, can data captured by sensors for traffic patterns serve purposes beyond smart parking? How can this information also help optimise waste collection and environmental monitoring? The implications of this data combination and cross-collaboration impact the decisions of city managers, cross-departmental collaboration and back-office operations.

At building level Coor Service Management utilise the IoT in their head office in Kista, Sweden. SmartUtilization is a system for measuring the utilisation of space in real time. Wireless sensors respond to body heat in space, transmitting data that can be presented visually in time and space in a web-based analysis tool. The analysis tool has pre-defined key performance indicators and charts for analysis, providing objective decision-support data for optimising the workspace. As a result, the company has been able to cut costs by up to 30% and at the same time increase both employee satisfaction and workforce productivity.

### 11.4.4.2 Machine learning and robotics

Samuel (1959) defined machine learning as 'a field of study that gives computers the ability to learn without being explicitly programmed'. Machine learning explores the study and construction of algorithms that can learn from, and make predictions about, data. It is a subset of artificial intelligence. Robotics has moved on from images of tin men and is making inroads into manual occupations.

Ford (2015) identifies artificial intelligence and machine-learning technology that allow computers to make decisions, recognise speech and visualise in 3D as the main drivers of the process. They are leading to the development of both algorithms and new robots that can perform all sorts of previously non-automatable tasks.

Research by McKinsey (Chui *et al.*, 2015) suggests that the impact of machine learning and robotics on jobs is best described in terms of activities rather than occupations, with very few occupations being automated in their entirety in the near or medium term. Instead the impact will see entire business processes transformed and the jobs performed by people redefined.

Susskind and Susskind (2015) challenge the granting of monopolies to today's professionals. They argue that our current professions are antiquated, opaque and no longer affordable, and are therefore unsustainable in an era of increasingly capable expert systems.

Jobs and activities in the built environment are vulnerable to this kind of technology. Styliano *et al.* (2015) for the BBC updated research by Frey and Osbourne (2013) using UK data and presented a list of occupations at risk. They estimated that valuers, for example, stood a 95% chance that their jobs would be automated by 2035; chartered surveyors generally saw a 63% chance.

### 11.4.4.3 Building data

Historically, data about buildings has been collected and maintained in silos with little attempt to construct a data model that runs in parallel to the lifecycle of a building. For example, architectural data would not be maintained post completion of construction and buildings would be measured multiple times during their life.

Building information modelling (BIM) is a process involving the generation and management of digital representations of the physical and functional characteristics of buildings. BIM brings together all of the information about every component of a building in one place. It makes it possible for that information to be accessed for any purpose. At the construction stage, for example, it reduces the risk of mistakes or discrepancies and minimises abortive costs.

BIM data can be used to illustrate the entire building lifecycle from design to demolition and materials reuse. Spaces, systems, products and sequences can be shown in relative scale to each other and, in turn, relative to the entire project. As buildings with BIM implementations age and move into the mainstream, the definitive BIM data will be available to support the optimal management of the building going forward.

Building management systems (BMS) are computer-based systems that manage, control and monitor building technical services (heating, ventilation, air conditioning, lighting etc.) and the energy consumption of devices used by the building. They provide sensor-based data and dashboard tools that allow building managers better to understand the energy usage of their buildings and to control and improve their buildings' operational performance.

BMS provide granular data about the operational performance of buildings in real time. In an ideal world, this would feed granular information about usage back into the design process. In practice, BMS has yet to move beyond operational control of space and there are few examples of buildings that integrate BIM data with BMS data to give a dynamic model of the building.

### 11.4.4.4 Distributed ledger technology

Algorithms that enable the creation of distributed ledgers are powerful, disruptive innovations that could transform the delivery of public and private services and enhance productivity through a wide range of applications.

A distributed ledger is a database that can be shared across multiple sites. All participants within a network have their own identical copy of the ledger. Any changes to the ledger are reflected in all copies in real time. The security and accuracy of the assets are maintained cryptographically to control who can do what within the shared ledger. Entries can also be updated by some or all of the participants, according to rules agreed by the network.

Distributed ledgers can underpin other software and hardware-based innovations such as smart contracts and the IoT. Furthermore, their underlying philosophy of distributed consensus, open source, transparency and community could be highly disruptive to many of these sectors.

Like any radical innovation, distributed ledgers create threats to those who are unable to respond. In particular, they may be perceived as threatening the role of trusted intermediaries in positions of control within traditionally hierarchical organisations.

Underlying this technology is the block chain. A block chain is a type of database that takes a number of records and puts them in a block. Each block is then 'chained' to the next block using a cryptographic signature. This allows block chains to be used like a ledger, which can be shared and validated by anyone with the appropriate permissions.

There are many ways to validate the accuracy of a ledger, but they are broadly known as 'consensus'. If participants in that process are preselected, that is, they are in a closed group, the ledger is permissioned. If the process is open to everyone, the ledger is unpermissioned.

The real advantage of block chain technology is that it can set rules about a transaction that are tied to the transaction itself. This contrasts with conventional databases, in which rules are set either at the database level or in the application, but not in the transaction.

Distributed ledgers have the potential to be radically disruptive. Their processing capability is in real time, very secure and increasingly low cost. They can be applied to a wide range of industries and services, including real estate. Proof of concept studies are in progress for land registration, for example.

A distributed ledger of properties, including validated building information and ownership, could make the sale of a building investment very efficient indeed, obviating the need for agency-style inputs.

# 11.5  Future scenarios

Any future is uncertain and the rapid pace of technology makes any long-term prognosis a challenge. During the course of writing this chapter at least two interesting social media platforms have disappeared, for example, having failed to gain sufficient traction or funding. Very few forecasters foresaw the rise of social media to its current level of prominence 10 years ago and, to a certain extent, the actual products and platforms are irrelevant going forward.

Technology is a great enabler and has facilitated significant change in the economic, political and social landscape. Social media has proved to be one channel through which change can be enacted. Examples of technology shaping the built environment physically abound from the role of lifts in the creation of skyscrapers, through the use of new materials in construction to the part played by IT in the configuration and location of space.

From the perspective of 2017, the largest and most potent change will be in the availability of real-time, granular data about the built environment generated by buildings themselves. As yet we have not assimilated this level of data into decision-making either philosophically or systematically. Data output from BIM in the design and construction processes is seldom made available to building managers at asset, property or facilities levels, for example. BMS are used to manage the operational parameters of space, but seldom used to inform decisions about the suitability of space for purpose, for example. All the scenarios developed here will have this significant resource underpinning them however space is used and by whom.

Three scenarios are developed here that reflect different potential futures not for technologies *per se* but for the reaction to them. The assumed time horizon is 2050 – a timespan of nearly 35 years. To put this in context the first IBM personal computer was introduced in 1981 – 35 years before the time of writing – and has undergone multiple generational changes since then. The iPad is around 6 years old and the iPhone 9 years old. Thirty-five years gives plenty of time for new machines, materials or applications to disrupt and change any outcome imagined here.

## 11.5.1  The first scenario: a creative divide

A company's most important asset is its creative capital. Creative employees pioneer new technologies and drive economic growth. Research for the Harvard Business Review (Florida and Goodnight, 2005) found that, in 2005, professionals whose responsibilities include innovating, designing and problem solving made up a third of the US workforce.

Yet not everyone is creative, nor does every situation require creativity. There is a clear divide between those who are active participants and those who are passive recipients. This divide extends into activities, splitting processes between creative and non-creative.

This scenario sees a growing digital divide emerging between these two groups. Active participants will drive creativity and innovation forwards, leaving passive recipients with a second-class service.

A good example of the divide is seen with television. Linear television broadcasting started in the UK in 1936 as public service free of advertising. Even as recently as 2000 the number of channels available to viewers without access to relatively expensive cable or satellite dishes was very restricted. In 2017, there is a collection of free-to-air, free-to-view and subscription services, with nearly 500 channels available to consumers.

Sitting on top of these channels are a raft of on-demand tools that classify content allowing time-shifted viewing. Despite these tools, for most viewers watching television remains essentially a passive pastime. Growth in interactivity, of adverts for example, has not emerged as quickly as forecast and remains at the experimental stage. In early 2016, the BBC switched one of its most innovative broadcast channels to online-only in response to cost pressures. BBC 3 is now available on demand only with no linear content. This moves viewing from wholly passive to active selection, and from a recipient audience to a participant one.

Hardware has already begun to follow this path. Gartner (2016) estimate that around half the computing devices shipped in 2015 (excluding phones) were tablet computers (i.e. devices geared around consumption of content rather than creation). With the exception of taking pictures, smartphones are also devices for consuming content as opposed to laptops or PCs, which are geared to content creation.

Social media platforms are flexible enough to cater for both participants and recipients, but some trends in technology may bear down disproportionately on the recipients group. In particular, machine learning will impact employment in those activities lacking any creative dynamic.

As far as the built environment is concerned, creative workspace is a different animal to space designed for consumption of content. Research by Harris (2015) for the City of London found that workplaces are powerful conveyors of messages to staff and clients about the values and culture of an organisation and consequently companies tend to value high specification and tailored fit-outs. As a result, this scenario sees the participants group leasing less Grade A office space, reflecting their need to keep rents to a minimum and spending more on the fit-out in order to encourage interaction and differentiate it from competitors.

The recipients group, under pressure from automation of the non-creative processes, are also less likely to pay premium prices for space.

### 11.5.2 The second scenario: technology backlash

Between 1811 and 1816, an uprising of workers swept the UK, igniting a number of armed raids. The so-called Luddites attacked mills and destroyed machinery. The Luddites were largely male textile workers concerned about machines replacing their jobs, or at least reducing the need for skilled workers with their enhanced rates of pay.

In *Rebels against the future*, Sale (1996) explores the lessons that may be learned from the Luddites with respect to the ubiquitous use of technology. Neo-Luddism can be described as any modern philosophy that is distrustful of the changes that will be brought about by technology. The principle theme is that the technology has evolved to control, rather than to facilitate, social interactions, threatening to dehumanise the process.

In this scenario, this backlash gains traction and begins to affect the number of technology users and the nature of their use. If sufficient scale were reached this could see falling sales of hardware and falling numbers of users of social media.

From the standpoint of the built environment this would be unlikely to generate a wholesale move back into conventional uses of space. Despite a backlash, engagement with technology at some level would be inevitable as it has permeated the very fabric of buildings. Growth of the IoT will make that ever more apparent and the impact of machine learning will continue to erode employment prospects in certain areas.

### 11.5.3   The third scenario: passive engagement

The idea of understanding a consumer's needs before they actually needed what Apple was making has remained a hallmark of the company throughout its history. The idea of empathising with a consumer before a market was even developed set the company on the path of always looking forward to find how people would behave and made it, in 2016, the world's largest company.

Over the last decade particularly, technology has moved from facilitating the automation of repetitive processes to becoming an integral part of life. Even the less technology literate cannot avoid interfacing with technology at some stage. Technology has become embedded in the fabric of society. Some commentators have heralded this as a fourth industrial revolution (see, for example, Schwab, 2016), arguing that the fusion of technologies and their interaction make the future significantly different from previous revolutions.

In this scenario, social media and the technology underpinning it continues to evolve, changing the built environment, working practices, and the number and quality of jobs.

The evolution of the IoT will deliver much better operational data on buildings and will make the built environment a much smarter place, increasing permeability between the public and private realms. The better data provided will feed better algorithms that in turn will make the management of the built environment significantly more efficient. The downside here is that activities built on those inefficiencies will become automated and jobs will disappear.

Distributed ledger technology will begin to disrupt processes built around the central control of data, democratising the process, reducing costs and leading to significant new opportunities to manage and control space.

### 11.5.4   In summary

These scenarios describe different ways that social media and the underlying technologies could evolve over the next decade. The embedded nature of technology in everything we do and everywhere we go makes the third scenario overwhelmingly the most likely outcome. Smartphones, for example, are just too useful to ignore and lightweight, long battery life tablets make mobility of work a given.

Social media platforms are the channels through which much of the change described here will be enacted. Although social media tools have grown to meet demand from people, they also provide a platform for devices to communicate exceptional events. The IoT, for example, makes it feasible for a sensor-equipped wastepaper basket to alert the building manager that its temperature was out of bounds long before any paper fire set off a smoke alarm – and it would probably use an instant messaging service to do it.

## 11.6   Conclusions

Perhaps uniquely in the history of work, social media has enabled individuals to brand themselves on an equal footing with corporates. This encourages individuals to see employment as a portfolio of jobs (Brown *et al.*, 2004) and moves the relationship between employer and employee away from monogamy. It may even presage the death of employment contracts, to be replaced by more specific service contracts.

This implies that there will be greater mobility in the workforce in the future than is seen even now, making it ever more important that the changing nature of the link between workspace and workplace is understood.

In terms of policy it is likely that control of the internet will become more explicit over time. However, this does not detract from the rich landscape of opportunity that it represents. It has always been, and will remain, difficult for policy to keep up with the exponential pace of change. Schwab (2016) notes that the second industrial revolution has yet to be experienced by the 17% of the world lacking electricity – 135 years on from the first power plant. By comparison the smartphone has reached 2 billion users in just 9 years.

Traditional economic models are likely to see significant change wrought by the fourth industrial revolution. The relatively low costs and high impact of new technologies mean that digital companies have marginal costs that tend towards zero and information goods being sold have storage and distribution costs that are virtually nil. Schwab (2016) highlights the differences between Detroit in 1990 and Silicon Valley in 2014. In 1990, the three biggest companies in Detroit had a combined market capitalisation of $36 billion, revenues of $250 million and 1.2 million employees. In 2014, the three biggest companies in Silicon Valley had 30 times higher capitalisation ($1.1 trillion), roughly the same revenues ($247 million) but 10 times fewer employees (137,000).

These changes are also likely to be manifested in the growth of small scale, high-technology, focused manufacturing and the collaborative economy that supports it. Customisation and customer service will continue to drive demand for products and communal culture will strengthen.

As far as technology is concerned, this horizon is likely to see processors getting faster, storage getting cheaper, devices becoming more capable, bandwidth getting broader and the advent of new materials, new techniques and more disruptive innovation.

The built environment will evolve to reflect these changes. Workplaces will become collections of individual workspaces that will ebb and flow according the need to interact face to face. Legal structures will adapt to reflect the links between work and place, and individuals will work where and when it is convenient to do so.

Neighbourhood high streets and city centres will grow leisure facilities and shrink retail space as online retailing takes a larger share of spending. Research from the British Retail Consortium (BRC, 2016) predicts that of 270,000 shops in the UK up to 74,000 could shut by 2020 due in large part to the impact of online retailing.

The widespread adoption of additive printing will see manufacturing polarise between small specialist fabricators and large, multifunctional factories with a parallel impact on the warehouse sector. In many cases, parts, for example, would be more cost-effectively printed locally than manufactured in Asia and shipped around the world.

Overall, the built environment will be smarter and better connected as BIM and BMS combine to increase operational efficiency across all sectors, including residential. Already interim solutions are available that allow BMS functionality in the home accessed through a smartphone app. Over the next 35 years full BMS functionality will be embedded in the design of all buildings – new and old.

Social media platforms are likely to remain a key interface between the internet and its user community over the next 35 years. This is not to say that the actual platforms used will not evolve over time. It took just over 10 years for Facebook to reach 1.6 billion users; this could reach 3.2 billion in another decade or the next new platform could replace it just as quickly.

## References

Azhara, S. and Abeln, J.M. (2014*)* Investigating social media applications for the construction industry. *Procedia Engineering*, 85, 42–51.

Barber, L. (2016) Globalisation 2.0 – an optimistic outlook, in *The Financial Times*, 14 January.

Botsman, R, and Rogers, R. (2010) *What's mine is yours*. Collins, London.

BRC (2016) Retail 2020, in *The Guardian*, 29 February.

Brown, M. (2012) Why the construction sector should engage with social media, in *The Guardian*, 16 February.

Brown, P., Hesketh, A. and Williams, S. (2004) *The mismanagement of talent: employability and jobs in the knowledge economy*. Oxford University Press, Oxford.

Bruns, A. and Burgess, J. (2013) Crisis Communication in Natural Disasters: The Queensland Floods and Christchurch Earthquakes, in Weller, K., Bruns, A., Burgess, J., Mahrt, M. and Puschmann, C. (eds) *Twitter and Society*. Peter Lang, Bern.

Burruss, J. and Kuettner, D. (2003) Forecasting for Short-Lived Products: Hewlett-Packard's Journey. *Journal of Business Forecasting Methods & Systems*, 21(4). Available at: https://www.questia.com/library/journal/1P3-305703281/forecasting-for-short-lived-products-hewlett-packard-s (accessed February 2016).

Chui, M., Manyika, J. and Miremadi, M. (2015) Four fundamentals of workplace automation. *McKinsey Quarterly*. Available at: http://www.mckinsey.com/business-functions/business-technology/our-insights/four-fundamentals-of-workplace-automation (accessed February 2016).

Cunningham, H. (1995) *Wiki Design Principles*. Available at: http://c2.com/cgi/wiki?WikiDesignPrinciples (accessed January 2016).

Florida, R. and Goodnight, J. (2005) Managing creativity. *Harvard Business Review*. Available at: https://hbr.org/2005/07/managing-for-creativity (accessed February 2016).

Ford, M. (2015) *The Rise of the Robots – Technology and the Threat of Mass Unemployment*. Basic Books, New York.

Frey, C.B. and Osbourne, M.A. (2013) *The future of employment: How susceptible are jobs to computerisation?* Oxford University, Oxford. Available at: http://www.oxfordmartin.ox.ac.uk/downloads/academic/The_Future_of_Employment.pdf (accessed February 2016).

Gartner (2016) *Forecast: PCs, Ultramobiles and Mobile Phones, Worldwide, 2012-2019, 4Q15 Update*. Gartner Group, Egham.

Harris, R. (2015) *Future workstyles and future workplaces in the City of London*. Ramidus/ City of London, London.

JISC (2016) *Strandlines Project*. JISC/King's College, London. Available at: http://www. strandlines.net/ (accessed January 2016).

Kaplan, A.M. and Haenlein, M. (2010) Users of the world, unite! The challenges and opportunities of social media. *Business Horizons*, 53(1), 59–68.

Kietzmann, J. and Hermkens, K. (2011) Social media? Get serious! Understanding the functional building blocks of social media. *Business Horizons*, 54, 241–251.

Macaulay, J., Buckalew, L. and Chung, G. (2015) *Internet of Things in Logistics*. CISCO/DHL.

Massolution (2015) *Crowdfunding industry report*. Available at: http://crowdexpert.com/ crowdfunding-industry-statistics/.

OECD (2008) Ministerial session, *The Seoul Declaration for the Future of the Internet Economy*. OECD Publishing, Paris.

Ofcom (2015) *The Communications Market Report*. Ofcom, London.

Ordanini, A. (2009) Crowd funding: customers as investors. *The Wall Street Journal*, 23 March, p. r3.

Pauley, N. (2014) *How the top UK construction companies are using social media marketing in 2014*. Available at: http://www.pauleycreative.co.uk/2014/01/how-the-top- construction-companies-are-using-social-media-in-2014/ (accessed March 2016).

Pew Research Center (2014) *Millenials in Adulthood*. Pew Research Center, Washington DC.

Sale, K. (1996) *Rebels against the Future: The Luddites and their War on the Industrial Revolution: Lessons for the Computer Age*. Addison Wesley, New York.

Samuel, A.L. (1959) Some studies in machine learning using the game of checkers. IBM Journal of Research and Development, 3, 210–229. Reprinted in E.A. Feigenbaum and J. Feldman (eds) (1963) Computers and Thought, 71–105. McGraw-Hill, New York.

Schmidt, E. and Cohen, J. (2013) *The New Digital Age: Reshaping the Future of People, Nations and Business*. Hodder & Stoughton.

Schwab, K. (2016) *The fourth industrial revolution*. World Economic Forum, Geneva.

Silberzahn, R. and Uhlmann, E.L. (2015) Crowdsourced research: Many hands make tight work. *Nature*, 526(7572). Available at: http://www.nature.com/news/crowdsourced- research-many-hands-make-tight-work-1.18508 (accessed February 2016).

Stokes, K., Clarence, E., Anderson, L. and Rinne, A. (2014) *Making sense of the UK collaborative economy*. NESTA/Collaborative Lab, London. Available at: http://www. nesta.org.uk/sites/default/files/making_sense_of_the_uk_collaborative_economy_14.pdf (accessed February 2016).

Stylianou, N., Nurse, T., Fletcher, G., Fewster, A., Bangay, R. and Walton, J. (2015) *Will a robot take your job?* BBC, London. Available at: http://www.bbc.co.uk/news/ technology-34066941 (accessed February 2016).

Susskind, R. and Susskind, D. (2015) *The Future of the Professions: How Technology Will Transform the Work of Human Experts*. Oxford University Press, Oxford.

Thompson, R. (2014) *FIGJAM – Personal branding in Real Estate Research*. Conference paper, ERES, Vienna.

Wearesocial (2015) *Digital, Social & Mobile Worldwide in 2015*. Available at: http:// wearesocial.com/uk/special-reports/digital-social-mobile-worldwide-2015 (accessed February 2016).

Part 3

Provocations about the Future: Practitioners' Viewpoints

# 12

# Sustainability through Collaboration and Skills Development

*Andy Ford and Aaron Gillich*

## 12.1 Introduction

Climate change is shaping the future of the built environment. Today everything from policy to skills development must be viewed through the lens of the UK 2050 carbon targets which have been passed into law. If one considers a timeline from early awareness of climate change in the 1980s to the much discussed 2050 horizon, then we are currently halfway along this journey. So where do we find ourselves? How does the industry today compare to 30 years ago? What corrections to this journey does the industry need in order to deliver the skills required for the carbon-free built environment that we're all counting on?

The nature of construction is all about change: changing relationships, changing structures, changing contracts, but with essentially the same skills. We've been creating buildings for thousands of years, and the same fundamental things need to happen now and in the future, but who works for whom has evolved and morphed. In a way, this comes down to the contracts and what people are paid to do under these established contracts. This poses a considerable challenge for a sustainable future because very few are truly paid to be sustainable and neither are they paid to collaborate. The very nature of a design team requires collaboration, which is a challenge in an increasingly sub-specialised industry that seems to favour silos over synergies.

This chapter considers how the idea of collaboration in the built environment has changed. It begins with the issue of complexity in contracts and how this 'marginalises' sustainability. It then considers how this leads to an industry driven by 'tick boxes' rather than collective vision. Next, the chapter discusses how these factors have created a built environment that largely externalises the concept of performance itself. Some believe that the course of innovation is self-correcting and that technology or the marketplace of ideas will save us. This idea is challenged as we look ahead to the steps needed to get the industry back on the path to a low-carbon 2050 that many in the construction industry are still trying hard to achieve.

*Sustainable Futures in the Built Environment to 2050: A Foresight Approach to Construction and Development*, First Edition. Edited by Tim Dixon, John Connaughton and Stuart Green.
© 2018 John Wiley & Sons Ltd. Published 2018 by John Wiley & Sons Ltd.

## 12.2   Complexity versus sustainability

As a generality, systems trend towards greater complexity, unless this is actively fought against. Complexity hinders sustainability, and this requires a call to arms.

Compared with 30 years ago, the industry is possibly slightly less aggressive, a little more diverse, than it used to be, but still entirely project and short-term money focused. Buildings have also changed, tending in the commercial sector to be larger (International Energy Agency, 2015), and much has been in the wrong direction from the point of view of simplicity of operation. Buildings are now far more complicated than they used to be, with complex controls that few understand, and the processes that deliver them are more complicated still. There has been a blossoming of project management, a previously under-acknowledged skill, which was generally the role of the architect in design and the main contractor in construction. But this advance has led to a breaking down of design into specialisms and delivery into small pieces, which need ever greater coordination and management.

Mechanical and electrical design engineers have gone from having close contact with subcontractors and manufacturers to rarely even setting foot on a building site. The subcontractors meanwhile are at the beck and call of the contractor, looking for a good price after they have won the project, which hampers their ability to invest with confidence. This is driving a culture of cost-cutting and more and more designers are finding themselves in similar circumstances.

This change in culture is largely a story of contracts. On an emotional and cultural level, buildings are about raising the earth and painting a skyline, but the unromantic truth is that the industry responds to what the contracts say should be done. To understand the modern building industry, we must look back over the timeline of contract structures and how those have changed into the relationships we see today.

### 12.2.1   Contracts in the built environment

The most common UK construction contracts have, since 1931, been developed by the Joint Construction Tribunal (JCT), although the use of so-called standard forms of contract goes back even further, to the 19th century. Most building work during this period was procured by approaches that today are described as the 'traditional' or 'conventional' method, placing the architect at the heart of the process. In 1903, a standard form was produced 'under the sanction of the Royal Institute of British Architects (RIBA) and in agreement with the Institute of Builders and the National Federation of Building Trades Employers of Great Britain and Northern Ireland'[1]. In 1931, the JCT was formed by RIBA and the first JCT standard form of building contract was issued. From 1967 JCT forms were issued and updated via the 11 constituent bodies which make it up, comprising representatives of architects, building employers, surveyors, consulting engineers, property developers, specialist subcontractors and local authority associations. The range of contracts has also increased over time, responding to changes in industry practice, new procurement methods and changes in legislation.

---

1  https://corporate.jctltd.co.uk/about-us/our-history.

The process of producing standard forms of contract came under review in the Latham report *Constructing the Team* (Latham, 1994). A key proposal was that only those bodies that would be called upon to the contract should approve the publication of new contracts. This has tended to influence behaviour to the benefit of the industry and its clients, although not in a deliberate sense. The industry as a whole, rather than the few key players, largely remains focused on operational needs and the day-to-day, with little attention to strategy. Latham focused on strategy for improving the business performance of the top end of an industry. Meanwhile we continue to rely on building regulations to ensure quality, and leave legislation to drive societal issue such as decarbonisation (Kwawu and Hughes, 2005).

The trend has become increasing complex because complexity favours the market leaders. If you are a project manager or a general contractor who wishes to be in complete control, you will use power to break down your suppliers into the smallest elements you possibly can. This then delivers to you the greatest possible influence to push their prices down and hence manage your own costs. And that's what's happened.

Because the big contractors, the consultants and developers, have been pushing their own agenda, and UK government have decided to step back from legislation, the needs of society are currently not well met. What has happened is that the UK industry is now made up of a few very big companies with a lot of power and lot of small, or micro, companies, some of which may be very good, but all of which, being small, are vulnerable to workload pressure and very sensitive to cash flow. This approach cascades down the chain, eventually reaching the most vulnerable. In an industry which is completely focused on project delivery for minimum cost, it has limited steady background work and goes through regular dramatic cycles, so small companies are vulnerable and, as a result, compliant. We would argue that this has suited the large contractors and they have exploited their supply chains (BIS, 2013a). This is the current status of the UK built environment from a contractual perspective. In terms of UK plc this is arguably quite successful, but whether it's where we need to be is another question. An overly complex building industry may help some company stock values, but it makes the delivery of sustainability more complex and inefficient.

In the context of the nature of UK construction, Harris led an analysis on behalf of the former UK Department of Business, Innovation and Skills (BIS, 2013a). It found that for a typical large building project (in the £20–25 million range) the main contractor may be directly managing around 70 subcontracts, of which a large proportion are small, £50,000 or less. For a regional project, the subcontract size may be even smaller, with examples of projects where 70% of subcontracts were below £10,000. This is clear evidence of the fragmentation of the industry and a real demonstration of the challenge of building integrated supply chains with a close focus on the end product and customer value (BIS, 2013a).

### 12.2.2   Collaboration in a fragmented industry

This trend for complex contract arrangements has had the practical impact of fragmenting construction supply chains. Good design which delivers what it sets out to do is about collaboration, and important relationships seem to have broken down. Clients have moved away from working closely with designers without a project management interface. Earlier contracts in the UK could typically require a contractor to employ a subcontractor of the client's choice (known as a 'nominated subcontractor'). In this arrangement, the subcontractors had a strong incentive as specialists to work closely with the client's engineering design consultant and to ensure their work was integrated because this is where their future recommendations, and hence project opportunities, came from. Now any work done in such a manner is largely a matter of goodwill. The designers have no way of saying who will deliver and have therefore retreated from the detail, leaving a gap. Suppliers have also done the same down the chain, leaving more gaps. Lawyers try to fill the 'responsibility' gaps, but, in our view, it is the relationships that are broken. These changes place the contractor in a role of considerable power, which contractors seem to use to a large extent for commercial purposes, and yet having thus positioned themselves they now must take considerable responsibility for our collective futures. The question is whether this will ever happen and, if it does, how?

## 12.3   Greenwashed change in an era of urgency

If sustainability is to compete among other contractual priorities it must somehow be measured in the same fragmented structure as the contracts themselves. This has led to well-intentioned schemes such as BREEAM. While positive on the whole, they are easily criticised as piecemeal tick-box exercises insufficiently tied to holistic performance outcomes. This approach to sustainability is ill-equipped to deal with the urgent reality of climate change. For example, we have claimed some of the 'easy wins' of insulting lofts and cavity walls, but we are nowhere near decarbonising our existing stock. We are short of houses. We are short of expertise. And we are short on time.

In our view, an insufficient number of built environment professionals truly understand what this industry needs to achieve in the long term and are focused on delivering it. The Zero Carbon Hub,[2] established in the UK in 2008, is a non-profit organisation that takes the lead in the day-to-day operational responsibility for achieving the government's target of delivering zero-carbon homes in England from 2016. However, this target is unfortunately now defunct as the idea of zero-carbon new buildings became the victim of politics.

Green building councils or independent, non-profit organisations made up of businesses and organisations working in the building and construction industry spread from the formation of the first in the USA and later in the UK.[3] The Better Buildings Partnership (Better Buildings Partnership, 2016) is a collaboration of the UK's leading commercial property owners, who are working together to improve the sustainability of existing commercial building stock. These are good signs. Yet, in general, the construction world appears to us still to be driven by tick boxes and compliance in design, and is short on innovation unless it is in how to make money. There also continues to be a close to zero understanding and engagement in research by industry (Royal Academy of Engineering, 2010) and a preference for somebody else to pay for training the workforce of the future.

---

2  http://www.zerocarbonhub.org.
3  http://www.ukgbc.org/about-us/our-history.

### 12.3.1 The 20-year cycle

To say that change happens slowly in the building industry is an understatement. One challenge that the industry faces is the illusion that 2050 is still a long way off.

In 1993 Fulcrum Consulting (the design consultancy that Andy Ford ran from 1984 to 2010) designed a seminal building in the history of low-energy design in the UK: the Elizabeth Fry building at the University of East Anglia in Norwich, UK. This was the vanguard for sustainable, simple buildings that actually performed as promised (Bordass *et al.*, 2001). Fulcrum thought at the time that within 5 years everyone would be producing buildings of comparable performance. But they were never able to do that, and we are only just beginning to be able to now, 20 years later. It's a quarter of the speed we need to progress if we are to achieve our current European Union new-build targets of near-zero energy for all new build by 2020 (European Commission, 2017).

### 12.3.2 Passive design and moving beyond tick-box sustainability

Since the beginning of this millennium, there has been a growing emphasis on sustainability and we have all had to learn rapidly what 'sustainability' means to us. In 2000 CIBSE created their first guide to sustainability, the *CIBSE Guide L* (CIBSE, 2000). It had received two revisions by 2007 and it is now under fundamental review because understanding across the industry has moved so fast. The changes to the Building Regulations Part L: Fuel and Power (DCLG, 2014) that have taken place over that same time period show just how quickly the concept of sustainability is changing. As the previous section described, the industry is not accustomed to change at this pace and many built environment professionals are struggling to keep up, let alone move beyond prescriptive definitions of sustainability.

Despite much talk about sustainability, there is still a lack of widespread delivery. As an industry, we are still following prescriptive paths to sustainability and looking to avoid the difficult issues rather than embrace their resolution in a fundamental way. The UK is legally bound to an 80% reduction in carbon emissions by 2050 compared to a 1990 baseline (HM Government, 2008). Yet in our view, we haven't really understood that this near-total decarbonisation of our energy supply is going to fundamentally alter our society, and the built environment is going to be at the sharp end of the change.

It is perhaps salient to revisit the origins of the term 'sustainable development'. The Brundtland definition of sustainable development, for example, helps to focus one's thoughts: 'development which meets the needs of current generations without compromising the ability of future generations to meet their own needs' (World Commission on Environment and Development, 1987). Also, looking back to the report *Our Common Future*, the comment by Per Lindblom (1985: 278) also bears repeating: 'The problems of today do not come with a tag marked energy economy or $CO_2$ or demography. The problems are multi-disciplinary and transnational or global. The problems are not primarily scientific and technological. In science we have the knowledge and in technology the tools. The problems are basically political, economic, and cultural.'

It is natural for us to move away from the hardest long-term problems and concentrate on the ones which feel closer: better those that are hard but more accessible. Human nature is to become bored with things that we cannot solve in a reasonably short time. If we try to engage society as a whole year after year with the same hectoring voice, we will fail. Hence new buzzwords get created to help us think that what we are doing is exciting. Currently perhaps 'well-being' might fit this idea. It is an increasingly used phrase representing a new perspective on comfort, but is at its core a traditional, and rather essential, idea.

All of these new names can distract from the long-term 'de-carbonisation challenge', a term which sounds rather obscure, hard to comprehend or internalise, but which must lie at the heart of all our efforts. In other words, we must achieve decarbonisation or we fail our world.

One could argue that the future of sustainability lies in creating simple, passive buildings. There needs to be a return to understanding what passive architectural design means. In the 1970s this was an architectural whim, a passing fashion. The designs had the right ideas but the technology was not up to the ambitions. Now passive design is real once again and this time technology, in terms of data, lighting, physics and simulation, is ready and capable of delivering. This will become, indeed must become, completely understood and implemented across all new buildings. It is time that the comfort of a building was as integral to its design, fabric and construction as structural stability and weather resistance.

This issue of fashion is at the core of the problem we face dealing with climate change. We are hardwired to think that things must move on so that after 5–10 years ideas are considered old-fashioned and not worth considering.

In summary, we have an industry driven by fragmented contract structures that has created an equally fragmented vision of sustainability. This creates a form of sustainability that insufficiently delivers sound design principles. To reach the ultimate goal of sustainability we must move this from the arena of ideas vulnerable to the fickle nature of fashion into the area of embedding the knowledge as core skills for all professionals: in other words, a natural part of what such professionals are and do. This leads to the concept of building performance: designing and delivering a built environment that is fit for purpose. Performance is essential to sustainability, but is very poorly incentivised by the modern building industry.

## 12.4    The externality of performance

The one thing that has escaped the modern contract structures is performance in use. Nobody really seems to want to 'own' building performance. But for the industry to work, it needs to be possible to not just say 'I'm going to design my part'. Rather, to have an industry that guarantees the product they deliver will do what it predicted. In this sense, the product should be seen as a building, not just part of a building.

### 12.4.1    The performance gap and the role of behaviour

The phrase 'performance gap' refers to the difference between what a building was designed to do and what it actually does. Even 'excellent' buildings have been found to consume two to three times their design estimates (Bordass *et al.*, 2004).

If demand reduction and control is ever going to work, then we must fundamentally limit the energy use of every building. It will require someone to 'own' building performance, establish a fair deal with regard to rewarding good design and good-quality build which genuinely results in long-term benefit. Australia, for example, has had some success with its NABERS Commitment Agreement for base buildings in new offices, which is based on actual energy performance (Energy Action, 2016). The behaviour of occupants is the most significant unknown, and prediction and modelling are highly dependent upon this behaviour after the technical aspects of the performance gap are resolved.

There has been much recent discussion about the performance gap in buildings. Arup produced a useful study to put this in context (Arup, 2013). Their work highlighted that unregulated energy and operational energy are well over half of a building's energy use, are largely under the control of the occupants and currently remain rather unpredictable. Understanding how people will behave in buildings has to date been very hit and miss, and largely down to surveys, instinct and experience. This is changing, with the expansion of mobile phones which locate occupants and techniques such as wide band radar (London South Bank University, 2016) that give information on where people are continuously and how they are influencing the conditions in a space. Their interaction with the building systems are beginning to be able to be studied with 'big data' analytics.[4] This will inform design and become embedded in the modelling and controls software (International Energy Agency, 2016). Industry and academia should be encouraged to collaborate more often to harness opportunities of sharing of data by understanding what additional data items may be collected and used by others (Sustainable Development Foundation, 2014).

### 12.4.2 Drivers for performance

In creating drivers for building performance, the correct role for government is at the strategic level. The UK Committee on Climate Change (CCC) and the introduction of budgets for the intervening period have been very useful instruments, following Nicholas Stern's review (Stern, 2010), which declared that there is 'a good economic case to invest early to avoid dangerous climate change'. UK emissions were 35% below 1990 levels in 2014 and provisional figures show emissions fell a further 3% in 2015. The first carbon budget has been met and the UK is currently on track to outperform the second and third carbon budgets, but not on track to meet the fourth, which covers the period 2023–27 (Committee on Climate Change, 2015).

In addition to strategic drivers at the policy level, there are market-led drivers as well. In 1990, we had the launch of BREEAM to the construction world. This was one of the first publicly available building environmental assessment systems, and now forms a common part of the planning and design process in the UK. This looked very broadly at sustainability and over time has considerably increased our understanding of the concept in the built environment. However, it suffers from the tick-box issues described in the previous section, tending to shift focus away from the deep challenge. Until 2008 it did not require evidence of success in anything other than prediction of performance. An extensive update introduced the requirement for a post-construction stage review in an attempt to verify the performance of the building rather than simply awarding certification based on design benchmarks.

---

4 http://www.demandlogic.co.uk.

While BREEAM takes this broader approach, another market-led driver exists in the Passivhaus model.[5] In this case, a gradual evolution had been taking place as researchers and pioneering practitioners built advanced buildings based upon the idea that buildings could be designed that simply remained comfortable without using fuel. This approach became known as Passivhaus and applied at first to a type of building that sort to avoid the need for heating. Early UK examples can be found at the University of East Anglia by Fulcrum Consulting (Standeven *et al.*, 1998).

The first pilot project was the Kranichstein passive house by Dr Wolfgang Feist (Passivhaus, 1990). This Passivhaus research group was a collaborative team focused on a clear, simple target. The University of East Anglia followed a traditional design team appointment for the first buildings, Constable Terrace and Nelson Court student residences, with the common arrangement of the engineer as consultant. This was a reasonable success, but frustrating to one of the authors as an engineer with a holistic building systems focus because of the separation of responsibility for the fabric and the services. This meant that the energy demand was determined by the architects and Fulcrum's appointment as engineers was to provide services to match whatever this demand might be.

When Fulcrum Consulting were invited to bid for the design of the Elizabeth Fry building it was strongly felt that it was necessary to take full responsibility for both building services advice and providing thermal detailing advice to the architect within the engineering appointment to really hit the targets. This approach enabled them to collaboratively engage with the fabric design. It also led to the structure being an integral part of the active ventilation, heating and cooling system through the use of ventilated precast concrete flooring. To enable this to happen required collaboration with the precast concrete suppliers at the earliest possible stage, with them involved as full members of the design team committed to delivering a warrantee for the building performance.

This is the Passivhaus approach rather than the broader ambitions of BREEAM. The narrower focus of Passivhaus has seemingly driven greater technical rigour faster where it has been introduced first. This is what is required to ensure we can deliver future design teams of project managers, architects, quantity surveyors, structural engineers and services engineers who can and are technically capable of guaranteeing building performance.

Over time there has been a shift in what the building services engineers do. It used to be that their fees were typically a percentage of the building services which were installed. Elizabeth Fry broke this mould as the fee was a percentage of the whole, removing any accidental incentive to include excess services in place of insulation.

The idea of fee structuring brings us to a recurrent theme in this chapter: contracts. There is, in our view, an insufficient contractual link between performance and profit margin. Ultimately a driver for change must link performance to profit in such a way that as the performance increases, the margin increases. This has to be over a short enough term to actually mean something to the people being paid. Our current challenge is this disconnect between property and construction that lies at the heart of the search for ways to link good building performance to increased profit.

---

5 http://www.passivhaus.org.uk.

Private finance initiatives (PFIs) bring together consortia including developers and investors, constructors and other service providers to finance, create and operate assets through long-term contracts. At first sight they should be a great mechanism for sustainability, but this has proven to be a naïve hope to date. These development consortia and the special purpose companies (SPCs) that they form are designed to deliver services according to strong contractual agreements that are negotiated with their public sector clients. These contracts typically last for between 15 and 50 years. These finance, design, engineer, construct and operate contracts are potentially the solution if the rewards for those delivering performance can be linked to the value of the asset over a long time. There is evidence that low-energy buildings and in particular net-zero buildings are a long-term excellent investment (Cortese, 2015). This just might deliver a route out of the never-ending cycle which is construction where profit is always from the current and next job rather than the success of past projects.

Things have continued to evolve and now because engineers are deemed to understand 'energy' they are increasingly appointed as 'sustainability technical' experts. This now includes both early and late stages, planning, pre-design stages and post design. This is a massive shift from the position in the 1990s of being brought in post tender for the design of services systems to being required to develop strategy to negotiate and deliver planning requirements for carbon and energy before pen has been placed on paper.

At one level, engineers have been at the forefront of the shift but alone they cannot deliver and they are still not generally well enough equipped through their education in creative design and problem solving to engage fully and collaboratively in design discussions with architects.

### 12.4.3   Collaboration and the performance gap

The idea of engagement across the design team is a fundamental step the industry needs to take in addressing building performance. The PROBE studies led by Bill Bordass and Adrian Leamann was a decade-long investigation into the causes of the performance gap (Bordass *et al.*, 2001). Most of the issues, such as excessive ventilation, window design, lighting and poor interfaces, could easily be addressed at the design stage through a more collaborative approach to how the building will actually be used, rather than designing to benchmarks such as Part L and BREEAM. Other factors, such as control and operation issues, were a direct result of designers not properly communicating the design intent to the building operators. The PROBE studies found that, in short, 'chronic occupant problems are widespread in British buildings. Many of these never come sufficiently high on anyone's priority list to get fixed, so slamming doors, and glare from sun and sky, hot offices, poor controls, noise disturbance and suchlike are the norms for occupants everywhere. They may seem trivial, but the effects on occupant satisfaction and perceived productivity are not.' (Leaman and Bordass, 2001: 142).

It could be said that building services engineers have been pushed very hard by the architects, who felt unable to advise effectively on how best to respond to these new client demands by passing them over to a specialist whose design decisions are apparently most affected even though their expertise was not in delivery of building fabric. But now the next stage is that the industry as a whole has to catch up.

We haven't completed the loop, but we've understood the extreme beginnings and the final ends and now we need to link them all back up again. Probably our next step is to understand people much better, both those we are designing for and those we work with. We didn't expect engineers to have to understand people in the early days. That was a surprise, but it turns out that comfort is highly subjective and energy use varies by a factor of three for the same building according to the way the occupants behave. Understanding society, human behaviour and interacting effectively with each other is by far the most important step beyond grasping basic thermodynamics. In our view, not enough designers or contractors grasp this quite yet.

## 12.5    Looking ahead to 2050

What does the building industry need to look like in 2050? One thing that hasn't changed anywhere is the need to deliver a project. This needs people to do different things, hold different skills and deliver an end product on time and to budget. There has been the introduction of a few new skills and the loss of old ones. Perhaps the greatest being the change in communication and its takeover by technology. Take the use of drawing to communicate. In the 1980s many architects would find that the very skill of working with pen and ink to draw that made them love their work was lost as computers arrived and CAD replaced hand drawing. Sketching at that moment became despised and yet this removed a core way of communication and shifted the load on to written words and those who could use them.

Despite changes in contracts and communication methods, to create a building all the same fundamental things still have to happen. Importantly an idea has to be formed, conceptualised, shared, engineered and constructed. Somebody has to be in charge of holding to the concept and making it work, but who employs who has moved around over time and their lines of responsibility have shifted.

The term 'novation' refers to a contract and duties being passed on, effectively nullifying an old agreement. This transfer of duties and obligations has become increasingly common in building design teams. The challenge is that if the design is incomplete at this point, then the new client or contractor has new pressures. The consultant's appointment is to work in the best interest of one's client. Having worked through the project from blank paper stage to tender, when 'sold on' to another client, with the first standing hopefully by, where do your responsibilities go? How do you achieve what you have evolved in intense discussion but as yet arguably incompletely described with the first client to whom you have a moral rather than entirely contractual responsibility? Collaboration in these circumstances faces significant challenges and such arrangements are far from ideal to deliver an integrated sustainable design. Perhaps this is the essence of 'professionalism', a topic explored by the EDGE commission on the professional institutions under Paul Morrell (Morrell, 2015).

Among Morrell's arguments was a critical need for education to break down the siloed nature of the built environment; more specifically that institutions should encourage greater integration and multidisciplinary working environments. By 'institutions', Morrell refers not only to higher education, but also to the professional institutions, arguing that their authority would increase considerably if they were to present shared views on critical matters of public interest, such as climate change.

Even the title of the Morrell report, *Collaboration for Change*, embodies the view of this current chapter: that the low-carbon path to 2050 that this industry seeks is one that we must walk together.

### 12.5.1 Motives for sustainability

Finding the right path to 2050 requires creating the right motives for sustainability. Construction and property will always be driven by money, so the question is how to use money to drive it in the right direction. How can we create a profit motive for sustainability? Well, part of the problem is that the construction industry is a relatively low profit margin industry. So, there has to be more profit in it. But the profit is not likely to be found in design and construction; it's in the long term. It is in property life-cycle management, managing the building and the property it occupies as an asset over many years. So, those things have to come together and optimisation will be the aim.

Good design means designing buildings that function properly, that deliver the experience that the client hoped for, giving them and society pride in their asset, that don't need tearing down and rebuilding too often, that can be changed and are flexible enough to cope with changes in the way we live and work. It's about this entire whole, and it's about filling in the gaps between the technology and the people at all stages. Essentially, construction is property, and property is construction.

To understand this is to realise we need to understand people and technology and how they interact, beginning with the design stage but not thinking any stage is an independent silo. Everyone must respect the skills and challenges faced at each point, and be willing to understand enough to trust.

Another aspect of creating motives is the issue of lobbying. Lobbying by the construction industry, and in particular the housing industry, to limit demands placed upon it has been extraordinarily successful. The Zero Carbon homes target introduced by the UK Labour Government in 2011 was an exciting thing. It got the housing industry very uptight. In response, they did two things: they set up the Zero Carbon Hub and they did a lot of lobbying. They lobbied well and at the change of government the first thing that happened was a change in the definition of zero carbon within weeks of coming into power. From there things seemed to go backwards. Politicians often speak of evidence-based policy, and certainly no government ever sets out to do the opposite, but the politics around sustainability on this occasion were undeniably clouded.

The 2008 UK Climate Change Act (HM Government, 2008) and wider efforts like the Paris Agreement (United Nations, 2015) are all positive progress, and they suggest that we can at least in principle come together to face big problems. But despite noble targets we have yet to create a stable long-term policy framework for climate change that brings industry along in ways that create virtuous cycles of innovation that still drive business interests. Unfortunately, the realities of climate change will continue regardless of how politicians define the phrase 'zero carbon'.

### 12.5.2 Building information modelling

One area in which the UK Government has taken a lead is in understanding their power as a client. In May 2011, the Cabinet Office published the *Government Construction Strategy* (Cabinet Office, 2011). The report announced the Government's intention to require collaborative 3D building information modelling (BIM; with all project and asset information, documentation and data being electronic) on its projects by 2016. The collaboration comes in the form of how the information is exchanged between different parties and is the crucial aspect of this level. Design information is shared through a common file format, which enables any organisation to be able to combine that data with their own in order to make a federated BIM model, and to carry out inter-rogative checks on it. Hence any CAD software that each party used must be capable of exporting to one of the common file formats such as Industry Foundation Class (IFC) or Construction Operations Building Information Exchange (COBie).

The UK Government having long viewed the construction industry as too hard to deal with but has recently decided that it has potential to contribute significantly more to UK growth if it can modernise and learn to collaborate. This is particularly true for expertise in digital and highly exportable processes, such as BIM. The UK construction industry indirectly employs over three million people. It is highly diverse with a number of subsectors that deliver around £100 billion to the UK economy anually. Its structure is a small number of internationally renowned large companies and an enormous tail of small and medium-sized enterprisess and micro organisations (HM Government, 2012).

Since 2011 the UK Government has embarked with industry on a 4-year program to modernise the sector with the key objective of reducing capital cost and the carbon burden from the construction and operation of the built environment by 20%. Central to these ambitions has been the adoption of information-rich BIM technologies and process to drive collaborative behaviours. The ambition is to unlock better, more effi-cient ways of working at all stages of the project lifecycle.

The process for the whole industry in 2016 is incomplete, and perhaps the scale of the challenge has been underestimated. Nevertheless, change towards a modern digital industry is clearly underway, with many projects, such as Crossrail (a major new rail infrastructure project) and the Olympics held in London in 2012, delivered very successfully. At the same time contractors and consultants are embracing the concept of BIM and looking for opportunities. With the government effectively procuring around 20% of all UK construction perhaps it is reasonable to anticipate that changes will make their way into private procurement.

Over the past 4 years, the BIM task force (BIS, 2013b) has refined its approach, delivered standards, methods and tools, and can reasonably claim to have demonstrated that significant learning and savings can be made through the use of digital technologies such as BIM. The UK Government has now declared that it will aim for level 3 BIM or Open BIM. Issues such as copyright and liability are intended to be resolved by developing robust appointment documents and traceable software originator/read/write permissions, and utilisation of shared-risk procurement routes such as partnering, which will require a considerable culture shift from construction's traditional linear thinking, embedded adversarial culture and focus on short-term cost.

### 12.5.3   Collaboration versus competition

The industry is well aware and very focused on coordination, as without it projects end up in a mess and not making money. We also regularly work in cooperation with others in design teams, but again this is focused on the delivery of a project or design. Both coordination and cooperation are a necessary part of a collaborative approach.

Cooperation takes place on any given project, while coordination is intrinsically long term and goal focused, beyond any individual project. It is about developing a relationship. The behaviour of a good collaborator will demonstrate openness and clear communication across boundaries, deliberately seeking to understand different approaches by the other experts and understand that it is always possible to learn better ways of working and contribute ideas from their own experience towards shared goals.

Expert knowledge is vital and validates things being done in a particular way, but there are multiple experts in a design and construction team. BIM is the opportunity to benefit and share a long-term aim of making things easier for each other, and using new work flow practices and blurring of boundaries, not only to allow open discussion in a respectful manner, but to also encourage sharing of expertise through commenting on each other's work and approaches without threat or discomfort.

Hoarding knowledge as a way to hold power is old-fashioned: it causes reciprocal negative behaviour and creates an atmosphere of distrust which is counterproductive and time-consuming. We know this, and yet it is the way our industry has behaved for a long time.

Clients are starting to observe and judge how teams behave, and create contracts which monitor and observe collaboration because it is a way to enable innovation, with savings in time and increases in efficiency. A well-structured collaborative team concentrates on the relationship beyond the project and the focus of the immediate task. Focusing on added value for a client, developing empathy to understand, wanting to embrace change and to understand how to influence for the greater good are all valid qualities for professionals. This requires sound knowledge and performing the traditional role of a professional as an expert, but it also requires a shift in the way such skills are deployed. Effective collaboration requires leadership and the skill to use knowledge creatively. Setting the right tone enables rapid change from confrontation to collaboration. Trust and respect has to be built within the team by explaining and debating in simple language, then doing what you say you will do and being tolerant in potential conflict situations.

People who display these behaviours are sometimes referred to as 'T-shaped people', working across boundaries trying to help each other (Guest, 1991). They see other companies as partners and look for ways to help each other, being comfortable to be seen to behave in this way openly. They discuss and establish common goals then look to find the simplest processes to get the information and the data needed to the right person so they tell each other what is useful and what is not.

In essence, the focus of this approach is not on the profession: it is on the role in the team. For example, the BIM Task Group have produced a Profession Map (BIS, 2013b) as a development tool to assist in developing and assessing the maturity of the individual and team behaviour in procurement. This matters a great deal if we are to develop a sustainable built environment in our country.

### 12.5.4 Sustainability as an infrastructure priority

The radical decarbonisation of the built environment must be approached as an infrastructure priority and planned in those terms. This argument has been advanced by many, including the UK Green Building Council (UKGBC). This strategy of decarbonisation calls for the UK building stock to be considered a public asset like the roads and bridges.

This would make the refurbishment or retrofit of UK buildings a long-term, consistently funded policy priority. This step would enable the private sector and government to collaborate and achieve a transformation not just of our industry, but of our country and the quality of life of the country's citizens. Treating buildings as infrastructure would also deliver the symbolic message that our built environment is something we experience together and share a collective responsibility in maintaining. It would also send long-term signals of stability to those wishing to invest in sustainability across the entire supply chain, from products to practitioners.

Sustainability is by its nature about sharing and collaborating to achieve a better long-term result. All the buildings we build from now on need to work first time and be low carbon, or near zero energy, from day one, and for their whole lifetime. Perhaps even more importantly most of the buildings that will be here in 2050 are already built and they will need radical refurbishment to achieve our carbon reduction targets. The UK has over 20 million homes, the majority of which do not perform to the needed standard. This is a huge long-term project, which will require a sophisticated and sensitive industry. Currently, however, this would not be how one would describe construction, despite some exemplars, but it can be achieved. Some of the best companies we have are in the infrastructure sector because they have the freedom to focus on large-scale projects, removing the constant focus on the need to bid for the next project that besets the majority of UK construction.

### 12.5.5 Balancing future supply and demand

A major challenge we face is the integration of the energy supply system with an energy demand system. In the UK coal is rapidly being phased out and the investment community is looking at post-carbon energy sources as the place for returns. The development of nuclear power in the UK is slow. Fracking is being promoted and we are increasingly reliant on imported natural gas. The National Grid plays out a minute-by-minute balancing act between supply and demand. This task is set to become increasingly challenging as this fossil fuel base load is replaced with intermittent renewables. The electrification of heat is a key strand of the UK decarbonisation strategy. Heating accounts for half the UK's overall energy use and 80% of homes are heated by natural gas (DECC, 2014). Shifting this considerable energy burden to electric sources such as heat pumps will further strain the National Grid. The UK is very close to rolling blackouts being a reality and has been for the past 3 years. The next 35 years will have to redefine how our buildings interact with energy grids. Buildings will no longer be standalone projects, but part of a balanced energy system.

Until recently our interaction as built environment professionals with energy suppliers has been through intermediaries and simply purchasing a supply of a suitable size. The grid itself has been remote from us. Now, however, our role is changing. Our interaction with electricity supply and generation is changing the way we design and operate our buildings, which is affecting the way our grid operates as our buildings become micro power stations. Traditional electricity generators and distributors are struggling to adapt to this more diffuse and less predictable generation system.

Meanwhile legislation, particularly through the planning regime, is forcing built environment professionals to take ever greater responsibility for predicting and controlling the amount of energy used by their buildings (DCLG, 2014). All this is within a changing planning and commercial environment. However, within this change lies the solution to much of the problem. We are developing building solutions that will allow much more flexibility in supply by introducing storage into both individual buildings and districts. However, we are not far away from energy rationing of some form, both in total quantity and in time of use.

Effective answers in the energy domain can, however, only be reached through a collaborative approach to problem solving by engineers and designers who understand the issues and how they can creatively be resolved. The issue of design as creative problem solving must be part of the education of our future professionals across all disciplines. If a building is to fit into a balanced energy system it requires building services engineers to work with urban planners, perhaps considering how one building can reject heat to serve another. The architect must work with the structural engineer to determine how the building's form and mass can be used as thermal storage to shift peak loads on the grid. And all of them must work with the building operators to both ensure and improve the performance over time.

In this world of energy and engineering we are dealing with people's health and comfort, and with all the complex issues they face in seeking to achieve a reasonable level of well-being equitably where comfort is not considered a privilege. Failure to provide comfort will be an issue which has a nationwide impact on our health and on our welfare budget. We therefore need people to be able to unpick and make sensible decisions that lead to better simpler and therefore sustainable solutions, rather than ever increasing complexity and instability.

Buildings individually will struggle to meet the zero-energy target, but groups of buildings can achieve this and we can expect to see various approaches seeking to find the optimum group size. This will be achieved through innovations such as district and community energy. Entire communities could potentially go off-grid as energy generation becomes localised. Such a community may generate all of their own energy with renewable resources, capturing and treating all of its water, and operating efficiently. Outside the UK, for example, the Australian town of Huntlee has set itself to be the country's first off-grid town, but a recent study identified 40 further towns located at the edges of existing grids which could find off-grid sustainability more cost effective (Renew, 2016).

This shift will be enabled by new ways of sharing and storing energy. This will also be assisted by a clear understanding that energy can be seen as both thermal and electrical power, which would also require a pipe network to collect and share heating and cooling, and smart grids to direct, control and share energy use.

Building professionals could be at the heart of the design and management of these networks and they will need to share and collaborate across industries rather than simply working within stages of design and delivery within the construction industry itself. However, failure to do so will see traditional professions and trades side-lined by new entrants, who see this area as a huge opportunity. For example, innovation might be in industrialisation of refurbishment for the home retrofit market utilising the robotics in use in the car industry.

All this will begin to shift the balance away from the current electricity supply grid, which is currently centrally controlled and manages by instruction. Instead, it will transition to a more distributed and negotiated relationship between smaller scale supply-side generators and the demand-side end users. Much of this negotiation and grid balancing will take place at the community level rather than the national level. The cost of locally generated solar and storage is, or soon will be, lower than the cost of generation in large centralised generators and transmitting the output across the network.

A project at London South Bank University called Balanced Energy Networks (BEN) points to a step in this direction (Balanced Energy Network, 2016). The project is designed to link buildings up thermally and electrically, and lets them share heating loads with each other and with underground storage. Perhaps one of the most fascinating things about what is happening now is that it is a network that can grow over time. It creates a viable system on a scale as small as two buildings, and further buildings can be added to the network without resizing or changing what has already been done. In fact, adding new load points actually increases the overall efficiency of the system by making it easier to balance out the different loads. In much the same way as a growing internet makes it easier to share information, a growing BEN system makes it easier to share heat.

### 12.5.6   The future of professional institutions

The challenges we face are huge and the timescale tight as we move towards 2050. We must also acknowledge that theoretical collaborative knowledge and skills alone will not save us, any more than skills in project management alone can deliver a project. Expertise is required and detailed understanding will also be essential, but the skills of collaboration and project management must prevent this expertise functioning in the traditional 'silos'.

Respect must be built across professions and trades to enable the rapid structural changes needed. This requires not just a technological shift, but a shift in the historic positions of professional institutions and trade associations. Much of this comes down to the need to communicate, share knowledge plainly without resort to arcane language and share information sources transparently.

Where might these shifts be formalised? They will need reference within the construction contracts to have any clout, and the status of a chartered professional through the associated professional institutions is perhaps the place to begin to address this.

We must in essence shift professional institutions from a position of creating and tightly holding unique knowledge, protecting it for members use only, towards creating and badging the 'trusted experts' who can use knowledge from the full cross-section of professional sources for the greater good, even when contractual pressure is applied. The professional must, of course, be held to account for such action, but also legally protected, and required to do so. Money counts, of course, so a way of contractual enforcement is required which must be jointly agreed.

## 12.6   Conclusions

If we stand back and look at the societal challenge required to achieve sustainability, two things are clear: things must work in practice not just in principle, and we need to be more comfortable with taking a long view to tackling big problems. The principles of a sustainable design are of little use if we can't tie them to performance in practice.

Governments following short-term election cycles must somehow create a long-term narrative that is both inspiring and consistent.

Key to achieving a sustainable built environment will be how the construction industry reacts. The promise put forward by BIM is a process and a technology that integrates the design, construction, performance and evaluation of a building project. If this promise is fulfilled, we will soon be in a position that is extremely different to where we are now. If construction can indeed modernise, and understand that it has the opportunity to lead the way to a sustainable future through collaboration and taking on the entire lifecycle of buildings, it will thrive and help take the lead for the UK around the world. If it does not, this modern connected world will deliver the opportunity to others, and UK construction will remain project deliverers with low profit margins and short horizons.

The construction industry is showing signs of growing up and being keen to take responsibility for the long term, including the education of those it needs for this future, for example developing its own curriculum for school children through the Design, Engineer, Construct programme, delivering a project-based curriculum that allows young people to discover architecture and engineering.[6]

At university level the Royal Academy of Engineering has also introduced Centres of Excellence for Sustainable Building Design to spread the understanding of the benefits in both architecture and engineering that these challenges provide. This is an important step in signalling the scale of transition that is about to occur and the academic excellence that will be required to deliver it. A modern building industry will be increasingly attractive to the world's top minds.

That brings us to where we are now. To summarise, the contracts that underpin the building industry have become more complex. Performance has been externalised, and we need a profit motive for performance to truly drive sustainability. Technology should help communication but we can't rely on a tech revolution. We have to rethink what we're building now and also renew our existing energy infrastructure. It is time to take the lead.

## References

Arup (2013) *Green Construction Board Buildings Working Group Final Report*, 4 March, 2013. Arup. Available at: http://www.greenconstructionboard.org/otherdocs/ Routemap%20final%20report%2005032013.pdf.

Balanced Energy Network (2016) *BEN Project*. London South Bank University, London. Available at: http://www.lsbu.ac.uk/research/research-interests/sites/ben-project.

Better Buildings Partnership (2016) *Industry to Design for Performance in New Pilots*. Available at: http://www.betterbuildingspartnership.co.uk/ industry-design-performance-new-pilots.

BIS (2013a) *Supply Chain Analysis into the Construction Industry – A Report for the Construction Industrial Strategy*. Research Paper No. 145. Department for Business Innovation and Skills, London.

---

6 http://designengineerconstruct.com/.

BIS (2013b) *Industrial strategy: government and industry in partnership.* Department for Business Innovation and Skills, London. Available at: http://www.bimtaskgroup. org/wp-content/uploads/2013/05/HM-Government-Industrial-strategy-government-and-industry-in-partnership-BIM-Building-Information-Modelling.pdf (accessed 30 January 2017).

Bordass, B., Cohen, R., Standeven, M. and Leaman, A. (2001) Assessing building performance in use 2: technical performance of the Probe buildings. *Building Research & Information*, 29(2), 103–113.

Bordass, B., Cohen, R. and Field, J. (2004) *Energy Performance of Non-Domestic Buildings: Closing the Credibility Gap.* Building Performance Congress. Available at: http://www. usablebuildings.co.uk/Pages/Unprotected/EnPerfNDBuildings.pdf.

Cabinet Office (2011) *Government Construction Strategy.* Cabinet Office, London.

CIBSE (2000) *CIBSE Guide L: Sustainability.* Chartered Institution of Building Services Engineering, London.

Committee on Climate Change (2015) *The Fifth Carbon Budget – The next step towards a low-carbon economy.* Committee on Climate Change, London.

Cortese, A. (2015) *Net Zero and Living Building Challenge Financial Study: A cost comparison report for buildings in the district of Columbia.* International Living Institute on behalf of District Department of the Environment.

DCLG (2014) *Conservation of Fuel and Power: Approved Document L.* Department for Communities and Local Government, London. Available at: https://www.gov.uk/ government/publications/conservation-of-fuel-and-power-approved-document-l (accessed 28 January 2016).

DECC (2014) *Estimates of heat use in the United Kingdom in 2013.* Department of Energy and Climate Change, London.

Energy Action (2016) *Commitment Agreements – UK Feasibility Review Report.* REP07083-A-001.1a. Usable Buildings Trust, London.

European Commission (2017) *Nearly zero-energy buildings.* Available at: https://ec.europa. eu/energy/en/topics/energy-efficiency/buildings/nearly-zero-energy-buildings (accessed 20 February 2017).

Guest, D. (1991) The hunt is on for the Renaissance Man of computing. *The Independent*, 17 September.

HM Government (2008) *Climate Change Act 2008.* HM Government, London.

HM Government (2012) *Industrial strategy: government and industry partnership: Building Information Modelling.* HM Government, London. Available at: https://www.gov.uk/ government/uploads/system/uploads/attachment_data/file/34710/12-1327-building-information-modelling.pdf.

International Energy Agency (2016) *Definition and Simulation of Occupant Behavior in Buildings.* Available at: http://www.iea-ebc.org/fileadmin/user_upload/docs/Facts/ EBC_Annex_66_Factsheet.pdf.

Kwawu, W. and Hughes, W. (2005) The impact of relational contracting on the construction industry, 21st Annual ARCOM Conference, University of London. *Association of Researchers in Construction Management*, 2, 1195–1204.

Latham, M. (1994) *Constructing the Team. Design, Drawing and Print Services.* ISBN 0 11 752994 X.

Leaman, A. and Bordass, B. (2001) Assessing building performance in use 4: the Probe occupant surveys and their implications. *Building Research & Information*, 29(2), 129–143.

Lindblom, P. (1985) *International Federation of Institutes of Advanced Studies.* WCED Public Hearing, Oslo.

London South Bank University (2016) *Ultra wideband radar developed to track home energy usage.* Available at: http://www.lsbu.ac.uk/case-studies/ultra-wideband-radar-developed-track-home-energy-usage.

Morrell, P. (2015) *Collaboration for Change.* EDGE Commission Report. Available at: http://www.edgedebate.com/wp-content/uploads/2015/05/150415_collaborationforchange_book.pdf.

Passivhaus (1990) The World's First Passive House. Available at: http://www.netzeronyc2020.net/Pages/firstpassiveHouse.aspx.

Renew (2016) *The 40 Australian towns that could, and should, quit the grid.* Available at: http://reneweconomy.com.au/2016/the-40-australian-towns-that-could-and-should-quit-the-grid-93813.

Royal Academy of Engineering (2010) *Engineering a low carbon built environment.* Royal Academy of Engineering.

Standeven, M., Cohen, R., Bordass, B. and Leaman, A. (1998) PROBE 14: Elizabeth Fry. *CIBSE Building Services Journal,* April.

Stern, N. (2010) *Stern Review: The Economics of Climate Change.* Available at: http://webarchive.nationalarchives.gov.uk/20100407172811/http://www.hm-treasury.gov.uk/d/Executive_Summary.pdf.

Sustainable Development Foundation (2014) *GCB Project 430 Knowledge Capture and Discussion – Report for the Green Construction Board, June, 2014.* Available at: http://www.greenconstructionboard.org/images/stories/Knowledge_and_Skills/SDF%20Exec%20Summary.pdf.

United Nations (2015) *Paris Agreement.* United Nations Framework Convention on Climate Change, Paris.

World Commission on Environment and Development (1987) *Our Common Future (Brundtland Rport).* Oxford University Press, Oxford.

## 13

# Built Environment Professionals as Sustainability Advocates

*Gerard Healey*

## 13.1   A view from 'the middle'

The urgency of improving the environmental performance of the world's building stock is increasing (WMO, 2016). Analysis of carbon mitigation strategies tends to focus on top-down or bottom-up approaches (IPCC, 2014). Examples of top-down include government regulation regarding energy efficiency or putting a price on carbon. In contrast, bottom-up approaches are driven by end-users or the market more broadly, such as office tenants only occupying buildings that meet particular sustainability criteria.

Janda and Parag (2013) expand on this binary view by arguing that building designers (or 'the middle') are also a legitimate actor for improving the energy performance of buildings. Examples of influence from the middle from the author's professional experience include contributing technical expertise to government regulation and policy, developing design standards for building owners, and designing buildings and systems that are more energy efficient than required by building code (without being requested to by the owner).

The fact that the middle can act as a driver of change is no surprise for design professions, with the opportunity and responsibility of the middle to influence the sustainability of the built environment being enshrined in professional codes of practice (Engineers Australia, 2010; Australian Institute of Architects, 2006; American Institute of Architects, 2012; CIBSE, 2015).

Janda and Parag (2013) describe three indicative modes of influence for 'the middle':

- enabling: allowing and possibly promoting a technology or strategy without altering it to suit the project circumstances
- mediating: adopting and adapting a technology, strategy or process to suit the project circumstances
- aggregating: harnessing cross-project opportunities, such as developing rules of thumb and defining best practice for particular building types based on experience on multiple projects, or aggregating projects to create sufficient scale to enable more cost-effective procurement.

One potential weakness of Janda and Parag's paper, however, is that it does not explicitly discuss the recognised need for built environment professionals to act as advocates

*Sustainable Futures in the Built Environment to 2050: A Foresight Approach to Construction and Development*, First Edition. Edited by Tim Dixon, John Connaughton and Stuart Green.
© 2018 John Wiley & Sons Ltd. Published 2018 by John Wiley & Sons Ltd.

for more sustainable solutions, with 'allowing (and possibly promoting) a technology or strategy' as part of the definition for 'enabling', being the closest they come to this (Janda and Parag, 2013: 45).

The opportunities for practitioners in 'the middle' to advocate for better sustainability outcomes has also been an area of active interest for the author, particularly in relation to how to increase the uptake of sustainability initiatives by developers and building owners (Healey, 2008, 2014, 2015).

This chapter adds to the discourse on opportunities for 'the middle' by sharing the outcomes of action-learning undertaken by the author to improve his own professional practice over 10 years working as a sustainable building design consultant. Methodologically, the action-learning approach is characterised by cycles of planning, acting, observing and critically reflecting in real-world settings in collaboration with stakeholders (Koshy *et al.*, 2011), making it well suited for research on building and consulting projects. It has the potential to simultaneously contribute to knowledge and practice, but because the learnings are situation and context specific, care needs to be taken in making generalisations (Koshy *et al.*, 2011). The chapter seeks to add to the understanding of 'the middle' by:

- arguing why built environment professionals need to view themselves as advocates, not just as professionals responding to a client brief or government regulation
- discussing some of the challenges in acting as an advocate
- sharing some communication techniques from literature that have influenced the author's approach to sustainability advocacy
- presenting examples from the author's professional practice in trying the techniques and reflecting on their effectiveness.

In doing so, the aim is to provide answers to the question 'How can built environment professionals be more effective advocates for sustainable buildings?'

## 13.2   Built environment professionals as sustainability advocates

Although Janda and Parag's categories in themselves suggest there is little role for built environment professionals as 'advocates', many built environment professional associations recognise the need for their members to promote sustainable outcomes.

For example, the Engineers Australia Code of Ethics requires members to 'promote sustainability' and 'practise engineering to foster the health, safety and wellbeing of the community and the environment' (Engineers Australia, 2010: 1), while one of Engineers Australia's required competencies for a chartered engineer is understanding stakeholder values, communicating in the terminology of the stakeholder, and ethically influencing stakeholders for the best overall interest of relevant communities (Engineers Australia, 2012). Similarly, the Chartered Institute of Building Services Engineers requires its members to 'promote the principles of sustainability and seek to prevent the avoidable adverse impact on the environment and society' (CIBSE, 2015: para 10).

Some professional architecture organisations set similar obligations for their members, including the Australian Institute of Architects ('encourage and maintain responsible ecologically sustainable and energy efficient design and development'; Australian

Institute of Architects, 2006: 1) and the American Institute of Architects ('In performing professional services, Members should advocate the design, construction, and operation of sustainable buildings and communities' (American Institute of Architects, 2012: 4)). Similarly, the Royal Institution of Chartered Surveyors has identified sustainability as a 'growing area of practice' for the future, with the need for members to develop more skills in this area (Cook and Chatterjee, 2015: 62).

In the background, however, human impact on the earth continues, with the World Meteorological Organisation noting that world leaders need to 'fast track' implementation of action (WMO, 2016: para 7). Built environment professionals therefore need to be advocates for sustainability.

## 13.3   Challenges in being a sustainability advocate

In the author's experience, there are a number of challenges that face built environment professionals in consciously acting as an advocate for sustainability at the same time as being a designer or advisor responding to client requests. These are now discussed in more detail.

### 13.3.1   Ethics

A significant challenge for professionals wanting to design more sustainable buildings is that clients and other project team members may not share the same vision. This can lead to moral dilemmas, with the individual potentially caught between their obligations to their client, employer, profession, broader society and/or their own sense of what is right (Van den Hoven *et al.*, 2012; Roeser, 2012). Another type of ethical challenge can occur if other project team members over-state the sustainability performance of a building or its features (Robb, 2016) – known as green wash – something which is both ethically wrong and, in Australia, potentially illegal (ACCC, 2011).

### 13.3.2   Lack of engagement

Many researchers note the challenges of engaging people in environmental issues, particularly climate change (Hoffman and Henn, 2008; Nisbet, 2009; Shome and Marx, 2009; Gromet *et al.*, 2013). The author has personal experience with this, having witnessed participants in a sustainability workshop become disengaged – demonstrated through lack of eye contact, body language, checking their phone – during discussion regarding melting ice caps. Reasons for lack of engagement, particularly in relation to climate change, could be because they do not believe it exists or do not think it will affect them (Shome and Marx, 2009; Nisbet, 2009).

Alternatively, stakeholder disengagement could be a result of a practitioner's attempts to engage (O'Neill and Nicholson-Cole, 2009; O'Neill *et al.*, 2012). O'Neill and Nicholson-Cole found that the shock- and fear-inducing images that '...made participants have the greatest sense of climate change being important were also dis-empowering at a personal level. These images were said to drive feelings of helplessness, remoteness, and lack of control' (O'Neill and Nicholson-Cole, 2009: 373). Conversely, the researchers found that the images '...making participants feel most able to do something about climate change did not hook their interest in the issue and were more likely to make people feel that climate change was unimportant...' (O'Neill and Nicholson-Cole, 2009: 373).

### 13.3.3   Stakeholder preconceptions

When advocating for sustainability, professionals may discover that stakeholders have preconceptions regarding specific initiatives or sustainability as a whole.

Cost is one powerful preconception and, in the author's experience, stakeholders often over-estimate the cost and complexity of implementing sustainability (World Green Building Council, 2013). It is the author's hypothesis that this perception persists, at least in part, because the construction industry is highly aware of the expensive, complicated or risky sustainability features (Healey, 2011) and is unaware of, or simply does not remember, the simple, cheap and reliable features. There is a scientific basis for this hypothesis, with psychologists noting that bad events are stronger than good in forming lasting memories (Baumeister *et al.*, 2001). The World Green Building Council (2013) suggests that people may overestimate the costs of green buildings because their views have become anchored by historical data and fail to account for price decreases (particularly relevant for photovoltaic panels in recent years), or anchored by widely publicised showcase buildings without considering how representative these buildings are of their own project.

Another common preconception is linked to the potentially political nature of sustainability and climate change action. For potentially polarising issues such as climate change, personal opinions can signal political ideology or other cultural affiliations. What people consider to be evidence and how they interpret it can be significantly affected by the accepted wisdom of their cultural group (Kahan, 2010, 2013; Kahan *et al.*, 2012). In such situations, opposing groups can become more polarised when presented with scientifically sound information (Kahan, 2010) and scientific literacy can potentially exacerbate the polarisation rather than diffusing it (Kahan *et al.*, 2012). As Hoffman and Henn (2008) note, the term 'green building' may be viewed negatively because some people associate it with the hippie movement, environmental activists or the political left. The author has witnessed this when the following question was asked as an ice-breaking question for a workshop: 'Is ecologically sustainable design tree-hugging or good business?' The designers in the room said 'good business', but the client's finance manager said 'tree-hugging'.

An environmental label may also be viewed negatively because of assumptions that environmental friendliness occurs at the expense of product quality (Hoffman and Henn, 2008; Newman *et al.*, 2014). For example, appliance manufacturer Whirlpool reportedly had to overcome a preconception in consumers that better water efficiency meant poorer washing performance for washing machines (Hoffman, 2006).

### 13.3.4   Double standards

Cost and payback are commonly viewed as the key to the success or failure of sustainable building initiatives. However, building projects involve a wide range of complex decisions that are not all made using the same process or quantitative and qualitative criteria. For example, Kinsley and DeLeon (2009) note that climate mitigation projects are generally subject to strict payback standards, whereas other building features (e.g. feature wood panelling) are not.

The author has witnessed this type of double standard in his own practice on many projects. For example, a hospital's finance director stated during a discussion regarding sustainability for a new hospital that all company investments were required to achieve a 3-year payback. However, the project had outdoor break areas for all staff rooms not subject to any payback period analysis. Instead they were seen as a functional require-ment related to attracting and retaining staff – a key risk for the project because of skills shortages in key professions in that location. In this hospital example, a key functional requirement overrides the payback period requirement. Similarly, on two high-rise office fit-outs, intra-tenancy stairs spanning six to seven levels were installed, costing approximately AU\$1.5 million each, which was approximately 5–10% of the project budget. The stairs arguably have positive environmental, health, social and productivity benefits, yet no cost–benefit study was undertaken to justify their inclusion. Instead it was a decision based on the expected benefits of staff interaction and business produc-tivity. Examples such as these begin to illustrate the diverse ways in which decisions are made and that payback is not always the driver or barrier.

### 13.3.5   Communicating in the language of the stakeholder

Engineers Australia requires chartered engineers to communicate in the terminology of the stakeholder. While speaking the language of the audience may seem self-evident, it can be poorly anticipated, even by high-level sustainability professionals. VOX Global *et al.* (2012) surveyed sustainability managers in large American companies and asked them what they thought would be the most critical success factor in their role before and after they took the job. Before starting, most thought that subject matter expertise would be most important, but once in their roles all agreed that communication and interpersonal skills were the most important factors. Even when a practitioner recog-nises the need to communicate in the language of the stakeholder, it can be difficult to do so in practice, with different people using their own professional jargon, using differ-ent words to describe the same thing, or the same word to describe different things (Hes, 2005; Shome and Marx, 2009). A further challenge can occur with terms such as climate change and global warming, which some people view as synonymous, but can '…activate different sets of beliefs, feelings, and behaviours, as well as different degrees of urgency about the need to respond' (Shome and Marx, 2009: 4).

## 13.4   Opportunities for more effective sustainability advocacy

A practitioner looking for guidance on how to better advocate for sustainable outcomes can find a range of reports that discuss the quantitative business case for green buildings (Kats *et al.*, 2003; GBCA, 2008; Slaughter, 2013; World Green Building Council, 2013). In the author's experience, quantitative financial arguments are only one technique of many that built environment professionals can use to better advocate for sustainability.

Table 13.1 summarises some studies that have influenced the author's approach to advocating for sustainable buildings. Each of the techniques is discussed further in the subsequent text.

**Table 13.1** Communication techniques and potential outcomes.

| Technique | Description | Difference in impact between more/less effective technique |
|---|---|---|
| Framing the message | In a laboratory experiment, compact fluorescent light (CFL) globes were labelled with a 'protect the environment' sticker or left blank<br><br>Factual information regarding the performance of the globes was presented in all cases | The proportion of people that chose the CFL over an incandescent globe varied by 20–30% depending on whether the sticker was attached, but the direction of change depended on political ideology (Gromet *et al.*, 2013). |
| Using social norms | Using descriptive social norms rather than environmental messages | Goldstein *et al.* (2008) found a 7–9% increase in towel reuse when a hotel used a sign with a descriptive norm compared to a standard environmental message<br><br>Similarly, Nolan *et al.* (2008) found that after 1 month, using social norms resulted in a 7–10% decrease in household energy consumption compared to the control group, compared to using a 2–3% decrease when using environmental messaging |
| Multiple techniques | Using vivid communication, personalised recommendations, encouraging commitment and framing the recommendations in terms of 'loss' rather than 'gain' | 30% increased applications for retrofit financing from homeowners who were visited by auditors trained using the techniques compared to those visited by the control auditors (Gonzale *et al.*, 1988) |

## 13.4.1 Framing tailored to the audience

Framing refers to the way information is presented and the context in which it is presented. A classic form of framing is emphasising losses rather than gains (Tversky and Kahneman, 1986; De Martino *et al.*, 2006).

When used purposefully, framing helps the audience engage with the decision in a positive way; emphasising the aspects of the design proposal that will most resonate with them and not distracting them with things they do not care about (Nisbet, 2009).

An example of the potential impact of framing (and preconceptions) comes from a study in the USA into purchasing preferences for energy-efficient light bulbs (Gromet *et al.*, 2013). Participants were given $2 to purchase a light bulb and any money they did not spend on the light bulb they kept for themselves. Their choice was between incandescent and compact fluorescent light (CFL) bulbs that produced equivalent brightness. Participants were split into four groups based on the relative cost of the bulbs and whether or not the CFL was labelled with a 'Protect the Environment' sticker. In one pair of tests the bulbs had the same price ($0.50), and in the other pair the CFL bulb was more expensive ($1.50) than the incandescent bulb ($0.50). All participants were given the same technical information about the two light bulb options (i.e. the CFL bulb lasts for 9000 more hours and reduces energy cost by 75%). Participants also completed a survey that ranked how politically conservative (right-leaning) or liberal (left-leaning) they were.

When the bulbs were the same price, the label had no effect. Almost all participants chose the CFL bulb, suggesting that long-term economic considerations dominated their choice. In contrast, when the CFL bulb was three times more expensive than the incandescent bulb, the sticker had a significant effect that varied with the respondents' political leanings (as measured by the survey). When the CFL was labelled as having environmental benefits, approximately 30% of people who were politically conservative (right-leaning) chose the energy-saving CFL. However, when the label was removed, 60% – twice as many conservative people – chose the CFL. The reduced uptake with the environmental label attached was also present for those who identified themselves as moderately left, with only the most politically left showing a reduction in uptake when the label was removed; from 70–80% with the label attached down to 50–60% uptake with no label (Gromet *et al.*, 2013).

### 13.4.2   Social norms

Descriptive social norms are descriptions of how most people behave in a particular situation (Goldstein *et al.*, 2008; Nolan *et al.*, 2008). As noted in Table 13.1 research regarding the reuse of towels in hotel rooms and household energy consumption has shown that messages using descriptive norms can have a larger effect on outcomes than environmental messaging. What is particularly interesting is that people may not be self-aware of this. For example, in their household energy study, Nolan *et al.* (2008) surveyed Californians about their underlying beliefs about what motivated energy conservation behaviour. They found, both before and after the campaign, that people expected that messages highlighting the financial, environmental or social benefits of saving energy would be more motivating than messages using descriptive norms. However, messages using descriptive peer norms (e.g. '99% of people in your community reported turning off unnecessary lights to save energy') resulted in the largest measured energy savings.

### 13.4.3   Multiple techniques

Finally, we should also consider the use of a range of techniques to help communications. For example, Gonzale *et al.* (1988) illustrate the potential impact of drawing on multiple communication techniques to better promote sustainability initiatives. They found that energy auditors trained to more effectively engage and motivate homeowners achieved a 30% greater implementation rate than equally experienced auditors who did not receive the communication training. The techniques included in the training were (Gonzale *et al.*, 1988):

- to communicate using vivid examples (e.g. comparing the total size of cracks under doors as equivalent to a hole in the wall the size of a football)
- to personalise the recommendations to the homeowners (e.g. by using the homeowners' own utility bills to illustrate current losses or potential savings)
- to encourage homeowner commitment (e.g. by involving them in the audit process and encouraging a verbal commitment to address the findings)
- to frame recommendations in terms of 'loss' rather than 'gain' (e.g. by highlighting the energy and money lost due to inaction rather than the energy or money saved by action).

## 13.5    Personal reflections on practice

The examples presented above show that various communication techniques can have significant impacts on the uptake of sustainability initiatives and behaviours. The following section shares some of the author's experiences in applying these techniques over the last 10 years of professional practice. These examples provide some insight into the author's experiences and opportunities for 'the middle' to influence the built environment beyond enabling, mediating and aggregating.

### 13.5.1    Communicating in the language of the stakeholder

One lesson learnt early on in the author's practice was that promoting sustainability initiatives primarily using environmental benefits was rarely the most effective way to engage with clients and stakeholders. The author's early attempts to use the language of the stakeholder were cumbersome and amounted to adding project-specific categories to a list of typical environmental impacts (e.g. energy, water and materials). For example, on a school project, a project-specific category was 'learning outcomes', while on a hospital project a project-specific category was 'patient well-being'. The result was the creation of sustainability frameworks that were overly complex and failed to engage stakeholders who were not already very interested in sustainability.

Over time, the author has developed a better understanding of the key drivers for different sectors (e.g. commercial offices, retail and universities). For example, in the Australian office sector, sustainability requirements are often driven by commercial rather than environmental reasons, including:

- leasing requirements of desirable tenants, including government and major corporations, many of which seek environmentally rated buildings (Department of Treasure and Finance, 2007; Conisbee and Leggett, 2011; Government Property Group, 2011)
- a desire for the building to be rated as 'A' or 'Premium' grade under the Property Council of Australia office quality guide (PCA, 2012), which sets minimum environmental performance requirements
- increased asset value and rents, and reduced vacancy rates (Newell *et al.*, 2011)
- reputation with investors (GPT, 2013; GRESB, 2015; McMahon, 2016).

In contrast, tenants in the Australian retail sector do not typically set sustainability lease requirements and, as such, the focus in retail tends to be on efficiency as a means for reducing operating costs (Talbot, 2012).

For universities, the motivation tends to be related to a sense of responsibility as part of being a public institution, as well as reputation with key stakeholders such as students, staff and benefactors (ULSF, 2016). In Australia, many universities use a rating system called Green Star to guide the design of facilities, typically to Australian or world's best practice levels (University of Melbourne, 2013; Monash University, 2013a; University of Tasmania, 2015).

### 13.5.2    Highlighting low-cost sustainable solutions

Another aspect where the author has refined his practice is in highlighting when projects incorporate low-cost sustainable solutions. The most common instance of this has been in relation to lighting design, where the author saw that it was common practice for (good) lighting designers to achieve lighting power requirements 20–40% lower than required by Australia's National Construction Code. For example, in a hospital project that the author was involved in as a sustainable design advisor, the lighting specialist's design required 40% less power than the National Construction Code maximum limits. The lighting designer made no attempt to highlight this to the client, however. Noting that the client was not motivated by environmental issues, but was very interested in operating costs, the author used the language of the client to highlight the lower operating costs of the lighting system.

### 13.5.3   Peer comparisons

The author has worked on projects for multiple clients who do not have strong environmental motivations. For these clients, the author has found that peer comparisons in the form of descriptive norms can be a useful influencing technique, provided that the comparison is framed in the right way.

For example, on an office refurbishment project, the client was based overseas and was unfamiliar with the Melbourne office market. This provided the author with an opportunity to speak the language of the client by talking about what tenants typical look for, as well as summarising the current trends in sustainability in competitor buildings. Through this use of peer and market norms the author was able to influence the sustainability targets for the project.

In contrast, on another project involving the construction of a grandstand for an international sporting event, the author deliberately avoided peer norms because the client's peer group had few examples of exemplary sustainability performance. Instead, for this comparison the author spoke the language of the client, who was interested in showing leadership and spectator experience, by highlighting the opportunity to take a leadership position in their sector and provide a world-leading experience to users. The author also noted the potential for enhancing the organisation's reputation by being a sustainability leader in their sector globally (in contrast to the previous example where the office client just wanted to keep up with market peers) and by highlighting areas where spectator experience and sustainability aligned (e.g. daylight, indoor air quality, thermal comfort, acoustics).

### 13.5.4   Reframing to emphasise client-specific values

The technique that the author has most practiced, which draws on many of those already discussed, is reframing environmental requirements to emphasise client-specific values.
The projects types where this occurs tend to fall into two broad categories:

- projects where a sustainability framework is imposed on the project, for example by the relevant planning scheme
- projects where the owner has a requirement for an overarching environmental rating without corresponding requirements for specific environmental impacts.

For both types of project, the author's approach to reframing begins by understanding how sustainability can enhance the core purpose of the building, reduce costs, support reputation or self-imposed corporate responsibilities, or manage risk (Healey, 2014).

The purpose of the reframing tends to be different, however, because the clients generally have different attitudes to sustainability.

For some projects in Melbourne, the planning scheme is the main driver of sustainability outcomes. For example, the City of Melbourne planning scheme clause 22.19 (Victoria Government, 2016) sets energy, water and waste performance requirements for a range of land-use types, while the Built Environment Sustainability Scorecard, which is referenced by many local governments across Victoria, sets requirements for energy, indoor environment quality, water consumption, stormwater, waste, transport and urban ecology (Municipal Association of Victoria, 2016).

The author has worked on a number of projects, typically apartment buildings and major retail developments, where the developer views the sustainability requirement as a cost burden and compliance risk rather than an opportunity to enhance the design. For these clients, reframing the environmentally focused planning requirements into business-case focused opportunities for the project was driven by an attempt to encourage the developer to embrace design initiatives that led to better environmental outcomes. It was found that this approach enabled a more engaged conversation with the developer about those initiatives where environmental and business outcomes align. In apartments, this tends to be related to resident amenity (e.g. daylight), which can more easily be translated into more saleable apartments, but less often to energy efficiency, which is generally not seen as saleable. For retail, the alignment tends to occur in relation to operating costs and shopper amenity, both of which can be strongly linked to the project business case. Despite these areas of alignment, engaging in this way did not seem to change the developers' perspective on sustainability as a whole.

The other type of projects where reframing has proved useful is when clients set overarching requirements based on multicriteria rating tools such as Green Star. Two sectors in Australia where this is common are commercial office towers and university buildings, as noted earlier.

Green Star is an environmental rating system for buildings and community developments (GBCA, 2013). It is used by many organisations in Australia to set standards and demonstrate commitment to environmental performance in the design, construction and operation of their buildings. Ratings are available for almost any building type in the design and construction of new buildings or major refurbishments, interior fit-outs, operations and maintenance, and communities. Star ratings are awarded for Best Practice (4 Star), Australian Excellence (5 Star) and World Leadership (6 Star). Projects are awarded a rating based on a multi-criteria assessment of environmental performance in the areas of management, indoor environment quality, energy, water, transport, materials, land use and ecology, emissions and innovation. Each of these categories has a number of credits, with points being awarded within each credit if set benchmarks are achieved. The design initiatives and mix of credits used to achieve a rating are at the discretion of the project team, which in the best case enables the design and rating to be aligned to the project objectives. In the worst case, the design and rating can be biased towards low cost and expedience, as noted by Monash University, when reflecting on its experiences with Green Star projects on campus: 'The project groups using the Green Star framework often select categories that are the cheapest and easiest to implement to achieve the star ratings, rather than implementing design features that would benefit the university in the longer term' (Monash University, 2013b: 2).

The purpose of reframing in these projects is to help clients get value for money from the Green Star rating. The success of this has varied, however. On one apartment project, this was unsuccessful because the apartments were sold off the plan before the sustainability strategy for the project could be finalised, leaving little incentive for the developer to align sustainability and the business case.

For an office project that was being designed at the time this chapter was written, the author facilitated workshops with the developer, design team, project manager and preferred head contractor. The author's technique was to estimate the extent (low, medium or high) that each Green Star credit could provide value to key stakeholders, along with the indicative cost of complying with the requirements of the credit (low, medium or high). This focus on value, as defined by the stakeholders, enabled a more engaged discussion and resulted in positive feedback from the project manager and developer.

The most detailed implementation of this technique by the author was on a project for the University of Melbourne called Arts West (Healey and Dean, 2015). For this project, the author mapped the environmental categories of Green Star to outcomes desired by the university: enhancing learning, saving money (upfront and long-term), maintaining reputation and responsibility, and managing risk. This helped the key stakeholders to understand the rationale for implementing particular design initiatives and better resolve disagreements about where money was prioritised on the project. The result on this project was a happy client and a sustainability strategy that remained intact from design through to implementation.

## 13.6   Conclusions

This chapter set out to add to the discourse on opportunities for 'the middle' and respond to the question: how can built environment professionals be more effective advocates for sustainable buildings?

It has shown that there are opportunities beyond the traditional economic focus to better engage with project stakeholders and influence outcomes towards sustainability. It has also shown, illustrated by the author's experiences, that learning how to be a more effective sustainability advocate requires focus and personal reflection across multiple projects (an example of aggregation).

As noted at the start of the chapter, the action-learning approach of planning, acting, observing and critically reflecting can be effective for those involved, but requires care when making generalisations to different contexts. For this reason, the author's experiences should be viewed as informed starting points that require testing. A key challenge for built environment professionals in helping us move to a sustainable future by 2050 is to reconfigure current practice by using improved sustainability communication techniques and to learn by doing to find what is effective in their own practice. In other words, for us to achieve a sustainable built environment by 2050 professionals need to complement their technical skills with effective sustainability advocacy skills. These skills go beyond the traditional focus on quantitative economic analysis, moralistic calls to action and information-based approaches, with a step change in our thinking needed if we are to succeed in our ambitions.

## Acknowledgements

The author would like to thank his colleagues and clients who, through real-world experiences, have inspired and contributed to this work. The author would also like to thank the editors for their helpful comments.

## References

ACCC (2011) *Green marketing and the Australian Consumer Law*. Australian Competition and Consumer Commission. Available at: www.accc.gov.au/system/files/Green%20marketing%20and%20the%20ACL.pdf.

American Institute of Architects (2012) *2012 Code of Ethics and Professional Conduct*. Available at: http://aiad8.prod.acquia-sites.com/sites/default/files/2016-04/AIA-Ethics-Code-of-Ethics-2012_0.pdf.

Australian Institute of Architects (2006) *Code of Professional Conduct*. Available at: http://architecture.com.au/docs/default-source/cpd/code-of-professional-conduct.pdf.

Baumeister, R., Bratslavsky, E., Finkenauer, C. and Vohs, K. (2001) Bad is stronger than good. *Review of General Psychology*, 5(4), 323–370.

CIBSE (2015) *Code of Conduct*. Chartered Institute of Building Services Engineers. Available at: www.cibse.org/About-CIBSE/Governance/Code-of-Conduct.

Conisbee, N. and Leggett, A. (2011) *Getting Your Building Ready for the Next Decade and Beyond*. Colliers International.

Cook, D. and Chatterjee, P. (2015) *Our changing world: let's be ready*. Royal Institution of Chartered Surveyors, London.

De Martino, B., Mukaran, D., Seymour, B. and Dolan, R. (2006) Frames, biases, and rational decision-making in the human brain. *Science*, 313(5787), 684–687.

Department of Treasure and Finance (2007) *Victorian Government Office Accomodation Guidelines*. State of Victoria. Available at: www.dtf.vic.gov.au/files/5f4b96df-d27b-4ae5-9f20-a1dc011530f6/Office-Accommodation-Guidelines-2007.pdf.

Engineers Australia (2010) *Our Code of Ethics*. Available at: www.engineersaustralia.org.au/sites/default/files/resource-files/2017-01/codeofethics2010.pdf.

Engineers Australia (2012) *Australian Engineering Competency Standards Stage 2 – Experienced Professional Engineer*. Available at: www.engineersaustralia.org.au/sites/default/files/content-files/2016-12/competency_standards_june.pdf (accessed 19 December 2016).

GBCA (2008) *The dollars and sense of green buildings*. Green Building Council of Australia. Available at: www.gbca.org.au/secure/GBCA_dollars_sense08.pdf.

GBCA (2013) *Introducing Green Star*. Green Building Council of Australia. Available at: http://www.gbca.org.au/uploads/212/34772/Introducing_Green_Star.pdf.

Goldstein, N.J., Cialdini, R.B. and Griskevicius, V. (2008) A room with a viewpoint: using social norms to motivate environmental conservation in hotels. *Journal of Consumer Research*, 35(3), 472–482.

Gonzale, M., Aronson, E. and Costanzo, M. (1988) Using social cognition and persuasion to promote energy conservation: a qasi-experiment. *Journal of Applied Social Psychology*, 18(12), 1049–1066.

Government Property Group (2011) *National Green Leasing Policy*. Australian Government. Available at: www.apcc.gov.au/ALLAPCC/GPG%20-%20National%20Green%20Leasing%20Policy.pdf.

GPT (2017) *Awards and Ratings*. The GPT Group. Available at: www.gpt.com.au/about-us/awards.

GRESB (2015) *GRESB Report*. Global Real Estate Sustainability Benchmark. Available at: https://gresb-public.s3.amazonaws.com/content/2015-GRESB-Report.pdf.

Gromet, D., Kunreuther, H. and Larrick, R. (2013) Political ideology affects energy-efficiency attitudes and choices. *Proceedings of the National Academy of Sciences*, 110(23), 9314–9319.

Healey, G. (2008) *Fostering technologies for sustainability: Improving strategic niche management as a guide for action using a case study of wind power in Australia*. PhD thesis. Melbourne: RMIT University.

Healey, G. (2011) *Intelligent buildings: Integrated systems and controls*. Available at: http://www.issinstitute.org.au/wp-content/media/2011/03/ISS-FEL-REPORT-G-HEALEY-low-res.pdf.

Healey, G. (2014) Winning hearts and minds: the role of emotion and logic in sustainable design decision making. *Environment Design Guide*, 81, 1–16.

Healey, G. (2015) Winning Hearts and Minds: The role of emotion and logic in the business case for sustainable building initiatives. *Journal of Design, Business & Society*, 1(1), 77–94.

Healey, G. and Dean, T. (2015) University of Melbourne's Arts West Redevelopment – A case study in value-for-money sustainability. *Tertiary Education Management Conference*. Wollongong, pp. 129–143.

Hes, D. (2005) *Facilitating 'green' building: turning observation into practice*. Available at: http://dtl.unimelb.edu.au/dtl_publish/research/24/67604.html.

Hoffman, A. (2006) *Getting Ahead of the Curve: Corporate Strategies that Address Climate Change*. Pew Center on Global Climate Change. Available at: www.c2es.org/docUploads/PEW_CorpStrategies.pdf (accessed 10 January 2014).

Hoffman, A. and Henn, R. (2008) Overcoming the social and psychological barriers to green building. *Organization Environment*, 21(4), 390–419.

IPCC (2014) Climate Change 2014, in Edenhofer, O. et al. (eds) *Mitigation of Climate Change. Contribution of Working Group III to the Fifth Assessment Report of the Intergovernmental Panel on Climate Change*. Cambridge University Press, Cambridge. Available at: www.ipcc.ch/pdf/assessment-report/ar5/wg3/ipcc_wg3_ar5_full.pdf.

Janda, K.B. and Parag, Y. (2013) A middle-out approach for improving energy performance in buildings. *Building Research & Information*, 41(1), 39–50.

Kahan, D. (2010) Fixing the communications failure. *Nature*, 463, 296–297.

Kahan, D. (2013) Making climate-science communication evidence-based – all the way down, in Boykoff, M. and Crow, D. (eds) *Culture, Politics and Climate Change*. Routledge Press. Available at: http://ssrn.com/abstract=2216469.

Kahan, D., Peters, E., Wittlin, M., Slovic, P., Ouellette, L., Braman, D. and Mandel, G. (2012) The polarizing impact of science literacy and numeracy on perceived climate change risks. *Nature Climate Change*, 2(10), 732–735.

Kats, G., Alevantis, L., Berman, A., Mills, E. and Perlman, J. (2003) *The Costs and Financial Benefits of Green Buildings – A report to California's sustainable building task force*. Available at: http://evanmills.lbl.gov/pubs/pdf/green_buildings.pdf.

Kinsley, M. and DeLeon, S. (2009) *Accelerating campus climate initiatives*. Rocky Mountain Institute and the Association for the Advancement of Sustainability in Higher Education.

Available at: http://www.chena.org/wp-content/uploads/climate/colleges/RMI_AcceleratingCampusClimateInitiatives.pdf.

Koshy, E., Koshy, V. and Waterman, H. (2011) *Action Research in Healthcare*. Sage Publications, London.

McMahon, E. (2016) Sustainable offices are the future. *The Sydney Morning Herald*, 13 May.

Monash University (2013a) *Sustainable New Building Design*. Available at: www.monash. edu/environmental-sustainability/campus-initiative/buildings/new-building-design.

Monash University (2013b) *Environmental Sustainability Stakeholder/Reference Committee Minutes of Meeting 1/2013*. Available at: fsd.monash.edu.au/ files/9-2013_130423_essrcminutes1_2013.doc.

Municipal Association of Victoria (2016) *Built Environment Sustainability Scorecard*. Available at: www.bess.net.au/about/.

Newell, G., MacFarlane, J. and Kok, N. (2011) *Building Better Returns – A study of the financial performanceof green office buildings in Australia*. Australian Property Institute. Available at: www.buildingrating.org/document/building-better-returns-study-financial-performance-green-office-buildings-australia.

Newman, G.E., Gorlin, M. and Dhar, R. (2014) When going green backfires: How firm intentions shape the evaluation of socially beneficial produt enhancements. *Journal of Consumer Research*, 41(3), 823–839.

Nisbet, M. (2009) Communicating Climate Change – why frames matter for public engagement. *Environment*, 51(2), 12–33.

Nolan, J., Schultz, P.W., Cialdini, R.B., Goldstein, N.J. and Griskevicius, V. (2008) Normative social influence is underdetected. *Personality and Social Psychology Bulletin*, 34(7), 913–923.

O'Neill, S. and Nicholson-Cole, S. (2009) 'Fear won't do it': Promoting positive engagement with climate change through visual and iconic representations. *Science Communication*, 30(3), 355–379.

O'Neill, S., Boykoff, M., Niemeyer, S. and Day, S. (2012) On the use of imagery for climate change engagement. *Global Environment Change*, 23, 413–421.

PCA (2012) *A guide to office building quality*. Property Council of Australia. www. propertycouncil.com.au/Web/EventsServices/ResearchData/Information__Products/Web/Events___Services/Research_Services/ItemDetail.aspx?iProductCode=0105065.

Robb, K. (2016) *Sustainable developments in question as off-the-plan buyers get greenwashed*. Domain. Available at: http://www.domain.com.au/news/sustainable-developments-in-question-as-offtheplan-buyers-get-greenwashed-20160722-gq8qw7/.

Roeser, S. (2012) Emotional engineers: Towards morally responsible design. *Science and Engineering Ethics*, 18(1), 2013–115.

Shome, D. and Marx, S. (2009) *The Psychology of Climate Change Communication*. Center for Research on Environmental Decisions. Available at: http://guide.cred.columbia.edu/pdfs/CREDguide_full-res.pdf (accessed 31 January 2017).

Slaughter, S. (2013) Making the case – Presenting sustainability investments to the C-suite. *Facility Management Journal*, November/December, 18–22.

Talbot, C. (2012) *Drivers of environmental sustainability in shopping centres*. AMP Capital. Available at: www.ampcapital.com.au/article-detail?alias=%2Fsite-assets%2Farticles%2Finsights-papers%2F2012%2F2012-11%2Fdrivers-of-environmental-sustainability-in-shoppin.

Tversky, A. and Kahneman, D. (1986) Rational choice and the framing of decisions. *Journal of Business*, 59(4).

ULSF (2016) *Talloires Declaration*. University Leaders for a Sustainable Future. Available at: http://ulsf.org/talloires-declaration/.

University of Melbourne (2013) *Sustainable Building Design*. Available at: http://sustainablecampus.unimelb.edu.au/key-areas/campus-grounds/buildings.

University of Tasmania (2015) *Sustainable Built Environment Designs Policy*. Available at: http://www.utas.edu.au/__data/assets/pdf_file/0006/39048/Sustainable-Built-Environmental-Designs-Policy-March-2015-minor-amendments-December-2016.pdf.

Van den Hoven, J., Lokhorst, G.-J. and Van de Poel, I. (2012) Engineering and the Problem of Moral Overload. *Science and Engineering Ethics*, 143–155.

Victoria Government (2016) *Melbourne Planning Scheme*. Available at: http://planningschemes.dpcd.vic.gov.au/schemes/combined-ordinances/Melbourne_PS_Ordinance.pdf.

VOX Global, Weinreb Group & Net Impact (2012) *Making the pitch: selling sustainability from inside corporate America*. Available at: http://voxglobal.com/wp-content/uploads/VOX-Global-2012-Sustainability-Leaders-Survey-Full-Report.pdf.

WMO (2016) *Globally Averaged $CO_2$ Levels Reach 400 parts per million in 2015*. World Meteorological Organisation. Available at: https://public.wmo.int/en/media/press-release/globally-averaged-co2-levels-reach-400-parts-million-2015 (accessed 22 November 2016).

World Green Building Council (2013) *The business case for green building – a review of the costs and benefits for developers, investors and occupants*. Available at: www.worldgbc.org/sites/default/files/Business_Case_For_Green_Building_Report_WEB_2013-04-11-2.pdf.

Part 4

Transformative Technologies and Innovation

14

# Energy Interactions: The Growing Interplay between Buildings and Energy Networks

*Phil Coker and Jacopo Torriti*

## 14.1   Introduction: energy interactions

The ways that we access, transport and use energy are changing dramatically in the face of technological advancement and evolving policy imperatives, not least the desire to decarbonise our energy system and wider economy. Electricity is now being generated from wind and solar energy, whilst ageing, centralised fossil and nuclear power stations are being decommissioned. New generating technologies can be installed at a local level, enlisting energy consumers as power generators. Energy applications are changing, with an explosion of new IT, communication and entertainment technologies accompanying dramatic efficiency gains with traditional technologies. There are signs of significant energy services transitioning from oil and gas to the electricity network, with a growth in electric heating and electric vehicles. These trends are bringing remarkable challenges and opportunities for existing and new entrant industry stakeholders.

The built environment sits at the forefront of these dramatic changes. The traditional concept of a centralised and separable energy system that delivers power to an unengaged energy user is losing relevance. Changes in energy use, energy production and energy management are playing out in our urban areas. The planning, design and operation of energy systems within buildings and cities is increasingly influenced by and influential on national energy systems. Energy transformation is taking place at national, city and building scales. Whilst there is ever-increasing interaction between these levels, design decisions are regularly made by distinct stakeholders isolated within a single frame of reference.

In navigating this complexity and change, there is a growing application for data and models that can help with planning and decision making. Alongside the rapid growth in information processing power, increasingly rich data is becoming available and modelling approaches are being advanced apace. This brings a rich opportunity for practitioners, but also an intense challenge. The ability to select the right analysis tool (or tools) with an appropriate frame of reference and capability is becoming an essential skill for professionals and analysts in the field of energy and the built environment.

In recent years, three recurring themes in energy policy have become commonly referred to as the 'energy trilemma'. Cost, security of supply and environmental

*Sustainable Futures in the Built Environment to 2050: A Foresight Approach to Construction and Development*, First Edition. Edited by Tim Dixon, John Connaughton and Stuart Green.
© 2018 John Wiley & Sons Ltd. Published 2018 by John Wiley & Sons Ltd.

sustainability are all receiving considerable attention, although the focus and interpretation of each is far from consistent across jurisdictions. The extension of 'dilemma' to 'trilemma' implies that these three themes represent unsatisfactory alternatives, and that it is highly challenging to satisfy all three simultaneously. It has also been noted that government and media attention can often highlight one at a time, resulting in a problematic lurch of focus from one to another.

- Attention to *cost* is typically focussed on either health and welfare or economic competitiveness. If home occupants cannot afford to keep their dwelling within an acceptable temperature range their health can be harmed. This is of particular concern for vulnerable consumers, for example the elderly and those with underlying health conditions. Where attention is devoted to business, high energy costs are deemed undesirable if they increase production costs and reduce the ability to compete.
- The need to reduce carbon emissions is often taken as the *environmental* aspect of the trilemma. However, decarbonisation is only one facet of environmental sustainability. Air quality has long been a factor and is now a resurgent issue in many global cities, including the UK. In developed countries attention falls mostly on transport fuels, but electricity generation and home heating cannot be neglected.
- *Security of supply* is often framed as a concern for 'keeping the lights on', supported by particular attention to the time of peak demand. Sufficient power stations and network capacity must be available to satisfy this need. There are many wider and arguably, subtler concerns here too. Energy systems must be resilient to shocks, whether plant failures, cyber threats or impacts from extreme weather events. Long-term fuel availability, whether satisfied by indigenous resources or established contracts, also offers a fundamental concern.

Considerable uncertainty surrounds the future supply of energy. Whilst there are still strong reserves of fossil fuels (BP, 2015), there is also an environmental imperative to switch away from fuels that lead to the greater share of mankind's carbon emissions. Future projections that address environmental concerns regularly point to a balance of renewables, nuclear and carbon capture and storage (CCS), as reflected in the work of the Intergovernmental Panel on Climate Change (IPCC). The IPCC seek to model a least-cost pathway that would meet our energy needs whilst reducing carbon emissions in line with various climate change scenarios (IPCC WG3, 2014). For a trajectory that keeps global temperature rise below 2 °C (by 2100), median 2050 projections of renewable generation (wind and solar combined) are seen that greatly exceed nuclear output. In turn, nuclear shows a similar energy output to fossil fuel with CCS (gas and coal combined). Dramatic uncertainty ranges are shown for all technologies and demand reduction.

In the nearer term, there is a good likelihood that recent momentum with renewable development will continue. Table 14.1 analyses National Grid's Future Energy Scenarios report, which outlines four scenarios for UK power system evolution, given varying socio-political assumptions (National Grid, 2015). Significant uncertainty is seen for nuclear deployment and especially for CCS, where expected growth is modest at best. Even in the worst case, stronger growth is seen in wind and solar, though growth in the 'No Progression' scenario is driven primarily by locked-in government incentives, currently drawing to an end. Significant growth for nuclear, CCS or wind is seen primarily in the 'Gone Green' scenario, which brings an implicit policy dependence.

**Table 14.1** Projection ranges of UK generating capacity growth.

| Electricity generation option | GW change in installed capacity (2014/15–2035/36) | | | | TWh energy output in maximum case 2035/36 |
|---|---|---|---|---|---|
| | Minimum case | | Maximum case | | |
| Nuclear | −4.2 | (NP) | 5.3 | (GG) | 92.5 |
| Coal | −18.1 | (GG) | −14.2 | (NP) | 0.0 |
| CCS coal | 0.0 | (NP) | 4.5 | (GG) | 21.2 |
| Gas | −4.1 | (GG) | 13.2 | (NP) | 22.3 |
| CCS gas | 0.0 | (NP) | 1.7 | (GG) | 6.3 |
| Onshore wind | 6.8 | (NP) | 11.9 | (GG) | 45.7 |
| Offshore wind | 8.8 | (NP) | 25.7 | (GG) | 100.8 |
| Solar | 7.6 | (NP) | 26.8 | (CP) | 24.7 |

Analysis of scenarios from National Grid (2015).
NP, No Progression; GG, Gone Green; CP, Consumer Power.
Only major generation types included for clarity.

By contrast, the 'Consumer Power' scenario posits significant growth in solar photovoltaic (PV) as well as modest growth of 5.4 GW for all types of combined heat and power (CHP). The 'Consumer Power' scenario is of particular note, assuming factors that are most likely to drive investment in urban areas; offshore wind in this scenario only grows by 11.3 GW, whereas onshore wind growth of 10.3 GW is similar to the 'Gone Green' projection.

There is a growing call for cities to play a greater role in the energy future (IPPR, 2014). Some cities already plan to achieve carbon neutrality through renewable energy, such as the ambitious Masdar City in the United Arab Emirates (UNEP, 2012). From the options considered above, only renewables, particularly wind and solar, are well suited to installation within or near to cities. Nuclear power stations are typically sited away from large population centres, not least given issues of public acceptability but also due to the need for access to large volumes of cooling water. Carbon capture and storage schemes will be more economic when sited close to large potential carbon stores, whether that be depleted oil/gas fields or salt caverns. Various factors limit the availability of other renewables. Wood fuel and other crop-based energy sources are restricted by land area and competition with food supply. Energy from waste is limited by waste supply, which is best reduced wherever possible. Ground heat will be harvested, but high temperature local geothermal sources tend to be rare. Harnessing low-grade ambient heat requires the addition of a heat pump, typically electrically driven.

As cities seek to source larger shares of energy from variable renewable energy (VRE) sources, a very significant challenge arises in achieving continual balance of supply and demand. For some time now, the assumed role of energy systems has been to satisfy users' demand. Demand has largely been treated as a given and generation sources managed to ensure that energy is available whenever required. Over recent years, this has been reframed as the need to provide energy services, bringing an initial emphasis on demand reduction through energy efficiency. Increasingly, flexibility of demand is being pursued, whereby the timing of demand can be shifted to ease pressures on supply. In whichever case, within electricity systems, absolute, real-time supply and demand must be kept in balance to preserve stable operation.

Much of this chapter is framed around the challenge of matching supply to demand. We first separate the factors that influence energy supply and energy demand. The sources and applications of data are described, before outlining some of the modelling techniques used to interpret this data. Alongside descriptions of variable renewable energy sources, we consider the challenges brought for energy systems and the roles of significant stakeholders. The chapter then considers techniques that are available to help balance supply and demand, before reviewing the role of current modelling approaches in valuing these techniques. Consideration is given to major emerging trends and uncertainties before we conclude by outlining some questions for energy systems that will need to be resolved on the way to 2050.

## 14.2 Emerging trends with energy supply and power system challenges

### 14.2.1 The growth of renewables

Recent trends support the projection of strong growth for wind and solar proposed above. Global investment in renewable energy rose dramatically through the previous decade, as shown in Figure 14.1. After peaking in 2011, annual investment levels have fallen but remain high. Global investment in solar energy overtook wind in 2010 and has remained somewhat higher since. By contrast, the UK has seen the greatest capacity developed in wind energy (see Figure 14.2), although solar installation accelerated markedly in 2014 and 2015. UK wind energy exhibits capacity factors some three times higher than solar, with the consequence that total energy generated by wind each year remains considerably higher, amounting to some 32,015 GWh for wind in 2014, compared with 4054 of solar (DECC, 2015).

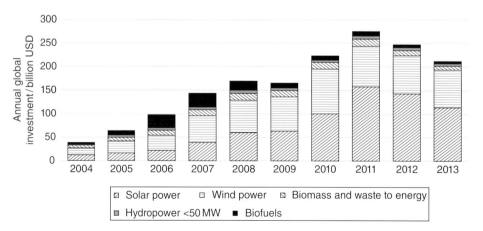

**Figure 14.1** Global investment in renewable energy. Geothermal power and ocean power omitted, as investment too low to be visible at this scale. Data from REN21 (2014).

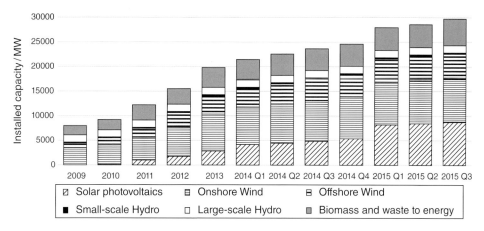

**Figure 14.2** Growth in UK installed renewables capacity. Wave/tidal omitted, as capacity too low to be visible at this scale. Data from DECC (2015).

A further consideration here lies in the location of energy installations. Any drive to install renewable generation within city limits, or even within a recognisable local support region, is likely to strongly favour solar. Wind generation has long favoured larger farms, typically remote from urban areas. This is influenced by a natural draw to areas where wind resource is highest, compounded by concerns about visual intrusion. By contrast, solar generation is seeing much higher uptake in urban areas, with installations more evenly spread between large-scale, standalone solar farms and more modest rooftop systems. However, even where remote wind generation proves more economically favourable there will be an imperative to match energy demand in our cities to this time-varying energy supply.

## 14.2.2 Data approaches for energy supply

Increasing generation from renewable sources, especially wind and solar, means an increased weather dependency within energy systems. System planning and design needs to take account of the time-varying nature of such resources as well as geographic variations. A range of methods are used that combine the engineering principles of energy conversion technologies with meteorological approaches of varying sophistication.

### 14.2.2.1 Surface station data

Data from surface weather stations has commonly been used to estimate the generation of proposed renewables installations. This approach was used by Coker *et al.* (2013) to explore the detailed statistical characteristics of renewable resources. Data can similarly be combined from multiple stations to simulate the generation of a possible UK wind fleet (Sinden, 2007). Poyry (2009) and SKM (2008) drew on similar datasets to Sinden in investigating the implications of different levels of VRE generation for the UK power system.

Care is needed when translating a meteorological record or estimate from one location to simulated renewable generation at another. The studies described above make a range of assumptions regarding the behaviour of energy conversion devices and the translation of weather features. For wind energy, wind speed must be corrected from height of measurement to an assumed hub height of the turbine. Manufacturers' power curves are regularly used to translate from wind speed to energy output. In the case of solar, corrections must be made for collector plate angle and orientation, whilst operating temperature should also be factored in for studies requiring higher accuracies. Various texts describe the detailed aspects of these steps, for example Twidell and Weir (2006). Fortunately, a growing range of renewable energy estimation tools incorporate such steps. The need for practitioners to make corrections from first principles is reducing, but the sensitivity of models to such assumptions should not be neglected.

### 14.2.2.2 Historic generation data

As renewable energy deployment has grown, so records from actual generation have brought increased representational accuracy for system-wide studies. Using data that directly represents energy output transferred to the electricity grid avoids many of the inaccuracies described immediately above. Whilst concerns regarding the commercial sensitivity of data have often restricted its availability, the value of shared data access for industry and research communities is increasingly being realised. Figure 14.3 shows recorded data from the GB power system, indicating the timing of wind generation set alongside electricity demand.

Publically available generation records are commonly used by system modellers, although they can exhibit a number of limitations:

- a lack of spatial granularity, for example for GB, data is only publicly available at aggregated system level: market participants can access higher resolution data and there is reason to hope that this will increasingly become more widely available
- invisible *embedded* generation: for the GB market, only large power stations (50 MW or larger in England) provide half-hourly metered data to National Grid
- a relatively short time record, with significant installation typically beginning late in the decade ending 2010
- poor representation of future fleet: the physical location of existing generators may not coincide well with future generation, especially where wind generation is set to move further offshore.

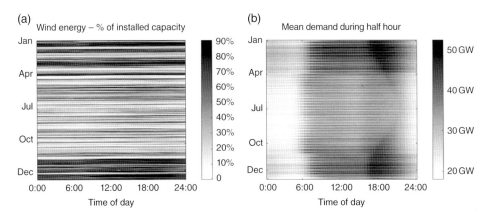

**Figure 14.3** GB wind generation and electricity demand, 2015. Data from Elexon (2016).

### 14.2.2.3   Modelled weather data

A growing range of data sets and tools are becoming available that harness meteorological numerical weather prediction (NWP) models, increasingly calibrated with historical energy generation records. NWP tools allow representation of a given section of the atmosphere, with a continuous spatial grid alongside (typically) a number of vertical layers.

Global 'reanalysis' models provide datasets of properties such as wind speed and solar irradiance by running NWP tools informed by long-term atmospheric records. Tools in common use draw on satellite data spanning more than 30 years, for example MERRA by NASA GMO (Rienecker *et al.*, 2011). In turn, datasets with finer temporal and spatial resolution can be generated by running localised NWP models, through approaches that 'downscale' the atmospheric representation, starting from either archived weather data or a reanalysis output. At the larger scale, NWP models are also used to simulate atmospheric behaviour with increased global temperature, and climate model outputs are now being used to explore the implications of a changing climate for large-scale renewable energy generation.

Continued, rapid improvement of meteorological approaches can be expected for renewable energy simulation. This reflects ongoing advances in computing power, but also an increased focus of meteorologists on energy applications. At the time of writing, NWP models typically represent cloud cover and state with lower confidence than parameters such as wind speed and temperature. The rapid growth of solar energy is bringing greater attention to this area. Improved methods are emerging that combine a range of approaches drawing on NWP models, energy generation data and other sensing techniques.

### 14.2.3   Planning and managing energy systems

A traditional, one-directional, physical representation of the electricity supply chain offers a helpful first step in understanding the actors in the electricity market. Electricity must be generated by conversion from some other energy source, conventionally in a fuel-based power station. This electricity can then be transported long distances through a high-voltage *transmission* network before passing to a denser network of local energy users through a *distribution* network. Commercial separation gives rise to the roles of *generator, transmission network owner, distribution network owner (DNO)* alongside the *end user. Energy suppliers* contract with end users to sell them electricity, but must therefore procure that electricity through a contract with a generator.

In practice, modern power systems are directly and indirectly influenced by a much broader range of stakeholders. System operators (SO) may have a role in controlling a network, with or without physically owning it themselves. In the UK, the GB SO, National Grid, controls the whole network, but only owns part of it, covering England and Wales. Further, a multitude of policymakers, regulators, market players, standards bodies, trade bodies, contractors, equipment suppliers etc. can bring influence to bear.

Whilst all electricity systems must have similar roles filled, many different models of market framework exist. Roles may be combined in a single company, especially in the case of large state-owned energy companies or small island networks. In the UK, the roles have been deliberately separated to pave the way for today's competitive energy market. Some notable responsibilities are as follows:

- The SO's main role is to maintain power balance and quality within certain mandated standards. They call on an array of ancillary services from contracted providers and have a limited trading role, but are not responsible for commissioning generation or procuring the majority of energy supply, which is a market function.
- Network owners must ensure that their networks have sufficient capacity to carry required power flows and that certain reliability standards are met.
- As well as contracting with customers and generators, energy suppliers must pay the SO and network owners for use of their services in conveying electricity to the end user.

The drive for decarbonisation and rapid adoption of new technologies in our energy systems brings new challenges for all of these actors:

- End users can now be generators too, with the emergence of small-scale local power generation. (Often known as *distributed* or *embedded* generation; the term *prosumers* has been coined to describe consumers who now also produce.)
- The SO has a new forecasting challenge, with the increase in weather-dependent supply compounding the traditional need to forecast demand. Emerging system characteristics exacerbate this challenge. Increased consumer application of power electronics, alongside the growth of non-synchronous generation, is reducing inherent system inertia. Small changes in supply and demand imbalance can lead to much more rapid changes in system frequency.
- Network owners are facing changing patterns of demand, as well as the potential for reverse power flows when the output from local embedded generation exceeds local demand for power.

Alongside dramatic technological change these roles and responsibilities are also set for change. In the UK there is currently no active distribution system operator (DSO) role, but this may be needed. Greater technological complexity brings debate on whether or not a DSO role will be required in many more markets and what form such a role might take.

### 14.2.4  Applications of data and models

This chapter primarily considers electricity balance at the scale of urban energy systems, also placing this in the context of wider regional or national energy systems. Power balancing tools draw predominantly from a technical/engineering perspective. There is a notable interaction with the energy system optimisation models described in section 3.4 below, which can be considered more economic in nature. It should be noted that building designers also have access to a plethora of tools to design specific components which are not covered here. The many and varied tools used to specify heating systems, or to develop operating strategies for equipment such as heat pumps or CHP systems, lie beyond the scope of this chapter.

For tools framed around the need to balance energy it can be the timescale of examination that sets models apart. A number of tools use a straightforward matching approach to ensure that sufficient supply is available to meet a requisite energy demand at every given time period. The DECC 2050 Pathways calculator (DECC, 2016), for example, seeks to achieve an annual energy balance at each of the 5-year intervals within the model analysis. More typically, models such as EnergyPLAN (Sustainable Energy Planning Research Group, 2016) harness higher resolution time series datasets to ensure power is balanced at much finer time steps, often hourly or half-hourly. Such tools are valuable for long-term visioning, but overlook many nuances that will be critical for the cost-effective and secure operation of future power systems.

More sophisticated power system models are routinely used in the energy industry and have been increasingly applied by the research community to examine the challenges of variability. These models will solve one or both of the *economic dispatch* (ED) and *unit commitment* (UC) problems. (See Wood *et al.* (2014) for an accessible explanation of these problems and their solution.) In combination, these help identify the least-cost operating regime for given power plant, considering fuel costs and operational constraints. One widely used tool, PLEXOS, has been applied to a range of national power systems, including the Irish and GB systems (Energy Exemplar, 2016). Many other bespoke tools are in use at specific research centres. Usually, electricity demand is taken as a given and these models calculate an appropriate operating regime for generating plant.

There are reasons for concern with the common practice of using single-year, half-hourly input data for power system models. With the growth of non-dispatchable renewables, it has become common practice to consider VRE as must-run plant. Therefore, annual data sets of winds and or solar generation are used as model inputs alongside demand data sets. However, closer examination of VRE behaviour reveals considerable variability at a range of timescales which cannot be effectively captured by a single-year approach. Figure 14.4 reveals the inter-annual variability in UK wind energy, derived from a reanalysis approach by Drew *et al.* (2015). Although running power system models with multiple data years can be onerous in terms of processing time and lead to outputs that are challenging to interpret, there is a clear need for improved representation of uncertainty.

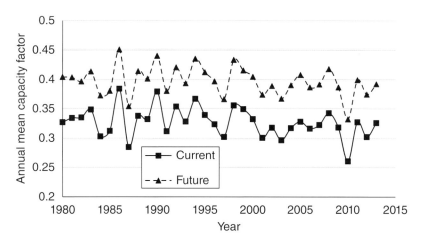

**Figure 14.4** Interannual variability of wind energy, shown by annual mean capacity factor. Here 'current' represents a UK wind fleet as installed in 2015; 'future' represents a fleet with significantly greater offshore installations in line with expectations post 2025. Data provided courtesy of D. Drew, as described in Drew *et al.* (2015).

## 14.3 Understanding energy demand

### 14.3.1 Trends in energy demand

In the UK energy use in housing amounts to just under a third of total energy use, having risen from a quarter in the 1970s. Figure 14.5 presents data from the Digest of UK Energy Statistics (DECC, 2014) showing a housing energy increase of some 16% from 1970 to 2012. Year-by-year variations have been attributed to alternating cold and mild winters. Over the same period, the number of homes also increased by more than two-fifths, whilst average household size has fallen. Hence, average energy use per home has fallen from 23,800 to 18,600 kWh, although the harsh winter of 2010 meant that energy use per home was higher that year (Palmer and Cooper, 2013).

Home heating requirements are influenced by a number of factors. Regional variations can be attributed to local climate, for example in the UK, Scotland and the north of England experience colder winters than the south and south-west, with additional heating needs. Buildings in denser urban areas typically consume less per meter (i.e. per household) than buildings in rural areas, attributable to building type and urban heat island effects. Building type influences heating demand, with variations in external wall area and window area. For example, flats are typically associated with less external wall area compared to their floor area, leading to lower heat loss in winter. On the contrary, detached houses tend to have greater external wall area and more windows than equivalent homes of other types (BRE, 2013). The ability to connect energy use with the detail of building type often relies on detailed surveys, such as the Household Electricity Survey of the UK, which collected metered data for hundreds of households in the UK in 2012 (Zimmermann *et al.*, 2012). The housing mix changes over time as new dwellings are built and demolished. Semi-detached and terraced houses have always been the most common house types in the UK. However, flats and detached houses have become more common in recent years, with flats now forming 20% of the housing stock and detached houses 17% (Boardman *et al.*, 2005).

### 14.3.2 Data on energy demand at the building level

Data on energy demand at the building level depends heavily on the accessibility of information on energy consumption by end users. In several countries by law it is only

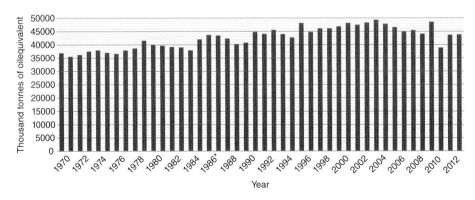

**Figure 14.5** Trends in household energy demand in the UK. Data from (DECC 2014), 11 months only for 1986.

required that traditional meter reading takes place on an annual or semi-annual basis. Consequently, most of the bills received by customers consist of estimates. This makes it difficult to derive any useful information from them.

In principle, more frequent and accurate bills would provide the basis for comparisons to historical consumption or to other consumers and could incentivise reduced energy consumption. The literature is mixed on the effectiveness of such approaches. For instance, Fischer (2008) finds that no energy savings originate from end-users knowledge about consumption.

In the future, consumers will have more information about their energy consumption and how much they are paying thanks to the introduction of smart meters. Smart meters *per se* cannot be expected to deliver any change in energy demand. However, smart meters will generate information (also known as direct feedback). When combined with human intervention, smart meters have been shown to trigger some level of change in energy demand. The effectiveness of smart meters in modifying energy consumption depends heavily on the type and medium of the feedback, for example McKerracher and Torriti (2013) show that large-scale energy savings effects from smart meters are in range of 3–5%.

Thus far, smart meters have only been rolled out in a limited number of countries. In 2010 the only European countries with double-digit percentages of implementation of smart meters *vis à vis* total electricity meters were Sweden (98%), Italy (93%), Finland (19%) and Denmark (13%) (Torriti *et al.*, 2010). The initial plan by the European Commission consisted of 80% penetration of smart meters by 2020 (2012/148/EU). In 2014, the EU-wide deployment target was decreased to 72%. This was necessary because only about half of the Member States committed to meeting the 2020 deadline.

These plans to roll out smart meters in the UK (and other European countries) up to 2020 will trigger monitoring studies aimed at detecting the electricity consumption of individual households via advanced metering technologies and thus deriving aggregate consumption at national (and European level). By harnessing two-way communication systems to record consumption at different times of the day, these monitoring studies should deliver a marked improvement to energy models based on occupancy records (Darby, 2010).

### 14.3.3 Planning for energy demand

The need to plan for secure and affordable energy supply has been central to the agenda of any developed country for almost a century, whereas demand issues, such as profiling, segmentation, differentiating tariffs according to time of day and peak demand, have received less attention. Yet the increasing importance of these issues in the so-called 'smart grid' accentuates the relevance of energy demand modelling. In this section, we present a brief taxonomy of existing modelling approaches with a view to assess how capable they are at forecasting energy demand at the building level.

#### 14.3.3.1 Engineering approaches to understand energy demand

The employment of engineering models to simulate residential energy demand can provide close to reality proxies to residential electricity demand without having to rely on historical consumption data. This means that in some cases the physical and behavioural data used as input in the model can be integrated with time of day or occupancy data, hence offering a breakdown of residential electricity loads which can be useful to balance demand and supply near real time, to differentiate tariffs and for demand-side response programmes. However, engineering models can be poorly suited for generalisation to wider population samples. As a consequence, models relying on either simulated or actual end-use data can be complex to implement and need to be validated.

Engineering models such as BREHOMES (Shorrock *et al.*, 1991) or the Cambridge Housing Model (Hughes, 2011) use data from the English Housing Survey as inputs to a physically based model such as the Building Research Establishment's Dwelling Energy Model (BREDEM). Similar approaches are taken in the UK Domestic Carbon Model (Lane *et al.*. 2005). These models explicitly account for the energy consumption of end-uses but require a large amount of input data and typically operate at a monthly or annual level, which does not provide sufficient resolution to assess the flexibility of demand at any point in time.

### 14.3.3.2 Understanding energy demand through price

Work looking at the extent to which aggregate residential electricity consumption profiles are shaped by changes in flat tariff prices typically relies on price information from bills. Models examining short-term elasticities (i.e. how loads change based on short-term variations in price) frequently rely on metered data. The success of a tariff is based on the price elasticity of demand (Filippini, 1995). Given the statistical properties of aggregate data on residential users' expenditure and variations in price, this formulation would yield a robust inverse relationship between consumption and changes in price. Several studies investigated this known relationship (Beenstock and Goldin, 1999; Bernard *et al.*, 2011; Borenstein, 2005; Garcia-Cerrutti, 2000; Shin, 1985; Silk and Joutz, 1997). The major problem which emerged in empirical research based on this hypothesis has arisen in fitting the part of the model that relates current and past observed income to expected future changes in prices. This calls for the re-formulation of the question of what, other than price, affects the timing of consumption.

### 14.3.3.3 Macroeconomic approaches

One of the criticisms moved against engineering-based and price-based approaches to understand energy demand is that they treat the household in isolation and overlook the relationship between the environment in which people live and wider dynamic socio-economic factors. A response to this problem is given by energy econometricians using aggregate macroeconomic models which rely on data about GDP, average income levels, population size and national energy prices, with a view to correlate socio-economic factors with energy demand. Models on residential electricity demand and macroeconomic data are particularly useful when they are based on large datasets. However, macroeconomic models tend to be resource intensive and lengthy. Cases which combine aggregate macroeconomic models with disaggregate energy demand can result in problems because of (i) the abovementioned multicollinearity effects and (ii) negative or unreasonable coefficients (Aigner *et al.*, 1984). For instance, the magnitude of coefficients indicating end-use consumption may change throughout the day along with load levels. However, the relationship between different appliances does not change. This means that coefficients characterising average end-use level are not representative of the daily electricity load.

#### 14.3.3.4 Models using physical non end-use data

Models using primarily physical non end-use data mainly rely either on external temperature data or daylight data. Studies looking at external temperature data generally find a significant relationship between electricity end-uses and external temperature (Hart and De Dear, 2004; Parker, 2003), although a methodological bias might be represented that existing studies are more representative of hot climates than temperate climates.

(Hill *et al.*, 2010) use support vector regression to estimate electricity demand on a half-hourly basis with a view to assessing the energy and costs savings associated with the change in time if the UK were to maintain daylight savings time over winter, instead of reverting to Greenwich mean time.

Biological data are used in networks models to simulate electricity consumption in residential buildings. Traditionally, the data originate from electric utility forecasts with the integration of input parameters which have an impact on residential electricity consumption. Input data are typically appliance ownership, appliance use, household income, type of dwelling and number of occupants (Aydinalp *et al.*, 2002). Neural network models frequently present problems in terms of multi-collinearity due to possible high levels of appliance saturation.

### 14.3.4 Applications of data and models

Most of the approaches described above are best suited to planning and policy targeted at single buildings, but bring less value at other scales. Least-cost optimisation models of energy use are supposed to represent the entire energy system, from primary resources to demands for energy services. These models are generally described as 'technology rich', with detail on both costs and other characteristics such as lifetime and efficiency. The assumptions are drawn from multiple sources and extensively peer-reviewed. These models have been applied to UK energy policy by imposing a cap on overall $CO_2$ emissions and then allowing abatement options to compete against each other, limiting those constrained by primary energy supply (e.g. biomass feedstock). Over the past 10 years UK energy policy has been significantly driven by a carbon reduction rationale, hence the widespread application of least-cost models.

MARKAL is arguably the most frequent application of cost-optimisation models in UK energy policy, although some limitations are widely recognised. MARKAL does not model non-$CO_2$ greenhouse gases such as methane, nor international aviation. This has resulted in some uncertainty as to the level of $CO_2$ cuts in the modelled sectors necessary to meet 80% overall. Second, the output generated by the model represents the least-cost option under the imposed constraints and presents the evolution of the least-cost options over time. The model implicitly assumes perfect foresight, therefore MARKAL outputs have been used prescriptively to inform policy choices. Third, whilst MARKAL has the merit of being 'technology rich', it was observed that its results are conservative when it comes to projecting certain technology capacities compared to other models (Morris *et al.*, 2002). For instance, MARKAL outputs imply a limited role for CHP in the period through to 2050, given the carbon emissions related to input gas use. However, this does not take account of wider benefits of CHP in a low-carbon energy system, described below.

## 14.4 Balancing supply and demand

### 14.4.1 Options to provide flexibility

Matching electricity supply to demand is a complex engineering challenge. Modern power systems display varying levels of inertia and incorporate a number of automated features to help maintain voltage and frequency within acceptable limits. Human oversight is used in maintaining these automated features and a broad range of additional technical and commercial actions are also taken. Whilst control has historically been applied on the supply side, increasing demand-side options are being used and an emergence of storage options is being seen.

#### 14.4.1.1 Modify supply

Power systems have traditionally been balanced by adjusting the supply side of the equation. Thermal power plant (whether oil, coal, gas or even nuclear or biomass) can be run at part load and its output modified in line with demand changes. Additional generating units can be started up or shut down to meet in-day variations, day-to-day swings or to balance longer term seasonal variation in demand. Flexible operation of thermal plant is not without problems, however. Part-loading plant brings an efficiency penalty with a requisite economic and carbon cost. Increased thermal cycling can also increase maintenance requirements and reduce reliability.

Reservoir-fed hydro-electric schemes have long been operated flexibly and pumped hydro schemes are even used to store electricity when demand is low. Significant future expansion may be limited, however, with most viable hydro schemes already exploited in many countries.

Weather-sensitive renewables can provide flexibility and, in some respects, are better suited to this than large thermal plant. Outputs can be readily controlled by adjusting wind turbine blade angles or through power electronic control of PV generation. Ultimately, however, potential is limited by the variable resource and flexibility comes at a cost. Preparing VRE plant to increase generation means that output must be reduced in advance, with subsequent loss of revenue.

CHP, long advocated as a low-carbon option, is finding a new role in power systems with increased variability. Coupling CHP with thermal stores (effectively large hot water tanks) can bring a range of flexibility benefits. This strategy has grown rapidly in countries such as Denmark (International Energy Agency, 2011), but has not yet seen universal adoption, with little attention to date in the UK. When VRE output is low, CHP output can be increased and heat stored. If VRE output increases, then CHP electricity output can be reduced and heat drawn from storage. It is even possible to incorporate electrical heating within the store to use cheap electricity at times of high supply excess.

#### 14.4.1.2 Modify demand

Until recently, demand management was largely restricted to either a service provided by very large energy users or through smaller users with static off-peak tariffs, such as the UK's long-established Economy 7 scheme. These tariff types typically provide a given amount of energy (7 hours in the case of Economy 7) at a time advantageous to the smooth running of the energy system, controlled by either a time switch or a remote signal. Large energy users, in contrast, may procure electricity through 'interruptible' contracts or agree specific demand response services with the SO.

Electricity markets have increasingly adopted incentives to reduce power use at times of system stress. Distribution network charges (distribution use of system, DUoS) in the UK are linked to three time bands with higher charges levied during amber and red periods, with the more expensive red bands usually falling in the later afternoon/early evening when electricity demand is highest. Transmission system charges are linked to peak demand, measured at three 'triads', the moments of highest demand in any given year. This provides an incentive to users to reduce their demand when triads are predicted.

### 14.4.1.3 Storage

The direct link between supply and demand can be broken by introducing energy storage. Stationary power applications have historically been limited by the high cost and bulk incurred, with grid-scale energy storage only deemed practicable for small-scale, remote power systems. This situation looks to be changing rapidly, with a profusion of energy storage technologies being proposed and rapid cost reduction being seen in established and novel products, from lead acid batteries, through modern chemistries (e.g. lithium ion) to flow batteries. Figure 14.6 shows a novel deployment of a lithium ion battery unit in Bracknell, UK, as part of a trial seeking alternatives to disruptive cable upgrades.

An alternative to storing electricity is to convert electricity to heat and harness thermal storage. This might be in the form of large-scale hot water storage, as mentioned with CHP above, or in smaller hot water tanks within buildings. Thermal storage offers one of the more promising routes to bring about true long-term storage, with seasonal heat stores now being deployed. This technology is enhanced when coupled with heat pumps, which can be especially effective where cooling is required in the summer and heating in the winter season (IRENA and ETSAP, 2013). Storing heat in the fabric of buildings also has a role. Whole-building solutions that increase insulation and thermal mass can help bring greater flexibility with timing of energy input.

**Figure 14.6** One of the energy storage management units installed on the streets of Bracknell as part of the Ofgem funded Thames Valley Vision smart grid trial. Image provided by Timur Yunusov.

Electric vehicles (EVs) have been advocated for some time as a potentially significant alternative to fossil fuel-based personal transport. At the time of writing, most major car manufacturers are bringing either electric and/or hydrogen powered cars to market. Whilst is it not clear whether one of these options will prove a winner and how quickly change will happen, it seems highly unlikely that new vehicles sold in 2050 will be powered by petrol or diesel. For now, vehicle cost is a deterrent, but vehicle prices are falling, vehicle ranges are increasing and EVs are beginning to emerge as an arguably attractive user proposition. Growing concerns around air quality in urban areas are helping to tip the balance in favour of such zero-emission options. Bloomberg have recently predicted that the 2020s will see mainstream EVs begin to 'cost less and perform better than their gasoline counterparts' (Bloomberg, 2016).

If EVs see a substantive uptake, their charging could place challenging demands on power networks, but could also prove a strong asset. Controlled charging solutions are being trialled that would at least mitigate the worst impacts on networks or could at best provide energy storage and grid services that help our energy system accommodate the vagaries of variable renewables and changing demand patterns. The term 'V1G' has been coined to cover the concept of controlled charging that could be interrupted or modulated to suit system need. 'V2G' encapsulates the concept of reversing power flow and returning power from vehicle batteries to the grid at times of need.

### 14.4.1.4   Hydrogen and natural gas

This chapter concentrates primarily on electricity as the means to distribute energy from a source to a user, with limited attention to the substantive role currently played by natural gas in many cities. Hydrogen could bring a striking alternative that serves something of the role of both electricity and gas. Whilst there are no naturally occurring reserves of hydrogen, it can be produced by electrolysing water. Hydrogen can be burned for heat or converted back into electricity using a heat engine or fuel cell. Fuel cell- based CHP systems bring the promise of small-scale and high electrical efficiency. This in turn conjures a vision where electricity can be turned into hydrogen at times of surplus, which can be stored and transported in urban areas. Local hydrogen networks could form the backbone of a high-renewable, sustainable energy future. Hydrogen could also serve as a transport fuel, with a hydrogen fuel tank and fuel cell effectively replacing the role of expensive chemical batteries in EVs.

The role that hydrogen will play is particularly unclear. At present, hydrogen is produced and transported/piped for use as a chemical feedstock. The vast majority is made from natural gas, with subsequent emissions of $CO_2$. City-scale hydrogen schemes are envisaged where carbon is captured at the city limits, bringing an extended life to natural gas transmission networks. In this possible future, natural gas distribution networks could be re-designated as hydrogen systems. A more pragmatic vision posits the injection of hydrogen into existing natural gas systems, which would serve to reduce the carbon intensity of gas use.

## 14.5   Characteristics of balancing options

The previous section has indicated a bewildering array of possible means to bring flexibility into urban energy systems. The role for these alternatives and success of their future deployment will be heavily influenced by commercial realities. Technical capabilities will govern this economic viability and also drive the suitability of different solutions for different niches.

The most fundamental characteristic, unit cost, must be seen in terms of both *energy cost* (price/kWh) and *power cost* (price/kW). The energy capacity of a store dictates the total amount of energy that can be held, whilst power dictates how rapidly the energy can be stored or released. Technologies with storage tanks, such as hydrogen systems and flow batteries, can offer the benefit of relatively cheap energy storage, even though power costs remain high. Conventional batteries may not compete strictly on energy cost, but offer a more balanced solution; energy or power can be increased by connecting additional battery units either in series or parallel.

The technical suitability of flexibility solutions is strongly driven by their speed of response and their sustain time: how long output (or input) capacity can be maintained. Intuitively, sustain time is linked to energy cost; lower cost increases the viability of larger capacity and thus longer sustain time. Broader technical characteristics must also be considered. Energy losses during charging and discharging (either one-way or round-trip efficiency) affect the economic case. Self-discharge can be irrelevant for a store required to cycle its output quickly, but technologies with high standing losses (e.g. flywheels and certain battery types) would be poorly suited for applications requiring energy to be stored over longer periods. Subtler characteristics, such as communications delay times and certainty of output (often represented as de-rated capacity), are becoming increasingly significant as more sophisticated applications are emerging.

### 14.5.1 New opportunities

Battery systems have long been used in smaller, isolated networks and their commercial use alongside VRE applications is growing. Numerous demonstration projects are seeking to establish the value of storage in larger scale energy networks, although this can be challenging in deregulated markets such as the UK, where the benefits of storage accrue to a number of separate market stakeholders. One of the great uncertainties at present concerns the speed at which fully commercial storage schemes will expand within larger, more developed power systems. The recent growth in PV installations has demonstrated the rate of change which can be achieved by small modular technologies, albeit aided by government incentives. We may be on the cusp of a similar growth in storage applications.

Representing the value of energy storage within deregulated energy markets is proving a particular obstacle. It is widely recognised that any single storage deployment can bring a range of separable benefits to multiple stakeholders. Storage studies that use bespoke methods to assess the value of a particular technology can struggle to capture the value to separate stakeholders or to effectively represent the possible competition between technologies. Similarly, modelling approaches aimed at estimating the value of demand-side response services thus far have failed to capture the multiple benefits associated with flexible demand (Bradley *et al.*, 2013).

#### 14.5.1.1 The rise of the aggregator

Alongside the profusion of new technologies seeking a business case, a new set of business models is arising. The opportunity for increasingly smaller energy users to participate in the demand response market has been enabled by the emergence of demand management aggregating companies. Aggregators enlist a number of energy users, deploy their own management or control solution and offer a combined service to the energy system operator. The revenue is then shared with the customers who own the energy-using appliances. Services offered by aggregators are increasingly seen as win–win solutions for different types of companies, including, for instance, hotels, telecommunication companies and warehouses.

Some aggregators have evolved their businesses as a natural progression from earlier roles as energy management providers to large energy users. Others initially offered energy efficiency services in the same way as energy service companies. Meanwhile energy suppliers and technology providers are also launching or considering providing aggregation services. Other firms are now entering the market with innovative and sometimes highly bespoke business models framed around specific types of energy-using appliance, end-user business or grid service product. Unsurprisingly, many aggregators have a strong interest in the expansion and potential of energy storage technologies.

## 14.6    Emerging challenges

The trends explored in this chapter point to the growing challenge of balancing energy supply and demand at a broad range of temporal and spatial scales. Renewable energy is expanding quickly, bringing many benefits, but also introducing increased supply-side variability. By 2050 it can be expected that wind and/or solar will provide a majority share of energy for many cities, with some approaching self-sufficiency from local resources. Much new generation will remain remote from cities, but the balancing challenge will be played out within our urban areas. System operators must manage this alongside varying demand, with numerous factors also set to change established demand profiles. Technology is already enabling more responsive consumers, presenting both opportunities and threats through the introduction of dynamic tariffs.

The transition to a low-carbon economy has been coupled with a high level of electrification of energy services, including heating and transport (Barton *et al.*, 2013). However, the likely pathway, extent and speed of transition is highly unclear. Where natural gas networks are established, they provide a great benefit in smoothing variability, reducing the cost of heating and providing specific utility that consumers value. It may be possible to decarbonise gas or switch to hydrogen supply, implying that full electrification of heat and transport is far from certain. The extent of electrification will be influenced by the global prices of other fuels (e.g. shale gas, oil and hydrogen), as well as ambition of decarbonisation policies. The evolution of energy-using technologies and energy networks is tightly intertwined. Wide-scale electrification of vehicles will necessitate changes in electricity networks, supply tariffs and system operation strategies. Investment in hydrogen supply infrastructure could enable a transition to hydrogen vehicles and new building technologies. These could be alternative or complementary routes.

Cities in particular will be confronted with complex decisions in relation to the mix of renewable sources, types of fuels and levels of automation in demand management. Decision makers, whether setting policy, planning for the future or operating in the present, must be able to navigate this complexity. This will require thinking across scales and across energy vectors, as well as understanding the interaction between users, buildings and energy systems. Accessibility, quality and application of data will be key to these challenges. Two imminent disruptions can be anticipated that will transform the way researchers and practitioners collect and analyse data:

i) Managing variable, weather-dependent renewables becomes more effective with access to high-quality and timely environmental data. We have described the progression from using limited weather records to rich model-based approaches and the advantages gained when integrating output data from real generation. Approaches can be expected to increasingly integrate environmental monitoring with energy-generation data. Enhanced monitoring and forecasting information is likely to open up new techniques for users, generators, traders and system operators.

ii) We are now seeing a massive roll out of two-way smart metering communication. Without this, most energy-demand data must be heavily averaged and aggregated in terms of volume, location and relationship with housing types. Smart metering data offers a dramatic improvement in resolution and timeliness of data, allowing much more meaningful understanding of patterns and variations in energy demand.

Synthetic representations of demand and supply play a significant role in terms of planning and designing energy systems. Energy supply and demand have long been treated as separate domains, overwhelmingly analysed in splendid isolation. This was helpful for analysts seeking to track trends, including (i) monitoring the $CO_2$ performance of macro-segments of the economy, (ii) linking energy demand or supply with economic growth and (iii) following the development of different domains and allowing longitudinal comparison across different years and different countries.

Holistic models integrating both demand and supply can present benefits in terms of (i) associating trends in energy demand with available supply, (ii) the opportunity to identify where flexibility of demand is based on the distribution of energy vectors and (iii) understanding not only which sectors consume more on average, but also how the supply mix can meet demand. An example of holistic approaches consists of the MARKAL model, a cost-minimisation tool originating from US academics and widely deployed by the UK Government to forecast demand and supply mix in energy policy appraisals. Alongside development of individual models, efforts are increasingly being seen to combine models through either soft-linking or tighter hybrid approaches. However, great care is needed. Whilst model users are frequently well versed in the limitations of their own tools, this can be challenging to communicate to policy makers. Increasing complexity of models can distract from the significance of model assumptions. Improvements in representation of uncertainty can lead to results that are hard to interpret and of limited apparent utility to decision makers.

The trends described above open up some fascinating uncertainties as urban energy systems evolve towards 2050:

- Distributed generation brings the possibility of local energy independence and the creation of island networks (especially for cities near the equator with rich solar resources and limited annual variability), whilst other approaches to manage variability point to increased interdependence with national and continental networks.
- Increased distributed control can be expected, but the level of autonomy is highly uncertain. New city-scale operators may be needed, taking either an active role in system balancing or setting rules for distributed automated intelligent systems.

- Increased management of energy demand and supply can be expected at the individual building/household level, with increasingly intelligent control of local generation and specific loads. A widely available time-varying price signal has been envisaged, although this might be visible to and acted on by end-users or serve as a behind-the-scenes signal triggering automatic controls.

Until now, resilience has been built into energy systems largely through engineering safety margins. Huge spinning machines in central power stations provide inertia, generous system margins became established with standby power stations available to meet demand peaks, cable size was planned for demand increases and networks were reinforced accordingly. Now, physical upgrades to infrastructure are becoming ever less desirable, given concerns of cost and congested highways. Increasingly, resilience is becoming reliant on active management, with a fundamental dependence on data and communications. In turn this will raise new challenges. This chapter has not dwelt on wider concerns such as the risks from data security, whether that be fears for security of personal data or the exposure of critical infrastructure to potential cyber attack. We have focused instead on the challenge of managing variability, but this is just one complex facet of our ever more complex energy systems.

## 14.7   Conclusions

Our energy system is in a state of rapid transformation, faced with the trilemma of maintaining secure, affordable energy supplies in a manner that is not damaging to our environment. Alongside rapid technological development, these factors are bringing major complexity and uncertainty for planners, designers and other built environment professionals. Against this background, this chapter has explored the techniques, data and models that are available to understand energy supply and demand, as well as to help balance the two. A particular trend has been seen for technologies and services to bridge the interface between energy use in buildings and national scale power system challenges.

Whilst there is an increasing trend towards local generation of energy, it is unclear to what extent cities and regions will establish energy independence and whether this is desirable. Where energy supplies are provided by remote, variable renewable energy supplies, the necessary balancing actions could still be enacted within the built environment. To take advantages of opportunities that arise, practitioners will need to develop a strong understanding of the over-arching energy system and the needs of disparate market stakeholders.

Models have been considered that can help to understand energy supply and demand, whilst modelling challenges have been revealed in assessing the value of energy flexibility services. Increasingly rich data is becoming available for practitioners and models are developing apace, both individually and in their combined use. To date, energy modelling research has played a largely normative role, valuable for assessing possible future trends and options in generation, transmission, distribution and demand of energy. With dramatic changes in information and communication technologies enabling increased automation, models and analytical insights become integral to design and operational decisions for the built environment. This is an increasingly interdisciplinary challenge that is blurring the boundaries of research and operational practice.

On the way to 2050, decision making within energy systems is set to become increasingly automated, although, once more, the level of autonomy that will be achievable and desirable is unclear. Concerns over protection of personal data and cyber security may be highly influential in setting the boundaries for automation. Business models and commercial roles are evolving rapidly; established players are finding tried and tested ways of working increasingly unfit for purpose, whilst opportunities for new entrants abound.

There is a strong need for practitioners who can integrate understanding of the wider energy system with understanding of building/building sub-system design. Practitioners will need to maintain an awareness of many types of model and develops skills in selecting the best tool for any specific decision. Computer-based tools will have a major role to play in decision making, but may not always meaningfully reflect the aspirations and actions of energy users and multiple stakeholders. In the face of rapidly evolving technology and a challenging policy landscape, designers and planners must develop skills in selecting energy options that make the most of today's technologies, deliver effectively for energy users and open the way for further beneficial change.

# References

Aigner, D.J., Sorooshian, C. and Kerwin, P. (1984) Conditional demand analysis for estimating residential end-use load profiles. *The Energy Journal*, 81–97.

Aydinalp, M., Ismet Ugursal, V. and Fung, A.S. (2002) Modelling of the appliance, lighting, and space-cooling energy consumptions in the residential sector using neural networks. *Applied Energy*, 71(2), 87–110.

Barton, J. *et al.* (2013) The evolution of electricity demand and the role for demand side participation, in buildings and transport. *Energy Policy*, 85–102.

Beenstock, M. and Goldin, E. (1999) The demand for electricity in Israel. *Energy Economics*, 21, 168–183.

Bernard, J.T., Bolduc, D. and Yameogo, N.D. (2011) A pseudo-panel data model of household electricity demand. *Resource and Energy Economics*, 33, 315–325.

Bloomberg (2016) *Here's How Electric Cars Will Cause the Next Oil Crisis*. Available at: http://www.bloomberg.com/features/2016-ev-oil-crisis/ (accessed 11July 2016).

Boardman, B. et al. (2005) Thermal comfort and control, in *40% House*. Environmental Change Institute, Oxford, p. 34. Available at: http://www.eci.ox.ac.uk/research/energy/downloads/40house/40house.pdf (accessed 1 February 2016).

Borenstein, S. (2005) The long-run efficiency of real-time electricity pricing. *Energy Journal*, 26, 93–116.

BP (2015) *BP Statistical Review of World Energy June 2015*. Available at: http://www.statista.com/statistics/263455/primary-energy-consumption-of-selected-countries/.

Bradley, P., Leach, M. and Torriti, J. (2013) A review of the costs and benefits of demand response for electricity in the UK. *Energy Policy*, 312–327.

BRE (2013) *The Energy Follow-up Survey 2011: Summary of survey findings*. Department of Energy and Climate Change, London.

Coker, P. *et al.* (2013) Measuring significant variability characteristics : An assessment of three UK renewables. *Renewable Energy*, 53, 111–120.

Darby, S. (2010) Smart metering: what potential for householder engagement? *Building Research and Information*, 38, 442–457.

DECC (2014) *Digest of United Kingdom Energy Statistics 2014*. Department of Energy and Climate Change, London.

DECC (2015) *Energy trends section 6: renewables*. Department of Energy and Climate Change, London. Available at: https://www.gov.uk/government/collections/energy-trends.

DECC (2016) *2050 Energy Calculator*. Department of Energy and Climate Change, London. Available at: http://2050-calculator-tool.decc.gov.uk/#/home (accessed 10 July 2016).

Drew, D. *et al.* (2015) The impact of future offshore wind farms on wind power generation in Great Britain. *Resources*, 4(1), 155–171. Available at: http://www.mdpi.com/2079-9276/4/1/155/.

Elexon (2016) Elexon Portal. Available at: www.elexonportal.co.uk (accessed 17 July 2016).

Energy Exemplar (2016) PLEXOS Integrated Energy Model. Available at: http://energyexemplar.com/software/plexos-desktop-edition/ (accessed 10 July 2016).

Filippini, M. (1995) Swiss residential demand for electricity by time of use. *Resource and Energy Economics*, 17, 281–290.

Fischer, C. (2008) Feedback on household energy consumption: a tool for saving energy. *Energy Efficiency*, 1, 79–104.

Garcia-Cerrutti, L.M. (2000) Estimating elasticities of residential energy demand from panel county data using dynamic random variables models with heteroskedastic and correlated error terms. *Resource and Energy Economics*, 22, 355–366.

Hart, M. and De Dear, R. (2004) Weather sensitivity in household appliance energy end-use. *Energy and Buildings*, 36(2), 161–174.

Hill, S.I. *et al.* (2010) The impact on energy consumption of daylight saving clock changes. *Energy Policy*, 38, 4955–4965.

Hughes, M. (2011) *A Guide to the Cambridge Housing Model*. Available at: https://www.gov.uk/government/publications/cambridge-housing-model-and-user-guide.

International Energy Agency (2011) *Energy Policies of IEA Countries: Denmark Review*. International Energy Agency, Paris.

IPCC WG3 (2014) *Climate Change 2014: Mitigation of Climate Change*. IPCC. Available at: https://www.ipcc.ch/report/ar5/wg3/.

IPPR (2014) *City Energy: A New Powerhouse for Britain*. IPPR. Available at: https://www.ippr.org/publications/city-energy-a-new-powerhouse-for-britain.

IRENA and ETSAP (2013) *Thermal Energy Storage*. Technology Brief, Available at: http://www.irena.org/DocumentDownloads/Publications/IRENA-ETSAP%20Tech%20Brief%20E17%20Thermal%20Energy%20Storage.pdf.

Lane, K. *et al.* (2005) *40% House Project – Background Material – A United Kingdom Domestic Carbon Model (UKDCM) Description, Method and Analysis*. Available at: http://www.eci.ox.ac.uk/research/energy/downloads/40house/background_doc_a.pdf.

McKerracher, C. and Torriti, J. (2013) Energy consumption feedback in perspective: integrating Australian data to meta-analyses on in home displays. *Energy Efficiency*, 6(2), 387–405.

Morris, S.C., Goldstein, G.A. and Fthenakis, V.M. (2002) NEMS and MARKAL-MACRO models for energy-environmental-economic analysis: a comparison of the electricity and carbon reduction projections. *Environmental Modelling & Assessment*, 7(3), 207–216.

National Grid (2015) *Future Energy Scenarios, UK gas and electricity transmission*. Available at: http://www2.nationalgrid.com/UK/Industry-information/Future-of-Energy/FES/Documents-archive/.

Palmer, J. and Cooper, I. (2013) *United Kingdom housing energy fact file 2013*. Available at: https://www.gov.uk/government/statistics/united-kingdom-housing-energy-fact-file-2013

Parker, D.S. (2003) Research highlights from a large scale residential monitoring study in a hot climate. *Energy and Buildings*, 35(9), 863–876.

Poyry (2009) Impact of Intermittency. How wind variability could change the shape of the British and Irish Electricity Markets. Available at: http://www.poyry.com/sites/default/files/impactofintermittencygbandi-july2009-energy.pdf.

REN21 (2014) *Renewables 2014 Global Status Report*. REN21 Secretariat, Paris.

Rienecker, M.M. *et al.* (2011) MERRA: NASA's modern-era retrospective analysis for research and applications. *Journal of Climate*, 24, 14.

Shin, J.S. (1985) Perception of price when price information is costly: evidence from residential electricity demand. *The Review of Economics and Statistics*, 67, 591–598.

Shorrock, L., Henderson, G. and Bown, J. (1991) BREHOMES : A Physically Based Model of the Energy Use of the United Kingdom Housing Stock, in *Building Simulation* (conference proceedings). International Building Performance Simulation Association, Nice, pp. 497–503.

Silk, J.I. and Joutz, F.L. (1997) Short and long-run elasticities in US residential electricity demand: a co-integration approach. *Energy Economics*, 19, 493–513.

Sinden, G. (2007) Characteristics of the UK wind resource: Long-term patterns and relationship to electricity demand. *Energy Policy*, 35(1), 112–127.

SKM (2008) *Growth Scenarios for UK Renewables Generation and Implications for Future Developments and Operation of Electricity Networks*. BERR, London.

Sustainable Energy Planning Research Group (2016) *Energy PLAN: Advanced energy system analysis computer model*. Aalborg University. Available at: http://www.energyplan.eu/ (accessed 10 July 2016).

Torriti, J., Hassan, M.G. and Leach, M. (2010) Demand response experience in Europe: policies, programmes and implementation. *Energy*, 35(4), 1575–1583.

Twidell, J. and Weir, T. (2006) *Renewable Energy Resources*. Taylor & Francis.

UNEP (2012) *Sustainable, Resource Efficient Cities – Making it Happen!* Available at: https://sustainabledevelopment.un.org/index.php?page=view&type=400&nr=1124&menu=35.

Wood, A.J., Wollenberg, B.F. and Sheble, G.B. (2014) *Power Generation, Operation and Control*, 3rd edn. IEEE Wiley.

Zimmermann, J.P. *et al.* (2012) *Household Electricity Survey: A study of domestic electrical product usage*. Available at: https://www.gov.uk/government/collections/household-electricity-survey.

# 15

# Sustained Innovation Uptake in Construction

*Graeme D. Larsen*

## 15.1  Introduction

Chapter 1 of this book highlighted the continued criticism of the construction sector regarding the alleged lack of innovation. This chapter seeks to offer an alternative perspective and to highlight how and where the construction sector can, in fact, be seen as 'innovative' (Winch, 2003). In doing so, the construction sector is championed as a place where innovative activity occurs if we seek to look in the right places and with the right methodology. Many of the studies claiming the construction sector is not innovative use approaches and criteria lacking suitable contextual sensitivity, developed for and derived from very different contextual settings, and thus do not enable the construction sector to shine.

The current chapter seeks to understand how the construction sector will need to evolve and change to meet the challenges outlined in the introductory chapter, and takes the stance that in order to either evolve or change then something 'different' and 'new' needs to happen. This 'newness' is therefore aligned with the need to innovate, together with understanding innovation and, most importantly, its sustained uptake within the sector continuing to 2050. Therefore, the things that will make us sustainable, that will allow us to move to a sustainable built environment by 2050 will be innovations. They may be innovations in materials, digital technologies, processes, working practices or perhaps procurement methods, for example, but they will be innovations.

This chapter uses relevant theoretical frames as touch points whilst mapping out what the author sees as the challenges associated with understanding sustained innovation uptake. 'Sustained innovation uptake' is defined here as the capability to continually access and adopt relevant innovation. Sustaining uptake is key as there is little point being able to improve sporadically where continuous improvement is possible. A network perspective of innovation is championed, whilst unpacking some of the attributes which are often oversimplified when considering sustained innovation uptake in other construction and development literature. In doing this, it presents a vision for the future whereby firms operate more openly as networks, procurement methods are designed to stimulate innovation uptake, and the shape of the market settings are nudged to help

*Sustainable Futures in the Built Environment to 2050: A Foresight Approach to Construction and Development*, First Edition. Edited by Tim Dixon, John Connaughton and Stuart Green.
© 2018 John Wiley & Sons Ltd. Published 2018 by John Wiley & Sons Ltd.

sustained innovation uptake. The chapter is based on three ongoing and interwoven interests focusing on understanding innovation uptake:

- the complex structural make-up of architectural, engineering and construction (AEC) firms
- the methods of procurement used through the supply network and, most importantly,
- the nature and potential impact a market (or stakeholders) network can play associated with sustained innovation uptake.

It is argued that each of the three interwoven interests can help us understand how we can help produce a sustained innovation uptake and thus what a construction sector might look like in 2050.

## 15.2   Background

Businesses within the UK are continually encouraged to be innovative themselves (and adopt innovations from others) to improve. Consideration needs to be given to the broader benefits that innovation can offer for sustainable cities and the broader built environment generally. Innovations (associated with the built environment) range from small advances in methods, materials and technologies right through to radical new procurement routes.

All innovations result in a change or adaptation to the manner in which professionals and operatives undertake their work and perhaps the work of the final users of the building. Therefore, tangible innovations typically require changes in an actor's behaviour or practices (which can be seen as a second-order innovation, a by-product innovation). Caution is required to ensure innovation occurs for the right reasons and within the right areas where there is the most room for improvement and benefit across the sector and to users of the built environment (e.g. energy and sustainability). This caution is needed to ensure the sector is not simply trying to adopt the latest fashion, something the sector could be accused of in the past. Thinking in strategic terms about innovation is not perhaps the UK construction sector's greatest strength as it often relies on being highly agile and responsive with a financial structure based around cash flow. Furthermore, it is argued that the very *term* 'construction sector' offers little help to our understanding, as the sector has become almost meaningless, including everything and nothing: from architects, housing surveyors, painters and lighting manufacturers etc. Readers are thus advised to be mindful of the countless innovations the UK construction sector has been encouraged to adopt over the years, only to realise that they did not fit the structure, operational routines or particular constituents of the sector. For example, Green *et al.* (2005), Fernie and Tennant (2013) and Fernie and Thorpe (2007) argue that supply chain management was conceived for a sector with high trust, a dominant player and a small number of suppliers, yet the construction sector has the polar opposite structure, thus raising concerns about its true suitability at a strategic level.

## 15.3   Central themes of innovation

If we are to understand innovation then we can think of it as something *new* to the adopting actor, with elements of risk and uncertainly inherent within it (Rogers, 2003). Furthermore, innovation is viewed as fluid, not fixed, but readily occurring during the uptake process (Boyd *et al.*, 2015). Thus, as practitioners and firms interact with a new material, process or tool they make changes, through negotiation of relevant networks of actors, and in order that it better fits their unique needs and context (Fleck, 1993; Pinch and Bijker, 1984). As such, it is through this uptake that additional change and innovation will be required (Boyd *et al.*, 2015). Similarly, to use a new material or tool the behaviour and practice of actors may need to change. As will become apparent later in this chapter, the focus of innovation can be described for illustrative purposes as a component, material or product. Importantly though, it is where the innovation and its uptake resides and manifests itself that is the real focus, thus in this chapter a network perspective is championed.

It is also true that the majority of construction work is undertaken by small to medium-sized enterprises (SMEs), yet this fact is often underplayed in research. Research into how SMEs operate and engage in the innovation uptake process is limited, with a few exceptions (e.g. Sexton and Barrett (2003) and Green *et al.* (2008)), thus leaving them with almost no voice within research and best practice initiatives. Importantly, the subtlety of how the firms are structured and function is key to any understanding offered. Simply continually targeting research or best practice agendas at the largest firms and assuming they have a unitary voice is foolish at best and incompetent at worst. However, a similar criticism is levied at those who argue research should instead focus upon SMEs. Such an argument simply replaces one context and set assumption with another. It is argued that we need to *unpack what makes up the real firm*, regardless of apparent size. This brings us to think further about the levels of analysis, whereby research associated with the construction sector will typically distinguish between industry, firm, project and actor levels (even if not explicitly or knowingly).

However, an even finer-grained analysis is required to get to the very heart of the issue. To simply state this is a 'firm' level understanding of sustained innovation uptake toward a more sustainable built environment in 2050 is not enough. Firms and stakeholders do what they do as a network with others and thus the sustained innovation uptake process occurs within a network of actors. Firms cannot operate in isolation from other firms (Kao *et al.*, 2009), meaning that innovation uptake occurs across networks of firms (Larsen, 2015). However, there is a dearth of research that considers networks of firms and the influence of the shape of these networks on innovation uptake. This view therefore helps us move beyond the reductionist view of the firm as a unit of analysis for understanding innovation uptake within the UK construction sector. In addressing this, the chapter seeks to offer insights into the importance of unique networks, from actor to sector level, within given contextual settings of an example client, supply network and market network (e.g. a Formula 1 venue).

In summary, the points of departure of the chapter and how it contributes to our understanding of sustained innovation uptake are as follows:

- the constituents that go to make up the 'construction firm' are unpacked: this goes beyond the typical literature dichotomising large AEC firms vs SMEs
- innovation of components, materials and products comes from within the supply network: currently the methods of procurement within the supply network offer little incentive for sustained innovation uptake
- the client, project type and thus market network all have agency in achieving sustained innovation uptake.

## 15.4    Where to look at the problem *from*

It is important to consider a starting point from which to view the problem and what literatures are seen to have purchase, even if problematic in practice. The agency-structure perspective (Archer, 1988; Giddens, 1979; Ritzer, 1996) can be used as a key touch point. Some perspectives privilege individuals at a micro level of understanding, with structural forces being subservient. Others emphasise structural forces and view individuals as subservient and with limited choice. However, the agency-structure perspective offers an alternative to that dichotomy. The approach involves championing that individuals (actors) are shaped and influenced by their contextual setting and the broader institutional logics, yet importantly it recognises that individuals in return shape and influence their contextual settings and broader institutional logics (Pettigrew, 1997). Thus, both actor and structure are not only privileged, but actually essential for any understanding offered. Those seeking sustained innovation uptake thus need to embrace this interplay, unpacking what constitutes the construction firm, the broader supply network and market networks. Indeed, this notion of a socio-technical approach is important in the wider *multi-level perspective* (MLP) literature. The MLP has been used as a touchstone to frame sustainability in the context of actor-networks, which are set within; from (Geels, 2011).

- a *landscape*: the overall socio-technical context and setting that encompasses social values, political beliefs and world views and more tangible facets, including institutions and the functions of the marketplace such as prices, costs, trade patterns and incomes
- a *regime*: the dominant practices, rules and technologies that underpin the prevailing socio-technical systems)
- the *niches*: the individual innovation experiments or grass root movements that may emerge over time (Geels, 2011).

It can therefore be argued that we need a better understanding of the firm, supply networks and market network (and the methods to achieve that understanding) if we are to move toward sustained innovation uptake. Put simply, this is not a study of one particular innovation, nor a study at project level, or firm level, but instead it is a multilevel study of the *elements/attribute/themes* that shape sustained innovation uptake, which at the time of writing are underplayed within the construction management community.

## 15.5    Sustained innovation uptake through networks

The organisational make up of AEC firms can be complex and certainly diverse. Put simply, AEC firms come in very different shapes and sizes, meaning that the very term 'AEC firm' is almost meaningless. This point is of course only further compounded by the fact that the firms servicing the sector cover such a broad spectrum of businesses, often including those supplying materials or perhaps key manufactured electrical or heating components to the sector.

Earlier, criticism was directed toward the tradition of research that has focused solely upon large AEC firms, typically seeking to offer a unitary voice for such firms. The notion of what constitutes an AEC firm is highly relevant. Such large firms typically have resources to engage with research projects, meaning research is often carried out with them for that very reason rather than that they are more important, more relevant or more interesting. Much of this tradition also focused on searching for ways to be more competitive through the uptake of innovation. This fact is compounded because the majority of the work undertaken within the construction sector is completed by its 125,000-plus SMEs – some 80% of total output (ONS, 2016). It can be argued that this is connected to the structural development of the sector, with increased specialization, and a growing gap between very large companies and SMEs. Such arguments are welcomed, as they bring to the fore the need for greater contextual understanding of AEC firms generally.

There is also a growing body of work, although still small at the time of writing, placing emphasis on more contextually sensitive research, leading authors to critique the repetitive focus on large AEC firms (Kao *et al.,* 2009). It is argued here that the call within the construction management literature for a shift to study SMEs over, and to the detriment of, research focused upon large firms is flawed. Yes, SMEs are highly relevant and should be an area of research, but it is argued here that the size is not the issue, it is our conceptualisation of firms. This chapter thus seeks not to set up yet another straw man by seeking to champion AEC SMEs at the expense of large AEC firms or vice versa. Instead, it is argued here that we need to unpack what makes up firms regardless of their size, looking at *the informally formed working networks of actors across firms.* Thus, we are looking within the firm, but also beyond the boundary of the firm at inter-firm networks. It is argued that such a stance will potentially reflect the reality experienced by practitioners far better, thus resulting in greater contextual sensitivity and improved understanding of sustained innovation uptake. This network approach dissolves the artificial boundaries created by the notion of firms and their structure, and privileges inter-firm networks (Larsen, 2015).

To elaborate, large AEC firms do not actually exist in any real sense, except perhaps on the stock markets or for shareholders. For the majority of staff, clients and associated supply networks the large AEC firm (as reported to Companies House and perhaps the stock market) is in fact completely irrelevant. However, what is highly relevant are the national, regional or local offices, driven either by business stream or geographical location, and the informally formed relevant social groups of both loosely and tightly knit networks of actors that champion or resist innovation uptake and how that is played out over time. So, in fact, it is not the notion of looking at either large AEC firms or SMEs that fails to help our understanding of sustained innovation uptake, it is in fact our conceptualisation of what forms AEC firms and where the agency for innovation uptake actually resides. The following section presents an example to help illustrate this argument.

A large AEC firm might have a head office in the USA, yet have national offices in nine separate countries. Each of these nine national head offices may then have a further four to nine regional offices and then those regional offices will have seven satellite offices. Consideration then needs to be given to what is undertaken at those offices, be it different market streams for civil, building, maintenance and so on. It is this unpacking of what makes up an AEC firm that is typically overlooked. Typically, the firm is seen as being reducible into having one unitary voice. It is argued here that is not the reality experienced by practitioners in these firms. Instead, the reality is closer to the various parts of the firm being embedded in local contextual networks with a high degree of autonomy and contested voices that suit those unique networks: all of which influences how we understand and thus strive for sustained innovation uptake. So, we need to look beyond these boundaries to loosely and tightly knit networks.

A closer inspection of AEC SMEs has revealed that they are often in fact part of a much larger AEC firm, although that larger firm appears somewhat of a silent player, thus blurring the lines and definitions. SMEs are not operating in isolation and thus their contribution to sustained innovation uptake should not be treated as such. The key message here is one of fine-grained analysis and seeking as great a depth and understanding of the context as possible even if it is methodologically difficult and results in a messy, ill-fitting and irrational version of what an AEC firm looks like. Often the networks have evolved organically rather than by some well-devised strategy. Similarly, the structures are typically in a state of flux, responding to both internal and external stimuli. Carrillo and Heavey (2000) note that a parent subsidiary business structure is one tactic to help AEC firms cope with the fluid network with myriad contextual considerations within which they must operate.

However, many firms also actually have a much larger parent or holding company (sometimes based in another country). The national or regional offices are used to gain access and embed what is an international company within a national or regional market place whilst also engaged with localised supply networks. The branches of the company and their geographically dispersed construction projects usually exhibit a high degree of autonomy and competition exists between different subsidiaries.

Sadly, such a 'fragmented' firm will struggle to find advice and support regarding sustainable innovation uptake that acknowledges this characteristic. We need research and methods that can cope with such messy situations. There is therefore a need for academics and practitioners seeking sustainable innovation uptake to first acknowledge this fact, then seek to understand the competing agendas across their firm and its branches as a whole. So far, the chapter has sought to view firms as not having a unitary voice, but rather being made up of contextually situated networks of actors (or indeed groups of actors with relevant interests) across different firms. It is argued that this network conceptualisation will help in the future by offering new insights into firms and their impact on sustained innovation uptake. The following section broadens the argument, moving to the supply network and methods of procurement impacting sustained innovation uptake.

## 15.6 Incentives for the supply network

The previous section made an argument for increased sensitivity when understanding how we think about AEC firms in order to understand sustained innovation uptake. This section moves toward thinking about where innovative components, products or materials come from, where the innovation occurs and thus the vast supply network servicing the AEC sector and what direction it might develop in the future.

Innovations come from a range of different places at different times depending upon what they are. Although design, consulting and contracting firms offer innovation around process, it is those firms producing the components, products (e.g. lighting or cladding systems) and materials (e.g. paints or cements) that go to form the parts of the finished building. The firms producing lighting systems, for example, may not be strictly seen as part of the AEC sector: a lighting manufacturer may consider themselves part of the electronics sector rather than the AEC sector. Nonetheless, it is argued that in order to understand sustained innovation uptake and how that might be achieved, we need to understand how the elements that go to make a 'whole building' are actually procured, and what motivates or enables those parties to innovative. Buildings typically consist of thousands if not millions of different elements, components, products or materials. Typically, firms supply those elements by 'selling' them to the contractor or sub-contractor on a project-by-project basis. It is accepted that sometimes such arrangements are complicated by how the contracting firm lets the work package, materials only or labour and materials. Yet, the question remains of how the suppliers of components, products and materials innovate and what role that has on achieving long-term innovation uptake.

Staying with the example of the lighting manufacturer; let us consider the practical situation where they are invited to supply lighting for a building at a sports venue. The successful bid by the UK to host the 2012 Olympics increased interest in mega sport venues: the varied facilities required, associated infrastructure and the importance of an *absolute* completion date for a construction project (Jenning, 2012). Research into the design and construction of large international sport venues and their associated facilities has typically focused on Olympic projects (Pitts and Liao, 2013). However, it is not the construction of Olympic facilities which are of focus here, but rather the sport that *claims* the highest global audience, that of Formula 1 (F1) motor racing. To add further context, hypothetically let us assume the sport venue client is the Silverstone F1 circuit in the UK. Such sports venues are particularly interesting because they are used for a whole range of leisure activities from motorsport right through to music concerts, exhibitions and conferences.

Let us assume then that this client is seeking lighting for their large media centre, the medical centre, the conference centre, service areas, the pit garages and the VIP facilities for spectators. Understandably, the client is concerned about energy costs and heat gain, yet also very mindful of the lighting quality required, service intervals, reliability and the need to demonstrate that they are a leading sports venue on a global stage of F1 racing.

Now, under current conditions within the AEC sector, Silverstone will (through their partners) attempt to source the best current option (which could be a minefield of competing and contradictory assessments), purchase the lights (through the construction contractor supply network) and then get them installed. With competition from other lighting manufacturers and developments in research within the lighting field, it is sadly quite possible for the lighting purchased by the client to be seen as costing too much to run, resulting in unacceptable heat gain and also insufficient illumination quality within a very short period of time, thus it has become outdated. This fact is in part due to the 'clouding' and misinformation surrounding what the right specification of light actually is, and there are numerous anecdotal stories reflecting this. Regardless, the client has purchased the lighting, owns the lights and is essentially stuck with them with no recourse.

Given the structural and financial norms of the AEC sector, the lighting manufacturer has sold a product to a specification. They have not designed and manufactured a specific product for a client (the client does not own the *patent* for the lighting). This is how things have evolved in the AEC sector over the years.

Within such norms, we can now question how the lighting manufacturer goes about improving their product; how they make their lighting more energy efficient, reduce heat gain whilst also improving lighting quality and thus how they innovate generally. This apparent short termism of selling lighting products on a project-by-project basis results in limited financial security, something that is typically required for high-end innovative activity. This in turn does not give the lighting manufacturer much long-term security for planning, or for planning research into new innovative ideas. Likewise, it does not give the lighting manufacturer much in the form of motivation to innovate or improve their products. There are few knowns about commitment from potential clients, meaning that the lighting manufacturer will find the financial planning for innovative developments problematic. A one-off payment gained from selling lights on a project-by-project basis offers the lighting manufacturer little certainty. It is argued that it is that very lack of certainly which in part hinders innovation and uptake. This is because the method of procuring the lighting yields very little long-term stability (organisational, financial or, importantly, technological) for the lighting manufacturer.

Now, let us imagine instead a scenario where Silverstone asks for the provision of lighting with a given specification. However, they don't ask to buy any lighting system or fittings. Silverstone simply wishes to buy the *right to lighting* at a given specification for a period of time. Then Silverstone goes one key step further by asking for a reduction in lighting energy costs, less heat gain and improvements in the light quality bi-annually for a 10-year period. This completely changes the rules of the game. This offers the potential for the lighting manufacturer to re-think their business model, now with much greater long-term certainty, long-term funding and an opportunity to invest more in research and innovation. This alternative long-term arrangement offers the lighting manufacturer the ability to plan a programme of innovation over a 10-year period with much greater certainty. Consideration can thus be given to where the intellectual property ownership of the lighting innovation rests. For example, within the automotive sector the ownership of the intellectual property of an innovative lighting design fitting to a car is open to negotiation, sometimes residing with the light specialist and sometimes with the car manufacturer themselves.

Given such examples, the AEC sector (and clients) should be questioning the procurement methods used and how these can be levered to strive for sustained innovation uptake. Certainly clients have a role to play, but so do the professionals and academics in guiding them regarding how to get the best out of the building they are procuring. Of course, versions of this business model are nothing new, and the model is typically referred to as *service-led procurement*. Other examples include aircraft manufacturers who source the engines for their planes by purchasing the *right to flight* in hours rather than purchasing actual engines. Larsen and Hughes (2013) draw upon such examples, including aerospace and electronic consumables sectors, where service-led procurement is seen as a key variable helping nurture sustained innovation uptake. It is thus argued that new procurement routes will play a greater role in ensuring the sustained innovation uptake in the future and by 2050 there will be totally new models of procurement (as yet not even conceived). It is argued that the procurement methods used at the time of writing will be looked back on as rigid, off-the-peg and stifling for innovation development and uptake.

## 15.7    Market networks

The argument has so far developed around the complexity of what constituents an AEC firm and the need to move beyond the rhetoric of isolated firms (with a unitary voice), moving to thinking about networks of firms innovating with a range of voices present. The chapter then discussed the challenges of stimulating innovation within the supply network within current institutional logics.

Attention is now turned toward clients and the markets that form around them. Literature champions why it is important for AEC firms to understand their clients and by doing so the markets they operate in (Kao, 2004). To get a handle on the complexity of this issue, building upon the example above of the lighting systems manufacturer and Silverstone F1 circuit as a client, a given market network is used for illustrative purposes.

Although once dominated by European F1 races and their associated venues, the changing world over the last 25 years, coupled with the opening of borders and increased internationalisation, has led to changes in the F1 race calendar and hence new venues. At the time of writing recent additions to the F1 race calendar include Abu Dhabi, Azerbaijan, Bahrain, China, Dubai, India, Korea, Russia, Singapore, Turkey and the USA. That equates to 11 new F1 venues being constructed since the year 2000. The drivers for such countries wishing to host a F1 race, and thus consider constructing a venue, are varied yet typically go well beyond the sport of motor racing. The reasoning behind such decisions is more aligned with putting the country on the map through the vast TV viewing audiences for either political benefits or the economic benefits of sports tourism.

F1 racing requires substantial significant built assets and infrastructure. Empirical case study evidence suggests an F1 racing venue will cost anywhere between $150 million up to $40 billion (if the associated development and infrastructure are included). It is thus not then surprising, with the stakes being so high, that such clients would demand innovative and long-term solutions. However, there have been a number of claims that some recently constructed F1 racing venues lack innovation and are following the same formulaic approach (Briggs, 2009; Stewart, 2011). There have been conflicting observations within academia, with some work taking a very positive stance (Abdul-Rahman *et al.*, 2014) whilst others have been more critical regarding challenges and areas for improvement (Larsen and Hughes, 2013; Larsen, 2016).

Rarely does a new F1 racing venue (or any project of significant size) get designed and constructed in isolation. On the contrary, F1 racing venues will typically form part of a larger redevelopment plan for a region within a particular country. An example of this is the Yas Marina F1 venue in Abu Dhabi, with total development cost estimated to be in the region of $40 billion. In Abu Dhabi, a large deserted area of the country was turned into the Yas Marina F1 project and includes the following: Yas Mall (blue chip shopping, 300,000 m$^2$), world-class links golf course, water theme park, residential units and the Ferrari theme park. The Yas Marina F1 project also includes the Yas 5-star hotel, which spans across the F1 race track and the construction of a new port suitable for mega yachts. The client for this undertaking was the Abu Dhabi's Ministry of Works and Housing (the country is effectively the client). The venue was designed in an incredibly short period of time, less than 3 years in total and took just 31 months of construction time. At its peak the Yas Marina F1 construction project reportedly had 45,0000 operatives on site, working day and night shifts.

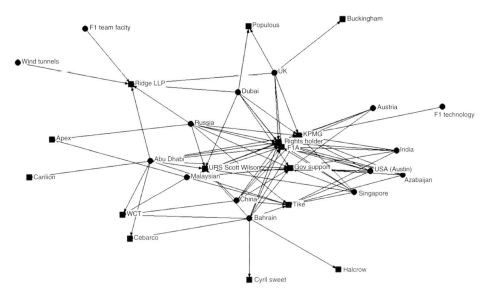

**Figure 15.1** Market networks of stakeholders and F1 venues since 2001 (Larsen, 2016).

To help understand this market a simple social network analysis diagram is offered below (Figure 15.1). Based on empirical data this shows the AEC firms servicing these types of clients as small dark squares, along with the regulators (FIA), commercial rights holders for the sport of F1 racing and host countries planning/regulatory bodies (Gov). The clients are denoted by the country where the F1 racing venue is located as small dark circles. Silverstone is thus represented by the UK.

By daring to open the 'black box' around a specific market through a network diagram, we can offer a range of observations and arguments. It is argued that this type of client and the stakeholders involved in the provision of the type of built facilities they want (leisure, sports and specifically an F1 racing venue) actually form a particular type of market, and that impacts our understanding of sustainable innovation uptake. It is argued that there are no *normal* markets, but rather that all markets have their own characteristics. If we are to understand how to achieve sustainable innovation uptake then we need to see the client and their market setting as an active variable for consideration. The following sections use the F1 example and Figure 15.1 to present a rationale for this call.

Given the network diagram in Figure 15.1, there are a limited number of stakeholders which form part of the market network. However, that could also be said for market networks constructed around, for example, a 100-floor multistory building built from the latest materials featuring smart facades in a city centre or perhaps a house built from straw bales and timber designed to be run totally off-grid. What is more relevant is that the diagram illustrates the issues of sustained innovation uptake from a network perspective and what this will mean for us as we look toward 2050. Granovetter's (1983) work on the strength of weak ties offers a useful initial launchpad for critiquing the network. Key to this critique is the relationship between the stakeholders and the venues/projects, and the directional orientation this gives the network. The network has a clear inward-looking, egocentric orientation.

It is suggested that this type of client, and the AEC firms connected with them, operate in a market setting that is potentially too inward looking, too dense and dominated by too few AEC firms, whereby those firms have a high amount of agency. This might be acceptable if you are one of the firms already in the market setting. However, the network shape of the market has adverse effects on sustained innovation uptake, as few new ideas can penetrate the inward-looking network. Using Granovetter as an influence, there has been a wealth of literature highlighting the negative impact overly inward-looking market networks can have on competitive and innovative activity (Maskell *et al.*, 1998; Kao *et al.*, 2009; Larsen, 2011, 2016).

For this example, attention needs to be given to the institutional logics if the market network is to become more open to sustained innovation uptake. Currently the market network points toward the agency held by the FIA (the governing body for motorsport), the CRH (commercial rights holder for F1 racing) and the host government's policy, laws and regulations. It is argued that in this example the FIA, the CRH and the governments of the countries are dominant, thus holding the majority of the agency. Possession of this agency means that entry into the market network needs to be supported by at least one of these institutional logics (it is unclear how this might be gained). These institutional logics may well stretch to shaping the methods of procurement deemed appropriate as previously discussed, thereby influencing the client's freedom to enter into service-led procurement arrangements to stimulate sustained innovation uptake. Of course, this is just one example of a market network, yet it is proposed that many others may be suffering a similar fate. As we attempt to look toward the year 2050 and how we might sustain innovation uptake it is argued that we will need to treat the market network as an active variable in that understanding. Whether we will be able to 'construct' a market network with a structure that does sustain innovation uptake is unclear, but that must surely be the goal.

Thus, hoping to achieve sustained innovation uptake without understanding the variables of the contextual setting is essentially a fruitless venture. Currently, research looking into how sustained innovation uptake occurs for such clients, their projects and the market does not even get off the starting grid. This is just one example market of the numerous different markets in the AEC sector (hospitals, schools, office, retail, commercial, leisure, infrastructure and so on). Thus, generic measures of sustained innovation uptake are meaningless as they underplay the very issues of importance (context) offering little reasoning for their claims. It is argued here therefore that we need a more contextualised view, taking into account the issues discussed here.

## 15.8   Summary: seeing both the wood and the trees

In the F1 case study in this chapter, the client, the stakeholders, procurement methods and market setting have been used for illustrative purposes. It is hoped that this example (although perhaps it is an unusual one in purely 'sustainable' terms) demonstrates the assumptions much of our current thinking is based on and their serious shortcomings. It is also hoped the example has demonstrated how the networks (at all levels) play numerous roles in understanding and potentially enacting sustained innovation uptake. Other markets may look very different, which is fine and accepted. The call here is not that all clients, projects and markets look like this, but precisely the opposite in that they are all unique, and we need to treat them as such and understand them as such. Currently we are failing to do this and instead we still live with an AEC sector that is dominated by acontextual approaches toward sustained innovation uptake, only to then complain that the sector is not innovative enough or fails to engage with change.

Sustained innovation uptake occurs across networks (operating at different levels of abstraction) with a project, and not just one specific isolated firm. So, just focusing on one AEC firm will prove fruitless and unrepresentative of how the process is enacted in practice. Thinking about the 'firm' in great detail is helpful, as illustrated earlier in the chapter, but we must also be able to consider that firm on the broader client, project, stakeholder and market network, and therefore see both the wood and the trees.

## 15.9   Concluding thoughts

This chapter has sought to shout about, rather than shy away from, many of the issues skirted over within the industry's current thinking and the majority of academic literature within the construction management field. It has been argued that to understand sustained innovation uptake we need to unpack some of our current assumptions in an effort to *see* both the wood and the trees. This means giving greater consideration to approaches that consider the multiple levels and their interrelationship (Geels, 2011). Currently, our thinking struggles to connect the dots across the levels of enactment, often focusing separately on actors, firms, supply networks, clients or best practice agendas with incorrect and outdated assumptions based on little empirical evidence.

The challenge for us at the time of writing is how we can consider these changing network shapes within the AEC sector. Attention is drawn to understanding how these networks will play out over time toward 2050; and thus how we might be able to influence the networks to suit particular interests and thus shape our future. This challenge manifests into improving our understanding of the interwoven attributes discussed, and to actually act on them in an instrumental manner to strive for sustained innovation uptake. This may sound trite, but it is an important step as the challenges discussed are typically oversimplified or worse still reduced to a box on a best practice diagram. So this is a big step in itself and one that illuminates the situation rather than keeping it in the shadows. There is no hiding it: understanding sustained innovation uptake is a messy and complex situation, across a number of interconnected levels, needing careful consideration.

The argument developed here sought to embrace the diversity of AEC firms in the broadest sense rather than simply stating research should focus on large international firms or SMEs. As a result, the false dichotomy (large firm vs SMEs) set up through much of the literature was challenged, offering instead a call for increased contextual understanding of what actually goes to make up the firms that might service the construction sector. The context is fluid, with practitioners within the firms and projects constantly changing; each firm's structure and approach to its business is reconsidered in response to a range of factors. Every stakeholder mentioned in this chapter has a role to play regarding achieving sustained innovation uptake. This is non-negotiable for everyone – actors may be completely unaware of the role they play or that they are even part of the innovation uptake process at all, but they are. The roles played are of course not fixed, but contextually situated and change over time, they are fluid. What guidance there is for stakeholders often over-simplifies the nature of 'the firm', often viewing it as being a unitary entity with one coherent voice and with little consideration regarding the complex structural organisation of firms; with regional subsidiaries, business units or even informal divisions due to acquisition. Firms are constantly refining and changing their structure (often contradicting each other) in an attempt to fit their changing market and this must surely be an active part of any understanding.

Likewise, the chapter sought to raise the relevance of the source of innovation associated with the components and products that go to form a completed building. In doing so, the short-sightedness in the current procurement arrangements within the supply network for achieving sustained innovation uptake was presented. Certainly there are efforts within the AEC sector to bring firms within the supply network together through best practice clubs, events and forums, but there is plenty of scope for improving this. It is hoped that readers will now begin to question how sustained innovation uptake occurs, where it might come from, who is driving it, what is there to motivate the innovators and who is involved in the negotiation process. For the example client and market networks discussed this supply network issue is potentially problematic and hinders innovation and uptake.

More practically, the UK construction sector would benefit from a more focused yet sensitive approach to understand sustained innovation uptake. As practitioners and academics we need the right mind set that can enable us to understand the messy situation described within this chapter. However, this means ensuring we have the right methodological tools or perhaps developing new methodological tools. Only then can any understanding reflect and resonate with the reality of where sustained innovation uptake is born and nurtured.

There are a number of messages to take away from this chapter. The key issue running through all of the messages is that until the structural make-up of the UK construction sector (across all levels) is used as an active part of our understanding, rather than falsely as a straw man, then we will struggle to understand, let alone achieve, sustained innovation uptake. Importantly, what the UK construction sector does not require is yet more judgement or advice concluding that the whole sector lacks innovation. Such claims are simply not the case and are not based on a fair criterion. The innovative activity in the construction sector may be difficult to trace and map for many of the reasons discussed, but it is there. What the UK construction sector actually needs is practical guidance that is context specific, localised and acknowledges that innovation occurs in networks and through networks, rather than generic best practice initiatives (which are typically geared toward simplistic conceptualisations of construction firms and the supply chain).

The next phase of sustained innovation uptake research associated with the built environment toward 2050 will hopefully take a marked step forwards, whilst fully acknowledging the socio-technical nature of the subject, considering the multiple levels of networks, and the unique and complex contextual setting described in this chapter.

## References

Abdul-Rahman, H. Wang, C. Wood, L.C. and Ismail, S. (2014) International joint venture between ASEAN and GULF: Bidding and delivering Bahrain International Formula 1 Circuit. *TRAMES*, 18(4), 357–382.

Archer, M. (1988) *Culture and agency: The place of culture in social theory.* Cambridge University Press, Cambridge.

Boyd, P., Larsen, G.D. and Schweber, L. (2015) The co-development of technology and new buildings: incorporating building integrated photovoltaics. *Construction Management and Economics*, 33(5), 349–360.

Briggs, G. (2009) *Tilke, tailor, circuit maker.* Available at: https://www.theguardian.com/sport/2009/mar/21/hermann-tilka-formula-one-designer (accessed 23 August 2017).

Carrillo, P. and Heavey, I. (2000) UK contractors' acquisitions strategy for Central and Eastern Europe. *Engineering, Construction and Architectural Management*, 7(3), 322–328.

Fernie, S. and Tennant, S. (2013) The non-adoption of supply chain management. *Construction Management and Economics*, 31(10), 1038–1058.

Fernie, S. and Thorpe, A. (2007) Exploring change in construction: supply chain management. *Engineering, Construction and Architectural Management*, 14(4), 319–333.

Fleck, J. (1993) Innofusion: Feedback in the innovation process, in Stowell, F.A. (ed.) *Systems Science: Addressing Global Issues.* Plenum Press, New York, pp. 169–174.

Geels, F.W. (2011) The multi-level perspective on sustainability transitions: Responses to seven criticisms. *Environmental Innovation and Societal Transitions*, 1(1), 24–40.

Giddens, A. (1979) *Central Problems in Social Theory: Action, structure and contradiction in social analysis.* Macmillan, Basingstoke.

Granovetter, M. (1983). The strength of weak ties: a network theory revisited. *Sociological Theory*, 1, 201–233.

Green, S.D., Fernie, S. and Weller, S. (2005) Making sense of supply chain management: a comparative study of aerospace and construction. *Construction Management and Economics*, 23(6), 579–593.

Green, S.D., Larsen, G.D. and Kao, C.C. (2008) Competitive strategy revisited: contested concepts and dynamic capabilities, *Construction Management and Economics*, 26(1), 63–78.

Jenning, W. (2012) Why costs overrun: risk, optimism and uncertainty in budgeting for the London 2012 Olympic Games. *Construction Management and Economics*, 6(30), 455–462.

Kao, C.C. (2004) *The briefing process: an organizational knowledge-creation perspective.* PhD thesis, School of Construction Management and Engineering, University of Reading.

Kao, C., Larsen, G.D. and Green, S.D. (2009) Emergent discourses of construction competitiveness: localised learning and embeddedness. *Construction Management and Economics – Special Issue on Informality and Emergence in Construction*, 27(10), 1005–1017.

Larsen, G.D. (2011) Understanding the early stages of the innovation diffusion process: awareness, influence and communication networks. *Construction Management and Economics*, 29(10), 987–1002.

Larsen, G.D. (2015) Innovation diffusion across firms, in Ørstavik, F., Dainty, A. and Abbott, C. (eds) *Perspectives on Construction Innovation.* Wiley-Blackwell.

Larsen, G.D. (2016) Mapping and understanding stakeholders within a niche market: Lessons from F1 circuits around the world. *Royal Institution of Chartered Surveyors Annual International Research Conference.* COBRA, Toronto.

Larsen, G.D. and Hughes, W. (2013) Revolutionary road: Innovative procurement methods for sustainable motorsport facilities. *Professional Motorsport Circuit*, Winter Issue, 34–38.

Maskell, P., Eskelinen, H., Hannibalsson, I., Malmberg, A. and Vatne, E. (1998) *Competitiveness, localised learning and regional development.* Routledge, London.

Office of National Statistics (2016) *Construction Statistics: No 17.* Office of National Statistics, London.

Pettigrew, A.M. (1997) What is a processual analysis? *Scandinavian Journal of Management*, 13(4), 337–348.

Pinch, T.J. and Bijker, W.B. (1984) The social construction of facts and artefacts: or how the sociology of science and the sociology of technology might benefit each other. *Social Studies of Science*, 14 August, 399–441.

Pitts, A. and Liao, H. (2013) An assessment technique for the evaluation and promotion of sustainable Olympic design and urban development. *Building Research & Information*, 41(6), 722–734.

Ritzer, G. (1996) *Sociological Theory.* McGraw Hill, London.

Rogers, E.M. (2003) *Diffusion of Innovations*, 5th edn. Simon & Schuster, New York.

Sexton, M. and Barrett, P.S. (2003) A literature review synthesis of innovation in small firms: insights, ambiguities and questions. *Construction Management and Economics*, 21(6), 613–622.

Stewart, J. (2011) Sir Jackie Stewart: Want more overtaking in F1? Make circuits punish drivers for their mistakes. *The Telegraph*, 26 February.

Winch, G.M. (2003) How innovative is construction? Comparing aggregated data on construction innovation and other sectors – a case of apples and pears. *Construction Management and Economics*, 23(6), 651–654.

# 16

# Humanising the Digital: A Cautionary View of the Future

*Ian J. Ewart*

## 16.1   Introduction

Forecasting the future of technology is fraught with difficulty, and we can easily look to the recent past and previous predictions of the future to judge the likelihood of getting it right. This is especially true now, as we find ourselves in the midst of a digital revolution, when digital technologies are changing so quickly that adoption in any specific sphere, such as the architecture, engineering and construction (ACE) industries, struggles to come to terms with one technology before it is superseded or becomes obsolete. Digital technologies are auxiliary to the practices of design and construction, which depend ultimately on the skills and activities of people engaging with their material environment. External drivers, emanating from the entertainment and communication industries, have meant that, to date, much of the use of digital technology in AEC has been based on adopting developments from outside the industry and trying make them fit into existing practices. This has created the position we now find ourselves, of constantly chasing the latest technology, rushed forward with limited attention, without the time to allow it to mature and disseminate throughout a heterogonous industry.

  My suggestion in this chapter is that the digital future in AEC has to be more 'human' than 'technological'. We will need to account more seriously for the human experience of the digital world, otherwise the apparent benefits of this revolution will prove to be illusory. The commercial and political agendas that are the driving force behind much of the digital revolution can only ever be convincing in tandem with a cultural acceptance of the technologies that are being produced. Technological choices are not based on simple decisions about resources and efficiencies, or the rhetoric of logic, but are heavily dependent on the socio-technical milieu in which they are presented (Lemmonier, 2002). So, by emphasising the social dimension of the digital world we need to be open to unpredictable behaviours, as real-world users subvert the digital practices intended by corporations, technical professionals and policy makers. Within AEC, this need not mean that the new socio-digital revolution becomes an uprising against the professional elite, or a rejection of the expert in favour of a democratic and technically-aware public. We should, however, start to consider how to embrace these changes and how they can act to the advantage of the industry, forsaking the notion of

*Sustainable Futures in the Built Environment to 2050: A Foresight Approach to Construction and Development*, First Edition. Edited by Tim Dixon, John Connaughton and Stuart Green.
© 2018 John Wiley & Sons Ltd. Published 2018 by John Wiley & Sons Ltd.

'technological determinism' and repositioning the digital revolution as one where society uses technologies for its benefit, rather than the technologies forcing society to bend to its will and adapt to its inherent limitations.

The digital world is currently accelerating away from the human world, driven by technological imperatives, in at least two key ways. The first is a popular notion of the power of science and technology to understand the world around us and to shape our future. This perception has been under critical scrutiny since sociological studies removed the veneer of neutrality from the world of science (e.g. Latour and Woolgar, 1986), and is currently facing a 'reproducibility crisis', which is questioning the accuracy of the majority of science experiments (Baker, 2016). The second is the exponential growth in the production of digital data, to an extent that is becoming increasingly difficult to contextualise, visualise and understand in any meaningful way (SINTEF, 2013). The digital world of the future will need to reject the idea that all data is good data, and include ways that this data can be presented on a human scale, in ways that people can understand.

These new trajectories will have consequences for the AEC industries in methods of working and ways of thinking, but we should as an industry view with optimism and excitement digital technologies as an enabler of emergent practices, allowing us to engage in the construction of a mutually beneficial future built environment. This chapter therefore adopts a cautionary approach to predicting digital futures, and instead considers the future of the relationship between society and the digital world.

## 16.2 Previous futures

Vincent Crapanzano, in his seminal philosophical treatise on the nature of imagination, used the trope of the constantly distant horizon as the location for our imaginative ambitions: drawing near as we move forwards and becoming more real as it does so, but yet, as we raise our eyes, presenting us with a tantalising new distant horizon. As he puts it 'Our constructions of the beyond are always slippery' (Crapanzano, 2004: 21). When we look to the future, and imagine what the world might look like, invariably we are drawn to technology as the yardstick by which we measure how far society could progress. In recent years, the concept of technology has shifted inexorably towards the digital and the view that the world, and reality itself, is no longer analogue, but is in some strange way made up of a digital representation of itself. This would have been difficult to predict 30 years ago, and as we attempt here to consider the future of construction 30 years from now, it is perhaps wise to reflect on previous predictions of the future. This is particularly resonant in this chapter, since it is concerned with digital futures, and quite clearly predicting the long-term future of something that throws up innovations and challenges almost daily is fraught with difficulty.

Despite our best efforts to trace the trajectory of the history of technology and extrapolate it into the future, the inevitable result is always a mix of fortunate hits and wildly inaccurate misses. Writing in 2017, and imagining the digital world three decades hence, it is salutary to cast our minds back the same amount of time and consider previously imagined futures of the technological world of today. A good starting point is the classic movie *Back to the Future 2* (*BTTF2*), made in 1989 but set in a contemporary 1985 and an imaginary vision of 2015, complete with what were seen as the technologies from 30 years in the future. Advances in transport feature heavily, including Marty McFly's hoverboard, and the ubiquitous flying car, ever present since the 1960s and the Jetsons cartoons. Of course, neither of these has come to pass, except at the fringes of personal transportation, and it seems unlikely they will in the next 30 years. Instead, transport has progressed in ways that were largely unanticipated, with the growing recognition of the effects of fossil fuels on the environment, and issues of congestion and safety coming to the fore. Interestingly, the finale of the first *Back to the Future* film ended with Emmett 'Doc' Brown filling his flying DeLorean with a handful of rubbish as fuel and heading off to the rousing assertion 'Roads? Where we're going, we don't need roads!' before landing in *BTTF2's* 2015, on a road. So perhaps we could have seen then, that the days of fossil fuels are numbered, and that sustainable sources of alternative fuels are on the rise, even if flying cars are somewhat fanciful.

Some of the other advances predicted in that previous future, such as self-tying boots and drying clothing are outside the scope of the current chapter, but of greater relevance is the popular perception of digital technologies that the film documents. Old Marty, complete with the latest fashion in double-tie neckwear, makes a video call to his colleague Doug Needles on a large flat-screen TV, which we then learn is being monitored by his boss Fujitsu-san, and results in him being fired there and then, ironically confirmed by a fax reading 'YOU'RE FIRED!!!' printed out on his table-top fax machine. This mix of communication technologies seems strange to us today, where faxes are virtually unused, and video calls are commonplace, enabled by the development of a digital infrastructure in the last decade or so, and forecast to continue with the planned rollout of 5G mobile networks.

Having predicted significant changes to communication technologies, albeit with mixed success, perhaps more surprising is *BTTF2's* prediction for the widespread use of head-mounted displays (HMDs) and augmented reality interactive technologies. Old Marty, in 2015, still wearing his double-tie, sits at the table with his future teenage children who are wearing what bears a remarkable resemblance to some of the recently launched virtual reality (VR) HMDs. The *BTTF2* prediction seems to take the concept of head-up displays, such as were then being used, for example, in fighter aircraft, and re-purpose them for use in entertainment, and particularly for teenagers. That type of immersive VR has been due for 'imminent arrival' since about the time of *BTTF2*, and after several false starts it seems that some significant developments in digital technologies over the last few years mean that VR really is about to happen. IT hardware has been developing at an exponential rate for several decades, as predicted by Gordon Moore, co-founder of Intel, who first wrote about this in 1965 when he noticed that the density of transistors had doubled every 2 years since their invention, and expected that trend to continue (Moore, 1965). However, it has taken until very recently for IT capabilities, and in particular graphics handling, to reach the point where it is possible to render complex images in real time. Moore's law can be seen in action in the ongoing development of graphics cards (most notably from Nvidia and Radeon), which are released annually at least with each one showing significant improvements over the last.

Similarly, the hardware technologies of immersive HMDs have improved rapidly in recent years, taking advantage of new generation graphics cards. The early market leader, and the device responsible for bringing this technology to the public, is the Oculus Rift. It was only in 2012 that Oculus launched their Kickstarter campaign to raise funds to develop the first commercially viable VR HMD, which led to the DK1 in 2013 (a device aimed at the knowledgeable enthusiast, rather than the everyday user), and the DK2 in 2014, a product which was impressive enough to interest Facebook, who that year bought Oculus for $2billion. The first consumer version (CV1) was launched in 2016, by which time a number of other immersive HMDs were being released, most notably the Vive, manufactured by the giant Taiwanese technology company HTC (also launched in 2016), and the Hololens, manufactured by Microsoft Corporation, as well as a gaming console headset from Sony.

*BTTF2's* predictions for digital interactions through HMDs, especially their potential in entertainment, has proved quite accurate, but the future for these technologies moves them beyond the home and outside the gaming industry, into other walks of life. The AEC sector looks likely to be one of the beneficiaries of this sphere of technological development as it is currently experimenting with the use of virtual environments and has a tradition of 3D architectural modelling that fits well with the capabilities of VR HMDs (Maftei and Harty, 2015; Moum, 2010). However, while it is usual in the gaming community to become individually immersed in a headset, the same will not be true of every other application. Whereas design, as a process of conceptualising the future built environment, can be seen to embrace a visually immersive future, the act of construction itself remains a process of skilled individuals interacting with the physical world around them in ways that serve to inform their judgement and suggest modes of behaving (Marchand, 2009). For those in the AEC sector, this means that the trajectory of development of this technology suits some activities, especially conceptual design, but not others, in particular the act of construction. However, in exposing new users to these developing technologies there is a process of overcoming the initial surprise and lack of familiarity before experimenting to find ways of interaction (Maftei and Harty, 2015). This is a useful starting point in imagining the future of VR in AEC: it is not just a tool for creating visual representations of the world in an ever more 'real' way, but a tool that allows people to become immersed in new ways. It may form the basis for new ways of analysing data, for example, and not simply be used as a design tool.

But, getting back to Marty McFly and Doc Brown, having celebrated their 'hits' (and there are others, such as fingerprint recognition and tablet computers), another notable 'miss' we should point out (whilst lamenting the lack of flying cars) is the use of mobile phones. Today digital communications are reliable, fast and cheap, much more so than was envisaged in 1985. Alongside possibly the biggest change to our digital world in the last three decades – the internet and World Wide Web – the connectivity that comes with new lightweight smartphones is allowing a whole host of new forms of social and technical interaction. The travails Doc Brown experienced as a lone genius, working against the odds to perfect his dream of time travel, might well have been eased if he had access to other academics or mad scientists working in geographically and theoretically disparate places. The so-called information age is now in full swing and almost at the point that any information is available to any person at any time and in any place. Such a high degree of connectivity, and the relatively unfettered access to almost unlimited data, is not without its problems of course, and as this is still a relatively new phenomenon we are yet to work through how we deal with a range of issues. The trend to the 'infinite archive' means that culturally we are confronted by issues to do with the use of language and concepts of memory, perception and truth, alongside more practical concerns such as notions of authorship and ownership, and the responsibilities of individuals and the state. However, within AEC, connectivity and the availability of data allows collaboration in the design and construction sequence, and the resulting built artefact can be supplemented with swathes of information about its capabilities and resources, the ultimate goal of the building information modelling (BIM) agenda (Azhar, 2011).

The future 2015 as portrayed by *BTTF2* fulfils a common trope of futurology, which is the perception of the future as one dominated by increased technology, and in recent years with an emphasis on particularly digital technologies as the marker of progress. This contrasts with the inertia of social change. Most of the social structures seen in previous futures are primarily reflections of the then existing social system, unless they are distorted to a dystopic vision of social atrophy, as was the case in *BTTF3*, with Biff's abuse of time travel leading to his maniacal acquisition of huge power. Such disturbing visions of the future are, of course, common, not only in the world of film and literature (e.g. from Huxley's *Brave New World* of 1932, to the *Hunger Games* film series of 2012–15), but also in science, for example in the debate about the environmental future of our planet. The message seems to be that technologies are constantly progressing in a positive way, but society is lagging behind, or if it changes in any significant way it is for the worse. This disconnect between our future technologies and our future social relations is worrying, and it should be at the forefront of our minds when considering what and how we relate to the digital world of the future, including, importantly, the built environment.

## 16.3 Social appropriateness of digital technologies

The debate about whether or not the construction sector is 'innovative' or 'conservative' depends on the terms of reference: whether construction is in some way a relative leader of innovation, or whether the sector is recklessly turning away from opportunities to improve. Usually this is framed in terms of the potential for improvements in economics or efficiency, on the basis that the construction sector is a major employer, user of materials, producer of waste and provider of essential human needs (e.g. infrastructure and housing). Construction is seen by some as being wedded to a traditional past, relying on trades and crafts, literally and metaphorically stuck in the mud (Carrillo and Chinowsky, 2006; Holt, 2015). Of course, this is far from the truth: many construction companies are modern and forward thinking, and continually experiment with new methods, materials and forms of organisation (Walker, 2016). As commercial entities they have a primary objective to improve their profitability, and keep a close eye on developments that they may be able to use to this end.

However, the frustrated proponents of the conservative construction agenda can point to a number of digital initiatives that are viewed with suspicion and largely eschewed by the AEC sector. A good example is the slow uptake of BIM, which has promised much but delivered little (Dainty *et al.*, 2015; Green, 2013). BIM has had the advantages of political champions, numerous forums and initiatives, and heavy promotion from the technology providers, and yet the dream of completely integrated digital models of building information remains stubbornly on a distant horizon. It is of course true to say that BIM, or at least that BIM dream, is not simply as a repository of information but also a way of working, of collaboration and co-production. In fact, one of the key issues facing the widespread adoption of BIM is the current difficulty in understanding exactly what BIM is (Davies and Harty, 2013). As a system of data integration intended to be used across a range of stakeholders, the reality is that different users are adopting parts of BIM that they see as suitable for their own requirements (Dainty *et al.*, 2015), somewhat defeating the objective of BIM as a single point of contact and dissemination from design, through construction and into operation.

The popular notion that social progress is inextricably linked to (and even depends upon) the uptake and development of digital technologies is in danger of adopting the rhetoric of technological determinism. In this view, regardless of the social context into which the technology is parachuted, the inherent benefits will automatically outweigh any social reservations, and ultimately a process of logical, linear progression will drive social change into acceptance. The experience of BIM with the AEC sector seems to offer yet another example of the need to take serious account of the role of social factors in planning for a digital revolution. The way that technologies are used is dependent on the social fit that they can carve out for themselves, either deliberately through political planning or organically as the community adopts and adapts them to align more or less with existing practices and beliefs (Lemonnier, 1992). New technologies come with attached meanings and frame their potential in relation to their existing uses. BIM has struggled to break free from a perception in some quarters that it is simply CAD+ and in others that its long-term benefits do not justify the initial investments in time and resources (e.g. Dossick and Neff, 2010). There is confusion in the distinction between developments in 3D modelling, improved structures of facilities management and the ability to use a 3D model as the basis for collaborative working and information sharing. Software suppliers such as Autodesk are continually developing their suite of programmes to increase function and performance, and indeed to supply what is ostensibly the BIM market. However, there is a fundamental philosophical difference between using 3D models in a traditional design-practice way and using the same software as part of an integrated information-sharing platform. Digital technologies do not come into AEC devoid of meaning, but bring with them suggested ways of working and notions of possibilities that are limited by tradition and inertia. This is enhanced by the inherent complexity of the sector, with variety of scale and purpose, and which often thwarts attempts to offer an overarching solution to service the needs of a community that is by no means homogenous (Davies and Harty, 2013).

More broadly within AEC, the intention to use digital technologies for collaborative working and engaging stakeholders in the design and construction process is predicated on the capabilities of the technologies being used and the relative skills and experience of the participants involved. In a typical co-design process, for example, where users are involved as participants, the conversation is directed by construction professionals, who curate the presentation of information within bounds that they deem most appropriate (Luck, 2007). Limits are placed on who can contribute to which parts of the process, and the extent to which their voices are heard. As an efficient way of involving non-technical users this makes sense, and there is no reason to expect them to contribute to the behind-the-scenes design work, let alone be competent in doing so. However, reducing digital technology to a forum for discussion demeans its potential and misses the possibilities for novel interventions. To change the industry so that it can relinquish substantial control of the design process depends on appropriating new technologies and applying them in innovative ways. Of course, as discussed above, there is some uncertainty in whether and how a community (such as the AEC sector, or parts of it) adopts a new technology, but by restricting the use of new technologies so that they maintain existing practices will reduce their potential for novel and surprising forms of exploitation. This seems to be happening in the case of emerging visualisation technologies that are currently migrating to AEC from gaming and entertainment, where they are being developed to create ever more realistic immersion, and are seen as an enticing future for the design side of AEC. However, if the industry accepts the concept of realism and immersion as it arrives from the gaming context, with its heightened and exaggerated realities, it risks accepting the digital human experience as somehow commensurate with the equivalent experience of the real world. We still do not really understand what the user is experiencing when they enter a VR environment (Kuliga *et al.*, 2015), and to begin to do so requires a social re-contextualisation of the technology to suit its new environment. In other words, we do not want successful use of new visualisation technologies to depend on the user's experience of gaming, nor do we want the experience of VR, for example, in an AEC context to be restricted by the paradigms of VR that come from gaming.

## 16.4   Socio-digital integration

As well as the need to consider how future digital technologies are contextualised in the AEC sector, with the aim of recognising their potential for novel practices, a second separation between the digital and the human is looming on the horizon: the incomprehensible vastness of the production of data. Making digital technologies relevant to the human experience depends on this vast body of data being rendered meaningful in real-world settings. As an industrial sector directly involved in the creation of that world, AEC organisations should be at the forefront of thinking about how we can reframe digital outputs.

It has been said that with the invention of the printing press, information became freely available on a scale unlike anything before, so that a typical daily newspaper contains as much information about the outside world as a pre-industrial farmer would come across in a lifetime. This might seem a massive leap, but it pales into insignificance when compared to the digital world today, and involves the invention of new words to describe it: the amount of data created in 2005 was estimated to be 130 exabytes (EB) (130 EB, about 130 billion gigabytes (GB)); by 2013 that figure had increased to 4.4 zettabytes (ZB) (4.4 ZB, about 4000 EB) and predictions for 2020 are around 44 ZB (40,000 EB), which is an increase of around 300-fold in 15 years (Hu *et al.*, 2014). According to research by the Swedish group SINTEF, in 2013 90% of the world's data had been generated over the previous 2 years (SINTEF, 2013). Further predictions suggest that the volume of data produced in the year 2017 alone will be greater than the combined volume of every previous year (Turner, 2014) and the rate of production of data is increasing exponentially. These figures are literally incomprehensible, even trying to reduce them to a human scale renders them only slightly less meaningless (e.g. 5 EB would account for all the words ever spoken by every human who ever lived). Even estimating these figures is proving difficult, and previous predictions are constantly updated, always upwards, when actual figures are calculated: the 2007 prediction for data produced in 2010 was 988 EB, which was revised to 1227 EB based on actual results (Turner, 2014).

Even more incredible is the fact that of all this data, only around 0.5% is actually analysed, a figure that is projected to drop as the rate of production increases (Gantz and Reinsel, 2013). The exponential growth in data production is causing a huge backlog of information, much of which is out of date before anyone has had a chance to look at it in any meaningful way. It may be true to say that we have already generated more digital data than we will be able to analyse in the rest of human existence (Turner, 2014). The path to the future therefore must include a means by which we can process data (past, present and future) in a way that can be sustained and made useable in the long term. If the digital revolution has been responsible for the generation of more data than we are able to use, there must be a shift in the paradigm in which we see our relationship with digital technologies, from data generators to social enablers. It is dangerous to continue to suggest uncritically that one of the benefits of the digital revolution is the production of 'big data', without recognising the gap between the proliferation of data and our limited ability to make use of it. What we are doing as a society is marvelling at the capacity of digital technologies to provide us with information about the world we live in, but which so far have contributed very little to resolving the major social challenges that we face today. There seems to be a politico-technical narrative that says that as long as we have data to analyse, then there is the potential to discover useful new things about the world, without ever encountering or confronting it.

If the most startling effect of the digital revolution to date has been largely to do with the production of 'unusable' data (Hu *et al.*, 2014; Turner, 2014), then we should question the extent to which this is also true within AEC. Traditional techniques of designing, planning and executing the construction of new buildings have been converted into, and enhanced with, digital versions. The example of BIM illustrates the problem of gathering data digitally and attempting to present it in a way that is useable to people in the world represented by that digital reality. As discussed above, a key reason for the slow uptake of BIM is a sense of bemusement at what to do with all that information, how and why to use it, as if data has been produced because it is possible to produce it, and not because it is inherently useful.

Coping with this overwhelming flow of data is going to be a key tenet of our digital future, which will involve greater automated data processing and/or innovative ways of involving people in the formatting of data in more accessible ways (e.g. Lanzeni, 2016). In an ironic tautology, the same political narrative that espouses the benefits of big data sees the solution to this problem in the development of digital infrastructures: faster internet connections, larger digital communities, improved hardware, smarter software, the 'internet of things' and so on, each of which opens up the potential for more new data. In effect the digital has been treated as a fundamental evolution of humanity, given an incontrovertible right to dominate our sense of progress and improvement.

All this may feed the fervent imaginings of filmmakers, but it is worth noting some disquiet among the scientific academic community about the potential for social degeneration at the hands of technologies: Stephen Hawking painted just such a picture for the future of artificial intelligence (MIT, 2015), including a warning that it could spell the end of the human race. My suggestion is that the most powerful tool we have at our disposal for the development of new ways of engaging with, analysing and understanding data is ourselves. The variety of human intuition and behaviours will never be replaced by an algorithmic analytical process, not least because of social resistance to the concept of AI. Therefore, we have to accept the need for new forms of human engagement with the data. I mean this literally: the ways that we physically interact with data have to be reduced to a human scale. This may mean, for example, innovative forms of visualisation that act as intermediaries between the vast repositories of data and the physical capabilities of individuals and communities, or forums for interaction that focus on problems and questions specifically relevant to a knowledgeable community.

## 16.5   Conclusions: the consequences for humanising the digital world

The ability of digital technologies to drive social change has always been questionable, and a greater acknowledgement of the role of social influences on the future of digital technologies seems beneficial. So, in the context of the AEC environment the relationship between the social and the digital is due a fundamental shift, away from the digital as a means of generating data controlled by intentional restrictions, and towards the affordances that these technologies allow for new forms of interaction between the digital and social worlds. This is where I see the future of digital technologies over the next few years and decades. If we can move away from the production of digital data to the co-production of socially relevant information, then the path of development for digital technologies will be allowed to meander in ways that we do not need to try to predict. There are always new technologies becoming familiar to the wider public in different contexts, but what the AEC sector currently lacks is the methods to adopt them in novel and disruptive ways.

Looking to 2050, I have argued in this chapter for a humanised future for digital technologies in AEC. This depends on two things: first, social appropriation within the context of a growing public awareness of new possibilities and the democratisation of technical skills, and, second, the practice of data generation will need to be re-thought to enable individuals and communities to envisage and understand data on a human scale. By way of a conclusion, it is also worth considering the consequences of such a shift.

First, there will need to be a re-thinking of the practices of co-production. We will need to accept that the democratisation of digital technologies shifts the balance of authority away from the expert. Not so much undermined, as changed to acknowledge states of uncertainty, generated by the complex interactions of disparate communities empowered in the process of design and production. New communication technologies (such as the proposed 5G mobile networks) and the relentless pace of development of digital hardware will make it easier for communities of knowledge to develop outside their traditional homes and create platforms for a multitude of voices.

Second, we should be enthusiastic about the potential for greater social inclusion in the design and construction of the built environment. Following on from the first point that improving communications will enable greater interaction, the consequent shared responsibility raises the spectre of interminable dispute and the sort of polarised opinions ubiquitous in discussion forums all over the internet. But that does not make it inevitable, and recognising the possibility at an early stage highlights the need to develop good practices to accommodate public expertise and see the co-creation of the future as essentially a positive path, which all contributors can see in an optimistic light.

Third, new technologies are enablers of emergent practices. The recent history of technologies has taught us that there are ingenious people with idiosyncratic views of the world who are willing and capable of turning technologies to alternative uses. Again, we could be fearful of this, but I remain optimistic that embracing unanticipated behaviours will lead to a more interesting built environment in the future.

Fourth, we need innovations in techniques for data engagement. The absurdity of the volumes and rate of data production will surely hit home soon, and the disparity between the maturity of the techniques of production and the underdevelopment of tools of analysis should soon become apparent. If the key issue is rendering data on a human scale, and in ways that are useful to communities of people, then a more direct and embodied engagement of people in that process will be essential.

Finally, we will need to address new moral and ethical dilemmas. Who bears the responsibility for truly co-created future built environments, and how are the risks and benefits apportioned? How can data be made accessible to knowledgeable communities in ways that are secure and free from abuse? As academics, how do we undertake research on the basis that we are co-participants, or even subjects, that our research questions are generated through interactions with our collaborators, who are themselves engaged in their own future-making?

This chapter began by describing the folly of predicting the future of technologies and especially digital technologies, and has explicitly avoided doing so, turning instead to the need for a re-thinking of the relationship between the fast-moving digital world and the relative inertia of social change. Most attempts to predict the material shape of the technological future have underestimated the pace of change, which is moving rapidly to begin with, and yet continues to accelerate relentlessly. However, without being specific about the type of digital technologies that might appear over the coming three decades, it is important to consider how the AEC sector can interact with and influence the digital world of the future.

It has been argued in the chapter that there is a growing separation between the digital world and the real world it purports to represent, and that this divide can only be bridged through social interventions. The AEC sector has an important role in leading and facilitating change since it stands at the vanguard of the construction of the future, and is becoming increasingly interested in the use of digital technologies to carry out its activities. This will undoubtedly continue and evolve, but to do so effectively there needs to be a recognition of the fluidity of social context for digital technologies, which are dispersing in novel and interesting ways; there also needs to be a more thoughtful approach to the use of digital data, bearing in mind the principle that for data to be useful it has to be rendered understandable on a human scale. Although these are generic problems, and there are undoubtedly serious issues to be resolved, it is well within the capacity of the AEC community to rise to the challenges and reframe social-digital relations to embrace an optimistic and fruitful digital future.

## References

Azhar, S. (2011) Building Information Modelling (BIM): Trends, benefits, risks and challenges for the AEC industry. *Leadership and Management in Engineering*, 11(3), 241–252.

Baker, M. (2016) 1500 scientists lift the lid on reproducibility. *Nature*, 533(7604), 452–454.

Carrillo, P. and Chinowsky, P. (2006) Exploiting knowledge management: The engineering and construction perspective. *Journal of Management in Engineering*, 22(1), 2–10.

Crapanzano, V. (2004) *Imaginative Horizons: An Essay in Literary-philosophical Anthropology*. University of Chicago Press, Chicago.

Dainty, A., Leiringer, R., Fernie, S. and Harty, C. (2015) Don't believe the (BIM) hype: The unexpected corollaries of the UK 'BIM Revolution'. *Proceedings of the EPOS conference, Edinburgh, June 24–26 2015*. Available at: http://personalpages.manchester.ac.uk/staff/christopher.neilson/files/3B1%20-%20Dainty%20Leiringer%20Fernie%20Harty%20-%20BIM%20Hype.pdf.

Davies, R. and Harty, C. (2013) Measurement and exploration of individual beliefs about the consequences of building information modelling use. *Construction Management and Economics*, 31(11), 1110–1127.

Dossick, C. and Neff, G. (2010) Organizational divisions in BIM-enabled commercial construction. *Journal of Construction Engineering and Management*, 136(4), 459–468.

Gantz, J. and Reinsel, D. (2013) The Digital Universe in 2020: Big data, bigger shadows, and the biggest growth in the Far East – United States. *IDC Review*. Available at: https://www.emc.com/collateral/analyst-reports/idc-digital-universe-united-states.pdf (accessed 13 March 2017).

Green, S. (2013) At it again. *Construction Research and Innovation*, 4(3), 12–15.

Holt, G.D. (2015) British construction business 1700–2000: proactive innovation or reactive evolution? *Construction Innovation*, 15(3), 258–277.

Hu, H., Wen. Y., Chua, T.-S. and Li, X. (2014) Towards scalable systems for big data analytics. *IEEE Access*, 2, 652–687.

Kuliga, S.F., Thrash, A., Dalton, R.C. and Hölscher, C. (2015) Virtual reality as an empirical research tool — Exploring user experience in a real building and a corresponding virtual model. *Computers, Environment and Urban Systems*, 54, 363–375.

Lanzeni, D. (2016) Smart global future: Designing affordable materialities for a better life, in Pink, S., Ardèvol, E. and Lanzeni, D. (eds) *Digital Materialities: Design and Anthropology*. Bloomsbury, London, pp. 45–60.

Latour, B. and Woolgar, S. (1986) *Laboratory Life: The Construction of Scientific Facts*. Princeton University Press, Princeton, NJ.

Lemonnier, P. (1992) *Elements for an anthropology of technology*. University of Michigan, Ann Arbor.

Lemonnier, P. (ed.) (2002) *Technological Choices: Transformation in material cultures since the Neolithic*. Routledge, London.

Luck, R. (2007) Learning to talk to users in participatory design situations. *Design Studies*, 28(3), 217–242.

Maftei, L., and Harty, C. (2015) Designing in Caves: Using Immersive Visualisations in Design Practice. *International Journal of Architectural Research*, 9(3), 53–75.

Marchand, T.H.J. (2009) *The Masons of Djenné*. Indiana University Press, Bloomington.

MIT (2015) *Our Fear of Artificial Intelligence*. Available at: https://www.technologyreview.com/s/534871/our-fear-of-artificial-intelligence/ (accessed 13 March 2017).

Moore, G.E. (1965) Cramming More Components onto Integrated Circuits. *Electronics*, 19 April, 114–117 (reprinted in the 1998 *Proceedings of the IEEE*, 86(1), 82–85).

Moum, A. (2010) Design Team Stories. Exploring interdisciplinary use of 3D object models in practice. *Automation in Construction*, 19, 554–569.

SINTEF (2013) Big Data, for better or worse: 90% of world's data generated over last two years. *ScienceDaily*, 22 May.

Walker, D.H.T. (2016) Reflecting on 10 years of focus on innovation, organisational learning and knowledge management literature in a construction project management context. *Construction Innovation*, 16(2), 114–126.

**Part 5**

**Conclusions and Common Themes**

# 17

# Understanding and Shaping Sustainable Futures in the Built Environment to 2050

*Tim Dixon, John Connaughton and Stuart Green*

'*There is nothing like a dream to create the future.*' Victor Hugo, Les Miserables *(1862)*
    '*Change is the law of life. And those who look only to the past or present are certain to miss the future.*' John F. Kennedy (US President, 1961–1963), address in the Assembly Hall at the Paulskirche in Frankfurt, 25 June 1963

## 17.1   Introduction

The overarching aim of the book has been to bring together leading thinking on issues of new professional practice and the future of a sustainable built environment within an integrated programme of foresight thinking to 2050. In doing this, the book has focused on three main areas which are important in a built environment context to 2050:

- sustainability and the built environment
- changing professional practice
- transformative technologies and innovation.

Primarily using a foresight-based approach for the majority of the chapters, and with a more qualitative, provocative practitioner-based element to supplement the thinking on professional practice, these chapters have sought to focus on both construction and development issues as key elements in the built environment.

If we are to understand the ways in which we need to move to a more sustainable future in construction and development, then we need to understand not only the speed and complexity of change in the wider world, but also the disruptive nature of this change. This is true whatever scale we look at in the built environment: buildings, neighbourhood or city level. 'Disruption', or the transformation of business models and networks driven by technology and business innovation (Ernst and Young, 2016), is at the heart of many of the changes that have been covered in this book. But this disruption can arise from political and policy trends, geopolitical forces and socio-economic trends, and can lead to wider repercussions for society and political systems.

Making sense of the future (and the present) can also be difficult when we experience what can be termed 'wild card' or 'black swan' events: unexpected, low-probability but high-impact events which could have long-term consequences for society, environment

*Sustainable Futures in the Built Environment to 2050: A Foresight Approach to Construction and Development*, First Edition. Edited by Tim Dixon, John Connaughton and Stuart Green.
© 2018 John Wiley & Sons Ltd. Published 2018 by John Wiley & Sons Ltd.

or the economy (e.g. the Fukoshima nuclear disaster in Japan in 2011). Certainly, in these uncertain times of Brexit and the US presidency of Donald Trump (or 'Trexit') we need to find ways of ensuring we build resilience and an enduring quality into the institutions and structures we have created to underpin a sustainable transition to the future.

In this concluding chapter, we look at the emerging lessons from this book and connect this to wider discourses on disruption, convergence and megatrends. We also examine what this tells us not only about understanding the future of construction and development, but also about helping to shape its future. The chapter therefore covers three main themes:

- **understanding the future**, where we explore the nature of disruption and convergence, and the interaction with 'megatrends' to 2050, with a particular focus on their impact on construction and development
- **what lies ahead for the built environment**, where we explore the emergent lessons from the chapters in this book
- **shaping the future: techniques, practice and policy**, where we examine the importance of futures-based techniques and black swans, and discuss the policy and practice implications of foresight in helping to shape the built environment of the future.

## 17.2   Understanding the future

### 17.2.1   The nature of technology disruption and convergence

Understanding future change means understanding the forces behind that change. As we saw in Chapter 1 there have been a number of attempts to identify the key drivers of long-term change in UK construction. At the heart of these drivers, and at the heart of many of the technological and business model changes we have covered, are disruptive technologies. The term 'disruptive technology' is used to describe a technology that results in a sudden change affecting established technologies or markets (Bower and Christensen, 1995). Therefore, whilst Chapter 15 highlighted the importance of understanding the nature of the construction sector and how its actor networks operate to create sustained innovation, we also need to understand the nature of innovation itself.

So, for example, in further work (see Christensen and Raynor, 2003) broadly within the field of disruptive innovation theory (DIT), the importance of disruptive technologies and their three critical elements of disruption is described. First, there is a rate of improvement that customers can utilise or absorb through, for example, better design of cars, although customers may not be able to use all of the performance capacity because of constraints such as road conditions, safety concerns and so on. Second, innovating companies can, through the improvement of products, offer advances in technology which may outstrip the ability of customers to use the technology. Third, sustaining innovations can contribute to better performance through either incremental or 'leap-frog' products designed for high-end customers. In contrast, disruptive technologies do not bring better products to established customers in existing markets: they tend to disrupt and redefine current trajectories by offering products that are not as good as those on offer, but may be more convenient or less expensive and which appeal to new or less-demanding customers. Therefore, once the disruptive product gains a foothold at the lower end of the market, an improvement cycle begins which results in the disruptors replacing the incumbents. Other types of disruption can be caused by reverse innovations which can bring well-developed technologies to markets or societies that did not have access or could not afford them, a characteristic which makes them appropriate for developing countries and emerging markets (National Research Council, 2010).

In contrast, incremental innovations are based on discoveries which occur within existing technology paradigms that do not significantly alter them (Foxon, 2003), for example increasing wind turbine efficiency through longer blades. Similarly, a radical or transformative technology involves fundamental changes to the way things are done, and require new knowledge bases and new infrastructures with perhaps even shifts in regime but which are not necessarily disruptive (e.g. fuel injection for the internal combustion engine). In comparison, a disruptive technology involves new knowledge bases that replace existing ways of doing things, but do not require significant regime change (e.g. replacing petrol with biofuels would disrupt business models based on petrol but would have minimal effect on social practices) (Greenacre *et al.*, 2011).

In further DIT work disruptive technologies are distinguished from sustaining (or incremental) technologies (Christensen, 2003). In this arena, sustaining innovations occur in the core market of a firm and result in a product which delivers better quality at lower prices, whereas disruptive technologies occur at the margins of established markets. At first these products (which may well not exhibit radical characteristics) are ignored by the majority of the market, although some consumers buy them because they may like a distinctive feature, and in time these niche markets may be extended as quality rises and costs fall. For example, using the DIT typology a more specific case of a potentially disruptive technology in urban retrofit is high-efficiency, cost-effective light-emitting diode (LED) lighting (Mulki and Hinge, 2010). LEDs, which rely on semiconductors, benefit from rates of improvement dictated by Moore's law, and software increases their value by adjusting their energy use based on required lighting levels. Other examples of disruptive technologies relevant to the energy retrofit domain include (i) phase change materials, which may offer advantages for thermal storage, air conditioning in buildings and load shifting of power demands, and (ii) plastic electronics, which have applications in lighting, photovoltaics and integrated smart systems. In the water sector, nanotechnology membranes have been highlighted as a disruptive innovation for water purification (including advanced treatment of grey water for portable use), and smart and biomimetic materials for a range of sectors (Dixon *et al.*, 2014). Moreover, such technologies can impact co-laterally on existing business models and the operation of broader networked infrastructures. Such secondary disruptive impacts could arise from the effect of disruptive technologies on both the energy efficiency of buildings and the operation of the electricity network. So, for example, as a result of improving building energy efficiency through urban retrofit, energy utilities' revenues and profits may be reduced, especially in markets where prices are high and where regulatory regimes underpin energy efficiency. Moreover, the large-scale deployment of distributed renewable generation technologies such as photovoltaics (PV) may impact the wholesale (peak) price of electricity (as has recently occurred in Germany). This would undermine current utility business and investment models, and at the same time drive the reconfiguration of existing top-down network (grid) infrastructures, creating a need both to reinforce local grids and provide new regional interconnections In the future, therefore, utility companies may need to cope with uncertainty and discontinuity by seeking new sources of revenue from new markets in building fabrics, decentralised systems and distributed generation, advanced metering infrastructure, and 'smart' appliances and applications (Dixon *et al.*, 2014).[1]

However, because disruptive technologies are so hard to predict and by nature occur infrequently, they are difficult to identify or foresee, particularly where performative consensus-based techniques (in a Foresight context), such as participatory road-mapping and backcasting are used to identify future transition pathways (National Research Council, 2010). There is a need therefore to develop hybrid methodologies which can also identify more unpredictable innovations (Dixon *et al.*, 2014).

More recently, we have also seen that the term 'disruption' can also have a wider meaning and focus than 'technology'. For example, disruption is also influenced (besides technological trends) by demographic shifts, globalisation and macro-economic trends (Ernst and Young, 2016). For example, the growth of globalisation through trade liberalisation and emerging market growth has created new competition and lower prices through an increasingly globalised market. In turn, this has created ramifications in some parts of the world where free movement and global choice has not benefited all parts of society, and so meant that some politicians have used this to argue against globalisation, and for a return to nationalism and perhaps even protectionism. Changing demographics in many parts of the globe have also played a part. In the developed world, ageing populations will have an impact on the built environment and how it evolves as well as healthcare, and migration and immigration will continue to impact on workforces and economic development. In the developing world, the continued growth of cities and urbanised populations with high birth rates will have huge ramifications for the way in which cities are developed in Latin America, Africa and Asia.

We are also seeing a new dimension to disruption through the convergence of different, but related, technologies. However, convergence and interaction are not new concepts. The basic premise is that different technologies come together or are integrated in the same system. An early example is the use of communication and imaging technologies on a mobile device designed to make calls and take pictures: two unrelated technologies that converge within a single device. As a recent UK government report pointed out (Government Office for Science, 2017: 7):

> 'The latest mobile telephony depends on a raft of technologies: transmitters, sensors, data storage, battery and power management, and user interfaces, among others. Some homes are already powered by solar cells and batteries, controlled by smart meters and appliances. The internet of things, however, has signaled the potential for technological interaction of a different order and scale – offering the prospect of literally billions of everyday objects communicating with each other to transform transport, home life and energy efficiency.'

The report points out the benefits and impacts of convergence around 'eight great' technologies (advanced materials, satellites, energy storage, robotics and autonomous systems, agri-science, regenerative medicine, big data and synthetic biology) and goes on to suggest how the impact of convergence could lead to better efficiencies in the built environment. For example, in new buildings and retrofits, where building information

---

1  See later in this chapter for a discussion of some of the emerging innovations in construction materials.

modelling (BIM) techniques are already starting to provide long-term efficiency gains, a wide range of convenient and money-saving applications could be made available. Access to buildings could be managed, for example, by mobile phone, with an electronic token, or could rely on face recognition. Sensor systems dependent on sound, temperature or movement could activate heat and light levels, and reduce them when rooms become unoccupied.

Disruption and convergence will continue to shape our world and impact on our future. Understanding how disruptive forces can influence (and be influenced by) the drivers for change, or the megatrends that will shape and influence our future to 2050, is therefore crucial to recognise.

## 17.2.2 Megatrends to 2050: the impact on construction and development

### 17.2.2.1 Global megatrends

As defined in the OED, a 'megatrend' is 'an important shift in the progress of a society or of any other particular field or activity; any major movement'. Alternatively, Eagar *et al.* (2014) define a megatrend as 'an inevitable evolution leading to a change of society, business, economics or environment'. As Chapter 1 suggests there has been quite a lot of work given to long-term drivers in the construction and development industry, but these can also be seen in the context of wider megatrends.

There has been no shortage of studies which have sought to identify megatrends and their shape and influence, both of which are heavily dependent on various forces of disruption. Work by Ernst and Young (2016), for example, suggests that eight megatrends are important to consider in a wider business context:

- industry redefined (the blurring of industry boundaries through convergence, which is caused by disruption)
- the future of smart applications (the use of technology and data analytics to create new layers of insight)
- the future of work (with increasing use of artificial intelligence (AI) and robotics)
- behavioural revolution (the growth of behavioural economics to understand and influence collective futures)
- empowered customers (the growth of the intelligent client who can also access data and information)
- the urban world (the increasing influence of cities and growing urbanisation)
- health reimagined (the growing importance of healthcare and health and wellbeing)
- resourceful planet (the continued importance of sustainability).

Of course, other writers and commentators have highlighted the importance of other factors. For example, PwC (2017a) suggest (besides rapid urbanisation) that climate change and resource scarcity, shifts in global economic power, demographic and social change, and technological breakthroughs will be important megatrends. Eagar *et al.* (2014) conducted a helpful review of the general megatrends highlighted by 20 'significant intelligent providers and observers'. The most common are summarised in Table 17.1.

Essentially, megatrends involve outlining a 'probable' future, but that is not to say there are no alternative futures which may also be possible. Indeed, megatrends can be altered or suddenly change direction through unexpected events, as we shall we see later in this chapter.

**Table 17.1** Most commonly-cited megatrends (adapted from Eagar *et al.*, 2014).

| Dimension | Megatrend | Overview and examples |
|---|---|---|
| Technology | Disruptive technology developments | New technologies such as the Internet of Things, AI and robotics |
| Energy and environment | Changing energy mix | New energy sources, including renewables |
| | Shortage of resources | Shortages of food, water, minerals and other resources |
| | Climate change | The influence and links with adaptation and mitigation |
| Economic and politics | Knowledge and information society | Increasing knowledge information and an educated society |
| | Economic shifts | Emerging markets and new middle classes |
| | Globalisation | A highly connected global economy and economic integration |
| | New normal | Lower interest rates, policy intervention and lower state spending |
| | Multi-polar | Diffusion of power, nationalism, populism and trade deals |
| Social and health | Demographic shifts | Population growth and ageing population |
| | Urbanisation and mobility | Growth of cities, large and small/medium sized |
| | Health and wellness demands | Growing importance of health and well-being agendas |

### 17.2.2.2 Interconnections between megatrends and global risks

As Eager *et al.* (2014) point out in their review of megatrends, it is striking to see how high a degree of consensus there is on identified megatrends. This may perhaps reflect the objective evidence, or perhaps an element of 'groupthink', where there is a tendency for observers to flock and coalesce around the key issues which might have already been raised.

The interconnections between megatrends are also important to consider. The recent report *Global Risks* by the World Economic Forum (WEF, 2017) suggested that the top five global trends over the next 10 years were (in rank order):

- rising income and wealth disparity: an increasing socioeconomic gap between rich and poor in major countries or regions
- changing climate: attributed directly or indirectly to human activity, and alters the composition of the global atmosphere, in addition to natural climate variability
- increasing polarisation of societies: the inability to reach agreement on key issues within countries because of diverging or extreme values, political or religious views
- rising cyber dependency: due to increasing digital interconnection of people, things and organisations
- ageing population: in developed and developing countries, driven by declining fertility and decrease of middle- and old-age mortality.

## Trend interconnection map

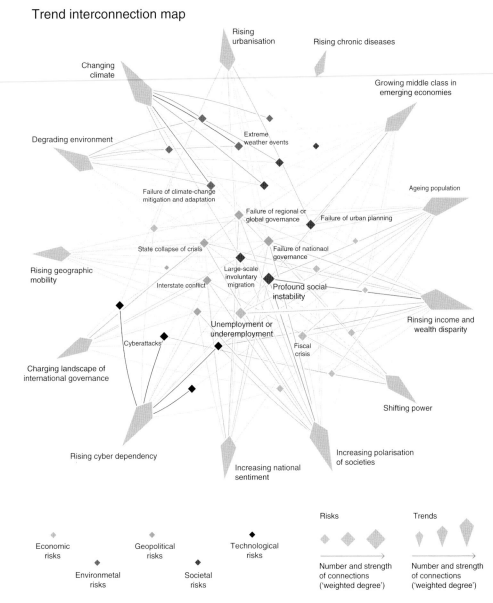

**Figure 17.1** The risks-trends interconnections map (WEF, 2017).

The report also suggested that it is important to recognise the 'interconnected nature' of these trends and the associated global risks. For example, the most interconnected pairing of risks in the 2017 survey was between 'high structural unemployment or underemployment and profound social instability'. The importance of considering interconnectivities between trends and associated risks is shown in Figure 17.1.

It is also interesting to note that whilst rising populist politics (*vox populi* risk) and the calls for deglobalisation persist, the environment continues to dominate the global risk landscape, with climate change ranked the number two underlying trend in 2017. Also, for the first time, all five environmental risks (extreme weather events, failure of climate change mitigation and adaptation, major biodiversity and ecosystem collapse, major natural disasters such as earthquakes, tsunami, volcanic eruptions and geomagnetic storms, and man-made environmental damage and disasters) in the survey were ranked both high-risk and high-likelihood, with 'extreme weather events' emerging as the single most prominent global risk.

Nonetheless, as the report points out (WEF, 2017):

> 'Although the world can point to significant progress in the area of climate change in 2016, with a number of countries, including the US and China, ratifying the Paris Agreement, political change in Europe and North America puts this progress at risk. It also highlights the difficulty that leaders will face to agree on a course of action at the international level to tackle the most pressing economic and societal risks.'

Moreover, it is interesting to note that the WEF global risk analysis, which covers a period of analysis from 2007 to 2017, showed asset price collapse and retrenchment from globalisation as the top two risks in terms of impact. By 2017 the top two risks were weapons of mass destruction and extreme weather events.

In summary, although megatrends continue to shape our world now, and will continue to do in the future, we also need to recognise the interdependencies of these forces, and the way in which they can translate into a complex array of risks which morph and flux in the short term, medium term and over a longer time period. Environmental challenges, however, continue to pose amongst the greatest risks of all.

### 17.2.2.3    Construction and development megatrends

Turning to construction and development, what are the specific megatrends that will play an important role in shaping the future of the built environment? Certainly, a number of the megatrends discussed above are highlighted in a recent Royal Institution of Chartered Surveyors (RICS) report on futures in the built environment (RICS, 2015), including:

- greater urbanisation and changing demographics
- shift in economic power – emerging markets
- growing middle class and increased consumption
- global inequality and instability
- increasing scarcity of resources
- increased need for sustainability in the built environment.

In turn these are seen as shaping and changing the way in which surveying professionals need to attract new talent, develop new skills and new understandings using, for example, technology and big data, and develop strong leadership skills in an increasingly complex world. The emphasis here then is on changing professional practice, reflecting the thrust of the RICS's aims and ambitions.

Clearly, climate change must also play a role in how we see the future. Significant asset value is locked into the built environment. For example, the UK's built environment includes 27 million homes, commercial and industrial properties, hospitals, schools, other buildings and the wider urban environment (DEFRA, 2012). Recent evidence for the Committee on Climate Change (CCC, 2017) also showed the importance of seeing people and buildings holistically. Therefore, we need to see our main policy areas for managing climate risks as focusing on the interrelationships between communities, buildings, the health and social care system, and population health and health protection. This is not surprising and reflects a growing focus on health and well-being in the built environment. For example, the UK CCC report (Kovats and Osborne, 2016) identified these key climate-related risks in the built environment:

- the risk of overheating of buildings requires urgent action: energy demand to cool buildings was projected to increase, possibly exceeding £1 billion by 2050
- flood risk was projected to increase, with damages rising from £1.3 billion now to £2.1–12 billion by the 2080s
- the urban heat island effect will mean that increases in temperature are exacerbated in urban areas
- between 27 and 52 million people could live in areas with water supply problems by 2050
- sewers were projected to fill and spill more frequently.

A recent WEF report (WEF, 2016) on the future of construction also highlighted four key megatrends which will shape the way the construction industry evolves over the next 10–20 years. These include the following.

- **Market and customer trends:** As demand from emerging economies increases (some 65% of construction growth in construction will occur in emerging economies), the industry needs to identify how these markets can best benefit from technological advances and increased safety standards in the developed world, although local market conditions will also need to be considered. Increasing competition in the industry is likely to weed out weaker companies, especially those where markets are highly fragmented and have low levels of innovation. Companies that are able to respond are likely to be able to take advantage of new markets arising from the substantial infrastructure gap in developed countries.
- **Sustainability and resilience trends:** Increasingly sustainability is being mainstreamed within both the construction process and the built environment. Currently, the construction sector is seen as the largest global consumer of materials, and buildings are the single most important consumer of energy. For example, the WEF (2016) suggest buildings and 'constructed objects' today account for 25–40% of the world's total carbon emissions and a similar amount of global energy use.[2] Moreover, the industry needs to react to the growing threats and risks associated with natural hazards and to enhance resilience or the ability to bounce back from shocks.
- **Societal and workforce trends:** Growing urban populations will place pressures on construction. The world's population is expected to be more than 6 billion by 2045, with more than 25% of people living in slums (UN, 2014). There is therefore a growing need for affordable housing in urban areas, where the existing space constraints can

---

2 Although the basis of calculation differs, the IPCC (Lucon *et al.*, 2014) suggested that 'buildings' accounted for 32% of total final energy use and 19% of energy-related greenhouse gases (primarily $CO_2$) emissions (including electricity-related) globally in 2010.

create complex conditions for construction. Also, an ageing population not only creates the need for adapting and converting existing buildings or constructing new buildings for older people, but also, despite technological innovation, reducing the available supply of construction workers.

- **Political and regulatory trends:** Changing regulatory impacts in health and safety requirements, financial and labour legislation, and environmental standards is likely to have an impact on business operations. Some may have a negative impact and others a more positive impact. WEF (2016) cites the new retrofit investments which have flowed from Germany's new Energy Saving Ordinance, which has been a major driver for innovation in the construction industry. The Energy Saving Ordinance (Energieeinsparverordnung, EnEV) came into force in 2002 and sets energy performance requirements for new buildings and for existing buildings in cases of major renovation. Related to this megatrend are issues connected with political risk (see above) and corruption in certain countries.

However, it is also important to consider the internal challenges that the construction industry faces in tackling these challenges. The WEF (2016) report highlighted the fact that dealing with these trends is impacted by the construction industry's low rates of innovation and innovation adoption. In the view of WEF this is linked with:

- informal processes and inconsistent process execution
- poor knowledge transfer between projects
- weak project monitoring
- little cross-function cooperation, based on sequencing
- poor supplier collaboration
- conservative company culture
- shortage of young talent.

Although there are tangible examples of innovation (see Chapter 15), the views above are confirmed by others, including Giesekam *et al.* (2016: 3), who describe construction as 'a highly fragmented, risk-averse, supplier-driven industry'. Managing these risks and developing strategies and policies to cope with future changes in construction and development will therefore be challenging but of paramount importance if we are to move to a sustainable future in the built environment. But what do the chapters tell us about the future of construction and development of the built environment, and how it could and should evolve in specific ways to 2050?

## 17.3  What lies ahead for the built environment? Lessons from the chapters

### 17.3.1  Cities, built environment and infrastructure

In the first part of this book we saw how, implicitly, it is important to understand sustainability in the built environment across scales. Therefore what we understand at building level (Chapter 3) can be transferred and is portable to neighbourhood (Chapter 4) and city level (Chapter 5) when action needs to be scaled up, and this process also operates down the scale from city to building level. In other words, there needs to be 'integration across scales' in terms of our understanding of the capacity for change in the built environment, and this is certainly true also of infrastructure in the built environment (Chapters 6 and 14).

Our understanding of what constitutes a 'sustainable built environment' varies, however, as we have seen in various chapters in this book. As with other related and contested concepts (Chapter 1) there is no single agreed definition. However, interesting work which has emerged from British Columbia in Canada suggests a sustainable built environment is one (Modus, 2015: iii): 'where people can have a great quality of life without undermining the natural systems that support us. It is a place that is resource efficient, resilient, prosperous, equitable, healthy, safe, attractive and authentic.' This definition also emphasises the importance of holistic thinking by identifying four important components of a sustainable built environment:

- integrated communities (e.g. land-use patterns, public space, density, urban form)
- housing (e.g. market, rental, non-market)
- buildings, energy and infrastructure (e.g. water/sewer/storm water infrastructure, energy infrastructure, building design)
- transportation (e.g. movement networks, roads, sidewalks, paths, vehicles).

The report also goes on to suggest that (Modus, 2015: iii):

> 'This sustainable built environment is a product of a society that values natural systems and people first and foremost. It functions in harmony with natural systems and cycles, respecting nature's limits and meets the diverse needs of our communities. It emerges from a social conversation that seeks to resolve trade-offs and drive innovation, so that development is aligned with core community values.'

This definition emphasises the importance of systems thinking and the interrelationship between the built environment and the people that use it. There is therefore also a need to understand sectoral interrelationships, for example the nexus between energy-water and waste, which is at the heart of urban metabolic thinking (i.e. where waste can be converted to energy or waste energy used to produce clean water). Although, as Green points out in Chapter 9, whilst systems thinking provides a useful framework for understanding sustainable construction, it falls significantly short as a means of providing practical guidance for implementation.

Nonetheless, this synergy also holds true in the context of systems interdependencies. For example, technologies such as ICT and increasing cross-sector demand will increase interdependencies between infrastructure sectors (Chapter 6), which can intensify uncertainty in the long-term planning of these systems. Understanding these interdependencies and being able to model them in a coherent way will not only help us to better understand the future consequences of current actions, but also how current actions can be modified to produce sustainable outcomes. This perspective also invites us to recognise the importance of 'complexity' in the context of systemic thinking, or the way in which complex systems (such as a city) feature a large number of interacting components (e.g. agents and processes) whose aggregate activity is non-linear, and which typically exhibit an element of self-organisation under selective pressures (see, for example, Batty (2013) and Chapter 5).

We also need to consider how resilience can complement and underpin sustainability (Chapter 1). As Barlow *et al.* show in Chapter 2, there are substantial technical and political challenges in designing energy-efficient and comfortable buildings that will be capable of withstanding climate change. A specific focus has been on designing buildings resilient to overheating, a growing risk in urban areas due to climate change and increasing urbanisation. Although techniques such as dynamic thermal simulation can help at the interface between engineering, planning and climate science, understanding the concept of resilience from the outset is important. This is vital given the growing focus on health and well-being across different scales of the built environment (UKGBC, 2017).

The origins of the word 'resilience' lie in the Latin word, *resilio*, meaning to 'bounce back' (Klein *et al.*, 2003; Meerow *et al.*, 2016), but in the academic literature the concept is open to different interpretations and nuances. Orr (2011) suggests resilience, which is a concept long familiar to engineers, mathematicians, ecologists, designers and military planners, means the capacity of the system to 'absorb disturbance; to undergo change and still retain essentially the same function, structure, and feedbacks' (Walker and Salt, 2006: 32). Therefore, for Orr (2011) resilient systems are 'characterized by redundancy so that failure of any one component does not cause the entire system to crash. They consist of diverse components that are easily repairable, widely distributed, cheap, locally supplied, durable, and loosely coupled.'

In another sense, resilience can be seen as operationalising sustainability, with the latter as the ultimate goal of sustainable development. In many ways, resilience is complementary to sustainability: resilience is about rebounding, withstanding shocks and re-establishing, whereas sustainability is about repairing, maintaining and the possession of endurance in the face of shocks. Orr (2016) suggests that sustainability implies a stable end state that can be achieved once and for all, whereas resilience is the ability and capacity to make ongoing adjustments to changing political, economic and ecological conditions. As Orr (2016: 23) suggests, the hallmarks of resilience 'are not just redundancy, adaptation, and flexibility, but also the foresight and good judgement to avoid the brawl in the first place.'

In the same way that sustainability can apply to different scales, resilience can as well. For example, Meerow *et al.* (2016: 39) offer a helpful definition of 'urban resilience':

> 'Urban resilience refers to the ability of an urban system-and all its constituent socio-ecological and socio-technical networks across temporal and spatial scales; to maintain or rapidly return to desired functions in the face of a disturbance, to adapt to change, and to quickly transform systems that limit current or future adaptive capacity.'

This means therefore that cities, as well as being smart and sustainable (Chapter 5), also need to have an underlying resilience.

Resilience is also at the heart of sustainable design (Chapter 7). However, as Farrelly also suggests, true 'sustainability is an action', or a response to everything that is unsustainable. Therefore, this concept needs to be constantly updated and informed by current and future thinking about new technologies and new materials. Design is about choice, a reaction to a condition or a problem, so sustainable (and resilient) design must react to the issues that face us in today's 'unsustainable' environment. In this respect Farrelly also highlights the importance of avoiding 'defuturing', or what Tony Fry's work has suggested is often the unintended effects of design, which can alter our collective futures in undesirable ways.

Finally, Farrelly's (Chapter 7) and Woodcraft and Smith's chapter (Chapter 4) also highlight the importance of understanding community in the context of sustainable development. They highlight the necessity of new models if the notion of sustainable futures in the built environment is to be taken seriously. Woodcraft and Smith, for example, argue for the adoption of a diverse, inclusive and sustainable understanding of prosperity as a guiding principle to consider alternative models of urban change, and use a scenarios and backcasting-based methodology to look at the future of sustainable communities (see below). This new prosperity model should reflect local aspirations for sustainable and prosperous communities, and by using two futures methods (scenario planning and backcasting) they connect current experience and future aspirations to identify pathways to change.

## 17.3.2 Changing professional practice and practitioners' viewpoints

In Chapter 8 we saw how vital the role of planning is in embedding sustainable development (although a contested concept) within the built environment. As Doak and Parker suggest, it has been argued that sustainable forms of urban development need to take their cue from the key components of sustainability, and that a planning framework is central to engaging with, mediating and coordinating the range of actors that produce and use the built environment. This necessary planning process, they argue, needs to work in an adaptable and multi-scalar way, embedding key agents of change and sources of knowledge in order to develop strategic visions and anticipatory intelligence.

This also raises the issue of what skills planners and other built environment professionals need to have at their disposal in an era when sustainable development and resilience are crucial concepts but where technological change is shaping and influencing the role of the built environment professional. In their practitioners' viewpoints, Ford (Chapter 12) and Healey (Chapter 13) both highlight the need for agility and relevance in professional training. Ford calls for greater collaboration across the built environment professions. In contrast, Healey suggests that design professionals need to complement their technical skills with effective sustainability advocacy beyond what he suggests is the traditional focus on quantitative economic analysis, moralistic calls to action and information-based approaches. In Healey's view there needs to be a focus on wider and diverse communication strategies based on behavioural economics, and expert judgment and decision-making. Moreover, as Thompson shows using scenarios (backlash, creative divide or passive engagement) in Chapter 11, built environment professionals will need to be aware of how social media and related innovations, including the Internet of Things, BIM and big data, will impact on professional roles in the future.

The focus on collaboration and the breaking down of professional silos was a point that formed the focus for the Edge Commission Report on the future of professionalism (Morrell, 2015). The report stressed the importance of professional bodies working together on strategies to tackle climate change, improve the performance of buildings and draw up a code of ethics to ensure they act in the public interest. In particular, the report urged collaboration on:

- industry reform: developing a shared vision of how to improve efficiency and the offer to clients and society
- climate change: developing the policies, industry capabilities and skills necessary to respond to the impact of the built environment on climate change

- building performance: tackling the divide between what is promised by the industry and what is delivered, developing common metrics, committing to measurement and evaluation, and the dissemination of findings
- ethics and the public interest: developing and standardising a national code of conduct/ethics across the built environment professions, building on shared experience in the UK and internationally
- education and competence: urging built environment institutions to commit to a cross-disciplinary review of the silo nature of the education system and establish a joint think tank that could pool the resources of the institutions to conduct research and develop policy for the industry.

That is not to say we will see the disappearance of the built environment professions, but rather their continued evolution. As Morrell (2015: 3) suggested:

> 'The questions that the professions face are not, for the most part existential, but rather evolutionary. What is of value will remain, but both the context and terms of trade will change as the professions adapt to keep themselves relevant to the needs of successive ages.'

It is also clear that recently the pace and scope of technological innovation has accelerated. The emergence of pervasive mobile technology and the availability of big data and open data sets have started to refocus the debate towards trying to understand the consequences of these and other related impacts on the future of work and the professions (Frey and Osborne, 2013; Citi GPS, 2016).

Certainly, professional work is not immune to such changes. Susskind and Susskind (2015) for example, talk about the way in which technological change (including artificial intelligence) is changing professional work in a variety of disciplines (including law, health and the built environment). There is therefore a trend from a craft-based activity, provided by human experts, towards a commoditised activity, as professional work becomes systematised and externalised (through online and web provision of services). Susskind and Susskind argue that the evolution of the professional era is characterised by four trends:

- the move from bespoke service (i.e. moving from tailoring for an individual to a standardised service)
- bypassing traditional 'gatekeepers' (e.g. BIM specialists rather than designers *per se*)
- a shift from a reactive to pro-active approach (e.g. from waiting for a client to anticipating needs)
- more for less (more professional service at less cost).

These trends are driven by technology, which stores, represents, shares and re-uses expertise in digital form, driven by automation and innovation. Importantly, these changes provide more access to expertise, and hence more power and autonomy, for clients rather than service providers (see also Bates (2016)).

Returning to key concepts and definitions, Green shows in Chapter 9 that universal definitions of sustainability remain elusive, with a significant disconnection between the debates that take place at the United Nations and the more mundane realities faced by construction professionals. For Green, many challenges of sustainability are characterised by conflicting objectives which defy technical solution. As he shows, sustainability is often seen to depend on professional notions of protecting the public interest.

Perhaps, as Green suggests, ultimately, if we take seriously the idea that sustainability is a 'wicked problem', we should also accept that such problems can never be solved in their own right. That does not mean we should abandon sustainability, but we must understand that the meaning of sustainability has evolved over time and will continue to do so. Moreover, our commitment to sustainability will always be shaped and constrained by the prevailing political discourse.

Finally, Connaughton and Hughes show in Chapter 10 how challenging it will be to transition to sustainable procurement by 2050. Yet, as the authors suggest, procurement is a key mechanism through which businesses and other organisations can not only help implement their sustainability goals, but also influence the behaviour and performance of others. In construction, with its traditions of price competitiveness, multi-tiered supply chains and exploitative practices, procurement therefore has a crucial role to play in putting the sector on a more sustainable footing through to 2050.

### 17.3.3  Transformative technologies and innovation

Some of the transformative changes in technological innovation that we will see in construction are likely to be based around such areas as drones, robots, augmented reality, the Internet of Things, virtual reality and 3D printing (Wakefield, 2016). Ultimately, given their importance, construction materials also offer an extremely powerful lever for innovation. The European Commission estimates that 70% of product innovation across all industries is derived from new or improved materials, and with about one-third of construction cost attributed to building materials, the scope for applying advanced building materials is substantial (WEF, 2016). The technological solutions emerging from the building material industry are numerous and wide-ranging: from the incremental innovation of traditional materials, to the creation of new material combinations with multi-functional characteristics, through to radically innovative materials with entirely new functionalities (see Arup (2016) and WEF (2016)) (Table 17.2).

**Table 17.2** Examples of new and advanced construction materials (adapted from WEF (2016), Arup (2016) and McPartland (2016)).

| Incremental innovation | →→→ | Radical innovation |
|---|---|---|
| Advances on traditional material and existing characteristics | New material combinations and multi-functional characteristics | Innovative materials with entirely new functionality |
| High insulation materials (e.g. Neopor) | Fast-setting cement and organic fibre | Rain-absorbing roof mats that imitate perspiration |
| Organically coated steel | Self-healing concrete | Phase-change materials using latent heat |
| Spray-on or paint-on PV | Self-cleaning materials | Super-repellent (liquid-infused and porous) surfaces |
| Building integrated PV glazing | Algal (or bio-reactive) walls to create energy and valuable algal bi-products | Graphene (a super light and super strong material) |

Categories based on WEF (2016). Technologies based on WEF (2016), Arup (2016) and McPartland (2016).

An interesting perspective on materials was also provided for the UK Future of Cities Foresight Programme by Purnell and Roelich (2015). They suggest that the bulk materials mix in cities will not change significantly in the future. However, an increased use of trace materials, which is crucial for low-carbon technologies, is likely to expose cities (and the wider construction industry) to critical materials supply issues. The low-carbon and resource conservation agendas are also likely to place pressure on supply and disposal of bulk materials, so that the reuse and recycling of components and urban mining (to extract rare compounds and elements from existing waste components) must be given equal prominence to traditional materials recycling.

However, as Larsen's chapter suggests, we must not let the allure of innovation get in the way of thinking holistically about meanings and context for the construction (or wider AEC) sector. Only by understanding the complexity of the sector can we seek to change it. As Larsen points out, despite a relatively bad press for lack of innovation, good examples of successful innovation in construction do exist. There is therefore a need to understand sustained innovation uptake within the construction sector rather than focusing upon the innovation act alone. In other words, construction firms are rarely innovative in isolation and for the uptake of an innovation to be sustained networks of stakeholders must work together, either knowingly or unknowingly. It is essential to gain a greater understanding of how all associated stakeholders operate in a wider market network and the potential impact these have on the uptake of innovations.

A cautionary approach is also adopted by Ewart in Chapter 16, who emphasises the difficulties and dangers of assuming that technological implementation in the construction sector can automatically produce beneficial results. In Ewart's view, technological determinism in the sector and in other industries holds great dangers. In the latter view, as Ewart suggests, regardless of the social context into which the technology is parachuted, the inherent benefits are seen as automatically outweighing any social reservations and ultimately a process of logical, linear progression drives social change into acceptance. The experience of BIM within the sector seems to offer an example of the need to take serious account of the role of social factors in planning for a digital revolution. In other words, we need to understand technology in the context of a sociotechnical perspective, which recognises the 'human' dimension. Moreover, the temptation to be overwhelmed by the allure of increasing amounts of data, and the emergence of big data, means we must think of new and innovative ways of handling this data and interpreting it wisely rather than blindly assuming big data analytics will provide us with all the answers to questions we seek. As Ewart suggests, this may mean, for example, innovative forms of visualisation that act as intermediaries between the vast repositories of data and the physical capabilities of individuals and communities, or forums for interaction that focus on problems and questions specifically relevant to a knowledgeable community.

In the context of the construction sector, understanding energy technologies is also becoming vital as markets change and evolve, and new decentralised systems become more feasible. As Coker and Torriti point out in Chapter 14, there is an increasing trend towards local generation of energy. However, it is unclear to what extent cities and regions will establish energy independence, and whether this is desirable. Where energy supplies are provided by remote, variable renewable energy supplies, the necessary balancing actions could still be carried out within the built environment. To take advantages of these new opportunities, built environment professionals will therefore need to develop a strong understanding of the over-arching energy system, and the needs of disparate market stakeholders (a point also highlighted by Ford and Gillich in Chapter 12).

## 17.4   Shaping the future: techniques, practice and policy

The chapters in this book also implicitly and explicitly carry lessons in practice and policy terms, and in how we need to develop our thinking for a sustainable built environment to 2050. This also applies to the techniques we can use to understand the future (Chapter 1). Within the built environment professions, perhaps planning, with its forward-looking nature, is closest to a 'futures' or 'foresight' view of the world (see Doak and Parker in Chapter 8).

Yet, as Freestone (2012) argues, the planning profession is also perhaps in need of a futures infusion to retain and strengthen its strategic relevance to policy-making. This is certainly also true of other built environment professions, including surveying, architecture and construction, where there has perhaps been a reluctance to engage in futures-based work outside the ambit of the professional bodies representing their members, academics and some other groups (Chapter 1). In this final chapter therefore, we examine the implications of the findings from this book for techniques, practice and policy in the built environment.

### 17.4.1   Futures-based techniques and black swan events

Identifying megatrends is crucial to successful horizon scanning as part of a foresight approach. This point was emphasised in Chapter 1, and we have seen the importance of identifying megatrends throughout this book. The OECD (2017) suggest that horizon scanning is:

> '...a technique for detecting early signs of potentially important developments through a systematic examination of potential threats and opportunities, with emphasis on new technology and its effects on the issue at hand. The method calls for determining what is constant, what changes, and what constantly changes. It explores novel and unexpected issues as well as persistent problems and trends, including matters at the margins of current thinking that challenge past assumptions.'

In this context, Newton (2007, 2008) argues that a three horizons approach can help us think coherently about the future. For example, Horizon 1 initiatives include those that are currently available, have demonstrable benefit, but have not been widely implemented. Horizon 2 initiatives, which are implementable over the next 2–3 years, already exist as model, prototype product or system, scoped process or equivalent but will require testing extension or real-world application to develop a convincing business case for implementation. Finally, Horizon 3 innovations (based on 15–20-year timelines) tend to be more radical, based on concepts and technologies which are very different from today and may involve significant barriers (see, for example, DEFRA (2010)).

**Table 17.3** A typology of hydrogen futures (McDowall and Eames, 2006).

| | |
|---|---|
| Descriptive | **Forecasts** use formal quantitative extrapolation and modelling to predict likely futures from current trends. |
| | **Exploratory scenarios** explore possible futures. They emphasise drivers, and do not specify a predetermined desirable end state towards which must storylines progress. |
| | **Technical scenarios** explore possible future technological systems based on hydrogen. They emphasise the technical feasibility and implications of different options, rather than explore how different futures might unfold. |
| Normative | **Visions** are elaborations of a desirable and (more or less) plausible future. They emphasise the benefits of hydrogen rather than the pathways through which a hydrogen future might be achieved. |
| | **Backcasts and pathways** start with a predetermined 'end' point – a desirable and plausible future. They then investigate possible pathways to that point. |
| | **Roadmaps** describe a sequence of measures designed to bring about a desirable future. Studies from the previous four groups, or elements of these groups, frequently form the basis for the identification of specific measures, but not always. |

This temporal dimension is helpful in terms of identifying potential risks and how particular technologies might be incorporated and deployed within the built environment. This also raises the issue of which foresight techniques can be used to examine the future, and link with evidence building and horizon scanning. As we saw in Chapter 1, scenario building and visions are two techniques which can be used. In recent years, a large number of futures-based studies have been developed in the field of low-carbon technologies. For example, McDowall and Eames (2006) identified six distinct, although overlapping, types of futures studies in the field of hydrogen. These are shown in Table 17.3 and are categorised according to whether they are 'descriptive' or 'normative'.

As McDowall and Eames (2006) suggest, forecasts are characterised by the use of quantitative methods to predict future trends based on current trends or surveys of expert opinion. Within foresight and futures studies, forecasts (as a standalone technique) are of limited value over longer time horizons because of their inherent deterministic view of the future and of technological change; on their own, therefore, such techniques fail to acknowledge changing technological regimes or paradigms, or disruptive impacts. Many therefore agree that other techniques offer greater opportunity and flexibility to explore a range of possible outcomes.

In a built environment context, there have been a number of examples of scenario-based and visioning approaches (Chapter 1). The UK Government Foresight programme, for example, contains some interesting examples of futures-based studies in particular contexts, including energy and the built environment (Government Office for Science, 2008), land use (Government Office of Science, 2010) and future cities (Government Office for Science, 2016). This has also led to the development of a futures toolkit (HM Government, 2014) for use by policy officials and analysts across government.

As Hunt and Rogers (2015a) point out in part of their work for the UK Future of Cities Foresight Programme, it has been argued that four historical archetypes exist across history in a range of geographical/cultural settings (Dator, 2002):

- business as usual: a society that continues on the same path
- disciplined: a society stabilised by ideological values

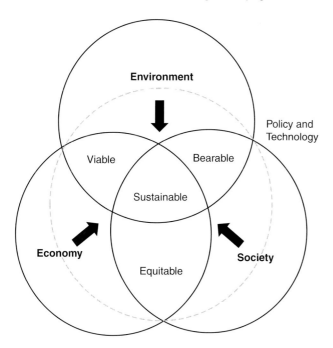

**Figure 17.2** Aspirational approaches to sustainability (Hunt and Rogers, 2015b).

- transformational: a highly transformative society beyond what we know and do now
- collapse: a less hopeful societal failure.

Interestingly, Hunt and Rogers (2015b) in a related report for the UK Future of Cities Foresight Programme developed three generic aspirational futures for cities. In their framework, the three sustainability pillars (Figure 17.2) appear as an interwoven structure that must balance aspects of city living requirements (and any change proposed) in order that they be sustainable, that is, viable, bearable and equitable in equal measures. Policy and technology (two other key drivers of change within a city) are seen as influential to this process. The alternative futures are referred to as Model 1 – Work and Economy, Model 2 – Environment and Resources, and Model 3 – People and Communities. Therefore, work and economy is based on a super-connected world in which the economy, trade and the world of work is prioritised. Environment and resources is based on an environmentally-aware world, in which the natural environment is valued for what it provides to cities, therein citizens and resources are marshalled to deliver greater resilience by fostering resource security and the avoidance of resource scarcity. Finally, people and communities is based on a world in which citizens and communities are mutually supportive and all other aspects of cities are shaped to facilitate this ideal.

Although such techniques offer us the comfort of at least thinking objectively about the future and what its implications for us and our world might be, they also recognise that we live in an uncertain world with an uncertain future. It seems that high-profile global incidents, such as 9/11, the Aceh tsunami and the Fukushima nuclear disaster, have made us realise that futures tools and techniques have their limitations (Wardman and Mythen, 2016). Taleb (2008) refers to these rare and unpredictable events as 'black swans', but others have used the terms, 'wild cards' and 'side swipes' to encapsulate similar events (Hunt and Rogers, 2015a).

For Taleb (2008) the origin of the term 'black swan' lies in the colonisation of Australia when until a black swan was discovered by settlers, everyone other than the indigenous population of Australia had thought all swans were white. So, black swans in other contexts are surprising (or outlier) events lying outside regular expectations which have extreme impact, and somehow seem explainable with hindsight (Taleb, 2008). In an era of what many suggest were unexpected events (e.g. Donald Trump's US presidency and Brexit) it is perhaps tempting to think of these as black swan events, but in fact the probability of each happening was approximately equal to the alternative, and therefore not completely unexpected (Kuznetsov, 2017).

That is not to say, however, that wider geopolitical turmoil will not create a future black swan event. Following the Trump election, for example, experts at the Bulletin of the Atomic Scientists moved the Doomsday Clock forwards 2 minutes and 30 seconds to midnight (Jamieson, 2017). Moreover, the real implications of events like Brexit remain uncertain. Recently two reports suggested that the UK would suffer a detrimental impact over the relatively short term (IFS, 2017; PwC, 2017b). However, the PwC report suggested over the longer term to 2050 that the UK would flourish as a growing global economy. Although this might seem an optimistic view, taking a long-term perspective is vital for planning housing, healthcare and other infrastructure requirements in the context of growing climate change and geopolitical turmoil.

Higgins (2013) and Perera and Higgins (2016) offer a useful classification of black swan events which links with three types of knowledge made famous by Donald Rumsfeld (former US Secretary of State for Defence):

- known knowns, which we can model with data, for example famine and the Y2000 bug
- known unknowns, which we can model but may have insufficient data, for example earthquakes, terrorism and the global financial crisis
- unknown unknowns, where we have no model and no data, for example asteroid attack and biological warfare.

Such categorisation is useful in the built environment in that it can help us to better understand the range of unexpected risks to the place and location, and space and operation of property and real-estate assets (Perera and Higgins, 2016). By understanding the impact of such risks, we can also improve resilience and reduce vulnerability in the built environment. Similarly, Iyer-Raniga (2012) shows how important black swan thinking is in the context of sustainability in the built environment, particularly in relation to extreme weather events: being prepared rather than being predictable can help us formulate tools and techniques to deal with unexpected events in a clear and rational way.

### 17.4.2   Policy and practice: shaping the future?

The UK Government's Foresight Programme is an example of how foresight thinking has attempted to influence public policy-making. The early roots of the programme go back to the 1960s, when a new focus on science and technology started to address what was widely conceived as an innovation problem in the UK (Habegger, 2010). This thinking eventually translated into the 1994 UK Foresight Programme, with a remit beyond technology to encompass broader societal and socio-economic or environmental problems. With the establishment of the UK Horizon Scanning Centre in 2004, there was a closer focus on cross-government priority setting, and there have been a number of foresight activities and futures projects relevant to the built environment, including intelligent infrastructure (2006), energy (2008), land-use futures (2010) and futures of citics (2016).[3]

This work has also been supplemented by horizon scanning activities (e.g. Delta and Sigma scans) (Habegger, 2010). However, in March 2014, the Cabinet Office's Horizon Scanning Secretariat and the Government Office of Science's Horizon Scanning Centre were merged to form the Horizon Scanning Programme team. This joint team now combines the two teams' expertise and networks to strengthen the programme, and its outputs. Essentially, in the UK, future analysis is used by government to think about long-term challenges and issues in achieving a particular goal or what our response needs to be. As HM Government (2014: 3) suggest:

> 'Futures analysis is designed to make uncertainty more tangible; to qualify and quantify the impact of abstract issues and trends that are often difficult to trans-late into near-term policy effects. By enabling more considered analysis, it can complement conventional forms of analysis and shape short- to medium-term policy responses in a way that is consistent with addressing major long-term challenges.'

On the face of it, the UK Foresight Programme has been considered effective in helping to inform policy-making in the UK government. However, there are genuine doubts as to the extent to which such studies genuinely influence and shape policy in the medium and long terms (Miles, 2010). Freestone (2012), for example, cites the case of the land-use futures foresight study which explored land-use change over a 50-year time period. The programme included a strong evidence base, state of the art science reviews, and scenarios and story-telling (Government Office for Science, 2010). However, Freestone (2012) points out that the project attracted criticism when some of the more radical scenarios were revealed (e.g. closure of Heathrow and its conversion to a reservoir). It also did not help that the UK coalition-led government, which came to power immediately after the report was published, considered planning to be a barrier on development.

In reality, it is hard to think of any integrated futures view of the built environment which has been formally endorsed by the government or the professions. Yes, there have been a number of futures studies, as we saw in Chapter 1, but these tend to treat the built environment in a fairly fragmented way, perhaps again reflecting the complex-ity and fragmented nature of the professions, and the construction and development sectors in general (see Chapter 1).

Thinking about the future of the built environment revolves around thinking about (i) the shape of the built environment, (ii) changing professional practices and (iii) techno-logical innovations. Yet, all are interrelated and interconnected, as we have seen in the earlier part of this chapter and in other parts of this book. Reports such as the Farrell report have attempted to emphasise the merits of an integrated approach to profes-sional training (e.g. Farrell's PLACE model (Planning, Landscape, Architecture,

---

3 See https://www.gov.uk/government/collections/foresight-projects.

Conservation and Engineering integration); Farrell, 2014), and the Edge report also pointed out the opportunities for built environment professions to reinvent themselves for the 21st century (Morrell, 2015).

It is, however, the integrated and complex nature of the built environment which makes it so challenging. As a recent report by the UK House of Lords (2016: 3) pointed out:

> 'The built environment affects us all. The planning, design, management and maintenance of the built environment has a long-term impact upon people and communities. It is widely acknowledged that the quality of life, prosperity, health and wellbeing of an individual is heavily influenced by the "place" in which they live or work. Policy towards the built environment in England is not the sole preserve of any one Government department; this both accounts for the diverse range of elements which comprise the "built environment", and reflects the diverse range of impacts which it has upon people and communities. There is an urgent need to co-ordinate and reconcile policy across numerous different areas and priorities.'

It is therefore difficult to see, without high‑level government intervention, how a more integrated foresight futures programme will emerge which would focus on a sustainable built environment in a holistic way (and encompass construction and development). That should not dissuade us from imagining and re-imagining the future, however, and we hope this book has gone some of the way towards seeing the possible futures that may emerge in this space to 2050.

We live in uncertain times, and having experts who can help us understand how to restructure contemporary institutions and structures to navigate towards a sustainable transition will be crucial. In their book, *Future Matters*, Barbara Adam and Chris Groves (2007) talk about the need for '21st century experts on the future' who have competencies and skills which include future-oriented action, knowledge and ethics, knowing where the public domains of science, economics and politics ends, knowing where responsibility will be 'inescapable' at the individual and collective level, and having the enthusiasm to inspire others. As Freestone (2012) suggests, their work carries powerful lessons if we are to engage with the future and 'populate' it (Adam and Groves, 2007: 15):

> 'It demands historical perceptiveness, asks for a thorough knowledge of temporal relations and calls for a trans-disciplinary outlook. At the practical level, it necessitates compassion with an eye for justice and an acute awareness of the interconnectedness, interdependence and interrelatedness of everything. As such it calls for conceptual skills and practical tools similar to those that ancient societies had honed to perfection: to understand processes and events in the wider scheme of things…Our contemporary situation entails that we understand ourselves not as objective observers and voyeurs but as implicated participants, inescapably responsible for that future in the making.'

## References

Adam, B. and Groves. C. (2007) *Future Matters: Action, Knowledge*, Ethics. Brill.

Arup (2016) *Cities Alive: Green Building Envelope*. Arup. Available at: http://publications.arup.com/publications/c/cities_alive_green_building_envelope (accessed March 2017).

Bates, T. (2016) *Book Review: The Future of the Professions (including teaching).* Available at: http://www.tonybates.ca/2016/01/04/book-review-the-future-of-the-professions-including-teaching/ (accessed January 2017).

Batty, M. (2013) *The New Science of Cities.* MIT Press, Cambridge, MA.

Bower, B.J.L. and Christensen, C. (1995) Disruptive technologies: catching the wave. *Harvard Business Review*, January–February, 43–53.

CCC (2017) *2017 Report to Parliament – Progress in preparing for climate change.* Committee on Climate Change, London. Available at: https://www.theccc.org.uk/publication/2017-report-to-parliament-progress-in-preparing-for-climate-change/.

Christensen, C. (2003) *The Innovator's Solution: Creating and Sustaining Successful Growth.* Harvard Business Press.

Christensen, C.M. and M.E. Raynor (2003) *The Innovator's Solution.* Boston, MA:

Christensen, C.M. and Raynor, M.E. (2003) *The Innovator's Solution.* Harvard Business School Press, Boston, MA.

Citi GPS (2016) *Technology at Work v2.0 The Future Is Not What It Used to Be.* Oxford Martin School/Citi GPS. Available at: http://www.oxfordmartin.ox.ac.uk/downloads/reports/Citi_GPS_Technology_Work_2.pdf (accessed February 2017).

Dator, J.A. (2002) *Advancing Futures: Futures Studies in Higher Education.* Praeger, Westport, CT, 409 pp.

DEFRA (2010) *The Built Environment: Futures Document.* Department for Environment Food & Rural Affairs, London. Available at: randd.defra.gov.uk/Document.aspx?Document=GA0403_9268_FRP.pdf (accessed February 2017).

DEFRA (2012) *UK Climate Change Risk Assessment: Built Environment – Summary.* Department for Environment Food & Rural Affairs, London.

Dixon, T., Eames, M., Britnell, J., Watson, G.B. and Hunt, M. (2014) Urban retrofitting: identifying disruptive and sustaining technologies using performative and foresight techniques. *Technological Forecasting & Social Change*, 89, 131–144. ISSN 0040-1625.

Eagar, R., Boulton, C., and Demyttenaera, C. (2014) The trends in megatrends: the most important megatrends and how to monitor them. *Prism*, 2, 12–23. Available at: http://www.adlittle.com/downloads/tx_adlprism/The_Trends_in_Megatrends.pdf (accessed February 2017).

Ernst and Young (2016) *The Upside of Disruption: Megatrends Shaping 2016 and Beyond.* Available at: http://www.ey.com/gl/en/issues/business-environment/ey-megatrends (accessed February 2017).

Farrell, T. (2014) *The Farrell Review of Architecture and the Built Environment.* Available at: http://www.farrellreview.co.uk/ (accessed February 2017).

Foxon, T. (2003) *Inducing innovation for a low-carbon future: drivers, barriers and policies.* Carbon Trust, London.

Freestone, R. (2012) Futures thinking in planning education and research. *Journal for Education in the Built Environment*, 7(1), 8–38.

Frey, C. and Osborne, M. (2013) *The Future of Employment: How Susceptible are Jobs to Computerisation?* Oxford Martin School, Oxford. Available at: http://www.oxfordmartin.ox.ac.uk/downloads/academic/The_Future_of_Employment.pdf (accessed February 2017).

Giesekam, J., Barrett, J.R. and Taylor, P. (2016) Construction sector views on low carbon building materials. *Building Research & Information*, 44(4), 423–444.

Government Office for Science (2008) *Foresight: Sustainable Energy Management and the Built Environment Project. Final Project Report.* The Government Office for Science,

London. Available at: https://www.gov.uk/government/uploads/system/uploads/attachment_data/file/293085/powering-our-lives-final-report.pdf (accessed February 2017).

Government Office for Science (2010) *Foresight: Land Use Futures Project – Final Project Report*. Government Office of Science, London. Available at: https://www.gov.uk/government/uploads/system/uploads/attachment_data/file/288843/10-631-land-use-futures.pdf (accessed February 2017).

Government Office for Science (2016) *Foresight: Future of Cities Project: Future of Cities: An Overview of the Evidence*. Government Office of Science, London. Available at: https://www.gov.uk/government/uploads/system/uploads/attachment_data/file/520963/GS-16-6-future-of-cities-an-overview-of-the-evidence.pdf (accessed February 2017).

Government Office for Science (2017) *Technology and Innovation Futures 2017* Government Office of Science, London. Available at: https://www.gov.uk/government/uploads/system/uploads/attachment_data/file/584219/technology-innovation-futures-2017.pdf (accessed February 2017).

Greenacre, P., Gross, R. and Speirs, J. (2011) *Innovation Theory: A review of the Literature*. ICEPT Working Paper, Imperial College, London.

Habegger, B. (2010) Strategic foresight in public policy: Reviewing the experiences of the UK, Singapore and the Netherlands. *Futures*, 42, 49–58.

Higgins, D. (2013) The black swan effect and the impact on Australian property forecasting. *Journal of Financial Management of Property and Construction*, 18(1), 76–89.

HM Government (2014) *Futures toolkit for policy-makers and analysts (Beta version)*. HM Government, London. Available at: https://www.gov.uk/government/publications/futures-toolkit-for-policy-makers-and-analysts (accessed February 2017).

House of Lords (2016) *Building Better Places: Report of Session 2015-16*. HL Paper 100, Select Committee on National Policy for the Built Environment.

House of Lords Select Committee on National Policy for the Built Environment (2016) *Building Better Places*. Stationery Office, London. Available at: https://publications.parliament.uk/pa/ld201516/ldselect/ldbuilt/100/100.pdf.

Hunt, D. and Rogers C. (2015a) *Aspirational City Futures: A short review of Foresight approaches*. Government Office of Science Foresight Report, London. Available at: https://www.gov.uk/government/uploads/system/uploads/attachment_data/file/516022/aspirational-city-futures-1a.pdf (accessed February 2017).

Hunt, D. and Rogers C. (2015b) *Aspirational City Futures: Three Models for City Living*. Government Office of Science Foresight Report, London. Available at: https://www.gov.uk/government/uploads/system/uploads/attachment_data/file/516031/aspirational-city-futures-1b.pdf (accessed February 2017).

IFS (2017) *Institute for Fiscal Studies Green Budget 2017*. Available at: https://www.ifs.org.uk/publications/8891 (accessed February 2017).

Iyer-Raninga, U. (2012) Applying Black Swan theory for achieving sustainability in the built environment. *International Journal of Environmental Science and Engineering Research*, 3(3), 108–113.

Jamieson, A. (2017) Doomsday Clock closer to midnight in wake of Trump presidency. *The Guardian*, 26 January. Available at: https://www.theguardian.com/us-news/2017/jan/26/doomsday-clock-closer-to-midnight-in-wake-of-donald-trump-election (accessed February 2017).

Klein, R.J.T., Nicholls, R.J. and Thomalla, F. (2003) Resilience to natural hazards: how useful is this concept? *Environmental Hazards*, 5(1), 35–45.

Kovats, R.S. and Osborn, D. (2016) People and the Built Environment, in *UK Climate Change Risk Assessment Evidence Report*. Report prepared for the Adaptation Sub-Committee of the Committee on Climate Change, London.

Kuznetsov, N. (2017) Debunking 'black swan' events of 2016. *Forbes*, 15 January. Available at: http://www.forbes.com/sites/nikolaikuznetsov/2017/01/15/debunking-black-swan-events-of-2016/#623bf6ab2166 (accessed February 2017).

Lucon, O., Ürge-Vorsatz, D., Zain Ahmed, A. et al. (2014) Buildings, in Edenhofer, O., Pichs-Madruga, R., Sokona, Y. *et al*. (eds), *Climate Change 2014: Mitigation of Climate Change. Contribution of Working Group III to the Fifth Assessment Report of the Intergovernmental Panel on Climate Change*. Cambridge University Press, Cambridge and New York.

McDowall, W. and Eames, M. (2006) Forecasts, scenarios, visions, backcasts and roadmaps to the hydrogen economy: A review of the hydrogen futures literature. *Energy Policy*, 34, 1236–1250.

McPartland, R. (2016) *10 material innovations shaping the buildings of tomorrow*. NBS website, 19 October. Available at: https://www.thenbs.com/knowledge/10-material-innovations-shaping-the-buildings-of-tomorrow (accessed February 2017).

Meerow, S., Newell, J.P. and Stults, M. (2016) Defining urban resilience: a review. *Landscape and Urban Planning*, 147, 38–49.

Miles, I. (2010) The development of technology foresight: A review. *Technological Forecasting and Social Change*, 77(9), 1448–1456.

Modus (2015) *Towards a Sustainable Built Environment for British Columbia: Synthesis of Findings*. Report for Real Estate Foundation, British Columbia. Available at: http://www.refbc.com/sites/default/files/Towards%20a%20Sustainable%20Built%20Environment%20for%20BC%20-%20FINAL%202015-10-13.pdf (accessed February 2017).

Morrell, P. (2015) *Collaboration for Change: The Edge Commission Report on the Future of Professionalism*. Ove Arup Foundation. Available at: http://www.edgedebate.com/?page_id=2829 (accessed February 2017).

Mulki, S. and Hinge, A. (2010) *Green Investment Horizons: Effects of policy on the market for building energy efficient technologies*. Working Paper, World Resources Institute, Washington DC.

National Research Council (2010) *Persistent Forecasting of Disruptive Technologies, Report 2*. National Academies Press, Washington DC.

Newton, P. (2007) Horizon 3 Planning: Meshing liveability with sustainability. *Environment and Planning B: Planning and Design*, 34(4), 571–575.

Newton, P. (ed.) (2008) *Transitions: Pathways Towards Sustainable Urban Development in Australia*. Springer.

OECD (2017) *Overview of Methodologies*. Available at: http://www.oecd.org/site/schooling fortomorrowknowledgebase/futuresthinking/overviewofmethodologies.htm (accessed February 2017).

Orr, D. (2011) *Security, Resilience and Community. Centre for Ecoliteracy*. Available at: https://www.ecoliteracy.org/article/david-orr-security-resilience-and-community (accessed February 2017).

Orr, D. (2016) *Dangerous Years: Climate Change, the Long Emergency and the Way Forward*. Yale University Press, New Haven and London.

Perera, T. and Higgins, D. (2016) *Black Swan Effects on the Real Estate Environment: A Conceptual Framework*. Paper Presented at the 5th World Construction Symposium 2016: Greening Environment, Eco Innovation & Entrepreneurship, July 29–31, Columbia, Sri Lanka. Available at: https://www.researchgate.net/publication/306228735_Black_Swan_Effects_on_the_Real_Estate_Environment_A_Conceptual_Framework (accessed February 2017).As per my note: Should be

Purnell, P. and Roelich, K. (2015) *Foresight Future of Cities Project: What will cities of the future be made of?* Briefing Note 3. Available at: https://www.gov.uk/government/uploads/system/uploads/attachment_data/file/452920/future-cities-materials.pdf.

PwC (2017a) *Megatrends: 5 global shifts changing the way we live and do business*. Available at: http://www.pwc.co.uk/issues/megatrends.html (accessed February 2017).

PwC (2017b) *The World in 2050*. Available at: http://www.pwc.com/world2050 (accessed February 2017).

RICS (2015) *RICS Futures: Our Changing World – Let's Be Ready*. Royal Institution of Chartered Surveyors, London. Available at: http://www.rics.org/uk/knowledge/research/insights/futuresour-changing-world/ (accessed February 2017).

Susskind, R. and Susskind, D. (2015) *The Future of the Professions: How Technology Will Transform the Work of Human Experts*. Oxford University Press.

Taleb, N.N. (2008) *Black Swan: The Impact of the Highly Improbable*. Penguin.

UKGBC (2017) *Building Places that Work for Everyone: Industry Insights into Key Government Priorities*. Available at: http://www.ukgbc.org/sites/default/files/08488%20Places%20for%20Everyone%20WEB.pdf (accessed February 2017).

UN (2014) *World Urbanization Prospects, 2014 Update*. United Nations, New York.

Wakefield, J. (2016) Tomorrow's Buildings: Construction industry goes robotic. *BBC News*, 4 May. Available at: http://www.bbc.co.uk/news/technology-35746648 (accessed February 2017).

Walker, B. and Salt, D. (2006) *Resilience Thinking*. Island Press, Washington, DC.

Wardman, J.K. and Mythen, G. (2016) Risk communication: against the Gods or against the odds? Problems and prospects of accounting for Black Swans. *Journal of Risk Research*, 19(10), 1220–1230.

WEF (2016) *Shaping the Future of Construction: A Breakthrough in Mindset and Technology*. World Economic Forum, Geneva. Available at: https://www.weforum.org/projects/future-of-construction (accessed February 2017).

WEF (2017) *Global Risk Report 2016*. World Economic Forum, Geneva. Available at: http://reports.weforum.org/global-risks-2017/ (accessed February 2017).

# Index

Note: page numbers in italics refer to figures; page numbers in bold refer to tables.

*Sustainable Futures in the Built Environment to 2050: A Foresight Approach to Construction
and Development*, First Edition. Edited by Tim Dixon, John Connaughton and Stuart Green.
© 2018 John Wiley & Sons Ltd. Published 2018 by John Wiley & Sons Ltd.